Contents

12th Edition

the dynamics
of mass
communication

Media in Transition

Joseph R. Dominick
University of Georgia, Athens

Mc Graw Hill

Connect
Learn
Succeed™

Published by McGraw-Hill, an imprint of The McGraw-Hill Companies, Inc., 1221 Avenue of the Americas, New York, NY 10020. Copyright © 2013, 2011, 2009, 2007, 2005, 2002, 1999. All rights reserved. Printed in the United States of America. No part of this publication may be reproduced or distributed in any form or by any means, or stored in a database or retrieval system, without the prior written consent of The McGraw-Hill Companies, Inc., including, but not limited to, in any network or other electronic storage or transmission, or broadcast for distance learning.

This book is printed on acid-free paper.

1 2 3 4 5 6 7 8 9 0 QVR/QVR 9 8 7 6 5 4 3 2

ISBN: 978-0-07-352619-5
MHID: 0-07-352619-3

Sponsoring Editor: *Susan Gouijnstook*
Marketing Manager: *Leslie Oberhuber*
Developmental Editor: *Julia Akpan*
Production Editor: *Holly Irish*
Production Service: *Anne Draus*
Manuscript Editor: *Margaret C. Tropp*
Text Designer: *Amanda Kavanagh*
Cover Designers: *Preston Thomas/Irene Morris*
Photo Research: *David Teitz*
Buyer: *Louis Swaim*
Composition: *10/12 Palatino by Laserwords*
Printing: *45# New Era Matte Plus, Quad Graphics, Versailles*

Vice President Editorial: *Michael Ryan*
Publisher: *David Patterson*

Cover photo credits: © Corbis; Ingram Publishing; PhotoAlto/Getty Images; Blend Images/Getty Images; Uppercut RF/Getty Images; flickr RF/Getty Images; Tetra Images/Getty Images; Nick White/Getty Images; Ingram Publishing; © Plush Studios/Blend Images LLC; Design Pics/Tim Antoniuk; © BananaStock/PunchStock; © Eyewire/Getty Images; © Fancy Photography/Veer; Ingram Publishing; Comstock Images/Jupiter Images; © Lars Niki; © The McGraw-Hill Companies Inc., Photo by Digital Light Source/Richard Hutchings.

Credits: The credits section for this book begins on page 460 and is considered an extension of the copyright page.

Library of Congress Cataloging-in-Publication Data
Dominick, Joseph R.
    The dynamics of mass communication : media in transition / Joseph R. Dominick. — 12th ed.
        p. cm.
    Includes bibliographical references and index.
    ISBN 978-0-07-352619-5
    1. Mass media. I. Title.
P90.D59 2012
302.23—dc23

2011048516

The Internet addresses listed in the text were accurate at the time of publication. The inclusion of a website does not indicate an endorsement by the authors or McGraw-Hill, and McGraw-Hill does not guarantee the accuracy of the information presented at these sites.

www.mhhe.com

For Meaghan and for Carole

about the author

Joseph R. Dominick received his undergraduate degree from the University of Illinois and his Ph.D. from Michigan State University in 1970. He taught for four years at Queens College of the City University of New York before going to the College of Journalism and Mass Communication at the University of Georgia where, from 1980 to 1985, he served as head of the Radio-TV-Film Sequence. Dr. Dominick is the author of three books in addition to *The Dynamics of Mass Communication* and has published more than 40 articles in scholarly journals. From 1976 to 1980, Dr. Dominick served as editor of the *Journal of Broadcasting.* He has received research grants from the National Association of Broadcasters and from the American Broadcasting Company and has consulted for such organizations as the Robert Wood Johnson Foundation and the American Chemical Society. He served as interim department head from 2005 until his retirement in 2008.

brief contents

contents

Contents   ix

Contents

boxed features

preface

Three things made me realize that a new edition of *The Dynamics of Mass Communication* was in order. The first was a news article that reported that (1) Facebook had nearly 700 million members worldwide (that means about 1 in every 10 people in the world is a member) and (2) the company was valued at about $100 billion dollars. Not bad for an idea that started in a dorm room.

Apps were the second thing. Apps weren't around when the 11th edition was written and the iPad had yet to come out. These days articles with cute titles about the growing popularity of apps for mobile media are appearing everywhere. Some of the more clever examples I found were "App-lause," "Planet of the Apps," "Get Appy," "What's App-ening?" "What's App Doc?" and my personal favorite, "App, App and Away." More than 10 billion apps had been downloaded by mid-2011. It was obvious that this app stuff was catching on.

The third thing had to do with the companies that now control most of the Internet's media commerce: Netflix, Apple, Google, Amazon, and Yahoo. When I first started working on the first edition of *Dynamics* (way, way back in 1980), Apple was only three years old and thanks to its early success as a computer builder, the company had revenues of about $330 million and employed around 50 people. In 2010, Apple had $65 billion in revenue and nearly 50,000 employees. Netflix, Google, Yahoo, and Amazon did not exist in 1980. In short, over the past 30 years, there has been a rearranging of the guard in mass communication. Traditional media companies, such as Harper-Collins, Condé Nast, Sony Music, Paramount Pictures, NBC, and Gannett, while still influential, have been joined by the new digital powers.

As you have probably deduced by now, these three developments—social media, apps, and the new media Goliaths—are major themes in the 12th edition.

The new edition also examines other events that have affected the media. The economic downturn that caused media revenues to shrink over the past couple of years has, it is hoped, bottomed out. Nonetheless, money is still tight and it is doubtful that some media industries will ever see their incomes rise to previous levels.

With the exception of YouTube and news/weather videos, the user-generated content craze has cooled off. Many bloggers have turned to Twitter or Facebook to express their thoughts. Most mass media are relying less on amateur content and more on professionally produced material. Even YouTube has put more emphasis on content produced by pros.

Video on the Web has exploded in the last couple of years. Internet-connected TV sets and DVD players are in many households. New software has made it ridiculously easy to add video to social media sites. Advertisers and public relations firms rely heavily on Web video in structuring their campaigns. Politicians declare their candidacies via Web video. The Online Video Guide lists numerous sites where a viewer can find videos in more than two dozen categories.

Finally, when I was working on the previous edition, Amazon's Kindle had been on the market for less than a year, and there were still doubts about its ultimate success. Amazon's e-reader sold about 400,000 units in 2008. As of this writing, experts estimate that the company has sold more than 8 million Kindles, and the device has gotten a lot of competition, including the iPad, the Nook, and Sony's e-reader. The book publishing industry is now feeling the same disruption that the recording industry felt when file sharing and digital downloading became the preferred way of acquiring music.

So much for the general overview. Here's a more specific look at what's new in the 12th edition.

New to the 12th Edition

Users of previous editions of the book will quickly notice that Chapter 18 ("International and Comparative Media Systems") in the 11th edition has been dropped from the 12th edition. Reviewers suggested that such a topic seemed too specialized in a basic introduction to media and should be left to a more advanced course. Nonetheless, key parts of that chapter are now included in the appropriate media chapters so that students who wish to take a course in the international area will be familiar with fundamental information on the topic.

Next, the organization of the book has been slightly rearranged. Chapter 12 ("The Internet and the World Wide Web") in the 11th edition is now Chapter 4 (retitled "The Internet and Social Media") and leads off Part II ("Media"). Since the Internet has had such a drastic impact on all of the mass media, it seems appropriate to discuss the Internet first rather than last. Consequently, Part II starts with the newest medium (the Internet), then looks at the oldest medium (print), and finally more recent media (sound and pictures).

In addition, Chapter 4 has undergone a major revision. The revised chapter has an expanded section examining the effects, economics, political implications, and dysfunctions of social networking sites such as Facebook, Twitter, YouTube, and MySpace. More specifically, the new Chapter 4 discusses, among other topics, the impact of social media on traditional media, the role of social media in the unrest in North Africa and the Middle East, and the problem of cyberbullying.

Here are some of the changes that you will find in individual chapters.

- Part I: Chapter 1 has been streamlined and contains additional discussion of mobile media and tablet computers. Chapter 2 has updated examples of the various media functions and Chapter 3 has an expanded discussion of the cultural impact of the social media.

- Part II: As mentioned above, the reworked Chapter 4 now leads off this section and is titled "The Internet and Social Media" to better reflect the increasing importance of social networks. This chapter now contains a look at the leading companies in the digital field: Apple, Amazon, Google, and Facebook. The newspaper industry is experimenting with new online models to generate revenue, and this development is discussed in Chapter 5 along with an examination of popular apps for newspapers. Speaking of apps, Chapter 6 looks at how magazines are using apps to bring digital versions to tablet computers and how the industry is using social media to increase readership. Chapter 7 now contains a new section on how e-readers are changing the book publishing industry. The Internet has paved the way for hundreds of new radio stations, and Chapter 8 examines the impact of this trend for traditional radio and looks at how radio networks and local stations are using apps to expand their listenership. The sound recording industry has been profoundly changed by the digital revolution. Chapter 9 now contains an expanded discussion of the impact of MP3 players and smartphones on the industry along with an analysis of the changing revenue streams. Chapter 10 has a new discussion of the rise (and potential fall) of 3-D movies and a revised section about how Hollywood relates to the home video industry. Chapter 11 describes how broadcasters have embraced social media and how apps have turned the iPad into a TV set. Chapter 12 describes the explosion of Web-based TV, including an updated analysis of its economic basis.

- Part III: Chapter 13 opens with a discussion of the most recent report on the news media from the Pew Research Center and looks at the newest trends in hyperlocal reporting. Chapter 14 opens with an analysis of the public relations problems for BP as the result of the Gulf oil spill. The chapter also contains an expanded section that considers how PR professionals are using the Web and social media in public relations campaigns. The advertising industry has also welcomed social media, and Chapter 15 illustrates how social media have been incorporated into modern advertising campaigns.
- Part IV: Chapter 16 contains an updated status of legal issues. Chapter 17 now includes a discussion of the ethical issues involved in the *New York Times*'s decision to publish documents it obtained from WikiLeaks.
- Part V: Chapter 18 brings up to date the latest findings from social science research, including a revised section on the impact of violent video games.

Box Score

As in past editions, the boxed inserts in each chapter provide background material or extended coverage of topics mentioned in the text and raise issues for discussion and consideration. The 12th edition includes more than 80 new or revised boxes.

The boxes are grouped into several categories. The Media Talk boxes refer students to the Online Learning Center and introduce important issues in mass communication. Instructors can use these as discussion starters.

The Social Issues boxes highlight matters of social concern that have generated some controversy. Examples include a discussion of how media coverage confers status on fringe groups and a consideration of whether we still need newsmagazines.

As the name suggests, Ethical Issues boxes raise questions about the proper way to act in difficult circumstances. For instance, what ethical problems are involved in "negative" public relations or in posting cell phone videos on video-sharing sites?

Critical/Cultural Issues boxes illustrate how this perspective can be used to further our understanding of mass communication. Examples include the influence of department stores on the development of radio and how the Food Network maintains traditional images of masculinity and femininity.

The Media Probe boxes take an in-depth look at subjects that have significance for the various media. Some examples include an examination of payola, how corporations are supporting rock groups, and the disappearing soap opera.

The Decision Makers boxes profile individuals who have made some of the important decisions that have had an impact on the development of the media. Examples include James Cameron, Tina Brown, and Catherine Hughes.

And, as before, the Soundbytes are brief boxes that highlight some of the strange, ironic, offbeat, and extraordinary developments that occur in the media, such as coffins made of newsprint and George Washington's overdue library books.

Continuity

The organization of the book has changed a bit since the 11th edition. Part I, "The Nature and History of Mass Communication," presents the intellectual context for the rest of the book and is unchanged from the 11th edition. Chapter 1 compares and contrasts mass communication with other types of communication and notes that the distinctions are becoming fuzzier. Chapter 2 introduces two perspectives commonly used to understand and explore the operations of the media: functional analysis and the critical/cultural approach. Chapter 3 takes a macroanalytic approach and traces the general history of media from the invention of printing to the explosion of social media.

Part II, "Media," represents the core of the book. Chapter 4, as noted earlier, is a revised and expanded version of Chapter 12 from the 11th edition, retitled "The Internet and Social Media." Chapters 5–12 then examine each of the traditional media. The organization of each chapter follows a similar pattern. First, there is a brief history from the medium's beginnings to how it is transforming itself in the digital age. This is followed by sections that describe how the medium is becoming more mobile, how it has been affected by user-generated content, and how it is using social media. Next comes a discussion of the defining characteristics of each medium and a description of the industry structure.

I have kept the emphasis on media economics. Since the major media in the United States exist to make a profit, it is valuable for students to appreciate where the money comes from, how it is spent, and why making a profit these days is harder than ever. This is even more important today with several media industries struggling to survive as traditional revenue streams dry up and their online efforts cannot make up the shortfall.

Part III, "Specific Media Professions," examines three specific professions closely associated with the mass media: news reporting, public relations, and advertising. Similar to the approach in Part II, each chapter begins with a brief history, examines the structure of that particular profession, considers the changes brought about by the digital revolution, and discusses key issues in the field.

Part IV, "Regulation of the Mass Media," examines both the formal and informal controls that influence the media. These are complicated areas, and I have tried to make the information as user-friendly as possible.

The concluding Part V, "Impact of the Media," continues to emphasize the social effects of the mass media. As noted earlier, Chapter 18 in the 11th edition, "International and Comparative Media Systems," has been dropped and its key sections distributed to the appropriate chapters.

Once again, I have tried to keep the writing style informal and accessible. Whenever possible, I have chosen examples from popular culture that I hope all students are familiar with. Technical terms are boldfaced and defined in the glossary at the end of the book. The book also contains a number of charts, graphs, diagrams, and tables that I hope aid understanding.

Supporting Materials

Online Learning Center
The Online Learning Center houses the Media Talk video clips, all of the instructor resources (Instructor's Manual, Test Bank, and PowerPoint slides), and the traditional student quiz materials. Access the Online Learning Center at **www.mhhe.com/dominick12e.**

Create
Craft your teaching resources to match the way you teach! With McGraw-Hill Create, you can easily rearrange chapters, combine material from other content sources, and quickly upload content you have written like your course syllabus or teaching notes. Arrange your book to fit your teaching style. Create even allows you to personalize your book's appearance by selecting the cover and adding your name, school, and course information. Order a Create book and you'll receive a complimentary print review copy

in 3–5 business days or a complimentary electronic review copy (eComp) via email in about one hour. Go to www.mcgrawhillcreate.com today and register. Experience how McGraw-Hill Create empowers you to teach your students your way.

CourseSmart e-Textbook

This text is available as an eTextbook at www.CourseSmart.com. At CourseSmart your students can take advantage of significant savings off the cost of a print textbook, reduce their impact on the environment, and gain access to powerful Web tools for learning. CourseSmart eTextbooks can be viewed online or downloaded to a computer. The eTextbooks allow students to do full text searches, add highlighting and notes, and share notes with classmates. CourseSmart has the largest selection of eTextbooks available anywhere. Visit www.CourseSmart.com to learn more and to try a sample chapter.

Tegrity

Tegrity Campus is a service that makes class time available all the time by automatically capturing every lecture in a searchable format for students to review when they study and complete assignments. With a simple one-click start and stop process, you capture all computer screens and corresponding audio. Students can replay any part of any class with easy-to-use browser-based viewing on a PC or Mac. Educators know that the more students can see, hear, and experience class resources, the better they learn. With Tegrity Campus, students quickly recall key moments by using Tegrity Campus's unique search feature. This search helps students efficiently find what they need, when they need it, across an entire semester of class recordings. Help turn all your students' study time into learning moments immediately supported by your lecture.

Acknowledgments

Thanks to all of those instructors who used previous editions of *The Dynamics of Mass Communication* and were kind enough to suggest improvements. Several colleagues deserve special mention: Professor Noah Arceneaux provided a boxed insert. Professor Scott Shamp was kind enough to share his blog page, and Professor Michael Castengera's newsletter, "Message from Michael," was a valuable resource. In addition, thanks to researcher Meaghan Dominick for her efforts with the Decision Makers boxes and to Carole Dominick for her efforts as a scrivener.

Once again I appreciate the sedulous efforts of all the reviewers who offered suggestions for the 12th edition:

Jane Campbell, Columbia State Community College
Susan J. De Bonis, Georgia Southern University
Donald G. Godfrey, Walter Cronkite School of Journalism
Dee Gross, Lorain County Community College
Susan Katz, University of Bridgeport
Candice Larson, Moorpark College
Robert M. Ogles, Purdue University
Jeff South, Virginia Commonwealth University
Emily Chivers Yochim, Allegheny College

And, as always, a big thanks to all the people at McGraw-Hill on publishing yet another edition: Vice President Editorial Michael Ryan, Sponsoring Editor Susan

Gouijnstook, Marketing Manager Leslie Oberhuber, Julia Akpan for her comprehensive editorial development, Director of Development Rhona Robbin, Production Editor Holly Irish, Media Project Manager Jennifer Barrick, Photo Researcher David A. Tietz, and Designer Preston Thomas.

The Audience

As most instructors will attest, the introductory course in mass communication attracts two types of students. One type is interested in following a professional career in some form of media (a career path made even more challenging by the current market conditions). This student wants to know the nuts and bolts of the media—how they are organized, how they work, who does what, and what career possibilities are out there. The second type of student will probably never pursue a career in the media but will become a member of the audience and consume a great deal of media content. These students are more interested in analyzing and understanding how the media operate and what impact they have on society. To use an overworked expression, they want to become "media literate."

An original goal of the first edition of *Dynamics* was to present an up-to-date, detailed, and comprehensive look at contemporary media that would benefit aspiring media professionals and at the same time provide a useful foundation for those who will end up in other careers. A second goal was to help both students and faculty understand and appreciate the fast-changing world of mass communication a little better. As has been the case 11 times before, it is hoped that this new edition still fulfills both of those goals.

Joseph R. Dominick
Dacula, Georgia

Your Guided Tour

Media in Transition:
  Where we were,
  where we are,
  where we're going.
Media today change in the blink of an eye, and being tuned into current and emerging media trends is crucial to becoming a savvy media consumer and—increasingly—a media producer as well.

The Dynamics of Mass Communication provides a forward-looking approach while continuing to supply critical information about the foundation on which the current media empires were built.

Chapter Opening

previews identify key goals for each chapter through learning objectives, while timely vignettes set the stage for what's to come.

media talk

Advertisers Gone Wild: New Ways to "Get the Message"

Clip 7: 2 minutes 15 seconds

You can watch Clip 7 *on the Online Learning Center home page,* www.mhhe.com/dominick12e. *Select* Student Center *and then* Chapter 2. This clip shows how advertisers are going out of their way to place ads in the strangest places. What functions does advertising serve for society? Why are advertisers resorting to placing ads in unusual places? Where is the oddest place you have seen an advertisement? Do you think advertisements located in odd places are more effective than traditional advertisements (such as billboards, television commercials, newspaper ads)? What types of ads are you least likely to respond to?

WWW

Media Talk

margin notes feature focus questions about the NBC videos found on the Online Learning Center that are pertinent to chapter topics.

Ethical Issues

boxes provide opportunities for critical thinking about ethical issues specific to mass communication industries.

ethical Issues *Naming Names*

There's nothing illegal about reporting the name of a juvenile who has been charged with a crime, but the news media have generally followed a policy of not revealing the suspect's name. The Code of Ethics of the Society of Professional Journalists urges that news media be cautious about naming juvenile suspects. The reasoning behind this policy is that juveniles lack the maturity of adults and often don't realize the consequences of their actions. Identifying youthful suspects may result in stigmatizing them for the rest of their lives. In short, the media give the juvenile a chance to go straight without carrying the baggage associated with an arrest.

Recently, however, there has been a trend toward naming juveniles, particularly if they have been involved in serious crimes. The decision to publish or not publish the name varies from newsroom to newsroom and illustrates an ethical philosophy called *situational ethics*. Situational ethics suggests that each individual problem or situation is unique and calls for a unique solution. There is no universal ethical principle that yields an unswerving path of action. For example, some media outlets will name

the juvenile suspect if he or she has been charged as an adult. Others will take the age of the person arrested into consideration. They may report the names of 16- or 17-year-olds but refrain from identifying younger individuals. Still others look at the severity of the crime; the more severe, the more likely they are to reveal the name of the suspect. The problem with this approach is that it sometimes leads to inconsistent results. A teen in one story may be named while a teen in another story is not identified.

The most extreme position argues that the name of anybody arrested for a crime should be reported. Not naming the suspect leaves a hole in the story. Somebody committed a crime. Somebody was arrested. Who? It makes no difference to the person whose car was carjacked if it was taken by a teen or an adult. The car is still gone. Suspects have the entire criminal justice system protecting them while the victims have no one to advocate for them. Finally, the proponents of this position argue that naming juvenile offenders might even encourage them to go straight and prevent future crimes.

Social Issues

boxes explore new developments in how mass media operate in a social context.

social Issues — Do We Need the Public Broadcasting Service?

The debate about PBS has been going on since the growth of cable television in the 1980s and 1990s. Many of the new channels featured content that was previously the province of PBS. The History Channel, the Discovery Channel, Animal Planet, Nickelodeon, the Hallmark Channel, and others fragmented the audience for PBS programs. PBS ratings have been declining (along with the ratings of many other networks) for the past decade. From 2000 to 2010, PBS's ratings dropped 37 percent.

What should be the role of PBS in a 500-channel television universe? A mission statement adopted by PBS stations in 2004 says in part that "public television is more essential than ever in the cluttered media landscape." It goes on to point out that in an age of conglomerate media ownership, PBS stations may be the only locally owned stations in the community and are better suited to responding to local needs. The document goes on to state:

> Public television . . . strives for impact and measures its success by the extent of its ability to educate and inform, to enlighten and entertain. In short, public television strives to:

- Challenge the American mind.
- Inspire the American spirit.
- Preserve the American memory.
- Enhance the American dialogue.
- Promote global understanding.

Those are lofty goals. Does the programming on PBS stations fulfill them? Critics suggest that PBS programs have grown musty with age. Nova, Masterpiece, and NewsHour have all been on the air for 30 to 40 years. The American version of Antiques Roadshow has been around for more than a decade. (The U.S. program was based on a British series that premiered in 1979.) Typical prime-time programming includes reruns of old British sitcoms such as Keeping Up Appearances and Are You Being Served? Critics also suggest looking at the schedule of the local PBS affiliate. How much local programming is aired during the typical week?

The programmers at PBS, however, face a dilemma. If their shows venture too far away from mainstream, such as programs that examine gay and lesbian lifestyles or global warming, PBS is criticized as being too liberal. If their shows stick with the familiar, they are branded as obsolete or redundant with those of the commercial networks.

A second issue concerns the drift of public television toward its commercial counterparts. That 2004 mission statement proclaims the goal of commercial television is to attract as many viewers as possible and expose them to advertising but suggests that PBS is different. In the past decade, however, PBS has opened up its programs to an expanded program of underwriting, whereby a sponsor donates money to a station or PBS in return for a 30-second message at the beginning of the program. Many of these messages look exactly like ads playing on commercial TV. In addition, underwriters would rather reach a large audience than a small one. This means that public TV, if it wants to continue to attract underwriting revenue, will try to air programs that attract a large audience, much like commercial TV.

The transition to digital makes the questions about the role of PBS even more complicated. Does PBS really need a Facebook fan page or a YouTube channel? Check out the PBS Twitter feed. Does it fulfill the goals of the mission statement? This is a debate not likely to end soon.

decision makers — Judy McGrath

For many of you reading this, Judy McGrath would seem to have the ultimate dream job. As president of the MTV Networks Music Group, she was responsible for MTV, MTV2, VH1, CMT, and all of the company's digital media services. Under her direction MTV has grown from a small niche cable network to an international brand that symbolizes a unique attitude and lifestyle.

Always a music fan, McGrath first tried to get a job writing for Rolling Stone. When her efforts proved unsuccessful, she turned to writing advertising copy and then went to work for Mademoiselle and Glamour. In 1981 she heard about a new cable channel launched by Warner Entertainment that would be devoted to rock music. Despite the fact that she could not even get the channel on her home TV, McGrath joined the newly created MTV as a copywriter and on-air promotion person. (She was one of the ones responsible for using all the space film footage to promote the channel.) To the surprise of many people, MTV was successful in attracting 16- to 24-year-olds, an audience coveted by advertisers. MTV became part of the huge Viacom conglomerate, and McGrath quickly moved up the ranks to creative director, executive vice president, and eventually chair and chief executive at MTV Networks. Under her direction MTV expanded all over the world.

When the music video novelty began to wear off in the mid-1980s and ratings started to sag, McGrath introduced programs that became popular culture icons: Beavis and Butt-Head, The Real World, The MTV Music Awards, MTV Unplugged, and Total Request Live. She also introduced political coverage to MTV and was instrumental in the development of the 1992 Choose or Lose get-out-the-vote campaign. More recently, McGrath has led MTV into other media: movies, books, and the Internet.

What does she see in MTV's future? Since a high proportion of MTV viewers are also Web surfers and spend a good deal of time on MTV.com, look for more integration of the music on MTV and MTV2 with the Web site. MTV.com will be used to highlight some of the artists or genres featured on the cable channels. In addition, plans are under way for more international expansion, particularly in Asia. Her plans will have to be carried out by someone else. McGrath stepped down from her position in 2011.

Decision Makers

boxes profile people who have had a significant impact on contemporary mass media.

Media Probe

boxes provide more in-depth information, illustrations, examples, and background to specific issues raised within each chapter.

Critical/Cultural Issues

boxes illustrate this approach to mass communication across a broad range of topics.

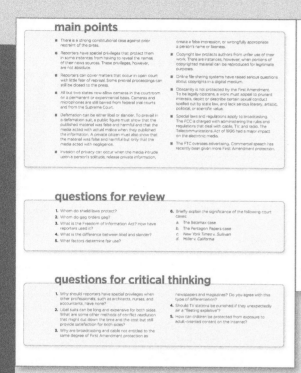

main points

- There is a strong constitutional case against prior restraint of the press.

- Reporters have special privileges that protect them in some instances from having to reveal the names of their news sources. These privileges, however, are not absolute.

- Reporters can cover matters that occur in open court with little fear of reprisal. Some pretrial proceedings can still be closed to the press.

- All but two states now allow cameras in the courtroom on a permanent or experimental basis. Cameras and microphones are still barred from federal trial courts and from the Supreme Court.

- Defamation can be either libel or slander. To prevail in a defamation suit, a public figure must show that the published material was false and harmful and that the media acted with actual malice when they published the information. A private citizen must also show that the material was false and harmful but only that the media acted with negligence.

- Invasion of privacy can occur when the media intrude upon a person's solitude, release private information,

create a false impression, or wrongfully appropriate a person's name or likeness.

- Copyright law protects authors from unfair use of their work. There are instances, however, when portions of copyrighted material can be reproduced for legitimate purposes.

- Online file-sharing systems have raised serious questions about copyrights in a digital medium.

- Obscenity is not protected by the First Amendment. To be legally obscene, a work must appeal to prurient interests, depict or describe certain sexual conduct spelled out by state law, and lack serious literary, artistic, political, or scientific value.

- Special laws and regulations apply to broadcasting. The FCC is charged with administering the rules and regulations that deal with cable, TV, and radio. The Telecommunications Act of 1996 had a major impact on the electronic media.

- The FTC oversees advertising. Commercial speech has recently been given more First Amendment protection.

key terms

First Amendment (p. 376)
prior restraint (p. 376)
injunction (p. 376)
shield laws (p. 380)
gag rules (p. 383)
Freedom of Information Act (FOIA) (p. 385)
USA Patriot Act (p. 385)

defamation (p. 386)
libel (p. 386)
slander (p. 386)
libel per se (p. 386)
libel per quod (p. 386)
trespass (p. 393)
Hicklin Rule (p. 396)
Internet neutrality (p. 399)

Equal Opportunities Rule (p. 400)
Fairness Doctrine (p. 401)
franchises (p. 402)
Telecommunications Act of 1996 (p. 403)
V-chip (p. 403)
consent order (p. 403)
cease-and-desist order (p. 403)

internet resources

Online Learning Center
On the Online Learning Center home page, www.mhhe.com/dominick12e, select Student Center and then Chapter 16.

1. Use the Learning Objectives, Chapter Outline, and Main Points sections to review this chapter.

2. Test your knowledge of the chapter using the multiple choice and flashcard features of the site.

3. Expand your knowledge of concepts and topics discussed in the chapter with additional Questions for Critical Thinking and Internet Exercises.

questions for review

1. Whom do shield laws protect?
2. Whom do gag orders gag?
3. What is the Freedom of Information Act? How have reporters used it?
4. What is the difference between libel and slander?
5. What factors determine fair use?

6. Briefly explain the significance of the following court cases:
   a. The Betamax case
   b. The Pentagon Papers case
   c. *New York Times v. Sullivan*
   d. *Miller v. California*

surfing the internet

Many Web sites deal with legal matters. The ones listed here seem most helpful for students.

www.fcc.gov
The FCC's home page. Contains an archive of recent speeches, a search engine, and consumer information, along with more technical data.

www.freedomforum.org
Contains a summary of recent First Amendment court decisions, relevant law articles, a First Amendment time line, and the full text of relevant Supreme Court rulings.

www.rcfp.org
The Reporters Committee for Freedom of the Press maintains this site, which contains recent court decisions, legal news, and a link to its publication, *The News Media and the Law.*

www.rtnda.org
Home page of the Radio and Television News Directors Association. Contains information about covering the courts, libel, copyright, and other legal issues.

questions for critical thinking

1. Why should reporters have special privileges when other professionals, such as architects, nurses, and accountants, have none?

2. Libel suits can be long and expensive for both sides. What are some other methods of conflict resolution that might cut down the time and the cost but still provide satisfaction for both sides?

3. Why are broadcasting and cable not entitled to the same degree of First Amendment protection as

newspapers and magazines? Do you agree with this type of differentiation?

4. Should TV stations be punished if they unexpectedly air a "fleeting expletive"?

5. How can children be protected from exposure to adult-oriented content on the Internet?

End of Chapter

review materials provide essential study aids, including clear, concise chapter summaries, review and critical thinking questions, key terms lists, and Internet resources.

Online Learning Center: www.mhhe.com/dominick12e

This book-specific Web site features practice tests, learning objectives, chapter main points, key terms, additional Questions for Critical Thinking, and an online glossary. For the instructor, the password-protected area of the Web site offers a teaching guide, detailed chapter summaries, and PowerPoint slides.

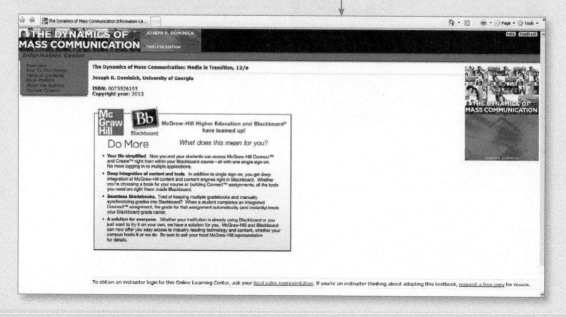

preface

Three things made me realize that a new edition of *The Dynamics of Mass Communication* was in order. The first was a news article that reported that (1) Facebook had nearly 700 million members worldwide (that means about 1 in every 10 people in the world is a member) and (2) the company was valued at about $100 billion dollars. Not bad for an idea that started in a dorm room.

Apps were the second thing. Apps weren't around when the 11th edition was written and the iPad had yet to come out. These days articles with cute titles about the growing popularity of apps for mobile media are appearing everywhere. Some of the more clever examples I found were "App-lause," "Planet of the Apps," "Get Appy," "What's App-ening?" "What's App Doc?" and my personal favorite, "App, App and Away." More than 10 billion apps had been downloaded by mid-2011. It was obvious that this app stuff was catching on.

The third thing had to do with the companies that now control most of the Internet's media commerce: Netflix, Apple, Google, Amazon, and Yahoo. When I first started working on the first edition of *Dynamics* (way, way back in 1980), Apple was only three years old and thanks to its early success as a computer builder, the company had revenues of about $330 million and employed around 50 people. In 2010, Apple had $65 billion in revenue and nearly 50,000 employees. Netflix, Google, Yahoo, and Amazon did not exist in 1980. In short, over the past 30 years, there has been a rearranging of the guard in mass communication. Traditional media companies, such as Harper-Collins, Condé Nast, Sony Music, Paramount Pictures, NBC, and Gannett, while still influential, have been joined by the new digital powers.

As you have probably deduced by now, these three developments—social media, apps, and the new media Goliaths—are major themes in the 12th edition.

The new edition also examines other events that have affected the media. The economic downturn that caused media revenues to shrink over the past couple of years has, it is hoped, bottomed out. Nonetheless, money is still tight and it is doubtful that some media industries will ever see their incomes rise to previous levels.

With the exception of YouTube and news/weather videos, the user-generated content craze has cooled off. Many bloggers have turned to Twitter or Facebook to express their thoughts. Most mass media are relying less on amateur content and more on professionally produced material. Even YouTube has put more emphasis on content produced by pros.

Video on the Web has exploded in the last couple of years. Internet-connected TV sets and DVD players are in many households. New software has made it ridiculously easy to add video to social media sites. Advertisers and public relations firms rely heavily on Web video in structuring their campaigns. Politicians declare their candidacies via Web video. The Online Video Guide lists numerous sites where a viewer can find videos in more than two dozen categories.

Finally, when I was working on the previous edition, Amazon's Kindle had been on the market for less than a year, and there were still doubts about its ultimate success. Amazon's e-reader sold about 400,000 units in 2008. As of this writing, experts estimate that the company has sold more than 8 million Kindles, and the device has gotten a lot of competition, including the iPad, the Nook, and Sony's e-reader. The book publishing industry is now feeling the same disruption that the recording industry felt when file sharing and digital downloading became the preferred way of acquiring music.

So much for the general overview. Here's a more specific look at what's new in the 12th edition.

New to the 12th Edition

Users of previous editions of the book will quickly notice that Chapter 18 ("International and Comparative Media Systems") in the 11th edition has been dropped from the 12th edition. Reviewers suggested that such a topic seemed too specialized in a basic introduction to media and should be left to a more advanced course. Nonetheless, key parts of that chapter are now included in the appropriate media chapters so that students who wish to take a course in the international area will be familiar with fundamental information on the topic.

Next, the organization of the book has been slightly rearranged. Chapter 12 ("The Internet and the World Wide Web") in the 11th edition is now Chapter 4 (retitled "The Internet and Social Media") and leads off Part II ("Media"). Since the Internet has had such a drastic impact on all of the mass media, it seems appropriate to discuss the Internet first rather than last. Consequently, Part II starts with the newest medium (the Internet), then looks at the oldest medium (print), and finally more recent media (sound and pictures).

In addition, Chapter 4 has undergone a major revision. The revised chapter has an expanded section examining the effects, economics, political implications, and dysfunctions of social networking sites such as Facebook, Twitter, YouTube, and MySpace. More specifically, the new Chapter 4 discusses, among other topics, the impact of social media on traditional media, the role of social media in the unrest in North Africa and the Middle East, and the problem of cyberbullying.

Here are some of the changes that you will find in individual chapters.

- Part I: Chapter 1 has been streamlined and contains additional discussion of mobile media and tablet computers. Chapter 2 has updated examples of the various media functions and Chapter 3 has an expanded discussion of the cultural impact of the social media.

- Part II: As mentioned above, the reworked Chapter 4 now leads off this section and is titled "The Internet and Social Media" to better reflect the increasing importance of social networks. This chapter now contains a look at the leading companies in the digital field: Apple, Amazon, Google, and Facebook. The newspaper industry is experimenting with new online models to generate revenue, and this development is discussed in Chapter 5 along with an examination of popular apps for newspapers. Speaking of apps, Chapter 6 looks at how magazines are using apps to bring digital versions to tablet computers and how the industry is using social media to increase readership. Chapter 7 now contains a new section on how e-readers are changing the book publishing industry. The Internet has paved the way for hundreds of new radio stations, and Chapter 8 examines the impact of this trend for traditional radio and looks at how radio networks and local stations are using apps to expand their listenership. The sound recording industry has been profoundly changed by the digital revolution. Chapter 9 now contains an expanded discussion of the impact of MP3 players and smartphones on the industry along with an analysis of the changing revenue streams. Chapter 10 has a new discussion of the rise (and potential fall) of 3-D movies and a revised section about how Hollywood relates to the home video industry. Chapter 11 describes how broadcasters have embraced social media and how apps have turned the iPad into a TV set. Chapter 12 describes the explosion of Web-based TV, including an updated analysis of its economic basis.

- Part III: Chapter 13 opens with a discussion of the most recent report on the news media from the Pew Research Center and looks at the newest trends in hyperlocal reporting. Chapter 14 opens with an analysis of the public relations problems for BP as the result of the Gulf oil spill. The chapter also contains an expanded section that considers how PR professionals are using the Web and social media in public relations campaigns. The advertising industry has also welcomed social media, and Chapter 15 illustrates how social media have been incorporated into modern advertising campaigns.
- Part IV: Chapter 16 contains an updated status of legal issues. Chapter 17 now includes a discussion of the ethical issues involved in the *New York Times*'s decision to publish documents it obtained from WikiLeaks.
- Part V: Chapter 18 brings up to date the latest findings from social science research, including a revised section on the impact of violent video games.

Box Score

As in past editions, the boxed inserts in each chapter provide background material or extended coverage of topics mentioned in the text and raise issues for discussion and consideration. The 12th edition includes more than 80 new or revised boxes.

The boxes are grouped into several categories. The Media Talk boxes refer students to the Online Learning Center and introduce important issues in mass communication. Instructors can use these as discussion starters.

The Social Issues boxes highlight matters of social concern that have generated some controversy. Examples include a discussion of how media coverage confers status on fringe groups and a consideration of whether we still need newsmagazines.

As the name suggests, Ethical Issues boxes raise questions about the proper way to act in difficult circumstances. For instance, what ethical problems are involved in "negative" public relations or in posting cell phone videos on video-sharing sites?

Critical/Cultural Issues boxes illustrate how this perspective can be used to further our understanding of mass communication. Examples include the influence of department stores on the development of radio and how the Food Network maintains traditional images of masculinity and femininity.

The Media Probe boxes take an in-depth look at subjects that have significance for the various media. Some examples include an examination of payola, how corporations are supporting rock groups, and the disappearing soap opera.

The Decision Makers boxes profile individuals who have made some of the important decisions that have had an impact on the development of the media. Examples include James Cameron, Tina Brown, and Catherine Hughes.

And, as before, the Soundbytes are brief boxes that highlight some of the strange, ironic, offbeat, and extraordinary developments that occur in the media, such as coffins made of newsprint and George Washington's overdue library books.

Continuity

The organization of the book has changed a bit since the 11th edition. Part I, "The Nature and History of Mass Communication," presents the intellectual context for the rest of the book and is unchanged from the 11th edition. Chapter 1 compares and contrasts mass communication with other types of communication and notes that the distinctions are becoming fuzzier. Chapter 2 introduces two perspectives commonly used to understand and explore the operations of the media: functional analysis and the critical/cultural approach. Chapter 3 takes a macroanalytic approach and traces the general history of media from the invention of printing to the explosion of social media.

Part II, "Media," represents the core of the book. Chapter 4, as noted earlier, is a revised and expanded version of Chapter 12 from the 11th edition, retitled "The Internet and Social Media." Chapters 5–12 then examine each of the traditional media. The organization of each chapter follows a similar pattern. First, there is a brief history from the medium's beginnings to how it is transforming itself in the digital age. This is followed by sections that describe how the medium is becoming more mobile, how it has been affected by user-generated content, and how it is using social media. Next comes a discussion of the defining characteristics of each medium and a description of the industry structure.

I have kept the emphasis on media economics. Since the major media in the United States exist to make a profit, it is valuable for students to appreciate where the money comes from, how it is spent, and why making a profit these days is harder than ever. This is even more important today with several media industries struggling to survive as traditional revenue streams dry up and their online efforts cannot make up the shortfall.

Part III, "Specific Media Professions," examines three specific professions closely associated with the mass media: news reporting, public relations, and advertising. Similar to the approach in Part II, each chapter begins with a brief history, examines the structure of that particular profession, considers the changes brought about by the digital revolution, and discusses key issues in the field.

Part IV, "Regulation of the Mass Media," examines both the formal and informal controls that influence the media. These are complicated areas, and I have tried to make the information as user-friendly as possible.

The concluding Part V, "Impact of the Media," continues to emphasize the social effects of the mass media. As noted earlier, Chapter 18 in the 11th edition, "International and Comparative Media Systems," has been dropped and its key sections distributed to the appropriate chapters.

Once again, I have tried to keep the writing style informal and accessible. Whenever possible, I have chosen examples from popular culture that I hope all students are familiar with. Technical terms are boldfaced and defined in the glossary at the end of the book. The book also contains a number of charts, graphs, diagrams, and tables that I hope aid understanding.

Supporting Materials

Online Learning Center

The Online Learning Center houses the Media Talk video clips, all of the instructor resources (Instructor's Manual, Test Bank, and PowerPoint slides), and the traditional student quiz materials. Access the Online Learning Center at **www.mhhe.com/dominick12e.**

Create

Craft your teaching resources to match the way you teach! With McGraw-Hill Create, you can easily rearrange chapters, combine material from other content sources, and quickly upload content you have written like your course syllabus or teaching notes. Arrange your book to fit your teaching style. Create even allows you to personalize your book's appearance by selecting the cover and adding your name, school, and course information. Order a Create book and you'll receive a complimentary print review copy in 3–5 business days or a complimentary electronic review copy (eComp) via email in about one hour. Go to www.mcgrawhillcreate.com today and register. Experience how McGraw-Hill Create empowers you to teach your students your way.

CourseSmart e-Textbook

This text is available as an eTextbook at www.CourseSmart.com. At CourseSmart your students can take advantage of significant savings off the cost of a print textbook, reduce their impact on the environment, and gain access to powerful Web tools for learning. CourseSmart eTextbooks can be viewed online or downloaded to a computer. The eTextbooks allow students to do full text searches, add highlighting and notes, and share notes with classmates. CourseSmart has the largest selection of eTextbooks available anywhere. Visit www.CourseSmart.com to learn more and to try a sample chapter.

Tegrity

Tegrity Campus is a service that makes class time available all the time by automatically capturing every lecture in a searchable format for students to review when they study and complete assignments. With a simple one-click start and stop process, you capture all computer screens and corresponding audio. Students can replay any part of any class with easy-to-use browser-based viewing on a PC or Mac. Educators know that the more students can see, hear, and experience class resources, the better they learn. With Tegrity Campus, students quickly recall key moments by using Tegrity Campus's unique search feature. This search helps students efficiently find what they need, when they need it, across an entire semester of class recordings. Help turn all your students' study time into learning moments immediately supported by your lecture.

Acknowledgments

Thanks to all of those instructors who used previous editions of *The Dynamics of Mass Communication* and were kind enough to suggest improvements. Several colleagues deserve special mention: Professor Noah Arceneaux provided a boxed insert. Professor Scott Shamp was kind enough to share his blog page, and Professor Michael Castengera's newsletter, "Message from Michael," was a valuable resource. In addition, thanks to researcher Meaghan Dominick for her efforts with the Decision Makers boxes and to Carole Dominick for her efforts as a scrivener.

Once again I appreciate the sedulous efforts of all the reviewers who offered suggestions for the 12th edition:

> Jane Campbell, Columbia State Community College
> Susan J. De Bonis, Georgia Southern University
> Donald G. Godfrey, Walter Cronkite School of Journalism
> Dee Gross, Lorain County Community College
> Susan Katz, University of Bridgeport
> Candice Larson, Moorpark College
> Robert M. Ogles, Purdue University
> Jeff South, Virginia Commonwealth University
> Emily Chivers Yochim, Allegheny College

And, as always, a big thanks to all the people at McGraw-Hill on publishing yet another edition: Vice President Editorial Michael Ryan, Sponsoring Editor Susan

Gouijnstook, Marketing Manager Leslie Oberhuber, Julia Akpan for her comprehensive editorial development, Director of Development Rhona Robbin, Production Editor Holly Irish, Media Project Manager Jennifer Barrick, Photo Researcher David A. Tietz, and Designer Preston Thomas.

The Audience

As most instructors will attest, the introductory course in mass communication attracts two types of students. One type is interested in following a professional career in some form of media (a career path made even more challenging by the current market conditions). This student wants to know the nuts and bolts of the media—how they are organized, how they work, who does what, and what career possibilities are out there. The second type of student will probably never pursue a career in the media but will become a member of the audience and consume a great deal of media content. These students are more interested in analyzing and understanding how the media operate and what impact they have on society. To use an overworked expression, they want to become "media literate."

An original goal of the first edition of *Dynamics* was to present an up-to-date, detailed, and comprehensive look at contemporary media that would benefit aspiring media professionals and at the same time provide a useful foundation for those who will end up in other careers. A second goal was to help both students and faculty understand and appreciate the fast-changing world of mass communication a little better. As has been the case 11 times before, it is hoped that this new edition still fulfills both of those goals.

Joseph R. Dominick
Dacula, Georgia

Your Guided Tour

Media in Transition:
Where we were,
where we are,
where we're going.
Media today change in the blink of an eye, and being tuned into current and emerging media trends is crucial to becoming a savvy media consumer and—increasingly—a media producer as well.

The Dynamics of Mass Communication provides a forward-looking approach while continuing to supply critical information about the foundation on which the current media empires were built.

Chapter Opening

previews identify key goals for each chapter through learning objectives, while timely vignettes set the stage for what's to come.

media talk

Advertisers Gone Wild: New Ways to "Get the Message"

Clip 7: 2 minutes 15 seconds

You can watch Clip 7 on the Online Learning Center home page, www.mhhe.com/dominick12e. Select Student Center *and then* Chapter 2. This clip shows how advertisers are going out of their way to place ads in the strangest places. What functions does advertising serve for society? Why are advertisers resorting to placing ads in unusual places? Where is the oddest place you have seen an advertisement? Do you think advertisements located in odd places are more effective than traditional advertisements (such as billboards, television commercials, newspaper ads)? What types of ads are you least likely to respond to?

WWW

Media Talk

margin notes feature focus questions about the NBC videos found on the Online Learning Center that are pertinent to chapter topics.

Ethical Issues

boxes provide opportunities for critical thinking about ethical issues specific to mass communication industries.

ethical Issues *Naming Names*

There's nothing illegal about reporting the name of a juvenile who has been charged with a crime, but the news media have generally followed a policy of not revealing the suspect's name. The Code of Ethics of the Society of Professional Journalists urges that news media be cautious about naming juvenile suspects. The reasoning behind this policy is that juveniles lack the maturity of adults and often don't realize the consequences of their actions. Identifying youthful suspects may result in stigmatizing them for the rest of their lives. In short, the media give the juvenile a chance to go straight without carrying the baggage associated with an arrest.

Recently, however, there has been a trend toward naming juveniles, particularly if they have been involved in serious crimes. The decision to publish or not publish the name varies from newsroom to newsroom and illustrates an ethical philosophy called *situational ethics*. Situational ethics suggests that each individual problem or situation is unique and calls for a unique solution. There is no universal ethical principle that yields an unswerving path of action. For example, some media outlets will name

the juvenile suspect if he or she has been charged as an adult. Others will take the age of the person arrested into consideration. They may report the names of 16- or 17-year-olds but refrain from identifying younger individuals. Still others look at the severity of the crime; the more severe, the more likely they are to reveal the name of the suspect. The problem with this approach is that it sometimes leads to inconsistent results. A teen in one story may be named while a teen in another story is not identified.

The most extreme position argues that the name of anybody arrested for a crime should be reported. Not naming the suspect leaves a hole in the story. Somebody committed a crime. Somebody was arrested. Who? It makes no difference to the person whose car was carjacked if it was taken by a teen or an adult. The car is still gone. Suspects have the entire criminal justice system protecting them while the victims have no one to advocate for them. Finally, the proponents of this position argue that naming juvenile offenders might even encourage them to go straight and prevent future crimes.

Social Issues

boxes explore new developments in how mass media operate in a social context.

social
issues   *Do We Need the Public Broadcasting Service?*

The debate about PBS has been going on since the growth of cable television in the 1980s and 1990s. Many of the new channels featured content that was previously the province of PBS. The History Channel, the Discovery Channel, Animal Planet, Nickelodeon, the Hallmark Channel, and others fragmented the audience for PBS programs. PBS ratings have been declining (along with the ratings of many other networks) for the past decade. From 2000 to 2010, PBS's ratings dropped 37 percent.

What should be the role of PBS in a 500-channel television universe? A mission statement adopted by PBS stations in 2004 says in part that "public television is more essential than ever in the cluttered media landscape." It goes on to point out that in an age of conglomerate media ownership, PBS stations may be the only locally owned stations in the community and are better suited to responding to local needs. The document goes on to state:

Public television . . . strives for impact and measures its success by the extent of its ability to educate and inform, to enlighten and entertain. In short, public television strives to:

- *Challenge the American mind.*
- *Inspire the American spirit.*
- *Preserve the American memory.*
- *Enhance the American dialogue.*
- *Promote global understanding.*

Those are lofty goals. Does the programming on PBS stations fulfill them? Critics suggest that PBS programs have grown musty with age. *Nova*, *Masterpiece*, and *NewsHour* have all been on the air for 30 to 40 years. The American version of *Antiques Roadshow* has been around for

more than a decade. (The U.S. program was based on a British series that premiered in 1979.) Typical prime-time programming includes reruns of old British sitcoms such as *Keeping Up Appearances* and *Are You Being Served?* Critics also suggest looking at the schedule of the local PBS affiliate. How much local programming is aired during the typical week?

The programmers at PBS, however, face a dilemma. If their shows venture too far away from mainstream, such as programs that examine gay and lesbian lifestyles or global warming, PBS is criticized as being too liberal. If their shows stick with the familiar, they are branded as obsolete or redundant with those of the commercial networks.

A second issue concerns the drift of public television toward its commercial counterparts. That 2004 mission statement proclaims the goal of commercial television is to attract as many viewers as possible and expose them to advertising but suggests that PBS is different. In the past decade, however, PBS has opened up its programs to an expanded program of underwriting, whereby a sponsor donates money to a station or PBS in return for a 30-second message at the beginning of the program. Many of these messages look exactly like ads playing on commercial TV. In addition, underwriters would rather reach a large audience than a small one. This means that public TV, if it wants to continue to attract underwriting revenue, will try to air programs that attract a large audience, much like commercial TV.

The transition to digital makes the questions about the role of PBS even more complicated. Does PBS really need a Facebook fan page or a YouTube channel? Check out the PBS Twitter feed. Does it fulfill the goals of the mission statement? This is a debate not likely to end soon.

decision
makers   *Judy McGrath*

For many of you reading this, Judy McGrath would seem to have the ultimate dream job: As president of the MTV Networks Music Group, she was responsible for MTV, MTV2, VH1, CMT, and all of the company's digital media services. Under her direction MTV has grown from a small niche cable network to an international brand that symbolizes a unique attitude and lifestyle.

Always a music fan, McGrath first tried to get a job writing for *Rolling Stone*. When her efforts proved unsuccessful, she turned to writing advertising copy and then went to work for *Mademoiselle* and *Glamour*. In 1981 she heard about a new cable channel launched by Warner Entertainment that would be devoted to rock music. Despite the fact that she could not even get the channel on her home TV, McGrath joined the newly created MTV as a copywriter and on-air promotion person. (She was one of the ones responsible for using all the space film footage to promote the channel.) To the surprise of many people, MTV was successful in attracting 16- to 24-year-olds, an audience coveted by advertisers. MTV became part of the huge Viacom

conglomerate, and McGrath quickly moved up the ranks to creative director, executive vice president, and eventually chair and chief executive at MTV Networks. Under her direction MTV expanded all over the world.

When the music video novelty began to wear off in the mid-1980s and ratings started to sag, McGrath introduced programs that became popular culture icons: *Beavis and Butt-Head*, *The Real World*, *The MTV Music Awards*, *MTV Unplugged*, and *Total Request Live*. She also introduced political coverage to MTV and was instrumental in the development of the 1992 *Choose or Lose* get-out-the-vote campaign. More recently, McGrath has led MTV into other media: movies, books, and the Internet.

What does she see in MTV's future? Since a high proportion of MTV viewers are also Web surfers and spend a good deal of time on MTV.com, look for more integration of the music on MTV and MTV2 with the Web site. MTV.com will be used to highlight some of the artists or genres featured on the cable channels. In addition, plans are under way for more international expansion, particularly in Asia. Her plans will have to be carried out by someone else. McGrath stepped down from her position in 2011.

Decision Makers

boxes profile people who have had a significant impact on contemporary mass media.

media *Probe*
Getting into College Thanks to Reality TV

Who could guess that all of those hours teens spend watching reality TV shows such as *Jersey Shore, Teen Mom, Project Runway,* and *Keeping Up with the Kardashians* could actually help them get into college?

All college students are familiar with the Scholastic Aptitude Test (SAT) that many colleges use as a tool in deciding admissions. The essay portion of one version of the 2011 SAT asked high schoolers to compose an essay about reality TV. Part of the actual assignment: *Do people benefit from forms of entertainment that show so-called reality, or are such forms of entertainment harmful?"*

Many SAT takers and their parents complained that they were at a disadvantage because the question assumes that students (1) watch TV and (2) watch enough reality TV to provide a meaningful response to the question. One father noted that he was proud that his child studied too much to watch TV and thought the question was unfair. A teen who took the test complained that kids who watched "crap TV" probably did better than he did.

SAT officials defended the question, arguing that the explanatory statement that preceded it *(These shows depict ordinary people competing in everything from singing and dancing to losing weight, or just living their everyday lives.)* should have been enough for students to write the essay. Or as one executive from the College Board put it: "Questions raised about a recent SAT essay [assignment] miss [the] basic point and confuse the literal topic with the task of writing the essay. If presented with a topic about balancing the risk of climbing a mountain with the reward of reaching the summit, for example, a good writer could compose a strong essay without ever having reached the summit of Mount Everest." Well, maybe, but it would certainly help if the good writer actually saw a mountain before assessing the risks of climbing one.

Some students who did not watch reality TV had to stretch in order to compose their essay. One wrote about 19th-century social critic Jacob Riis and the absence of an objective reality. That's a long way from Snooki and The Situation.

critical cultural *Issues*

Cultural Meaning and Trade Characters

Tony the Tiger, Mr. Clean, the Maytag repairman, Ronald McDonald, the Jolly Green Giant, Betty Crocker, the Keebler Elves—these are examples of trade characters, fictional beings, played by actors or animated, created to help sell a product, service, or idea. Like slogans, trade characters are popular because they are an effective way of linking the product and its advertising so that consumers can easily remember the message. But trade characters do more than slogans; they give a product personality, style, and depth by creating an image with a clear cultural meaning with which the audience can identify.

An article by Barbara Phillips in a 1996 issue of the *Journal of Popular Culture* examines the role of trade characters in American culture. Phillips notes that mass-produced products have little cultural meaning. A Duracell battery is hard to distinguish from an Eveready battery, and neither is likely to arouse any emotional response. Trade characters, however, give meaning and significance to otherwise indistinguishable products by linking a product to an image that has a cultural meaning. One way that trade characters create this meaning is by employing commonly accepted mythical symbols—images that convey cultural meaning. Take the Jolly Green Giant, for example. The giant is a common mythical figure whose size connotes strength, power, and authority. His green color is associated with freshness, while his hearty "ho-ho-ho" imparts warmth and humor. The giant's image on a can of peas makes the product less remote and more friendly.

Created by the Leo Burnett Agency, the Jolly Green Giant has been ho-ho-ho-ing for more than 50 years.

The use of mythical symbols gives trade characters another quality: They communicate messages without having to state them explicitly. Mr. Clean, for example, immaculate in his all-white costume, symbolizes cleanliness and purity. His image suggests that using his product will produce these results, but he never actually says so. In contrast, an ad that proclaims, "Our cleaner will leave your countertop spotless and pure," might be met with some degree of doubt. Since trade characters do not directly state that a product has specific attributes, their "claims" are less likely to be rejected.

There are, of course, some drawbacks to the use of trade characters. Cultural meanings shift over time, and advertisers must be careful to monitor changing attitudes in society. Perhaps the best example of this potential is Aunt Jemima. The Quaker Oats Company started using this trade character in 1889. Over the years, however, the image became an unacceptable stereotype. In 1968, during the civil rights movement, her image changed: She lost 100 pounds and became younger; her red bandana was replaced by a headband. In 1990 she was made over again into an image that was the black equivalent of Betty Crocker, an image the company hoped was more positive. Some trade characters may be entirely inappropriate. Joe Camel, for example, was the subject of much criticism because the cartoon character seemed designed to encourage children to smoke. Camel eventually phased him out.

Trade characters have become an established part of American culture. Their ranks will undoubtedly increase in the future.

Media Probe boxes provide more in-depth information, illustrations, examples, and background to specific issues raised within each chapter.

Critical/Cultural Issues boxes illustrate this approach to mass communication across a broad range of topics.

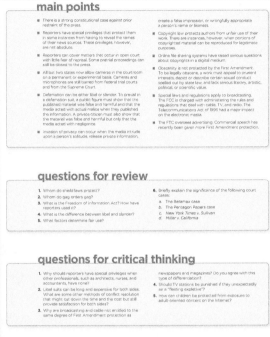

main points

- There is a strong constitutional case against prior restraint of the press.

- Reporters have special privileges that protect them in some instances from having to reveal the names of their news sources. These privileges, however, are not absolute.

- Reporters can cover matters that occur in open court with little fear of reprisal. Some pretrial proceedings can still be closed to the press.

- All but two states now allow cameras in the courtroom on a permanent or experimental basis. Cameras and microphones are still barred from federal trial courts and from the Supreme Court.

- Defamation can be either libel or slander. To prevail in a defamation suit, a public figure must show that the published material was false and harmful and that the media acted with actual malice when they published the information. A private citizen must also show that the material was false and harmful but only that the media acted with negligence.

- Invasion of privacy can occur when the media intrude upon a person's solitude, release private information,

create a false impression, or wrongfully appropriate a person's name or likeness.

- Copyright law protects authors from unfair use of their work. There are instances, however, when portions of copyrighted material can be reproduced for legitimate purposes.

- Online file-sharing systems have raised serious questions about copyrights in a digital medium.

- Obscenity is not protected by the First Amendment. To be legally obscene, a work must appeal to prurient interests, depict or describe certain sexual conduct spelled out by state law, and lack serious literary, artistic, political, or scientific value.

- Special laws and regulations apply to broadcasting. The FCC is charged with administering the rules and regulations that deal with cable, TV, and radio. The Telecommunications Act of 1996 had a major impact on the electronic media.

- The FTC oversees advertising. Commercial speech has recently been given more First Amendment protection.

key terms

First Amendment (p. 376)	defamation (p. 386)	Equal Opportunities Rule (p. 400)
prior restraint (p. 376)	libel (p. 386)	Fairness Doctrine (p. 401)
injunction (p. 376)	slander (p. 386)	franchises (p. 402)
shield laws (p. 380)	libel per se (p. 386)	Telecommunications Act of 1996 (p. 403)
gag rules (p. 383)	libel per quod (p. 386)	V-chip (p. 403)
Freedom of Information Act (FOIA) (p. 385)	trespass (p. 393)	consent order (p. 403)
USA Patriot Act (p. 385)	Hicklin Rule (p. 396)	cease-and-desist order (p. 403)
	Internet neutrality (p. 399)	

questions for review

1. Whom do shield laws protect?
2. Whom do gag orders gag?
3. What is the Freedom of Information Act? How have reporters used it?
4. What is the difference between libel and slander?
5. What factors determine fair use?

6. Briefly explain the significance of the following court cases:
   a. The Betamax case
   b. The Pentagon Papers case
   c. New York Times v. Sullivan
   d. Miller v. California

questions for critical thinking

1. Why should reporters have special privileges when other professionals, such as architects, nurses, and accountants, have none?
2. Libel suits can be long and expensive for both sides. What are some other methods of conflict resolution that might cut down the time and the cost but still provide satisfaction for both sides?
3. Why are broadcasting and cable not entitled to the same degree of First Amendment protection as

newspapers and magazines? Do you agree with this type of differentiation?

4. Should TV stations be punished if they unexpectedly air a "fleeting expletive"?
5. How can children be protected from exposure to adult-oriented content on the Internet?

internet resources

Online Learning Center

On the Online Learning Center home page, www.mhhe.com/dominick12e, select Student Center and then Chapter 16.

1. Use the Learning Objectives, Chapter Outline, and Main Points sections to review this chapter.
2. Test your knowledge of the chapter using the multiple choice and flashcard features of the site.
3. Expand your knowledge of concepts and topics discussed in the chapter with additional Questions for Critical Thinking and Internet Exercises.

surfing the internet

Many Web sites deal with legal matters. The ones listed here seem most helpful for students.

www.fcc.gov
The FCC's home page. Contains an archive of recent speeches, a search engine, and consumer information, along with more technical data.

www.freedomforum.org
Contains a summary of recent First Amendment court decisions, relevant law articles, a First Amendment time line, and the full text of relevant Supreme Court rulings.

www.rcfp.org
The Reporters Committee for Freedom of the Press maintains this site, which contains recent court decisions, legal news, and a link to its publication, The News Media and the Law.

www.rtnda.org
Home page of the Radio and Television News Directors Association. Contains information about covering the courts, libel, copyright, and other legal issues.

End of Chapter

review materials provide essential study aids, including clear, concise chapter summaries, review and critical thinking questions, key terms lists, and Internet resources.

Online Learning Center: www.mhhe.com/dominick12e

This book-specific Web site features practice tests, learning objectives, chapter main points, key terms, additional Questions for Critical Thinking, and an online glossary. For the instructor, the password-protected area of the Web site offers a teaching guide, detailed chapter summaries, and PowerPoint slides.

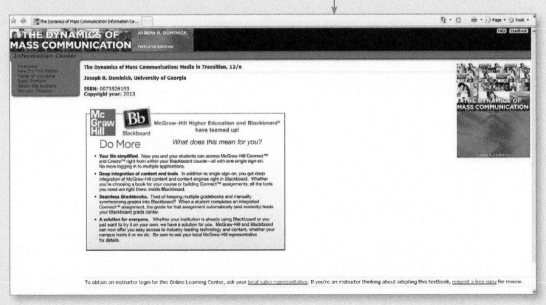

The Nature and History of Mass Communication

Part I

The Nature and History of Mass Communication

The marriage of Prince William and Kate Middleton, watched by more than a billion people, is a clear example of mass communication.

Chapter**1**

communication:
mass and other
forms

This chapter will prepare you to:

- recognize the elements of the communication process
- understand the different types of communication settings
- identify the function of gatekeepers
- describe how the Internet has changed mass communication
- explain the various types of mass media convergence
- understand the technological, economic, and social forces that are transforming mass media

This is a book about mass communication. Great, you might say, but what's mass communication? Well, that question is getting more difficult to answer all the time. Consider the following:

- More than a billion people watched on television as Prince William married Kate Middleton in 2011. In the United States, about 23 million people got up before dawn to watch the ceremony, carried by 11 U.S. TV networks. Across the globe, another few hundred million watched it via online streaming over the Internet.

- A teenage girl sends an average of 100 text messages per day.

- *Avatar*, a 2009 film directed by James Cameron, took more than four years to produce, including about a year for a University of Southern California professor to invent a new language spoken by the Na'vi characters in the film. *Avatar* cost around $300 million to produce and at least another $100 million to market. As of 2011, more than 130 million people had seen the film, which has grossed more than $2 billion worldwide at the box office.

- As of 2010, there were more than 150 million blogs on the Internet.

- Rebecca Black is an American teenager whose mother paid a record label a few thousand dollars to produce a music video of Rebecca singing a catchy tune called "Friday." The video was posted on YouTube and as of mid-2011 had received more than 146 million views. (Of the 3.2 million people who rated it on

YouTube, about 90 percent disliked it. Nonetheless, the song made it onto *Billboard* magazine's Hot 100 chart, peaking at number 58.)

■ Facebook reports its members post more than 60 million status updates per day.

■ Google (the owner of YouTube) is an American company that receives about 95 percent of its revenue from advertising. Much of that revenue comes from the sponsored links that pop up next to the results of a Google search. (Precise numbers are hard to come by, but Google reports that it handles more than a billion searches a day.)

■ In 2010, some 124 million Skype users spent 88.4 billion minutes on Skype-to-Skype phone calls.

■ An unsuspecting information specialist in Pakistan unknowingly reported about the raid that killed Osama Bin Laden over his Twitter account. The first credible confirmation of Bin Laden's death came from the chief of staff of former Defense Secretary Donald Rumsfeld, who broke the news via Twitter about 20 minutes before it was reported by the major news networks and an hour before President Obama confirmed it. In the minutes after the networks announced Bin Laden's death, Twitter recorded as many as 5,000 tweets per second.

■ Live Messenger, Windows instant message service, has more than 300 million active users a month and carries billions of messages every day.

Some of these examples would probably fit anybody's conception of mass communication: the billion people who watched the royal wedding, the 130 million who saw *Avatar,* Rebecca Black's video. In contrast, some of these examples would seem to fall outside a common-sense definition of mass communication: the teenage girl with her text messages, the Skype phone calls, an instant message. But what about all those blogs, or Facebook status updates, or the ad on a Google search page, or the news events that break on Twitter? Mass communication or something else?

We'll try to answer those questions, but first we need to back up and look at the basic process of how humans communicate. This examination will help us clarify the differences between mass and other forms of communication.

the communication process

Figure 1-1 depicts the communication process. We will refer to this figure as we examine the process more fully.

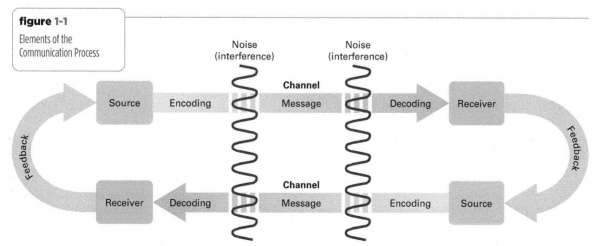

figure 1-1

Elements of the Communication Process

media Probe   *Sniff This*

Conventional advertising relies on sight and sound channels. We use our eyes and ears—we read the text, hear the announcer, and see the images. But now advertisers are zeroing in on the nose.

Perfumes, naturally enough, rely most heavily on the olfactory channel. In the past whenever a reader opened a magazine such as *Allure*, he or she might be hit with a blast of fragrances. New technology has minimized this problem as magazines now embed scent strips on their ad pages. A reader has to scratch the strip to unleash the scent.

Scent strips are not confined to magazines. Kraft, the maker of DiGiorno pizzas, handed out scent strips in supermarkets so shoppers could get a whiff of its new garlic bread pizza. Avon encases scent strips in its product catalogue.

Premium movie channel Showtime caused a "scentsation" with a promotional campaign for its series "Weeds," which features a drug-dealing soccer mom. Showtime added scent strips that smelled of marijuana to its magazine ads. Not everybody was pleased with that.

Encoding: Transmitting the Message

To begin with, the **source** initiates the process by having a thought or an idea that he or she wishes to transmit to some other entity. Naturally, sources differ in their communication skills ("Garçon, I will have the Boeuf Haché Grillé au Charbon de Bois" versus "Gimmea-burger"). The source may or may not have knowledge about the receiver of the message. Sources can be single individuals, groups, or even organizations.

Encoding refers to the activities that a source goes through to translate thoughts and ideas into a form that may be perceived by the senses. When you have something to say, your brain and your tongue work together (usually) to form words and spoken sentences. Encoding in a communication setting can take place one or more times. In a face-to-face conversation, the speaker encodes thoughts into words. Over the telephone, this phase is repeated, but the phone subsequently encodes sound waves into electrical energy.

The **message** is the actual physical product that the source encodes. When you talk, your speech is the message. When you write a letter home, what you put on the paper is the message. When a television network presents *The Voice* or *American Idol*, the programs are the message. Human beings usually have a large number of messages at their disposal that they choose to send, ranging from the simple but effective "No!" to something as complicated as Darwin's *On the Origin of Species*. Messages can be directed at one specific individual ("Dude!") or at millions (*People* magazine). Messages can be cheap to produce (the spoken word) or very expensive (this book). Some messages are more under the control of the receiver than others. For example, think about how hard or easy it is for you to break off communication (1) in a face-to-face conversation with another person, (2) during a telephone call, and (3) while watching a TV commercial.

Channels are the ways the message travels to the receiver. Sound waves carry spoken words; light waves carry visual messages. Air currents can serve as olfactory channels, carrying messages to our noses—messages that are subtle but nonetheless significant. Touch is also a channel (such as braille). Some messages use more than one channel to travel to the receiver. For example, radio signals travel by electromagnetic radiation until they are transformed by receiving sets into sound waves that travel through the air to our ears.

Decoding: Receiving the Message

The **decoding** process is the opposite of the encoding process. It consists of activities that translate or interpret physical messages into a form that has eventual meaning for a receiver. As you read these lines, you are decoding a message. If you are playing the radio while decoding these lines, you are decoding two messages simultaneously—one aural, one visual. Both humans and machines can be thought of as decoders. The radio is a decoder; so is a DVD playback unit; so is the telephone (one end encodes and the other end decodes); so is a film projector.

What we said earlier about encoding also applies to decoding: Some people are better at it than others. Many of you will not be able to decode "¿Dónde está el baño?"; others will. Some people are able to read 1,500 words a minute; others struggle along at 200.

The **receiver** is the target of the message—its ultimate goal. The receiver can be a single person, a group, an institution, or even a large, anonymous collection of people. The receivers of the message can be determined by the source, as in a telephone call, or they can self-select themselves into the audience, as with the audience for a TV show. It should also be clear that in some situations the source and receiver can be in each other's immediate presence, while in other situations they can be separated by both space and time.

Feedback

Now let us examine the bottom half of Figure 1-1. This portion of the figure represents the potential for **feedback** to occur. Feedback refers to those responses of the receiver that shape and alter the subsequent messages of the source. Feedback represents a reversal of the flow of communication. The original source becomes the receiver; the original receiver becomes the new source. Feedback is useful to the source because it allows the source to answer the question "How am I doing?" Feedback is important to the receiver because it allows the receiver to attempt to change some element in the communication process. Communication scholars have traditionally identified two different kinds of feedback—positive and negative. In general terms, positive feedback from the receiver usually encourages the communication behavior in progress; negative feedback usually attempts to change the communication or even to terminate it.

Feedback can be immediate or delayed. Immediate feedback occurs when the reactions of the receiver are directly perceived by the source. A speech maker who hears the audience boo and hiss while he or she is talking is getting immediate feedback. On the other hand, it might take weeks to determine the effectiveness of a multimillion-dollar advertising campaign.

Noise

The final factor we will consider is **noise.** Communication scholars define *noise* as anything that interferes with the delivery of the message. A little noise might pass unnoticed, while too much noise might prevent the message from reaching its destination. There are at least three different types of noise: semantic, mechanical, and environmental.

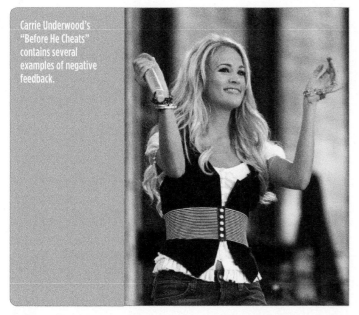

Carrie Underwood's "Before He Cheats" contains several examples of negative feedback.

Semantic noise occurs when different people have different meanings for different words and phrases or when the arrangement of words confuses the meaning. If you ask a New Yorker for a "soda" and expect to receive something that has ice cream in it, you'll be disappointed. The New Yorker will give you a bottle of what is called "pop" in the Midwest. An article in a college newspaper included the following: "A panel of representatives from the sports world met to discuss performance-enhancing drug use at the Journalism School last night."

Noise can also be mechanical. This type of noise occurs when there is a problem with a machine that is being used to assist communication. A TV set with a pixillated picture, a pen running out of ink, and a static-filled radio are all examples of mechanical noise.

media Probe   *Communication Gone Awry*

Communication between people is a fragile thing. Sometimes things go wrong. Examples:

- A prankster reprogrammed a digital video billboard on a main road in the heart of Moscow to show a two-minute clip from a pornographic movie. The result: a miles-long traffic jam.

- Customers using HTC Smartphones were surprised to receive text messages from the future. An apparent software bug dated all messages from the year 2016.

- A customer called a local pastry shop and ordered a cake for a going-away party. The customer said, "Please write on the cake 'Best Wishes Suzanne' and underneath that 'We Will Miss You.'"

  When the customer picked up the cake, it read:
  Best Wishes Suzanne
  And Underneath That
  We Will Miss You

- The Government Printing Office mistakenly posted on its Web site a confidential 266-page report that included maps showing the precise locations of stockpiles of fuel for nuclear weapons.

- In early 2011, a computer malfunction in a bank's ATM in Sydney, Australia, allowed customers to withdraw hundreds of dollars more than they had in their accounts. News of the free money spread on Twitter and soon some ATMs had lines with 30 to 40 people waiting to take advantage of the glitch. (Bank executives reminded customers that they could look at withdrawal records to identify those who fraudulently withdrew cash.)

- Chef Wolfgang Puck's restaurants are pricey, but imagine the surprise of a Texas man when he got a Visa credit card statement indicating that he spent more than $23 quadrillion on a meal at one of Puck's eateries. Another man in New Hampshire was also charged $23 quadrillion after buying a pack of cigarettes at a gas station. A spokesperson for Visa said the charges were caused by, you guessed it, a technical glitch.

- On the other hand, nearly 10,000 residents of Ohio got a notice from the state tax department that they were due a tax refund of $200 million. The letter stated that the amount of the refund was too large to be paid by direct deposit so they would be sent a check. Once again, a software problem caused the mega-overpayment.

- In South Carolina, one of those electronic message boards that usually flash messages about traffic delays was reprogrammed to read "Zombies Ahead."

A third form of noise can be called environmental. This type refers to sources of noise that are external to the communication process but that nonetheless interfere with it. Some environmental noise might be out of the communicator's control—the noise at a restaurant, for example, where the communicator is trying to hold a conversation. Some environmental noise might be introduced by the source or the receiver; for example, you might try to talk to somebody who keeps drumming her or his fingers on the table.

As noise increases, message fidelity (how closely the message that is sent resembles the message that is received) goes down. Clearly, feedback is important in reducing the effects of noise. The greater the potential for immediate feedback—that is, the more interplay between source and receiver—the greater the chance that noise will be overcome.

communication settings

Interpersonal Communication

Having considered the key elements in the communication process, we next examine three common communication settings, or situations, and explore how these elements vary from setting to setting. The first and perhaps the most common situation is **interpersonal communication,** in which one person (or group) is interacting with another

sound byte

Beware Autocorrect

Machine-assisted communication works great—unless the machine screws up. Many smartphones and other devices have an autocorrect function where the machine corrects spelling errors and predicts intended words before they are fully typed. If a person doesn't proofread his or her messages, confusion can result. Here are a few examples taken from Damnyouautocorrect.com:

Intended message: "I'm going to be in the poor house."

Sent message: "I'm going to be in the outhouse."

Intended message: "I just found out I made the varsity cross country team."

Sent message: "I just found out I made the varsity cross dressing team."

Intended message: "I have to meet for a group project now."

Sent message: "I have to meet for a groin project now."

person (or group) without the aid of a mechanical device. The source and receiver in this form of communication are within each other's physical presence. Talking to your roommate, participating in a class discussion, and conversing with your professor after class are all examples of interpersonal communication.

The source in this communication setting can be one or more individuals, as can the receiver. Encoding is usually a one-step process as the source transforms thoughts into speech and/or gestures. A variety of channels are available for use. The receiver can see, hear, and perhaps even smell and touch the source. Messages are relatively difficult for the receiver to terminate and are produced at little expense. In addition, interpersonal messages can be private ("Whassup?") or public (a proclamation that the end of the world is near from a person standing on a street corner). Messages can also be pinpointed to their specific targets. For example, you might ask the following of your English professor: "Excuse me, Dr. Iamb, but I was wondering if you had finished perusing my term paper?" The very same message directed at your roommate might be put another way: "Hey, Space Cadet! Aren't you done with my paper yet?" Decoding is also a one-step process performed by those receivers who can perceive the message. Feedback is immediate and makes use of visual and auditory channels. Noise can be either semantic or environmental. Interpersonal communication is far from simple, but it represents the least complicated setting.

Machine-Assisted Interpersonal Communication

Machine-assisted interpersonal communication (or technology-assisted communication) combines characteristics of both the interpersonal and mass communication situations. The growth of the Internet and the World Wide Web has further blurred the boundaries between these two types of communication. This section focuses on those situations that are closer to the interpersonal setting. The next section examines how the computer and the Internet have redefined many of the features of mass communication.

In the machine-assisted setting, one or more people are communicating by means of a mechanical device (or devices) with one or more receivers. One of the important characteristics of machine-assisted interpersonal communication is that it allows the source and receiver to be separated by both time and space. The machine can give a message permanence by storing it on paper, disk, or some other material. The machine can also extend the range of the message by amplifying it and/or transmitting it over large distances. The telephone, for example, allows two people to converse even though they are hundreds,

Microsoft's Bill Gates uses machine-assisted communication to get his point across at the annual meeting of the World Economic Forum. (Raymond Reuter/Sygma/Getty Images)

even thousands, of miles apart. A letter can be reread several years after it was written and communicate anew.

The source in the machine-assisted setting can be a single person or a group of people who may know the receiver or not have firsthand knowledge of the receiver.

Encoding in this setting can be complicated or simple, but there must be at least two distinct stages. The first occurs when the source translates his or her thoughts into words or symbols. The second occurs when one or more machines encode the message for transmission or storage. When you speak on the telephone, for example, you choose and pronounce your words (stage 1), and a machine converts them into electrical impulses (stage 2).

Channels are more restricted in the machine-assisted setting. Whereas interpersonal communication can make use of several channels simultaneously, machine-assisted settings generally rely on only one or two. E-mail, for instance, relies on sight; a phone call uses electrical energy and sound waves.

Messages vary widely in machine-assisted communication. They can be tailor-made for the receiver (such as e-mail) or limited to a small number of predetermined messages that cannot be altered once they are encoded. Messages in this setting can be private or public and relatively cheap to produce.

Decoding can go through one or more stages, similar to the encoding process. Reading a letter requires only one stage, but reading a text message requires two: one for the phone to decode electrical energy into patterns of light and dark, and another for your eyes to decode the written symbols.

The receiver in this setting can be a single person, a small group, or a large group. Receivers can be in sight of the source or out of view. They can be selected by the source (as with a Skype phone call) or self-select themselves into the audience (as when taking a pamphlet from somebody on the street).

Feedback can be immediate or delayed. A band playing at a concert will hear the audience applaud following a song. A band that provides streaming audio of a new song on its Web site might have to wait for days to see if people liked it. In many situations feedback is limited to one channel, as in a phone conversation. In some situations feedback can be difficult if not impossible. If the automatic teller gives you a message that says, "Insufficient funds," you cannot tell it, "I just made a deposit this morning. Look it up."

Noise in the machine-assisted setting can be semantic and environmental as in interpersonal communication, but it can also be mechanical. Interference with the message might be due in part to difficulties with the machine involved.

In the future, machine-assisted communication will become more important. Mobile media, such as cell phones and laptop and tablet computers, will become more and more popular and continue to expand the scope and impact of personal communication (see Chapter 3). The Internet may come to function more as an aid to interpersonal communication than as a mass medium (see Chapter 4). Finally, the differences between machine-assisted communication and mass communication will continue to blur. All of these trends will hasten the transition of traditional mass media into new forms of communication channels.

Mass Communication

The third major communication setting is the one that we will be most interested in. The differences between machine-assisted interpersonal communication and mass communication are not that clear. Here is a traditional definition: **Mass communication** refers to the process by which a complex organization with the aid of one or more machines produces and transmits public messages that are directed at large, heterogeneous, and scattered audiences. There are, of course, situations that will fall into a gray area. How large does the audience have to be? How scattered? How heterogeneous? How complex must the organization be? For example, suppose a billboard is constructed on a busy street in a small town. Obviously, this would qualify as

sound byte

Punctuation Matters

From the cover of *Tails* magazine: "Rachel Ray finds inspiration in cooking her family and her dog."

machine-assisted communication (a machine was used to print the billboard), but is this better defined as mass communication? An automatic letter-writing device can write thousands of similar letters. Is this mass communication? There are no correct answers to these questions. The dividing line between machine-assisted interpersonal communication and mass communication is not a distinct one.

The line is even less distinct when the Internet and the Web are considered. Take an e-mail message, for example. It can be addressed to one person, much like machine-assisted interpersonal communication, or it can go to thousands, a situation closer to mass communication. Or take the case of a post on Facebook that might be seen by tens of thousands or only by a few friends, depending on privacy settings. The first case resembles mass communication; the second is more like machine-assisted interpersonal communication. In both cases, feedback is limited, a feature of mass communication, since the usual clues of tone of voice, gestures, and personal appearance are not present.

Source   Until the advent of the Internet and the Web, the source in the traditional mass communication situation was typically a group of individuals who acted in predetermined roles in an organizational setting. In other words, mass communication was the end product of more than one person's efforts. For example, think about how a newspaper is put together. Reporters gather news; writers draft editorials; a cartoonist draws an editorial cartoon; the advertising department lays out ads; editors lay out all these elements on a sample page; technicians transfer this page to a master; other technicians print the final paper; the finished copies are given to the delivery staff; and, of course, behind all this is a publisher who has the money to pay for a building, presses, staff, trucks, paper, ink, and so on. This institutional nature of mass communication has several consequences that we will consider later in this book.

The advent of Internet-based mass communication changes this situation. Thanks to the World Wide Web, one person can become a mass communicator. The implications of this change are discussed further in Chapter 4.

For both traditional and Internet-based mass communication, the source usually has little detailed information about its particular audience. The author of a blog has little detailed information about individuals who visit the site. Traditional mass media may have collective data, but these are typically expressed as gross audience characteristics.

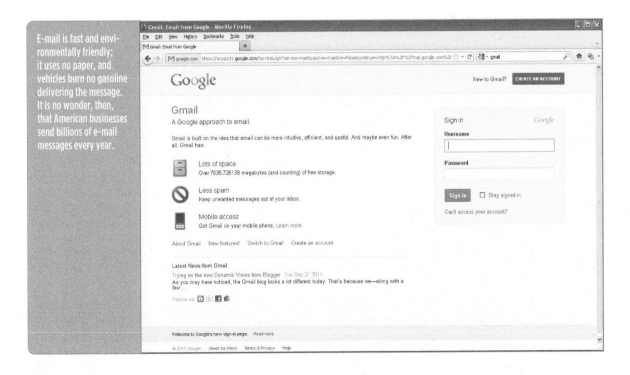

E-mail is fast and environmentally friendly; it uses no paper, and vehicles burn no gasoline delivering the message. It is no wonder, then, that American businesses send billions of e-mail messages every year.

The newspaper editor, for example, may know that 40 percent of the readers are between 25 and 40 years old and that 30 percent earn between $20,000 and $50,000, but the editor has no idea about the individual tastes, preferences, quirks, or identities of these people. They are an anonymous group, known only by summary statistics.

Encoding/Sending Encoding in mass communication is always a multistage process. Suppose a film producer has an idea. He or she explains it to a screenwriter. The writer goes off and produces a script. The script goes to a director, who translates it for the camera. Cinematographers capture the scenes on film. The raw film goes to an editor, who splices together the final version. The film is copied and sent to theaters, where a projector displays it on the screen, where the audience watches it. How many examples of encoding can you find in that oversimplified version of moviemaking?

Mass communication channels are characterized by the imposition of at least one, and usually more than one, machine in the process of sending the message. These machines translate the message from one channel to another. Television makes use of complicated devices that transform light energy into electrical energy and back again. Radio does the same with sound energy. Unlike interpersonal communication, in which many channels are available, mass communication is usually restricted to one or two.

Decoding/Receiving Messages in mass communication are public. Anyone who can afford the cost of a newspaper or a movie ticket or a TV set can receive the message. Additionally, the same message is sent to all receivers. In a sense, mass communication is addressed "to whom it may concern." Of all the various settings, message termination is easiest in mass communication. The TV set goes dark at the flick of a switch; an automatic timer can turn off the radio; the newspaper is quickly put aside. There is little the source can do to prevent these sudden terminations other than bullying the audience ("Don't touch that dial!") or trying to stay interesting at all times ("We'll be back after these important messages").

Mass communication typically involves multiple decoding before the message is received. The radio decodes patterns of electromagnetic radiation into sound waves for our hearing mechanism. The TV receiver decodes both sight and sound transmissions.

Receiver One of the prime distinguishing characteristics of mass communication is the audience. First, the mass communication audience is a large one, sometimes numbering in the millions of people. Second, the audience is also heterogeneous; that is, it is made up of dissimilar groups who may differ in age, intelligence, political beliefs, ethnic backgrounds, and so on. Even in situations where the mass communication audience is well defined, heterogeneity is still present. (For example, consider the publication *Turkey Grower's Monthly*. At first glance, the audience for this publication might appear to be rather homogeneous, but upon closer examination we might discover that members differ in intelligence, social class, income, age, political party, education, place of residence, and so on.) Third, the audience is spread out over a wide geographic area; source and receiver are not in each other's immediate physical presence. The large size of the audience and its geographic separation both contribute to a fourth distinguishing factor: The audience members are anonymous to one another. The person watching the *CBS Evening News* is unaware of the several million others in the audience. Lastly, in keeping with the idea of a public message, the audience in mass communication is self-defined. The receiver chooses which film to see, which paper to read, which Web site to visit, and which program to watch. If the receiver chooses not to attend to the message, the message is not received. Consequently, the various mass communication sources spend a great deal of time and effort to get your attention so that you will include yourself in the audience.

Feedback Feedback is another area where there are differences between interpersonal and mass communication. The message flow in mass communication is typically one-way, and feedback, in many instances, is more difficult than in the interpersonal setting. This situation, however, is rapidly changing because of the Internet. Newspapers often

Encoding at the movies. Director Tim Burton on the set of *Alice in Wonderland*. A motion picture goes through several stages of encoding before it gets to the audience: concept, story, script, filming, and editing.

include e-mail addresses of reporters to encourage reader feedback. Producers of TV shows scan Web sites and blogs to glean the latest reaction to their episodes. People tweet (send Twitter messages) while they attend newsworthy events. Systematic, large-scale feedback conducted by media research companies, such as the Audit Bureau of Circulations for newspapers and MRI for magazines, tends to be more delayed, but there are exceptions. Nielsen Media Research, for example, provides overnight ratings for network TV shows.

Noise   Finally, noise in the mass communication setting can be semantic, environmental, or mechanical. In fact, since there may be more than one machine involved in the process, mechanical noise can be compounded.

Table 1-1 summarizes some of the differences among the three communication settings that we have talked about.

Defining Mass Media

In the broadest sense of the word, a *medium* is the channel through which a message travels from the source to the receiver ("medium" is singular; "media" is plural). Thus in our discussion we have pointed to sound and light waves as media of communication. When we talk about mass communication, we also need channels to carry the message. **Mass media** are the channels used for mass communication. Our definition of a mass medium will include not only the mechanical devices that transmit and sometimes store the

table 1-1

Differences in Communication Settings

Element		Settings		
		Interpersonal	Machine-Assisted Interpersonal	Mass
	Source	Single person; has knowledge of receiver	Single person or group; has great deal of knowledge or no knowledge of receiver	Organizations or single person; has little knowledge of receivers
	Encoding	Single stage	Single or multiple stage	Multiple stages
	Message	Private or public; cheap; hard to terminate; altered to fit receivers	Private or public; low to moderate expense; relatively easy to terminate; can be altered to fit receivers in some situations	Public; can be expensive; easily terminated; same message sent to everybody
	Channel	Potential for many; no machines interposed	Restricted to one or two; at least one machine interposed	Restricted to one or two; usually more than one machine interposed
	Decoding	Single stage	Single or multiple stage	Multiple stages
	Receiver	One or relatively small number; in physical presence of source; selected by source	One person or small or large group; within or outside physical presence of source; selected by source or self-defined	Large numbers; out of physical presence of source; self-selected
	Feedback	Plentiful; immediate	Somewhat limited; immediate or delayed	Highly limited; usually delayed
	Noise	Semantic; environmental	Semantic; environmental; mechanical	Semantic; environmental; mechanical

message (TV cameras, radio microphones, printing presses) but also the institutions that use these machines to transmit messages. When we talk about the mass media of television, radio, newspapers, magazines, sound recording, and film, we will be referring to the people, policies, organizations, and technologies that go into producing and distributing mass communication. A **media vehicle** is a single component of the mass media, such as a newspaper, radio station, TV network, or magazine.

In this book we will examine eight different mass media: radio, television, film, books, sound recordings, newspapers, magazines, and the Internet. Of course, these eight are not the only mass media that exist. Billboards, comic books, posters, direct mail, matchbooks, and buttons are some other kinds of mass media one could choose to examine. The eight types of media we have chosen, however, have the largest audiences, employ the most people, and have the greatest impact. They are also the ones with which most of us are most familiar.

mass media in transition

It doesn't take a genius to see that the mass media five years from now will be significantly different than they were five years ago. A combination of technological, economic, and social factors has made some traditional business models obsolete, and several media are struggling to reinvent themselves for the digital era. Other media are dealing with a fundamental shift in the ways they reach their audiences.

Technology

On the technology level, the emergence of the Internet has created a new channel for mass communication. In the beginning, traditional media companies, such as newspapers and magazines, were unsure how to use this new medium and many posted content for free on their Web sites in an effort to promote the print editions. This ultimately siphoned off potential readers of the print edition, especially young readers, and circulation fell along

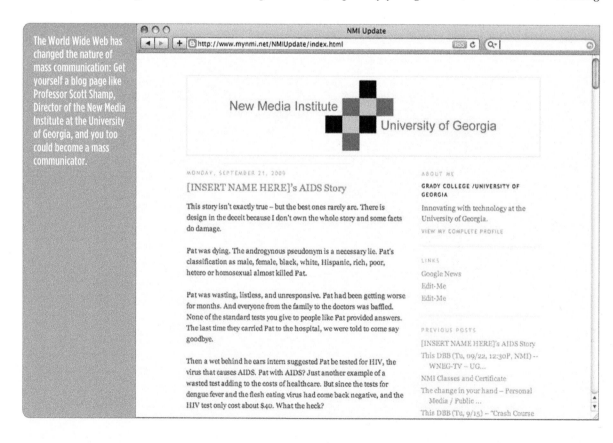

The World Wide Web has changed the nature of mass communication: Get yourself a blog page like Professor Scott Shamp, Director of the New Media Institute at the University of Georgia, and you too could become a mass communicator.

with advertising revenues. Consequently, the traditional print media are looking for new ways to prosper in the digital age. Publishers are hoping that mobile media, such as the smartphone and the tablet computer, will offer new sources of revenue (see below).

At the same time, the Internet opened the door for a host of new competitors for traditional media. Some Web sites simply replaced functions served by traditional media. Classified ads that might have gone to the newspaper went to Web sites such as Craigslist or autotrader.com. Online video sites, such as YouTube and hulu.com, cut into the audience and revenue of traditional TV networks and stations. Internet radio stations captured listeners at the office that previously had listened to broadcast stations. Other Web sites created new functions that captured audience attention and time. Instead of watching TV, many young people spent time on Facebook or Twitter or other social network sites. This increased competition forced the traditional media to reexamine their usual ways of doing business.

The primary reason behind this growth in competition is easy to see: The Internet brings down the cost of mass communication to a level at which almost anybody can afford it. A single individual can start a Web site for a relatively small sum (Facebook started in a Harvard dorm; Craigslist started as a hobby) and reach a potential audience of millions. Furthermore, the low cost means that individual sites can be supported solely by those who create them, thus removing the profit consideration from the equation. It's probably fair to say that the vast majority of bloggers, for example, blog for reasons other than profit. To sum up, in the past, established media companies were shielded from new competition because the costs to enter the market were so high. That is no longer the case. A whole new type of mass communicator has emerged to compete with traditional media organizations, and the choices available for the audience have mushroomed.

Of course, not everybody who puts up a Web site is engaging in mass communication. If nobody or only a few people visit the site, no mass communication takes place. The fact that Uncle Harold publishes a blog does not mean that Uncle Harold is on the same level as the *New York Times* as a mass communicator. The *Times* has a lot more resources with which to draw a mass audience. But technically speaking, the same could be said about traditional media. If no one reads the *New York Times,* then no mass communication takes place. In short, although the potential to be a mass communicator exists for everybody—including Uncle Harold and the *New York Times*—actually becoming one is more difficult for Uncle Harold.

Economics

This transition was further accelerated by the economic downturn during the last years of the decade. Advertising money dried up, and as noted above, competition from Web sites siphoned off the profits of traditional media. Organizations that expanded during an era of easy credit all of a sudden found themselves burdened by massive debt. Not surprisingly, cutbacks, layoffs, and severe cost-cutting followed. Several media organizations went bankrupt; others struggled to find new revenue streams; still others totally joined the digital era by ending their traditional forms and going online. By 2011, the economic situation had improved somewhat, but mass media companies still faced financial challenges.

Social Trends

Social change also hastened the transition. Consumers became accustomed to receiving their information and entertainment for free, and efforts to charge for Internet content met with resistance. Traditional passive media exposure was replaced by active participation in new social media such as Facebook, YouTube, and Twitter. The recording industry watched as person-to-person file sharing skyrocketed and sales of CDs plummeted. People began to spend their time creating media content (more than half of teens have created a social networking site; more than 150 million people have started blogs) and less time consuming media content.

The chapters in Parts II and III of this book will provide more details about how the various media are coping with this transitional era.

characteristics of media organizations

Describing the characteristics of mass media organizations was a lot easier before the Internet came along. As mentioned above, thanks to the Internet, the distinction between machine-assisted interpersonal communication and mass communication has become fuzzy. When we try to identify the typical characteristics of mass communication organizations, the distinctions become fuzzier. Some Web sites engage in mass communication; some don't. The *New York Times* Web site gets more than 19 million unique visitors every month; we would expect the *Times'* Web site to possess the typical characteristics of a mass media organization (and it does). At the other end of the spectrum, the average blog has about 10–20 regular readers; most would agree that this is more like machine-assisted interpersonal communication. It is unlikely that these sites would share the same distinguishing features as www.nytimes.com. Nonetheless, at the risk of oversimplifying, and recognizing that some Web operations may represent exceptions, below are five features that have been traditionally used to define organizations that produce mass communication:

1. Mass communication is produced by complex and formal organizations.
2. Mass communication organizations have multiple gatekeepers.
3. Mass communication organizations need a great deal of money to operate.
4. Mass communication organizations exist to make a profit.
5. Mass communication organizations are highly competitive.

Let's examine each of these characteristics in turn and then examine how each has been transformed by the Internet and by the economic and social forces mentioned above.

Formal Organizational Structure

Publishing a newspaper, making a movie, or operating a TV network requires control of money, management of personnel, coordination of activities, and application of authority. Accomplishing all of these tasks requires a well-defined organizational structure characterized by specialization, division of labor, and focused areas of responsibility. Consequently, traditional mass communication has been the product of a bureaucracy. As in most bureaucracies, decision making takes place at several levels of management, and channels of communication within the organization are formalized. Thus, many of the decisions about what gets included in a newspaper, TV program, or movie are made by groups. Further, decisions are made by several individuals in ascending levels of the bureaucracy, and communication follows predictable patterns within the organization.

Turning now to the Web, a formal organizational structure is found with some Web operations but not with others. Web sites can be produced and maintained by a single individual or a small group, and decisions do not have to be filtered through a hierarchy. The Drudge Report, for instance, has only a handful of employees. Keep in mind, however, that many Web sites that attract a large audience have organizational structures that resemble those of a traditional mass media organization. To illustrate, Facebook has more than 2,000 employees and offices in 15 countries. YouTube has 13 separate departments.

Gatekeepers

Another important factor that characterizes the traditional mass communication organization is the presence of multiple **gatekeepers.** A gatekeeper is any person (or group) who has control over what material eventually reaches the public. Some gatekeepers are more obvious than others, such as the editor at a newspaper, the news director at a TV station, or the acquisitions editor at a book publishing company. More complex organizations have more gatekeepers.

The dismal economic climate has had an impact on gatekeeping. When newspapers and magazines lay off employees, editors are likely to be included among those losing their jobs. When media companies consolidate and simplify their corporate structure, it usually means fewer gatekeepers.

Getting past the gate-keepers in network television is difficult. ABC's hit series *Desperate Housewives* was first turned down by HBO, CBS, NBC, Fox, Showtime, and Lifetime.

Gatekeepers are far less numerous on the Web, but that doesn't mean they are nonexistent. Most newspapers, for example, have someone who scans comments posted on their Web sites and removes offensive or libelous posts. YouTube has several people who screen videos and remove the ones that are inappropriate or violations of copyright. Facebook removes illegal, offensive, and pornographic content, as does YouTube. These sites exemplify a feature of gatekeeping that is unique to the Web—they rely on audience members to do the monitoring. Facebook and YouTube, for example, have links that allow members to report content that they find objectionable.

In general, however, gatekeeping is not a principal feature of many Internet sites, a situation that has both positive and negative consequences. On the one hand, individuals have the freedom to post whatever they want without too much fear of censorship. On the other hand, there is no guarantee that what is made available will be accurate or worthwhile. Rumors, conspiracy theories, vitriol, and truly tasteless content abound on the Internet. There are no editors to sort out the credible from the lies or to distinguish merit from the trash.

Large Operating Expenses

Traditionally, it has taken a lot of money to get into the mass communication business and more money to keep going. In 2009 cable giant Comcast acquired NBC Universal for about $14 billion, and in 2011 Access Industries paid more than $3 billion to buy Warner Music Group, the world's third-largest recording company.

Once the organization is operating, expenses can also be sizable. A radio station in a medium-size market might spend around $1 million in operating expenses. A medium-market TV station probably spends $5–10 million annually.

As we have already noted, the Internet has reduced start-up and operating costs, but this does not mean that Web operations don't need cash in order to grow and prosper. Indeed, if an entrepreneur wants his or her Web site to reach a mass audience, somebody has to pay the bill. YouTube, for example, might not have gotten off the ground without an $11.5 million investment from a venture capital company. Facebook followed the same route, accepting about $40 million from two venture capital companies. Evan Williams, one of the founders of Twitter, raised $22 million from outside investors. (On the other hand, if your plans are less grandiose, Google gives members free blog space and Yahoo charges only $10 a month to host a Web site.)

Companies that have strong financial resources are the likeliest to survive high operating expenses and are more likely to survive in a down economy. In 2010, a number of global media giants dominated the field. Table 1-2 lists these "megamedia" companies; these names will turn up frequently in succeeding chapters.

Competition for Profits

In the United States, mass communication organizations exist to make a profit. Although there are some exceptions (the Public Broadcasting Service, for example), most newspapers, magazines, record companies, film studios, book publishers, and TV and radio stations strive to produce a profit for their owners and shareholders. Broadcast stations are licensed to serve the public interest and newspapers assume a watchdog role for their readers, but if they do not make money, no matter how noble their goals, they go out of business (as was illustrated several times during the recession of the late 2000s.)

table 1-2 Global Media Giants	Company (home country)	2010 Revenue (in billion U.S. dollars)*
	Vivendi (France)	$38.3
	Walt Disney Co. (United States)	38.0
	Comcast (United States)	37.9
	News Corp. (United States)	32.8
	Time Warner (United States)	27.0
	Bertelsmann (Germany)	22.0

*To give some perspective to these data, Wal-Mart revenue for the same period was $422 billion; General Electric's was $135 billion.

Profit ultimately comes from the consumer. When you download a song from iTunes or buy a movie ticket, part of the price includes the profit. Newspapers, radio, TV, and magazines make most of their profit by selling to advertisers the attention their audiences give them. The cost of advertising is then passed on to the consumer. The economics of mass communication is an important topic, and we will explore it throughout this book.

Since the audience is the source of profits, mass communication organizations compete with one another to attract an audience. This should come as no surprise to anyone who has ever watched television or passed a magazine stand. The major TV networks compete with one another for ratings, spending millions of dollars to promote their programs. Radio stations compete with other stations in their market. Record companies spend large sums promoting their recordings, hoping to outsell their competitors. Motion picture companies may gamble millions on films to compete successfully. As we have seen, the Internet has made competition even more severe.

As for Web sites, many exist to make a profit. Perezhilton.com contains advertising and sales pitches for merchandise, as does gawker.com. Amazon.com makes its profit by selling hundreds of different products. Other Web sites do not share the profit motivation; some exist to serve the public (such as the .gov sites) or to gain attention and/or prestige for their owners (blogs). In this latter case, competition will not be much of a factor.

To sum up, the Internet is home to millions of Web sites. Many of them fit the definition of mass communication and exhibit all of the traditional characteristics of mass communication organizations (such as CNN.com, ESPN.com, nytimes.com). Other operations also engage in mass communication and exhibit some but not all of the five traditional features. (Thesmokinggun.com strives to make a profit. It attracts about 4 million unique views a month but has only a handful of employees and relatively small operating expense since it gets all its material from public records.) Other sites are better defined as machine-assisted interpersonal communication. Once again, the Internet has forced us to reexamine the way we traditionally think about mass communication and mass communicators.

the internet: mass and interpersonal channel?

As the Internet evolves, two distinct developments are becoming clear. The first suggests that the Web will become more important for interpersonal and social functions, as evidenced by the tremendous rise of social media. The operations that have been most successful on the Web most resemble interpersonal or machine-assisted communication. Blogs, e-mail, Skype, eBay, Facebook, Twitter, instant messages, Wikipedia, and all of the Napster-like file-sharing programs are not so much examples of mass communication as they are of machine-assisted interpersonal communication, facilitating communication between single individuals (writing on someone's "wall" in Facebook) or among relatively small groups of people (such as occurs with Google Groups). In addition, virtually none of the successful operations mentioned above were started by a big media company (but big media companies bought in when these sites became successful).

Second, many experts have predicted that traditional mass media content (TV, movies, newspapers, magazines, sound recording, books, radio) will eventually be distributed mainly over the Internet, making the Net the single most important channel of mass communication. This trend is already taking shape with online newspapers and magazines; TV networks making their programs available on the Web (for example, hulu.com); movie studios making films available for download (for example, Netflix); downloadable books (for example, Amazon's Kindle e-book reader); and music (iTunes). There are dangers, however, associated with this development. If we become too dependent on the Internet, what happens if a natural disaster (such as a hurricane) or human-made calamity (such as a terrorist cyber attack) disables the system? In any event, the Internet is fostering both mass and machine-assisted communication at the same time.

Whatever its ultimate direction, the Internet has prompted mass communication scholars (and textbook writers) to rethink conventional definitions and categories of mass communication. It has also necessitated fresh models to describe the communication process, a topic that we will turn to next.

models for studying mass communication

The traditional model of mass communication was a "one-to-many" model. It suggested that information from the environment (both news and entertainment) is filtered through a mass media organization (newspaper, TV network, movie studio) where it is decoded, interpreted, selected, and finally encoded into a message that is reproduced many times over and distributed through the appropriate channel. For example, newspaper reporters cover events and encode stories that are evaluated by editors (gatekeepers) to see if they should make it into that day's edition of the paper.

Once through the gate, the paper is reproduced and physically distributed to readers. The readers, the receivers of the message, decode and interpret the message. Some audience behavior (buying a product, watching a TV show, subscribing to a magazine) is monitored by the media organization and is used as feedback to help shape future messages. Under the traditional model there is little direct interaction between sources and receivers.

Figure 1-2 is a rough attempt to represent Internet communication, a new arrangement that makes possible several different levels of communication: one source communicating with one receiver (e-mail), one source communicating with many receivers (CNN.com), a few sources communicating with a few receivers (chat rooms, blogs), and many sources communicating with many receivers (YouTube, eBay).

Note that in this simplified model, content is provided not only by organizations but also by individuals. In this circumstance there are no organizational gatekeepers. A single individual performs the decoding, interpreting, and encoding functions. Also note that Figure 1-2 is not a one-way model. Communication doesn't proceed from left to right but flows inward. The traditional mass communicator no longer necessarily initiates the process. Instead, it is possible for the receiver to choose the time and manner of the interaction. Suppose you want to find out what happened in a game involving your favorite baseball team that went into extra innings and finished late at night. With the traditional media you have to wait for a newspaper to be published or for your favorite TV station, cable network, or radio station to report the score. With the Internet you can visit a sports news Web site and find the information immediately.

Another area of contrast between the traditional and Internet models is that the messages that flow to each receiver are not identical. For example, you have many different choices about what you can use as your starting page when you access the Internet. In addition, it's possible to customize the information you receive. MSN.com, for example, offers many different configurations that allow you to choose specific sports scores, news headlines, stock market reports, weather forecasts, and entertainment news. Each receiver can customize the information that he or she receives. Some writers have characterized the traditional mass communication model as a "push" model (the sender pushes the information to the receiver), whereas the Internet model is a "pull" model (the receiver pulls only the information that he or she wants).

figure 1-2

Internet Mass
Communication Model

Finally, Figure 1-2 shows that both individuals and organizations are linked through a computer-mediated environment. This makes interaction and feedback much easier. The online magazine Slate.com, for example, has a site titled "The Fray," where readers can comment on stories in the magazine. This environment allows people and organizations to be linked in unprecedented ways, in totally new forms of interaction. The auction site eBay joins buyers and sellers all over the world. The Facebook "Causes" page brings together people who were probably never aware of one another and lets them unite in such endeavors as The Nature Conservancy (nearly a half-million members). All in all, the new model, incomplete as it might be, suggests a new way of conceptualizing communication in the age of the Internet.

transition: emerging media trends

As media continue to evolve, several trends are already apparent: (1) audience segmentation, (2) convergence, (3) increased audience control, (4) multiple platforms, (5) user-generated content, (6) mobile media, and (7) social media. We will present a brief discussion of each term below, and subsequent chapters will point out additional examples.

Audience Segmentation: The End of Mass Communication As We Know It?

Media audiences are becoming less "mass" and more selective. For example, in the 1930s nearly everybody tuned their radios to *Amos 'n' Andy*. Today the top-rated radio station in a major market is lucky if it captures 10 percent of the audience. In the 1950s *I Love Lucy* was a top-rated TV show with about 50 percent of viewers tuning in. In the 1980s *The Cosby Show* was number one with about a 33 percent share, and in 2011, top-rated *American Idol* got about 13 percent.

About three out of every four adults read a newspaper in the 1960s; today that's down to about one out of two. *Reader's Digest* had a circulation of 18 million in 1976; today it's down to around 7 million.

All of these numbers illustrate the segmentation or fractionalization of the mass audience. What are some of the reasons for this change? First, for many in today's audience, time has become a scarce commodity, with much of it devoted to commuting, working, and child rearing. All of this means less time available for media, and when audience members do spend time with the media, they tend to look for content geared to their special interests.

Second, there are more media today to choose from: From just three TV networks in the 1950s to hundreds of cable and satellite channels, as well as DVDs, video games, and YouTube; from single-screen movie theaters to 18-screen multiplexes and movies on demand; and from a dozen or so local radio stations to hundreds of channels on satellite radio. Finally, advertisers have turned from mass to target marketing, paying a premium to reach those people most likely to buy their product or service. The ultimate consequence of all these factors is that the audience for any single media vehicle is reduced.

Does all of this mean that mass communication is no longer a meaningful term? Should this book be retitled *The Dynamics of Segmented Communication*? Or maybe just drop the "mass" and call it *The Dynamics of Media Communication*? Well, it may be too early to assign the notion of mass communication to the annals of history. First, the definition of mass communication given earlier still applies: Complex organizations use machines to transmit public messages aimed at large, heterogeneous, and scattered audiences. Consider the examples at the opening of the chapter. The billion people who watched the royal wedding, the 130 million or so who saw *Avatar*, and the 140 million plus YouTube views certainly justify the term *mass communication.* True, these are rare events, but even a flop TV show can reach more than a million households.

Second, the channels of mass communication are unchanged, but there are more and more mass media vehicles using these channels: a few hundred TV networks today compared to four in the 1980s; about 14,000 broadcast radio stations today compared to about 9,000 in the early 1980s; about 255 million Web sites today compared to 3 million in 1998. The messages sent by these mass media through the channels of mass communication have become more specialized as traditional and new media are aiming their content at defined audience niches, in part to meet demands of advertisers and in part because it's more cost-efficient. Consequently, it's harder for any one media vehicle to reach a large number of audience members. Nonetheless, the potential is still there for the right message in the right medium (such as the 2011 Super Bowl that brought 111 million people to the Fox TV network) to transcend the limits of specialized content and attract a mass audience in the broadest sense of the term.

Convergence

The dictionary defines *convergence* as the process of coming together or uniting in a common interest or focus. Convergence is not a new idea (some past examples are sporks, clock radios, and brunch), but the word has enjoyed renewed popularity in recent years and has become the centerpiece in discussions about future trends in mass communication. It is a difficult term to discuss, however, because it has been used to refer to several different processes.

At one level it refers to **corporate convergence.** This trend started in the 1980s with synergy. Companies that were content providers, such as movie studios and record labels, acquired distribution channels such as cable TV. As digital technologies emerged, synergy turned into convergence, a vision of one company delivering every service imaginable.

The early years of the new century saw several attempts at corporate convergence, but most were unsuccessful. For example, the merger between "old" media Time Warner and "new" media AOL didn't fulfill expectations. They finally split up in 2009. In France the

social issues

Too Much?

Alvin Toffler used the term "information overload" in his 1970 best-seller *Future Shock*. Information overload refers to the difficulty a person has in making a decision or understanding an issue in the presence of too much information. Or, as Toffler put it, "When the individual is plunged into a fast and irregularly changing situation, or a novelty-loaded context . . . his predictive accuracy plummets. He can no longer make the reasonably correct assessments on which rational behavior is dependent."

Toffler wrote this a couple of decades before the Internet appeared, and information overload has only increased with the advent of new technologies. We are regularly plunged into fast-changing situations and novelty-loaded contexts. In the modern world, all of us are showered with information from the traditional print and electronic media, along with e-mail, text messages, tweets, Facebook postings, video links, smart phones, apps, Skype, and countless Web sites, all vying for our attention.

Some preliminary research suggests that dealing with this constant stream of information may not be good for us. One study noted that high usage of cellular phones and social network sites hindered long-term memory and mental performance. Another study discovered that multitasking, such as watching TV, playing games on a smartphone, and texting, also impeded short-term memory.

Some authors worry that the flood of available information is decreasing our attention span. Many people report that it is difficult for them to get through a book, a movie, or a long conversation without checking e-mail, Facebook status updates, or their Twitter accounts.

The problem may be more pronounced among the younger generation. A study by the Kaiser Family Foundation found that 8- to 18-year-olds devote an average of 10 hours and 45 minutes to the media each day and for much of that time they are multitasking—for example, listening to an iPod while texting and checking Facebook.

Here's the problem. People with short attention spans cannot solve many of the issues that face modern society. Some problems demand uninterrupted focus, long study, and undisturbed contemplation. As with many other things, when it comes to using communication technology, moderation may be the best strategy. (P.S. If you've read this far without checking your Facebook page, I'm very impressed.)

---

convergence between "new" media company Vivendi and "old" media Universal Studios and Universal Music failed. In 2005 Viacom "de-converged," spinning off "old" media CBS, Infinity Radio, and a publishing house into a separate company while keeping "new" media MTV networks and a home video company.

Convergence made a mild comeback during 2010–2011. Software giant Microsoft acquired Skype for more than $8 billion. Experts predict that Microsoft will use Skype's calling capability to enhance the Xbox 360. In addition, satellite broadcaster Dish network bought Blockbuster, primarily to use Blockbuster's streaming movie service to compete with Netflix.

Another type of convergence is **operational convergence.** This occurs when owners of several media properties in one market combine their separate operations into a single effort. For example, in Florida, TV station WFLA, the *Tampa Tribune,* and TBO.com operate a converged news department. In 2010, the *Deseret News* merged its newsroom with its sister stations, KSL TV and radio. All in all, an estimated 50 examples of this kind of convergence are currently under way. And if cross-media ownership rules are relaxed, this trend may accelerate.

The advantages of this type of convergence are obvious. It saves money because, rather than hiring a separate news staff for each medium, an operation can have the same reporters produce stories for the paper, Web site, and TV station. In addition, each medium can promote its partners. For instance, the TV newscast can encourage readers to visit the Web site or the print newspaper.

There are, of course, disadvantages as well. First, convergence may be synonymous with cutbacks as most merged newsrooms use smaller staffs. When the *Deseret News* merged with KSL, it cut its workforce by more than 40 percent. Second, reporters require additional training to master various media. This has generated some controversies among print reporters who are not eager to become "backpack journalists" (see Chapter 13) carrying around video cameras and audio recorders as part of their reporting tools. Further, many critics worry that converged operations mean fewer independent and diverse forms of journalism. Some conclude that, although operational convergence may be good for the media companies, it may not be good for consumers. In any case, the jury is still out on the merits of operational convergence.

media *Bad Career Choices*
Probe

A market research firm analyzed the revenue earned by 700 industries in 2010 and came up with list of 10 businesses that will probably not be around much longer:

1. Wired communication carriers
2. Mills
3. Newspaper publishing
4. Apparel manufacturing
5. DVD, game, and video rentals
6. Manufactured home dealers
7. Video postproduction services
8. Record stores
9. Photofinishing
10. Formal wear and costume rental

Note that six of the ten are media-related.

Finally, what may be the most important type of convergence is **device convergence,** combining the functions of two or three devices into one mechanism. Apple's iPhone, for example, is a phone, an MP3 player, and a camera, and it can connect to the Internet. The latest model video game platforms can also play DVDs. Some cell phones incorporate navigation systems. Experts predict that eventually the home PC will converge with the TV set in one information appliance that will include e-mail, phone, Internet, DVD playback, and TV functions. Of course, the fact that the functions of more than one device can be combined doesn't mean that consumers will buy it. (There probably isn't much demand, for example, for a combination cell phone/electric razor.) In addition, there is always the danger that convergence will result in a piece of equipment that is too complex for consumers to operate.

Device convergence is manifesting itself in yet another way. All media seem to be converging on the Internet as a major channel of distribution. Newspapers and magazines have online editions. Music downloads are fast replacing CDs as the preferred delivery method. TV networks are making their episodes available for downloading as well as starting their own broadband channels. Movies and books are also available in digital download forms.

Increased Audience Control

Audience members are more in charge of what they want to see and/or hear and when they want to do it. Let's take television as an example. For many years viewers had to watch programs broadcast by local stations and the major networks according to the media's schedule. However, recent technological advances have given more power to the consumer. The VCR allowed time shifting, or recording a program to be viewed at a more convenient time. Remote controls made it easier for viewers to select what they wanted to watch. Cable and satellite channels offered hundreds of new viewing opportunities. Home video gave individuals the chance to make their own videos. In the past few years, digital video recorders (DVRs) such as TiVo have made time shifting easier and more efficient. Viewers can pause live TV, fast-forward through commercials, and store up to 80 hours of programming. Many cable companies now offer video on demand, enabling viewers to select content that they can watch at their convenience. In short, power has shifted from the source to the receiver.

The same trend is apparent in news. For many decades most Americans were dependent on the news provided by their local newspaper or TV network. Today audience members can choose from 24-hour cable news networks, Internet sites such as CNN.com that are devoted to news, and sites such as Google News that aggregate news from many different sources. If an audience member is not content with the traditional news outlets, she or he can read one of the hundreds of blogs that discuss news events.

Until recently, consumers were forced to buy recorded music packaged according to the wishes of industry executives. If an audience member wanted to buy just one or two songs by an artist, he or she was out of luck. The consumer had to buy an entire album. The success of Napster and other file-sharing programs clearly demonstrated that individuals were not satisfied with that arrangement. The music industry was slow to respond, but now consumers can download individual tracks from iTunes and other online sources.

Before the Internet, consumers with something to sell had to rely on the local newspaper's classified ad section. Now they can create their own ads on eBay or Craigslist. Similarly, employers once had to depend on the "Help Wanted" section of the paper. Now, however, they can scan the résumés of hundreds of potential employees on Monster.com.

Subsequent chapters will contain other examples of this trend, but by now the point is probably clear: The audience is gaining more control over the mass communication process. As one expert put it, mass communication has gone from a sit-down dinner with a fixed menu to a Vegas-style buffet.

Multiple Platforms

"Everything. Everywhere." This has been the mantra at many media companies as they try to adapt to the changing world of media technology. The strategy is to make content available to consumers using a number of delivery methods to a number of receiving devices (or multiple platforms, in the industry jargon).

Music videos may be the best illustration of this trend. For many years music video fans had to be content watching videos on MTV, VH1, Fuse, or one of the other cable/satellite networks. Then Web sites began streaming music videos. Recall that Rebecca Black's music video got more than 140 million views on YouTube. Recording companies realized that consumers were watching more videos on their computer screens than on their TV screens. Apple's video iPod, cell phones, and tablet computers opened up other possibilities. Today music videos still run on traditional TV screens, but the record labels have also struck deals with Apple and phone companies, such as Verizon, to take advantage of the new screens.

Television companies have also moved in this direction. NBC partnered with Fox to start hulu.com, where visitors can watch hundreds of current and past TV series as well as dozens of shorter video clips. ABC has selected episodes of its shows on ABC.com and has an application for the iPad. In short, the networks are trying to make their content available on as many screens as possible.

Other media are also taking advantage of multiple platforms. Almost all major newspapers and magazines have Web sites for their digital versions that usually include video clips. The *Atlanta Journal-Constitution* and the *Seattle Post-Intelligencer,* like many other newspapers, deliver news to smartphoners and tablet computers. Entertainment and news can be heard on a traditional radio set, a satellite receiver, or a computer and downloaded to an iPod.

We may not be quite there yet, but having everything available everywhere may not be that far in the future.

User-Generated Content

User-generated content or peer production was a hot trend during the last few years but has recently slowed down. Of course, some Web sites such as YouTube, Flickr, and Wikipedia depend heavily on user-generated content. Members generate posts on Twitter and Facebook. Many news organizations accept video, photos, and audio sent in by citizen journalists. CNN, for example, has iReport and Fox News has a similar feature called uReport. On the other hand, magazine and book publishing, motion pictures, radio, sound recording, and entertainment television make relatively little use of user-generated material.

Mobile Media

Much of modern mass communication involves people looking at screens. For the past couple of decades, the two main screens have been the TV screen and the computer screen. Now a parade of small screens has joined the lineup: the screens on smartphones, iPods,

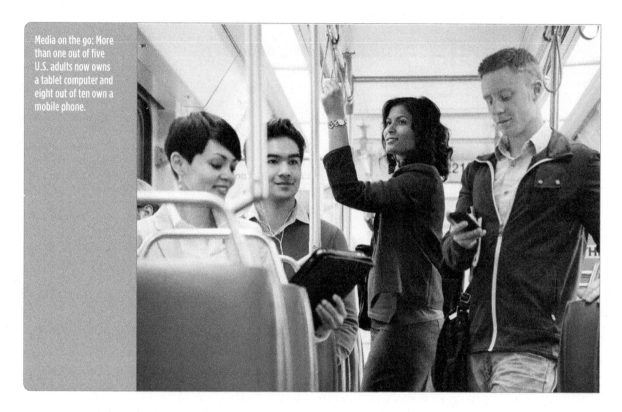

Media on the go: More than one out of five U.S. adults now owns a tablet computer and eight out of ten own a mobile phone.

tablet computers such as the iPad, e-readers, and handheld gaming devices. More than 45 million people have smartphones; more than 15 million have an iPad or other tablet computer; and more than 3 million have the Kindle e-reader. In short, mass media have become increasingly mobile.

Mobile media can access the Internet through programs called applications (apps) rather than through the traditional Web browser (more on apps in Chapter 4). Media companies, especially newspaper and magazine publishers, are hoping that apps for mobile media will provide them with a new source of revenue.

Examples of mobile media are everywhere. People can watch movies and TV shows, read books, newspapers, and magazines, and surf the Internet on their smartphones or iPads. In addition to playing games, owners of Sony's PSP (PlayStation Portable) can download movies for later viewing. The iPod contains enough memory for thousands of songs and can play video. As suggested earlier, mobile media are another manifestation of the "anywhere" characteristic of multiple platforms.

The implications of this trend are of such great consequence that it is included in Chapter 3 as one of the significant milestones in the development of communication. In addition, the chapters in Part II of this book contain a section that details how each element of the mass media is becoming more mobile.

Social Media

The last trend that is shaping the transition of the mass media goes by the name "social media." Although the label is simple, the concept is hard to define in a few words. At the risk of making things too simple, **social media** are online communications that use special techniques that involve participation, conversation, sharing, collaboration, and linkage.

Participation is the simplest technique that defines social media. It involves soliciting feedback from people about various issues or items. A news Web site that asks for opinions

media *Probe*   *Desperately Seeking Sockets*

Charging your electronic gadgets is no big problem when you're at home since there are usually plenty of electrical outlets around. But what about when you're not at home? People carry iPhones, iPads, Nooks, Kindles, Evos, BlackBerrys, laptop computers, and many other electronic devices. According to a wireless industry trade group, there were more than 300 million wireless devices in the United States in 2010 and they all had one thing in common: They needed to be plugged into an electrical outlet to be recharged. This situation has led to a new travel phenomenon: the pursuit of the plug.

Visit any Starbucks or Barnes & Noble store and you'll probably see several sockets in use. At one Barnes & Noble store in Manhattan, so many people were plugging in that customers were tripping over the power cords. Fearing that someone might get hurt, the manager finally covered the outlets with metal plates.

Airports present a real challenge. Now that most provide WiFi service, travelers are bringing more gadgets that need charging. At many older airports the demand for sockets usually exceeds the supply and you often see travelers lining up to use the available outlets. Some airports have recognized the problem and are quickly adding outlets. The newly remodeled Terminal 5 at JFK Airport in New York boasts 806 outlets. Installing new plugs is pricey: about $200 per plug in a terminal under construction but about $1,000 in an old terminal where walls have to be torn up.

Travelers, of course, are learning to cope with the socket shortage. Some carry battery packs that can be plugged in to provide additional power (of course the battery packs eventually have to be recharged). Some have become skilled at sniffing out hard-to-find plugs, usually behind a row of seats or on the backside of a pillar. Other travelers choose to fly first class where most seats have built-in power ports. One frequent traveler may have the most creative solution. He carries a multi-plug extension cord and if all the outlets are in use, he asks if he can share.

about a proposed new program and a Web operation such as Digg that lets people vote for their favorite online article or image are examples of participation.

Blogs and other Web sites that allow people to comment and to respond to one another are examples of the conversation function. Sharing is illustrated by YouTube, Flickr, and other sites where individuals can create and upload content for others to see. Wikis are social media that exemplify collaboration. The most elaborate social media involve linkage (more about linkage in Chapter 2). These are sites such as Facebook, MySpace, Google Groups, and Twitter where people can link up with friends (both close and distant) and form their own social networks and communities.

There is no doubt that social media have become popular. At the start of 2011, Facebook had more than 500 million users. If Facebook were a country, it would rank third in the world.

In addition to the Internet operations mentioned above, the Web sites of traditional media companies have incorporated the techniques of social media. About 75 percent of all newspapers allow readers to comment on stories, and about 60 percent allow readers to upload pictures and other content to their Web sites. The Web is filled with articles that explain how advertisers and public relations firms can use social media to promote their products and causes.

Businesses are turning to social media to market their products. Home Depot, for example, sponsored a video contest that asked consumers to illustrate the home improvement project that they would like to undertake. The company created a Web site where people could view all the entries and discuss their projects on a home improvement bulletin board. Social media may also reshape politics. The 2008 presidential campaign of candidate Barack Obama relied extensively on social media. The future president created a Web site, my.barackobama.com, that encouraged people to post blogs and link with other supporters (more than 2 million did); he also accumulated nearly a million MySpace friends, placed videos on YouTube, and started his own photostream on Flickr. After his election, he continued to rely on social media with a new Web site, Change.gov, where people shared their opinions about important issues.

Social media have become influential in the mass communication process, and we will have more to say about them in Chapter 4 and subsequent chapters.

main points

- The elements in the communication process are a source, encoding process, message, channel, decoding process, receiver, feedback, and noise.

- The three types of noise are semantic, environmental, and mechanical.

- The three main settings for communication are interpersonal, machine-assisted interpersonal, and mass communication.

- Each element in the communication process may vary according to setting.

- *Mass communication* refers to the process by which a complex organization, with the aid of one or more machines, produces public messages that are aimed at large, heterogeneous, and scattered audiences.

- Traditionally, a mass communicator was identified by its formal organization, gatekeepers, expensive operating costs, profit motive, and competitiveness. The Internet has created exceptions to these characteristics.

- New models have been developed to represent Internet mass communication.

- Communication content has become more specialized in the past 40 years, but the channels of mass communication still have the potential to reach vast audiences.

- Seven trends that characterize modern mass communication are audience segmentation, convergence, increased audience control, multiple platforms, user-generated content, more mobility, and social media.

questions for review

1. What are the main elements in the communication process?

2. What are the three types of noise?

3. Compare and contrast interpersonal communication with machine-assisted interpersonal communication.

4. How has the Internet changed the characteristics of the sources of mass communication?

5. As far as the mass media are concerned, what is the difference between a fixed-menu dinner and a Vegas buffet?

questions for critical thinking

1. What's the most embarrassing communication breakdown that's happened to you? Analyze why it happened. Was it due to semantic noise? Environmental noise? Mechanical noise?

2. Keep a media diary for a day. Tabulate how much of your time is spent in interpersonal, machine-assisted interpersonal, or mass communication. What conclusions can you draw?

3. What are some of the shortcomings of the communication model in Figure 1-2? Are there some elements that are missing?

4. Find additional examples of the seven trends that characterize modern mass media. Are there some media that will be less affected by these trends? Do you think these trends are positive or negative developments?

key terms

source (p. 5)
encoding (p. 5)
message (p. 5)
channels (p. 5)
decoding (p. 5)
receiver (p. 6)
feedback (p. 6)

noise (p. 6)
interpersonal communication (p. 7)
machine-assisted interpersonal communication (p. 8)
mass communication (p. 9)
mass media (p. 12)
media vehicle (p. 13)

gatekeepers (p. 15)
corporate convergence (p. 20)
operational convergence (p. 21)
device convergence (p. 22)
social media (p. 24)

internet resources

Online Learning Center

On the Online Learning Center home page, www.mhhe.com/dominick12e, *select* Student Center *and then* Chapter 1.

1. Use the Learning Objectives, Chapter Outline, and Main Points sections to review this chapter.

2. Test your knowledge of the chapter using the multiple choice and flashcard features of the site.

3. Expand your knowledge of concepts and topics discussed in the chapter with additional Questions for Critical Thinking and Internet Exercises.

surfing the internet

Listed here are sites that deal with interpersonal and mass communication.

www.aber.ac.uk/media/Documents/Short/trans.html
A thorough and lucid review and critique of the transmission model of communication. Contrast this model with the one in Figure 1-2.

www.mymissourian.com
As the site's slogan indicates ("Grassroots Journalism by Mid-Missourians"), a good example of user-generated content.

http://dcc.syr.edu
The latest research on and experiments about convergence, sponsored by the Convergence Center at Syracuse University.

http://social-networking-websites-review.toptenreviews.com
As the URL says, a site that reviews the top 10 social networking sites. Includes a side-by-side comparison and reader comments.

The Apprentice can be analyzed from a variety of perspectives.

Chapter**2**

perspectives on mass communication

This chapter will prepare you to:

- understand the differences between the functional approach and the critical/cultural approach to studying mass communications

- explain the value of each approach in the analysis of the mass communication process

- describe the functions mass media perform for society

- explain uses-and-gratifications analysis

- recognize the dysfunctions of mass communication

- understand the concepts of *meaning, hegemony,* and *ideology*

People study mass communication for a variety of reasons. Scholars study it to better comprehend the process and to develop theories that explain and predict how the media operate. Critics study it to offer insights about its influence and to suggest improvements. Media consumers study it to become media literate, to be able to understand the elements involved in the mass communication process, and to analyze and critically evaluate information presented in the mass media. Those in the media industry study it in order to increase their operating efficiency and maximize their profits when they sell news and information products to the general public.

No matter what the reason for study, it is helpful to use a **paradigm** (a model or pattern used to analyze something) to guide the way we think about the mass communication process. A paradigm is useful for several reasons:

- It provides us with a consistent perspective from which to examine mass communication.

- It generates concepts that are helpful in understanding media behavior.

- It helps us identify what is or is not important in the process.

There are many paradigms that we could use to study, understand, and appreciate mass communication. This book will introduce three that provide different ways of analyzing media and society: the functional approach, the critical/cultural approach, and the empirical approach. The **functional approach** emphasizes the way that the audience uses mass communication and looks at the various benefits and detriments that come from media consumption. The **critical/cultural approach** uses the techniques of the humanities, such as the analysis of texts and the deconstruction of messages, to examine the underlying power relationships in media exposure and stresses the many meanings and interpretations that audience members find in media content. The **empirical approach** uses the techniques of the social sciences, such as experiments and surveys, to investigate the cognitive, attitudinal, and behavioral effects of mass communication. Just as the mass media are in transition, so are the paradigms used to study them, as all three of these techniques have to take into account the changes brought about by the Internet and social media.

This chapter will introduce the functional approach and the critical/cultural approach. We will postpone discussion of the empirical approach until the last chapter of the book. This is not because the empirical approach is somehow better or more difficult to understand than the others, but because it's the one that has been most used in setting media policy, has generated the most popular controversy, and highlights some key issues that make a fitting ending for a book such as this one. For the present, however, let's examine the functional and the critical/cultural perspectives.

A recent example can serve to highlight the difference between these two approaches. *The Apprentice,* a reality TV show starring tycoon Donald Trump, first aired in 2004 and as of mid-2011 a celebrity version was still on the NBC prime-time schedule. The program features individuals who form teams to complete specific business-related tasks. At the end of each program someone is fired, until only one person remains. The winner is then rewarded with a desirable job (or a donation to charity in the celebrity version).

A functional analysis would inquire why people choose to view this program. Do they watch it for its entertainment value? Do they take away information that might be helpful to them in their own occupations? Do they learn anything about the way business operates? Do they like to "play along" with the contestants and try to figure out who is going to get fired? Do males and females watch for different reasons? Do they talk about the show with others?

A critical/cultural researcher would look at the show as a text and deconstruct its various elements. For example, what casting and editing techniques were used to make the show appear real? How does the program portray capitalism, the profit motive, and business in general? Does it glorify competition over cooperation? Does it reinforce the paternalistic nature of the business world to have Trump as the ultimate arbiter of who stays or who goes? Does it suggest that accumulating wealth is an important value? What is the cultural significance of using the O'Jays' "For the Love of Money" as its theme song? From the critical/cultural perspective, the program appears to carry an ideological message that legitimizes private enterprise and capitalistic social values.

All in all, this program could serve as the springboard for many contrasting avenues of inquiry. We'll start this chapter with a look at functional analysis and then examine the critical/cultural approach.

functional analysis

In its simplest form the functional approach holds that something is best understood by examining how it is used. In mass communication this means examining the use that audiences make of their interactions with the media.

By way of introduction, here are some actual responses given by college students to the question, Why do you use Facebook?

- I use Facebook because it is a good way to keep in touch with people I otherwise wouldn't see. (It also lets me see how cute people are, if I was drunk when I met them.)
- I use Facebook because I have no life and I'm compulsive about who my ex-boyfriends are conversing with.
- I use Facebook because it gives me a way to put off studying.
- I like to see the incriminating photos that people put up there.

Responses such as these, varied though they are, have led to several generalizations about the functions that media have for a society and for its individual members. This section will focus on cataloging and describing those functions.

The Role of Mass Communication in Society

The mass media are a pervasive part of our lives. Just how pervasive might become clear if we charted the various functions the media perform for us. Before we do this, however, we need to realize that different media have different primary uses. Not many people, for example, listen to CDs to find out the latest news or read the newspaper while driving their cars. Moreover, different groups of people use the same mass media content for different reasons. History professors, for example, might read articles in scholarly journals in order to keep up with their profession. Others who pursue history as a hobby might read the same journals in order to relax and be diverted from their normal routine.

One more qualification needs to be mentioned before we begin examining the functions and uses of mass communication. It is possible to conduct this analysis on at least two levels. On the one hand, we could take the perspective of a sociologist and look through a wide-angle lens to consider the functions performed by the mass media for the entire society (this approach is sometimes called **macroanalysis**). This viewpoint focuses on the apparent intention of the mass communicator and emphasizes the manifest purpose inherent in the media content. On the other hand, we could look through a close-up lens at the individual receivers of the content, the audience, and ask them to report on how they use mass media (this approach is called **microanalysis**). Sometimes the end results of these two methods are similar in that the consumer uses the content in the way that the source intended. Sometimes they are not similar, and the consumer uses the media in a way not anticipated by the mass communicator—a phenomenon noted by both the functional and critical/cultural paradigms. Let's begin our analysis by using the wide-angle lens.

Functions of Mass Communication for Society

For a society to exist, certain communication needs must be met. Primitive tribes had sentinels who scanned the environment and reported dangers. Councils of elders interpreted facts and made decisions. Tribal meetings were used to transmit these decisions to the rest of the group. Storytellers and jesters entertained the group. As society became larger and more complex, these jobs grew too big to be handled by single individuals. Throughout the following discussion we will examine the consequences of performing these communication functions by means of mass as opposed to interpersonal communication. Furthermore, there may be instances in which these consequences are undesirable from the point of view of the welfare of the society. These harmful or negative consequences are called **dysfunctions**. We will consider some of these as well. Lastly, these functions are not mutually exclusive; one example might illustrate several different categories.

This public-service campaign is an example of the warning function of the media.

Surveillance   **Surveillance** refers to what we popularly call the news and information role of the media. The media have taken the place of sentinels and lookouts. The output of the thousands of media journalists in this country is impressive. The four major television networks provide about 600 hours of regularly scheduled news programs, and CNN, Fox, and MSNBC provide similar services. Web sites such as CNN.com update news continuously, and many big-city radio stations broadcast nothing but news. Newsmagazines reach nearly 4 million people, and approximately 1,500 daily newspapers and 7,000 weeklies also spread the news. The size of the news audience is equally impressive. On any given day about 60 million Americans are exposed to mass-communicated news.

The surveillance function can be divided further into two main types. Warning, or **beware surveillance**, occurs when the media inform us about threats from terrorism, hurricanes or volcanoes, depressed economic conditions, increasing inflation, or military attack. These warnings can be about immediate threats (a television station interrupts programming to broadcast a tornado warning), or they can be about long-term or chronic threats (a newspaper runs a series about air pollution or unemployment). There is, however, much information that is not particularly threatening to society that people might like to know about. **Instrumental surveillance** has to do with the transmission of information that is useful and helpful in everyday life. News about films playing at the local theaters, stock market prices, new products, fashion ideas, recipes, and teen fads are examples of instrumental surveillance.

Note also that not all examples of surveillance occur in what we traditionally label the news media. *People* magazine and *Reader's Digest* perform a surveillance function (most of it instrumental). In fact, the surveillance function can be found in content that is primarily meant to entertain. HBO's *Sex and the City* performed a surveillance function for fashions and designer footwear.

What are some of the consequences of relying on the mass media to perform this surveillance function? In the first place, news travels much faster, especially since the advent of the electronic media. It took months for the news of the end of the War of 1812 to travel across the Atlantic. In contrast, more than 90 percent of the U.S. population knew about the terrorist attacks of September 11, 2001, within 2 hours of the events. The initial air strikes in Operation Iraqi Freedom were reported on television minutes after they happened. Speed sometimes leads to problems, however; inaccuracies and distortions travel just as fast as truthful statements. In 2011, NPR erroneously reported that Congresswoman Gabrielle Giffords had died following a shooting incident in Tucson, Arizona.

The second consequence is a bit more subtle: Much of what we know about the world is machine-processed, hand-me-down information. News is prescreened for us by a complex arrangement of reporters and editors, and our conception of reality is based on this second-generation information, whose authenticity we do not usually question. For example,

social issues *Twitter and the News*

As many of you may already know, Twitter is a free social messaging service that allows people to communicate brief messages, called "tweets," in real time. Subscribers can read the tweets on their cell phones or Twitter Web site. Twitter has many interesting uses, but the one that is most relevant to this chapter is its role in breaking news events. In short, Twitter is taking over part of the surveillance process from traditional media.

When a U.S. Airways flight crash-landed in the middle of the Hudson River, many people first learned of the event from Twitter. Within minutes of the crash, there were hundreds of messages posted along with a picture of the crash sent by a person on a nearby ferry boat hurrying to rescue the passengers. The deadly attacks in Mumbai, India, were reported on Twitter before the traditional media got hold of the story. During the height of the crisis there were about 80 posts every 5 seconds from eyewitnesses and from others pleading for help. Much of the news about the postelection violence in Iran came from Twitter. In 2011, a Twitter user unknowingly reported about the attack that killed Osama Bin Laden. For news junkies, Twitter has a site called Breaking News On, which, as the name suggests, is devoted only to breaking news.

Does this mean we no longer need journalists? Twitter opens up the journalistic process to anybody with a cell phone or computer and can replace traditional reporting. As we shall see in Chapter 13, this trend toward citizen journalism is reshaping the news business. Twitter allows almost instantaneous coverage of a news event and can get information out to the public before the traditional news media arrive on the scene.

Moreover, Twitter can be hyperlocal in focus. Friends can send news reports to friends. When a tornado warning was issued for portions of Colorado, one resident in Boulder heard about the warning not from the traditional media but from a tweet from a friend in California. During the rash of tornadoes in the Southeast in 2011, Twitter users became local reporters describing the damage and the efforts of relief workers.

Although Twitter has obvious strengths, we shouldn't be hasty in dismissing traditional journalism. When a news story breaks on Twitter, a torrent of unfiltered information comes at the user and it is difficult to keep up with the flow. There are no editors to make it manageable. In addition, tweets can be in error and quickly spread false information. Further, tweets of a breaking news story represent the fragmented views and comments of eyewitnesses who were fortunate enough (or unfortunate enough) to be at the scene of a breaking story. There are no journalists who could provide context and separate the meaningful from the trivial. And, of course, it's difficult to provide much thoughtful analysis in 140 characters.

Moreover, Twitter's popularity as a news source does not alter the point made in the text. We are still highly dependent on others for news. We still have to have a certain amount of trust in the media (or Twitterers) that do our surveillance. Credibility is still a chief concern. Just as with traditional media, we have to decide how much faith to invest in Twitter and behave accordingly.

human beings have allegedly walked on the moon. Millions saw it—on TV. Not many saw it in person. Instead, we took the word of the TV networks that what we were seeing was fact, not fiction. However, some people believe that television staged the whole thing somewhere in Arizona as part of a massive, government-inspired publicity stunt. The same phenomenon occurred in 2004 with the rovers landing on Mars, as some people thought the pictures received from Mars were fakes. The point is this: In today's world, with its sophisticated system of mass communication, we are highly dependent on others for news. Consequently, we have to put a certain amount of trust in the media that do our surveillance. This trust, called **credibility**, is an important factor in determining which news medium people find the most believable. We will discuss this concept at length in Chapter 13.

The widespread use of the Internet to transmit news does not change this basic idea. The stories posted on CNN.com or other news-oriented Web sites have been screened by several reporters and editors. Other Web sites that deal with news, such as the Drudge Report or the many blogs that have recently appeared, may not have a layer of editors, a circumstance that may affect the sites' credibility. Information that is spread through e-mail and by lesser-known Web sites may be especially suspect, as is news spread by social media. Whether the news is filtered or unfiltered, we still have to decide how much faith we invest in the media that provide it.

On the dysfunctional side, media surveillance can create unnecessary anxiety. In 2004 the media began reporting on an impending epidemic of bird flu that could kill anywhere from 5 million to 150 million people worldwide. As of early 2011, the epidemic had yet to materialize. (Of course, if an epidemic eventually occurs, this is a really bad example.)

Interpretation   Closely allied with the surveillance function is the interpretation function. The mass media do not supply just facts and data. They also provide information on the ultimate meaning and significance of events. One form of interpretation is so obvious that many people overlook it. Not everything that happens in the world on any given day can be included in the newspaper or in a TV or radio newscast. Media organizations select those events that are to be given time or space and decide how much prominence they are to be given. Stories that ultimately make it into the paper, onto the newscast, or onto a media organization's Web site have been judged by the various gatekeepers involved to be more important than those that did not make it.

Another example of this function can be found on the editorial pages of a newspaper. Interpretation, comment, and opinion are provided for the reader as an added perspective on the news stories carried on other pages. A newspaper might endorse one candidate for public office over another, thereby indicating that, at least in the paper's opinion, the available information indicates that this individual is more qualified than the other.

Interpretation is not confined to editorials. Articles that analyze the causes of an event or that discuss the implications of government policy are also examples of the interpretation function. Why is the price of gasoline going up? What impact will a prolonged dry spell have on food prices? When the president broadcasts a major political address, network correspondents usually appear afterward to tell us what the president "really said." In 2011 experts offered their opinions on the future of the struggle against terrorism after the death of Osama Bin Laden.

Interpretation can take various forms. Editorial cartoons, which originated in 1754, may be the most popular form. Other examples are less obvious but no less important. Critics are employed by the various media to rate motion pictures, plays, books, and records. Restaurants, cars, buildings, and even religious services are reviewed by some newspapers and magazines. One entire magazine, *Consumer Reports,* is devoted to analysis and evaluation of a wide range of general products. Political "spin doctors" try to frame the way media cover news events in a way that is positive for their clients. Many blogs interpret news events in line with their own political philosophy. Facebook offers the option to recommend or "like" certain items.

What are the consequences of the mass media's performing this function? First, the audience is exposed to a large number of points of view, probably far more than they could come in contact with through personal channels. Because of this, a person (with some effort) can evaluate all sides of an issue before arriving at an opinion. Additionally, the media make available to the individual a wide range of expertise that he or she might not have access to through interpersonal communication. Should we change the funding structure of Social Security? Thanks to the media, a person can read or hear the views of various economists, political scientists, politicians, and several hundred bloggers.

There are, however, certain dysfunctions that might occur. First, there is no guarantee that opinions by experts are accurate and valid. One 2011 study examined the predictions of 26 pundits who wrote newspaper columns or appeared on the Sunday morning news shows; it found that half of the time the predictions were wrong. Second, there is the danger that an individual may, in the long run, come to rely too heavily on the views carried in the media and lose her or his critical ability. Accepting without question the views of the *New York Times* or Rush Limbaugh may be easier than forming individual opinions, but it might lead to the dysfunctional situation of audience passivity and of people allowing others to think for them.

Linkage   The mass media are able to join different elements of society that are not directly connected. For example, mass advertising attempts to link the needs of buyers with the products of sellers. Legislators in Washington may try to keep in touch with constituents' feelings by reading their hometown papers. Voters, in turn, learn about the doings of their elected officials through newspapers, television, radio, and Web sites. Telethons that raise money for the treatment of certain diseases are another example of this **linkage** function. The needs of those suffering from the disease are matched with the desires of others who wish to see the problem eliminated.

media
Probe
A Matter of Interpretation

Here's how two newspapers covered the same story: a report on minority home ownership released by the Pew Hispanic Center.

Headline in the conservative *Wall Street Journal:* "Housing Boom Aided Minorities"

Headline in the liberal *New York Times:* "Home Ownership Losses Are Greatest Among Minorities, Report Finds"

Both headlines are accurate. Minorities did increase home ownership from 1995 to 2004, but they also lost their homes at a disproportionate rate once the housing bubble burst. The *Journal* and the *Times* chose to interpret the facts differently.

Another type of linkage occurs when geographically separated groups that share a common interest are joined by the media. Publicity about the sickness known as Gulf War syndrome linked those who claimed to be suffering from the disease, enabling them to form a coalition that eventually prompted government hearings on the issue.

The best examples of linkage, however, are on the Internet. The online auction site eBay lets a person who wants to sell a bronze cremation urn link up with potential buyers across the world. WebMD offers subscribers various "communities" where they can discuss their problems with others who have similar maladies. Craigslist.org lets users find jobs, roommates, dog walkers, and motorcycles for sale. Match.com boasts that it "gets singles connected to the millions of romantic possibilities out there, and often, to one very special someone." After a person finds that special someone, she or he can check out thenest.com, a blog where newlyweds share their experiences about the ups and downs of married life.

Facebook is another prime example of linkage. Facebook members can link up with friends, old and new, create interest groups, and share photos, videos, and links to stories. The fastest-growing application of Facebook in 2009 was "Causes," which links people to causes and benefits.

Rachel Maddow offers her interpretation of events on MSNBC.

On the other hand, this linkage function may have harmful consequences. In 2011 it was estimated that there were more than 1,000 "hate" sites on the Internet. Terrorists can use these sites to spread hate propaganda and to recruit new members. Some Web sites provide password-protected online discussion groups in which veteran terrorists can persuade new members to join their cause.

Transmission of Values   The transmission of values is a subtle but nonetheless important function of the mass media. It has also been called the **socialization** function. *Socialization* refers to the ways an individual comes to adopt the behavior and values of a group. The mass media portray our society, and by watching, listening, and reading, we learn how people are supposed to act and what values are important. Consider the images of an important but familiar concept as portrayed in the media: motherhood. The next time you watch television or

social issues
Status Conferral and the Fringe

One of the by-products of the surveillance function of the media is status conferral—individuals or issues that receive media attention achieve a certain amount of social prominence. The reasoning behind this phenomenon is rather circular: The audience evidently believes that if you *really* matter, you will be the focus of media attention, and if you are the focus of media attention then you *really* matter. Knowing this fact, many groups or individuals go to extreme measures to get media attention for their causes so that the status-conferral effect will occur.

In 2010, Terry Jones, the Pastor of the Dove World Outreach Center in Florida, a church that has fewer than 100 members and a history of engaging in anti-Muslim rhetoric, announced that he was going to burn the Quran, the Muslim holy book, on September 11th as a commemoration of the 2001 attacks on New York and Washington, D.C. In the pre-Internet age, Jones would probably have burned the book and only a few people outside his congregation would have noticed.

The Internet, however, has changed things. Jones had a Twitter account and one of his messages called for an international "burn a Koran day." Jones also started a Facebook group and posted a video on YouTube. An organization called EuroIslam Info that monitors social media for anti-Islam content discovered Jones's plans and condemned them in a press release that was noted by Yahoo and other Web sites. CNN picked up the story and did a short interview with Jones. Other news media quickly followed suit, and Terry Jones and his Quran burning became a national news story. The media attention was magnified because Jones's anti-Islam demonstration came amid a controversy about building an Islamic center near the site of the September 11 attacks in New York.

Jones gave about 150 media interviews in the weeks preceding September 11. The story appeared on the front page of more than 50 major newspapers. It was the lead story on several network newscasts and the number one topic on cable news and opinion programs. As the story spread across the world, it inspired protests in many Muslim nations. Secretary of Defense Robert Gates personally called Jones and asked him to call off the burning. Even President Obama condemned the plan. As the story continued to grow, several people, including Secretary of State Hillary Clinton and presidential press secretary Robert Gibbs, criticized the media for giving too much attention to a small fringe group. Salon's Justin Elliott summed it up this way: "In short, the U.S. media [have] given a global platform to a fringe pastor with a tiny flock, elevating him to a level of significance that would make most members of Congress jealous." Eventually Jones canceled his plans to burn the book and media attention quickly faded away.

If the story ended there, it would make a neat example of the dysfunctional effect of media surveillance. Jones, however, changed his mind, burned a copy of the Quran, and posted a video of the event on the group's Web site. This time the U.S. media paid scant attention to the event, but the earlier controversy had brought Jones's Web site to the attention of many Muslim groups that began to monitor its content. When the groups saw the video, they immediately spread the word to the Muslim world. Violent demonstrations broke out in Afghanistan and several people died. Perhaps the lesson to be learned here is that once the media give prominence to an issue, the status-conferral effect lingers after the story dies down.

Started in 1995 by Craig Newmark, craigslist.org gets about 3 billion page views per month.

media *Probe*   *Facebook and Instant Messages*

When a new form of social media becomes popular, it seldom replaces an existing form. Instead, the two forms tend to serve different communication functions. A study by Anabel Quan-Haase and Alyson Young published in the October 2010 issue of the *Bulletin of Science, Technology & Society* demonstrates this phenomenon.

The researchers were interested in two questions: (1) Why do students join Facebook and what gratifications do they receive from its continued use? (2) How do gratifications from using Facebook compare with those obtained from instant messaging (IM)? As is usual with uses-and-gratifications studies, the researchers provided their respondents with a list of possible reasons for using Facebook and for using IM.

After analyzing the data, the study concluded that students joined Facebook for a half-dozen reasons: to pass time, to share problems, to be sociable, to be part of the crowd, to express affection toward others, and to share social information. In contrast, although some IM motivations overlapped with those of using Facebook, instant messages were more utilitarian and included relationship development and maintenance. IM usage was seen as a channel suited for more intimate conversations and for sharing problems. As the authors summed it up, "Overall, we can conclude that sociability is a central gratification obtained from both forms of social media. However, the kinds of needs that each medium fulfills are different in nature and directly linked to their functionality."

thumb through a magazine, pay close attention to the way mothers and children are presented. Mass media mommies are usually clean, pretty, cheerful, and affectionate. Ivory Snow laundry detergent typically adorns the packages of its products with a wholesome-looking mother and healthy child smiling out across grocery aisles. (Incidentally, the company was embarrassed back in the 1980s when one of their clean-cut, all-American types went on to star in X-rated films.) The Clairol company sponsored an ad campaign that featured the "Clairol Mother," an attractive and glamorous female who never let raising a child interfere with maintaining her hair. When they interact with their children, media mothers tend to be positive, warm, and caring.[1] Consider these media mommies drawn from TV: Marge Simpson, Alicia Florick (*The Good Wife*), Claire Dunphy (*Modern Family*), and Lynette Scavo (*Desperate Housewives*). All are understanding, reasonable, friendly, and devoted to their children.

These examples show that the media portray motherhood and child rearing as activities that have a positive value for society. Individuals who are exposed to these portrayals are likely to grow up accepting this value. Thus, a social value is transmitted from one generation to another.

Mass Media and Socialization   Sometimes the media consciously try to instill values and behavior in the audience. Many newspapers report whether accident victims were wearing seat belts at the time of impact. In 1989, TV writers voluntarily agreed to portray alcohol usage more responsibly in their programs and to include references to designated drivers whenever possible. The next time you watch current TV shows, see if you can find anyone smoking a cigarette. The health concerns regarding smoking have prompted its virtual disappearance from prime-time TV.

There are probably countless other examples of values and behavior that are socialized, in part at least, through the media. Let us examine some of the consequences of having the mass media serve as agents of socialization. At one level, value transmission via the mass media helps stabilize society. Common values and experiences are passed down to all members, thereby creating common bonds among them. On the other hand, values and cultural information are selected by large organizations that may encourage the status quo. For example, the "baby industry" in this country is a multimillion-dollar one. This industry advertises heavily in the media; it is not surprising, then, that motherhood is

---

[1]OK, Evelyn Harper, Charlie and Alan's mother on *Two-and-a-Half Men,* might be an exception.

media *Probe*   *Unlinking via Text Message*

According to a research study done in Australia, text messages sent via cell phone play a big part in young couples' romantic relationships. Women were more likely to send text messages detailing to their partner how they were feeling. Men, on the other hand, stuck to practical messages such as "I'll pick up some food."

The volume of texting picked up when the relationship was under stress. Apparently, people wanted to refrain from face-to-face interactions when things were going badly, preferring to send less confrontational text messages.

Evidently, you can also unlink using text messages. The research noted that 15 percent of the sample had dumped a partner with just a text message. "We r thru," maybe?

media talk

Advertisers Gone Wild: New Ways to "Get the Message"

Clip 7: 2 minutes 15 seconds

You can watch Clip 7 *on the Online Learning Center home page,* www.mhhe.com/dominick12e. *Select* Student Center *and then* Chapter 2. This clip shows how advertisers are going out of their way to place ads in the strangest places. What functions does advertising serve for society? Why are advertisers resorting to placing ads in unusual places? Where is the oddest place you have seen an advertisement? Do you think advertisements located in odd places are more effective than traditional advertisements (such as billboards, television commercials, newspaper ads)? What types of ads are you least likely to respond to?

WWW

depicted in such an attractive light. To show mothers as harried, exhausted, overworked, and frazzled would not help maintain this profitable arrangement.

Mass media can also transmit values by enforcing social norms. A 2010 story in the *Los Angeles Times* reported that city officials in the small town of Bell, California, had voted themselves exorbitant salaries. Eight of the officials were later arrested and charged with misappropriation of funds.

Not every attempt by the media to enforce social norms is successful. In an effort to combat binge drinking by college students, several campuses launched media campaigns designed to show that excessive alcohol consumption was not as widespread or normal as many students might think. The idea behind the campaign was to show college students that most of their peers drink only moderately or less, thus reducing pressure on them to drink to excess. A report released in 2003, however, found no drop in student binge drinking on university campuses that used a social norms media campaign in their prevention efforts.

TV and Socialization   Of all the mass media, television probably has the greatest potential for socialization. By the time an individual is 18, he or she will have spent more time watching television than in any other single activity except sleep. A prime-time program that is popular with young people might draw an audience of 6 million 6- to 11-year-olds. Because of this wide exposure, several writers have warned of possible dysfunctions that might occur if television is the most important channel of socialization. For instance, since so many TV programs contain violence, it has been feared that young people who watch many such programs might be socialized into accepting violence as a legitimate method of problem solving. In one survey among grade schoolers, heavy TV viewers were more likely than light TV viewers to agree with this statement: "It's almost always all right to hit someone if you are mad at him or her." Another possibility is that the pervasiveness of television violence will encourage fearfulness about the "real world." One study, for example, found that children who were heavy TV viewers were more fearful of going out at night than were light TV viewers. We will discuss this topic at greater length in Chapter 18.

Finally, it has been argued that for many years the image of minority groups transmitted from one generation to the next by the mass media reflected the stereotypes held by those in power: white, Anglo-Saxon, Protestant males. As a result, members of minority groups endured many years during which, for example, Native Americans were seen as savages who murdered civilized whites and African Americans were depicted in menial and subordinate roles. These stereotypes were slow to change, partly because it took a long time for members of these minority groups to influence the workings of large media organizations.

Entertainment   Another obvious media function is that of entertainment. Two of the media examined in this book, motion pictures and sound recordings, are devoted primarily to entertainment. Even though most of a newspaper focuses on the events of the day, comics, puzzles, horoscopes, games, advice, gossip, humor, and general entertainment features usually account for around 12 percent of the content. (If we considered sports news as entertainment, that would add another 14 percent to this figure.) Television is primarily devoted to entertainment, with about three-quarters of a typical broadcast day falling into this category. The entertainment content of radio varies widely according to station format. Some stations may program 100 percent news, while others may schedule almost none. In like manner some magazines may have little entertainment content (*Forbes*), while others are almost entirely devoted to it (*National Lampoon*). Even those magazines that are concerned primarily with news—*Time* and *Newsweek,* for example—usually mix some entertainment features with their news reporting.

The scope of mass media entertainment is awesome. By 2011 more than 50 million people in the United States had seen *Avatar* at a theater. About 110 million people watched the 2011 Super Bowl on the Fox Network. Satellite radio boasts 21 million subscribers. Eminem's *Recovery* album sold more than 3.5 million copies. In a typical month about 2 million people read (or at least look at) *Playboy*. The video game *Call of Duty: Black Ops* sold more than 5 million copies the first day it was on sale.

The importance of the entertainment function of mass media has grown as Americans have accumulated more leisure time. The workweek has decreased from about 72 hours at the turn of the 20th century to the current 40 hours.

The emergence of mobile media (discussed in more detail in Chapter 3) has also amplified the entertainment function of the media. Specially equipped vehicles let children watch DVDs as they go on family trips. Travelers in airport terminals can play games on their cell phones or watch movies on their laptops or iPods while they wait. Commuters can play video games on handheld devices while they travel.

The Internet has enlarged our options for entertainment. Surfing the Web has become a national pastime. Americans spend about 3 hours a day on the Internet and much of that time is spent on activities—such as watching video, playing games, and listening to music— that fall into the entertainment category. In a recent survey respondents were asked, "What sources of entertainment do you turn to most often?" The Internet came in second, behind only television. In addition, the Internet has changed how we define entertainment. About 60 percent of respondents considered social networking sites to be a form of entertainment and the percentage was even higher among 18- to 24-year-olds. Video sharing sites, such as YouTube, contain more than 250 million videos, about 75 percent of them made by amateurs. These numbers suggests that Americans are relying more on their friends, particularly their friends on social networking sites, for diversion and less on the traditional entertainment media.

Troubadours, storytellers, court jesters, and magicians fulfilled the entertainment function in the centuries before the media. What are the consequences of having this task now taken over by mass communication? Clearly, the media can make entertainment available to a large number of people at relatively little cost. On the other hand, entertainment that is carried by the mass media must appeal to a mass audience. As a result, media content is designed to appeal to the lowest common denominator of taste. More programs that resemble *Survivor* and *Jerry Springer* will find their way to TV than will opera performances. Newsstands are filled with more imitators of *Playboy* than imitators of *Saturday Review.* We are more apt to see sequels such as *Star Trek VIII, Wes Craven's New Nightmare,* and *Saw VI* than we are to see *Much Ado About Nothing II* and *More King Lear.* Rock stations outnumber classical stations 20 to 1.

One other consequence of the widespread use of media for entertainment is that it is now quite easy to sit back and let others entertain you. Instead of playing baseball, people might simply watch it on TV or play it on their Xbox. Instead of learning to play the guitar, an adolescent might decide to listen to a recording of someone else playing the guitar. Critics have charged that the mass media will turn Americans into a nation of watchers and listeners instead of doers.

How People Use the Mass Media

It is probably clear by now that statements made about the functions of mass communication in society could be paralleled by statements about how the media function at the level of the individual. Consequently, we will now focus on how the individual uses mass communication (in other words, we are moving from macro- to microanalysis). At the individual level the functional approach is given the general name of the **uses-and-gratifications model**. In its simplest form the uses-and-gratifications model posits that audience members have certain needs or drives that are satisfied by using both nonmedia and media sources. This discussion will be concerned more with media-related sources of satisfaction. The actual needs satisfied by the media are called media gratifications. Our knowledge of these uses and gratifications typically comes from surveys that ask people questions about how they use the media (much like the questions at the beginning of this chapter). We can classify the various uses and gratifications into a six-category system: (1) cognition; (2) diversion; (3) social utility; (4) affiliation; (5) expression; and (6) withdrawal.

Cognition   Cognition is simply the act of coming to know something. When a person uses a mass medium to obtain information about something, he or she is using the medium in a cognitive way. Clearly, the individual's cognitive use of a medium is directly parallel to the surveillance function at the macroanalytical level. At the individual level researchers have noted that two different types of cognitive functions are performed. One has to do with using the media to keep up with current events, while the other has to do with using the media to learn about things in general or things that relate to a person's general curiosity.

Several surveys have found that many people give the following reasons for using the media:

- I want to keep up with what the government is doing.
- I want to understand what is going on in the world.
- I want to know what political leaders are doing.

These reasons constitute the current-events type of cognitive gratification. At the same time, many people also report the following reasons for using mass media:

- I want to learn how to do things I've never done before.
- I want to satisfy my curiosity.
- The media make me want to learn more about things.
- The media give me ideas.

These statements illustrate the second type of cognition—using the media to satisfy a desire for general knowledge.

Diversion   Another basic need of human beings is for diversion. Diversion can take many forms. Some of the forms identified by researchers are (1) stimulation, or seeking relief from boredom or the routine activities of everyday life; (2) relaxation, or escape from the pressures and problems of day-to-day existence; and (3) emotional release of pent-up emotions and energy. Let us look at each of these gratifications in more detail.

Stimulation   Seeking emotional or intellectual stimulation seems to be an inherent motivation in human beings. Psychologists have labeled these activities "ludic behaviors"— play, recreation, and other forms of activity that seem to be performed to maintain a minimum level of intellectual activity. Many people report that they watch, read, or listen simply to pass the time. The media have taken advantage of this need to avoid boredom in many creative ways. Airlines provide audio and video entertainment during long flights. Supermarkets have grocery carts with video screens that display the latest bargains. Restaurants and coffeehouses offer free WiFi to allow customers to surf before they sup. Special magazines are distributed only to doctors' waiting rooms. And advertisements can be found on walls and the backs of stall doors in restrooms.

sound byte

What . . . No Metallica?

Researchers who study the diversion function of the mass media focus on the process by which people seek rewarding media content. No less important is the opposite process: avoiding those forms of entertainment people cannot stand. For example, an Illinois high school teacher was looking for a way to cut down on the number of students who were kept after school as punishment. He started playing Frank Sinatra albums during detention. School behavior improved dramatically.

Relaxation   Too much stimulation, however, is undesirable. Psychological experiments have indicated that human beings are negatively affected by sensory overload, in which too much information and stimulation are present in the environment. When faced with sensory overload, people tend to seek relief. The media are one source of this relief. Watching *American Idol* or reading *People* magazine represents a pleasant diversion from the frustrations and problems of everyday life. The choice of material used for relaxation might not always be apparent from surface content. Some people relax by reading articles about Civil War history; others read about astronomy or electronics. Still others might relax by listening to classical music, and some might check their Facebook page. The content is not the defining factor, since virtually any media material might be used for relaxation by some audience members.

Emotional Release   The final manifestation of the diversion function is the most complex. On the one hand, the use of the media for emotional release is fairly obvious. For instance, the horror movie has had a long history of popularity in America. Starting with *Dracula* and *Frankenstein* and continuing through *The Creature from the Black Lagoon, Them,* and *The Thing* right up to *Nightmare on Elm Street, Friday the 13th, The Ring,* and *Scream,* people have sat in dark theaters and screamed their lungs out. Tearjerkers have also drawn crowds. *Broken Blossoms, Since You Went Away, The Best Years of Our Lives, Terms of Endearment, Titanic, The Notebook,* and *Marley and Me* have prompted thousands, perhaps millions, to cry their eyes out.

On the other hand, emotional release can take more subtle forms. One of the big attractions of soap operas, for example, seems to be that many viewers are comforted by seeing that some people (even fictional people) have troubles greater than their own. Other individuals identify with media heroes and participate vicariously in their triumphs. Such a process evidently enables these people to vent some of the frustrations connected with their everyday lives.

Emotional release was probably one of the first functions to be attributed to media content. Aristotle, in his *Poetics,* talked about the phenomenon of **catharsis** (a release of pent-up emotion or energy) occurring as a function of viewing tragic plays. In fact, the catharsis theory has surfaced many times since then, usually in connection with the portrayal of violence on TV. Chapter 18 contains a discussion of research that has dealt expressly with the catharsis notion.

Social Utility   Psychologists have also identified a set of social integrative needs, including our need to strengthen our ties with family, friends, and others in society. The media function that addresses this need is called **social utility**, and this usage can take several forms. Have you ever talked with a friend about a TV program? Have you ever discussed a current movie or the latest song you downloaded? If so, then you are using the media as **conversational currency**. The media provide a common ground for social conversations, and many people use things that they have read, seen, or heard as topics for discussion with others. There is a certain social usefulness in having a large repository of things to talk about so that, no matter where you are, you can strike up a conversation and be fairly sure that the person you are talking to is familiar with the subject. ("What did you think of the Super Bowl?" "How did you like *Bridesmaids?*")

Social utility is apparent in other instances as well. Going to the movies is probably the most common dating behavior among adolescents. The motion picture theater represents a place where it is socially acceptable to sit next to your date in a dark room without parental supervision. In fact, many times the actual film is of secondary importance; the social event of going out has the most appeal.

Viewers who watch *American Idol* often form parasocial relationships with the contestants.

Other people report that they use the media, particularly television and radio, as a means to overcome loneliness. The TV set represents a voice in the house for people who might otherwise be alone. Radio keeps people company in their cars. In fact, some viewers might go so far as to develop feelings of kinship and friendship with media characters. This phenomenon is called a **parasocial relationship**, and there is some evidence that it actually occurs. For example, one study that examined parasocial relationships between the audience and TV newscasters found that more than half the people surveyed agreed with the statement "The newscasters are almost like friends you see every day."

Affiliation   This use is the individual counterpart to the linkage function mentioned earlier. Psychologists have recognized that one of the central needs of human beings is the need for affiliation. First described in the 1930s, the need for affiliation refers to a person's desire to feel a sense of belonging or involvement within a social group. The Internet is the primary medium that fulfills this function for many people. Facebook, Twitter, Linkedin, and Google Groups are the most obvious examples. Others include online gaming, instant messaging, dating and matchmaking Web sites, and text messaging. The need for affiliation is a powerful one as evidenced by the more than 500 million members on Facebook, the more than 200 million Twitter accounts, and the 100 million professionals on Linkedin. How many Facebook friends do you have?

Expression   Self-expression refers to individuals' need to express their inner thoughts, feelings, and opinions. The first examples of the need for self-expression are the cave drawings done by early human beings. Since that time, the need for self-expression has been fulfilled primarily by creative and artistic activities such as music, painting, writing, dance, and sculpture. The Internet has opened up new vistas for self-expression. Bloggers can express their opinions. Many sites let visitors comment on stories. Epinions.com is a site that is composed entirely of people's opinions. Budding musicians, actors, and filmmakers can post their efforts on YouTube or other photo- and video-sharing sites. MySpace and Facebook pages can be personalized to express a person's individuality. Several sites exist where budding digital artists can post their handiwork. The millions of blogs that have sprung up in the last few years suggest that expression is an important function for the individual.

Many people turn to the media for breaking news events such as the Ebola outbreak in West Africa.

Withdrawal   At times, people use the mass media to create a barrier between themselves and other people or activities. For example, the media help people avoid certain chores, as children are quick to learn. This hypothetical exchange might be familiar:

"It's your turn to let the dog out."
"I can't. I want to finish watching this program. You do it."

In this case attending to mass media content was defined as a socially appropriate behavior that should not be interrupted. In this manner other tasks might be put off or avoided entirely.

People also use the media to create a buffer zone between themselves and others. When you are riding a bus or sitting in a public place and do not want to be disturbed, you bury your head in a book, magazine, or newspaper. If you are on an airplane, you might pop in your iPod ear buds and tune everybody out. Television can perform this same function at home by isolating adults from children ("Don't disturb Daddy; he's watching the game") or children from adults ("Don't bother me now; go into the other room and watch *Sesame Street*").

Content and Context   In closing, we should emphasize that it is not only media content that determines audience usage but also the social context within which the media exposure occurs. For example, soap operas, situation comedies, and movie magazines all contain material that audiences can use for escape purposes. People going to a movie, however, might value the opportunity to socialize more than they value any aspect of the film itself. Here, the social context is the deciding factor.

sound byte

A Real Turnoff

The text mentions that the mass media can be used as a withdrawal mechanism that lets people isolate themselves from other people. But what if you're in a laundromat or a waiting room and there's a TV set blaring away? Suppose you want to withdraw from the mass media? One solution is TV-B-Gone, a device about the size of a package of gum that is really a universal remote control that turns off all TVs within a radius of 50 feet. Just don't use it at a sports bar.

It is also important to note that the functional approach makes several assumptions:

- Audiences take an active role in their interaction with various media. That is, the needs of each individual provide motivation that channels that individual's media use.
- The mass media compete with other sources of satisfaction. Relaxation, for example, can also be achieved by taking a nap or having a couple of drinks, and social utility needs can be satisfied by joining a club or playing touch football.
- The uses-and-gratifications approach assumes that people are aware of their own needs and are able to verbalize them. This approach relies heavily on surveys based on the actual responses of audience members. Thus, the research technique assumes that people's responses are valid indicators of their motives.

A great deal of additional research needs to be done in connection with the uses-and-gratifications approach. In particular, more work is needed in defining and categorizing media-related needs or drives and in relating those needs to media usage. Moreover, additional research is needed to understand the functions performed by social media. Nonetheless, the current approach provides a valuable way to examine the complex interaction between the various media and their audiences.

critical/cultural studies

The uses-and-gratifications approach relies on methods common to the social sciences. Researchers who use this approach ask people questions and tabulate the results or enumerate characteristics of media content. In contrast, critical/cultural researchers use a more qualitative and humanities-oriented approach. Although they use different methods, functional analysis and critical/cultural studies share some similarities. Both take a macroanalytic view of mass communication, both acknowledge that the media can be powerful forces in society, and both recognize that the media can operate in ways that can be dysfunctional. Unlike functional analysis, however, the critical/cultural approach examines such concepts as ideology, culture, politics, social structure, and hegemony as they relate to the role of media in society. Some background on this school of thought may be helpful.

A Brief History

Most scholars suggest that the origins of the critical/cultural model can be traced to the Frankfurt School during the 1930s and 1940s. The Frankfurt School was a group of intellectuals committed to the analytical ideas of Karl Marx. (Keep in mind that we are discussing Marxism as a philosophical system and an analytical tool. Marxism as a political and economic system has fallen on hard times of late.) In simplified terms the core of this Marxist approach was that the best way to understand how a society worked was to examine who controlled the means of production that met the basic needs of the population for food and shelter. Marx noted that many Western countries had adopted a system of industrial capitalism in which mass production created wealth for the capitalists—the ones who owned the factories where the goods were produced. Mass production ensured that the basic needs of a society were met, but at a cost: tension between the haves (the wealthy) and the have-nots (the workers who labored in all those factories). In other words, the capitalist system exploited the working class and guaranteed their domination by the wealthy. Because capitalists were interested in creating more capital (or wealth), they had a vested interest in ensuring that the system stayed in place. Marx suggested that life would be better for all if some other, more equitable system of sharing wealth were in place.

The members of the Frankfurt School extended Marxist analysis into the cultural life of a society. They noted that, just as big firms controlled the production of economic goods, other big companies controlled the production of cultural goods. The radio industry, motion picture studios, newspaper and magazine publishers, and later the television business all adopted the capitalist model of production. According to the Frankfurt School, the culture industry exploited the masses just as capitalists did. They published and broadcast products based on standardized formulas that appealed to the mass audience and at the same time glorified and promoted the capitalist culture. For example, during the Depression of the 1930s, Hollywood did not make films that advocated a different economic or political system. Instead, the studios churned out glitzy musicals and comedies that portrayed common people who get a break and make it big despite bad economic times. The television sitcoms of the 1950s showed well-off families content with their lives in the suburbs: Ozzie and Harriet never agitated for a new economic system.

Much of the writing of members of the Frankfurt School was designed to show the exploitative character of mass culture and the way the culture industry helped destroy individuality by promoting the social dominance of large corporations. The object of the critical theory espoused by these writers was resistance to this mass culture and exploitation. The media were so powerful and pervasive, however, that critical resistance to these forces was nearly impossible. The media continued to reinforce the status quo.

The viewpoint of the Frankfurt School was criticized for being pessimistic and gloomy and for underestimating the power of the audience. Nonetheless, this perspective caused many to analyze the impact of the media industries on the political and economic life of society and to use interdisciplinary theories and methods in their investigations.

The next important stage in the development of the critical/cultural approach took place in Great Britain during the late 1950s and early 1960s. Scholars at the Centre for Contemporary Cultural Studies at Birmingham University noted that members of the British working class used the products of mass culture to define their own identities through the way they dressed, the music they listened to, the hairstyles they favored, and so forth. The audience did not seem to be manipulated by the media, as the Frankfurt School argued; instead, the relationship was more complicated. Audience members took the products of mass culture, redefined their meaning, and created new definitions of their self-image.

This emphasis on meaning was reinforced by studies of film and television. A theory developed by British film critics suggested that cinematic techniques (camera angle, editing, imagery) subtly but effectively impose on the audience the meanings preferred by the filmmaker.

This theory was later amended to acknowledge that, although films and TV shows could try to impose their preferred meanings on people, audience members were free to resist and come up with their own meanings. For example, although the dominant theme in a documentary about efforts to control pollution might be how hard industry is trying to control the problem, some in the audience might see the program as nothing more than an empty marketing gesture by big companies.

Moviegoers can find emotional release when they watch movies such as *Toy Story 3*.

During the Depression most Hollywood films refrained from making social or political statements about the hard times. Instead, films like *My Man Godfrey*, shown here, suggested that things were fine and that, with a little luck, everyone could afford the good life portrayed in the film.

Important to the cultural studies group were the values that were represented in the content. Again drawing from Marx, the group noted that the values of the ruling class became the dominant values that were depicted in mass media and other cultural products. Marx analyzed dominant values in economic terms, but the cultural studies scholars extended the perspective to class, race, and, with the growth of feminist studies, gender. In Britain, and later in the United States, the dominant values that were represented were those of white, upper-class, Western males. The media worked to maintain those values by presenting versions of reality on TV and films that represented this situation as normal and natural, as the way things should be.

The audience, however, was not passive. The dominant values may have been encoded in complex and subtle ways (much critical/cultural research is aimed at describing and analyzing these subtle depictions), but viewers can supply their own meanings to the content (much critical/cultural research tries to catalogue how various audience members interpret content in different ways). One of the classic studies examined how the audience made sense of a British TV program, *Nationwide.* One group of viewers seemed to accept the dominant message of the program that British society was harmonious and egalitarian; another group "negotiated" their own, somewhat different interpretation; and a third group, young blacks who were not part of the mainstream, rejected it altogether.

The critical/cultural approach gained prominence in the United States during the 1970s and 1980s and was adopted by communication researchers and scholars engaged in feminist studies. Like Marxist analysis, feminist analysis saw inequalities in the way that wealth and power were distributed in society. Marx, however, argued that this inequality stemmed from industrial capitalism; feminist scholars suggested that it stemmed from male domination of women in society (sometimes referred to as *patriarchy*). Feminist critics examined how the media and other forms of culture contributed to the oppression of women. Advertising, for example, might suggest that the proper (or natural) place for a woman is in the home or that looking good is the preferred way for women to achieve success.

Not all critical/cultural scholars, however, emphasize power relationships. James Carey, for example, contended that researchers should study how communication creates, maintains, or modifies a culture. He argued that it is valuable to look upon communication as a ritual—how it draws people together and how it represents a sharing of beliefs. Someone interested in the ritual role of mass communication, for instance, might examine the cultural meanings of men gathering to watch *Monday Night Football* and how this rite illustrates the social bonds that help maintain society. Other critical/cultural scholars have examined how cultural myths are embodied in mass communication. A myth is an expressive story that celebrates a society's common themes, heroes, and origins. Studying the way popular media programs utilize the collective myths of a culture might help us understand their success. *Star Trek,* for example, has spawned a cult following, four TV series, and at least a half-dozen movie sequels. A mythic analysis of the TV show suggests that it draws upon a myth deeply rooted in American history—the myth of the frontier where a wagon train heads hopefully into uncharted and potentially dangerous territory in search of better horizons. Note that the *Star Trek* prologue describes space as "the final frontier," the *Enterprise* takes the place of the wagon train, Klingons take the place of hostile Indians, and Kirk becomes the wagon master while Spock serves as trusty sidekick.

As is probably obvious by now, the critical/cultural perspective is multidimensional and encompasses a wide variety of topics and analytic methods. It is difficult to summarize the important notions of such an eclectic approach, but the ones listed next have general relevance.

Key Concepts

Like most other specialized ways of examining the audience, the critical/cultural approach has developed its own specialized vocabulary. We will examine some of the key terms.

Cultural studies, naturally enough, broaden the study of mass communication to encompass the notion of **culture**. Culture is a complex concept that refers to the common values, beliefs, social practices, rules, and assumptions that bind a group of people together. Hence, it is possible to identify a street culture or an Asian American culture or even a college student culture.

Culture is studied through the practices and texts of everyday life. A **text** is simply the object of analysis. Texts are broadly defined: They can be traditional media content such as TV programs, films, ads, and books, or they can be things that do not fit into the traditional category, such as shopping malls, T-shirts, dolls, video games, and beaches.

Texts have **meaning**, the interpretations that audience members take away with them from the text. In fact, texts have many meanings; they are **polysemic**. Different members of the audience will have different interpretations of the same text. Some may interpret it the way the source intended; others may provide their own unique meanings.

Ideology is contained in texts. Broadly, an ideology is a specific set of ideas or beliefs, particularly regarding social and political subjects. Mass communication messages and other objects of popular culture have ideology embedded in them. Sometimes the ideology is easy to see. Commercials, for example, illustrate the belief that consumption is good for you and for society. Other times the ideology is subtler and harder to detect.

Hegemony has to do with power relationships and dominance. In the United States, for example, those who own the channels of mass communication possess cultural hegemony over the rest of us. Groups with political and economic power extend their influence over those groups that are powerless or at the margins of society. Hegemony, however, is not based on force. It depends on the dominated group's accepting its position as natural and normal and believing that the status quo is in its best interest. Media rules, regulations, and portrayals all help the dominant class present the status quo as customary and desirable. Hegemony creates the positions of the superior and the inferior. This division is unstable and continuously being negotiated through interpretations of meaning.

A couple of examples will illustrate how these concepts are used in the critical/cultural approach. One critical/cultural study used the long-running TV show *60 Minutes* as its text. The analysis found predictable themes and formulas in the program. One common type of *60 Minutes* segment can be interpreted as the classic American detective story. Somebody, maybe a business that is ripping off consumers, is committing a crime. The *60 Minutes* reporters have to hunt down clues and gather information. They may sneak in a hidden camera to catch the wrongdoers in the act. The reporters become the heroes; the businesspeople are the villains. The story is eventually resolved, and those who were committing the bad deeds are exposed or brought to justice.

This seems to be a meritorious service to the public. But upon closer inspection, this kind of *60 Minutes* story seems to be reinforcing the hegemony of the dominant class. Note that these stories go after companies or businesses that have violated some basic values of

critical ⊕ cultural issues

PE Teachers in the Movies

Over the past two decades many local school boards have cut physical education (PE) programs. In 2005 it was estimated that only about one in four students in the United States attended a daily physical education class. At the same time, teenage obesity has become a serious problem. In 2011 about 30 percent of children and teens were considered overweight, a 100 percent increase since 2002.

Is it possible that the deemphasis of PE programs could somehow be linked to the way that PE is portrayed in popular culture? A study in a 2003 issue of *Sports, Education and Society*, by Bryan McCullick, Don Belcher, Brent Hardin, and Marie Hardin, provided relevant information on this question by examining media portrayals of PE instructors.

The authors noted that popular culture can be meaningful in shaping how students and others view their relationship to education and educational programs. The article used a conceptual framework called *symbolic convergence theory*, which suggests that mass media provide stories with overarching themes that are shared by most members of a culture. These themes become part of the audience's notion of reality and can be more powerful than the "real thing." With this as a foundation, the researchers set out to find if there were common themes in the way PE instructors are depicted in the motion picture medium.

The authors identified 18 movies from 1990 to 2000 that portrayed physical education teachers. They included many that will probably be familiar to readers of this text: *Clueless, Mr. Holland's Opus, The Faculty, Scary Movie, Never Been Kissed,* and *Whatever It Takes.* The next step was to view the videotape of each movie and to identify common themes and representations.

Several themes emerged. First, PE teachers were seldom shown teaching. Instead, they were on the sidelines "cheering, chiding or deriding the students for lack of ability or machismo. The message is clear: teachers might be found in the classroom but not in the gymnasium."

Second, PE teachers were bullies. In several of the films, they enjoyed humiliating and verbally and physically embarrassing their students. In *Never Been Kissed* the main character becomes fatigued while running and drags herself to the teacher and asks for a drink of water. The teacher responds with "What do I look like, a waitress?" and threatens the student that if she doesn't finish running she will fail PE. In another movie the PE teacher repeatedly hits a male student with a baseball. Similar scenes occur throughout the film, and each time the teacher verbally abuses the student by calling him a girl.

Finally, there was a vast difference in how male and female PE teachers were depicted. Female teachers were portrayed as lesbians. In *Clueless* the main character describes her PE teacher as "in the grand tradition of PE teachers, same-sex oriented." In *Scary Movie* the teacher, Miss Mann, is a female with heavy facial hair and broad shoulders. On the other hand, male PE instructors were portrayed as sex-obsessed heterosexuals. In *Mr. Holland's Opus,* for example, the PE teacher continually talks to the main characters about sex.

The authors speculate about some of the possible consequences these stereotypes might have. The connection between physical education and sexuality might stop both males and females from entering the field because they might want to avoid what they might perceive as the negative connotations that go with the profession. Negative portrayals of PE might also reinforce an unfavorable image that school boards and school officials might have of the topic. As the authors put it: "If school administrators voted for the elimination of physical education after viewing . . . *Clueless, Sidekicks,* and *Never Been Kissed,* they could hardly be blamed."

The researchers acknowledge that their study provides no evidence of a causal link between their findings and the attitudes of audience members toward physical education. They argue, however, that their study provides students, educators, and administrators with information that might help them design strategies to combat these stereotypes and to help PE professionals develop more positive approaches for their chosen vocation.

American capitalism: "Thou shalt not cheat the customer" and "Thou shalt not promise more than thou canst deliver." The stories never question the basic ideology that capitalism is good for you. Instead, they imply that life would be fine if we could just expose all those companies that do not play by the rules of free enterprise and bring them back into the fold. Further, note how the program stands up for the "little person." The reporters are our friends and champions. Everything is fine with the system, and CBS can continue to make money selling ads in a top-rated program. It is easy for viewers to come away with an interpretation that simply reinforces the economic and social hegemony of the powerful.

A second example concerns arcade video games as a text. These games are typically played by a relatively powerless segment of society—younger teenagers. Nonetheless, these players can find a meaning in the games that lets them resist, for a rather short time, forms of social control, allowing them to form their own cultural identity. The arcade games, for instance, reverse the traditional relationship between machine and machine operator. In industry the two work together to produce some commodity; in the arcade the player plays against the machine. The idea is to consume, not to produce.

Playing arcade games is regarded by some with a certain amount of disapproval; some games are violent, and others have mature themes. There is also the view that game playing is a waste of time, and this disapproval on the part of *non*players probably plays a role in the games' attraction for those who *do* play. In addition, the joystick or steering wheel offers the player a direct means to control his or her environment, something that may not be possible in much of everyday life. These factors may account for the continuing popularity of this type of entertainment. Nonetheless, a closer look suggests that, although video games allow the player some freedom of cultural interpretation, the games still work to reinforce the dominant ideology—the social values contained in the games are the common ones in society. Thus, arcade players get a chance to blow away monsters, aliens, drug runners, thugs, and other assorted bad guys; there is no opportunity to show disfavor with the prevailing social norms. And, of course, many of those quarters from the arcade go back to the video game companies, which maintain their economic hegemony and make more games that teens can play to make them feel as though they are resisting the dominant ideology while they are actually supporting it.

This book presents a series of boxed inserts that illustrate the critical/cultural approach and demonstrate the range and diversity of critical/cultural topics. For example, see the boxed insert "PE Teachers in the Movies" in this chapter; in Chapter 6 you will find a critical/cultural analysis of teen magazine Web sites.

Some friction exists between those who choose the functional approach and those who adopt the critical/cultural approach. This discord seems unnecessary since these two paradigms ask different questions about media and society and use different tools to look for answers. In addition, each approach can learn from the other. No single technique is somehow better than the rest. All are useful in the quest to understand the complicated relationships between mass communication and its audience.

main points

- Functional analysis holds that something is best understood by examining how it is used.

- At the macro level of analysis, mass media perform five functions for society: surveillance, interpretation, linkage, transmission of values, and diversion. Dysfunctions are harmful or negative consequences of these functions.

- At the micro level of analysis, the functional approach is called *uses-and-gratifications analysis*.

- The media perform the following functions for the individual: cognition, diversion, social utility, affiliation, expression, and withdrawal.

- The critical/cultural approach has its roots in Marxist philosophy, which emphasized class differences as a cause of conflict in a society.

- The critical/cultural approach suggests that media content helps perpetuate a system that keeps the dominant class in power. It also notes that people can find different meanings in the same message.

- The key concepts in the critical approach are text, meaning, ideology, and hegemony.

- Although they are different approaches, both functional and critical/cultural studies can be valuable tools for the analysis of the mass communication process.

questions for review

1. What is the difference between macroanalysis and microanalysis?

2. What is a dysfunction? What are some examples?

3. What is parasocial interaction? How does it work?

4. What is meant by the uses-and-gratifications approach? What are its assumptions?

5. What are the key terms in the critical/cultural approach?

questions for critical thinking

1. Compare and contrast the functional and the critical/cultural approaches. How does each view the audience? How does each view the media?

2. Compare your own reasons for using Facebook with those that appear at the beginning of the chapter. Are there any similarities?

3. Can you find any more current examples of status conferral? Linkage? Media dysfunctions?

4. As mentioned in the text, one of the assumptions of the uses-and-gratifications approach is that people can

verbalize their needs. Suppose this assumption is false. Is the uses-and-gratifications approach still useful?

5. Review the boxed insert "PE Teachers in the Movies," an example of the critical/cultural approach. Are movie portrayals of teachers in general more positive than the portrayal of PE teachers? Why does Hollywood continue to perpetuate these stereotypes? Is it related to profits? *Glee* is a hit TV show. How does it portray PE teachers?

key terms

paradigm (p. 29)

functional approach (p. 30)

critical/cultural approach (p. 30)

empirical approach (p. 30)

macroanalysis (p. 31)

microanalysis (p. 31)

dysfunctions (p. 31)

surveillance (p. 32)

beware surveillance (p. 32)

instrumental surveillance (p. 32)

credibility (p. 33)

linkage (p. 34)

socialization (p. 35)

uses-and-gratifications model (p. 40)

catharsis (p. 41)

social utility (p. 41)

conversational currency (p. 41)

parasocial relationship (p. 42)

culture (p. 47)

text (p. 47)

meaning (p. 47)

polysemic (p. 47)

ideology (p. 47)

hegemony (p. 47)

internet resources

Online Learning Center

On the Online Learning Center home page, www.mhhe.com/dominick12e, *select* Student Center *and then* Chapter 2.

1. Use the Learning Objectives, Chapter Outline, and Main Points sections to review this chapter.

2. Test your knowledge of the chapter using the multiple choice and flashcard features of the site.

3. Expand your knowledge of concepts and topics discussed in the chapter with additional Questions for Critical Thinking and Internet Exercises.

surfing the internet

The following are useful sites that are related to the material in this chapter. In addition, scan some of the newsgroups on the Net to see some of the special-interest topics that bring people together.

http://eserver.org
Page contains links to works using the critical/cultural approach in many disciplines.

www.aejmc.net/ccs
Home of the Critical and Cultural Studies division of the Association for Education in Journalism and Mass Communication.

www.tandf.co.uk/journals/titles/07393180.asp
The Web site of one of the prominent journals that publishes critical/cultural research: *Critical Studies in Media Communication.*

Hieroglyphics, an early form of picture writing, was developed by the Egyptians nearly 5000 years ago.

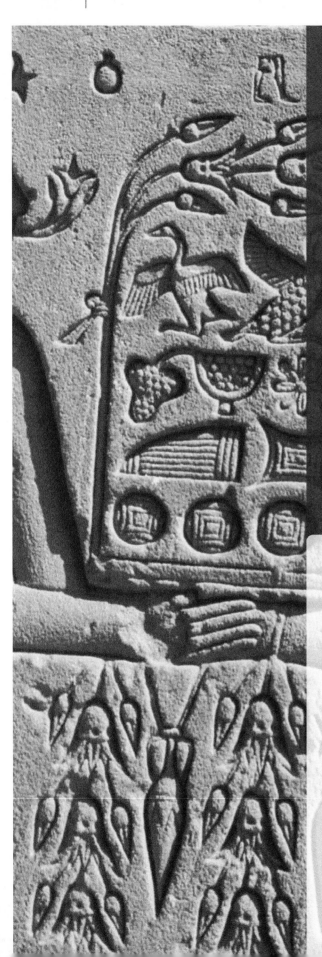

Chapter**3**

historical and cultural context

This chapter will prepare you to:

- describe the major events and general trends in media history
- recognize the milestones in the development of human communication
- understand the role that these advances played in prompting significant changes in our culture and society
- learn that the emergence of new communication technologies changes but does not make extinct those communications that came before
- understand that each advance in communication increases our power to convey and record information

The Yir-Yoront were a tribe that lived in relative isolation for hundreds of years in a sparsely settled part of Australia. A central part of the tribe's life revolved around the manufacture and use of a crude stone axe. Only the older adult men in the tribe possessed the knowledge of how to construct the axe and they were the ones who used it most often. If a woman or young man needed to use the axe, he or she first had to get permission to borrow it from the elders.

Then, in the 1900s, missionaries arrived and decided that they could improve the lives of the Yir-Yoront by giving them mass produced steel axes. The crude stone axes quickly lost their value and women and children began doing tasks that had previously been done solely by men. All of a sudden the elders of the tribe found that they were now dependent on young people and women, who worked much more efficiently using the steel axe. In addition, younger members of the tribe no longer depended upon older members to teach them how to make stone axes. Since the elders' advice no longer carried the importance it once had, their privileged position in society evaporated and the tribe's power structure fell apart. To make a long story short, the tribe eventually disappeared. The moral of this detour into anthropology: New technology often has significant impact on a society's culture.

figure 3-1

Media Time Line

In like manner, the development of new communication technologies has had a significant impact on the tribe we might refer to as Americans. Understanding the history of these technologies will help us comprehend how they have shaped our culture, and since history tends to be cyclical, understanding the past will also help us predict what may happen in the future.

You have probably heard the old joke about the guy who was annoyed because he couldn't see the forest because of all the trees, or couldn't see the blizzard because of all the snow, or couldn't see the city because of all the tall buildings (you probably get the idea by now). Well, sometimes it can be hard to see history because of all the names, places, dates, and events. Consequently, this chapter steps back and takes a broad view of media history, emphasizing major events and general trends.

Specifically, this chapter discusses seven milestones in the development of human communication: printing, telegraph and telephone, photography and motion pictures, radio and television, digital media, mobile media, and social media (see Figure 3-1). This overview of the historical and cultural context of mass communication will supplement and make more meaningful the specific histories of the various media presented in Parts II and III of this book.

before mass communication

Language developed about 200,000 years ago and led to the development of an oral culture—one that depended on the spoken word. Such a culture is tremendously dependent on memory. The history and folklore of the culture was transmitted by individuals who memorized large amounts of information and recited it to those in the next generation who, in turn, passed it on to their offspring. Because there is a practical limit to what one person can remember, the growth of information and knowledge in an oral society was slow.

As humans developed further, it became harder to rely on oral communication to fulfill society's communication needs. The need to keep more detailed, permanent, and accessible records spurred the next big development in communication—writing.

Writing probably developed in Sumeria (present-day Iraq) about 3500 B.C. A few hundred years later other systems of writing sprang up in Egypt and China. The emergence of the written word had many implications for early societies. It created a privileged class—those who could read and write—that had greater access to information, which led to greater access to power. Information was recorded on scrolls or eventually bound into books. Books and scrolls were stored in libraries, permanent repositories of knowledge that endured from one generation to the next. Writing helped establish empires by making it easier to keep records and to coordinate the movement of armies.

Books became more numerous during the Middle Ages. Most were hand-copied by scribes or monks working in monasteries. As trade and travel increased, the demand for information grew. Universities were founded in Paris around 1150 and in Oxford a few years later, making the demand for books even greater. There were not enough monks or scribes, however, to meet the demand, and books became expensive and even more a medium of the elite.

This situation changed dramatically around 1450 with the invention of the printing press and movable type—the first of the communication milestones that we will examine.

printing

The invention of printing is actually a story of many inventions. One of these was the development of paper by the Chinese. China was also responsible for the development of block printing—character outlines were carved out of a block of wood, and the raised parts were inked and pressed against a piece of paper. The oldest surviving block-printed book was published in 868. The Chinese also perfected a system of movable type, using first clay and later blocks of wood for individual characters. The Koreans were experimenting with movable metal type by the beginning of the 15th century.

The next major invention occurred in Germany, where Johann Gutenberg is generally credited with developing a printing press that used movable metal type. Gutenberg published his famous Bible around 1453, and his new printing method quickly spread across Europe. Only 30 years after Gutenberg's Bible appeared, there were printing presses in more than 110 towns in western Europe alone. The total increase in the number of books available in Europe is impossible to calculate, but it is probably safe to say that by 1500 there were hundreds of times more books available than in 1450. As books proliferated, their cost went down. Although still expensive, books were no longer the exclusive possession of the very rich. The printed book could now be afforded by those who were simply relatively prosperous.

The consequences of the printing revolution are so far-reaching and extensive that it is impossible to discuss all of them. Most scholars seem to agree, however, on the most significant results.

Effects of the Gutenberg Revolution

The printing press facilitated the development of vernacular (everyday) languages across the European continent. Most of the pre–printing press, hand-lettered books had been written in Latin—the language of the Catholic Church and of higher education. Reading these works therefore required the knowledge of a second language, which restricted potential readership to the educated elite. Many early printers, however, recognized that a broader market for their books would be available if they were published in French, German, or English. Many printers also felt closer ties to their home country than to the church, further encouraging the printing of books in native languages. This trend had other consequences. Bodies of information now became more accessible to more people, further encouraging the growth of literacy and, in turn, prompting the publication of more books. Finally, the use of the vernacular probably helped pave the way for the nationalism that swept Europe in succeeding centuries.

Johann Gutenberg was a wine connoisseur as well as a metallurgist. His design for the printing press was borrowed from a similar device used in wine making.

The printing press played a role in the religious upheaval that swept Europe in the 16th century. Before the press, those clerics who disagreed with the doctrines and policies of the church had limited channels for expression. Handwritten copies of their views were few, had limited circulation, and could easily be censored or confiscated by authorities. The situation was forever changed after Gutenberg. Theologian and religious reformer Martin Luther's writings were translated from Latin into the vernacular, printed as pamphlets, and distributed all over Europe. It has been estimated that it took only a month for his famous Ninety-five Theses (the ones he nailed to the church door in Wittenberg, Germany) to be diffused across Europe. One of his later pamphlets sold 4,000 copies in a month. Despite efforts by the church to confiscate and burn Luther's writings, the Reformation movement continued. In addition, the printing of the Bible in the vernacular meant that individuals now had direct access to the core of their religious belief system. The Bible could be read directly and interpreted individually; there was no need for clerical intervention. This increased access to information further weakened the power of the Catholic Church and helped the spread of Protestantism.

Moreover, the arrival of printing speeded up the publication of scientific research. Although it would still be considered agonizingly slow in the era of e-mail and the Internet, printing a book of scientific findings took far less time than it did when manuscripts were handwritten. Printing also ensured that identical texts would be read by scientists in different countries and helped them build on the work of others. Galileo and Newton made their contributions to science in the 17th century, after 16th-century advances in printing.

The printing press even helped exploration. The travels of the Vikings are little known, in part because they explored during a time when it was difficult to record and publicize their exploits. Columbus visited America after printing developed, and his deeds were widely known in Europe a year after his return. Printed accounts of the discoveries of early explorers found a ready audience among those eager to find wealth and/or bring religion to the New World. Many early developers published glowing (and sometimes overly optimistic) accounts of life in the new lands, hoping to promote investments and help business. The journeys of the early voyagers were helped by printed books that contained navigational and geographic information about the Americas.

Further, the printing press had a profound effect on the growth of scholarship and knowledge. Whereas access to handwritten textbooks was difficult, university students now had printed texts. (Think how hard it would be to take this course if everybody in the class had to share just one textbook.) As the number of books increased, so did the number of students who studied at a university. Literacy increased further. Interest in the classical works of Greece and Rome revived as these works appeared in printed books available to many. Books based on the scholarship of other countries appeared. The advances in mathematics made by Indians, Muslims, and Arabs were disseminated. Without the printing press the Renaissance of the 16th century might not have occurred.

Finally, the printing press led to the dissemination of what we would today call *news*. As will be discussed in Chapter 5, newspapers sprang up in Europe at the beginning of the 17th century. These early publications were primarily concerned with foreign news. It wasn't long, however, before these papers focused on domestic news as well. This development did not sit well with some monarchies, and government attempts to suppress or censor news content were not unusual. It took until the end of the 17th century to establish the notion of a press free of government control (more on this topic in Chapter 5). The early newspapers made government and political leaders more visible to the public and helped create a climate for political change in both Europe and America.

Technology and Cultural Change

Before leaving this topic, we should note that it is easy to ascribe too much significance to the printing press, to assume that the printing press was the prime mover behind all the effects mentioned. Such a view is called **technological determinism**—the belief that technology drives historical change. A more moderate position suggests that technology functions with various social, economic, and cultural forces to help bring about change.

Printing did not cause the Reformation, but it probably helped it occur. And vernacular languages were growing in importance before Gutenberg, but his invention certainly helped them along. In any case, the birth of printing marks the beginning of what we have defined as *mass communication,* and it is certainly a momentous event in Western history.

The next centuries brought further refinements to printing. A metal press was developed by the late 1790s; steam power to drive the press was added shortly thereafter. Advances in printing technology helped usher in the penny press, a truly mass newspaper (see Chapter 5). A better grade of paper made from wood pulp came into use in the 1880s, about the same time as the Linotype machine, a device that could compose and justify a whole line of metal type. Photoengraving brought better visuals to the paper in the 1890s, as did the development of halftone photography a few decades later. Hot-metal type gave way to photocomposition and offset printing in the 1970s and 1980s, and the computer ushered in an age of relatively cheap desktop printing a few years later. Printing has changed a great deal over the years, but its consequences are still very much with us.

The next two communication milestones occurred during what many have called the age of invention and discovery, the period roughly encompassing the 17th–19th centuries. The reasons behind the many achievements of this period are several. The great explorations of previous centuries had brought different cultures together, and scholars were able to share ideas and concepts. Further, there was a change in the way people generated knowledge itself. The traditional authority of the Catholic Church was eroding, and intellectuals looked less to faith and revelation as a source of knowledge and more toward reason and observation. Philosophers such as Bacon, Descartes, and Locke argued for systematic research based on what the senses could perceive. In addition, scientific societies in Italy, France, and Great Britain helped advance the frontiers of knowledge. And, as already mentioned, the printing press helped distribute news of current discoveries to all, prompting others to achieve new breakthroughs. Whatever the reasons, these three centuries saw such advances as Galileo's use of the telescope and notion of a heliocentric solar system, the theory of blood circulating through the body, Newton's theory of gravitation, the roots of modern chemistry, the utilization of electricity, and the discovery of microscopic bacteria. Inventions came along at a dizzying rate: the steam engine, the locomotive, the tractor, the internal combustion engine, the automobile, the sewing machine, the dynamo, and a host of others. Not surprisingly, the field of communication also saw major developments, as the next two milestones demonstrate.

conquering space and time: the telegraph and telephone

It is appropriate that we spend some time discussing the telegraph and telephone, two related technologies that presaged many of the features of today's media world. For instance, the telegraph harnessed electricity; it demonstrated the technology that would eventually be used in radio. It was also the first medium to use digital communication (dots and dashes). The telephone, with its interconnected network of wires and switchboards, introduced the same concept now at the core of the Internet: Everybody was linked to everybody else.

Development of the Telegraph

It is difficult for people raised in an age of smart phones, cable TV, tablet computers, e-mail, and the Internet to appreciate the tremendous excitement that greeted the development of the telegraph. Before the appearance of the telegraph in the early 19th century, messages could travel only as fast as the fastest form of transportation (with some minor exceptions). A messenger on horseback would clop along at around 15–20 miles per hour. A train carrying sacks of mail could travel about 30 miles per hour. The fastest form of message transportation was the carrier pigeon, which could cover more than 35 miles per hour. Then along came the telegraph, which sent messages traveling over wires at the almost unbelievable speed of 186,000 miles per second, the speed of light itself. No wonder that,

The detected image is the media Probe icon at bottom left.

sound byte

Skeptic

Some were skeptical about the benefits of the telegraph. Maine might be able to talk to Texas, but, as Henry David Thoreau pointed out, what if Maine and Texas have nothing important to talk about?

when it first appeared, the telegraph was described as the great "annihilator of time and space." It was the first device that made possible instantaneous point-to-point communication over huge distances. Today's text messages can be thought of as instant telegraphy.

The technology necessary for the telegraph dates back to the discovery of electricity. Many early inventors realized that electricity could be used to send messages simply by varying the time the current was on and off. Experiments with early versions of the telegraph (*telegraph* comes from Greek words meaning "to write at a distance") were performed in the late 1700s. By the 1830s and 1840s, workable telegraph systems had been developed in England and the United States.

Samuel Morse was the principal force behind the creation of the telegraph in America. His device consisted of a sending key, a wire, and a receiver that made marks on a paper tape in concert with changes in the electrical current. Later versions did away with the paper tape and let the operator read messages by listening to the clicks made by the receiver. To simplify message transmission, Morse developed a code consisting of dots and dashes that is still in use today.

Morse demonstrated his device in the late 1830s and eventually received a grant from the government to continue his work. He constructed a line between Baltimore and Washington, D.C., and opened the nation's first telegraph service with the famous message "What hath God wrought?"

The Cultural Impact of the Telegraph

Public reaction to the new machine was a combination of awe and amazement. The telegraph wires that swayed between poles were called *lightning lines.* The early telegraph offices set out chairs so that spectators could watch as messages came in from distant cities. Some people refused to believe that the new invention worked until they traveled to the source of the telegraphic message and verified it with the sender. Some were afraid that all that electricity flowing around above them posed a danger to their health, and they refused to walk under the wires.

Despite these fears the telegraph grew quickly, and lightning lines soon criss-crossed the nation. By 1850 almost every town on the expanding Western frontier could communicate with every other city. Maine could talk to Texas at the speed of light. By 1866 a cable had been laid on the floor of the Atlantic Ocean, linking Europe and America. Four years later, the overland wires and undersea cable carried more than 30 million telegraphic messages (telegrams).

media *Probe*   *End of an Era*

After 155 years in the telegraph business, Western Union has pulled the plug. The yellow telegram with words typed on strips of paper no longer exists. In January 2006 the company discontinued its telegram service.

Western Union started sending telegrams back in 1851 when it was called the Mississippi Valley Printing Telegraph Company. It took the Western Union name after it acquired a number of competing telegraph services. For decades the telegram brought news, both good and bad, to millions of Americans. In 1929 alone, Western Union handled more than 200 million messages.

Advances in technology, however, ensured the telegram's demise. Faxes and cheaper long-distance telephone rates provided alternatives. The rise of e-mail, text messaging, and instant messages was the last straw.

Western Union, however, is still around. The company has refocused its efforts into the financial area. Its formal name is now Western Union Financial Services, and it specializes in money transfers for businesses. Interestingly, the company chose to announce the end of its telegram service by posting a notice on its Internet site, taking advantage of the medium that helped make the telegram obsolete.

The telegraph was changing communication at about the same time another invention was changing transportation—the railroad. Interestingly, the telegraph wires generally followed the railroad tracks, and stationmasters were often the first telegraphers. The telegraph made it possible to keep track of train locations and coordinate the complex job of shipping goods to various parts of the country—particularly to the West. The telegraph helped the train bring settlers to the frontier and played a role in the country's westward expansion.

The conduct of war was also changed by the telegraph. Troops could be mobilized quickly and moved, usually by railroad, in response to tactical and strategic developments. The significance of the telegraph for the military was demonstrated many times during the Civil War.

Morse's invention had an impact on commerce as well. It sped up communication between buyers and sellers, reported transactions, and organized deliveries. Instant communication brought about standard prices in the commodity markets. Before the telegraph the price of corn varied with local market conditions and might be several dollars cheaper in, say, Chicago than in St. Louis. After the telegraph connected all markets, local variations were evened out.

Further, as we will discuss in more detail in Chapter 5, the telegraph greatly enhanced newspapers' ability to transmit news. Information from distant places had previously taken weeks to reach the newspaper office. With the telegraph and Atlantic cable, even news from Europe could make the next day's edition. Newspaper publishers were quick to recognize the potential of this new device and used it heavily. Many incorporated the word "Telegraph" into their name. The telegraph also helped the formation of news agencies, or *wire services* as they were also called. The Associated Press made great use of the expanding telegraphic service to supply news to its customers. Finally, the telegraph changed the style of reporting. Because the early telegraph companies charged by the word, news stories became shorter. Rather than wordy, reflective, and interpretive reports, scoops, breaking news, and the bare facts began to characterize news reports.

Government and Media

The telegraph also set the precedent for the relationship between the government and large media companies. In many other countries, since the telegraph was used to deliver messages, it seemed an extension of the post office, and the government agency that assumed responsibility for the postal service also administered the telegraph. However, this model was not followed in the United States. Although some in the government endorsed a federal takeover of the telegraph system, the prevailing sentiment was in favor of private, commercial development. By the end of the 19th century, telegraphic communication was dominated by one company, Western Union. As we will see in later chapters, other mass media—motion pictures, radio, television—were also developed as private rather than government enterprises and were dominated by one or a few large companies.

Alexander Graham Bell demonstrates a version of his telephone for representatives of the business community. Bell and his colleagues eventually received 30 patents for telephone-related inventions.

A Change in Perspective

Another consequence of the telegraph was subtler and harder to describe. In some ways the telegraph changed the way people thought about their country and the world. By erasing the constraints of space, the telegraph had the potential to function as an instant linkage device (see Chapter 2) that tied people together. Morse wrote how the telegraph would make a neighborhood of the whole country. A Philadelphia newspaper, shortly after the successful demonstration of the device, wrote that the telegraph destroyed the notion of "elsewhere" and made everywhere "here." The paper declared that the telegraph would "make

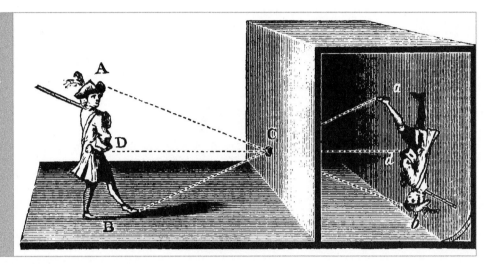

In the camera obscura a small opening containing a lens produces an inverted and reversed image of an object. Many artists used the camera obscura to help them draw precise images of people, landscapes, and buildings.

the whole land one being." An article in a magazine of the period was even more expansive: The telegraph "binds together by a vital cord all nations of the earth." It may not be too much of an overstatement to contend that the telegraph introduced the notion of a global village that was to be popularized a century later by Marshall McLuhan. It created a sense of unity among Americans and encouraged them to think in national and international terms.

The telegraph was joined by a companion invention, the telephone. Like the Morse invention the telephone conquered time and space and had the added advantage of requiring no special skills, such as Morse code, for its use. It transmitted the human voice from point to point. There was some confusion over the precise role the telephone would play in society, but the notion of linking phone users by wires and the development of the switchboard eventually made it possible to connect one place with many others. This arrangement helped the telephone become a fixture in businesses and homes across the nation. The telephone made private communication easier to achieve. It was now possible for people to converse away from the watchful eyes of parents, bosses, and other authority figures. Finally, like the telegraph industry the telephone industry would be dominated by a large corporation, AT&T, which would eventually gain control of Western Union.

In sum, the telegraph and the telephone enabled people to communicate over vast distances in what we now call *real time* and had a far-reaching impact on the political, economic, and social development of the United States and the rest of the world. We will discuss this impact in detail throughout the book. In many ways it is still making itself felt today.

capturing the image: photography and motion pictures

The telegraph and the telephone drew upon advances in the science of electricity. The next communication advance we will examine could not have occurred without advances in the field of chemistry.

Early Technological Development

Two things are required to permanently store an image. First, there must be a way to focus the image on a surface. Second, the surface must be permanently altered as a result of exposure the image. The first requirement was fulfilled in the 16th century with the creation of the camera obscura, a dark chamber with a pinhole in one wall. The light rays

Mathew Brady's famous 1864 photo of a war-weary Abraham Lincoln. Part of this portrait was later used on the five-dollar bill.

that entered the chamber through the small hole projected an image on the opposite wall. The second requirement took longer to achieve. In the 1830s two Frenchmen, Joseph Niepce and Louis Daguerre, experimented with various substances that changed upon exposure to light rays. Silver iodide provided the best results, and Daguerre sold this discovery to the French government. An English scientist, William Fox Talbot, working at about the same time as Daguerre, refined the process by capturing his images on paper in the form of negatives, permitting copies to be made. Other advances quickly followed, including the use of flexible celluloid film. George Eastman's company introduced the Kodak box camera in 1888 with the slogan "You press a button. We do the rest." The Kodak was designed for the mass market. Amateur photographers simply aimed the camera, pressed the button, and then sent the camera off to Kodak, where the film was developed and printed.

There were several long-range consequences of these technological advances. Early photos (called *daguerreotypes*) required long exposure times, making them particularly suitable for portraits, for which the subject could remain still. These early portraits provided a way to preserve and humanize history. Our images of George Washington, for example, are from paintings that show him in an idealized manner, usually in noble poses making him appear distinguished and powerful. Our images of Abraham Lincoln, however, come from the many photographs that were taken of him during his term in office. The early photos, taken around 1860, showed him in flattering poses. The later photos, taken after years of war, showed a man grown visibly older, with lines creasing his forehead and tired eyes.

Photorealism and Mathew Brady

The Civil War was the first American war to be photographed extensively. Before the camera the public's view of war was probably shaped mostly by paintings and etchings that showed magnificent cavalry charges and brave soldiers vanquishing the enemy, not the horror and carnage of actual combat. Mathew Brady persuaded the U.S. government to give him access to the battlefield. (Brady apparently thought the government would cover the costs of his venture, but his expectations were never met, and many of his photos were lost.) Because early photography was not able to capture action scenes, Brady was limited to photographing scenes of the aftermath of a battle. These images, however, were powerful enough. In 1862 Brady's colleagues photographed the battleground at Antietam just two days after the battle and before all the dead had been buried. The resulting photographs were the first to show the actual horrors of war. When the photos went on view in a New York gallery, they caused a sensation. The carnage of battle was revealed to all. As Oliver Wendell Holmes remarked, "Let him who wishes to know what war is like look at this series of illustrations." A hundred years later, other communication advances would bring scenes of horror from the Vietnam War directly into American living rooms.

Photography had an impact on art. Now that a means had been developed to preserve realistic images, artists were free to experiment and develop different ways of portraying the world. Again, although it is hard to say how much of a role photography played in influencing painting, the impressionist, postimpressionist, and cubist schools of painting came to prominence at about this same time. At the other end of the spectrum, photography itself became a fine art, as virtuosos such as Alfred Stieglitz, Margaret Bourke-White, and Edward Steichen created masterpieces of graphic reproduction.

Photography's Influence on Mass Culture

One did not have to be an artist, however, to take pictures—everybody could and did. Advances in film and camera technology put cameras in the hands of the masses. Ordinary people took photos of significant people, objects, and events: marriages, new babies, new cars, pets, vacations, family reunions, proms, and so on. Photo albums quickly became a part of each family's library. Photography enabled each generation to make a permanent record of its personal history. Today's camera-equipped smartphones build upon and expand this tradition.

Advances in the printing process, such as halftone photography, also made it possible for photographs to be published in magazines and newspapers. By the beginning of the 20th century, dozens of illustrated dailies and weeklies were being published in the United States. This development created a new profession—**photojournalism**—and changed America's conception of news. Photojournalism reached new popularity in the 1920s when the pace of life quickened, and many innovations cropped up that promised to save time for the consumer—lunch counters for fast meals, express trains, washing machines, vacuum cleaners, and so forth. When it came to news reporting, the biggest time-saver was the photograph. Readers could look at photos much more quickly than they could read the long text of a story. As a consequence, printed columns decreased and space devoted to pictures increased, helping popularize the tabloids and picture magazines such as *Life* (see Chapter 6).

Photojournalism had subtler effects as well. First, it changed the definition of news itself. Increasingly, news became that which could be shown. Accidents, natural disasters, demonstrations, and riots were natural photo opportunities. This visual bias in news reporting remains a topic of concern even today. Second, as photo historian Vicki Goldberg put it, photography created "a communal reservoir of images." Certain historic events were fixed forever in the minds of the public by their photos: the fiery crash of the *Hindenburg*, the young girl screaming over the body of a dead student at Kent State, the smoking remains of the World Trade Center, the bubbling undersea BP oil leak. All of these images have been etched permanently on the national consciousness.

Modern cell phone cameras have made photographers of everybody, and that, in turn, has raised privacy issues. Cell phones with cameras are banned in many locker rooms and health spas. Nearly every state has a law governing photographic voyeurism. Compounding the problem are the many Internet sites that showcase user-generated content, such as Flickr, Fotolog, and Phanfare. Unsuspecting people might be shocked to find that photos taken without their knowledge or permission all of a sudden show up on the Internet.

Pictures in Motion

The technology behind photography led to the development of another way to capture an image. The goal behind this new milestone, however, was to capture an image in motion. Chapter 10 details the early history of the motion picture medium and traces how it evolved from a series of toys into a giant entertainment industry. It is significant that this new medium evolved while three significant trends were occurring in the United States. The first was industrialization. In the Industrial Revolution, which began in the early 19th century and continued into the 20th, production and manufacturing both increased significantly. Along with industrialization came the second trend, urbanization, as people moved into the cities to be near the plants and factories where they could find jobs. In the United States one-fourth of all Americans lived in an urban area by 1914. The third trend was immigration. About 25 million people immigrated to the United States between 1871 and 1914, and most of them wound up in cities where they went to work in manufacturing plants.

The culmination of these trends was the creation of a huge audience that was drawn to the new medium of motion pictures. The first movie houses sprang up in the cities.

Edwin S. Porter's *The Great Train Robbery* was the first American film to tell a story. This classic Western was actually shot in New Jersey.

Called *nickelodeons*, they were storefronts that had been turned into makeshift theaters, with uncomfortable benches or folding chairs for the audience, a tinkling piano, and poor ventilation. Nonetheless, nickelodeons were big hits among the newly arrived immigrants. By 1910 there were more than 10,000 of these nickelodeons around the country, and film exhibitors and filmmakers quickly recognized that there was a market for filmed entertainment. The motion picture business had started. Film eventually moved to plusher theaters and tried to appeal to the middle class, but it left its mark on the immigrant population. Many learned the customs and culture of their new country from nickelodeons.

Motion Pictures and American Culture

The long-range impact of the motion picture lay mainly in the areas of entertainment and culture. As the demand grew for feature-length films, only very large companies were able to come up with the money needed to pay production costs. As will be noted in Chapter 10, these large companies came to dominate the production, distribution, and exhibition of movies. Today's film industry is controlled by global conglomerates that still follow many of the patterns established in the 1920s.

Movies forever altered America's leisure time. Vaudeville soon died out. Going to the movies became an important social activity for the young. Saturday afternoons that once were spent going to parks and friends' houses were now spent inside a darkened theater.

The movies became a major cultural institution. Photography and the mass-appeal newspaper had made it easier for people to recognize and follow the fortunes of their favorite celebrities, but motion pictures raised this process to a new level. Hollywood produced cultural icons, the movie stars. The popularity of motion pictures was based on their appeal to all social classes. Unlike serious drama, opera, and ballet, which appealed to the elite, movies attracted the masses. The movies helped bring about the notion of a popular culture, a phenomenon whose benefits and liabilities are still being debated.

In 1915 American poet Vachel Lindsay published *The Art of the Moving Picture*, which signaled the beginnings of a new popular art form. Lindsay's book was the first of many serious attempts to develop a theory of film. Although a popular entertainment form that blended business and art, film soon became a topic worth serious study, a trend still with us today as evidenced by the many universities that teach film as part of their curricula.

Finally, although film played its most prominent role as a medium of entertainment, it is important to note that it had an influence on journalism as well. Started around 1910, newsreels appeared weekly or semiweekly and pictured the major events of the period. The big movie studios eventually controlled the production of newsreels. They standardized the content of the 10-minute reels so that audiences could expect to see something from Europe, some national news, some sports, a feature or two, and perhaps a human-interest story. The newsreels were discontinued in the 1950s and 1960s as pictorial journalism moved to television. These early news films, however, influenced many of the conventions and expectations of broadcast news reporting.

ethical issues   *Images of War*

Mathew Brady's decision to photograph dead soldiers on the Antietam battlefield started a controversy that persists even today: What is the proper way to cover the carnage caused by a war? Is it fitting to show dead American soldiers on the nightly newscast or in the newspaper? How about dead enemy soldiers or civilian casualties?

For many years the U.S. government forbade the photographing of dead U.S. soldiers for fear that it would demoralize the home front. Franklin Roosevelt reversed that policy during World War II when he felt that those at home had become too complacent and too removed from the realities of combat. Accordingly, in 1943 *Life* magazine published a photograph of the sand-covered bodies of three unidentifiable U.S. soldiers on an invasion beach in New Guinea. A short time later, John Huston's classic documentary film *The Battle of San Pietro* contained scenes of actual combat and resulting casualties. Decades later, during the Vietnam conflict, filmed scenes of wounded and dead GIs found their way onto the network news.

Operation Iraqi Freedom reopened the controversy. Since many reporters were embedded with combat troops, battlefield coverage was sometimes shown live or shortly after it occurred. For the most part the reporting on the part of the U.S. media was restrained. This led some observers to charge that the media were sanitizing the war and avoiding its harsh realities. On the other hand, when *USA Today* published a front-page photo of the bodies of two dead Iraqis, the paper received dozens of letters and more than a hundred phone calls criticizing the newspaper for its lack of judgment and accusing it of being antiwar.

Media professionals expressed different viewpoints concerning their responsibilities in time of war. Quoted in the *Washington Post*, ABC's Ted

Koppel argued in favor of showing dead bodies: "One thing you cannot do is leave people with the impression that war is not a terrible thing." CNN's Walter Rodgers apparently felt the same way. During a live broadcast from outside Baghdad, Rodgers showed the body of a dead Iraqi soldier next to a burned-out personnel carrier. Said Rodgers in a story in *Newsday*, "You ought to show even more than taste allows so no one has any illusions how terrible carnage and war are."

But does the audience really need to see grisly scenes to be reminded of the horrors of war? Doesn't everybody already know that war is horrible? Steve Capus, an NBC news producer, contended that a newscast should communicate the reality of war without wallowing in death or injury. News anchor Charles Gibson went further: "Any time you show dead bodies, it is simply disrespectful."

John Szarkowski, former director of photography at the Museum of Modern Art, offers another perspective. He argues that editors and reporters should not show every bloody scene they come across. After a while people become inured to the violence in the images, and each successive scene has less power than the one before it.

This issue is still with us today. For nearly two decades the Pentagon imposed a policy that forbade the taking of pictures of the caskets of returning war dead. This rule was relaxed in 2009 to allow photos and video footage as long as the families of the deceased agreed.

In sum, this debate will go on as long as reporters cover wars, and journalists will continue to struggle with their ethical obligations to their profession and to the audience.

news and entertainment at home: radio and television broadcasting

Radio, the first medium that brought live entertainment into the home, would not have been possible without advances in physics. The discovery of electromagnetic waves caught the attention of many scientists, who looked for ways to use this new discovery to send messages. Advances in wire telephony in the United States made it possible to send voice and music over the air and prompted AT&T to fund a massive research program in the area. Radio development, however, was stymied by patent problems. Had it not been for World War I, radio's development might have taken far longer. The war had a couple of major consequences for radio's development. The U.S. Navy solved the legal problem by asserting control over all patents that made possible major advances in technology. Further, a large number of soldiers went into the Signal Corps, where they learned the fundamentals of the new medium. When they came back from the war, these men kept interest in radio alive, helping popularize many amateur radio clubs, and provided the basis for a ready-made audience for early broadcasting.

Radio Broadcasting

The shift from using radio as a point-to-point communication device (like the telegraph) to using it as a point-to-many broadcasting medium caught many by surprise. Thanks to the popularity of early radio stations, broadcasting became a national craze, and by the early 1920s the stage was set for the emergence of another mass communication milestone. Radio was the first mass medium that brought sports, music, talk, and news into the living room.

In addition to World War I, other historical circumstances influenced radio's development. It is easy to overlook today, but when radio first started out, there was no system in place that permitted it to support itself. Many radio stations went on the air simply for the novelty of it, with little thought as to how to fund their operations. Significantly, modern radio emerged in the Roaring Twenties, when economic conditions were vigorous, consumer goods were easily available, stocks were soaring, and many people in the business world were accumulating fortunes. In the midst of this climate, it was easy for radio broadcasting to turn to commercials for its economic base. Accepting advertising brought quick profits and was in tune with the business-is-good philosophy of the times. Business was so good, in fact, that the federal government generally kept out of it. Radio, however, needed government intervention. Overlapping signals from too many radio stations broadcasting on too few frequencies was a serious problem. In 1927 Congress created a Federal Radio Commission (FRC), whose main task was to regulate the technical side of the medium. Unlike the situation in some European countries, the FRC and its successor, the Federal Communications Commission, took a generally light-handed approach to regulation and favored the fortunes of commercial broadcasters.

It was also the era when newspaper chains and many other businesses were consolidating their operations. The development of radio networks fit nicely into this model, and it was not long before national programming was supplied by two, and later three, national radio networks. Further, tabloid newspapers were capturing readers, and Hollywood films were booming. These trends were to have an impact on the future of radio programming. In concert with its evolution as an advertising medium, radio moved toward mass-appeal programming that provided an audience of consumers for those who bought commercial time on the new medium.

Ironically, the Depression of the 1930s, which did some financial damage to radio, also helped its programming. Many performers from vaudeville, the recording industry, and the theater, rendered unemployed by the Depression, took their talents to radio, particularly network radio. As a result, the level of professionalism and the caliber of entertainment improved, and the networks solidified their grasp on the industry. By 1937 almost every powerful radio station in the country was a network affiliate. News broadcasting came of age about this same time, and radio soon became a more important source of news than the newspaper.

The Cultural Impact of Radio

In terms of the long-term impact of this medium, several elements stand out. First, and most obviously, radio helped popularize different kinds of music. One of the early radio stations with a powerful signal was WSM in Nashville, which carried broadcasts of *The Grand Old Opry*, a program that introduced country music to many thousands. Broadcasts of black rhythm-and-blues music crossed the race barrier and gained listeners among whites. In more recent years radio helped popularize rock and roll, reggae, and rap.

Radio made its own contributions to the popular culture. Although early programs recycled many vaudeville acts, genres original to the medium soon developed. One of these was the soap opera, whose familiar formula later made the transition into television. In 1940 soaps accounted for more than 60 percent of all network daytime programming. Entertainment series aimed at children introduced youngsters to *Jack Armstrong—The All-American Boy* and *Captain Midnight.* The significance of these programs may be less in their style or content and more in the fact that they signaled the radio broadcasters' attitude that children were a viable market and that it was acceptable to send advertising their way. Situation comedies such as *Amos 'n' Andy* and action-adventure programs such as *Gangbusters* were other formats that persisted into television.

After a somewhat shaky start, radio news came of age in the 1930s and 1940s. Audiences tuned to the new medium for live coverage of the events leading up to World War II. Listeners could hear live the voices of world leaders, such as Adolf Hitler and British prime minister Neville Chamberlain. Commentators would then provide what in a more modern

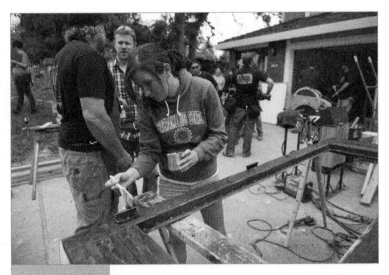

The cultural influence of television is sometimes subtle. Shows such as cable network HGTV's *Color Splash* revived interest in home remodeling and interior design.

era would be called *instant analyses* of what was said. Radio personalized the news: Unlike newspapers, where a byline might be the only thing that identified a reporter, radio news had commentators and reporters with names, distinctive vocal styles, and personalities. A list of famous radio news personnel of the period includes H. V. Kaltenborn, Edward R. Murrow, and Lowell Thomas. These individuals became celebrities and introduced a new component into journalism—the reporter as star. This trend would also carry over into television as network anchors and reporters were able to command multimillion-dollar salaries, just like movie stars and sports heroes.

Finally, like the movies, radio changed the way Americans spent their free time. Radio was the prime source of entertainment and news. Families would faithfully gather around the radio set in the evenings to listen to the latest episodes of their favorite programs. By the 1940s household radio listening time averaged more than 4 hours per day, most of it in the early evening hours. A new phrase emerged to describe this period of peak listening activity. It was called *prime time*, another concept that passed over to TV.

Television Broadcasting

Television, as will be discussed in Chapters 11 and 12, also had its beginnings in the 1920s and 1930s, and, as was the case with radio, a war interrupted its development. World War II halted the growth of TV as a mass medium. Early transmitting stations went off the air during the war, and TV receivers were no longer manufactured. The technology behind TV, however, received a substantial boost from the war effort, as new discoveries in the field of radar were translated into an improved TV broadcast system.

Also, like radio, television became popular during an age of relative prosperity. After a period of postwar retooling, American industry began churning out consumer goods. The self-denial of the war years gave way to a fulfillment of long-repressed desires, as Americans bought new cars, dishwashers, barbecue grills, and air conditioners. But the TV set was the most sought-after appliance. Television swept the country during the 1950s. It took the telephone about 80 years to reach 85 percent of the country's homes, and the automobile did it in 49 years. Television did it in 10. Approximately 10 million homes had TV in 1950; by 1959 that number had more than quadrupled. As new labor-saving appliances increased leisure time, more often than not that leisure time was spent watching TV. Household furniture had to be rearranged to accommodate the TV set in the living room.

The Cultural Impact of TV

Television grew up surrounded by other dramatic social trends and events. Americans were moving into the suburbs, and commuting thus became a ritual. Women were beginning to enter the workforce in greater numbers. The 1960s saw the emergence of the civil rights movement, the escalation of the war in Vietnam, and the growth of the counterculture. Television brought these happenings into the nation's living rooms.

Today, television is in 99 percent of all households, and the set is on about 8 hours every day. In an astoundingly short period, TV replaced radio as the country's most important entertainment and information medium and became a major cultural and social force. In fact, television probably has not been with us long enough for us to see all of its ultimate consequences. Some, however, are fairly obvious. Television has become a major consumer of time. Sleeping and working account for the most time in a person's day, but

media *Probe*   *The Rise of the Intangibles*

As Negroponte predicted, the shift from atoms to bits continues to accelerate. It may not be long before all of the traditional media forms (atoms) shift to intangible form (bits). The trend is easy to see.

- The popularity of the Kindle, the iPad, and other e-book readers has prompted publishers to release more books in digital form. In 2011, Amazon reported that Kindle e-books were outselling print books.

- The sale of CDs is in sharp decline, down 23 percent from 2007 to 2009. Conversely, sales of digital music are increasing.

- Sales and rentals of DVDs are plummeting; wholesale revenue dropped 44 percent from 2009 to 2010. Netflix and other services that offer direct download of movies to the home TV set are flourishing. More than 25 percent of U.S. homes equipped with broadband subscribe to Netflix.

- Newspapers and magazines are struggling to keep their paper versions alive, and most are providing apps that allow readers to subscribe to digital versions over their smartphones or tablet computers.

- Microsoft and Apple are offering video games via direct download to the Xbox 360, iPhone, and iPod Touch.

Of course, this transition will not happen overnight and some traditional media forms will survive, but its implications are profound. Many traditional media companies will have to find new business models to survive. New digital companies such as Apple, Google, and Amazon will become more important in mass communication. Advertisers will rethink their strategies for reaching consumers. Media professionals will need to develop new ways of performing their jobs. Subsequent chapters of the book will provide more details on how this transition is transforming mass communication.

TV watching ranks third. Television also has transformed politics. Political conventions are staged for TV; candidates hire TV consultants; millions are spent on TV commercials; candidates debate on TV; and so on. TV has exerted a standardizing influence on society as well. Clothing, hairstyles, language, and attitudes seen on TV pervade the nation and, for that matter, the rest of the world. Further, television news became the most important and believable source of information. And, like the motion picture, television created a whole new slate of stars and celebrities. It has also been suggested that television has become an important source of socialization among children and that TV programs inspire antisocial and other undesirable behavior. (Chapter 18 reviews the evidence for these assertions.)

Although the telegraph was the first to be called the "great annihilator of time and space," television might be a better candidate for that title. Audiences have seen TV pictures live from Baghdad, Earth's orbit, the moon, and Mars (well, as live as they can be from a place so far away). In fact, today's TV viewer expects to see live reports of breaking stories, no matter where they are; no place seems far away anymore.

Photography was credited with creating a reservoir of communal experience. Television, however, has widened and deepened that reservoir. For example, televised images of President Kennedy's funeral, the *Apollo 11* moon landing, the *Challenger* explosion, the planes striking the World Trade Center, and the aftermath of Hurricane Katrina have all been indelibly impressed upon the national consciousness.

the digital revolution

In his book *Being Digital*, Nicholas Negroponte, director of MIT's Media Laboratory, summed up the digital revolution as the difference between atoms and bits. Traditionally, the mass media delivered information in the form of atoms: Books, newspapers, magazines, CDs, and DVDs are material products that have weight and size and are physically distributed. Negroponte maintains that this is rapidly changing: "The slow human handling of most information in the form of [recorded music], books, magazines, newspapers, and videocassettes is about to become the instantaneous transfer of electronic data that move at the speed of light." In short, atoms will give way to bits.

As an example, consider the difference between e-mail and traditional paper mail. In the traditional system a letter must be placed in an envelope with a postage stamp and

social issues *Are We Making Progress?*

All the communication milestones discussed in this chapter changed the way information was stored or transmitted. Starting with the printing press, they all expanded the scope of human communication by making it possible for people to share information with other people in other places or at other times. This achievement prompted a rather optimistic attitude toward the social benefits of the media. For example, the telegraph was viewed as a force for morality, understanding, and peace. Both radio and TV were touted as means of bringing education, high culture, and refinement to the masses. Cable TV was supposed to bring new forms of entertainment to minority groups and open the way for two-way TV that would aid the democratic process by making possible electronic polling. None of these things has yet come to pass. Nonetheless, the Internet, with its ability to connect everybody to everybody, is currently being touted as an information revolution that will affect society as deeply as the printing press. Whether this will happen is a matter of debate, but for now it might be useful to ask if new communication technologies automatically carry with them social benefits. Have they been liberating or constrictive?

A number of social critics have pointed out that new communication media expand the potential for freedom of expression and have greatly enlarged the scope of human culture. The cost of sending messages over long distances has dramatically decreased. Thanks to the telegraph, telephone, and Internet, people can do business, socialize, and argue with people all over the world. The new media have made information available to all. And, if information is power, the new media will empower more individuals. New means of communication make it easier for democracy to

function. Film, radio, and TV have opened up new art forms and patterns of entertainment.

Others suggest a different interpretation. The new communication media have spurred the growth of large conglomerates whose main goal is profit, not cultural enrichment. Further, new communication media create an overload of information, some of it overpowering and pervasive, such as commercials, junk e-mail, and telemarketing. The information made available by the new technologies may be neither interesting nor useful nor profound, and it may interfere with people's attempts to identify the truly significant.

Moreover, although technological advances—such as the telegraph, telephone, and Internet—have expanded the scope of communication, is any of the communication worthwhile? Check out any chat room or Facebook page, and you will probably find that much of the communication consists of greetings, good-byes, flirting, and "how-are-you's." Twitter messages can't exceed 140 characters. How much real dialogue actually occurs? Is it possible to have a meaningful conversation with people whom you can't see and who may not even be who they say they are? The new media have done little to promote political participation. Political apathy continues to increase. Most people would rather stay at home and watch TV than go to a political forum. Further, many critics would argue that the new media have provided little that is new and fresh in the arts and entertainment. Expanded TV channels have brought us more of the same.

In sum, advances in communication media have the potential for both positive and negative consequences.

given to the U.S. Postal Service, whose employees sort it, transport it, and deliver it a few days later to its recipient. E-mail needs no paper, no postage, and no delivery by postal carriers. It is a series of bits of information that travels electronically and is delivered in seconds rather than days. With e-mail the same message can be copied a thousand times and sent to a thousand different people much more quickly and cheaply than with paper mail.

At the risk of oversimplifying a rather complicated topic, we can describe **digital technology** as a system that encodes information—sound, text, data, graphics, video—into a series of on-and-off pulses that are usually denoted as zeros and ones. Once digitized, the information can be duplicated easily and transported at extremely low costs.

As will be discussed in Chapter 4, the computer was the first device to use the digital system to process information. The innovation quickly spread to other media. Digital technology makes possible the special effects now common in motion pictures and television, as well as digital audio, digital video, digital photography, and digital equivalents of newspapers, magazines, and books.

The development of the Internet meant that computers could send digital information to all parts of the globe. All of a sudden, a new distribution medium was available that permanently changed the media environment. In short, digital technology and the Internet triggered a revolution in the way information is stored and transmitted. As a result, the traditional mass communication media found themselves in uncharted waters and had to figure out how to cope with this drastic development. Newspapers, for example, used to exist only on paper (atoms). Now they exist in both paper and

media
Probe   *Martin Cooper*

Almost everybody knows that Alexander Graham Bell was the inventor of the wired telephone, but not too many people know about Martin Cooper, the person generally given credit for inventing the cell phone. Cooper received a degree in electrical engineering and, after a stint in the Navy, went to work for the Motorola Company in 1954. During his early years at Motorola, Cooper worked on developing portable communication devices. In 1967 he perfected a portable handheld police radio.

Motorola then gave Cooper the task of leading its research into cellular communication technology. At the time, Motorola was in a heated competition with rival Bell Labs to come up with a workable system. While the scientists at Bell worked to develop a bulky car phone, Cooper convinced Motorola to develop a personal phone, one small enough and light enough for people to carry around. After several years of experimentation, Motorola was ready to unveil its invention to the public. In April 1973, on his way to a press conference in New York City, Cooper decided to give the phone one last test. Standing outside a New York hotel, Cooper pulled out his prototype cell phone, which looked like a white brick with a number pad and an antenna. To the amazement of passersby, Cooper dialed a number and began talking out loud into his phone, thus making the first private personal cell phone call. Who was at the other end of Cooper's call? His rival at Bell Labs. Cooper can't remember his first words, but they were probably something like "Guess what? We did it." He does remember that there was a long period of embarrassed silence at the other end.

As of this writing, Cooper, now in his seventies, is still active in cellular technology. He is chairman of a company that is trying to improve wireless access to the Internet.

digital form (bits). Big recording companies used to distribute music on tape or on disk (atoms). Napster and other music-sharing sites proved that individuals could download music files (bits) from other individuals on the Internet, totally bypassing the recording companies. The chapters in Parts II and III of this book discuss how the media are adapting to the digital age.

The digital revolution, of course, has had a profound impact not only on the mass media but also on other institutions. It has, for example, transformed business. Even companies that deal in atoms rather than bits have found that they have to devise whole new marketing and distribution schemes to capitalize on the new digital age. It is not possible (yet) to have a tennis racket physically delivered over the Internet, but you can go online, search the various sporting goods sites for bargains, and order one that appeals to you. The Postal Service or a package delivery company, however, still has to deliver the racket (atoms) to you. The importance of this new form of buying and selling has added a new noun, *e-commerce,* to our vocabulary.

Of course, for most people reading this book, the digital revolution is no longer a revolution—it's their life. Access to powerful information processing and storage tools is no longer earthshaking; it's taken for granted. Today's college students do most of their research online, store their music and photos digitally, communicate via text messages and Facebook, make their travel arrangements through the Web, and entertain themselves with video games, digital TV, streaming video, iPods, and iPads.

The aftermath of this revolution, as has been mentioned previously, has been the empowerment of the individual audience member. Fledgling writers no longer need a publisher; they can create a blog, discussed in Chapter 4. New bands can bypass music companies and make their music available online. People with items to sell no longer have to pay a newspaper to run classified ads; they can find buyers for free on the Internet. Traditional news media no longer have monopolies over information. Many pictures of the 2009 U.S. Airways crash landing in the Hudson River and the postelection violence in Iran were taken by witnesses with digital cameras or cell phones and shared over the Internet. All in all, the digital age has made technology accessible and cheap so that information may be obtained and shared.

The potential social and cultural implications of the digital age are considerable.

First, as mentioned in Chapter 1, digital technology has made it possible for everyone to be a mass communicator. This, in turn, is having a huge impact on how people are getting news, opinion, and entertainment. The trend toward user-generated content is one

critical⊕cultural issues

The Meaning of Media

Cell phones, laptops, and tablet computers belong to that broad class of devices known as *mobile information devices*. It's possible, however, that lumping these devices under one umbrella label may obscure differences in the way audience members perceive their functions. Communication scholars point out that communication technologies may be socially constructed in different ways by their users.

In an article in the June 2003 issue of *Critical Studies in Mass Communication*, Paul Leonardi argues that culture plays a major role in how media are perceived. Leonardi conducted focus groups (structured group interviews guided by a moderator) among Latinos living in the United States. He asked participants to discuss how cell phones, computers, and the Internet were perceived in Latino culture.

His results were somewhat surprising. Latino culture places a high value on consistent and close interpersonal contact, and the cell phone was seen as consistent with that value. Focus group participants revealed that the cell phone was an important tool for communication and was becoming a necessity for daily life. More than 90 percent of respondents had used a cell phone. Almost all of those who didn't currently own a cell phone planned to buy one within a year. Respondents recognized the utility of the cell phone in an emergency and the fact that cell phones represent an alternative way of reaching someone when the land lines are busy. Cell phones had become so ingrained in their daily lives that some participants mentioned that their children used cell phones to call them from another room in the house to ask what was being prepared for dinner. In short, the cell phone fit nicely with cultural values.

On the other hand, computers and the Internet were not such a good fit. Only 40 percent of the respondents had used a computer, and even fewer (27 percent) had ever used the Internet. Respondents appeared to think of computers and the Internet in the same way, treating them as similar. They did not see the Internet as a communication medium.

Instead, the Latinos in these focus groups perceived it as a tool with which to find information. The use of e-mail, chat rooms, and message boards as communication channels was seldom mentioned. Although computers were perceived as useful devices, they were also seen as inhibiting interpersonal communication among family members and friends. Surfing the Internet was perceived as a solitary activity that isolated people from each other. In short, respondents felt that computers and the Internet did not keep people connected. As a result, interpersonal values were jeopardized by these technologies.

Language also played a role in participants' preference for the cell phone over the computer. Spanish-language cell phones are readily available; Spanish-language computer platforms are harder to find. In addition, only a small portion of Internet content is in Spanish. This posed a cultural problem for Latinos. In order to access the Internet, it was necessary to forgo the use of one's native language.

Although many of the respondents said that they planned to purchase a computer in the near future, their stated reasons for buying a computer had nothing to do with the computer's communication potential. Instead, the Latinos in Leonardi's study recognized that those who didn't have a computer would be in an inferior position to those in mainstream U.S. culture.

Leonardi's findings highlight that Latinos living in the United States do not view these information devices as homogeneous. Instead, they have distinct perceptions based on how cell phones, computers, and the Internet relate to their cultural values regarding communication. As Leonardi sums up: "[T]he communication goals of a particular group of users always play a crucial role in their uses and perceptions of technology. If we forget this, we may blindly adopt technologies because we believe they are a sign of progress without making sure they help us progress."

manifestation of this. In a typical month more than 60 million people visit YouTube to watch videos posted by other people—that's a much bigger audience than most hit prime-time TV shows attract. And YouTube is not the only video-sharing site. At last count there were more than 60 similar Web sites. It would appear that we are all trying to entertain each other.

The number is hard to pin down, but there are probably more than 130 million blogs on the Internet. Bloggers have become citizen journalists, reporting live from the scene of major news events such as the inauguration of President Barack Obama. They have also influenced debates on such topics as Social Security reform and party politics. Many blogs, such as Power Line and The Daily Kos, have become powerful editorial voices.

Second, consider what the digital age might mean for politics. A huge amount of political information—party platforms, candidates' positions, text of speeches—is available in digital form on the Web. A Pew Foundation survey found that the number of Americans who got campaign information online doubled from the 2000 to the 2004 election. Ideally, this should result in a better-informed electorate. Indeed, the Internet raises the possibility of true direct democracy. Our current representative democracy was conceived in part as a solution to the practical problem that all the people could not be physically present in one place to debate and vote. The Internet now makes it possible for computer owners to debate and cast a ballot at home. Do we still need representatives? Should we institute "digital democracy"?

Americans are already living in digital homes. They talk on digital telephones, play digital video games, watch digital TV, save programs on digital video recorders such as TiVo, stream movies, listen to digital music, take pictures with digital still and video cameras, and interconnect home computers via digital networks. The digital world touches everyone's life every day.

Finally, the arts have entered the digital age. There's a Digital Art Museum online that exhibits the work of leading artists. There are many other Web sites that feature digital artwork. Musicians, sculptors, and graphic artists have also embraced digital technology.

On the downside, now that the digital age has torn down the barriers to accessing and producing information, there is a whole lot of it. Enter "digital revolution" into a Google search, and you'll get about 7 million hits. The information is organized into not what you think is relevant but what the search engine thinks is relevant. Consequently, the results of the search seem chaotic, and you may have to scroll through several pages before you find something that is even remotely connected to what you are looking for. The digital revolution has resulted in an information glut. As scholar Neil Postman describes it in an article in the *Harvard International Journal of Press/Politics,* "Like the sorcerer's apprentice, we are awash in information without even a broom to help us get rid of it. Information comes indiscriminately, directed at no one in particular, in enormous volume, at high speeds, severed from import and meaning."

Finally, there is the problem known as the "digital divide." In the United States, although the gap shows signs of narrowing, families making more than $50,000 per year are more than twice as likely to have Internet access compared to those earning $30,000 or less. And whereas about 77 percent of the population of North America is connected to the Internet, in Africa it is about 11 percent. In the future those who have access to information will also have more access to power than those who do not. Will this digital divide translate into more serious social, economic, and political divisions?

mobile media

Sometimes it's hard to see a milestone when you're in the middle of it, but the signs are getting hard to miss. Walk around campus or on a busy main street, and see how many people are talking on cell phones. Check out any airport waiting lounge, and see how many people are laboring over laptop computers or reading on a Kindle or playing Angry Birds on an iPad. What you see are indications that the next wave of communication technology is breaking over us.

About 250 million people in the United States own cell phones. Of these, about 46 million are smartphones—phones that let you make calls but also incorporate features found on a computer such as Internet connectivity and the ability to send e-mail. More than 60 million people carry laptops and another 12 million or so have iPads or other tablet computers. All of these devices share common characteristics.

- They depend on wireless technology.
- They are portable, making it possible for people to access information from anywhere. The new portable media are the best illustration of one of the major themes of this book: increased media mobility.
- They are interconnected, making it possible for people to hook into the Internet or the worldwide phone network.
- They are blurring the distinction between mass and interpersonal communication.

Before the cell phone, two screens dominated American lives: the TV screen and the computer screen. Cell phones and tablet computers have become the third screen—a

sound byte

screen that has the potential to drastically transform traditional media and American culture. Let's first take a look at how mobile media are serving some of the traditional media functions discussed in Chapter 2.

We'll start with surveillance. Radio and TV stations have been providing traffic reports for decades, but now subscribers to a company called Traffic411 can hear the latest information tailor-made for their particular commute over their cell phone. Sports fans can receive scores, standings, and the latest news about games in progress over their phones if they subscribe to ESPN wireless. Several services offer the latest stock prices to their phone customers. Need to check ski conditions before heading out to the slopes? Motorola offers an Internet-ready cell phone that allows you to stay informed.

The newest generation of cell phones lets users take still pictures or video clips and post them on the Web in seconds. Imagine millions of Americans walking around with video-equipped cell phones. When breaking news occurs, people in the area can take video and still photos before the media even arrive on the scene. Striking images of the 2010 earthquake and tsunami in Japan were placed directly on the Web by local individuals. The news was transmitted without a traditional reporter or news organization. A cell phone video of Saddam Hussein's execution made its way onto the Web. In the future we will all be reporters.

Entertainment is firmly entrenched on the small screen. Comcast offers Xfinity, an application for the iPad, iPhone, and iPod touch, which features a selection of video-on-demand programs. HBO To Go offers a similar app for the iPad. Hundreds of game apps are available for tablet computers and smart phones. The Angry Birds app has been downloaded 100 million times. Millions listen to music on smartphones. Netflix subscribers can stream movies to their mobile devices. E-readers, such as the Kindle, are becoming increasingly popular.

Turning now to linkage, it's obvious that being connected to millions of other people all over the world makes everyday life easier. What was once considered wasted time can now be used productively. Laptops enable people to read documents, send e-mail, prepare reports, and analyze data while waiting for a plane or even sitting on the plane itself. Businesspeople trapped in a traffic jam can make calls and stay in touch with the office through their smartphones. A special use of the linkage function is achieving safety and security. A *Consumer Reports* survey found that security was the number-one reason people buy cell phones. Cell phone users can report accidents and other emergencies in seconds, no matter where they occur. More than 30 percent of all 911 calls come from a cell phone.

If you're late, you can call or send a text message alerting those at your destination. If you're lost, you can call for directions. If you're buying groceries for dinner, you can check

The cell phone is now the primary mode of socializing for teenagers. More than half of teens in the United States have their own phone.

to see if people want fish or chicken. There are many other examples, but the words of one 17-year-old pretty well sum it up: "With my cell phone I can order pizza from anywhere." This use vividly illustrates how wireless portable media are serving the linkage function of communication; thanks to the Internet and the cell phone network, everybody can be linked to everybody.

The cell phone has taken on symbolic properties. Users

media *Probe*   *This Is Your Brain on a Cell Phone*

Ever since cell phones first made their appearance there has been concern about health risks associated with long-term use. Scientists are concerned that radiation from the phone might cause brain tumors or other problems.

A 2011 experiment looked at how regions of the brain reacted to prolonged cell phone use. The subjects held cell phones to their left and right ears for 50 minutes on two different days. On one day the cell phones were off. On the second day the cell phone held to the right ear was on while the other was off. The study found that regions of the brain close to where the cell phone was held showed increased activity, but it was unknown if such increased brain activity posed any health hazards. Nonetheless, the experiment demonstrated that the human brain is sensitive to the electromagnetic radiation coming from cell phones, a finding likely to prompt more investigation.

The World Health Organization is being cautious about possible health hazards. In 2011, it labeled cell phones as a possible cancer-causing agent. The agency stressed that the link is far from clear and that more research is needed before a reliable conclusion can be drawn. Nonetheless, for those who are worried about the risks of prolonged cell phone use, experts advise keeping calling time to a minimum, using the speaker phone, or wearing headphones.

customize their phone's appearance and ring tones to reflect their own individuality and/or status. Having the latest, thinnest model with all the bells and whistles has become "cool."

Family life has been forever altered because of cell phones. About 75 percent of all teenagers now have access to a cell phone, and more than 50 percent own one. The increasing number of teens with cell phones is due in part to parents who want their children to be prepared in case of an emergency or who want to check up on them when they are out of the house. In a family in which parents are on the go because both hold jobs and children have to get to soccer or gymnastics or band practice, the cell phone provides a way for parents to monitor offspring by phone rather than in person. This new phenomenon is called **mobile parenting.**

Cell phones have even changed our culture's conception of time, a phenomenon called **time softening.** You've probably experienced this scenario several times. You're supposed to meet a friend at a restaurant at eight. A few minutes after eight, your friend calls you on your cell phone and says he's in his car only a couple of miles away and should be there in 10 minutes. If you're in contact, can you really be late?

Of course, like most revolutions mobile media have a downside. Most important, driving and talking on a cell phone don't mix. A study done at Harvard in 2002 suggested that cell phone use while driving might be linked to as many as 2,600 traffic deaths a year. Another study concluded that drivers on cell phones contribute to as many as 1.5 million accidents a year. It's no surprise, then, to find that as of 2010, 30 states had passed laws to limit cell phone usage while driving.

The linkages provided by cell phones can be used for evil purposes. The attacks in Mumbai, India, were reportedly coordinated by individuals in Pakistan who guided the gunmen by cell phone and even in some cases decided the fate of hostages.

Camera-equipped cell phones have also raised privacy issues. Celebrities have to put up with star-obsessed fans (dubbed the "snaparazzi") taking their photos while they are eating, shopping, or walking down the street and posting them on the Web. In New York City several restaurants, clubs, and gyms frequented by celebrities have banned cell phones.

For every person who appreciates the convenience of a cell phone, there's another person who wishes that they would just shut up. Most professors are not amused by cell phones ringing during lectures. People eating at restaurants find their dining experience marred by people at other tables chatting loudly into their phones. Commuters relaxing or reading on trains and buses are disturbed by the loud conversations of cell phone users.

Finally, wireless mobile media can be expensive. A 64-gigabyte Apple iPad 2 with WiFi and 3G connectivity retails for about $830. The BlackBerry Torch 9800 costs nearly $500. An iPhone 4 runs about $300. If it turns out that only the rich can afford these devices, the digital divide between rich and poor will only increase.

The Facebook Web site: "Giving people the power to share and make the world more open and connected." Facebook has more than two billion active users worldwide.

social media

We are in the midst of the last communication milestone that we will examine—social media. We will discuss social media in more detail in the next chapter. In this section, we will take a macroanalytic view and trace their history and cultural impact.

The first tool for social media was the telephone. It connected friends and family and kept people in touch. When Bell Labs invented speed dialing, the telephone became an instrument of community building. The speed dial numbers programmed into a phone became a de facto community of people (and emergency services) that you felt were important to you. Speed dialing even introduced the notion of a preferred place within the community; if you were number one on a person's speed dial, you were probably number one in that person's life. (There is a classic *Seinfeld* episode about competing for the top spot on a person's speed dial.)

The birth of the Internet opened up new channels for social media. As we shall learn in Chapter 4, when the Internet first developed it was designed as a tool for the sharing of scientific data. Instead, scientists sent e-mails to their friends and colleagues. Linking several computers together made possible instant messaging, and in 1988 Internet Relay Chat allowed users to send real-time messages to others on the same channel.

The primary impetus behind the growth of social media was the development of the World Wide Web. The origins of social media on the Web can be found in the mid-1990s when personal Web pages became popular. A means of self-expression, these were pages where people could post photos, brief autobiographies, poems and essays, and links to other sites that they enjoyed. Visitors could sign a guest book, leave a brief message, and send e-mail to the site's owner, but personal pages did not lend themselves to building a social network.

The Web site that is generally acknowledged as the first social network site was SixDegrees.com. The site advertised itself as a tool to help people connect. It attracted a large audience but couldn't sustain itself and went under in 2000. Ryze.com debuted in 2001 as a site aimed at linking together business professionals and entrepreneurs but never achieved mass popularity. Friendster launched in 2002 and was originally designed to compete with online dating sites. The theory behind Friendster was that people would feel more comfortable dating friends of friends than they would strangers that they met online. It was immediately successful and soon had more than 3 million users. The quick growth led to technical problems, and its servers could not keep up with the demand. In addition, people began creating fake profiles and posting fake photographs. These problems led many to abandon the site.

Many social media sites launched in 2003. The most successful was MySpace, originally designed to appeal to those who had dropped Friendster. MySpace let users personalize

sound byte

Did Kramer Invent Facebook?

Seinfeld fans might remember the episode in which Kramer decided to post pictures and names of all the people in his apartment building on the lobby wall so that residents would socialize more with one another. His idea worked so well that Jerry insisted that Kramer take the photos down because all the elderly female residents of the apartment building kept greeting him with kisses.

It seems that Facebook uses the same concept but on a much bigger scale (and without the actual kisses).

their spaces and was a favorite of independent bands who used the service to promote their music. Teenage fans of these musical groups were then attracted to the site and encouraged their friends to join. By 2005 MySpace had millions of members and was purchased by the News Corporation for $580 million.

Facebook started in 2004 and was originally designed to serve only those at Harvard University. The service quickly expanded to other colleges (members had to have an .edu e-mail address to belong), and the service was seen as a private community. This did not last long as Facebook expanded to include high school students and corporate members and eventually was open to everybody. YouTube began operation in 2005, quickly became a popular site for user-generated content, and was acquired by Google for $1.65 billion. Twitter came on the scene a year later. The success of these sites is well-known, as evidenced by the hundreds of millions of people who visit them.

Keep in mind that digital social media are a relatively new phenomenon and constantly evolving. Consequently, it's risky to make generalizations about their effects. Some preliminary observations, however, are possible. First, social media have changed the idea of community. In the past, people developed friendships based on local geography. Social media make possible virtual communities based on shared needs, experiences, and interests rather than locale.

The notion of virtual community varies by age group. People over 55 constitute the fastest growing demographic segment on Facebook. This group uses social media to maintain existing relationships and to re-establish friendships with old high school or college classmates or people from their original hometown. In contrast, younger people are more apt to use social media to form new friends and communities based on mutual interests. Thus, aspiring teen goths may identify more with the G.O.F. (Goths of Facebook) than with their high school classmates. They might "friend" a fellow goth in Bulgaria rather than another teen living across the street.

Second, social media have changed how we define privacy. Some have accused social media of fostering a peephole culture. Digital cameras make everybody a reporter. When Christian Bale launched into a rant against a crewmember on a movie set, he probably never expected to see it on YouTube. When fashion designer John Galliano made bigoted remarks in a Paris bar, he probably never expected a video of his slurs to become an Internet sensation. Additionally, social media make it ridiculously easy to make public what was once private. Many young people will post personal information on their Facebook pages without considering the consequences. Photos posted on social media sites have come back to haunt many unsuspecting partygoers.

Finally, social media have made history more permanent. Digital media are easily archived and easily accessible. Your tweets, blog entries, Facebook postings, and photos are all probably saved somewhere on some hard drive. Today's teenagers who apply for jobs in the next few years may find that much to their chagrin those embarrassing old party photos posted on Facebook have resurfaced. Candidates running for president in 2036 might have to explain why they made those controversial blog postings back in 2010. Keep an eye on social media over the next few years and see what other consequences might develop.

concluding observations: the impact of new media

In 1839 the director of the Paris Observatory, François Arago, was speaking to the French Parliament about a new technology that was then sweeping Europe: the daguerreotype, the ancestor of the modern photograph (see page 61). Many critics were hostile to the new technique because they feared it would have a harmful effect on French society by destroying the livelihood of thousands of French portrait painters and perhaps even put an end to the art of painting itself.

critical ⬤ cultural issues

Cell Phones, Religion, and Culture

Professor Heidi Campbell has studied the cultural implications of the widespread adoption of the cell phone.[1] She points out that the cell phone is more than a phone. It is a means of individual expression (personal ring tones, wallpaper, phone covers) as well as a tool for business, creating a social network of employees and clients. In fact, the cell phone has the potential for generating unexpected cultural impact.

The impact of the cell phone has spread to religion. Campbell describes how religious groups are using the cell phone to incorporate religious practices into society's new on-the-go lifestyle. For example, religious groups in many countries offer daily Bible text messages. Pope Benedict XVI sent out an inspirational text message to subscribers just a few days after his elevation. Catholics in the Philippines can receive the "Mobile Way of the Cross" and the "Mobile Rosary" on their cell phones. Muslims can buy a special phone that reminds them of prayer times and a digital compass that indicates the direction of Mecca. A British youth group uses cell phones to create a national prayer chain. All members receive a text message at specific times encouraging them to pray.

Of course, new technologies and religious culture do not always mesh smoothly. Muslims have criticized those who send text messages during Ramadan rather than making traditional personal visits. Hindus objected to an image of a Hindu god talking on a cell phone.

[1]See Heidi Campbell, "Texting the Faith: Religious Users and Cell Phone Culture," in A. Kavoori and N. Arceneaux (eds.), *The Cell Phone Reader* (New York: Peter Lang, 2006).

As Campbell points out, religious groups are receptive to those aspects of new technology that support their traditions but tend to resist those advances that cause friction with the traditional culture and beliefs. This process is a dynamic one, and often a new technology is shaped by a culture in order to fit in. Campbell presents a prime example of this process by analyzing the reactions of one ultra-orthodox religious group to the cell phone.

The average Israeli spends about 450 minutes per month talking on a cell phone, one of the highest rates in the world. Not all segments of Israeli society, however, have taken to the device. Ultra-orthodox Jews belong to a community that rejects modernity and its secular values. The cell phone is seen as a device that could be harmful to this community because it could easily deliver materialistic content to its users. At the same time, however, ultra-orthodox Jews note that the cell phone could possess certain benefits for the community.

What grew out of this tension is the "kosher phone," a specially designed handset that preserves the phone's calling function but disables text messaging, Internet access, video, and voice mail applications. The kosher phone emerged after long negotiations between cell phone manufacturers and a council of rabbis. The council also drafted guidelines about how the technology would be used.

As Campbell concludes, if a technology with questionable features is deemed valuable to a community, a "culturing process" takes place. This culturing process may involve changes in both the culture of a community and the technology itself. In short, culture can influence both the form and function of any new technology.

In defending the daguerreotype, Arago maintained that these fears were shortsighted. He voiced what we can call Arago's rule of technology: The greatest potential impact of a new invention is not how it changes or replaces old things but how it generates things that are entirely new. Arago's rule certainly held true for photography. It may have put a few portrait painters out of work, but more important, it led to the development of mechanically reproduced images, photojournalism, and the motion picture—developments that helped usher in the age of mass communication, something that the members of the 1839 French Parliament could not even have imagined.

One lesson we can learn from these milestones in the development of human communication is that, as Arago realized, it is impossible to predict the ultimate use of a new medium. When the telegraph was invented, many people thought it would have a profound effect on the world order. Since nations were linked by the telegraph and could send instant messages to one another, it was predicted that misunderstandings would cease, prejudices would vanish, and peace would reign. Things did not quite go in that direction. Alexander Graham Bell suggested that the telephone be used as a means of communication among the various rooms of a house or that phones be sold only in pairs, linking just two specific points, such as a person's office and home. The phonograph was first used to record business dictation. When radio first started, most thought it would be used as a substitute for telegraph or telephone communication. All of these inventions became mass communication media that their creators never envisioned. We may be at the same point with the digital and wireless mobile milestones. We can see some of their possibilities, but their ultimate evolution is impossible to predict. Arago's rule may be validated all over again.

It appears that the emergence of a new communication technology changes *but does not make extinct* those advances that came before it. The telegraph and the telephone did not kill the printed word; nor did film, radio, TV, and the Internet. Television did not make radio extinct, but it did cause a major change in the way the medium was used. Likewise, the computer, the Internet, and mobile media will probably not cause any of the traditional media to evaporate, but they will probably change the way we use these "old" media.

Figure 3-1 (see page 54) is a time line that displays when each of the milestones occurred. A quick examination of the figure makes clear that the pace of communication innovations has accelerated. It took humans dozens of centuries to get from language to writing. The jump from writing to printing took about 5,000 years. The telegraph and telephone cropped up only 300 years later, followed quickly by photography and motion pictures. Radio was invented only a few years after that, as was TV. The computer followed on the heels of television. In fact, a person born in 1912 and who lived a hundred years (an accomplishment becoming increasingly more common) would have lived through several milestones: radio/TV, computers, mobile wireless media, and social media. Each advance in communication increases our power to convey and record information, and each has played a role in prompting significant changes in our culture and society. It is becoming difficult to digest fully the impact of one communication medium before another comes on the scene.

main points

- Printing made information available to a larger audience. It helped the development of vernacular languages, aided the Protestant Reformation, and contributed to the spread and accumulation of knowledge.

- The telegraph and telephone were the first media to use electricity to communicate. They marked the first time the message could be separated from the messenger. The telegraph helped the railroads move west and permitted the newspapers to publish more timely news. The telephone linked people together in the first instance of a communication network.

- Photography provided a way to preserve history, had an impact on art, and brought better visuals to newspapers and magazines. Motion pictures helped socialize a generation of immigrants and became an important part of American culture.

- Radio and TV broadcasting brought news and entertainment into the home, transformed leisure time, and pioneered a new, immediate kind of reporting. Television has an impact on free time, politics, socialization, culture, and many other areas as well.

- The digital revolution changed the way information was stored and transmitted and made e-commerce possible.

- Mobile media have changed American culture and taken over some of the functions of mass media.

- The next communication milestone is the expanding use of social media.

- In general, it is difficult to predict the ultimate shape of a new medium. New media change but do not replace older media. The pace of media inventions has accelerated in recent years.

questions for review

1. Why was the telegraph labeled "the great annihilator of time and space"?

2. What exactly is the "communal reservoir of images" created by photojournalism? Can you think of other examples of images that are forever fixed by photographs?

3. What digits are used in digital technology? Why could the telegraph be considered the first digital device?

4. How have mobile media changed how we think about time?

questions for critical thinking

1. Suppose Henry David Thoreau (see page 58) were alive today. What do you think he would say about the Internet?

2. Many people would argue that, of all the communication media discussed in this chapter, television has had the greatest impact on society. Do you agree?

3. When the Internet was first developing, the term *information superhighway* appeared frequently in news stories about it. Now that the Internet has been around for a while, news stories rarely contain that term. Why is this so?

4. Do you have a Facebook page? If so, how has it changed your life?

5. Consider the boxed insert "Cell Phones, Religion, and Culture." Can you think of other technological devices that have been subjected to a "culturing" process? How does the "kosher phone" relate to the concept of a community? Who should decide what features of a new technology are introduced to a particular culture?

key terms

technological determinism (p. 56)

photojournalism (p. 62)

digital technology (p. 68)

mobile parenting (p. 73)

time softening (p. 73)

internet resources

Online Learning Center

On the Online Learning Center home page, www.mhhe.com/dominick12e, *select* Student Center *and then* Chapter 3.

1. Use the Learning Objectives, Chapter Outline, and Main Points sections to review this chapter.

2. Test your knowledge of the chapter using the multiple choice and flashcard features of the site.

3. Expand your knowledge of concepts and topics discussed in the chapter with additional Questions for Critical Thinking and Internet Exercises.

surfing the internet

Here are some sites that provide information on media history. Some of the sites mentioned in Chapters 4–12 are also of relevance here.

http://fi.edu/franklin/inventor/bell.html
Reconstructs Bell's path to the invention of the telephone.

http://mediahistory.umn.edu
The best all-around site for media history. Contains an extensive time line, other links, book reviews, articles, archives, chat boards, and pages on the history of specific media.

www.archive.org
Home of the Wayback Machine. Surf the Web the way it used to be.

www.digitalhistory.uh.edu/historyonline/hollywood.cfm
Provides links to many sites that contain information about film history.

www.gutenbergdigital.de
Gutenberg's Bible on the Web.

http://inventors.about.com/od/tstartinventions/a/telegraph.htm
Page devoted to Samuel Morse and telegraphy. Contains diagrams of early telegraphs and relevant links.

Media

Part II

Media

http://www.google.com/

Web   Images   Videos   Maps   News   Shopping   Gmail   more ▼

Go

Google Search

I'm gonna be your friend. Listen and learn how

Advertising Programs   Busine

© 2011 -

Digital companies such as Apple, Google, Microsoft, and Amazon have reshaped modern mass communication.

Done

Chapter**4**

the internet
and social media

This chapter will prepare you to:

- describe how computers were invented
- explain how the Internet and the World Wide Web were developed
- understand the advantages of broadband Internet access
- realize the potential impact of Web 2.0
- recognize the economic impact of the Internet
- discuss the social concerns raised by the Internet

"The Internet changes everything." When Microsoft founder Bill Gates wrote those words back in 1999 he was specifically talking about business but, as it turns out, the Internet has changed much more than business. It has changed the economy, politics, science, education, communication, and American culture. Most relevant to this chapter is the fact that the Internet has transformed mass and interpersonal communication. As we shall see in future chapters, the mass media are in a state of transition as they struggle to adjust to the disruptions caused by the Internet. Moreover, digital companies such as Google, Apple, and Amazon have become major players in today's mass communication arena. Finally, social media such as Facebook, Twitter, and YouTube have opened up new channels of communication among members of the audience and between the media and the audience. Again, as we shall see, social media have created new opportunities and challenges for the media industries.

Consequently, we will begin our look at the various mass media with the most recent innovations: the Internet and social media.

a brief history of the computer

Before there could be an Internet, there had to be a computer. The first computers were adding machines that took the drudgery out of repetitive arithmetical calculations, such as the *arithmetique*, a machine invented by French mathematician Blaise Pascal that could add numbers up to a million. A German mathematician, Gottfried Wilhelm von Liebnitz, explored binary arithmetic, a system with just two possible values, 0 and 1, which eventually became the system used by modern computers.

In the United States, in the 1880s, Herman Hollerith developed a machine that used punched cards and electrical circuits to do calculations. His machine was so successful that he started his own company, International Business Machines (IBM). Howard Aiken, a Harvard professor, developed the first computer using the binary system in 1940. A few years later, researchers at the University of Pennsylvania constructed the first all-electronic computer called ENIAC. Although ENIAC was a huge improvement, it weighed two tons and was two stories tall.

In the 1950s, the invention of transistors, integrated circuits, and silicon chips led to computers that were smaller, cheaper, and easier to maintain. Personal computers (PCs) designed for home use and using prepackaged software appeared in the 1970s.

The invention of the modem in 1980s enabled computers to converse with one another over phone lines. The development of local area networks (LANs) allowed several computers to be linked together, setting the stage for the Internet. By the 1990s, the trend toward miniaturization continued. Laptop computers and wireless modems became popular.

By the turn of the century, personal computers and laptops were in the vast majority of American homes, and most people were using them as communication devices utilizing the Internet. People used their computer to get news, send e-mail, watch video online, and keep up with their friends.

At the end of the first decade of the 21st century, computers became more portable. Netbooks, small laptop computers designed for Internet access and some basic functions, appeared in 2009, followed by Apple's iPad and other brands of small tablet computers. In addition, smartphones that provided Internet access were increasingly common. The creation of social networks such as Facebook and YouTube caused a further explosion of computer communication.

The hottest topic of the past few years has been **cloud computing.** (The cloud is a symbol that represents the Internet.) At the risk of oversimplifying, cloud computing refers

ENIAC, completed in the late 1940s, was the world's first general-purpose, digital, all-electronic computer. The device took up most of the space in a good-sized room. ENIAC is a far cry from today's laptop computers.

to applications and services offered over the Net. Rather than being stored on your computer, the programs reside on a network server connected to the Internet. Examples of cloud computing include online data storage, Google's online suite of office applications, and Apple's new iCloud content retrieval system.

Every day Americans send millions of e-mails, check in with social networks, comment on news stories, upload video, and spend idle time surfing the Web. For many people, it's hard to imagine life without a computer.

the internet

The Internet is a network of computer networks. Think of it as a system that combines computers from all over the world into one big computer that you can operate from your own PC. Some computers are run by government agencies (like the National Aeronautics and Space Administration), some by universities, some by libraries, some by school systems, some by businesses, and so on. The connections among these networks can be ordinary phone lines, microwaves, fiber optic cables, or wires built specially for this purpose. A related example might be the phone system. When you call somebody in Cleveland, the call is routed through several different phone networks in different parts of the country. You really do not care what route it takes or what companies handle it as long as your call gets there. So, too, with the Internet. When you search for information, send e-mail, or chat online, several different networks may handle your messages. Just as there is no one phone company, there is also no one Internet company.

The Internet's seemingly chaotic structure arose from its somewhat fractured history. A little background will help to clarify.

From ARPANET to Internet

Back in the early 1970s, when the Cold War was still raging, the U.S. Department of Defense was concerned about the vulnerability of its computer network to nuclear attack. The Pentagon did not want to lose all its computing and communication ability to one well-placed atomic bomb. Consequently, defense computer experts decentralized the whole system by creating an interconnected web of computer networks. The system was designed so that every computer could talk to every other computer. The computers themselves then figured out how to send the packet. Thus, if one portion of the network happened to be disabled, the rest of the network could still function normally. The system that the Pentagon eventually developed was called ARPANET.

At about the same time, companies developed software that enabled computers to be linked to local area networks (LANs). Not surprisingly, many of these LANs were also connected to ARPANET, causing the network to grow even more.

The users of this early network were primarily scientists and computer experts, and most observers thought that it would continue to be of interest only to high-tech types. (The network was once uncharitably labeled a "Disneyland for geeks.") In the late 1980s, however, the National Science Foundation, whose own network was already connected to ARPANET, created supercomputing centers at U.S. universities. Since they were so expensive, only five could be built. This meant that they had to be shared and interconnected. The ARPANET seemed like the obvious choice for interconnection, but there were too many problems involved. Instead, the National Science Foundation built its own system and hooked together chains of regional networks that were eventually linked to a supercomputer. Thus, the Internet, or Net, was born.

Now that students, scientists, government workers, and others had access to supercomputers, the amount of information at their disposal increased tremendously. The Internet also served as a communication link that enabled scientists from all over the country

sound byte

to share data. Doctors, lawyers, journalists, authors, and business owners recognized the potential of the Net, and traffic increased.

The Internet was still used by only a small fraction of computer owners. Three developments, however, contributed to a meteoric rise in the Internet's popularity.

The first was the development of the World Wide Web (WWW, or Web) in 1990. Engineers working at a physics laboratory in Switzerland created an interconnected set of computers on the Net that all used the same communication program. This program took advantage of **hypertext,** a navigational tool that linked one electronic document, either text or graphics, with another, thus creating a virtual web of pages. The Web started off as an electronic information resource for scientists but was quickly discovered and utilized by the entire Internet community. Any organization or individual could create a page on the Web as long as the person or organization used the communication rules developed in Switzerland. It was not long before conventional media companies, businesses, organizations, and individuals got involved with the Web. By 1998 it was estimated that there were more than a million Web sites in operation.

The second development made it easier for consumers to find what they were looking for on the Web. This happened in 1993 with the creation of user-friendly navigation tools that helped further spur the growth of the Web. The first of these **browsers,** called Mosaic, was able to retrieve data, determine what they were, and configure the data for display. Mosaic created a graphical display for users that simplified navigating the Internet. In 1994 one of the developers of Mosaic formed a commercial company that was eventually named Netscape. Software giant Microsoft introduced its own browser, Internet Explorer, a few years later.

The third development was the **search engine,** a utility that scans the Internet for terms selected by the user and displays the results according to some predetermined criterion, such as relevance. Some well-known search engines are Google and Yahoo!. These advances helped users make sense of the Internet and turned it into a useful information tool.

The mid-2000s saw the development of easy-to-use software programs that made it simple to upload content to the Internet. This encouraged the growth of blogs (see below), social networking sites, and video-sharing sites, all of which combined to make the Internet more popular than ever.

The new century saw the Internet continue to grow at a fast pace. More Americans were accessing the Internet using high-speed broadband connections, and WiFi hot spots made the Net more mobile. As of 2010, about 80 percent of U.S. adults were Internet users. The average American was online more than 32 hours in a month and viewed more than 1,600 Web pages. Obviously, the Internet has grown into a powerful mass communication medium.

Structure and Features of the Internet

Individuals gain access to the Internet through an Internet service provider (ISP), a company that connects a subscriber to the Net and usually charges a fee (many companies, including some local phone and cable companies, function as ISPs). As of 2011, the biggest ISPs were AT&T and Comcast with about 15 million subscribers each.

Once connected to the Internet, an individual can make use of a variety of tools for information, entertainment, and communication. Three of the more popular uses are (1) e-mail, (2) the World Wide Web, and (3) specialized applications, called apps.

E-Mail   Millions of people are connected to the Internet, and you can send mail to one of them or to many of them. **E-mail** works on the client/server arrangement. To send and

media *Tweeting and the City*
Probe

If you are a big user of Twitter, then you would fit right in with the socially connected folks in Washington, D.C. According to survey by *Men's Health* magazine, the nation's capital ranked number one in the number of people using Twitter to stay in touch. Atlanta ranked second, followed by Denver. Texans apparently have yet to embrace Twitter. The two bottom-ranked cities were Laredo and El Paso.

read e-mail, users (clients) must access another computer (the server), where their mailbox resides. E-mail messages are not limited to text. Attachments, such as graphics or spread-sheets, can also be sent.

E-mail is usually fast, cheap, and reliable. It is the most widely used Internet resource. In 2010, more than 107 trillion e-mail messages moved through the Net.

E-mail is helpful, but it also has some drawbacks. First, it is not as formal as a printed letter, so there may be some tasks for which it is inappropriate (like telling someone he or she has been fired). Second, e-mail is not as private as a letter in an envelope. Your message may travel through several computers where others might have access to it. At some com-panies employee e-mail might also be available to management. Third, e-mail comes with the ever-present nuisance called **spam.** Spam, the cyber equivalent of junk mail, includes unsolicited messages touting low mortgage rates, porno sites, and miracle cures; clogs up people's mailboxes; and takes time to delete. Fourth, there is the problem of information overload. In many businesses, memos that used to go to a small group of people now get sent to everybody, and every decision—no matter how small—gets circulated via e-mail.

World Wide Web   As mentioned earlier, the **World Wide Web (WWW)** is a network of information sources incorporating hypertext that allows the user to link one piece of information to another. Note that the Web is *part* of the Internet; the two terms are not synonymous.

Some terminology might be useful at this point. The structure of the Web is based on the Web server, a computer connected to the Internet that facilitates the transfer of hyper-text pages. One server can hold thousands of hypertext pages. A **Web site** is a complete set of hypertext pages linked to each other that contains information about a common topic. A **Web page** is a hypertext page that is contained within a Web site. The home page of a Web site is the entry or doorway to the site that might contain links to other pages or to various sections of the site.

The protocols for navigating the Web assign each Web page a uniform resource locator (URL) and an Internet address. URLs are structured as follows:

protocol://server.subdomain.top-level domain/directory/filename

For example, the URL for this book is:

http://www.mhhe.com/dominick12e

This means that the page is in the hypertext transfer protocol, the server is linked to the WWW, the subdomain name is *mhhe,* the top-level domain is *com,* and the directory name is dominick 12e.

Their tremendous variety makes it nearly impossible to categorize the types of sites on the Web, but we'll try anyway. Below is a list of some of the more popular types of Web sites:

- *Commercial sites* are maintained by various businesses in order to promote or sell their products. They may contain product descriptions, consumer information, advertising, spe-cial offers, and other material. Tide.com, for example, is the home of Tide detergent and ups.com is the home of United Parcel Service. Commercial sites typically end in .com.
- *Organizational sites* are created by many nonprofit groups whose main goal is to pro-vide information to their members and to the general public. Some examples include

ethical issues
Ethical Obligations and the Internet

In late 2008, a Florida teenager televised his own suicide over the Internet. The teenager had announced his intention to commit suicide earlier that day in an online forum and linked his Web cam to Justin.tv, a live video-streaming Web site. Estimates vary, but at least a couple of hundred people watched the teen take an overdose of drugs and lie back on his bed. After several hours of viewing his motionless body, one of those watching the video feed finally called the police, who arrived on the scene too late to save his life.

This tragic episode is troubling enough, but the behavior of those who read the teen's blog and who watched the video is even more upsetting. Many egged him on and urged him to commit suicide. Some doubted he could do it and called him a coward if he didn't go through with it. Some were convinced that the whole thing was a fake and did nothing. After watching the teen's immobile body for several hours, bloggers speculated that they were seeing a still photo or maybe a recorded tape. Some failed to acknowledge that the scene was authentic even after police broke down the door and unsuccessfully tried to revive the teen. One blogged that the cops looked fake because they didn't have any handcuffs hanging from their belts.

Why does the Internet bring out the malice, cruelty, and cynicism in people? People on the Internet can hide behind a cloak of anonymity. It's easy to spew nastiness when you don't have to own up to your remarks. Anonymity breeds irresponsibility. Then, there is the herd instinct. When they act as part of a group, some people will do and say things that they never would do or say as an individual. Being part of a crowd makes it easy to avoid responsibility. Also, there is the well-documented bystander effect. People in a crowd are less likely to offer help in an emergency if other people are also present. The same phenomenon probably occurs online as well. Finally, there is a lack of connection on the Internet. The person in front of the Web cam can be seen as an object; there is no personal connection between viewer and subject. To many who watched this tragedy, it may have aroused as much emotional connection as a typical YouTube video.

In fairness, this was a complicated case. The teen was obviously suffering from mental problems and had threatened suicide before but never went through with it. Not everybody online egged him on; some took the teen seriously and tried to talk him out of it. Nonetheless, it does bring up the question of what are the ethical obligations of people who are part of forums or online social networks. As we shall see in Chapter 17, there is an ethical principle called the *categorical imperative* that seems to apply here. Simply put, the categorical imperative resembles what we generally call the *Golden Rule:* "Do unto others as you would have them do unto you."

If you were having psychological problems, how would you want others to respond? With jeers, taunts, and callousness? Or would you want them to be understanding and helpful? The same reasoning should apply online. All of us should feel a responsibility to others. If someone is talking about suicide, the matter should be treated seriously and with sympathy. Our obligations to other human beings do not change simply because we are online.

the sites of the American Medical Association, the National Education Association, the American Association of Retired People, and UNESCO. Organizational sites typically end in .org.

- *Education sites* typically belong to colleges and universities. Harvard.edu and Stanford .edu are examples. Educational sites end in .edu.
- *Government sites*, as the name suggests, are restricted to government entities from the federal to the local level. Thus, USA.gov is the U.S. government's official Web site and Atlanta.gov is the official Web site of the city of Atlanta. Most but not all government sites end in .gov.
- *E-commerce sites* are designed to sell products or services directly from a Web site. Examples are Amazon.com, Overstock.com, and Fandango.com.
- *Personal sites* include information about a person, family, or small group. Genealogy pages, personal pages, blogs, and many other kinds of sites would fall into this category.
- *News and information sites* might be specific in focus—such as globalwood.org with news about the lumber industry and perezhilton.com with entertainment news—or more general, such as CNN.com or abcnews.go.com.
- *Entertainment sites* provide pleasure and amusement. There are a huge number of these sites including hulu.com, youtube.com, jokes.com, and collegehumor.com.
- *Social networking sites* are places such as MySpace, Facebook, Linkedin, and Twitter where people link up with friends and share information.
- *Search engine sites* display lists of sites related to a user's search term. Google, Yahoo!, MSN, and several others are popular search engines.

Many Web sites function as **portals.** A portal, as the name suggests, is an entryway, the first page a person looks at before zooming off into the Web. The strategy behind a successful portal is to offer visitors useful information, such as news headlines, weather, stock information, and bargains, so that they do not go looking for these items at some other site. The longer a person stays at the portal, the greater the chance that she or he might see some of the advertising on the site. Some of the best-known portals are those provided by Yahoo!, Excite, MSNBC, and AOL.

How big is the World Wide Web? The answer is hard to come by because the Web grows every day. As of 2009, the search engine Google estimated that there were more than a trillion unique pages on the Web. However, although it is called the *World Wide Web,* it is primarily a Web for industrialized nations. About 85 percent of the pages on the Web are in English, Japanese, French, or German.

Apps   Apps are special computer programs designed for mobile devices such as smartphones and tablet computers. At the risk of oversimplifying, a person using an app uses the Internet to transport data from a Web site, but the Web site is not displayed by a Web browser. In other words, apps take people to a site that is different from the same site accessed via a browser. Apps are designed to provide a more satisfying experience. For example, type CNN.com in your browser and you'll arrive at a conventional-looking Web site with numerous thumbnails, some video, and many bulleted headlines. Those who use the CNN app with their iPad or other tablet device see something totally different: a visually striking exhibit of photos and video clips displaying headlines. Touch-scrolling reveals other stories and other photos and video. Tap on a photo and you're taken to the full story. There are no bothersome pop-ups or intrusive ads or spam messages. Some experts refer to apps as a "walled garden" where you are shut out from the wider Web.

Apps are extremely popular. As of 2011, iPad users had downloaded more than 60 million apps. Experts estimate that worldwide more than a billion apps have been downloaded for smartphones and tablet computers. There are apps for nearly everything, from finding the nearest Starbucks to tracking the stock market. Games are the most popular app. *Angry Birds* has been downloaded more than 300 million times. As we shall see in the following chapters, many mass media companies are hoping that apps will bring them more visitors and increased revenue.

Applications for mobile media are a big business, accounting for almost $4 billion in revenue in 2010.

88

the evolving internet

The Internet changes so fast that it is hard to predict its future. Nonetheless, here are several trends that most experts agree will significantly affect the Net in the next few years.

Broadband

Broadband refers to any of the several ways to connect to the Internet that carry information many times faster than conventional dial-up modems. The tremendous gain in speed makes it possible to send huge files in much less time. Downloading a typical music file might take more than half an hour with a dial-up modem but only a minute or so with a broadband connection. In addition, broadband makes it practical to send video over the Internet.

Consumers can access broadband through a satellite modem, a cable modem, or a digital subscriber line (DSL) through their telephone. All three methods are more costly than a dial-up connection, averaging anywhere from $40 to $75 per month.

In addition to facilitating high-speed Internet access, broadband makes possible many other desirable things, including video-on-demand, interactive television, live streaming video, and downloadable movies.

Thanks to increased marketing efforts and special pricing plans, the number of broadband subscribers has increased over the past few years. At the beginning of 2011, about 70 percent of U.S. households had a broadband connection. Nonetheless, the United States lags behind several other countries in broadband penetration. South Korea, for example, has 93 percent of its subscribers connected to broadband.

Going Mobile: The Wireless Web

Wireless technology will become more and more common during the next decade. There were more than 20 million laptop computers with wireless Net access in 2010, and thanks to the iPhone and other smartphones, more than 50 million people used their cell phone to connect to the Internet and 20 million access the Net via tablet computers. Easier-to-use interfaces and faster networks will probably increase this number in the near future. Fairly soon, the Internet will be available everywhere.

What makes all of this possible is the development of **WiFi,** or **wireless fidelity,** technology. WiFi uses low-power radio signals to connect devices to one another and to the Internet. A base station serves as a transmitter, and computers and cell phone customers can use special hardware and software to hook into the system.

Many WiFi public access locations or "hot spots" have sprung up all over the country—in airport waiting rooms, cafes, and even parks. People who frequent these hot spots can link up with the Internet at no cost. Experts estimate that there are about 250,000 hot spots across the globe.

As mentioned in Chapter 1, mobility is one of the emerging characteristics of modern mass communication. WiFi was the first step in that direction for the Internet. The next step will be **WiMax,** a technology that will bring wireless Internet access to entire metropolitan areas. WiMax works a lot like WiFi, but instead of a short range of 200 feet or so, WiMax permits access across a range of approximately 10 miles. This means an individual could log onto the Net while riding on a commuter train or in the back seat of a car. Wireless companies hope that eventually the WiMax network will be as pervasive as today's cell phone net.

Monetizing the Web

As new Web sites attract big numbers of visitors, investors and Web site operators are interested in converting all of these visitors into some form of monetary reward. Hence the emergence of the rather clumsy term *monetizing,* the process of converting something to money. Some solutions are novel. My Second Life sells virtual real estate to real companies so that they can market their products in a virtual world. Shutterfly offers subscribers a chance to upload, edit, and share their photos and charges a small fee for prints. Others are more conventional. Facebook sells display advertising on its pages. Google sells sponsored links next to its search results (see "Social Issues: Counterfeit Clicks"). Hulu runs ads before its programs. YouTube does the same for some of its videos.

social
Issues   *Counterfeit Clicks*

Internet advertising is big business, generating more than $26 billion in 2010. One of the most common forms of Internet advertising is "pay per click." Whenever you do a search on Google, for example, on the right side of the results page you will see a number of sponsored links to products or services related to what you are looking for. Search for "satellite radio," and you get nine sponsored links to places that sell satellite radio receivers and hardware. Google gets paid every time someone clicks on one of those links—hence pay per click.

On top of that, Google charges advertisers to feed their sponsored links to various Web sites. (The "Ads by Google" heading usually appears near such links.) These links might appear in blogs, on recipe sites, on the home pages of businesses, and so on. The advertisers also pay Google for each click on these sites. Google, in turn, shares that money with the publisher of the Web page (the blogger, recipe compiler, business owner, and so on).

This system has obvious benefits for advertisers, Web page publishers, consumers, and search engine companies, but it also creates tempting possibilities for abuse—such as "click fraud." Click fraud can work in two ways. The simplest is for a person to generate a lot of false clicks on a competitor's link. Suppose Bob and Barb sell toothbrushes. Barb pays Google $1 every time someone clicks on her sponsored links on a Google search results page. Bob buys a cheap online robot program that repeatedly clicks on Barb's link, costing her $1 each time. Pretty soon, Barb is paying a big chunk of her budget for fraudulent clicks.

The second way is more complicated but no less dishonest. Suppose Barb hires Google to place a sponsored link to her toothbrush site on relevant sites throughout the Web (oral hygiene sites, dental health sites, and so on). She pays Google $1 for every click on her links on these sites. Google passes 50 cents of this fee on to the Web page publisher (the oral hygiene site, dental health site, and so on). Now suppose Bob starts a bogus Web site called "Bob's Bright Smile Blog," and Google places Barb's sponsored link on Bob's blog. Bob next uses his online 'bot program to generate thousands of clicks on Barb's link on his Web site, thus defrauding Barb out of a lot of money.

How prevalent is this kind of fraud? It's hard to say. One 2006 report estimated that around 15 percent of all clicks are false. Google, Yahoo!, and other popular search engines are aware of these scams and have installed click fraud filters that look for patterns and delete phony clicks. Nonetheless, many advertisers claim that the big search engine companies aren't doing enough. Lane's Gifts and Collectibles, for instance, was part of a class action lawsuit that eventually resulted in Google's agreeing to a $90-million settlement over charges of click fraud.

No matter what the technique, one thing is certain: Commercialization will continue to increase on the Internet. First, as big companies snap up promising sites, they will be looking for ways to find a return on their investment. The folks at Yahoo! didn't pay $40 million for Flickr simply because they like to look at pictures. Second, as the traditional media continue to lose audience, advertisers and marketers are looking to the Net to increase the reach of their ads. Heinz, for example, sponsored a contest on YouTube with a $57,000 prize to the person who made the best TV commercial for its catsup.

Blogs

Blog is short for "web log." Blogs are journals in which people write about whatever they want: news, politics, sports, music, movies, quilting, or any other interest. Readers can post comments and engage in virtual conversations with the blog author. Blogs often contain links to other blogs, news reports, music clips, and video-sharing sites. The book you are reading has its own blog site. Check out http://dynamicsmasscomm.blogspot.com for updates, examples, and discussions of topics covered in this text.

Blogs got their start in the late 1990s but didn't become popular until free software programs made it easy for anybody to put a blog online. And a lot of people did. Technorati, a Web site that tracks these things, reports there were about 130 million blogs in 2009. Recently, the popularity of blogging has decreased, especially among young people. A study done by the Pew Research Center found that in 2010 half as many teenagers blogged as in 2006. The percentage of people in the 20–40 age group who blog also declined. The Pew study suggested that young people have turned to Facebook and Twitter to express their opinions rather than start a blog.

Nonetheless, some blogs have become successful and have many readers. The *Daily Kos* and *Powerline,* for example, have become influential in politics while *TMZ* and *Perez Hilton* are leading blogs devoted to entertainment.

Mashable.com is one of the most popular blogs on the Web.

internet economics and new online mega-companies

We will now take a brief look at the impact of the Internet on the national economy, examine the new mega-companies that now dominate the digital landscape, and then focus on the financial arrangements of individual Web sites.

The Internet and the National Economy

The Internet has had a significant impact on the national economy. Experts estimate that the Internet has created about 1.2 million jobs. Economists value the direct economic value of the Internet at around $185 billion. That includes about $26 million in advertising, around $90 billion in retail sales (Amazon.com had revenues of $34 billion in 2010), and about $70 billion paid to Internet service providers. Analysts estimate that the indirect financial benefit of the Internet's impact on the rest of the economy is about $440 billion.

Advertisers now spend more money on online advertising than they spend on newspaper advertising. Online ad spending now accounts for about 15 percent of all advertising expenditures and this percentage is expected to grow.

New Mega-Companies

Although the Internet has been cited as a model of a free market driven by pure competition, it has become dominated by the big companies listed in Table 4-1. Note that these companies didn't exist a few decades ago. Note also that each of the new digital powerhouses dominates the market in certain areas. Google dominates search, accounting for 83 percent of all searches; Amazon dominates online retail selling; Facebook dominates social media; Apple dominates online music delivery; Netflix dominates online movie delivery.

Note yet again that when it comes to mass communication, these companies are primarily in the content distribution business; they produce little in the way of original media content. (Apple once owned Pixar, a company that makes animated films, but sold it to Disney.) Google's YouTube draws mainly on user-generated video to draw an audience. It then makes money by selling advertisers access to this audience. In short, it profits from

table 4-1	Rank	Company	Estimated revenue 2010
Leading Digital Mass Media Companies	1.	Google	$14 billion
	2.	Yahoo!	$4.4 billion
	3.	Apple	$4.1 billion
	4.	Facebook	$1.6 billion
	5.	Netflix	$1.5 billion
	6.	Amazon	$1.0* billion

* Estimated revenue from Kindle sales and media downloads. Amazon's total revenue from all retail sales was about $34 billion.

the work of others. Facebook does essentially the same thing. Netflix distributes movies made by movie studios; Apple distributes music, books, movies, and TV shows made by others, as does Amazon. In short, there has been a shift in media power from the traditional content creators in New York and Hollywood to Silicon Valley and Seattle, the homes of the content distributors.

Now let us take a more specific look at the financial side of individual Web sites.

Web Site Economics

The tremendous variation in the kinds of people and organizations found on the Internet makes it hard to summarize its economic arrangements. Suffice it to say that the profit motive matters more to some than to others. A company that sells merchandise over the Internet is probably much more concerned with generating revenue than is a government agency or university that maintains a site as a service to its clients. Likewise, Uncle Max is probably not worried whether his blog ever generates a profit.

The rest of this section examines those online operations for which making money is an important consideration. There are three basic ways to make a profit over the Internet.

The first is to create a site with content so compelling that people will pay to see it. One type of company that follows this model offers specialized information that has value for a large number of customers. The *Wall Street Journal,* one such example, charges a subscription fee to access its online edition. The *New York Times,* as we shall see in the next chapter, is also charging for content. *Consumer Reports* offers access to its product evaluations for $26 a year.

The other type of business that uses this pay-for-content model is pornography. At last count there were thousands of these sites, and some were among the most profitable on the Web. Sex sells, even on the Internet.

The second way to make money on the Net is to sell merchandise or services online. Amazon.com, the site that sells everything from laptops to lawn mowers, is the best example of this business model. Although many online retailers went bust in the early years of the new century, many of those that remain are profitable. For example, Amazon had a profit of about $1 billion in 2010.

The third moneymaking method is for the site to sell advertising. Advertisers spent more than $26 billion in 2010 for online exposure. Online advertising can be broken down into three main categories: (1) paid search ads, (2) display ads, and (3) classified ads. Of these three, paid search ads (such as those sponsored links that show up on the right side of a Google search) account for the most revenue, followed by display ads (banner ads, pop-ups) and classifieds.

One way to make money with a Web site is to sell merchandise online as does ecost.com.

media *Probe*
Owe Money? Be Careful What You Post on Facebook

Bill collectors have learned how to use Facebook to collect past due debts. It's easy for a collector to scan a person's Facebook page to see if the person is wearing expensive jewelry or driving a new car or has just returned from a vacation in Hawaii. Such information tells a collector that the person has assets that might be used to pay past bills.

Some collectors have gone further. In an attempt to use embarrassment as a weapon, they have impersonated a person's friends and have posted messages asking that the person call the debt collection agency. Others have used Facebook to contact a person's family and ask them to persuade the person to pay his or her debts. These techniques are probably illegal, but that doesn't stop some collectors from using them.

Display ads are becoming more sophisticated and harder to avoid. Most now employ some form of "rich media," using color, motion, and clever layouts to attract attention. Video display ads are becoming more common, and many are displayed as soon as a user visits a Web site.

Well-known Web companies with Web sites that attract lots of visitors dominate online advertising revenue. Google, for example, accounted for about 66 percent of gross online revenue in 2011 while Yahoo! accounted for about 16 percent.

Of course, some Web sites use some combination of one or more of these techniques. For instance, eBay charges for its services, sells advertising, and markets its own customized merchandise.

the internet audience

Sources of Feedback

As with the other media that will be described in Part II, independent companies provide information about the Internet audience. Reliable data about audience size are important for advertisers who want to place banner ads on Web sites. The two companies that

comScore Inc. measures what Internet sites are most popular.

ethical
Issues   *Black Hats Versus White Hats*

Suppose you sell shoelaces. Suppose further that you want to sell a lot of your shoelaces online. Suppose even further that you design an attractive, informative, and easy-to-use Web site that shows off your product in the best way possible. It's only a matter of time before people from all over the world are visiting your Web site and buying your shoelaces, right? Not exactly. Even the best-designed Web site is useless if people can't find it.

And how do people find it? Most use search engines like Google and Yahoo!. And the cold fact of the matter is, your site needs to show up near the top of a shoelace shopper's search results page if you expect to make any money.

Just to illustrate: A search for "shoelaces" on Google returned 519,000 hits. If your Web site was number 502,000 in Google's results, it's unlikely that many people would find it. On the other hand, if you were number one (as was Ian's Shoelace Site in this example), you would probably do much better. (Statistics show that the first screen of a search results page accounts for 70 percent of all user clicks.) But what does it take to get a Web site into the top ranks? The answer to that question takes us into the rather arcane world of "search engine optimization," and a consideration of "white hat" versus "black hat" techniques raises ethical questions about online marketing and advertising.

Search engines such as Google and Yahoo! use an algorithm (a set of specific instructions) that determines how their results are ranked. "Spider bots" follow these complex and secret algorithms as they race around the Web at dizzying speed compiling their results for individual searches. If a person knew something about how these algorithms worked, it would be possible to design a Web page that would score high in the ultimate results. Enter a new professional: the search engine optimizer (SEO).

SEOs know that the factors that Google and other search engines use in their algorithms include the number of times search terms turn up in the content of the site, whether the search terms match the key words that describe the site, the number of links to the site, and the "credibility" of those linking sites. Armed with this knowledge, the SEOs redesign the site using "white hat" or legitimate methods, such as making everything on a page visible to the search engine. Product listings, for instance, are moved from an unsearched database to the site itself. Another white-hat technique is participating in a Web ring with other high-quality sites, thus increasing the number of links to the site. A third is making sure that each page has plenty of text that includes relevant terms (search engines don't pay much attention to pictures or graphics).

On the other hand, black-hat techniques are generally considered unethical. These might include "cloaking," creating two versions of a site, one that people see and a bogus site that is visible only to search engines that includes popular search terms, such as "sex." Another is using text containing popular search terms, such as "sex," that users can't see (the background and the foreground colors are the same) but that are visible to spider bots. Yet another is "link farming," using software that automatically generates a huge number of pages with links back to the original site. There are even illegal software programs that can forcibly inject links into sites that search engines score as more credible (such as universities).

Naturally, Google, Yahoo!, and the other search engines are well aware of these scams and do their best to minimize the rigged rankings that result from black-hat techniques. Companies that get caught can have their sites delisted from search results. In 2006, for example, Google accused automaker BMW of using the cloaking technique to enhance its search rankings and dropped the company from its results until the offending procedure was removed. Nonetheless, as revenues from Internet search marketing continue to increase, the struggle between the black hats and the white hats will no doubt continue.

dominate the audience measurement field are comScore and Nielsen/NetRatings. Both organizations use a panel of consumers to generate their data. comScore samples about 2 million people in the United States, using software that works with a computer's operating system to monitor Internet activity at home and at work. Nielsen uses a similar setup with a sample of about 70,000 people. Both services issue periodic reports that list the most popular Web sites. For example, in March 2011, comScore reported that Google, Facebook, Yahoo!, Microsoft, and AOL were the parent companies of the top five Web sites.

Nearly 2 billion people worldwide now use the Internet. The Pew Foundation has sponsored a number of surveys that have focused on the Internet and the people who use it. As one of its reports put it, "At the infant stage, the Internet's user population was dominated by young, white men who had high incomes and plenty of education. As it passed into its childhood years in 1999 and 2000, the population went mainstream; women reached parity with men online, lots more minority families joined the party and more people with modest levels of income and education came online." In short, by 2011 the Internet population resembled the general population.

The Pew report calls the Internet the "new normal" in the American way of life. About two out of three adults use the Internet. On a typical day more than 100 million U.S. adults go online to use e-mail, get their news and weather, search for specific information, or simply browse for fun. Teenagers use the Internet even more, with about 8 out of 10 reporting that they go online on a regular basis. The first "Internet generation" has come of age, and many of them can't recall what things were like before the Web became a reality.

Social Media

Trying to define social media is an incommodious task. A quick search of the Web will yield many definitions (thesocialmediaguide.com lists 50), most of them variations of the Wikipedia version (an example of using a social medium to define social media): "Social media are media for social interaction, using highly accessible and scalable communication techniques. Social media is the use of web-based and mobile technologies to turn communication into interactive dialogue." (This was the definition as of mid-2011; it might be different now. It also appears that Wikipedia can't agree on whether "social media" is singular or plural.) Of course, the people who use social media probably aren't interested in a formal definition. They are more interested in what they can do with social media. In short, social media allow us to:

- participate (such as voting for a favorite online article on Digg)
- converse (posting a comment on someone's blog)
- share (creating and posting material to a blog or to sites such as Flickr and YouTube)
- collaborate (creating content with other members of a group, such as Wikipedia)
- link up (forming social networks with friends and those who have similar interests on sites such as Facebook, Twitter, and Linkedin)

No matter how we define social media, it is obvious that they are immensely popular. Facebook has about 600 million members and has more than 150 million unique visitors in a typical month. Seventy-five percent of all U.S. teenagers are on social media networks. More than half the people in the United States are members of Facebook. Twitter has 200 million registered accounts and 23 million unique visitors. Twitter reports that it averages about 140 million "tweets" a day. MySpace, although not nearly as popular as it was a few years ago, still draws about 50 million unique visitors a month and Linkedin about 26 million. If all the time people in the United States spend on the Internet could be condensed into one hour, visiting social network sites and blogs would account for the most time, about 13½ minutes. Playing games would be next, accounting for about 6 minutes, followed by sending/receiving e-mail at 5 minutes.

Social media users are getting older. The number of adults on social media has doubled from 2007 to 2011. The average age of a user has increased from 33 in 2008 to 38 in 2010. Women are more likely than men to belong to a social network.

Social media are popular because they can be accessed on a variety of platforms—PCs, laptops, netbooks, tablet computers, and smartphones. The average smartphone user spends about 20 percent of his or her usage time visiting social network sites. Facebook reported that more than 150 million members access the site via mobile media.

Effects of Social Media

We have already discussed the history and some of the cultural consequences of social media in Chapter 3. The remainder of this section will focus on their more practical effects. First, as we shall see in more detail in subsequent chapters, traditional media have incorporated social media into their efforts to attract and hold an audience. Newspaper stories typically have an option that lets readers share the story on Facebook, Twitter, and other sites. TV programs have their own Facebook pages, and many movies (*Paranormal Activity,* for example) depend heavily on social media for promotion. Many aspiring singers got their big break thanks to a YouTube video.

Interestingly enough, using social media does not seem to have much impact on the time spent with traditional media, probably because many social media users are multitasking—posting on Facebook or Twitter while watching TV or listening to music.

sound byte

Follow the Leader

As of mid-2011, the five people who had the most followers on Twitter were (1) Lady Gaga, (2) Justin Bieber, (3) Britney Spears, (4) Barack Obama, and (5) Kim Kardashian. Draw your own conclusions.

decision makers

Mark Zuckerberg

Contributed by Meaghan E. Dominick

Mark Zuckerberg is one of the few 20-somethings to be the subject of a major motion picture. *The Social Network* traced Zuckerberg's trials and tribulations during the early years of Facebook.

Zuckerberg was interested in computers at a young age. His parents supported his interests and hired a computer programming coach to hone his talents. At 12, he began to create computer games based on board games that he enjoyed playing as a child. About a year before the widespread availability of computer networking software, Zuckerberg created a computer network that linked all of the computers in his house. In high school, he co-wrote a music recommendation program called Synapse. AOL and Microsoft tried to purchase the program for around a million dollars and Microsoft tried to recruit him to join their company. Zuckerberg declined both offers. Instead, he enrolled in Harvard University in September 2002.

While a student at Harvard, Zuckerberg created a Web site called CourseMatch, allowing Harvard students to see what courses their classmates were taking. After the success of CourseMatch, Zuckerberg then developed Facemash. To build the program, Zuckerberg first hacked into the dormitory ID photos at Harvard. Facemash then displayed ID photos

of two students and allowed the Web site user to choose the more attractive person. The site attracted 450 visitors within its first hour online but was shut down within a few days.

Zuckerberg quickly moved on to his next project. In early 2004, as a 19-year-old college sophomore, Mark Zuckerberg created what is now the largest social networking site on the Web in his college dorm room. Originally called thefacebook, the program was created in order to connect college students to one another. At first, thefacebook only allowed Harvard students to join. Slowly other Ivy League schools were added. By the end of 2004, thefacebook allowed registration from students at universities and colleges across the United States. Eventually, Zuckerberg shortened the name to Facebook. By 2005, high school students and international universities could join Facebook by invitation only. By 2006, Facebook expanded to include anybody above the age of 13. Currently, Facebook has more than 700 million users and is still growing.

At the time of thefacebook's creation, other social networking sites existed, but they allowed the user to manipulate their identities and representations of themselves. Zuckerberg's innovation was to create a site where people represented themselves truthfully, allowing social networking to take place.

Facebook now incorporates many features in addition to social networking. The site allows users to share pictures (currently it hosts more than 15 billion user-uploaded photos) and video. In addition, millions of Facebook members play interactive games with their friends on the site.

Zuckerberg's latest vision of Facebook's future is to connect its users to all things on the Internet. Certain Web sites allow Facebook users to log in to their sites and "like" the article, product, or whatever they are reading and share it with their Facebook friends.

Since Facebook is not a publicly traded company, it is hard to pinpoint an exact valuation. The estimated valuations, however, have always been greater than $50 billion. In 2010, *Time* magazine named Zuckerberg its Person of the Year.

Second, in a subtle way, social media have changed the way we think about entertainment. A recent survey revealed that about 60 percent of its respondents considered social media sites to be a form of entertainment. Among young people, the percentage was even higher. This finding holds significance for the established entertainment media since it seems that people are relying more on their friends, especially friends on social networking sites, for their entertainment and less on traditional media.

Video-sharing sites, such as YouTube, further reinforce this trend. New digital cameras and software make it easy to shoot, edit, and post a video on the Web. YouTube has more than 120 million videos, and amateurs produce about 75 percent of them. In addition, it has become simple to embed videos in Facebook pages or in blogs. In short, thanks to social media, friends, neighbors and acquaintances are supplying a significant amount of our entertainment.

Third, in addition to entertainment, social media have become an indispensible part of news gathering. Postings on Twitter and Facebook are often a key source of information when news breaks, as was demonstrated during the earthquakes in Haiti and Japan. The mainstream media often rely on Twitter and Facebook during the early stages of a news event. In Haiti, many of the early images of the devastation came from videos survivors had posted to YouTube that were subsequently shown on TV news programs. During the

Japanese quake, one woman in England reported that she was chatting on Facebook with her cousin in Japan while the earthquake was going on.

Next, as was probably inevitable, social media have become commercialized. It seems that every big marketing campaign now has some social media component. The Carnival Cruise Lines Web site permits cruisers to form communities, share cruise photos, and give advice about cruises. Major brands have Facebook pages (BMW has more than 50 pages, one for each country where the car is sold) and Twitter accounts (Snickers has more than 2,500 followers). Old Spice (and many other brands) has its own YouTube channel (the commercial "Should your man smell like an Old Spice Man?" has been viewed more than 19 million times). Dr. Pepper has a fan base of 8.5 million people who checked that they "like" the soft drink on Facebook. A Google search for "public relations" and "social media" returned more than 14 million results. Many brands now employ people whose only job is to direct the company's social media efforts. It's possible that this commercialization may cause a backlash among users. Much of the time, Twitter seems to function as a marketing device for celebrities who want to stay in touch with their fans or promote their latest efforts.

Monetizing Social Media

Advertising on social media is big business, generating about $2 billion in 2010, projected to rise to $8 billion in 2016. Facebook dominates the social media advertising business, collecting more than $1.5 billion in 2010, mostly for display advertising on its pages. Investors are bullish about social media. When Linkedin offered stock for sale, it raised $9 billion. If Facebook goes public, experts predict it will be valued at between $50 and $100 billion.

Social Media as Mobilizers

Social media can mobilize people into showing up at a certain place at a certain time. Flash mobs—groups of people called together by social media who appear suddenly in a public place, perform some seemingly meaningless activity for a short time, and then disperse—have been around since the early days of social media. In 2006, flash mobs gathered at various London Underground stations and danced to disco music. Hundreds of people showed up at a mall in Bristol in the United Kingdom to participate in a *Star Wars* light saber battle. (More recently, in a disturbing trend, flash mobs have assembled to commit crimes, as happened in London during the summer of 2011.)

In 2010—2011, however, the mobilizing power of social media was put to more serious use as unrest spread across the Middle East. Interestingly, it started in Tunisia, a country that is among the most Internet-connected in the Arab world, after an unemployed young man immolated himself in a gesture of protest. In spite of heavy government censorship, young people spread the news of his suicide and plans for further protests against the government on Facebook and posted video of the demonstrations on YouTube. Despite government restrictions on Internet use, protesters still managed to use Facebook and other social media sites to keep the demonstrations alive. Eventually, the protests led to the government's downfall. The aftermath, however, was not as positive as some had hoped. Sectarian rivalries emerged, the economy faltered, and demonstrations against the temporary provisional government occurred in parts of the country.

The mobilization power of social media was dramatically demonstrated during the 2010–2011 unrest in North Africa.

The unrest next spread to Egypt. The trigger event in that country was the death of Khaled Said resulting from a beating by Egyptian police. Using Tunisia as a model, young people set up a Facebook page titled "We Are All Khaled Said" that quickly attracted 400,000 members. In addition, those dissatisfied with the regime of Hosni Mubarak used social media to mobilize, coordinate, and publicize

media *Probe* The Importance of a Real Place in a Virtual World

Much of the analysis of the 2010–2011 uprisings in North Africa examined how the Internet and social media led to the fall of several governments. Somewhat overlooked was the role physical spaces played in the process.

With a little imagination, it's possible to trace the origins of social media back to the Greek agora, a designated area of the city where people could congregate, hear civic announcements, and discuss the latest news. The agora became the focal point of the political, cultural, and economic activity that defined city life. In modern times, the agora has been transformed into the city square, such as Times Square in New York, Trafalgar Square in London, and St. Peter's Square in Rome.

When the protests began in Tunisia, it is not surprising that the demonstrators came together in Kasbah Square in Tunis. In Egypt, the protesters assembled in Tahir Square; in Bahrain, it was Pearl Square. The situation was reversed in Libya, with supporters of the government gathering in Tripoli's Green Square, but once again the square figured prominently in the conflict.

The importance of the square is easy to understand. One hundred thousand people massed in one place makes a stronger statement than 10,000 people gathered in each of 10 separate places. Moreover, unlike social media such as Facebook, Twitter, or Skype, where individuals are connected only by virtual means, those who assemble in a public square can feel the power that comes with numbers, personally share their grievances and passions with others standing next to them, and join together to achieve a social revolution.

protests and demonstrations. As one young activist summed it up, "We use Facebook to schedule the protests, Twitter to coordinate, and YouTube to tell the world." The Khaled Said Facebook page called for large-scale protests in January 2010, and hundreds of thousands of protesters turned out. The Mubarak government, unsure of how to respond, eventually resorted to shutting down the Internet in Egypt. With help from Google and Twitter, dissidents were able to work around the blackout and get their messages publicized. The government shortly reversed course and reopened Internet access. The protests mounted across the country until Mubarak, under both internal and external pressure, stepped down and a military council took over the government. Demonstrations did not stop, however, as marchers once again took to the streets to protest the slow pace of political reforms.

As of mid-2011, social media had helped spread the unrest to other Middle Eastern countries but the results were not as benign. Libya erupted into a civil war. In Syria, dozens died in clashes between demonstrators and the government. At least 20 persons were killed during protests in Bahrain.

The mixed results highlight some of the strengths and weaknesses of the social media when used for political purposes. First, although social media may be the catalyst for a revolution, there is no guarantee that their revolutionary mobilization will be successful. In 2009, in the aftermath of the disputed elections in Iran, social media got people into the street but their protests did not result in regime change as the government used violence to suppress the uprising. The same scenario seemed to be unfolding in Libya and Syria in mid-2011. Second, authoritarian governments are becoming more sophisticated in dealing with protests organized via social media. In Syria, the government ostensibly lifted a ban on Facebook and YouTube as a concession to protesters, but critics note that the government could easily monitor Facebook postings to identify the ringleaders of any protests. In other countries, the authorities have used social media to distribute false information about planned protest rallies and then arrested all those who showed up for the bogus event. Russia and China have even set up alternative social media (Vkontakte in Russia and Kiaxin in China) where dissidents are more easily monitored. Finally, social media may empower young people to assemble and throw off the reins of an oppressive regime, but the real test comes afterward when a new, more responsive government has to be created. So far, social media have not been as successful in promoting this more difficult task.

Negative Impact

In addition to the cautions mentioned in the previous paragraph, we should not close this section without mentioning more about the downside of social media. First, social media interfere with productivity in the workplace. According to one 2009 survey, employees spent an average of about 45 minutes per week on social networking sites while at work. This may not sound like much, but over a year it could cost employers millions of dollars.

Further, digital media are easily duplicated, archived, and shared. Your tweets, blog entries, Facebook postings, and photos are probably saved somewhere on somebody's hard drive and may come back to haunt you. Items that a person might think were private might be shared with everybody thanks to ex-boyfriends and ex-girlfriends. Those party pictures that you posted might not go over so well with a prospective employer. (Many companies report that they routinely check the Facebook pages of job applicants.) Candidates running for office in 2036 might have to explain why they made those controversial blog postings back in 2012.

Next, there is the potential for **cyberbullying.** Cyberbullying can take many forms, including posting derogatory messages on a person's Facebook page, posting embarrassing or unflattering photos, or harassing someone via instant messages, texts, or e-mails. Bullying has been around a long time, but social media have made its effects more serious. Online bullying spreads quickly and easily, and it has the potential to reach a large audience. A recent study done by the Pew Foundation's Internet Project contained some troubling findings:

- One in three teenagers had experienced some form of cyberbullying.
- Online bullies were generally the same age as their victims.
- Girls reported more online harassment than boys.
- Those who experienced online bullying were more likely to be depressed and were more apt to miss school.

There have been several reports of teens who committed suicide following episodes of sustained cyberbullying. Teens in particular may lack the maturity and patience to cope with online bullies. In sum, social media connect us to all sorts of people, some of whom may not be very nice.

Finally, Facebook communication is not face-to-face communication. Updating your Facebook status every couple of hours, sending dozens of text messages a day, and posting clever tweets do not develop a person's interpersonal communication skills.

the social implications of the internet

Now that you know some details about the Internet and social media, let's examine some of the implications. Keep in mind, however, that the Internet and social media are still evolving, and much has yet to be discovered about their impact on society. Nonetheless, a few consequences are already apparent.

A New Model for News

To begin, the Internet supplements the traditional surveillance function of the mass media. As we have seen, when a news event happens, involved or interested parties can report on the event via Twitter or Facebook or post videos to YouTube. News about the earthquake and tsunami in Japan and the raid that killed Osama Bin Laden first appeared on social media. This represents a shift in traditional journalism in which decisions are made by editors and flow from the top down. Now the news can start at the source and go "sideways" to all who are interested. As some experts have put it, traditional news used to be a lecture; now it's a conversation.

Blogs have questioned the accuracy of news stories in the traditional media and have exposed several instances of sloppy or inaccurate reporting. In response, the news media have attempted to make their techniques more transparent. In short, the Internet provides additional checks and balances to the traditional news media and makes them more accountable to the public.

The Internet has also expanded the interpretation function. Social media in particular have made it possible for everyone to chime in with his or her opinion on news topics and controversial issues. Moreover, many politicians and prominent policy makers read blogs magnifying their influence even more.

Lack of Gatekeepers

As mentioned in Chapter 1, traditional mass media have a number of gatekeepers. On the Internet, however, there are none. This situation has several implications.

First, the risk of overloading the system with unwanted, trivial, worthless, or inconsequential messages is increased. Do we really need 130 million blogs or 140 million daily tweets?

Second, gatekeepers also function as evaluators of information. Newspaper editors and television news directors consider the authenticity and credibility of potential news sources. Gatekeepers, however, are not infallible. As detailed in Chapter 13, many mistakes can slip through the gates of even the most established TV networks, newspapers, and magazines. Nevertheless, if the system works properly, bogus news tips, unsubstantiated rumors, and false information are filtered out before they are published or broadcast. Information obtained on the Internet, however, comes without a guarantee. Some of it might be accurate; some of it you must use at your own risk.

Third, having no gatekeepers means having no censorship. The Internet is like a huge city. There are some streets where the whole family feels comfortable and other streets where you probably would not want to take your children.

Of course, there are some potential positive benefits from a lack of gatekeepers. Take blogs, for example. Topics that might be considered too controversial or unfavorable to the economic interests of traditional media can be publicized by bloggers. Further, blogs are not bound by the traditions of mainstream journalism. They can be partisan, in questionable taste, and totally individualistic. This makes for lively and exciting content.

Information Overload

The Internet represents an information retrieval tool that is unparalleled—provided a person knows how to use and understand it. In the days before the Net, students doing research would have to look things up in a text, reference book, or encyclopedia—sources that had some recognized authority. Today, students can use a search engine to look for the topic. A Web search indiscriminately displays a list of "sources," which may number in the millions. Every source on the screen seems to have the same credibility, even though some may be scientific documents and others comic books.

For example, while doing research, I used Google to look for references to "virtual reality." My search turned up 32,100,000 matches, including some that were about virtual reality games, quite a few that were XXX-rated, a large number from multimedia companies that produce virtual reality software, some that described technical background, and one about the use of virtual reality techniques for law enforcement and explosive ordnance training. (Of course, I might have narrowed my search using some advanced techniques, but the fact remains: There is so much on the Web that it is sometimes more overwhelming than useful.) Further, other than making a reasoned guess from the titles, I had no clue as to which sources were more authoritative than the others. (Students doing a conventional search would also have to assess the credibility of their sources, but the profuseness of information and the sheer size of the Net make this extremely difficult to do.)

Privacy Concerns

The Internet also raises a number of privacy concerns. Maintaining a person's privacy in the electronic age is not a new problem, but before the advent of the Internet, compiling a detailed dossier on someone required days or even weeks of searching through records scattered in dozens of places. Today,

media talk

How the Web Lures Children into Pornography

Clip 2: 7 minutes 57 seconds

You can watch Clip 2 *on the Online Learning Center home page,* www.mhhe.com/dominick12e. *Select* Student Center *and then* Chapter 4.

This clip is an unusual interview of a man who operated a child pornography site. He describes his battle on Capitol Hill to make the public more aware of the sexual exploitation of children over the Internet. Do you think parents need to be more involved in monitoring their child's Internet use? What can parents do to protect their child on the Internet? Is there any way to enforce laws on the Internet, or is the Net like the "wild wild west"?

WWW

computerized databases enable a person to accomplish the same things with only a couple of clicks of a mouse. What follows are some illustrations of this growing problem:

- In 2011, Sony discovered that a hacker had stolen the names, birth dates, and possibly credit card numbers of 77 million people who played online games using Sony's PlayStation.
- In 2009, a list of the names of 250 Los Angeles Police officers under investigation for alleged misconduct was mistakenly posted on the Internet.
- Some states have put the names and addresses of sex offenders on Web sites. Although the motives behind this practice may be understandable, the potential for harm due to incorrect or outdated information is substantial. In North Carolina a family was harassed because their address was listed online as the home of a known sex offender. The sex offender had actually moved away many months earlier, but the entry was never removed from the database. Many companies now charge as much as $150 to do online searches that will disclose someone's current address, Social Security number, bank account number, criminal record, and work history.
- Another growing concern is identity theft. A person can obtain someone's name, Social Security number, and date of birth from the Internet and can then apply for credit cards, get loans, and even commit crimes under another name. Even more unsettling is the fact that the victim may not even know what has been done in his or her name.

For the past few years, the government has wrestled with this privacy problem, and several bills have been introduced in state legislatures as well as the U.S. Congress that would restrict the availability of personal information. The issue is complicated because of concerns that government regulation might be so rigid that legitimate searches for information would be difficult. Many people prefer voluntary guidelines to laws.

Escapism and Isolation

Finally, does the Internet detach people from other people? Many individuals already spend lots of time engaging in sending e-mail, instant messaging, online chatting, game playing, online shopping, updating their Facebook and Twitter pages, and maybe even cybersex. As more and more attractions go online, will we spend even more of our lives staring at computer screens? Some psychologists have identified a condition known as *Internet addiction,* similar to drug or alcohol addiction. Early studies of Internet users revealed that those who spent many hours online also showed signs of isolation and depression. Subsequent studies have not found such a link, but these studies were done before social networking sites became popular.

the future: the evernet

Computers and computer chips keep shrinking. Before long, tiny computers will be part of our household appliances and maybe even our clothes. These devices will be so small that we probably will not even realize they are there. Moreover, experts predict that in the next 10 years advances in technology will enable these microcomputers to carry Web addresses and be connected continuously to the Internet. Imagine a furnace that automatically orders new filters over the Internet whenever it senses that the old ones are dirty. Imagine wearing a tiny computer that automatically unlocks your car, opens your garage door, pays your toll and parking fees, and reminds you that your tires need to be rotated. If you can imagine all of this, you have some idea what the **Evernet,** the successor to the Internet, will be like.

The Evernet (also called the Supranet or Internet II) will mark the convergence of wireless, broadband, and other devices, resulting in your being connected continuously to the Internet anywhere using any information device. You will no longer have to "log on" to the Net; you and all of the other devices that have computer chips will be automatically "online" all the time and all connected to one another. The Evernet will merge the virtual world with the physical world.

The implications of the Evernet are staggering. A person could send or access information instantly from anywhere in the world. What does that mean for consumers? You could order anything from anywhere at any time. Impulse buying would take on a whole new meaning. Further, shoppers could access price comparison search engines and find out if there was a better deal across the street. What about the implications for business? A manufacturer's assembly lines could be connected to cash registers all over the country. When sales go up, the assembly line works overtime.

What about daily living? "Smart houses" that run themselves would be possible. A smart house would inform you about your daily appointments and chores, monitor security systems, schedule maintenance and repairs, order food when supplies were low, regulate temperature and lighting, start the coffee brewing, and even run a hot bath.

What about health? People wearing pacemakers could have their heart rate and other medical data transmitted continuously to their physicians. If something were amiss, a person would get a call from his or her doctor's computer: "Your blood pressure is too high. Are you taking your pills?"

Granted, all of this sounds a bit like science fiction, and there is always the possibility that new technology will not impress consumers. Nonetheless, just 50 years ago, the Internet also sounded a lot like science fiction.

the internet and social media

The Internet and social media are still evolving, so it is difficult to describe specific career paths. As we shall see in later chapters, there are opportunities for students skilled in online advertising and online public relations techniques. People who can design and manage Web sites will be in demand. Several media companies have hired social media directors who oversee the company's presence in and use of social media. In fact, in the future there may be jobs in social media that don't exist yet.

The career outlook in the various media industries changes quickly. For a more current description of conditions in the Internet industry and a more detailed look at career options, please consult the book's Web site: www.mhhe.com/dominick12e.

main points

- The computer's ancestors were machines that performed mathematical calculations.

- By the 1970s, personal computers using packaged software were on the market.

- The Internet is a network of computer networks. It was started by the U.S. Department of Defense and in its early years was used primarily by scientists. The current Internet started in the 1980s thanks to the efforts of the National Science Foundation.

- The main features of the Internet are e-mail, the World Wide Web, and apps.

- The introduction of broadband Internet connections has encouraged the growth of streaming video and microcasting.

- The Internet has had a beneficial impact on the national economy, and e-commerce continues to grow.

- Social media have become important sources of news and entertainment.

- Social media can mobilize political movements.

- The Internet has created social concerns about lack of gatekeepers, information overload, lack of privacy, and isolation.

- The Evernet may be the successor to the Internet.

questions for review

1. How did the Internet come into being?
2. Distinguish between a Web site, a Web page, and a portal.
3. What are tablet computers? How will they affect your life?
4. What are the main functions performed by social media?
5. What are some of the social implications of the Internet and social media?

questions for critical thinking

1. Check out some of the blogs available on the Net. How many did you find useful?
2. Do a Web search for your name. See how much personal information you can find out about yourself on the Web. How easy was it for you to find the information? Could others have found it as well?
3. Do you use social media? How influential are they among your friends?
4. Some critics (Roger Ebert among them) have suggested that the era of free information on the Internet is almost over and that ultimately we will pay for most of the content we get over the Net. Do you agree? Would you pay to access a search engine? Or a Web site such as CNN.com?
5. Speculate on the future of social media.

key terms

cloud computing (p. 83)
hypertext (p. 84)
browsers (p. 84)
search engine (p. 84)
e-mail (p. 84)

spam (p. 85)
World Wide Web (WWW) (p. 85)
Web site (p. 85)
Web page (p. 85)
portals (p. 87)

broadband (p. 88)
WiFi (wireless fidelity) (p. 88)
WiMax (p. 88)
cyberbullying (p. 98)
Evernet (p. 100)

internet resources

Online Learning Center
On the Online Learning Center home page, www.mhhe.com/dominick12e, *select* Student Center *and then* Chapter 4.

1. Use the Learning Objectives, Chapter Outline, and Main Points sections to review this chapter.
2. Test your knowledge of the chapter using the multiple choice and flashcard features of the site.
3. Expand your knowledge of concepts and topics discussed in the chapter with additional Questions for Critical Thinking and Internet Exercises.

surfing the internet

www.isoc.org/internet/history/
An interactive history of the Internet provided by the Internet Society.

http://www.yahoo.com
The address of one of the many popular Web portals.

www.pewinternet.org
The latest news about how people use the Internet as determined by the Pew Internet and American Life Project.

www.socialmediawebsites.com
A directory of the best social networking and media Web sites.

www.technorati.com
Want to read a blog? Want to read 130 million? This is the site that tries to track them all.

www.twitter.com
What are you doing right now? Tell everybody in just 140 characters.

OME PAGE | TODAY'S PAPER | VIDEO | MOST POPULAR | TIMES TOPICS

:he New York Times
:hursday, October 13, 2011

Today's Paper

:he Times in Print for Thursday, October 13, 2011

:ump to: Front Page | International | National | Obituaries | Editorials, Op-Ed and Letters | New York | Business Day | Sports Thursday | The Arts | Home | Thursday Styles | Corrections |

:HE FRONT PAGE

:ongress Ends 5-Year Standoff on Trade Deals in Rare Accord

:y BINYAMIN APPELBAUM and JENNIFER STEINHAUER

.pproval of long-awaited free trade agreements with :hree countries offered a rare moment of bipartisan :greement in Washington.

Jnlikely Turn for a Suspect in a Terror ?lot

:y ROBERT F. WORTH and LAURA TILLMAN

Mansour J. Arbabsiar, suspected in an alleged Iranian lot to kill a Saudi diplomat in Washington, seems to .ave been more a stumbling opportunist than a :alculating killer.

With Three 9s, Cain Refigured Math for :axes

:y TRIP GABRIEL and SUSAN SAULNY

Herman Cain's 9-9-9 plan for taxes is getting .ntensive new scrutiny as Republicans continue to :irt with their candidates.

.ACE REMIXED

.n Strangers' Glances at Family, :ensions Linger

:y SUSAN SAULNY

:or one family, being mixed-race is not a defining .ssue, but outside the home, strangers gawk and make .acist comments, in what has become part of life for .nany families like theirs.

▸ Video: Just a Family
▸ Slide Show: Meet the Greenwoods
▸ Graphic: A Mixed-Race Family Tree

:d, Trainer

Today's Front Pages

NYT - New York Edition

🔍 Enlarge This Image

▸ **NYT - National Edition**

▸ **IHT - Europe**

▸ **IHT - Asia**

Chapter**5**

newspapers

This chapter will prepare you to:

- describe the challenges newspapers face in today's digital age
- recognize the conditions that had to exist before a mass press could come into existence
- understand the significance of the penny press
- explain the features that define both online and print versions of newspapers
- recognize the convergence of online and print newspapers
- understand the function of the Audit Bureau of Circulations (ABC)
- identify the various methods newspapers are using to stay in business

After March 28, 2011, reading articles posted on the *New York Times* Web site became a little more complicated and maybe a bit more expensive. Prior to that date access to news articles was unlimited and free. However, like most newspapers, the *Times* was searching for ways to increase its revenue. The solution: Build a "paywall" and charge readers for access to online stories.

Here's how the *Times* explained its new system, which cost about $20 million to develop. If you subscribe to the print edition, you can access all online content without additional charges. If you do not subscribe, you can still view 20 articles on NYTimes.com every month free of charge. If you want to read more, you have to become a digital subscriber (digital subscription packages range from $195 to $455 per year depending on what mobile device you use for access). If, however, you access a *Times* article via a link on Facebook, Twitter, a blog, or other social media, you can still read those articles even though you are over your monthly limit. If you come to a *Times* article via one of the five major search engines (Google, Bing, Yahoo!, Ask, AOL), you face a daily limit of five free articles per search engine, for a grand total of 25 per day in addition to the 20 per month. The home page at nytimes.com and all section fronts are free for all users to browse at all times.

Computer-savvy readers quickly found ways to bypass the paywall altogether by clearing the cookies that track the number of stories or by deleting characters from the URL or adding a few lines of computer code. In short, the *Times* built a $20 million wall with many holes in it.

A spokesperson for the newspaper stated that the paywall was deliberately designed to be porous. The *Times* endorses the idea of an open Internet and did not want to discourage the casual reader. Newspaper executives believe that many people will opt for the full access that comes with a digital subscription. And, of course, the *Times* wants all of those page views that come via Facebook, Twitter, and Google so that advertisers will still find the site attractive.

Will paywalls solve the economic problems of the newspaper industry? Will readers pay for content that used to be free? That remains to be seen, but other papers are closely watching the *Times* experiment.

This chapter looks at the history, structure, economics, and future of the newspaper industry as it struggles to find its way in the digital age.

a brief history

Journalism in Early America

Before we get to the details, it might be helpful to identify some general features of newspapers in early America:

- There were few papers.
- Printers and postmasters did most of the early publishing.
- News was not as timely as it is today.
- The idea of a free press was not endorsed by colonial governments.

In 1690 Boston printer Benjamin Harris published the first American newspaper, *Publick Occurrences both Foreign and Domestick.* One of the items in the paper alleged an affair between the king of France and his son's wife. This news story infuriated the Puritan officials of the colony, and they shut down the paper after one issue. The notion of a free press had yet to surface in America; most colonists believed that a paper had to have royal consent to be published.

Fourteen years later, John Campbell, the local Boston postmaster, put out the *Boston News Letter.* Published with royal permission, the paper was dull and lackluster, with many news stories simply reprinted from European papers. Campbell's paper had only about 300 subscribers and never made a profit.

A few years later, another Boston paper, the *New England Courant,* came on the scene. It was published by James Franklin, Ben's older brother, without government permission. Eventually, the elder Franklin's paper got him into trouble with the local authorities, and he was thrown into prison. Ben took over, and the paper prospered under his leadership. Ben eventually moved on to Philadelphia, where he started the *Pennsylvania Gazette,* which boasted such innovations as more legible type, headlines, and a cleaner layout.

Ben Franklin retired from a successful publishing career at the age of 42. During his career, he had started several papers, published one of America's first magazines, run the

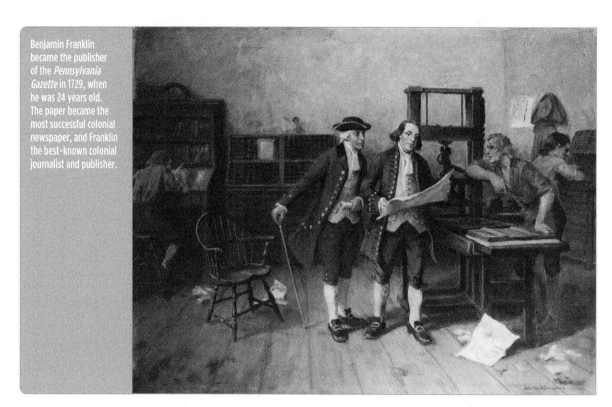

Benjamin Franklin became the publisher of the *Pennsylvania Gazette* in 1729, when he was 24 years old. The paper became the most successful colonial newspaper, and Franklin the best-known colonial journalist and publisher.

first editorial cartoon, proved that advertising copy could sell merchandise, and, perhaps most important, demonstrated that journalism could be an honorable profession.

The Beginnings of Revolution

Newspapers grew in numbers during the Revolutionary War, and most were partisan, siding with the colonies or with the Crown. This period marked the beginnings of the **political press,** which openly supported a particular party, faction, or cause.

In 1776, when the Continental Congress adopted the Declaration of Independence, the text of the document was published in the *Pennsylvania Evening Post* on July 6. The next year the Continental Congress authorized Mary Katherine Goddard, publisher of the *Maryland Journal,* to print the first official copies of the Declaration with the names of the signers attached. Under Goddard's direction the *Journal* became one of the leading colonial papers during the war. Goddard was one of about 30 women who printed or published colonial newspapers.

The Political Press: 1790–1833

The politicization of newspapers did not end with America's victory in the Revolutionary War. Instead, partisan leanings of the press were transferred into another arena—the debate over the powers of the federal government.

At the vortex of this debate between Federalists and anti-Federalists was the Constitution of the United States. Although the original document made no mention of the right of a free press, the Bill of Rights did contain such a provision. The **First Amendment** held that "Congress shall make no law . . . abridging the freedom of speech, or of the press." Thus, the idea of a free press, which had emerged during the Revolutionary period, became part of the law of the new nation when this amendment was ratified in 1791.

Newspapers grew with the country in the first 20 years of the 19th century. The daily newspaper began in 1783 and developed slowly. By 1800, however, most large cities had

Two early examples of the black press: *Freedom's Journal* was started in 1827 by John Russwurm, the first black person to graduate from a college in the United States, and Samuel Cornish. Cornish later edited the *Colored American*, a paper that had subscribers from Maine to Michigan.

at least one daily paper, and by 1820 there were 24 dailies, 66 semi- or triweeklies, and 422 weeklies. These newspapers were read primarily by the upper socioeconomic classes; early readers had to be literate and possess money to spend on subscriptions (about $10 per year or 6 cents per issue—a large sum when you consider that during those years 5 cents could buy a pint of whiskey). The content typically included commercial and business news, political and congressional debates, speeches, acts of state legislatures, and official messages.

During this period several newspapers were formed in response to the needs and interests of minority groups. *Freedom's Journal*, the first of more than 40 black newspapers published before 1860, was founded in the late 1820s by the Reverend Samuel Cornish and John Russwurm. Written and edited by blacks, the paper championed the cause of black people by dealing with the serious problems arising from slavery and by carrying news of foreign countries such as Haiti and Sierra Leone that appealed to its black audience.

At about the same time, in 1828, another minority group, the Cherokee Nation, published the *Cherokee Phoenix*, written in both Cherokee and English. When the Cherokees were evicted from their home in Georgia and forcibly resettled in Oklahoma, a new paper, the *Cherokee Advocate*, was started and continued to operate until 1906. The *Advocate* was revived in the 1970s and now publishes a monthly edition.

Birth of the Mass Newspaper

Front page of the *New York Sun:* Benjamin Day's reliance on advertising for revenue is illustrated by the several columns of classified ads appearing on the front page.

Several conditions had to exist before a mass press could come into existence:

- A printing press had to be invented that would produce copies quickly and cheaply.
- Enough people had to know how to read to support such a press.
- A mass audience had to be present.

In 1830 the U.S. manufacturing firm R. Hoe and Company built a steam-powered press that could produce 4,000 copies per hour. This and subsequent steam-powered presses that were even faster made it possible to print an extremely cheap newspaper that everybody could afford.

The second element that led to the growth of the mass newspaper was the increased level of literacy in the population. The first statewide public school system was established during the 1830s. The increased emphasis on education led to a concomitant growth of literacy as many people in the middle and lower socioeconomic groups acquired reading skills.

The final element was subtler and harder to explain. The mass press appeared during an era that historians call the age of Jacksonian democracy, an age in which ordinary people were first recognized as a political and economic force. Property requirements for voting had died out. Every state but one chose presidential electors by popular vote. In addition, this period was marked by the rise of an urban middle class. The trend toward democratization of business and politics fostered the creation of a mass audience responsive to a mass press.

The Penny Press

Development of the Penny Press   Benjamin Day was only 22 years old when he launched the mass-appeal *New York Sun* in 1833. Day's idea was to sell his daily paper for a penny (a significant price reduction from the 6 cents a copy for other big-city dailies). Moreover, the *Sun* contained local news, particularly those items that featured sex, violence, and human-interest stories. Conspicuously absent were stodgy political debates. Day's gamble paid off as the *Sun* attracted readers, and the **penny press** was launched.

Others imitated the *Sun*'s success. The colorful James Gordon Bennett launched the *New York Herald* in 1835, which was an even more rapid success than the *Sun*. The *Herald* introduced a financial page, a sports page, and an aggressive editorial policy that emphasized reform.

Another important pioneer was Horace Greeley. His *New York Tribune* appeared in 1841 and soon ranked third behind the *Herald* and *Sun* in circulation. Greeley used his editorial pages for crusades and causes. He opposed capital punishment and gambling and favored trade unions and westward expansion.

Greeley also supported women's rights. In 1845 he hired Margaret Fuller as literary critic for the *Tribune*. In addition to providing commentary on the fine arts, Fuller wrote articles about the hard lot of prostitutes, female prisoners, and the insane. Greeley's decision to hire Fuller is typical of his publishing philosophy: Like Fuller he never talked down to the mass audience but rather attracted readers by appealing to their intellect more than to their emotions.

The last of the major newspapers of the penny-press era that we will consider began in 1851 and, at this writing, is still publishing. The *New York Times*, edited by Henry Raymond, promised to be less sensational than the *Sun* or the *Herald* and less impassioned than Greeley's *Tribune*. The paper soon established a reputation for objective and reasoned journalism.

All these publishers had one thing in common: As soon as their penny papers were successful, they doubled the price.

Significance of the Penny Press   At this point, we should consider the major changes in journalism that were prompted by the success of the mass press during the period from 1833 to 1860. We can identify several key changes:

- The basis of economic support for newspapers
- The pattern of newspaper distribution
- The definition of what constituted news
- The techniques of news collection

William Randolph Hearst, the successful publisher of the *San Francisco Examiner* and later the *New York Journal*, employed sensationalism (yellow journalism) to win the circulation wars of the late 1800s. He created a major publishing empire consisting of a chain of newspapers, a wire service, and four syndicates.

Prior to the penny press, most of a newspaper's economic support came from subscription revenue. The large circulation of the penny papers made advertisers realize that they could reach a large segment of potential buyers by purchasing space. Moreover, the readership of the popular papers cut across political party and social class lines, thereby assuring advertisers a broad-based audience. As a result, advertisers were greatly attracted to this new medium, and the mass newspapers relied significantly more on advertising revenues than did their predecessors. As we shall see, the Internet would eventually dismantle this 180-year connection between advertising and news.

Older papers were distributed primarily through the mail; the penny press, although relying somewhat on subscriptions, also made use of street sales. Vendors would buy a hundred copies for 67 cents and sell them for 1 cent each. Soon it became common to hear newsboys hawking papers on street corners in the larger cities. Since these papers had to compete with one another in the open marketplace of the street, editors went out of their way to find original and exclusive news that would give their paper an edge.

The penny press also redefined the concept of news, hiring people to go out and look for stories. Reporters were assigned to special beats: police, financial, sports, and religion, to name a few. Foreign correspondents were also popular. And newspapers changed their emphasis from the affairs of the commercial elite to the social life of the rising middle classes.

This shift meant that news became more of a commodity, something that had value. And, like many commodities, fresh news was more valuable than stale news. Any scheme that would get the news into the paper faster was tried. Stories were sent by carrier pigeon, Pony Express, railroad, and steamship. The Mexican War of 1846 made rapid news transmission especially desirable, and many newspapers first used the telegraph to carry news about this conflict. All in all, the penny papers increased the importance of speed in news collection.

Newspapers as Big Business

A new reporting technique emerged during the Civil War as telegraphic dispatches from the war zones were transformed into headlines. Because telegraph lines sometimes failed, the opening paragraphs of the story contained the most important facts. If the line failed during transmission of a story, at least the most important part would get through. Thus, the "inverted pyramid" style of reporting was developed.

After the war, from about 1870 to 1900, the total U.S. population doubled, and the urban population tripled. Newspapers grew even faster than the population; the number of dailies quadrupled, and circulation showed a fivefold increase. The thriving newspaper business also attracted several powerful and outspoken individuals who had a profound influence on American journalism. We will consider three: Pulitzer, Scripps, and Hearst.

Joseph Pulitzer came to the United States from Hungary and turned the *St. Louis Post-Dispatch* into a success. In 1883, he bought the *New York World.* In a little more than three years, Pulitzer increased the paper's circulation from 15,000 to 250,000.

What was Pulitzer's formula for success? Pulitzer stressed accuracy. He also introduced practices that appealed to advertisers: more advertising space and ads priced on the basis of circulation. Moreover, he aimed his paper at the large population of immigrants then living in New York by stressing simple writing and many illustrations. Pulitzer also reintroduced the sensationalized news format of the penny press, as the *World*'s pages carried stories about crime, violence, and tragedy. Finally, Pulitzer endorsed the notion that a paper should promote the welfare of its readers, particularly the underprivileged.

Attempts to reach a working-class audience were not confined to the East. In the Midwest, E. W. Scripps started papers in Cleveland and Cincinnati, both growing industrial cities with large populations of factory workers. The Scripps papers featured concisely edited news, human-interest stories, editorial independence, and frequent crusades for the working class. Scripps pioneered the idea of a newspaper chain. By 1911 he owned 18 papers.

Perhaps the best-known of these three newspaper giants, thanks to the film *Citizen Kane,* is William Randolph Hearst. While Pulitzer was succeeding in New York and Scripps was acquiring papers in the Midwest, the 24-year-old Hearst was given control of the *San Francisco Examiner,* thanks to the generosity of his wealthy father. Hearst went after readers by appealing to their emotions. Fires, murders, and stories about love and hate were given splashy coverage. Hearst banked heavily on sensationalism to raise his readership level. His strategy worked: The *Examiner* shot to the number-one position.

Yellow Journalism

Hearst, like Pulitzer before him, then invaded the big league—New York City. In 1895 he bought the *New York Journal.* Soon, Pulitzer and Hearst were engaged in a fierce circulation battle as each paper attempted to outsensationalize the other. As one press critic put it, the duel between these two spread "death, dishonor and disaster" all over page one. Sex, murder, self-promotion, and human-interest stories filled the two papers. This type of reporting became known as **yellow journalism,** and whatever its faults, it sold newspapers.

The battle between Pulitzer and Hearst reached its climax with the Spanish-American War in 1898. When the battleship *Maine* was blown up in Havana harbor, the *Journal* offered a $50,000 reward for the arrest of the guilty parties. Circulation promptly jumped over the 1 million mark. War was finally declared in April, and the *World* and the *Journal* pulled out all the stops. Hearst chartered a steamer and equipped it with printing presses. He also brought down his yacht and sailed with the U.S. fleet in the Battle of Santiago. The *Journal* put out 40 extras in a single day.

Although the period of yellow journalism was not the proudest moment in the history of the American newspaper, some positive features did emerge from it. First, it brought enthusiasm, energy, and verve to the practice of journalism, along with aggressive investigative reporting. Second, it brought wide exposure to prominent authors and led to some fine examples of contemporary writing. Stephen Crane, Frank Norris, Dorothy Dix, and Mark Twain all wrote for newspapers during this period (1880–1905). Further, yellow journalism helped popularize the use of layout and display devices—banner headlines, pictures, color printing—that would go on to characterize modern journalism.

The Early 20th Century

From 1900 to 1920, consolidation characterized the newspaper business. Although circulation and profits went up, the number of daily newspapers decreased, and the number of cities with competing newspapers dropped by 60 percent. What happened?

First, the cost of new technology—Linotype machines, high-speed presses—proved too much for many marginal papers. Second, advertisers showed a preference for the paper with the largest circulation in the market. Smaller-circulation papers saw their revenues shrink to the point at which they could no longer compete. Third, consolidation had increased profits in the railroad, grocery, and hotel businesses, and newspaper publishers decided it could do the same for them. Consequently, newspaper chains—companies that owned several papers—grew quickly. By 1933 six chains—Hearst, Scripps-Howard, Patterson-McCormack, Block, Ridder, and Gannett—controlled 81 dailies with a combined circulation of more than 9 million, about one-fourth of all daily circulation.

Appearing with the consolidation trend and enjoying a short but lively reign was **jazz journalism.** At the end of World War I, the United States enjoyed a decade of prosperity known as the Roaring Twenties. The radio, Hollywood, the airplane, Prohibition, and Al Capone all captured national attention. The papers that best exemplify jazz journalism all sprang up in New York between 1919 and 1924. All were characterized by two features: (1) They were **tabloids,** printed on a page that was about one-half the size of a normal newspaper page; and (2) they were richly illustrated with photographs. The best example of this trend was the *New York Daily News.*

The Impact of the Great Depression

The Depression had a huge social and economic impact on newspapers and magazines. During the 1930s total daily newspaper circulation increased by about 2 million; the total population increased by 9 million. The total income of the newspaper industry, however, dropped about 20 percent in this decade. Marginally profitable papers were unable to stay in business, and approximately 66 dailies went under.

Although worsening economic conditions were one cause of the newspaper's decline, more important was the emergence of radio as a competitor for national advertising dollars. From 1935 to 1940, newspapers' share of national advertising revenues dropped from 45 to 39 percent, while radio's share jumped from 6 to more than 10 percent. By 1940, however, thanks to increased revenue from local advertisers, newspaper revenues had rebounded. Nevertheless, the economic picture was not rosy, and the number of daily papers declined to 1,744, an all-time low, in 1945.

Postwar Newspapers

The postwar economy forced the newspaper industry to move even further in the direction of contraction and consolidation. Although newspaper circulation rose from approximately 48 million in 1945 to about 62 million in 1970, the number of dailies stayed about the same. There was actually a circulation loss in cities with populations of more than a million, and several big-city papers went out of business. Moreover, the number of cities with competing dailies dropped from 117 to 37 between 1945 and 1970. This meant that about 98 percent of American cities had no competing papers.

In 1945, 60 chains controlled about 42 percent of the total daily newspaper circulation. By 1970 approximately 157 chains accounted for 60 percent of total circulation. Why had the number of chains continued to grow? One factor was the sharp rise in costs of paper and labor. Newspapers were becoming more expensive to print. The large chains were in a position to share expenses and to use their presses and labor more efficiently. For instance, several papers could share the services of feature writers, columnists, photographers, and compositors, thus holding down costs.

The consolidation trend was present across media, as several media conglomerates controlled newspapers, magazines, and radio and TV stations. Black newspapers were also caught up in the trend toward concentration. In 1956 the *Chicago Defender* changed from a weekly to a daily, and its owner, John Sengstacke, started a group of nine black papers, including the Pittsburgh *Courier* and the Michigan *Chronicle.*

Another continuing trend was the competition among media for advertising dollars. The total amount of advertising revenue spent on all media nearly tripled between 1945 and 1970. Although the total spent on newspapers did not increase at quite this pace, the amount spent on television increased by more than threefold. The rising TV industry cut significantly into the print media's national advertising revenue.

The biggest development of the 1980s was the birth of *USA Today,* whose content was characterized by shorter stories, splashy graphics, and lots of charts and tables, innovations that were imitated by many local papers.

Contemporary Newspapers: Struggling to Survive

The problems of the newspaper industry became apparent during the 1990s and intensified as the new decade progressed. Readership started a slow but steady decline; the Internet siphoned away advertising revenue, especially classified ad dollars, and young people in particular deserted the paper and went online for their news.

media *Ethel L. Payne*
Probe

When Lyndon Johnson signed the Civil Rights Act of 1964, he invited leaders of the civil rights movement to join him in the Oval Office. Only one woman was among the group that witnessed the historic moment—Ethel L. Payne, an African American journalist who had reported on civil rights issues for more than a decade.

Payne was the granddaughter of slaves. She originally wanted to become a lawyer but was denied admission to law school because of her race. In 1948 she went to Japan to work with African American troops who were stationed there. Two years later Payne showed excerpts from her personal journal about the problems of black soldiers to a reporter for the *Chicago Defender* who was visiting Japan. Her stories became a series in the newspaper and launched Payne on a journalism career.

Based in Chicago, Payne won awards for her coverage of problems in the African American community. She went to Washington in the mid-1950s to cover the beginnings of the civil rights movement. She wrote stories analyzing the historic *Brown* v. *Board of Education* Supreme Court

decision. Payne made her presence felt at White House press conferences when she asked President Dwight Eisenhower pointed questions about the lack of progress on civil rights during his administration.

In 1956 Payne covered the arrest of Rosa Parks in Montgomery, Alabama, and the subsequent bus boycott. She reported the big stories of the civil rights movement, including the efforts to integrate the University of Alabama; the violence in Little Rock, Arkansas; the confrontation at Selma, Alabama; and the march on Washington in 1965. She was one of the first reporters to interview Dr. Martin Luther King Jr.

In 1966 she traveled to Vietnam to cover African American troops, who were involved in much of the fighting. She later accompanied Secretary of State Henry Kissinger on a six-nation tour of Africa. In 1978, at age 67, she ended her career with the *Chicago Defender* to write a syndicated column. Seven years later she became a leader in the effort to free South African leader Nelson Mandela.

Ethel Payne died in 1991. The *Washington Post* published a tribute to her on its editorial page. It praised her for being fair, straightforward, and independent, an assessment probably shared by her millions of readers.

In addition, the industry was hurt by several bad management decisions. First, publishers did not know what to do with the Internet. Papers created online editions as an afterthought and used them primarily to steer readers to the print edition. From the beginning Web sites were seen as tangential to the paper's core business. Second, the online editions were free; readers paid nothing for the content. Predictably, some readers stopped subscribing to the print edition and circulation declined further. Moreover, the free content created an expectation that news online was free for the taking. Any future attempts to charge for this content would be met with resistance. Finally, the easy credit available during the middle part of the new decade prompted many papers to expand and to buy up existing properties. As a result, a number of newspaper companies were saddled with huge debts. (See "Media Probe: The Debt Trap" on page 125.) During prosperous times this would have been a manageable situation, but the economic collapse during the last years of the decade cut into the bottom line and many papers could not meet their debt obligations.

All of this came together in 2008–2009 and resulted in a deluge of unfortunate developments. At the risk of spreading too much gloom and doom, here is just a partial sampling of the bad news:

- The Tribune Company, publisher of the *Chicago Tribune* and the *Los Angeles Times*, declared bankruptcy.
- The *Christian Science Monitor* stopped its daily print edition.
- Newspapers in Detroit and in several other cities cut home delivery to three times a week.
- The *Seattle Post-Intelligencer, Rocky Mountain Times,* and about 100 other daily and weekly papers shut down.
- From 2007 to 2008, newspaper advertising revenue dropped an alarming 23 percent.
- In early 2009, the cost of a share of stock in the New York Times Company was under $5, less than the cost of a Sunday edition of the *Times*.

The current state of the newspaper industry is a good example of the old good-news, bad-news refrain: The bad news is that the industry is still losing readers and revenue.

social issues

Comment Boards: Meaningful Discussion or Just Mean?

Comment boards on newspaper Web sites were created in part to encourage readers to share their viewpoints with other readers and to engage in meaningful dialogue about the topic under consideration. Much of the time that is exactly what happens, but sometimes things can get out of hand.

Below are a few sample comments that appeared in a major metropolitan newspaper on an opinion piece about teaching cursive writing in public schools—not exactly a hot-button topic. (Screen names have been changed.)

8:32 am (Posted by A referring to an earlier comment)

Maybe you could use spell check before you post sarcasm. It's "unintelligible" not "unintelligable." Have a nice day, low IQ.

9:14 am (Posted by B)

A: Do you represent the cursive lobby, or are you just a d**k?

9:16 am (posted by A)

"Do you represent the cursive lobby, or are you just a d**k?"

B: Do you have anything relevant to write or are you just a drive by retard?

9:36 am (posted by C)

Printing is the best kind of writing, and a lot of us uses the computer.

9:39 am (posted by A)

"Printing is the best kind of writing, and a lot of us uses the computer.'

Yet you can't even use the word "uses" correctly. USE the computer, not uses the computer, Gump.

Most of you have probably read other exchanges where the discussion deteriorated into snarkiness, name-calling, insults, and rants. Print newspapers don't have this problem since most papers require people who write letters to the editor to provide their real name and address. The problem with newspaper Web sites is that those who comment can post their observations using some made-up handle or screen name, thus rendering them anonymous responders. This cloak of anonymity allows people to make rash and even hate-filled statements that they probably wouldn't make if their names were attached to them. As a result, newspapers must make sure their comment boards welcome serious discussions and offer readers a chance to voice their opinions without offending others or getting the paper into legal trouble.

Papers use several techniques to keep a civil level of discourse on their comment boards. Many require people to register and provide a valid e-mail address before they can post comments. *The Wall Street Journal* even requires posters to use their real names.

Other papers have assigned a staff member to read all comments and delete inappropriate ones. This solution requires some degree of subjectivity on the part of the moderator, but typically comments containing hate speech, personal attacks, racial slurs, spam, and copyright violations are deleted. The moderator may also limit the number of comments that one person may make per story in order to eliminate the back-and-forth squabbling that sometimes takes place between two readers.

The law has generally protected newspapers from lawsuits that stem from comments made by others that were posted on online newspaper comment boards. Nonetheless, newspapers can get embroiled in defamation suits brought by individuals who claim they were defamed by anonymous comments on the Web site. Those who were allegedly defamed can ask a court to compel the newspaper to reveal the name of the anonymous poster who made the damaging remarks. Although some state courts have refused to force a newspaper to disclose user names, others have ruled differently. Each newspaper must decide for itself if it is willing to go to court to defend the anonymity of someone who is unwilling to put his or her own name on a comment.

The good news is that the industry is not losing them quite as badly as before. From 2008 to 2009, print newspaper advertising revenue dropped nearly 29 percent. From 2009 to 2010, total print ad revenue dropped again, but this time only by 8 percent. After declining for two years, online ad revenue jumped nearly 11 percent from 2009 to 2010, but the increase was not nearly enough to compensate for the losses suffered by the print version. Circulation continued to fall, dropping 6 percent from 2008 to 2009, and the decline continued into 2010—but, on the bright side, no major newspaper closed in 2010.

newspapers in the digital age

Transitions

Newspapers are experimenting with ways to stay afloat in the digital age. Their efforts are directed at two areas: cutting costs and increasing revenue. Cost-cutting efforts have ranged from the mild to the extreme. At one end of the spectrum, many newspapers are sharing content, something that would have been unheard of a decade ago. The *Washington Post*, for example, shares certain stories with the *Baltimore Sun*. Fierce competitors *Dallas Morning*

News and *Fort Worth Star-Telegram* trade sports coverage. Content sharing helps keep down the cost of news gathering. Numerous papers have cut costs by laying off employees or asking staff members to take unpaid furloughs.

Several big-city papers have stopped delivery to outlying areas, saving printing and delivery costs. Other papers have stopped home delivery on certain days of the week, suggesting that readers buy a newspaper at the newsstand or read the online edition to fill in the gaps. The most drastic cost-cutting step of all is dropping the print edition altogether and becoming an online-only publication. In Michigan, for example, the *Ann Arbor News* stopped its paper-and-ink operation and became AnnArbor.com, and as mentioned earlier, the century-old *Christian Science Monitor* dropped its daily print edition in 2009 and shifted to online.

At the same time, newspaper publishers are searching for new ways to make money. Some, like the *New York Times*, are instituting a paywall. Others are attempting to charge readers a small sum for content, called a micropayment, which would imitate the business model pioneered by iTunes. Others are looking for ways to generate more income from advertising on cell phones and other mobile media. Finally, the industry is trying to figure out how to make more money from news aggregators, such as Google News, that use newspaper content to draw readers to their sites. We will examine the economics of the newspaper industry in more detail below.

Since it appears that the future of the newspaper business is closely tied to its online efforts, let's take a more detailed look at newspapers online.

Online Newspapers

Online papers have certain advantages over traditional newspapers:

- Printed newspapers are limited by the **newshole,** the amount of news that can be printed in one edition. Online papers have no such limitations. The full text of lengthy speeches, transcripts of interviews, and extensive tables and graphs can be accommodated easily.
- Online papers can be updated continuously; there are no edition deadlines.
- Online papers are interactive. E-mail addresses, comment boards, and chat rooms allow readers to provide quick feedback to the paper. Many have searchable archives and links to other sites.
- Online papers can provide photos and video and audio clips to accompany news stories and advertisements. Some even offer social networking opportunities.
- Online papers can feature user-generated content.

In 1994 about 20 daily papers had Web sites. By 2010 it was rare for a paper not to have one.

During the early years of the Internet, online newspaper sites were slow to innovate. There was a fear that the Web site would steal readers from the print version. Thus, many of them simply took their print stories and placed them online, updating them only once a day. Some even withheld stories until they were published in the print edition. Newspapers, however, now realize that if they want to compete with other news sites such as CNN and CBS News, their Web sites have to do more.

Mobile Media

In golf, a "Mulligan" is like a "do-over": It gives a player a chance to re-hit a bad shot. Newspapers look upon mobile media as their version of a Mulligan. The newspaper industry's equivalent of a bad golf shot was its decision to put its content on the Web for free, a move that hurt its bottom line. Now with the growing popularity of mobile media, the industry is betting that more people will want to read news on e-readers, smartphones, or tablet computers rather than on their home or laptop computers. Chapter 1 has described the amazing growth of mobile media. As of mid-2011, about 45 million people have smartphones; more than 15 million have iPads or other tablet computers; and more than 4 million have the Kindle or other e-readers. The tremendous potential of mobile media has given the industry a chance to alter its online business model. Consequently, newspapers are using mobile media to make their product more appealing to advertisers and/or charging consumers to pay for news.

For example, newspaper subscriptions are available for the Kindle and Nook e-readers. In 2011, the Kindle edition of the *Washington Post* cost about $12 a month and the *Chicago Tribune* was $10 a month. The Nook subscription to the *New York Times* cost about $20 per month.

Many newspapers have developed apps for mobile media that take them to a special newspaper site that offers a different experience from reading the online version of the paper at its usual Web address. To illustrate, readers who go to the *USA Today* Web site (www.usatoday.com) see a typical newspaper Web site crammed with options. A reader can choose from about 100 links that lead to more detailed stories. Readers who have the iPad app go to a different *USA Today* site. The design is cleaner, easier to navigate, graphically pleasing, and features the familiar *USA Today* blue and white logo. Readers can scroll through story summaries or tap the logo to choose one of several sections, such as "Money" or "Sports," where they can choose to read further. Video and photos are smoothly integrated with the stories, and the readers can enlarge images with their fingers. Tapping on the "Weather" section brings up national and local temperature maps and radar images.

Rupert Murdoch's News Corp. owns the distinction of offering *The Daily*, the first online paper designed exclusively for the iPad. Readers can download the app for free but must pay a fee to subscribe or read a single issue. Annual subscriptions cost about $40.

Speaking of subscriptions, a few major newspapers have struck a deal with Apple to sell subscriptions through Apple's App Store. For example, in mid-2011 a person could subscribe to the *New York Daily News* iPad edition for $12 a year. Apple's usual deal is to take 30 percent of the subscription fee revenue plus a chunk of the advertising revenue that comes from the apps. Some papers, dissatisfied with Apple's terms, have designed and sold their own apps. It's too early to tell how many papers will take advantage of Apple's offer.

Although apps may eventually represent a significant revenue stream, they have a downside. They can be expensive to develop, and apps have to be designed for each specific operating system used by mobile devices. In other words, a newspaper must develop an app for the iPhone and a different app for the Android.

In sum, look for newspapers to be designed for multiple digital platforms, not just paper. As *New York Times* publisher Arthur Sulzberger Jr. put it, "Newspapers cannot be defined by the second word—paper. They've got to be defined by the first—news."

User-Generated Content

Newspapers are incorporating user-generated material into their print and digital versions but are doing so with caution. Most will allow readers to post comments on stories but are careful about relying too heavily on citizen journalists for original reporting because citizen-produced journalism carries some risk. The competence, credibility, and objectivity of the average citizen reporter may be suspect. It is difficult to know if citizen journalists are knowledgeable or if they are pursuing some personal agenda. The person who submits a story about a new school board policy might have children directly affected by the policy. The citizen journalist who calls *Little Fokkers* the best comedy film he ever saw may have only seen three comedy films in his life. Consequently, newspapers rely on user-generated content mainly for news tips, eyewitness accounts, or photos and videos of certain news events.

Some newspapers have created separate sites to house user-generated content. The publisher of the *Denver Post* created YourHub.com, a series of local Web sites that feature user-generated content. The Tribune Company in Chicago manages ChicagoNow, a site that features user-written blogs and other content generated by readers. The *St. Louis Post-Dispatch* has a similar site, MySTLtoday. Other papers are investigating other ways to make the most of user-generated content. Couples can post a 1- to 3-minute video version of their wedding announcement on the Weddings/Celebrations page of the *New York Times* Web site. Tackable allows news editors looking for a photo to go with a news story to post a photo request for a specific area. Users who have the Tackable app on their smartphones can view a map that shows all the potential photo opportunities in their area, take a photo, and submit it to a news editor for possible publication.

Social Media

It took a while but newspapers now realize that it is an economic advantage to spread awareness about themselves and their news stories on social media. Consequently, it is the rare newspaper site that does not contain a link to its Facebook page or Twitter feed. The *New York Times* has about 3 million Twitter followers; *USA Today* has about 53,000 Facebook fans. The *Chicago Tribune*'s Facebook welcome page has a number of news section subpages, a discussion tab, a subdivision that asks readers to respond to interesting questions, and links to local shopping bargains.

Many papers, including the *New York Times,* provide live headline feeds to Twitter. Others have created separate Twitter accounts for each section of the newspaper, and others use Twitter to communicate with readers. Following newspapers on Twitter is becoming more popular. The *Washington Post* nearly doubled its Twitter followers from 2010 to 2011. Other top papers saw gains of 15 to 50 percent. More than 200 newspapers post videos on YouTube, including the *Chicago Tribune,* the *Miami Herald,* and the *Boston Globe.*

Many newspapers, along with other news organizations, are hiring social media editors whose job consists of monitoring social media, alerting the newspaper when social media break a story, developing apps for the paper's digital edition, and managing the paper's Twitter and Facebook sites. The social media editor will become more important as more readers come to the paper from outside links rather than going directly to the paper's home page.

defining features of newspapers

The online and print editions of the newspaper share some defining features. First, the newspaper is made up of diverse content. Newspapers contain international, national, and local news. In addition, they feature editorials, letters to the editor, movie listings, horoscopes, comics, sports, film reviews, recipes, advice columns, classified ads, and a host of other material. Their range of content is extensive.

Second, newspapers are conveniently packaged. Both the print and online versions are organized according to content. There are sections devoted to general news, financial news, sports, and entertainment. In addition, each story contains a headline that makes it easy for readers to decide if they want to peruse the rest of the story.

Third, newspapers are local. Reporters cover meetings of the local school board, the city council, and the zoning commission. They cover the local police station and tell about the newest store openings in the local mall. Sports sections cover the hometown Little League and high school teams. Local people with merchandise to sell use the classified ads. Newspapers are the only medium with the resources to report all the neighborhood activities in a community.

Fourth, more than any other medium, the newspaper serves as a historical record. One writer described newspaper journalism as "the first draft of history." The typical paper contains a record of daily events, some profound, some not so profound, that influence our lives. If a person wants to get a sense of what life was like in the 1940s, for example, he or she can flip through some old issues of the paper and see what events were on people's minds, what movies they were seeing, and what products were being advertised.

Fifth, newspapers perform the watchdog role in our society. They monitor the workings of government and private industry for misdeeds and wrongdoings. They alert the public to possible threats and new trends.

Finally, newspapers are timely. News is not useful if it is stale. Recognizing this fact, the largest-circulation newspapers in the United States publish daily and online editions that can break news any time of the day. Getting the news out fast has always been one of the characteristics of the newspaper business.

	2010 Circulation (millions)	2008 Circulation (millions)	Percent Change
table 5-1 Top 10 Newspaper Circulation (Print) — **Paper**			
Wall Street Journal	2.06	2.01	+2
USA Today	1.83	2.29	−20
New York Times	0.88	1.00	−12
Los Angeles Times	0.60	0.74	−19
Washington Post	0.55	0.62	−11
New York Daily News	0.51	0.63	−19
New York Post	0.50	0.63	−21
Chicago Tribune	0.44	0.52	−15
Houston Chronicle	0.34	0.45	−24
Newsday	0.31	0.38	−18

Note: With few exceptions, newspaper circulation has seen a slow but steady decline.

organization of the newspaper industry

This section will first examine the organization of the traditional ink-and-paper newspaper industry and then consider the online versions. The print newspapers that are published in this country are many and varied. They range from the *Wall Street Journal*, a nationally oriented financial daily, to the *Daily Journal of Commerce*, a small financial paper published in Portland, Oregon; from the *National Enquirer* to the *Daily Lobo*, the college newspaper of the University of New Mexico; from the million-plus-circulation *New York Times* to the 6,000-circulation Gallipolis *Daily Tribune* in Ohio. Obviously, there are many ways to categorize an industry as diverse as this one. For our purposes we will group papers by frequency of publication (dailies and weeklies), by market size (national, large, medium, small), and by their appeal to specialized groups. Table 5-1 shows the top 10 newspapers by circulation and the percentage change in circulation between 2008 and 2010.

Print Dailies

To be considered a daily, a newspaper has to appear five times a week. In 2009 there were 1,387 dailies, down 3 percent from 2008 (see Figure 5-1) and about 6,500 weeklies. Whether a daily or a weekly, the chief concern of a newspaper is **circulation,** the number of copies delivered to subscribers, newsstands, and vending machines. Circulation figures reflect the crisis in the newspaper industry. Weekday morning circulation has decreased 14 percent since 2000, evening circulation has dropped 40 percent, and Sunday circulation is down 22 percent (see Figure 5-2). In addition, since the U.S. population has grown, the

figure 5-1

Number of Daily Newspapers in the United States, 1950–2010

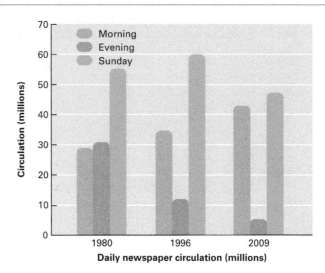

figure 5-2

Daily Newspaper Circulation, 1980–2009

Daily newspaper circulation (millions)

ratio of newspapers per household has dropped precipitously. In 1960, about 111 newspapers were sold per 100 households. In 2010, that number had declined to 40 newspapers sold per 100 households. The overall trend does not inspire optimism.

The circulation crunch, however, has not hit all papers with equal force. This becomes apparent when we divide daily newspapers into market groups.

National Newspapers   Only a few papers fall into this category. These are publications whose content is typically geared not for one particular region or city but for the entire country. These papers use satellites to transmit images and text to regional printing plants, where the papers are assembled and distributed. Gannett's *USA Today,* the *New York Times,* and the *Wall Street Journal* are the three national newspapers in the United States. Circulation for this group has not declined quite as much as in other segments.

Large Metropolitan Dailies   These are newspapers based in communities with a population of 500,000 or more. They are the group that is in the biggest trouble. Competition for readers from the Internet, a loss of advertising revenue to online sites, and the migration of young readers to the Web have all combined to hurt circulation and profits. From 2006 to 2010, total print circulation of the 10 largest metropolitan dailies dropped more than 40 percent. As we have already noted, several big-city papers have folded.

Medium-Sized Dailies   Papers in this segment have circulations that range between 100,000 and 500,000, and their fortunes, particularly the papers at the top end of this range, are declining about as fast as their big-city counterparts. This group also lost about 40 percent of its print circulation from 2006 to 2010. There were, however, bright spots. Some medium-sized papers, particularly those in Florida and Arizona where the population is older, did not see such steep losses.

sound byte

R.I.P. (Rest in Paper?)

A British company has found a novel way to use recycled newspapers: They make coffins from them. The biodegradable coffins come in two sizes and four colors with optional printed designs. For those choosing cremation, the company also makes urns from recycled paper.

Small-Town Dailies   Papers in this category generally have circulations under 100,000, and they are the ones that are doing the best job weathering the storm. Circulation loss in this group from 2006 to 2010 was about 20 percent. Some smaller papers even managed to gain circulation. The Madison, Wisconsin, *State Journal* increased circulation by more than 10 percent from 2007 to 2008. Why has the downturn been less severe in this group? They face

120

decision

makers   *Al Neuharth*

Al Neuharth got into the newspaper business when he was 11 years old, delivering the *Minneapolis Tribune*. At 13 he had a part-time job in the composing room of a local weekly.

After serving in the military, he took a job as a reporter for a paper in South Dakota and later moved to the *Miami Herald*. Neuharth moved up rapidly through the ranks and eventually entered management. In 1960 he was appointed an assistant executive editor of the *Detroit Free Press*. His achievements there brought him to the attention of executives of the Gannett Company, who persuaded him to leave Detroit to manage two of Gannett's papers

in New York. Neuharth's success there earned him a promotion to the position of chief of Gannett's operations in Florida. By 1970 Neuharth had become CEO of the company.

His emphasis was on the bottom line. During his tenure Gannett's annual revenue increased from $200 million to $3.1 billion. Neuharth continued the strategies of his predecessors by acquiring small- and medium-market dailies that enjoyed monopoly status in their markets and keeping costs down while raising ad rates. Stung by criticism that his papers emphasized profit at the expense of journalism, Neuharth strengthened the editorial operations of Gannett papers, and by 1980 many had won awards for excellence in reporting.

Neuharth's biggest gamble came in the early 1980s when he decided to use a network of communication satellites and regional printing plants to produce *USA Today*, a national general-interest newspaper. The new paper was greeted with derision by critics, who dismissed it as a "McPaper" that served up flavorless "fast-food" journalism. *USA Today* was an immediate hit with readers, however, and quickly garnered more than a million readers. Advertisers took a little longer to get on board, but the paper eventually turned a profit.

Now most experts agree that, after more than 25 years on the newsstands, *USA Today* has had a significant impact on the industry. Most newspapers have incorporated color, splashy page makeup, more charts and graphics, and shorter, more tightly written stories.

Neuharth retired in 1989 to become chair of the Freedom Foundation, an organization dedicated to furthering the cause of a free press in society. He also continues to write a syndicated newspaper column. The *Washington Journalism Review* named him the most influential person of the 1980s in print media.

■ Al Neuharth, the man responsible for making Gannett the nation's biggest newspaper company.

less competition from other media outlets, their classified ad revenue is less likely to be hurt by sites such as Monster.com or Craigslist, and their emphasis on local news is more likely to keep readers.

Print Weeklies

The number of weekly newspapers in the United States has remained fairly stable at about 6,500 over the past 10 years. The circulation of weeklies, however, increased from 29 million in 1970 to more than 45 million in 2009. Despite this increase in circulation, the rising costs of printing and distribution have made weekly publishers more cost-conscious.

Special-Service and Minority Newspapers

Special-service newspapers are those aimed at several well-defined audience segments. There are, for example, many newspapers published specifically for the African American community. The African American press in this country has a long history, dating back to 1827. Most early papers were started to oppose discrimination and to help gain equal rights and opportunities. The African American press reached its circulation peak in the 1960s when approximately 275 papers had a circulation of about 4 million. Since that time the African American press has seen a significant decline in both numbers of papers and circulation.

In 2011 approximately 190 African American papers, mostly weeklies, were publishing in 35 states and the District of Columbia. Papers such as the *Chicago Defender* and the

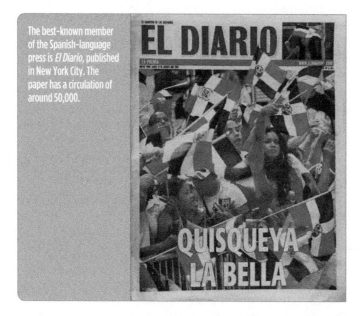

The best-known member of the Spanish-language press is *El Diario*, published in New York City. The paper has a circulation of around 50,000.

Philadelphia Tribune are leading voices in their communities. Like their mainstream counterparts, African American papers are increasing their online presence.

Hispanics are the fastest-growing minority group in America, and the Spanish-language press has grown with them. According to the National Hispanic Media Directory, the number of daily Spanish-language newspapers grew from 14 in 1990 to more than 25 in 2010, while the number of weeklies increased from 152 to nearly 420. Some of the prominent Hispanic newspapers include *El Diario* in New York and *La Opinion* in Los Angeles. Like newspapers in general, the Hispanic press saw some circulation declines from 2006 to 2009 but not nearly as much as English-language papers.

There are many other ethnic newspaper publishers in the United States. Twelve cities have at least one Chinese-language newspaper, and eight cities have papers targeted to Polish Americans.

Another special type of newspaper is exemplified by the college press. Although numbers are hard to pin down, as of 2011 there were about 1,800 college papers published at four-year institutions, with a total circulation of more than 6 million. College newspapers are big business; consequently, more and more papers are hiring nonstudent professionals to manage their operations. Two of the largest college papers in terms of circulation are the University of Minnesota's *Minnesota Daily* and Michigan State University's *State News*, both with circulations of approximately 30,000. College newspapers get high readership scores. A 2005 survey found that 71 percent of college students read at least one issue of their college newspaper in the past week. The comparable number for the mainstream press was 41 percent. Even so, college papers are suffering from revenue losses.

Organization of Online Newspapers

There are three main types of online newspaper Web sites: (1) news aggregators, (2) online Web sites associated with a local or national print newspaper, and (3) online-only sites.

News aggregators are sites that take information from many sources and meld it into a new presentation. There are two types of news aggregators: (1) sites that use an automatic formula to scan news publications and group related stories together (such as Google News and Yahoo!News), and (2) sites that use humans to scan and select the stories (such as The Drudge Report and The Huffington Post). The sites typically carry headlines, photos, video, a lead sentence or two, and links to the full story. The newspaper industry has mixed feelings about aggregators. On the positive side, some readers will read a short summary of a story on Google news and click on the link that takes them to the newspaper or magazine where the full story appears. On the negative, many people simply scan the aggregator's summaries and never visit the original source.

The vast majority of online newspapers are affiliated with traditional print newspapers, either dailies or weeklies. Their structure varies: Some sites have a stand-alone organization with staffers who work only for the online site. Other sites combine the print and online operations so that one person may work for both. Most of these Web sites have a small number of employees, averaging about 5–10 people. The most popular newspaper Web sites are those that have a print counterpart (see Table 5-2).

Online-only sites have proliferated in the last couple of years. Many were started by journalists who were laid off from their print newspaper jobs. Others are the remnants of a print publication that went out of business, such as seattlepi.com, the online site of the

table 5-2	Rank	Newspaper Web Site	Unique Visitors 2009–2010 (in millions)
Most Popular Newspaper Web Site, 2010	1	USA Today	239
	2	New York Times	217
	3	Wall Street Journal	122
	4	Los Angeles Times	95
	5	Washington Post	91

defunct *Seattle Post-Intelligencer.* Most online-only sites focus on local community news and events. Some examples are Patch.com, owned by AOL, which specializes in local community news in about 1,000 towns, and the Voice of San Diego, a nonprofit site staffed by 10 former journalists that gets about 60,000 unique visitors a month. So far, finding a profitable business model has been a challenge for most of these sites.

newspaper ownership

For many years the ownership story in the newspaper industry was big fish gobbling up smaller fish as large companies got bigger by acquiring smaller ones. The newspaper industry is still dominated by several large group owners, but the economic downturn has at least temporarily reversed the trend toward consolidation. The top five newspaper group owners are listed in Table 5-3. The biggest is the Gannett Company with 83 daily newspapers and a combined circulation of about 7 million.

The trend away from consolidation began in 2007 when the then second-largest newspaper chain, Knight Ridder, was purchased by the McClatchy Company, which in turn sold off a dozen of the papers to private owners. The Tribune Company was taken over in 2008 by real estate tycoon Sam Zell, who then sold off one of the company's biggest papers, *Newsday,* to a cable TV company. The Dow Jones Company sold six papers to a small newspaper company in Alabama.

Why the reversal? Newspapers are no longer the profit centers they were before the Internet. Their long-term prospects seem dim, and so far nobody has come up with a plan that would turn things around. Stock values have plummeted and shareholders have pressured management to sell papers that were losing money. In any event, for the short term at least, the trend is toward becoming smaller rather than getting bigger.

producing the print and online newspaper

Departments and Staff

The departmental structure and staffing of a newspaper vary with its size. At the most general level, all papers are divided into three departments: (1) business, (2) production, and (3) news-editorial. The business department is in charge of selling advertising space in both the print and online editions and building the paper's circulation and Web site traffic. As the title implies, the production department handles the physical and electronic tasks necessary to get the news printed on paper and available on the Web site.

table 5-3	Name	Number of Papers Owned	Top Paper
Biggest Newspaper Groups, 2010, by Revenue	Gannett Company	83	USA Today
	Tribune Co.	26	Chicago Tribune
	New York Times Co.	20	New York Times
	McClatchy Co.	30	Miami Herald
	Advance Publications	25	Cleveland Plain Dealer

ethical issues *What's the Appropriate Job Description for a Converged Reporter?*

As the text makes clear, newspaper reporters are expected to do much more today than before the Internet, when a reporter's job description was fairly basic: Gather information, and write and edit stories for a print newspaper. Now a reporter has many other duties, including writing and updating Web stories; taking and posting photos, video, and audio to go with online stories; and blogging. Is it ethical for newspapers to require this increased workload of their employees?

It will come as no surprise that these added duties have sometimes caused problems: increased time demands on reporters, management problems for publishers and editors, and difficulties with unions over compensation. Many newspapers have started 24-hour newsrooms and now require reporters to come in early or stay late, well beyond normal working hours. Some reporters complain that they are expected to write blogs for the paper or do online interviews and participate in chat rooms. They argue that these activities are beyond the call of duty and should carry extra pay. Reporters also complain that the added time demands make it difficult to

step back and reflect on the deeper implications of a story. Further, these time demands make it harder for reporters to do "enterprisers," stories that require them to go beyond their daily routines and do original research and investigation. Enterprisers are often stories that win awards and help establish a reporter's reputation; reporters naturally want time to develop them.

Newspaper managers are aware of these problems but argue that newspaper journalism has changed forever. Executives suggest that reporters must accept that they are now newspaper/Web correspondents and adjust their priorities accordingly.

The Newspaper Guild, the union representing journalists, does not agree. The Guild argues that reporters who perform these extra duties should be given extra compensation. As newspapers' Web sites become more complex and ambitious, reporters likely will have even more online responsibilities and an increased workload. This will probably be a prime topic of future contract talks between labor and management.

The most complex department is news-editorial. Note that these two functions—news and editorial—are kept separate in both the online and print versions. The editorial pages contain opinion, while the news pages contain objective reporting.

In the past, newspapers maintained separate departments for the print and online versions. At some papers the online staff was on a different floor or even in a different building. The current trend is toward merging the two.

There are several arrangements for a combined newsroom. One traditional arrangement is a newsroom directed by a managing editor who oversees and coordinates the day-to-day operations of the department. A city editor supervises local coverage, assigns reporters to beats (such as city hall, police, and health), and directs general-assignment reporters to handle a variety of stories. A wire editor edits international and national news from the Associated Press and other major news services. Most newspapers also have one or more people who are responsible for preparing the editorial pages.

A newer arrangement uses four defined roles: (1) a newsflow editor who manages the progress of a story through both the print and online version; (2) a storybuilder who combines print, audio, and video elements for a story; (3) a news resourcer who specializes in information, providing background, depth, and context to stories in both the print and online versions; and (4) "backpack" journalists (see Chapter 13) who conduct interviews, take photographs, and record audio and video footage for dissemination in print and online formats.

The growing number of people who receive news via a mobile device has further complicated a newspaper's organizational structure. In 2010, *USA Today* announced a new arrangement that puts less emphasis on print and more on Web and mobile operations. The revised system relies more on teams and less on traditional departments. In the new setup, the content-creation teams are organized by topic and their stories flow to a production desk where different presentations of the stories are prepared for the print, Web, and mobile editions.

Prepublication Routine

Operational convergence is evident in the way the print and online editions are prepared. The traditional print newsroom had one deadline when all stories had to be ready. The modern converged newsroom is a 24/7 operation in which news on the paper's Web site is updated continuously.

sound
byte

Who?
Beat reporters need to know the jargon of the area they cover lest embarrassing things happen. A case in point: A new reporter covering the legal circuit for a Virginia paper did not know that FNU (first name unknown) and LNU (last name unknown) were common abbreviations in Virginia law enforcement. Unaware of this jargon, the newcomer dutifully reported that a Mr. Fnu Lnu had been indicted by a grand jury.

There are two basic sources for news: local reporting and wire services. Early in the day the wire editor scans the outputs from the wire services and flags possible stories for the print and online editions. At the same time, the city editor is assigning reporters to various stories that will appear in print and online, and the managing editor is gauging the available space, the newshole, that can be devoted to news in that day's print edition. The greater the number of print ads, the greater the number of pages that can be printed, and the larger the newshole. The online edition, of course, has no such limitations.

Convergence is also showing up at the individual level. As the day progresses, reporters file stories for print, mobile, and online editions. Many reporters also shoot and edit video for the Web site or record audio for a podcast. Since the Web mobile versions are continuously updated, some online stories may be rewritten several times. But this isn't all that is expected of the 21st-century newspaper reporter. She or he may be expected to write a blog, participate in chat rooms, and respond to reader e-mail. (These new duties have caused some problems; see "Ethical Issues: What's the Appropriate Job Description for a Converged Reporter?")

Editors for the print edition edit stories and design page makeup. Photos and graphics are added, and the finished pages are sent to a composing room. Eventually, the pages make their way to the press room, where they are printed and bundled together for delivery.

These procedures, of course, do not apply to the online version. Web editors post and update stories when needed. They also decide what photos and video and audio clips will accompany the day's stories. Many papers have instituted "early teams," an editor and one or more reporters who start work around daybreak and work into the early afternoon reporting, writing, and posting stories exclusively for the Web and mobile editions. About 8 out of 10 big newspapers have created early teams for their Web sites. The concept is less likely to be found in smaller papers, with only about 3 in 10 using early teams. When everything is in order, the story and related graphics are posted to the Web or mobile site. There is no need for a composing room, printing press, paper, or delivery truck.

the economics of newspaper publishing

As mentioned earlier, the business model that has sustained the newspaper industry for the past few centuries is falling apart. Circulation is declining, but a far more serious problem is the decline in advertising revenue. In order to understand the situation, we need to take a close look at the economics of newspaper publishing. We'll start by examining revenues and expenses.

Revenue

The traditional print newspaper has two sources of revenue: selling advertising space and circulation income—money from subscriptions and newsstand sales. Of these two sources, advertising is by far the more important, accounting for about 85 percent of income.

There are four main types of advertising revenue:

- *Local retail:* advertising by local specialty stores, auto dealerships, grocery stores, and other local businesses
- *Classified:* employment ads, real estate ads, for-sale ads, and so forth, usually published in a special section of the paper
- *National:* ads bought by advertisers who need to reach a mass audience, such as ads for food, cell phones, and financial services
- *Prepaid inserts:* supplements put together usually by national chains such as Best Buy or Target that are inserted into the paper

media *Probe*   *The Debt Trap*

Note that the list of expenses below refers to expenses incurred by a newspaper. If the list referred to newspaper companies, we would have to add another significant item: debt. In fact, many individual newspapers are still profitable while many big newspaper companies are mired in debt.

When the economy was strong and credit easy to get, many newspaper owners, following the philosophy that bigger is better, expanded their holdings and financed their expansions by borrowing large sums of money. Then the economy went sour, advertising dried up, and the companies were left with declining revenues and a mountain of debt.

The numbers can be overwhelming. The Journal Register Company borrowed heavily to buy papers in the Detroit area right before the slump in auto sales. The result: The company owes about $620 million. Gatehouse Media, whose business plan involved acquiring small to medium-sized papers, wound up $1.2 billion in debt. The McClatchy Company, which acquired the Knight Ridder Company a few years ago, has a long-term debt obligation of $2.39 billion.

And, of course, the interest charge on these loans keeps accumulating. In 2007, Morris Communications had to sell 14 of its papers to meet a debt payment and was still more than $400 million in debt at the end of the year. The *New York Times* had to sell part of its building and take a $250 million loan from a Mexican businessman to meet one of its recent debt payments. The Tribune Company couldn't meet its obligations and declared bankruptcy.

All of this money going to pay off debt means that there is less money to pay reporters, cover operating expenses, and invest in improved news coverage—not a good trend for an already struggling industry.

Of these four types, classified and local retail are the most important. Historically, local retail has accounted for about 50 percent of all ad revenue and classified ads about 40 percent. Unfortunately for the newspaper industry, these two categories of advertising have been hit hard by increased competition and the economic downturn. Local retail advertising revenue dropped about 40 percent from 2006 to 2010. Much of this loss occurred because many local stores went out of business because they couldn't compete with companies such as Wal-Mart, an organization that does little newspaper advertising. Classified ad revenue fell a staggering 66 percent over the same period. Employment ads, real estate ads, and auto ads declined the most as competition from sites such as Monster .com and Craigslist and the bad economy ate into newspaper revenue. In other words, the industry's top two revenue streams have dropped by more than 50 percent over a four-year period. That spells trouble.

Expenses

The costs of running a typical print newspaper can be viewed in several ways. One common method is to classify the costs by function:

- *News and editorial costs:* reporters and editors who cover and report the news
- *Printing costs:* such as newsprint (the paper), ink, and the cost of running the press
- *Mechanical costs:* composing and production expenses
- *Circulation and distributions costs:* gas, trucks, and delivery people
- *General administration costs:* clerical, secretarial, accounting, and so forth

These expenses are related to the circulation size of the paper: the more copies printed, the more the cost of ink, paper, delivery, and so on.

Newspapers have tried to cut these costs as much as possible by laying off people, shrinking the physical size of the paper, cutting delivery to outlying regions, and adopting more efficient production techniques. Costs, however, can be reduced only so far; long-term survival depends on increased revenue.

Are Online and Apps the Answer?

About the only bright spots for newspapers in the last few years have been the increasing popularity of their Web sites and mobile apps. Overall, the newspaper industry averages about 71 million unique visitors to its Web sites, compared to the 46 million or so who get the print versions. The number of unique visitors to the top 10 newspaper Web sites

Newspapers are turning to automation to save money. These robot movers handle tons of paper.

increased by more than 15 percent from 2008 to 2010, and some individual newspaper sites scored impressive gains: Washingtonpost.com saw a 28 percent increase in unique visitors in just one month in 2009.

The difficulty is that the increasing numbers of online readers are not translating into enough advertising dollars to stem the bleeding from the print version. Because the supply of online advertising opportunities is abundant, the price on online ads is cheaper. For every dollar advertisers pay to reach a print newspaper reader, they pay about 5–10 cents to reach an online reader. Consequently, the print version still supplies most industry revenue.

Even so, digital advertising revenue continues to increase, totaling about $26 billion in 2010, surpassing newspaper advertising for the first time. The problem is that much of the growth in digital ads is not associated with newspaper sites. In 2010, newspaper sites accounted for only 6 percent of online display revenue. (Interestingly enough, the one news site that has been most successful in generating digital ad revenue is the Huffington Post, a site that depends heavily on free content.) Not surprisingly, newspapers are exploring other ways to make money such as charging for content and generating revenue from mobile apps.

Will readers pay to read the news? The jury is still out on that question, but initial indications aren't encouraging. In the first place, it's hard to get consumers to start paying for something that they used to get for free. One survey of paywalls at three dozen newspapers found that 1 percent of their readers were willing to pay a fee to read the newspaper online. As of this writing, it's still too early to assess the results of the *New York Times* pay system mentioned at the beginning of the chapter. In its first month, about 100,000 people signed up (at a low introductory price), but total traffic to the site declined.

What about mobile media? There are more than 45 million smartphone owners in the United States, and a recent survey found that half of its sample used their phones to get news from a Web site, 39 percent read a local paper on their phones, and 35 percent read a major newspaper. The *USA Today* and *New York Times* apps are among the most downloaded apps for the iPhone and iPad.

As of mid-2011, News Corp., the company behind *The Daily*, the digital paper designed for the iPad, had yet to release official subscription figures. Experts estimate that the free app

social issues

A Nonprofit Newspaper?

The traditional business model of newspapers is in trouble, and the industry is looking for different ways to structure the industry. There is no lack of suggestions.

One of the most interesting is the Low-Profit Limited Liability Company (L3C for short). An L3C is a business that strives to make a profit but is allowed to take investments from foundations and charities because the L3C is recognized as having a socially desirable benefit. The newspaper, say L3C supporters, performs in a way that benefits society: It promotes democracy by keeping its readers informed and encourages contributions to the marketplace of ideas. The big advantage of the L3C is that it opens up new investment potential. Big foundations, for example, are required to pay out at least 5 percent of their wealth every year into program-related investments. They can invest this money in for-profit organizations, such as an L3C, if they have a social benefit. The newspaper, of course, would still have to run a successful operation. The L3C structure has been approved in several states, but the Internal Revenue Service does not yet recognize newspapers as qualifying for that status.

Another alternative is to have newspapers adopt the model currently used by many universities: an endowed institution. Such an institution would not exist to make a profit but to serve society by promoting the general welfare. A huge advantage of this structure is that organizations that qualify are exempt from income tax and any donations made to the organization are tax deductible. Of course, the start-up costs for such an endeavor would be formidable. A newspaper might have to raise $1 billion or more just to cover the annual costs of publishing a paper. In addition, as an endowed institution the paper could no longer endorse political candidates.

A third alternative would keep newspapers as profit-making endeavors but would give them certain legal advantages. For example, the government could exempt newspapers from current antitrust laws, enabling a group of papers to negotiate among themselves to fix their prices. (Major League Baseball has gotten a similar break.) Or the government could do away with regulations that restrict papers from owning TV and radio stations in the same market or prevent two newspapers in the same market from merging.

Of course, there are compelling arguments against these arrangements. Why should a newspaper be given special privileges? All-news radio stations also promote social benefits. How about giving them special status as well? Further, do we really want to protect newspapers from the reality of the marketplace? The marketplace provides valuable feedback; it tells papers what is working and what isn't. Insulating papers from the marketplace makes it hard to tell if they are really serving their readers. Lastly, all of these solutions assume that the newspaper is something worth keeping. A survey conducted by the Pew Center for Excellence in Journalism found that 42 percent of respondents would not miss their newspapers. If that's the case, it's going to be hard for any ownership model to succeed.

Maybe the most creative suggestion is for newspapers to declare themselves a religion and ordain reporters as priests. This would free newspapers from tax obligations and also qualify reporters for the priest-penitent privacy privilege. (It's rather unlikely that this will happen.)

---

had been downloaded about 1 million times but only 90,000 or so had bought a subscription. If subscriptions continue to grow at the same rate as sales of new iPads, it will take several years before *The Daily* breaks even.

The situation may change if more newspapers follow the magazine industry and offer subscriptions via Apple's app store (see next chapter). Also, if newspapers ask readers to pay for their news, there may be competitors who offer it for free. It may take a few years before the situation becomes clearer.

Will advertisers pay a premium to reach consumers who read newspaper on their smartphones or tablet computers? The mobile advertising model holds some potential for increased revenue. Surveys suggest that consumers are more receptive to ads on mobile media than they are to ads on Web sites. In 2010, about $740 million was spent on mobile advertising, a whopping 79 percent increase over 2009. On the downside, the $740 million represented only 3 percent of all digital advertising. Projections suggest that mobile ads will bring in more than $2.5 billion by 2015. On the other hand, it's more difficult for an advertiser to place ads in apps than on traditional Web sites because advertisers might have to buy a separate ad for each mobile device. Advertisers also must deal with the device makers and software providers (such as Apple and Google) that have their own rules regarding how ads are purchased, adding more complexity to the process. In sum, mobile advertising offers some hope for the industry, but it is still too early to tell how much benefit it will be.

Will Newspapers Survive?

The Pew Center's State of the News Media Report 2011 put it this way: "[T]he destination that newspaper organizations are trying to reach is pretty clear now—more robust digital enterprises to pick up the slack as print advertising and circulation fall. The path from here to there, unfortunately, once again is not clear at all."

Some newspapers will survive; some won't. Those that are in the best position are owned by big companies whose overall profits can offset the newspaper losses. Those that are most at risk are those whose parent companies took on large amounts of debt during the easy-credit years of the past decade. Newspapers that can find creative and innovative ways to market their mobile products will also have an advantage.

The newspaper of the future will probably be a hybrid version that appears in print only a few days a week but with a Web site and mobile app that are constantly updated. It's likely the online version will be delivered to a number of platforms including cell phones, iPods, iPads, and e-book readers such as Amazon's Kindle. Its main revenue source will be advertising, but it might also charge for specialized content. It will still employ journalists, but their daily routines will be unlike those in past decades. They will be audio reporters, photographers, video reporters, and bloggers.

All in all, it may be several years before new business models for the print and online newspaper industries are fully established. As the transition continues, look for more disruption and further challenges for this troubled industry.

global newspapers

Many newspapers provide foreign-language or international editions. The popular ones fall into two categories: general newspapers and financial newspapers. As far as the United States and Great Britain are concerned, the following were the leaders at the end of 2010:

1. *The Economist,* based in London, carries a mixture of financial and political news. Readily available in the United States, the weekly is printed in Virginia, London, and Singapore. It reaches about 1 million readers.

table 5-4	Year	All Daily Papers	Daily Circulation per 1,000 Adults
Daily Newspaper Circulation	1960	58,882,000	475
	1970	62,108,000	428
	1980	62,201,840	360
	1990	62,327,962	329
	2000	55,772,847	287
	2009	45,653,000	195

Source: Compiled by author.

2. *The Wall Street Journal*'s international editions reach about 1 million readers, mainly in Europe, Asia, and South America.

3. *The Financial Times* of London, as its name suggests, specializes in economic news; it has a worldwide circulation of about 390,000.

4. *The International Herald Tribune,* published by the *New York Times* and headquartered in France, has a worldwide circulation of about 240,000, mostly in Europe. The paper is printed in 36 locations around the world.

5. *USA Today*'s International Edition reaches more than 60,000 readers in 60 countries. Its main audience consists of U.S. businesspeople who are traveling or working abroad.

Other papers that enjoy international status are *The New York Times, Le Monde* (France), *El Pais* (Spain), *The Times* (Great Britain), *The Statesman* (India), and *Al Ahram* (Egypt).

the newspaper audience

Sources of Feedback

The best-known feedback system for newspapers is that connected with the **Audit Bureau of Circulations (ABC).** During the early 1900s, with the growth of mass advertising, some publishers began inflating the number of readers in order to attract more revenue from advertisers. In an effort to check this deceptive practice, advertisers and publishers joined to form the ABC in 1914. The organization's purpose was to establish ground rules for counting circulation, to make sure that the rules were enforced, and to provide verified reports of circulation data. The ABC audits about three-fourths of all print media in the United States and Canada—about 2,600 publications.

The ABC functions in the following manner: Publishers keep detailed records of circulation data. Twice a year, publishers file a circulation statement with the ABC, which the ABC in turn disseminates to its clients. Once a year, the ABC audits publications to verify that the figures that have been reported are accurate. An ABC representative visits the publication and is free to examine records and files.

In 2010, the ABC announced a new formula for calculating circulation. Newspapers that publish "branded" editions, such as a Spanish language version, can now include them in their total average circulation figures. In addition, the new ABC rules let newspapers count a subscriber more than once if he or she pays or registers to access content via a print subscription, Web site, mobile media, or e-reader. Although these changes reflect the current reality of the newspaper business, it makes it difficult to track historical trends because the data collected under the new rules will not be directly comparable to older data.

Those publishers who want more detailed feedback on their online audience size can subscribe to Nielsen/NetRatings (see Chapter 4). The company releases monthly reports on the number of unique visitors to various popular Web sites.

Audiences

As of 2011 approximately 45 million copies of morning and evening papers, either purchased at the newsstand or delivered to the doorstep, found their way into American homes every weekday. Daily newspaper circulation, in absolute terms, has decreased since 1990, as a glance at Table 5-4 shows. The population, however, has been increasing.

media *Probe*

Number of Daily Newspapers per Capita

According to United Nations data, here are the five countries in the world with the most daily newspapers per capita.

Rank	Country	Number of Dailies per 1 million inhabitants
1.	Norway	16
2.	Italy	13
3.	Sweden	10
4.	Finland	10
5.	New Zealand	9

Newspapers and democracies seem to go together; all of the top five countries are democracies as well as 9 of the top 10. The United States ranked 14th on this list with about five dailies per 1 million residents.

To reflect this fact and to provide additional perspective, the final column of the table presents the ratio of daily circulation to the total adult population of the United States (expressed in thousands). As can be seen, daily newspaper circulation is not keeping pace with the overall growth of the population.

The percentage of adults reading one or more papers every day has declined from about 80 percent in the early 1960s to about 50 percent in 2010. The most pronounced decline has occurred in the 18–29 and 30–44 age groups and among those who have not attended college. The overall drop in daily circulation has been most noticeable in urban areas.

Why the overall decline? Some have attributed it to the increased mobility of Americans, the increase in single-person households, more expensive subscription and per-copy prices, a general decline in the literacy of young people, and competition from other media, especially the Internet.

Print newspapers are losing readers to online media. In 1995 about 4 percent of the U.S. population went online at least once a week to get their news. By 2010 the figure was more than 40 percent. A recent survey by the Pew Research Center found that one in seven Internet users have reduced the amount of time they spend with daily newspapers. The key demographic group that reads most of its news online is young adults—the same group that reads print papers the least. When people go online for news, however, they do not necessarily go to online newspapers. Many visit portals such as Excite or Yahoo!; some go to search engines such as Google; others check CNN.com or a TV network news Web site.

the newspaper industry

It's probably obvious by now that the traditional print newspaper is not a great place to look for a job. Since 2000, the total number of people employed in the news industry (newsroom employees, press operators, composers, delivery people, and so on) has declined by about 20 percent. The number of editorial employees (reporters, photographers, and editors) has decreased slightly more, and additional layoffs and paper closings are likely.

On the bright side, the online news area is one that will probably grow in the near future. Anybody who wants to become a reporter should make sure that his or her online skills are up-to-date and that he or she can report for a variety of platforms: audio, video, Web, mobile, and print.

The career outlook in the various media industries changes quickly. For a more current description of conditions in the newspaper industry and a more detailed look at career options, please consult the book's Web site: www.mhhe.com/dominick12e.

main points

- Newspapers in colonial America were published with permission of the local government. A free press did not appear until after the Revolution.

- The mass newspaper arrived in the 1830s with the publication of Benjamin Day's *New York Sun,* the first of the penny-press papers.

- The era of yellow journalism featured sensationalism, crusades, and human-interest reporting and introduced more attractive newspaper designs.

- Many newspapers were merged or folded during the early 1900s, as tabloid papers became popular. The trend toward consolidation would continue into the years following World War II.

- The newspaper industry is currently in a crisis as declining circulation and advertising revenue have made it difficult for many papers to stay in business.

- There are four types of daily papers: national newspapers, large metro dailies, midsize dailies, and small-town dailies. Other major types of papers are weeklies, special-service newspapers, and minority newspapers.

- All papers now have online versions and many have apps for mobile media.

- The trend toward consolidation in the newspaper industry has ended.

- Newspapers are reexamining their business model and converging their print and online operations.

- Newspaper audiences are measured by the Audit Bureau of Circulations. Newspaper readership has declined for the past several decades, but online readership is growing.

questions for review

1. Trace the changes in the definition of *news* from the 1600s to the 2000s.
2. What are the defining characteristics of newspapers?
3. What are some of the advantages the traditional ink-and-paper newspaper has over the online version?

What are some of the advantages the online version has over the print version?

4. Why are newspapers in trouble?

questions for critical thinking

1. Why don't young people read newspapers? What, if anything, could newspapers do to recapture this audience segment?
2. Should newspapers be allowed to own broadcast stations in their markets? Why or why not?
3. Will the online version eventually replace the print version of a newspaper? Why or why not?
4. What will the newspaper industry look like in 10 years?
5. Do we still need newspapers?

key terms

political press (p. 107)
First Amendment (p. 107)
penny press (p. 109)

yellow journalism (p. 111)
jazz journalism (p. 111)
tabloids (p. 112)

newshole (p. 115)
circulation (p. 118)
Audit Bureau of Circulations (ABC) (p. 129)

internet resources

Online Learning Center

On the Online Learning Center home page, www.mhhe.com/dominick12e, *select* Student Center *and then* Chapter 5.

1. Use the Learning Objectives, Chapter Outline, and Main Points sections to review this chapter.

2. Test your knowledge of the chapter using the multiple choice and flashcard features of the site.

3. Expand your knowledge of concepts and topics discussed in the chapter with additional Questions for Critical Thinking and Internet Exercises.

surfing the internet

The following are examples of sites that deal with the newspaper industry. All listings were current as of late 2010.

www.decaturdailydemocrat.com
A good example of a slick online paper published by a small-town daily.

www.huffingtonpost.com
One of the most successful news aggregator sites

www.naa.org
Site of the Newspaper Association of America, a major industry trade organization. Contains information on newspaper circulation, public policy, and diversity, as well as links to the organization's *presstime* magazine.

www.ojr.org
The *Online Journalism Review,* published by the Knight Digital Media Center, the best single source for the latest information on Internet journalism.

www.theonion.com
Looks like an authentic online paper but is actually satirical.

www.usatoday.com
Colorful site of the national daily *USA Today*. Note the emphasis on video, photos, and blogging.

Mobile Media
Check out the apps for *The Daily,* the *News York Times, Flipboard,* and *The Pulse.*

Condé Nast, the publisher of *The New Yorker* and many other magazines, reported that there have been almost 4 million downloads of the apps for Condé Nast magazines.

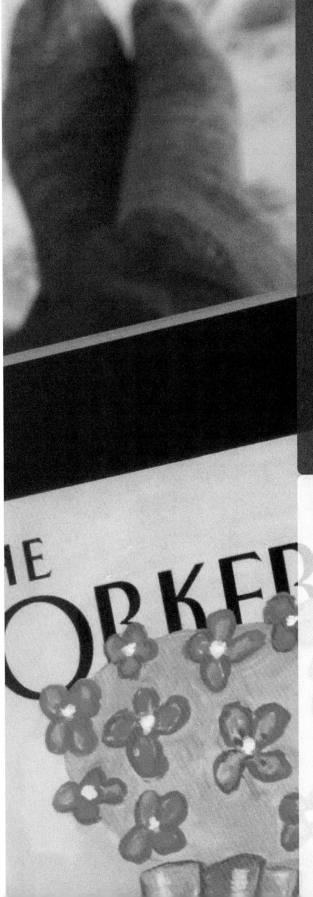

Chapter**6**

magazines

This chapter will prepare you to:

- discuss the characteristics of magazines
- understand how the magazine industry is divided
- understand the function of Mediamark Research Inc. (MRI)
- appreciate the efforts of magazine publishers to incorporate the Internet and tablet computers into their business model
- understand the current financial situation of the magazine industry
- identify the five main magazine content categories
- describe the departments that produce magazines

The magazine industry has been in a slump and is looking for a way to revitalize itself. The industry is hoping that its fortunes will improve thanks to an electronic device about the same size and weight as a typical magazine: the tablet computer. Magazine publishers are betting that readers are willing and eager to read magazines in digital form and that tablet computers, such as the iPad or the Motorola Xoom, are the perfect delivery platforms. In the next few years, about 100 million people will own tablet computers. It's not surprising that publishers are eager to reach this growing audience. To quote a press release from Zinio, a company that develops digital magazine technology: "With the Tablet PC . . . leading magazine publishers will fundamentally change the way people experience magazines."

Well, that remains to be seen. A viable business model is still being worked out, and it is unlikely that the print version of the magazine will vanish. One thing, however, is certain: The tablet computer will be an important factor in the future of the magazine industry.

This chapter will explore the history, structure, economics, and organization of this industry as it progresses through a transitional period.

a brief history

The Colonial Period

In colonial times *magazine* meant "warehouse" or "depository," a place where various types of provisions were stored under one roof. The first magazines printed in America were patterned after this model; they were to be storehouses of varied literary materials gathered from books, pamphlets, and newspapers and bound together under one cover.

It was Ben Franklin who first announced plans to start a magazine in the colonies. Unfortunately for him, a competitor named Andrew Bradford got wind of his idea and beat Franklin to the punch. Bradford's *American Magazine* was published a few days before Franklin's *General Magazine* in 1741. The two publications carried political and economic articles aimed at an intelligent audience.

Both Franklin's and Bradford's magazines were ambitious ventures in that they were designed for readers in all 13 colonies and deliberately tried to influence public opinion; both quickly folded because of financial problems. The next significant attempt at magazine publishing occurred in Philadelphia when another Bradford (this one named William) started the *American Magazine and Monthly Chronicle* in 1757. This publication also contained the usual blend of political and economic articles mixed with a little humor; it was well edited and able to support itself for a year.

As America's political relations with England deteriorated, magazines, like newspapers, assumed a significant political role. Thomas Paine, who in his rousing pamphlet *Common Sense* argued for separation from England, became editor of the *Pennsylvania Magazine.* This publication strongly supported the Revolution and was a significant political force during the early days of the war. It became an early casualty of the conflict, however, and closed down in 1776.

All these early magazines were aimed at a specialized audience—one that was educated, literate, and primarily urban. Their overall impact was to encourage literary and artistic expression and to unify the colonies during America's struggle for independence from England.

After the Revolution

Magazines popular during the late 18th and early 19th centuries contained a mix of political and topical articles directed primarily at an educated elite. The birth of the modern newsmagazine can be traced back to this period. *Niles Weekly Register,* which reported current events of the time, was read throughout the country.

Politics was also reflected in other magazines of the period. One of the most influential was the *Port Folio,* edited by the colorful nonconformist Joseph Dennie. Dennie's intended audience was a select one; he wished to reach "Men of Affluence, Men of Liberality, and Men of Letters." Although the major thrust of the magazine was political, Dennie interspersed travelogues, theater reviews, satirical essays, and even jokes.

The Penny-Press Era

While the penny press was opening up new markets for newspapers (see Chapter 5), magazine publishers were also expanding their appeal and coverage. The *Knickerbocker, Graham's Magazine,* and the *Saturday Evening Post,* all established between 1820 and 1840, were written not so much for the intelligentsia as for the generally literate middle classes. By 1842 *Graham's,* under the direction of Edgar Allan Poe, had a circulation of 40,000. The growing social and economic importance of women was illustrated by the birth of *Godey's Lady's Book* in 1830 and *Peterson's* in 1842. These two magazines offered articles on fashion, morals, diets, and health, and printed elaborate, hand-colored engravings in their pages. *Godey's,* under the editorship of Sara Hale, was a pioneer for women's rights and was the first magazine to campaign for wider recognition of women writers (see "Media Probe: Sara Josepha Buell Hale").

media *Probe* Sara Josepha Buell Hale

Sara Josepha Buell Hale was responsible for having Thanksgiving declared an annual holiday and was the author of the popular nursery rhyme "Mary Had a Little Lamb." She was also one of the women who left a lasting impression on 19th-century American journalism.

Sara Josepha Buell married David Hale, a New Hampshire lawyer, who encouraged her to write articles and poems for local magazines. By the time she was 38, she had published 17 poems, many magazine articles, two short stories, a literary review, and a novel.

Her literary accomplishments brought her to the attention of Louis Godey, publisher of *Godey's Lady's Book,* who offered her the position of editor. She brought to the magazine an intimate editor-reader relationship that proved so popular that the magazine had a circulation of 150,000 by 1860, a remarkable figure for the time.

Sara Hale not only edited *Godey's Lady's Book* but also wrote about half of every issue. In addition, she found time to champion women's rights and was influential in persuading Matthew Vassar to start the college that still bears his name.

She spent 40 years editing the magazine and finally retired at age 89. Thanks to her efforts, *Godey's Lady's Book* is credited with being the best women's magazine of the period.

In 1850 *Harper's Monthly* was started as a magazine that would present material that had already appeared in other sources (rather like the *Reader's Digest,* except that the articles were reprinted in full). *Harper's* also included elaborate woodcut illustrations along with its articles in double-sized issues. *Harper's Weekly* was instituted seven years later and was to become famous for its illustrations of the Civil War. In 1863 this magazine began publishing reproductions of Mathew Brady's war photographs.

The most famous example of the crusading approach of the penny press was the *Harper's Weekly* campaign against the corrupt political administration in New York in 1870. Under the control of William "Boss" Tweed, a group of unscrupulous politicians managed to bilk the city out of approximately $200 million. The editorial cartoons of Thomas Nast were credited with helping to bring down this ring.

The Magazine Boom

In 1860 there were approximately 260 magazines published in the United States; by 1900 there were 1,800. Why the surge? The primary factors were more available money, better printing techniques that lowered prices, and especially the Postal Act of 1879, which gave magazines special mailing rates. It became possible to aim for a national market on a mass scale, and several magazines set out to do just that.

This political cartoon, titled "Under the Thumb," was created by Thomas Nast and appeared in *Harper's Weekly* during the summer of 1871.

The most successful of the magazines seeking a mass market was the *Ladies' Home Journal,* founded by Cyrus Curtis in 1881. The first issue, eight pages long, contained an illustrated short story, an article on growing flowers, fashion notes, child care advice, needlework hints, and recipes. Curtis was the first to recognize the potential for national advertising in the magazine industry.

The general crusading spirit of the press spilled over onto the pages of leading magazines of the late 1800s and early 1900s. Theodore Roosevelt dubbed the magazines that embraced this reform movement **muckrakers.**

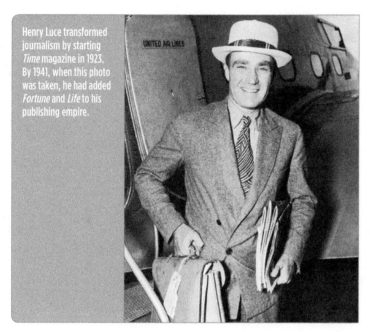

Henry Luce transformed journalism by starting *Time* magazine in 1923. By 1941, when this photo was taken, he had added *Fortune* and *Life* to his publishing empire.

Corrupt practices in big business was the first issue to activate the muckrakers' zeal. *McClure's* ran an exposé of Standard Oil Company by Ida M. Tarbell. Although it carried the innocuous title "History of the Standard Oil Company," the article was filled with dynamite, for it revealed bribery, fraud, unfair business practices, and violence. Shocking stories on political corruption in big cities and another series on crooked practices in the railroad industry followed Tarbell's initial effort. Other magazines joined in. *Cosmopolitan* published "The Treason of the Senate" in 1906 and followed up with attacks on the International Harvester Company. By 1912 the trend toward crusades and exposés had spent itself. Many of the problems uncovered by the muckrakers had been remedied. Most important, the public had grown tired of the crusades, and magazines had to search for other ways to attract readers.

Between the Wars

Shifting economic conditions and changing lifestyles in the decades following World War I also influenced magazine development. Three distinct types evolved in the years between World War I and World War II: (1) the digest, (2) the newsmagazine, and (3) the pictorial magazine.

The finest example of the digest genre, *Reader's Digest,* appeared in 1922. Although this magazine reprinted articles that had appeared elsewhere, it first condensed and edited the material so that it could be read by people in a hurry.

The idea of a newsmagazine was not new—examples could be found in the 19th century. *Time,* however, borrowed little from its predecessors. From its beginning in 1923, *Time* based its format on an original concept: the distillation and compartmentalization of news under various departments. Other innovations included the use of the narrative style to report news stories; group journalism produced by the pooling of the efforts of reporters, writers, and editors into anonymous articles; the institution of a large research department; and a brash, punchy, jargonish writing style. The magazine grew slowly, but by 1930 it was turning a substantial profit. Two imitators, *Newsweek* and *U.S. News,* appeared in 1933.

In the mid-1930s two magazines, *Life* and *Look,* revived the tradition of the pictorial weekly originated by *Harper's. Life* was launched in 1936 and had almost a quarter-million subscribers before it even had a name. It featured public figures caught in unguarded moments, photo essays, occasional glamour shots, and articles on the arts. In this format *Life* would live for 36 years (it would reappear in the

The beginning of life for *Life:* The magazine's first cover was shot by famous photographer Margaret Bourke-White.

media Probe

Ebony *Magazine: Adjusting to the Digital World*

John H. Johnson started *Ebony* magazine in 1945, and it became one of the most successful magazines designed for an African American audience. In the days when most magazines, along with other media, ignored the black audience, *Ebony* showcased the entertainers, the politicians, the preachers, and the scholars that black America wanted to read about. In the segregated South, the magazine was the main source of news about what was happening to black Americans in the rest of the country. Aimed at a black, middle-class audience, *Ebony*, along with its sister publication, *Jet*, helped shape the attitudes and aspirations of a generation of African Americans.

In the 1960s, during the civil rights movement, *Ebony* was criticized for being too moderate and out of touch with the feelings and politics of the time. Although never losing its temperate editorial focus, *Ebony* covered the marches and the demonstrations. Indeed, the first African American man to win a Pulitzer Prize for photography worked for *Ebony*. His prize-winning photo showed Coretta Scott King at her slain husband's funeral.

Throughout the next three decades, *Ebony* fared well. Its circulation was nearly 2 million and it managed to turn a respectable profit. Then in the late 2000s, *Ebony* was hit by the same economic and social changes that affected the entire magazine industry. Young people gravitated away from print and toward the Internet, and *Ebony*'s readers were primarily over 50. Circulation dropped to about 1 million. Advertisers followed the young audience to the Internet and revenue declined. Advertising pages declined almost 40 percent in 2009. By 2010, *Ebony* was in serious financial difficulty.

Although the magazine started a Web site, it seemed that *Ebony* did not yet recognize the importance of the digital platform. President-elect Barack Obama (whose victory in the 2008 election may have been helped by social changes inspired by the magazine) granted his first postelection interview to *Ebony*. Afraid that immediately posting the interview on its Web site would hurt the sale of the print version, it appeared online many days later, after it was published in the magazine. In the meantime, the president-elect granted an interview to 60 *Minutes* and *Ebony* lost its scoop.

In 2011, *Ebony* announced that it was introducing what it called a cover-to-cover redesign, the biggest revamp since its inception in 1945. Changes include a cleaner design, a new section devoted to empowerment and inspiration, and more color. The Web site was updated, with more emphasis on social media. *Ebony* also has an app for the iPad. Will the changes be enough to keep the venerable magazine afloat? It will be a tough struggle because it faces competition from *Essence*, a periodical owned by magazine powerhouse Time Warner. In addition, younger readers can choose from many African American Web sites, including the blog Afro-Netizen that contains political and cultural articles. In sum, *Ebony* is searching for its niche in today's media landscape.

late 1970s in a totally different format). *Look* hit the newsstands in 1937, just a few months behind *Life. Look* lacked the current-affairs emphasis of its forerunner and concentrated more on personalities and features. Over the years it evolved into a family-oriented magazine. *Look* expired in 1972.

The Postwar Period

Magazines of the postwar era reflected publishers' firm belief that the one way to become profitable was to specialize. Increased leisure time created a market for sports magazines such as *Field and Stream, Sports Afield, Golf Digest, Popular Boating,* and *Sports Illustrated.* Scientific advances also generated a resurgence of a popularized version of *Scientific American.*

The rapid expansion of urban communities and urban lifestyles gave rise to many specialized publications. Liberalized attitudes toward sex prompted such ventures as *Confidential* (1952) and the trendsetting *Playboy* (1953). During the 1960s the rebirth of an interest in urban culture encouraged the rise of "city" magazines, of which *New York* is probably the best example. For the black press the most significant development in the 1950s was the expansion of black magazines. John Johnson had started *Negro Digest* back in 1942 and used his profits to publish *Ebony*, whose format imitated that of *Life*, in 1945. In the early 1950s he added *Jet*, a weekly newsmagazine, and *Tan*. These were followed later by *Black World* and *Essence*.

Contemporary Magazines

After a couple of dismal years that saw the death of the print versions of many magazines, including *House and Garden, Domino,* and *Portfolio,* the magazine industry saw some improvement in 2010, thanks to a recovering economy and the proliferation of apps for tablet computers (more on apps later), resulting in about a 3 percent increase in revenue over 2009.

Despite this good news, the magazine industry still faced an uphill battle. First, they had marketing problems. Supermarkets and big discount stores, such as Wal-Mart, were

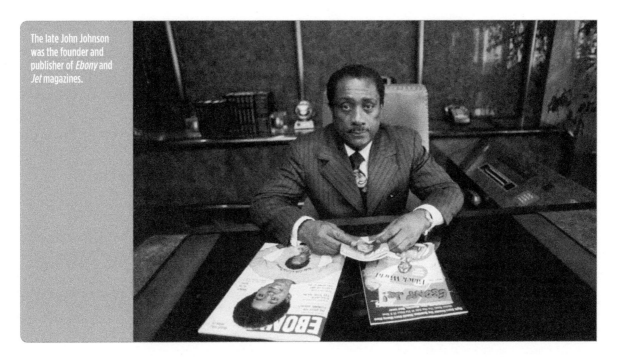

The late John Johnson was the founder and publisher of *Ebony* and *Jet* magazines.

becoming more selective about the number of magazines they would display on their shelves. Sweepstakes competitions, such as the one sponsored by Publisher's Clearing-house, have nearly disappeared because of legal problems, and the national do-not-call list has made it more difficult to recruit subscribers over the phone.

Second, cable TV and the Internet have encroached upon magazines' biggest selling point—attracting a specialized audience. Targeted cable channels, such as the Food Network and Oxygen, offer advertisers an alternative and sometimes more efficient way to reach their audiences. The Internet offers even more precise targeting. Doityourself .com., for example, is a natural place for Lowe's and Home Depot to advertise.

Publishers have been trying several strategies to improve their fortunes. They are strengthening their Web and mobile media presence in an attempt to offset print advertising shortfalls. Other companies are branching out into ancillary activities, such as sponsoring conferences and trade shows. All are becoming more cost-conscious.

Circulation held steady or declined slightly for most magazines from 2009 to 2010. There were some bright spots, however, as some individual magazines saw noteworthy gains. *Food and Family* quadrupled its circulation. *Game Informer* jumped 27 percent while the circulation of *Food Network Magazine* was up 16 percent. There were some big losers as well. *Playboy* lost 30 percent of its circulation while *Reader's Digest* lost 24 percent. New magazines continued to arrive on the scene. MediaFinder.com reported that 193 new magazines launched in 2010 while 176 ceased publication. Compare that number with 2009, when 596 magazines went out of business.

The trend in magazine publishing for the last few decades has been to find a hot topic and quickly launch a magazine to take advantage of it. If the topic cools, then the magazines devoted to it are in trouble. For example, the booming real estate market during the middle of the decade prompted a host of home styling and decorating magazines. When the real estate market crashed, it took with it many of these publications (*Domino, Home, Country Home,* to name a few).

Finally, the magazine industry continues to be dominated by a few big companies that publish best-selling magazines (see Table 6-2 on page 151).

critical ⊕ cultural issues

Teen Magazine Web Sites: What's the Message?

More and more teenage girls are going online, and among their top destinations are the Web sites of teen magazines. Much like their print counterparts, these Web sites contain articles on beauty, fashion, and relationships, but the Web sites offer additional features. They are interactive. Most have chat rooms, bulletin boards, and quizzes with instant feedback. In addition, they are private. Teenage girls looking for information about sexuality, for example, might feel more comfortable looking at this information online rather than reading it in a magazine. Finally, the information on the Internet can remain available indefinitely.

What are the messages that these Web sites are presenting to young women? Feminist theorists suggest that teen magazines may play an important part in teaching young girls about what it means to be feminine. They may emphasize the importance of physical appearance and stress that attracting men is the most important goal for teenage girls. Are teen Web sites doing the same?

This question was the focus of an article by Magdala Labre and Kim Walsh-Childers in the fall 2003 issue of *Mass Communication and Society*. The researchers analyzed the Web sites of *Cosmogirl, Teen People, Seventeen,* and *Teen* and identified the major themes present in the Web sites. One theme was that beauty was a requirement to be successful and to feel good about oneself. The researchers were quick to point out that the beauty presented in these Web sites was not natural beauty but beauty that had to be created. Young girls' body parts were portrayed as problem areas to be fixed. The underlying message seemed to be, "You are not OK as you are." As an illustration the authors pointed to a magazine Web site that offered help for eyebrows; another had an online poll that asked what girls hated most about their hair.

A second theme followed naturally from the first: Beauty is achieved through products. The Web sites offered a wide array of beauty products for those girls who were dissatisfied with the way they looked. Moreover, the sites portrayed the use of these products as the natural and accepted mode of behavior. The *Cosmogirl* site, for example, featured a survey that asked readers to name their favorite beauty products and to say why they love them. Another part of the site asked, "What's in your make-up bag?" The Web site seemed to assume that all its readers had favorite products and that owning a makeup bag was the norm.

A third theme, not unexpectedly, was that the Web sites could help teenage girls find the right products to make them beautiful. The sites took on the role of best friend or big sister, someone who knew about beauty problems and how to solve them. Some of the Web sites had experts, usually identified by just a first name, who offered tips on what to buy. The underlying lesson appeared to be that buying lots of cosmetics is the natural way for a young woman to become beautiful.

The authors conclude that the notion that beauty equals success sends the wrong message. Young women are being taught that they can gain power and happiness by purchasing the right brand of cosmetics, and not through personal achievements. The content of the Web sites also supports one of the criticisms frequently voiced by feminist critics: These sites polarize gender roles by promoting the idea that women in society have roles restricted to making their bodies beautiful in order to attract male attention. Finally, the researchers point out that these sites capitalize on teenage girls' insecurities about their bodies to stimulate consumption. By defining beauty as physical perfection and urging the purchase of products to achieve that perfection, these sites (as well as their print counterparts) are creating unrealistic expectations in their young readers. Many young women may spend a good deal of time and money pursuing an ideal that can never be achieved.

magazines in the digital age

Magazines are still learning how best to use the Internet. In the early days of the Web, many magazines simply took articles from the print edition and posted them online. The main purpose of the online edition was to encourage people to subscribe to the print edition. Today, however, magazine Web sites have become more sophisticated and are treated as equal to their print counterparts. Many online magazines now have their own original content.

For readers a digital version of a magazine has obvious advantages. First, it may be available days before the print version arrives. Second, readers can easily e-mail articles to friends, order products advertised on the Web site, and search back issues. For the publisher the biggest advantage is cost. Producing and distributing an online edition is far cheaper than putting out a print edition.

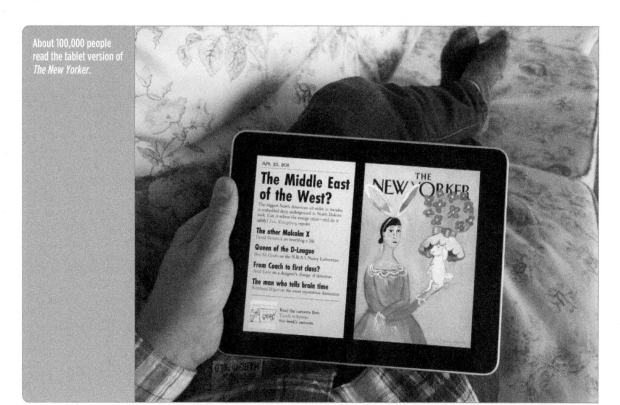

Transition

The digital future of the magazine industry is slowly beginning to take shape. It seems apparent that the Web will play a more important role in both the publishing and marketing of magazines. More than 8,000 consumer magazines have Web sites, up about 50 percent from 2006. Every month these Web sites attract more than 75 million unique visitors, but the print version continues to bring in the bulk of the revenue. As of 2010, the magazine industry received less than 15 percent of its income from its digital efforts. The digital part of the equation is likely to grow in the next few years as magazines increase their efforts to

ethical issues   *Airbrushing and Ethics*

Airbrushing is a general term that refers to touching up a photograph to remove imperfections or to enhance the image. Digital photography has made it extraordinarily easy to retouch photos. In fact, if you buy a digital camera and related software, it's likely that the software contains retouching tools that eliminate red-eye or make an image thinner or thicker.

An ethical issue arises when, without disclosing the alterations to the viewer, airbrushing is used to create images that are too ideal or too much of an improvement on reality. Magazines have been the source of several controversial examples. *GQ* admitted that a photo of Kate Winslet was airbrushed before appearing on its February 2003 cover. *Men's Fitness* thickened the biceps on a photo of tennis star Andy Roddick to promote a story about building stronger arms. *Glamour* was accused of slimming *Ugly Betty* star America Ferrera on its cover (the magazine denies any airbrushing was done). Perhaps the most famous example was *Redbook*'s retouching of the cover photo of singer Faith Hill on its July 2007 cover. A Web site got hold of the original unretouched photo and ran it along with the airbrushed version. The differences were striking. In 2011, many Web sites showed an airbrushed photo of Katy Perry used on the cover of *Rolling Stone* along with the original version.

The ethical issue involved here is one of deception. Do readers have a right to know when photos have been digitally altered? The fashion magazine industry would argue that there's nothing wrong with airbrushing. After the Faith Hill controversy, a spokesperson for *Redbook* asserted that the retouching it did on her photo was "completely in line with industry standards." This admission suggests that deception is the industry standard and everybody does it. Of course, the fact that everybody does it does not make it right.

Another defense is that fashion photography should never be expected to tell the truth. Fashion is part fantasy and part art. Or as one fashion magazine executive put it, "They're not really photographs. They're images."

Others ask, What's the big deal? So cover girls (and guys) aren't as perfect as they are pictured. Where's the harm? Well, the harm may be to young girls' self-images. Several studies have found that women feel worse about their own body image after looking at fashion magazines. Further, these images might create unreal expectations. One survey found that almost half of third-grade girls wanted to be thinner, a wish brought on perhaps by hundreds of exposures to airbrushed models.

For its part, the American Society of Media Photographers makes its position clear. From its Code of Ethics: "Disclose any alteration and manipulation of content or meaning in editorial feature or illustrative photographs and require the publisher to disclose that distortion or any further alteration."

deliver magazines to tablet computers, e-readers, and smartphones. A 2010 survey done for the MPA—Association of Magazine Media found that about 60 percent of U.S. consumers planned to buy an e-reader or tablet computer in the next three years. Another survey disclosed that four out of five consumers wanted to read magazines on their tablets and e-readers and were willing to pay for the content.

Individual magazines are also integrating print subscriptions with Web subscriptions. For about $48 a year, *Sports Illustrated* offers a subscription that includes the print version and access to the digital version on several platforms. *The Economist* offers a print plus digital package for $127. As we shall see in this chapter, more magazines are using apps to sell their digital editions.

Replica Editions

The print version of many magazines is available digitally in replica form. A replica edition tries to duplicate the paper magazine reading experience as closely as possible. Unlike an online edition, where a reader can choose from a menu of stories and other features created expressly for the Web, a digital replica contains all the stories, graphics, fancy layouts, headlines, ads, and page numbers—and even those annoying little subscription cards—that the reader would find in the print edition. The replica version is displayed one page at a time, and the pages are side by side, just as in the print version.

Several companies offer electronic delivery of replica editions to subscribers. The biggest is Zinio Systems with about 750 titles available, including *Popular Science, TV Guide,* and *PC World.* Zinio's biggest competitor is Texterity, whose offerings include *Smart Money, Vibe,* and *Spin.*

Apps for Mobile Platforms

The magazine industry is experimenting with business models using apps to bring digital magazines to tablet computers and other mobile devices. Although consumers have shown a reluctance to pay for access to online content on the Web, they have been

critical ⊕ cultural issues

Digital and Print Magazines and the Reading Experience

Will digital editions of magazines eventually replace the print edition? An article by Brita Ytre-Arne in a 2011 edition of *Media, Culture and Society* examines this question using a critical/cultural approach.

The author looked at readers of a weekly Norwegian women's magazine, *KK*, who also were familiar with the magazine's Web site. The results of her study revealed that magazine readers may like magazine Web sites but they still feel that Web sites will never replace the print magazine because there are experiences associated with print that a digital equivalent can't duplicate.

This conclusion is not due to the fact that print magazine readers were not technologically skilled or novices when it came to the Internet. All her informants were skilled Internet users and often surfed the Web. They were all familiar with magazine Web sites but showed little interest in them.

Second, content differences between the digital and print versions did not prompt readers to prefer one over the other. Most agreed that the same stories and pictures appeared in both versions.

What did cause the difference in preference? Ytre-Arne posited two factors. The first was that magazines were read in certain contexts in which computers had no place. The second was that the interface (to use a computer term) of the print version was preferred over the Web interface.

With regard to the first factor, print magazines were read in specific situations—for example, at the end of the day in bed, with a glass of wine, in a relaxing chair, or at the dining table. Informants believed that computers had no place in these circumstances. One informant pointed out that even a laptop computer was impractical for relaxed reading, "It's just not comfortable to sit with the computer *on* you. [It's] just too hot to keep on one's lap." Indeed, many readers thought the computer was inimical to the whole notion of relaxation, probably because people associated the computer with work. As one put it, "I just don't enjoy myself when I am sitting in front of a computer screen." And another: "It's easier to leaf through magazines. You get a different overview and a different feeling."

As for the second factor, the interfaces of digital magazines were not suited to an enjoyable reading experience. Readers mentioned that there was movement on the screen as ads popped up, that clicking and scrolling were distracting, and that navigating back and forth between pages was bothersome. In contrast, the informants liked to have something that they could hold in their hands and something that was permanent. They also liked the fact that articles could be clipped and saved. The tactile dimension was also important. Readers liked the feel and the texture of a print magazine. They also thought that high-quality glossy photos looked better on the printed page.

Before we close, take note of two things about Ytre-Arne's work. First, unlike many critical/cultural analyses of media, it does not examine a text; instead, it examines the experience of interacting with mass media, an approach that is used less often. Second, the research for the article was conducted before the iPad and various magazine apps became popular. Would her conclusions differ if her informants were reading magazines on their iPads? That's a question for a subsequent study.

willing to pay for an app that supplies content to their smartphone, iPad, or other tablet device. Publishers have also discovered that readers spend more time with a magazine obtained through an app than when they visit a Web site. Consequently, industry executives look at the tablet computer as another chance to remake the digital version of the magazine. A magazine app would be able to offer a richer content experience that advertisers would find more appealing. For example, instead of the somewhat cluttered and busy look of www.people.com, the *People* magazine app for the iPad is clean and easy to navigate.

Magazine publishers turned to Apple and its App Store as a way to get their magazines on iPads. Their first efforts were less than successful because the apps only allowed for the purchase of a single copy of the magazine rather than an annual subscription. Moreover, consumers balked at the price of a single edition, which was almost as much as a print copy sold at the newsstand. Apple also declined to share data about the consumers who downloaded the apps with publishers; such information would be highly useful to publishers in their efforts to sell advertising.

After much negotiation, Apple announced a subscription plan in 2011. Most of the sales would be handled through Apple's App Store and Apple would take a 30 percent cut of every sale. Consumer data would be shared with publishers only if the subscribers volunteered to share their information. Many publishers were less than enthusiastic about the arrangement but still signed on with Apple. Major magazine publisher Hearst struck a deal with Apple to make available iPad subscription apps for *Esquire, Popular Mechanics,* and *O, the Oprah Magazine* for about $20 per year. Condé Nast publishing also struck an agreement with Apple, as did the publisher of *Elle* and *Popular Science.*

Google has announced a similar app plan for tablets that use its Android system. Google's One Pass system gives publishers a better economic deal—Google only takes 10 percent—and publishers have access to subscribers' information. Despite the better terms, most publishers expect that Apple will dominate the tablet app market for the next few years. To sum up, magazine companies have high hopes that the tablet will revitalize their industry but it's too early to gauge the tablet's long-term impact.

User-Generated Content

Publishers are cautiously experimenting with user production of content. Part of their caution stems from their desire to maintain editorial control over the content on their Web site and to ensure that offensive or distasteful content does not appear. A second concern is the lack of a clear way to turn this content into a revenue generator. Food magazine sites let readers post their own recipes, cooking hints, and photos. *New York* magazine's Web site publishes reader reviews of local restaurants. Nonetheless, user-generated content does not play a big role in magazine publishing.

Social Media

The magazine industry is becoming more skilled at using social media. Check out the stories on any magazine's Web site. At time.com, readers can click on icons that will post a link to a story to their Twitter or Facebook accounts, allowing them to share the stories with their social contacts. The more readers directed to that story by social media, the more time .com can charge for advertising. Most magazines have their own Facebook and Twitter accounts. *Time* magazine, for example, has about 2 million Twitter followers; *Elle* has more than 700,000. On Facebook, *Maxim* has 310,000 people who indicated they like the magazine.

Further, many magazines, such as *Cooking Light* and *Prevention,* have established reader communities. Feedback from these communities helps the magazine plan future issues and keep current on reader likes and dislikes. Another creative use of social media by several magazines involves real-time conversations between readers and experts in the magazine's editorial area. *Traveler* magazine, for example, used Tumblr to let readers ask questions of travel experts. Other magazines use social media to enhance the reading experience. They may include reader polls, simple video games, and real-time chat on their social media sites. *Time,* for example, let its Facebook community members create a fake "Person of the Year" image to share with friends.

Maybe this promotional announcement from *Field & Stream* magazine best summarizes how magazines have seized upon social media: "[O]n our Facebook page, you'll find fun extras (outtakes from photo shoots, status updates from writers on assignment, and the occasional contest with cool prizes) that you won't find anywhere else. Even better, our Facebook page is a chance for you to reach out to other F&S readers. Who knows? One of them might just be an old flame."

defining features of magazines

The first defining feature of both print and digital magazines is that, of all the media discussed in this book, they attract the most specialized audiences. There are publications designed to reach specific demographic groups (*AARP Magazine, Maxim*), specific occupational groups (*Pointe,* the magazine for ballerinas, or *Builder*), specific interest groups (*Cigar Aficionado, American History*), specific political groups (*National Review, Mother Jones*), specific geographic groups (*Southern Living, Arizona Highways*), and a host of other very specific groups (*Latin CEO*).

The second defining feature is magazines' relationship with social, demographic, economic, and social trends. Of all the media, magazines are most in tune with such trends. As consumer and business needs change, some new magazines emerge, some old magazines cease publication, and others fine-tune their content. To illustrate, the Hispanic population in the United States rose more than 10 percent from 2000 to 2004, about four times the increase of the overall U.S. population. Magazine publishers were quick to offer publications aimed at this growing segment of U.S. society. *People en Espanol, Reader's*

Digest's Selecciones, Shape en Espanol, and *Healthy Kids en Espanol* were just some of the titles launched in the past few years. To take another example, a poker craze swept the United States in 2004–2005. Magazine publishers were quick to respond with titles such as *All In* and *Bluff.* (Keep in mind that trendiness is a two-edged sword. Should the poker craze fade, so will the magazines.) Magazines also spring up along with political movements. The *Tea Party Review* debuted in 2011.

The third feature is that, as we have seen, magazines can *influence* social trends. Magazines helped fuel the American Revolution. The muckrakers at the turn of the 20th century prompted social reform. In the 1950s *Playboy* launched the sexual revolution in the United States. In the 1970s *Ms.* helped usher in the women's movement.

Will the digital magazine spell the end of the traditional print edition? As the preceding discussion suggests, probably not. Despite the advances in mobile technology, the print magazine is still the most convenient form to take with you. You can roll it up, or fold it, and it doesn't depend upon a wireless or a WiFi connection. Second, as noted in Chapter 1, audience segmentation is becoming more and more pronounced. Magazines were the first medium to adapt to this changing condition, and they remain well situated for the future.

This is not to say that there won't be changes. Magazines that aim for a large, undifferentiated audience, such as *TV Guide* and *Reader's Digest,* will have a harder time staying profitable. Some magazines will shift entirely to the Web. Finally, the magazine industry may find a totally different business model. The app subscription model discussed earlier is one possibility. One thing is clear: The next few years will be challenging ones for magazine publishers.

organization of the magazine industry

One of the problems in discussing the magazine industry is deciding what exactly is a magazine. The dictionary defines *magazine* as a "periodical publication, usually with a paper cover, containing miscellaneous articles and often with illustrations or photographs." This definition is broad enough to include *Reader's Digest,* with a circulation of more than 8 million; *Water Scooter,* a magazine for boating enthusiasts; *Sky,* given away to airline passengers by Delta Airlines; *Successful Farmer,* the magazine of farm management; *Go,* distributed to Goodyear tire dealers; *The Journal of Social Psychology;* and the *Bird Watcher's Digest.* There are around 20,000 magazines published in the United States. Both the number and the diversity of these publications are staggering. For example, Wikipedia lists about 80 art magazines and 7 periodicals devoted to wildlife. There are more than 6,000 magazines sold regularly on newsstands, and the number of new consumer titles continues to rise. Obviously, classifying the magazine industry into coherent categories is a vexing problem. For our purposes we will employ two organizational schemes. The first classifies print and online magazines into six main content categories: (1) general consumer magazines, (2) business publications, (3) custom magazines, (4) literary reviews and academic journals, (5) newsletters, and (6) public relations magazines. The second scheme divides the magazine industry into the three traditional, functional components of manufacturing: production, distribution, and retailing.

A glance at any newsstand will illustrate that consumer magazines fall into major general-interest categories such as sports, health, computers, business, and women's interests.

Content Categories

General Consumer Magazines   A consumer magazine is one that can be acquired by anyone, through a subscription or a single-copy

media *probe*

Convergence: A Magazine Gets into the TV Business—Sort Of

In 2011 *Glamour* magazine announced plans to produce a reality TV series called *Glamour Girls* that would be shown exclusively on the iPad. Described as a cross between *Mary Tyler Moore* and *The Hills*, the series follows the lives of four young professional women as they work in the fashion industry. Each episode would last about 10–12 minutes.

Why would a magazine produce a program for the iPad? Product placement. *Glamour* readily admits that the series would be a showcase for

sponsors' products. During one episode, for example, the main characters might wear clothing and accessories from the Gap. If viewers like an outfit or outfits that one of the characters is wearing, they can tap the iPad screen and scroll through a selection of all the Gap outfits shown on that episode. Another tap of the screen takes viewers to Gap.com, where they can immediately buy the clothing and get discounts on other Gap products.

Although *Glamour Girls* is an interesting experiment, it faces an uphill road to success. More than 2 million people subscribe to the print version of *Glamour*. Fewer than 10,000 have downloaded the *Glamour* iPad app.

purchase or as a free copy. These magazines are generally shelved at the corner newsstand or local bookstore. (Other types of magazines are usually not available to the general public.) These publications are called *consumer magazines* because readers can buy the products and services that are advertised in their pages. One noticeable trend in the content of consumer magazines is, as mentioned, the movement away from broad, general-appeal to more specialized publications. Some of the better-known consumer magazines are *People, Time, Reader's Digest, TV Guide, Sports Illustrated,* and *Woman's Day* (see Table 6-1). Note that consumer magazines can exist in both print and online versions and that some magazines exist only online without a print counterpart. Salon.com, for example, covers politics and culture while Slate.com, owned by the Washington Post Company, usually focuses on current affairs. A more recent entry is *The Huffington Post*, published by author-columnist Arianna Huffington.

Business Publications   Business magazines (also called *trade publications*) serve a particular business, industry, or profession. They are not sold on newsstands, and their readership is limited to those in the profession or business. The products advertised in these publications are generally those that would be purchased by business organizations or professionals rather than by the general public. *Business Publications Rates and Data* lists approximately 4,000 titles of business magazines. Most of these magazines are published by independent publishing companies that are not connected with the fields they serve. For example, PennWell and Penton are two private publishing companies that publish business magazines in a variety of areas. Other business publications are put out by professional organizations, which publish them as a service to their members. The degree of specialization of these magazines is seen in the medical field, which has approximately 375 publications serving various medical specialties. Some business publications are called

table 6-1	Title	Circulation (millions)	Percent Change from 2008
Top 10 Consumer Magazines, 2009, by Circulation	*AARP Magazine*	24.5	+1.4
	Reader's Digest	7.6	−8.2
	Better Homes and Gardens	7.6	−0.4
	Good Housekeeping	4.6	−0.8
	National Geographic	4.6	−0.2
	Woman's Day	3.9	—
	Family Circle	3.9	—
	Ladies' Home Journal	3.8	—
	People	3.6	−0.2
	Time	3.3	—

Note: With a few exceptions, magazine circulation has been declining.

social issues *Do We Need Newsmagazines?*

The three major news weeklies, *Time, Newsweek,* and *U.S. News and World Report,* have been publishing for more than 70 years and have been influential forces in American politics, entertainment, and culture. Their choices of which people graced their covers even made news. Recent developments, however, have put their future in doubt. For many decades, the newspaper, radio, and later television provided the bare details and the newsmagazines provided context, background, analysis, and interpretation of news events. It was a successful formula and huge media companies, such as Time Inc., grew out of the idea.

Today, however, with cable news operating around the clock, news Web sites that are updated frequently, cell phones, bloggers, Twitter, and other social networks that can provide instant coverage, the concept behind the news weeklies is no longer as compelling as it once was. This fact is reflected in declining circulation numbers and loss of ad revenue to competitors.

The situation is so gloomy that *U.S. News and World Report* dropped out of the mix in 2008 and became a monthly magazine devoted primarily to consumer guides. *Newsweek* downsized by about 20 percent and announced plans to run more opinion and analysis pieces in an attempt to attract a more elite subscriber base that would be more appealing to advertisers. Of course, concentrating on opinion pieces also saves money. It costs less to write opinions than to cover news. *Time* was in the best situation of the three, but it also went through a round of layoffs and staff reductions and has indicated that it will also become more opinion centered.

Is the weekly newsmagazine relevant anymore? Some would argue in the affirmative. Over the years the newsmagazines have cultivated a number of columnists (for example, Joe Klein and Jonathan Alter) whose analyses have proven perceptive. Many would trust their views more than those of the countless bloggers who now populate the Internet. The news weeklies have also encouraged the publication of minority views and the observations of people who don't normally get to publish their thoughts (see, for example, *Newsweek*'s "My Turn" column). Moreover, shifting from reporting to opinions and analyses means that magazine investigative journalism, which dates back to the muckrakers in the 1900s, will no longer appear. International news, not well reported on television or by newspapers, might also be hard to find.

Naturally, others disagree and think that news weeklies are simply dinosaurs. When the editor of *Newsweek* gave a speech at Columbia University's journalism school, he closed by asking how many of the hundred or so people in the audience read *Newsweek.* Nobody raised a hand. That was not a good sign. In 2010, *Newsweek* was sold to audio magnate Sidney Harman for $1 (plus the assumption of the magazine's sizable debt). *Newsweek* then merged with *The Daily Beast,* a news/culture/entertainment/opinion Web site overseen by well-known magazine editor Tina Brown. As of this writing, it is unclear if the revamped magazine will be successful.

vertical because they cover all aspects of one field. For example, *Pulp and Paper* reports on all segments of the paper mill industry. Other publications are called *horizontal* because they deal with a certain business function, no matter in what industry it exists. *Selling,* for example, would be targeted at salespeople in all industries. Leading business magazines include *Computerworld, Oil and Gas Journal,* and *Medical Economics.* Business publishers are also active in supplying databases and computer bulletin board systems to their clients. Like consumer magazines, business publications can exist in print and online.

Custom Magazines   Custom magazines are published by corporations that try to keep existing customers satisfied while attracting new clients. Some are distributed for free at various business locations; others can be purchased at newsstands. Lexus, for example, publishes a magazine that promotes its automobiles, while Hilton publishes *Grand Times,* enticing people to vacation at its resorts.

Custom magazines have been around for a while. Airlines have published them for decades, but in the last few years custom magazines have become more visible primarily because businesses have discovered that they are an effective marketing tool.

Custom magazines present at least two problems for the traditional magazine industry. First, they siphon off advertising dollars from more conventional magazines. If Lexus can target its potential customers with its magazine, it might reduce its advertising buys in *Time, Newsweek,* or other consumer publications. Second, a custom magazine editorial staff may have less independence than a traditional magazine. It would be highly unlikely that a story in Hilton's *Grand Times* would say something negative about the company. Be that as it may, custom magazines likely will be a more important factor in the years to come.

decision makers   *Tina Brown*

Contributed by Meaghan E. Dominick

Tina Brown enrolled at Oxford University at age 17. As a student, she wrote for *Isis*, the literary magazine of her university. Graduating with a BA in English literature, Brown pursued her dream of a journalism career by doing freelance reporting for various publications including *The Sunday Times* and *The Sunday Telegraph*. She also wrote a weekly column for Punch magazine. Her freelance reporting earned Brown the Catherine Pakenham Award for best journalist under 25.

At 25, Brown became the editor-in-chief of *Tatler* magazine. At the time, *Tatler* was a small society magazine. Brown developed it into the preferred magazine for fashion, photography, and coverage of Prince Charles and Lady Diana's wedding. Brown left Tatler magazine in 1982 to pursue full-time writing. The break, however, was not long.

In 1984, Brown became the editor-in-chief of *Vanity Fair*. At the time, *Vanity Fair* was a struggling publication. Brown hired writers such as Dominick Dunne and photographers such as Annie Leibovitz to cover both celebrities and "serious" journalism. Brown's insight and leadership turned around the failing magazine and launched *Vanity Fair* as one of the nation's thriving magazine publications.

In 1992, Brown left *Vanity Fair* to become the editor of *The New Yorker*. One of Brown's first controversial decisions was to hire a staff photographer. Until her tenure, *The New Yorker* did not take photography as a serious art. In addition, Brown approved several controversial covers. With Brown at the helm, *The New Yorker* increased sales every year. Brown left the magazine in 1998.

Following her departure, Brown became the chairperson of a new multimedia company with Miramax Films, with the intention of starting a new magazine. In 1999, she created *Talk magazine*. *Talk* garnered success, but fell victim to the advertising recession following the September 11, 2001, attacks and stopped production in January 2002.

Brown then moved on to host a television show called *Topic [A] with Tina Brown* in 2003. Brown interviewed a variety of guests ranging from celebrities to political figures. In 2005, Brown was offered a book deal to write a biography of Princess Diana. She accepted the deal and production of her show ceased. Brown went on to write *the New York* Times best-selling book *The Diana Chronicles*, published in 2007.

In October 2008, Brown and Barry Diller founded *The Daily Beast*. *The Daily Beast* is an online newsmagazine that offers original news articles with news summaries. Brown filled the role of editor-in-chief. *The Daily Beast* garnered much critical acclaim, winning various online journalism awards. In August 2010, *Time* magazine named *The Daily Beast* one of the 50 Best Websites of 2010. In November 2010, *Newsweek* merged with *The Daily Beast* to create The Newsweek Daily Beast Company. Brown is currently serving as editor-in-chief for both *The Daily Beast* and *Newsweek*. Throughout her long career, Brown has managed to keep in tune with American culture and has been one of the leading figures in magazine journalism.

Literary Reviews and Academic Journals   Hundreds of literary reviews and academic journals, generally with circulations under 10,000, are published by nonprofit organizations and funded by universities, foundations, or professional organizations. They may publish four or fewer issues per year, and a large number do not accept advertising. These publications cover the entire range of literary and academic interests, and they include such journals as the *Kenyon Review, Theater Design and Technology, European Urology, Journalism and Mass Communication Quarterly, Poultry and Egg Marketing*, and the *Journal of Japanese Botany*. Most literary reviews and journals have online versions.

Newsletters   When some people hear the word *newsletter*, they think of a club, PTA, or church bulletin filled with helpful hints. Although these newsletters are important to their readers, we are talking about newsletters typically four to eight pages long and usually created by desktop publishing. They are sold by subscription, and in recent years they have become big business. In fact, there is even a *Newsletter Newsletter*, published for those who edit newsletters. The coverage area of a newsletter may be broad or narrow. It might deal with one particular business or government agency, or it might report on a business function that crosses industry lines. The *Federal Budget Report*, for example, reports on just the president's budget and appropriations. On the other hand, the *Spear Report* covers financial developments that have an impact on many industries.

Newsletters are extremely specialized, with small circulations (typically under 10,000) but high subscription prices. Typical fees are about $200–300 a year, but fees of $600–800 are not unheard of, and some daily newsletters cost as much as $4,000 annually. Some influential newsletters are *Aerospace Daily & Defense Report, Oil Spill Intelligence Report*, and *Drug Enforcement Report*. Most newsletters are available online, and some can be delivered to mobile devices.

Public Relations Magazines   These are magazines published by a sponsoring company and intended specifically for one of its publics. An internal public relations (PR) magazine is aimed at employees, salespeople, and dealers. An external PR magazine is directed to stockholders, potential customers, and technical service providers.

These publications typically carry little advertising, apart from promotional items for the sponsoring organization. These publications also have their own professional organization, the International Association of Business Communicators. Most PR magazines exist only in print, but some have online counterparts.

Functional Categories

A second useful way of structuring the print magazine industry is to divide it by function into the production, distribution, and retail segments.

The Production Function   The production phase of the industry, which consists of approximately 3,000–4,000 publishers, encompasses all the elements necessary to put out a magazine—copy, artwork, photos, titles, layout, printing, and binding. A subsequent section will describe in more detail how a magazine is produced.

The Distribution Function   The distribution phase of the industry handles the job of getting the magazine to the reader. This is not a simple job. In fact, the circulation department at a large magazine may be the most complex in the whole company. As with newspapers, circulation of magazines means the total number of copies that are delivered through subscriptions or bought at the newsstand. There are two main types of circulation. In **paid circulation,** readers pay to receive the magazine, either through a subscription or at the newsstand. Paid circulation has two main advantages: (1) Periodicals that use paid circulation qualify for lower, second-class postal rates; and (2) paid circulation provides a revenue source to the publisher in addition to advertising. On the negative side, paid-circulation magazines must undertake expensive promotional campaigns to increase subscriptions or to sell single copies. Paid-circulation magazines have the added expense of collecting subscription payments and keeping records. Most consumer magazines use paid circulation.

The alternative to paid circulation is **controlled circulation.** Controlled-circulation magazines set specific qualifications for those who are to receive the magazine. Magazines that are provided to airline passengers or hotel/motel guests are examples. Controlled circulation has two main advantages: (1) Publications using it can reach all the personnel in a given field, and (2) these publications avoid the costs of promoting subscriptions. On the negative side, controlled-circulation magazines gain no revenue from subscriptions and single-copy sales. Further, postage for these publications costs more. Controlled circulation has generally been used by business, custom, and public relations magazines.

No matter what method is chosen, the circulation of a magazine is an important number. The larger the circulation, the more the magazine can charge for its advertising space.

For a paid-circulation magazine, distributing copies to subscribers is a relatively simple affair. The complicated (and expensive) part of this process is getting subscribers. There are no fewer than 14 methods used by magazines to build subscription lists. They include signing up subscribers via the Web; employing cash-field agencies, which have salespeople make house-to-house calls to sell subscriptions directly to consumers; employing direct-mail agencies; mounting direct-mail campaigns sponsored by the publisher; and, finally, using what are called *blow-in cards,* those annoying little cards that fall out of a magazine as soon as you open it.

The tremendous diversity of the magazine industry is illustrated by this magazine display in a bookstore. Magazine publishers compete vigorously for prime space (front row, eye level) in such a display.

Single-copy distribution to newsstands and other retailers is a multistep process. The publisher deals with only one party, the national distributor. The national distributor handles from a dozen to 50 or more titles. At least once every month, representatives of the magazine sit down with the national distributor and determine the number of magazines to be distributed for an upcoming issue. The national distributor then delivers the magazines to wholesalers who sell magazines and paperback books within specified areas. In any given month a wholesaler might receive 500–1,000 magazines to distribute to dealers.

The particulars of online distribution are much different. Mobile users can download apps from the publisher to purchase single copies of a magazine or go to Apple or Google and use their apps for an annual subscription. They can also download replica versions from companies such as Zinio. Alternatively, readers can access the online versions of magazines through their Web browsers.

The Retail Function   The retailer is the last segment of the industry. The best available figures indicate that there are approximately 140,000 retail outlets in the United States. Supermarkets accounted for about 33 percent of all sales in 2009. Supermarket sales have become so important that publishers pay the stores a premium of about $25 per checkout rack to have their titles prominently displayed. When a dealer receives a magazine, he or she agrees to keep the magazine on the display racks for a predetermined length of time (usually a week or a month). At the end of this period, unsold copies are returned to the wholesaler for credit. Supercenters, such as Wal-Mart, accounted for 16 percent.

magazine ownership

Recent mergers and acquisitions have resulted in a magazine industry dominated by large corporations. Many of the conglomerates (Time Warner, Hearst) have extensive holdings in other media. Table 6-2 contains a ranking of the top consumer magazine publishers by 2009 revenue and lists their well-known titles.

producing the magazine

Departments and Staff

The publisher is the chief executive officer at a magazine. He or she is responsible for budgeting, maintaining a healthy advertising position, keeping circulation high, and making sure the magazine moves in a consistent editorial direction. The publisher oversees four main departments:

1. *Circulation:* This department is responsible for keeping current readers satisfied and attracting new readers.
2. *Advertising and Sales:* As the name suggests, this department is responsible for selling space in the magazine to advertisers.
3. *Production:* This department oversees the actual printing and binding of the magazine.

table 6-2	Rank	Company	Revenue (billions)	Top Magazines
Leading Magazine Publishers, 2009, by Revenue	1	Time Warner	$2.7	*People, Time*
	2	Advance Publications	2.6	*Vogue Glamour*
	3	Hearst Corp.	1.8	*Cosmopolitan, Good Housekeeping*
	4	Meredith Corp.	.81	*Ladies' Home Journal, Better Homes and Gardens*
	5	Reader's Digest Assn.	.72	*Reader's Digest*

4. *Editorial:* The head of this department supervises the editorial staff, plans topics for upcoming issues, and helps out with various public relations activities. The managing editor handles the day-to-day operation of the magazine, such as making sure articles are in on time, choosing artwork, and changing layouts.

Some magazines might have a separate department to handle their online operations, but declining revenues have compelled many publications to converge the online and print operations.

The Production Process

Everything moves in cycles. Early magazine publishers were printers as well as writers, but during the 19th century the production function was divorced from the editorial function. Many magazines have now gone full circle: Computers enable writers and editors to set their words into type and make up pages, reuniting the production and editorial functions.

The first step in all print magazine production is preliminary planning and idea generation for upcoming issues. Once the overall ideas are set, the next step is to convert the ideas into concrete subjects for articles. At this point preliminary decisions concerning article length, photos, and accompanying artwork are made. Then the managing editor assigns certain articles to staff writers or freelancers.

The next step involves putting together a miniature **dummy,** a plan or blueprint of the pages for the upcoming issue that shows the contents in their proper order. This phase can now be done electronically, thanks to computer programs that allow editors to view 32 pages at a time.

At about this same time, schedules are drawn up to ensure that an article will get to the printer in time to be included in the forthcoming issue. A copy deadline is set—this is the day the writer must hand in the story to the editor. Time is set aside for editing, checking, and verifying all copy. A timetable is also set up for illustrations and artwork.

Articles are written and edited at the computer. Once they are in acceptable form, a computerized typesetter sets the copy in body and display-size type, and the articles are sent to the press or posted on the magazine's Web site.

The production process is different for the online version. One of the advantages of the Web version of a story is that it can contain more information than the print story. As a result, the transcript of lengthy interviews, background facts, and time lines may be incorporated into a Web story. Deadlines for weekly or monthly publications don't make sense for an online publication. Articles are frequently updated when new angles or new information appears. In addition to writers and editors, others also contribute to the process. A Web producer may incorporate audio and video into an online story. A graphics expert may look for the best screen layout for the story. Another editor may look for ways to include social media in the story. In short, publishing an online version requires additional skills and creates different challenges.

economics

There are four basic sources of print and digital magazine revenue: (1) subscriptions, (2) single-copy sales, (3) advertising, and (4) ancillary services such as e-commerce, custom publishing, and database assistance. This section will concentrate on the first three.

The magazine industry was facing lean times as the decade came to an end. Advertising revenue dropped about 15 percent from 2007 to 2010. In addition, there were troubling signs on the horizon. Thanks to deeply discounted subscriptions, single-copy sales of magazines continued to fall, down about 30 percent from 2007 to 2010. Moreover, magazine circulation has declined about 14 percent from 2000. A glance at Table 6-1 shows that, of the top 10 consumer magazines, only 1 increased circulation from 2008 to 2009. Things were so bad that the publisher of the venerable *Reader's Digest* filed for bankruptcy in August 2009.

Hay There

Hay & Forage Grower, the only national publication devoted to alfalfa, demonstrates how almost all magazines are using social media. The publication has a Facebook page (with 375 fans) and a Twitter feed (with 224 followers).

Another significant trend is the growing importance of advertising in the revenue mix. In 1995, advertising accounted for about 56 percent of all revenue with subscription income and newsstand sales making up the rest. In 2010, among the top consumer magazines, advertising accounted for about 71 percent. As is obvious, any slowdown in advertising, as happened in the latter part of the decade, will spell trouble for magazines. Magazines are increasingly turning to their online editions to help improve their bottom lines, but so far, as we have seen, the results have not been encouraging, with online revenue accounting for less than 15 percent of the typical magazine's income.

The relative importance of subscriptions, single-copy sales, and advertising varies tremendously from magazine to magazine. *Reader's Digest* gets almost all of its money from subscriptions and advertising. On the other hand, *Woman's World* gets only a small proportion from subscriptions and relies mainly on advertising and newsstand sales. To gain some perspective on advertising, in 2010 it cost about $275,000 for a full page in *People magazine*. A full-page ad in *Fortune* cost about $130,000, but you could buy an ad on Forbes.com for much less.

Yet another economic problem for the industry was a shift in the marketing environment. Big retailers such as Wal-Mart and supermarkets want to display only those titles that are best-sellers; cluttering up their shelves with unsold copies hurts their bottom line. As a result it was becoming more difficult for new magazines to find shelf space.

From the perspective of the consumer, it makes sense to subscribe to a magazine rather than to purchase it regularly at the newsstand. From 1996 to 2010, average annual subscription rates actually dropped from about $30 to $26. On the other hand, average cover prices during that same period shot up from $1.71 to about $4.50. Some publishers are opting to bundle print and digital subscriptions together. *Sports Illustrated* offers a print, Web, and Android app subscription package for $48 a year.

Where does the money go? The typical dollar breaks down approximately as shown in Table 6-3. Two items included in the manufacturing and distribution category of Table 6-3 have increased at the fastest rate: paper and postage.

global magazines

Magazines are popular the world over, and many American magazines have counterparts in other countries. *Reader's Digest* publishes more than 40 international editions read by nearly 20 million people. *Time* distributes its international edition in more than 150 countries. Hearst oversees the distribution of editions of *Redbook* and *Good Housekeeping* in more than 100 countries. There are Japanese, Polish, and Russian versions of *Cosmopolitan*.

Small, special-interest magazines are also growing internationally. A Spanish-language version of *Popular Mechanics* is sold throughout Latin America. *Men's Health* publishes editions in Britain and Russia. *Business Week* and *Fortune* have significant foreign readership. Publishers think that Russia and China will be major growth markets in the near future.

table 6-3	Expense	Amount
Breakdown of a Consumer Magazine's Dollar	Advertising expenses	$0.08
	Circulation costs	0.31
	Editorial costs	0.10
	Manufacturing and distribution	0.40
	Other costs	0.01
	Administration	0.10

the magazine audience

Sources of Feedback

The print magazine industry, like the newspaper industry, depends on the Audit Bureau of Circulations (ABC) for information about who is reading the publication. The ABC audits most consumer magazines and issues two reports a year. The ABC counts both print and digital circulation, including circulation on tablet computers, but does not count visits to free magazine sites on the Web. The report includes the magazine's average paid circulation and its rate base. The rate base is the number of buyers guaranteed by the magazine and is also the number the magazine uses to compute its advertising rates.

Another company, Business Publication Audit (BPA), specializes in business and trade magazines. It issues reports similar to those of the ABC, with additional information concerning the occupations of readers who receive controlled-circulation publications.

Although it is helpful to know the total circulation figure for a magazine, that number does not tell the whole story. Circulation measures the **primary audience,** those people who subscribe to the magazine or buy it at the newsstand. In addition, there is the **pass-along audience,** those people who pick up a copy at the doctor's office, at work, on the road, and the like. **Mediamark Research Inc. (MRI)** provides data on the total audience for magazines. This company selects a large sample of the magazine-reading public and conducts personal interviews with individuals to get an exposure score for each magazine. The reports issued by MRI are extremely detailed and encompass many volumes. They contain such specific information as the percentage of a particular magazine's readers who make more than $50,000 per year and detailed product use data, such as how many readers used a headache remedy in the past month.

Several companies supply feedback about online readership. These reports usually tabulate the "unique visitors" to a Web site in some period of time, usually a month. The number of unique visitors to a magazine Web site may be much larger than its print circulation. *Sports Illustrated,* for example, has a print circulation of about 3 million; in contrast, si.com often receives more than 7 million visitors in a month. *Business Week* has a print circulation just under 1 million, but businessweek.com typically sees about 9 million visitors a month.

Audiences

Although data on the audience of a particular magazine are readily available, information about the total audience for magazines is hard to come by, primarily because of the difficulty in defining what qualifies as a magazine. Nonetheless, some figures are available. In 2010, as reported to the ABC, total circulation of the top 589 magazines exceeded 325 million copies. Of these, about 11 percent were bought at the newsstand, while the remaining 89 percent were delivered as part of a subscription.

Almost everybody does some type of print or online magazine reading. In an average month, 85 percent of U.S. adults read at least one copy of a magazine. Most read more. One study reported that adults read or look through an average of 10 magazines per month. About 28 percent read a magazine on an average day, and the typical adult spends about 25 minutes daily reading magazines. As far as demographics are concerned, the typical magazine reader is more educated and usually more affluent than the nonreader. Magazine readers also tend to be joiners. One survey found them far more likely than nonreaders to belong to religious, scientific, and professional organizations.

the magazine industry

The job outlook for the magazine industry is not as bad as it was a few years ago, but it is still far from optimistic. According to the Bureau of Labor Statistics, overall employment in the publishing industry dropped 15 percent from 2007 to 2010 but employment picked up slightly during early 2011. Online jobs were more plentiful and individuals with social media skills had an advantage in the job market. The long-term employment picture is expected to improve if the economy recovers.

Those wishing to pursue careers in this area should develop strong writing and editing skills. Knowing how to prepare stories for the print and Web versions of a magazine is a big plus. Multimedia expertise is also an asset.

The career outlook in the various media industries changes quickly. For a more current description of conditions in the magazine industry and a more detailed look at career options, please consult the book's Web site: www.mhhe.com/dominick12e.

main points

- The first American magazines appeared during the middle of the 18th century and were aimed at an educated, urban, and literate audience.

- The audience for magazines increased during the penny-press era as mass-appeal publications became prominent.

- Better printing techniques and a healthy economy helped launch a magazine boom during the latter part of the 19th century.

- The muckrakers were magazines that published exposés and encouraged reform.

- Magazines began to specialize their content following World War I. Newsmagazines, digests, and picture magazines became popular.

- The magazine industry is experiencing a difficult time due to declining advertising revenue.

- Magazine publishers hope that the tablet computer will reenergize the publishing business.

- Magazines are specialized, current, influential, and convenient.

- The magazine industry is dominated by large publishing companies.

- The magazine industry can be divided into the production, distribution, and retail divisions.

- A typical magazine publishing company has several main departments, including circulation, advertising, production, and editorial.

- Magazines get revenues from subscriptions, single-copy sales, and print and online advertising.

- MRI is a company that measures magazine readership.

questions for review

1. What are the four defining features of contemporary magazines? Should any other features be added to this list?

2. Why did the general-interest magazines *Look* and *Life* go out of business?

3. How is the magazine industry learning to coexist with the Internet?

4. What are the major departments at a magazine?

questions for critical thinking

1. Are there dangers in having large corporations dominate the magazine publishing industry?

2. *Playboy, Cosmopolitan,* and *Ms.*—three magazines that influenced social trends—all came on the scene before 1980. Are there any more current magazines that have been influential in shaping American culture and society? If not, why not?

3. Is it possible for a magazine to become too specialized? How big does a specialized audience have to be to support a print magazine? A Web-only magazine?

4. Muckraking by magazines never reappeared after its heyday in the early 20th century. Why not?

5. Read "Critical/Cultural Issue: Teen Magazine Web Sites: What's the Message?" (page 141), and consider the following: Do these Web sites have a responsibility to present a more realistic and well-rounded view of young womanhood? How might the emphasis on beauty and beauty products affect young women who may not be able to afford the "right" cosmetics? Would the same messages be contained in Web sites for magazines targeted at adult women?

6. What's the future for magazines on the iPad and other tablet computers?

key terms

internet resources

Online Learning Center

On the Online Learning Center home page, www.mhhe.com/dominick12e, *select* Student Center *and then* Chapter 6.

1. Use the Learning Objectives, Chapter Outline, and Main Points sections to review this chapter.

2. Test your knowledge of the chapter using the multiple choice and flashcard features of the site.

3. Expand your knowledge of concepts and topics discussed in the chapter with additional Questions for Critical Thinking and Internet Exercises.

surfing the internet

The following are examples of sites of or related to magazines. All sites were current as of late 2010.

http://money.cnn.com
A cooperative venture between CNN and *Money* magazine, both owned by Time Warner. Note the interactive tool you can use to look up a stock price.

www.people.com
Makes extensive use of photos and video. Also available on iPhone, Blackberry, and iPad.

www.magazine.org
The site of MPA—the Association of Magazine Media, the major trade association of the industry. Contains statistics, FAQs, press releases, and research reports.

www.zinio.com
Provides digital delivery of magazines. Download the software and a sample issue to see for yourself how this process works.

www.apple.com/ipad/from-the-app-store
Check out some of the apps available for various magazines.

Amazon's Kindle e-book reader can hold about 3,500 average-size novels.

chapter7

books

This chapter will prepare you to:

- understand that books are the oldest form of mass communication
- recognize the factors that led to the commercialization of book publishing
- explain how the digital revolution may change the underlying structure of the book industry
- identify the main parts of the book industry
- understand how economics affects the book industry

Recently while browsing the shelves in a local bookstore I noticed a man who would pick up a book, take out his iPhone, type something, and replace the book on the shelf. When I courteously inquired as to what he was doing, he replied, "I come here to see what new books are out and then I order them from Amazon over my iPhone to be delivered to my Kindle. I haven't bought a print book in months." That concisely says a lot about today's book industry: (1) Traditional brick and mortar bookstore are going to find it difficult to stay in business (as we shall see below, one major chain declared bankruptcy in 2011); (2) the Kindle, the iPad, and other e-readers are redefining the way we read books; and (3) online booksellers, such as Amazon and Apple, have drastically changed the way books get to their readers.

Although it took a while for the digital revolution to catch up with the book publishing industry, things are changing rapidly. This chapter will look at the history, structure, economics, and future of this evolving mass medium.

a brief history

Early books were inscribed by hand and lavishly decorated; many were valued as works of art. Until approximately the 12th century, most books in Europe were produced by monks in monasteries. As noted in Chapter 3, all this changed with the invention of movable type that worked with a printing press.

The invention of movable metal type suitable for printing is generally credited to Johann Gutenberg. Trained as a metalworker, Gutenberg developed a way to cast metal type and to encase it in a wooden mold that could then be attached to a printing press. In about 1455 Gutenberg printed his first book—the Bible. First put on sale at the Great Frankfurt Fair, the book cost the equivalent of three years of wages for the typical laborer of that time.

Gutenberg's innovations spread quickly throughout Europe. The Protestant Reformation and the writings of Martin Luther spurred the printing of religious books. Printed books appeared in England in 1476. Although book publishing was not considered a socially important force, Henry VIII recognized its potential as a political force and required all printers to obtain government approval before setting up shop.

Colonial America

By the early 17th century, book publishers had followed the early immigrants to North America. In

Many early medieval manuscripts, such as this hymn book, were "illuminated" with colorful drawings and graphics.

1640 the Puritans in Cambridge, Massachusetts, printed the *Bay Psalm Book*. About 90,000 other titles were to follow it as book publishing took hold in the American colonies. Early publishers functioned as printers and sometimes as authors. One of the early printer-publishers who went on to fame was Benjamin Franklin. His *Poor Richard's Almanack* sold about 10,000 copies a year. Most book content was religious, such as that in *The Practice of Piety* and *Day of Doom.* Sentimental novels, many of them imported from England, also sold well. As the Revolutionary War approached, many book printers turned out political pamphlets. Thomas Paine's *Common Sense* sold 100,000 copies in just 10 weeks.

The Penny-Press Era

The change in printing technology and the growth of literacy mentioned in Chapter 5 also helped the book publishing industry. Many of the publishing companies still active today can trace their roots to the early 1800s. Many publishers specialized in professional and educational books, while others addressed their efforts to the general public. Book prices declined and authors such as James Fenimore Cooper and Henry Wadsworth Longfellow became popular, as did the works of English authors. Public education and the penny newspaper created a demand for reading materials. The number of public libraries tripled between 1825 and 1850. Book reading became a symbol of education and knowledge.

The novels of Charles Dickens and Walter Scott were best-sellers during this period, as were books by Herman

sound byte

But He Never Told a Lie

George Washington, the father of our country, had many commendable virtues but he was really bad at returning library books. Washington checked out a couple of books from the New York Society Library in 1789. Apparently he got distracted by serving as president of a new country and forgot to return the books. Librarians who were digitizing records from the late 1700s uncovered Washington's transgression. The library estimates that Washington owed about $300,000 in late fees.

Melville and Henry David Thoreau. Specialized books also appeared. In the late 1840s textbooks were profitable, as were reference, medical, and engineering books. The most significant book of the period, however, was probably Harriet Beecher Stowe's *Uncle Tom's Cabin,* published in 1852. It sold 300,000 copies in its first year and was credited with converting many readers to an antislavery position.

The Paperback Boom

During the Civil War soldiers turned to reading to fill the idle time between campaigns. This created a demand for cheap reading materials, and before long a series of paperbacks priced at 10 cents apiece flooded the market. These "dime novels" included the popular Frank Merriwell and Horatio Alger stories. By 1880 about one-third of all books published in the country were paperbacks, and 15 firms were selling the softbound volumes at prices ranging from 5 cents to 15 cents. Many of the best-selling paperbacks were pirated editions of best-sellers in England and other European countries. By the late 1880s this problem was so bad that a new copyright law was adopted. This new law, combined with years of cutthroat competition and price cutting, spelled the end of this era of paperback popularity.

The Early 20th Century

The period from 1900 to 1945 saw the commercialization of publishing. Prior to this time, many publishing companies had been family-owned and specialized in publishing one particular kind of book. Publishers had been a close-knit group, and their dealings with one another resembled what might take place in a genteel private club. However, several events altered this situation. First, a new breed of literary agents, concerned with negotiating the best bottom line for their authors, entered the scene. Forced to pay top dollar for the rights to books, the publishing business became more businesslike. Second, many publishing houses expanded into the mass market, publishing popular works of fiction. To compete in the mass marketplace, these publishing houses introduced modern promotion and distribution techniques to the book industry. Third, a depression in the 1890s and a subsequent sluggish economy meant that the book industry was forced to depend more on banks for finance capital. The banks, of course, insisted that the book companies be run with the utmost efficiency, with an eye toward increasing profits. By World War II all these factors combined to make the book industry more commercially oriented.

The content of popular books was highly variable during this period. Outdoor adventures written by such authors as Jack London and Zane Grey were popular at the turn of the century. During the Roaring Twenties light fiction such as *The Sheik* and P. G. Wodehouse's Jeeves stories were best-sellers. Detective fiction by Erle Stanley Gardner (Perry Mason was his hero) and Ellery Queen sold well during the Depression. In 1936 two books broke the 2-million mark in sales: Dale Carnegie's *How to Win Friends and Influence People* and Margaret Mitchell's *Gone with the Wind.*

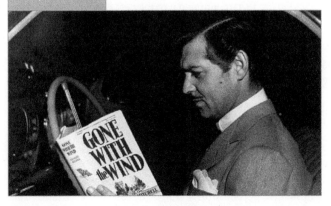

Margaret Mitchell's *Gone with the Wind* was turned down by 25 publishers before Macmillan published it.

Postwar Books: Paperbacks and Consolidation

Shortly after the end of World War II, new paperbacks published by Bantam, Pocket Books, and New American Library appeared. These books were popular because of their 25-cent price and because new channels of distribution were used to market them. Wire racks filled with paperbacks appeared in train stations, newsstands, drugstores, and tobacco shops. A whole new audience was thus exposed to paperbacks. In 1950 the "quality" paperback appeared. These were serious nonfiction or literary classics that found their prime markets in education.

social Issues   *The Case of the Disappearing Book Reviewer*

The cutbacks at newspapers have caused collateral damage to the book industry. As a cost-saving measure, many papers have downsized or completely eliminated the book review section. The *Chicago Tribune*, for example, shrank its book section and moved it from its high-circulation Sunday edition to low-circulation Saturday. The *Los Angeles Times* dropped its stand-alone book section, and the *Atlanta Journal-Constitution* eliminated the position of book review editor.

Part of the reason for the disappearance is money. Economic times are tough, and book publishers have cut back on print advertising in favor of point-of-purchase displays. Consequently, book review sections don't bring in much revenue and are the first to be chopped when things get tough.

What are the consequences of this trend? For one, it might ultimately hurt the newspaper even more in the future. Book readers are also newspaper readers. Encouraging reading, especially book reading, encourages reading the newspaper as well. The trend also signals that newspapers see their societal function differently. Newspapers initially carried book review sections not because they were profitable but as a public service to their readers. The book section was a contribution to the country's ongoing intellectual and cultural conversation.

There are some observers who suggest that the loss of newspaper book reviewers is not something to bemoan. In recent years, many blogs devoted to book reviewing have emerged (such as curledup.com). The authors of these blogs argue that reviewing has become less elitist and more democratic. Motivated readers can seek out dozens of different opinions rather than relying on the viewpoints of a privileged few. (Note that this is another example of how the interpretation function is shifting from the traditional media to the Internet.)

Can bloggers do the job as well as traditional reviewers? It's difficult to tell. Bloggers need no special training or education to write a review. You can have more confidence that a review in a newspaper was written by somebody who has some experience and expertise in the area. Book sections also tried to present a wide range of reviews, including books from all genres, from well-known and not-so-well-known authors and from major and not-so-major publishers. Bloggers may not display that same range.

The disappearance of the book review section is especially hard on authors. In the past, getting a book reviewed by a prestigious newspaper usually meant increased sales, visibility, and prestige. Getting reviewed by a blogger in Boise does not have the same cachet.

Moreover, expanded leisure time and more disposable income made book reading a popular means of recreation. In short, the book publishing business looked like a good investment for the future. Consequently, large corporations began acquiring book companies. Between 1958 and 1970, there were 307 mergers or acquisitions of publishing companies. These mergers brought new financial and management resources to the book industry, which helped it stay profitable during the 1970s.

The content of popular books during this period was varied. The first big paperback best-seller following World War II was Dr. Benjamin Spock's *Baby and Child Care*. Other notable paperbacks followed. Mickey Spillane's Mike Hammer was a hard-boiled private eye who appeared in six novels during the 1950s that sold 17 million copies. *Peyton Place*, a novel famous for its racy (for the time) parts, sold 10 million in paperback. All in all, from 1946 to 1970, paperback sales were dominated by light fiction and an occasional how-to book.

The Contemporary Book Industry

The wave of consolidation that began in the 1970s continued into the new century. Bertelsmann acquired Random House, and HarperCollins bought Morrow. Consequently, as of 2009, book publishing was dominated by a few big companies.

The 1990s and early 2000s ushered in major changes in the way books are marketed. Amazon.com was the first major company to offer books for sale online direct to consumers, with no trip to the bookstore necessary. Barnesandnoble.com and bordersstores.com provided similar services. In 2010 online sellers sold more than $4 billion worth of books.

Along with other mass media, book publishing suffered from the economic downturn at the end of the decade. From 2007 to 2009, book industry income declined about 7 percent but revenue increased slightly from 2009 to 2010. Traditional brick-and-mortar bookstores were having trouble making a profit as more people ordered books online or **e-books.** Book retailer Borders declared bankruptcy in 2011.

E-readers such as Amazon's Kindle, Barnes and Noble's Nook, and Apple's iPad were becoming increasingly popular. Experts estimate that Amazon has sold more than

3.5 million Kindles and readers have downloaded millions of e-books. Research from eMarketing suggests that 28 million people will own dedicated e-readers (such as Kindle, Nook, or Kobo) by 2013. Consequently, revenue from e-books has increased over the past few years while revenue from traditional print books has declined.

The content of contemporary books is remarkably varied. As the new decade began, fiction books by Stephanie Meyer (the Twilight series featuring vampires), Nora Roberts (romance stories), and Stieg Larsson (mystery stories) were on the best-seller lists. In nonfiction, Sarah Palin, Bill O'Reilly, and Mitch Albom had best-sellers. Diet and self-help books continue to be popular. All in all, the varied content of the book industry reflects the specialized tastes of today's reading public.

books in the digital age

Transition

For many years, books were the last stronghold of the analog age. Digital technology had made changes in the way books were produced but readers still purchased a tangible object, ink on paper bound between covers. In the last few years, however, the digital revolution has caught up with the book industry and it is well on the way to shifting away from atoms to bits.

E-Readers and E-Books

Early e-book readers were expensive, difficult to use, and had poor image quality. On top of that, there weren't enough e-book titles available to spur consumers into trying the new technology.

The situation changed in 2006 when Sony introduced its e-book reader with better graphics and an online store where customers could purchase e-books for 20 percent less than the print version. Books first had to be downloaded to a computer and then side-loaded to the Sony reader. Sony sold a respectable number of the devices but not enough to cause waves in the industry.

The next year online retailer Amazon introduced its Kindle e-book reader. Able to hold more than 1,000 average-size books, the Kindle featured wireless connectivity that enabled a book to be downloaded directly to the device in about a minute. The Kindle started slowly but eventually became Amazon's best-selling product ever. In 2011, Amazon announced that it sells more e-books via Kindle than print books. Amazon's online bookstore has nearly 1 million books available in digital form, and its 2011 revenue from the Kindle and downloaded Kindle products topped $5 billion. Other companies offer competing devices, such as the Nook, the Touch, the Kobo, and the Jetbook. Tablet computers such as the iPad can also serve as e-readers.

E-reader prices continue to drop, with Amazon's Kindle with Special Offers retailing at $114. Some e-books can be downloaded for free, but the price of the typical book ranges between $9 and $13. E-reader owners can also borrow digital books from public libraries.

E-book revenue is still far less than traditional print books revenue, but the trend is unmistakable. From 2009 to 2010, e-book sales increased by about 370 percent. Experts predict that this upward trend will continue for the next few years.

No one is suggesting that the e-book will ever totally replace the traditional ink-and-paper book. The people who like to read books will likely gravitate to the Kindle or other e-book readers. On the other hand, many people not only like to read books, they like to own them as well. These people appreciate the feel and the texture of a physical book and the sense of satisfaction that comes with a well-stocked library. They will continue to buy traditional books.

Printing on Demand

Another possibility thanks to digitization is **printing on demand**. This publishing method is a little less radical than that of the e-book. In this approach traditional publishers are still part of the mix, but books are printed and distributed differently.

media *Probe*   *How About a Book for $125,000?*

If you think textbooks are expensive, you probably haven't heard about Kraken Opus, a publisher of what can only be described as luxury literature. Of course, the books that Kraken publishes are not the same as what you would find in your library. Kraken throws in additional unique features that make its products more than mere books.

If you happen to be a fan of Indian cricket star Sachin Tendulkar, you can purchase a book reviewing his career that includes a signature page that was made by mixing in a pint of Tendulkar's blood with paper pulp. The book carried a price tag of $75,000 and only 10 copies were produced. They quickly sold out.

Another luxury publisher, Taschen Books, published 12 copies of a book of photos about the *Apollo* moon landing that contained a piece of moon rock. One of the books sold for $125,000.

Who buys such expensive items? Many collectors think that these books will increase in price just like rare coins or paintings. One hedge fund manager bought 20 copies of a $40,000 book about Ferrari racing cars and stored them in a climate-controlled facility.

One thing is certain: You probably won't see these kinds of books on a Kindle.

Here's how it works: Publishers create a huge database of books in digital form. A customer goes to a bookstore, browses through a catalogue, and selects a book. A machine in the bookstore then downloads the book and prints it while the customer waits.

Printing on demand has led to the growth of self-publishing. An author can upload a book to a company that specializes in printing on demand for free and pay only when someone downloads a book. University presses, which generally have many books that sell only a few hundred copies, have welcomed printing on demand because it allows them to keep all their special-interest titles available.

Mobile Books

The e-book is just as portable as the paper-and-ink version. Digital books can be downloaded to a dedicated book reader, such as Sony's e-book reader or Amazon's Kindle, or to other handheld devices, including cell phones. The Kindle has a feature that synchs it to an iPhone so that readers can start reading on the Kindle and continue reading on their iPhones. Amazon also announced plans to make their books available for BlackBerrys and other brands of phones.

User-Generated Content

The book publishing industry has experimented with user-generated content but has not been impressed with the results. The British Division of Penguin Books published a wiki-novel in 2007 but the effort was not well received. For the near future, at least, professional writers will be the main source of book content.

Social Media

The book publishing industry is experimenting with social media in a variety of ways. In the marketing area, several publishers have utilized social media to promote their books. Many books have their own Facebook pages. Authors are also using social media. An author's Facebook page or Twitter account can be used to promote a new book, stay in touch with fans, and keep people up-to-date on works in progress. For example, in mid-2011, mystery writer Patricia Cornwell's Facebook page contained a video plugging her newest book, an author biography, status updates, and an extensive photo album. Her Twitter page had more than 4,000 followers.

Social networking sites for people who write and read books have also sprung up. Shelfari.com, for example, describes itself as "a gathering place for authors, aspiring authors, publishers, and readers, [that] has many tools and features to help these groups connect with each other in a fun and engaging way." Library Thing and GoodReads are similar sites. HarperCollins recently started Authonomy, a Web site where aspiring

media *Probe*   *Kindle or Traditional Textbooks?*

Fans of the Kindle and other e-readers have suggested that the devices should be a perfect fit for college textbooks. E-readers are more environmentally friendly, easier to carry than big, bulky textbooks, and e-books are cheaper than paper-and-ink books.

Interestingly, students prefer the old, traditional text to the Kindle. At least, that's the finding of a recent study done by the Book Industry Study Group. About 75 percent of students reported that they liked the printed text more than the e-reader. When asked to explain their choice, students reported that traditional books had more permanence and that it was easier to make marginal notes. Moreover, it was easier to quickly skim through pages and jump from place to place in a print textbook. Finally, students thought that printed books had more resale value.

Keep in mind that e-readers will continue to improve and the situation may change, but for now college students still prefer the paper-and-ink book.

authors could submit manuscripts and ideas and have them critiqued by other members of the community.

defining features of books

Books are the least "mass" of the mass media. It took about 40 years to sell 20 million copies of *Gone with the Wind,* but more than 50 million people watched the movie version in a single evening when it came to television. Even a flop TV show might have a million people in its audience, whereas a popular hardcover book might make the best-seller list with 125,000 copies sold. Even a mass-market paperback might sell only about 5 million copies.

Books, however, can have a cultural impact that far outweighs their modest audience size. *Uncle Tom's Cabin* is credited with helping to change a nation's attitude toward slavery. Dr. Spock and his *Baby and Child Care* altered the way parents brought up their children and became the target of critics who blamed him and his methods for the social unrest of the 1960s. Rachel Carson's *Silent Spring* changed the nation's attitudes toward the environment.

Finally, books are the oldest and most enduring of the mass media. Gutenberg printed his first book in the 15th century. Public libraries have been around for hundreds of years. Many individuals have extensive collections of books in their own home libraries. People throw away newspapers and magazines shortly after reading them, but most save their books.

sound byte

Quick Reads

Don't have time to slog through all those novels for your English lit class? Check out rinkworks.com and its Book-a-Minute Link for a really bare-bones summary.

Here, with apologies to F. Scott Fitzgerald, is the hyper-condensed version of *The Great Gatsby:*

Gatsby: Daisy, I made all this money because I love you.

Daisy: I cannot reciprocate because I represent the American Dream.

Gatsby: Now I must die because I also represent the American Dream. *(Gatsby dies)*

Nick: I hate New Yorkers.

organization of the book industry

The book publishing industry can be divided into three segments: publishers, distributors, and retailers.

Publishers

The publishing segment consists of the 2,500 or so establishments that transform manuscripts submitted by authors into books that are sought by readers. Every year these companies publish 100,000 to 150,000 new titles. Book publishing is a highly segmented industry. Publishers have developed a classification system for the industry based on the market that is served. The following are the 10 major divisions suggested by the Association of American Publishers:

Big publishers, such as McGraw-Hill, use Facebook to promote their products.

1. *Trade books:* Titles aimed at the general consumer and sold primarily through bookstores. They can be hardbound or softbound and include works for juveniles and adults. Trade books include fiction, nonfiction, biographies, cookbooks, and art books.

2. *Religious books:* Includes Bibles, hymnals, prayer books, theology, and other literature of a devotional nature.

3. *Professional books:* Titles aimed at doctors, lawyers, scientists, accountants, business managers, architects, engineers, and all others who need a personal reference library in their work.

4. *Book club and mail order:* These may at first sound more like part of a distribution channel than a division of the publishing segment, but some book clubs publish their own books and almost all prepare special editions for their members. Mail-order publications consist of books created for the general public and marketed by direct mail. These are different from book clubs because the books are marketed by the publisher and customers do not incur any membership obligations in an organization.

5. *Mass-market paperbacks:* Softbound volumes on all subjects that achieve their major sales in places other than bookstores. Typically, these are the books sold from racks in supermarkets, newsstands, drugstores, airports, chain stores, and the like.

6. *Elementary and secondary textbooks:* Hard- and softcover books, workbooks, manuals, and other printed materials intended for use in the classroom. Logically enough, schools are the primary market for these publishers. (This division is also referred to as *elhi*—from *el*ementary and *hi*gh school.)

7. *Higher education:* Texts and workbooks for the college market.

8. *Audiobooks:* Books released on disc that consist of a person reading the text of a book.

9. *E-books:* As mentioned above, those digital versions available for downloading to computers or special readers.

10. *Other:* These include university presses, reference books, and standardized tests.

Table 7-1 shows the relative importance of each of these segments to the industry. As can be seen, trade, professional, and textbook publishing are the major divisions, accounting for 79 percent of sales.

table 7-1 Sales by Publishing Industry Division, 2010	Division	Percentage of Sales
	Trade	31
	Professional	22
	Elhi	14
	Higher education	12
	Book club/mail order	1
	Mass-market paperback	4
	E-books	4
	Audio books	1
	All other	11

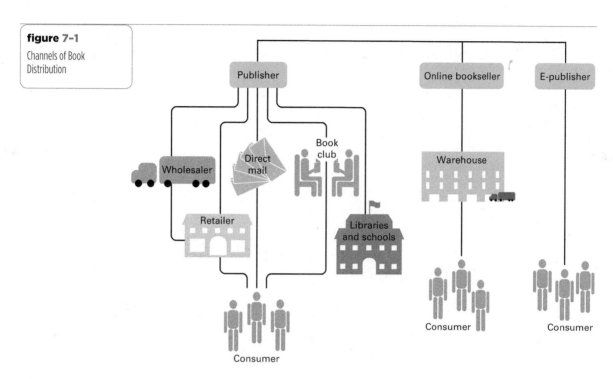

figure 7-1

Channels of Book Distribution

Distributors

The Internet has drastically changed the book distribution system. There are now three main channels by which books get to consumers. In the traditional method the publisher usually ships copies of the book to a wholesaler or distributor who, in turn, sends the books to a retail outlet where consumers can buy them. Online booksellers such as Amazon.com use a different approach. The consumer orders a book from the Web site, and the book is shipped from the seller's warehouse directly to the consumer, bypassing the distributor and retail outlet. E-books, of course, go directly from publisher to consumer, bypassing everything in between. Figure 7-1 illustrates these distribution arrangements.

Retailers

There are around 9,000 bookstores in the United States plus the big online booksellers. As of 2010, Amazon.com was the biggest bookseller in the United States and the rest of the world. The Barnes and Noble chain was in second place. Borders/Waldenbooks went into bankruptcy in 2010 and by 2011 closed all of its stores. In 2010, these three big chains accounted for about $13 billion in revenue (this figure includes magazine sales, stationery, coffee, and so on). Other retail channels include college bookstores and direct-to-consumer sellers such as book clubs.

ownership in the book industry

The book industry is dominated by large conglomerates with interests in other media. The top five companies as of 2010 were the following:

1. *Pearson Publishing:* A global media company that is the world's largest educational publisher, with imprints such as Scott, Foresman and Prentice-Hall. It also owns the Penguin Group of consumer publishing firms (Penguin, Dutton, and Viking) as well as the *Financial Times* business newspaper.

2. *Random House:* Part of the Bertelsmann media empire, which includes interests in 600 companies in 63 countries and is engaged in books, magazines, TV, and radio.

media *Wizardry and E-books*
Probe

J. K. Rowling, author of the Harry Potter series of books that have sold millions of copies in their print format, was shrewd enough to retain the rights to the e-book edition of the novels. The author recently announced the launch of Pottermore, a Web site that will be the only place where readers can download e-book versions of the Harry Potter novels. By retaining e-book rights, Rowling stands to make far more money than if she had sold them along with rights to the print version. The site promises to make the e-editions compatible with all e-readers.

In addition, Pottermore will offer new illustrations, interactive online games, and social networking. It is expected that the Web site will not only help e-book sales but will also inspire new interest in the print version.

3. *HarperCollins:* Rupert Murdoch's worldwide communications company, which owns HarperCollins as well as 20th Century Fox, the Fox TV network, and various newspapers and magazines.

4. *Simon & Schuster:* Part of the CBS Corporation, a conglomerate that has TV networks, radio stations and a radio network, and cable networks.

5. *Hachette Book Group:* Formed in 2006, when a French company, Hachette Livre, acquired Time Warner Books. The book group includes Little, Brown and Company, Grand Central Books, and Hachette Digital.

producing the book

Departments and Staff

There are four major departments in a typical publishing company: (1) editorial, (2) production, (3) marketing, and (4) general administration or business.

The editorial department is in charge of dealing with authors; it is responsible for selecting manuscripts and preparing them for publication. Some editors specialize in procuring new manuscripts, and some read manuscripts, write reports on them, and recommend acceptance, revision, or rejection. Other editors work with accepted manuscripts, checking grammar, language, accuracy, and so on.

As its name suggests, the production department oversees the physical design of the book. This department is responsible for type style, composition, paper, printing, and binding.

The marketing department supervises sales, promotions, and publicity. The actual type of marketing depends on the book and its intended audience. Publishers of elhi textbooks sell mainly to school systems. Mass-market paperbacks are sold to retailers who, in turn, sell them to the public. Advertising in trade magazines, television interviews, and reviews in respected publications and blogs are common marketing tools.

The business manager at a publishing company is responsible for several functions. One of the most important is accounting. Further, this department prepares budgets and makes long-range financial forecasts. Other responsibilities include dealing with internal personnel policies and supervising the general day-to-day operational needs of the company.

The Publication Process

Editors get their books in three ways: (1) through submissions by agents, (2) as unsolicited books sent in by authors, and (3) as book ideas generated by the editor. Most trade manuscripts are submitted through literary agents. Agents are known quantities and will not generally submit manuscripts that they know are unacceptable to the editor. Unsolicited manuscripts are given an unflattering name in the business: "slush." As they come in, these manuscripts are put in the slush pile and eventually read, if the author is lucky, by an editorial assistant. Most of the time they are rejected with a form letter, but every

media *Probe*   *Meet the Author (Virtually)*

In years past, authors would promote a book by going on multicity book tours, where they might be interviewed on local TV and hold book signings at local bookstores. With the cost of travel going up and the number of bookstores available to host a signing going down (especially after Borders closed its stores in 2011), publisher Simon & Schuster and its authors have developed a new way to connect with readers and promote their products: video interviews on the Web. The publisher thinks that these videos will help authors cultivate a one-to-one relationship with their readers, something important in today's book publishing arena.

Here's how they do it. Readers submit e-mail questions to an author. The author scans the questions, chooses the ones to be answered, and responds with a video message made on the author's personal Web cam. The questions and the video answers are then displayed on a Web page,

where the questions appear under a video player. Visitors to the site simply click on a question that interests them and the corresponding author video plays on the screen.

A recent visit to the Simon & Schuster Web site found video interviews with a dozen authors, including thriller author Brad Thor and teen novelist Lisa McMann. Sample questions for Thor: "How does it feel being banned in Saudi Arabia?" "Do you still live in Utah?" Readers asked McMann, "What's your favorite book (other than your own of course)?" and "You've got nice hair. Would you ever shave your head?" Her answer: Probably, but it would have to be for the right thing.

In addition to answering questions, the videos give authors a chance to build a closer connection with readers. Some authors include a video tour of their office or a look at their bookcase while other authors just mug for the camera. McMann's video, for example, showed off her dancing ability.

once in a while an author gets through. For instance, E. D. Baker's *The Frog Princess* has sold well and has been translated into several languages. Editors also generate ideas for books. If an editor has a good idea for a book, he or she will generally talk to one or more agents who will suggest likely candidates for the assignment. This is another good reason that writers should have agents. In any case, the author typically submits a proposal consisting of a cover letter, a brief description of the planned book, a list of reasons it should be published, an analysis of the potential market, an outline or a table of contents, and perhaps one or two sample chapters. The proposal usually goes to an acquisitions editor and is evaluated. If the publishing decision is favorable, a contract is signed, and the author begins work in earnest.

Editorial work starts as soon as the author submits chapters to the publisher. Editors look at the overall thrust of the book to make sure it makes sense and achieves its original intent. Moreover, the mechanics of the book are checked to make sure that the general level of writing is acceptable, that all footnotes are in order, that all necessary permissions to reproduce material from other sources have been obtained, and that all artwork is present. Eventually, both author and editors will produce a manuscript that is mutually satisfactory.

While all this editing is going on, other decisions are being made about scheduling, designing the interior look of the book, and designing the cover. At the same time, other editors are preparing the files for the e-book edition. When everything is in order, the book is printed, bound, and sent to the warehouse to await distribution, or it is distributed online.

the economics of book publishing

The book industry is slowly recovering from the recession at the end of the decade. Revenue increased slightly from 2009 to 2010 (see Figure 7-2). Revenue from e-books was increasing but publishers were worried that it would not be enough to offset future losses from traditional hardback and paperback books.

At the consumer level, it is obvious that books have become more expensive. In 2011, a hardcover copy of *Bossypants* by Tina Fey had a list price of $27 while best-selling paperbacks retailed for about $10. E-books have also gotten more expensive, with prices in the $12–14 range.

decision
makers   *Jeff Bezos*

Jeff Bezos was always tinkering with things. When he was three, he took apart his bed. Eleven years later, he tried to make a hovercraft out of a vacuum cleaner. Sixteen years after that, he tinkered with the way books were sold and totally revolutionized the business by starting Amazon.com.

After growing up in Houston and Miami, Bezos enrolled at Princeton, where he studied computer science and engineering. After a couple of jobs in the financial marketplace, he wound up at a Wall Street investment company. One day in 1993, while doing financial research, he came across a startling statistic: The Internet was growing at a rate of 2,300 percent a year. Bezos recognized the tremendous selling potential of the Net and decided to launch an online business. He reasoned that things that are big mail-order sellers should also do well online. Accordingly, he made a list of the top 20 mail-order products and determined that books would be the best item to sell. A virtual bookstore would have the space to list all the millions of books in print; no brick-and-mortar store could do that. Further, book wholesalers had already produced CD-ROMs that listed all available titles. Bezos recognized that the existing book databases could easily be put online.

Bezos's family and friends invested $300,000 in his idea, and Bezos moved to Seattle, the home of many Net-savvy programmers who would be needed to get the business online. Seattle was also the home of one of the biggest book wholesalers in the country.

Working out of his garage, Bezos created a Web site that he tested among his friends. It seemed to work well, and Bezos decided to open the site to everybody. But what to call it? He originally wanted to call it Cadabra .com, as in "abracadabra," the magic incantation. When he tried this name out on his lawyer, however, the lawyer thought Bezos said "Cadaver.com" and wanted to know why he would name his site after a dead body. Bezos went back to the drawing board and eventually settled on Amazon.com, after one of the world's longest and most powerful rivers.

The rest, as they say, is Internet history. The company grew quickly. In 1996 Amazon.com had 300 employees. In 2010 it had about 33,000. From a few thousand customers in its first year, it now has more than 20 million in about 150 countries. Sales in 2010 exceeded $34 billion. Its brand name is more recognizable than Burger King or Barbie. Amazon .com has also branched out from books and now sells CDs, toys, electronics, and gifts from its Web site. Amazon.com is now the biggest bookseller in the world.

Bezos shook things up once again by introducing the Kindle e-book reader, Amazon's best-selling item of all time. Additionally, Amazon now offers downloadable music and movies. Amazon has reached iconic status as a marketing channel.

---

figure 7-2

Book Publishing Revenue, 1983–2010

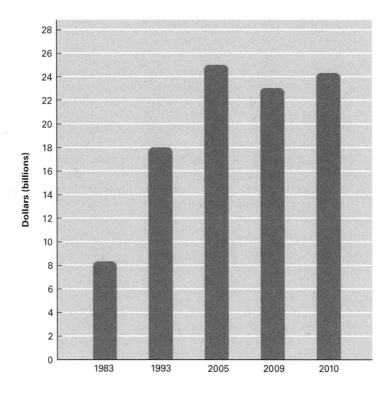

table 7-2	Hardcover Book		E-Book	
Cost Breakdown of a Hardcover Book and an E-book	**Item**	**Amount**	**Item**	**Amount**
	Retail Price	$26.00	Retail Price	$12.99
	Retailer	$13.00	Apple Distributor Fee	$3.90
	Printing and Shipping	$3.25	Converting Text to Digital File	$0.50
	Cover, Typesetting, Copy Editing	$0.80	(Not Applicable)	
	Marketing	$1.00	Marketing	$0.80
	Author Royalty*	$3.90	Author Royalty**	$3.25
	Publisher Overhead and Profit	$4.05	Publisher Overhead and Profit	$4.54

* Assumes 15 percent of retail price. This percentage may vary.

** Calculated at 25 percent of retail cost. Other publishers might use a different formula.

A publisher has two main sources of income: (1) the money that comes from book sales and (2) money from **subsidiary rights** (sales to book clubs, foreign rights, paperback rights, and reprint permissions). Of these two the income from book sales is more important. It should be noted, however, that the publisher does not get all the money from the sale of a book. The list price is discounted for wholesalers and booksellers. These discounts might amount to 40 percent for many books.

Table 7-2 contains a breakdown of the revenue generated by a hardcover edition of a book priced at $26 and its e-book version priced at $12.99. (We're assuming the e-book is purchased from Apple for viewing on an iPad.) It appears that publishers make slightly more from e-books, but keep in mind that at present e-books account for only a small portion of a publisher's revenue. Also keep in mind that a publisher can receive more revenue by publishing a paperback edition of the hardcover book. As yet, there is no paperback equivalent of an e-book.

Advances and acquisition rights are two of the big expenses in publishing. For example, Tina Fey reportedly received about $5 million for *Bossypants* and Hillary Clinton was paid $8 million for her autobiography.

the book publishing audience

Sources of Feedback

The most important form of audience feedback in the book industry is the best-seller lists compiled by newspapers such as the *New York Times* and *USA Today* and the trade publication *Publisher's Weekly*. These organizations use slightly different methods to tabulate a rank ordering of the best-selling books, but all involve collecting data from a sample of the various channels of book distribution—chain bookstores, independent bookstores, newsstands, and e-books—and then assigning various weights to the numbers to come up with the rankings. Making the best-seller list is important because many bookstores automatically order large numbers of all books that make the list. Consequently, appearing on the list can mean added sales for a book.

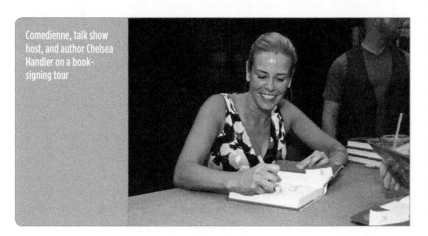

Comedienne, talk show host, and author Chelsea Handler on a book-signing tour

critical🌐cultural issues

Labor versus Management in Journalism Textbooks

As mentioned in Chapter 2, the critical/cultural approach examines texts, broadly defined. In a paper presented at the 2000 convention of the Association for Education in Journalism and Mass Communication, Dr. Jon Bekken took a more literal approach and examined textbooks—in this case, journalism textbooks—to discover if these texts were instilling a professional ideology in their readers.

Bekken notes that studies of the coverage of business conflicts have generally found that the media cover these disputes from a perspective that does not favor labor or labor unions. For example, labor reporting focuses on the inconvenience strikes cause for consumers rather than on the issues that lead to a strike. Wages rather than health and safety are portrayed as the central concern of labor. In addition, there is a trend toward ignoring labor news altogether. Fewer than a dozen newspapers employ even one full-time labor reporter.

Bekken wondered if these attitudes might have been fostered during a reporter's academic training. He was specifically interested in the way organized labor was portrayed in 29 media writing and reporting textbooks. After performing a critical/cultural analysis, he concluded that the texts marginalized labor, making it seem unimportant. For instance, he noted that some textbooks have exercises that ask students to write articles about layoffs or hiring freezes based on press releases or notes from interviews with corporate or government officials. The subtle lesson conveyed in these exercises is that the important perspectives do not include those of labor. Other texts simply make little or no mention of labor or labor unions even though many newspaper workers belong to the International Typographical Union and several newspapers have been plagued by labor-management troubles.

Most texts gloss over labor problems in the newspaper industry itself. Health risks such as carpal tunnel syndrome, poor working conditions, and inadequate pay are seldom mentioned. The idea that joining a union might help address some of these issues is not discussed.

Bekken chronicles other examples of how labor is almost trivialized. One textbook devotes as many words to covering labor as it does to covering weddings. Another urges reporters to avoid an antibusiness attitude in their stories and to rely on corporate officials, financial analysts, and government regulators as sources for business news. When textbooks do discuss how to cover labor, their emphasis is on covering strikes, violence connected with strikes, or unfair labor practices.

What are some of the results of the way these texts depict labor? As Bekken says,

> Students carry blind spots towards labor inculcated in their academic training into newsrooms across the country. Editors and publishers have slashed the number of labor reporters. . . . Reporters and editors typically do not look to the labor movement for news—rather they wait for strikes, or include labor in discussions of special interest groups said to dominate the political system.

Bekken ends his analysis by noting that in recent decades textbook authors have tried to remove sexist language and pay more attention to cultural sensitivity. Moreover, newer editions of reporting texts have been expanded to cover topics such as religious news and consumer news. Nonetheless, he points out, most journalism textbooks do not do a good job covering the large number of Americans who labor for a living. The fact that many of the students who read these books go on to ignore labor in their own reporting ought not surprise us.

In addition to best-seller lists, the industry uses Nielsen BookScan, a service that measures actual sales data from about 6,500 major retailers across the United States, including big chains and independent stores. In a typical week the service tabulates sales figures on more than 300,000 different titles. Companies that subscribe to BookScan can access sales data broken down by region, subject, and format.

Audiences

According to a 2008 survey by the National Endowment for the Arts, about 119 million Americans reported reading at least one book in the past year. In 2002, the comparable number was about 116 million. The increase, however, did not keep pace with the increase in the adult population for those years. In percentage terms, about 54 percent of Americans read books in 2008, down from 57 percent in 2002.

Literary reading—defined as reading novels, short stories, plays, and poems—jumped about 4 percent from 2002. Interestingly, the survey found that the biggest increase in literary reading was among 18- to 24-year-olds, reversing an earlier trend. In addition, the survey found that about 15 percent read some form of literature online.

ethical issues   *"Truthiness" or Consequences?*

Comedy Central's Stephen Colbert introduced the word *truthiness* to the American people during one of his reports. As defined by the *Urban Dictionary, truthiness* means the quality of stating concepts that one wishes or believes to be true rather than the facts. Odd as it may seem, truthiness was at the core of one of the most publicized controversies in the book publishing industry in 2006.

At issue was James Frey's *A Million Little Pieces,* a powerful memoir about the author's struggles with addiction, the law, and himself, concluding with his eventual rehabilitation. The book was published in 2003 and became a huge best-seller when Oprah Winfrey chose it as one of her book club selections. Shortly thereafter, thesmokinggun.com reported that it was unable to find any record of Frey's alleged run-ins with the law and subsequent prison time. Faced with these discrepancies, Frey admitted that parts of his memoir were, in fact, fictional. For example, Frey wrote that he spent three months in jail; the actual police records showed that he spent only a few hours in custody. He also admitted that he lied when he wrote about running over a police officer and undergoing a root canal without Novocain, nor could he produce any records that supported his claims of struggles in rehab.

The reaction to these revelations ran the gamut from condemnation to support. Oprah Winfrey initially supported Frey, claiming that, even with the fabrications, the "underlying message" of the book was still valid. Other literary types sounded a similar theme. They argued that a memoir was based not on what actually happened but on how the author remembered what had happened. It was the "essential message," or the "essence of the experience," or "the larger truth," or the "inner core of the story" that counted, not factual matters.

Readers, however, thought otherwise. Many said they felt betrayed. Even Oprah changed her stance, removed the book from her reading list, and berated the author for his transgressions during an episode of her program. Two readers even filed a lawsuit against the publisher for breach of contract and deceptive advertising for calling the book a work of nonfiction.

What are the ethical implications of this situation? Does the author of a personal memoir have an ethical obligation to his or her readers to inform them that what they are reading might contain some exaggerations or embellishments or even outright fiction? What about the publisher? Should it publish a disclaimer about the accuracy of a memoir? Is it under any ethical obligation to check on the veracity of the information it publishes? (Interestingly, courts have held that publishers are not legally bound to check facts, but what is their ethical obligation to their readers and to other memoirists who actually write the truth and whose reputation may be sullied by those who don't?)

In the aftermath of the scandal, several things occurred. Some publishers conceded that they will be looking more closely at some of the more extreme claims made by authors who submit memoirs. James Frey was dropped by his publisher and his contract for additional books was canceled. Plans for a movie based on the book (Brad Pitt and Jennifer Aniston bought the film rights) were put on hold. Despite all of these developments, "truthiness" can still be profitable. Frey's royalties for *A Million Little Pieces* amounted to more than $4 million.

It appears, however, that the lessons of the James Frey saga were not taken to heart. Truthiness, unfortunately, is still around. In 2008, it was revealed that *Love and Consequences,* published by Penguin, was a fake. The book purported to be about a racially mixed woman, raised in poverty by an African American mother, who sold drugs for a tough Los Angeles street gang in order to survive. In truth, the author was a middle-class white woman who went to private school and admitted making up the whole story. The publisher recalled all the books and canceled a proposed book tour. It is not known if the author got to keep any advance money.

More recently, a *60 Minutes* report questioned the veracity of parts of *Three Cups of Tea,* Greg Mortenson's story of his adventures in Pakistan. Truthiness lives on.

the book publishing industry

 >>

Book publishing is a relatively small industry. There are only about 70,000–75,000 jobs in the entire business. Like the other print media, the book industry has been hard hit by the economic downturn. Consequently, the career outlook, at least for now, is depressing. On the bright side, despite all the pundits who keep saying that reading is a lost art, the recent readership figures released by the National Endowment for the Arts show that book reading is still holding its own. If the economy bounces back, then career prospects should improve.

The career outlook in the various media industries changes quickly. For a more current description of conditions in the book publishing industry and a more detailed look at career options, please consult the book's Web site: www.mhhe.com/dominick12e.

main points

■ The book is the oldest form of mass communication. Early books were printed by hand until the invention of movable type and the printing press.

■ In early America publishers were also printers. Books became more popular during the 17th and 18th centuries.

■ From 1900 to 1945, the book publishing industry became more commercialized. Continuing consolidation has resulted in a modern book industry that is dominated by a few large companies.

■ E-books and e-book readers are becoming more popular.

■ The book industry consists of publishers, distributors, and retailers. The emergence of online booksellers has changed the way books are sold and distributed.

■ The book publishing industry is trying to cope with unfavorable economic conditions.

questions for review

1. How has the content of popular books changed from the 17th to the 21st century?

2. What are the defining features of books?

3. What are the main revenue sources for book publishers?

4. What is the difference between a trade book and a mass-market paperback?

questions for critical thinking

1. What would you prefer—a traditional ink-and-paper book (such as this one) or an e-book? Why?

2. Book sales have not increased in the last couple of years. What might be some of the reasons? What impact, if any, do you think the Internet has had on book reading?

3. What advantages and disadvantages are connected with a book industry dominated by a few big firms?

4. Read "Critical/Cultural Issues: "Labor versus Management in Journalism Textbooks" on page 172, and then consider the following: To what extent—and why—does it matter whether such texts avoid discussing labor problems in the media industry or carry a promanagement bias? If you are taking a course in writing/reporting, look at the text you are using. Does it marginalize or trivialize labor? What can students do to raise awareness of these issues in class?

key terms

e-book (p. 162)
e-reader (p. 162)

printing on demand (p. 163)

subsidiary rights (p. 171)

internet resources

Online Learning Center

On the Online Learning Center home page, **www.mhhe.com/dominick12e,** *select* **Student Center** *and then* **Chapter 7.**

1. Use the Learning Objectives, Chapter Outline, and Main Points sections to review this chapter.

2. Test your knowledge of the chapter using the multiple choice and flashcard features of the site.

3. Expand your knowledge of concepts and topics discussed in the chapter with additional Questions for Critical Thinking and Internet Exercises.

surfing the internet

Remember, Web sites change all the time; some move, some evaporate, and some transform.

www.amazon.com/kindle-store-ebooks-newspapers-blogs/
Check out this site even if you don't own a Kindle. Browse more than 950,000 items.

www.bookweb.org
The home page of the American Booksellers Association, the trade group representing independent bookstores. Contains the current best-sellers list.

www.bookwire.com
Takes a look inside the book business. Includes news, features, and links to other related sites.

www.bisg.org
The home page of the Book Industry Study Group. Provides research information about the industry.

www.publishersweekly.com
The online version of *Publisher's Weekly,* the leading trade magazine. Includes job listings.

Chapter**8**

radio

This chapter will prepare you to:

- explain how radio broadcasting developed in the 1920s
- recognize how television affected radio
- discuss the defining features of radio
- understand that radio gets programming from local stations, networks, and syndication companies
- explain how the digital age is affecting radio
- appreciate the potential of HD radio
- understand how the Internet and tablet computers have affected the radio industry

In early 2011, if you did a Google or a Bing search for the term "radio," the first item that popped up on both search engines was Pandora Internet Radio—not bad for a company that just a few years ago was on the verge of bankruptcy.

Pandora got its start in 2000 as part of an academic project by Pandora founder Tim Westergren to analyze all types of music and to classify them according to several criteria including lyric content, rhythm, instrumentation, melody, and harmony. After a few years of categorization, Westergren realized that his database could create a customized radio station for an individual listener based on the listener's musical tastes. Tell Pandora that you like Stevie Nicks and Pandora might recommend Fleetwood Mac or Tom Petty. Thus Pandora Internet Radio was born.

Pandora Internet Radio quickly became popular but the company struggled financially. Subscribers could opt for a free, ad-supported version that limited the number of songs they could listen to, or they could pay a fee and listen to all the songs they wanted. As an Internet radio station, Pandora had to pay performance royalties on the music it played. In 2007, the Copyright Royalty Board raised the rates and Pandora was near bankruptcy. Some employees worked for months without being paid.

Then two things happened that changed everything. The first was the iPhone. Pandora became the second-most downloaded app for the iPhone. In two years, its audience nearly doubled. As of 2010, it had about 80 million subscribers. Next, Pandora negotiated a new royalty payment arrangement with the Copyright Royalty Board that kept it in business.

The company also realized that the future of Internet radio depended on having the service available on as many platforms as possible. Pandora is the number-one down-loaded app for the iPad. It is also available on Internet-connected TV sets and Blu-ray disc players. Pandora is also bundled with other Internet services such as Netflix and Flickr. It's even available on a WiFi-equipped refrigerator made by Samsung.

Pandora's latest venture involves getting into the family car. More than half of all radio listening occurs in the car and the company is eager to tap this market. Pandora has already made deals with GM, Ford, and Mercedes-Benz to have its service available on the dash-board of new models. Traditional AM and FM stations, the ones that dominate in-car listen-ing, are looking at these developments with great interest.

In mid-2011, Pandora also caught the attention of Wall Street. Its initial public offering of stock brought the company about $235 million.

The growth of Pandora demonstrates that the traditional radio business will never be the same. The radio business today is actually several businesses: the traditional terrestrial broadcasting stations such as WGN in Chicago or WABC in New York; Sirius XM and satellite radio; and online radio stations such as Pandora.

Let's start by getting some historical perspective on radio, beginning with the terrestrial kind.

a brief history

In 1887 Heinrich Hertz, a German physicist, successfully sent and detected radio waves. Guglielmo Marconi used Hertz's efforts to build a wireless communication device that could send Morse code—dots and dashes—from a transmitter to a receiver. Marconi started a wireless telegraphy company that would play an important part in early radio's development.

Reginald Fessenden and Lee De Forest provided the breakthroughs that would make broadcasting—as opposed to sending dots and dashes—possible. Fessenden, with the help of General Electric (GE), built a high-speed, continuous-wave generator that could broadcast the human voice and music. De Forest invented the vacuum tube, originally called the *audion*, which made it much easier to receive radio signals.

The development of early radio was hampered by legal battles over patent rights to various inventions. When World War I broke out, the U.S. Navy assumed responsibility for all relevant patents, and radio made great technical strides during the war.

The Birth of Commercial Radio

Big Business After the war corporate America recognized the potential of radio. A new company, the Radio Corporation of America (RCA), was formed and acquired the assets of the U.S. division of the Marconi Company. Stock in RCA was held by some of the biggest companies of the period: AT&T, GE, and Westinghouse. Note that these companies thought RCA would be in the wireless telegraphy business. Despite the efforts of Fessenden and De Forest, it was hard to envision that broadcasting news and entertainment to the general public could make money.

Some individuals, however, were more prescient. David Sarnoff, an employee of the Marconi Company who later became head of RCA, suggested that one day this new invention would become a "radio music box." Sarnoff himself would be one of the central figures in the development of this new medium.

A young boy listens to an early radio set.

A Mass Audience   Frank Conrad, an engineer for Westinghouse in Pittsburgh, tinkered with radio as a hobby. He built a radio transmitter in his garage and started broadcasting recorded music, reporting sports scores, and showcasing the musical abilities of his sons. In a short time he had attracted an enthusiastic audience of radio fans. A local department store started selling radio sets so that more people could hear Conrad's programs. Westinghouse built a station so that Conrad's signal would be heard by more people. Westinghouse also built the radio sets and received "free" advertising because of its connection with the station. The station, KDKA, signed on in 1920 and is still on the air, making it the country's oldest station.

KDKA was a success. In response, RCA, GE, and AT&T, along with many other companies and organizations, started radio stations. Radio listening became a national craze. By discovering that an audience existed for broadcast programs intended for the general public, radio found the role it would play for the foreseeable future.

Better Receivers   Early radio receivers were not user-friendly. They were powered by an assortment of large, bulky, and sometimes leaky batteries. Tuning required patience, a steady hand, and a knowledge of electronics.

By 1926, however, set manufacturers had improved their product. New radios ran on household current, could be tuned with just two knobs, had better antennas, and looked like a fashionable piece of furniture. Between 1925 and 1930, 17 million radio sets were sold, and radio was becoming truly a mass medium.

The Commercialization of Radio

One of the curious things about early radio broadcasting was that very little of it was done by broadcasters. The early stations were owned by a polyglot of organizations. WLS in Chicago was owned by Sears, Roebuck (*World's Largest Store*); WGN by the *Chicago Tribune* (*World's Greatest Newspaper*); WSM in Nashville by the National Life and Accident Insurance Company (*We Shield Millions*); and WHB in Kansas City by the Sweeney Automotive and Electrical School.

Early broadcasting was not expensive, and radio station owners figured they got their money's worth through the exposure they received through the station. Before long, however, operating expenses began to pile up, and stations searched for a way to have their stations turn a profit.

Nobody knew quite how to do it. Some people thought listeners should send in voluntary contributions; others wanted a tax on radio tubes. It was the phone company that finally came up with a workable plan. AT&T began selling time on WEAF, their flagship station in New York, to anybody who wanted to broadcast a message. The most logical customers for this new service were companies that had things to sell. Thus, in 1922 the Queensboro Realty Company paid $300 for five radio talks that extolled the benefits of living in the country, preferably on a lot bought from Queensboro Realty. Other companies quickly recognized the advertising potential of this new medium and bought time on WEAF and other stations. The problem of financing radio broadcasting was solved—broadcasting would be supported by advertising.

Networks   Linking radio stations into a **network** made good economic sense. Rather than having each individual station pay the costs of producing its own program, it was much cheaper for all stations to share the cost of a single program and broadcast the same show on all stations. Moreover, a linked network of stations gave advertisers the ability to reach a larger audience in a wider geographic area.

critical ⊕ cultural issues

Department Stores and the Early Days of Radio

Contributed by Noah Arceneaux, Assistant Professor of Media Studies, San Diego State University.

In 1922, the year of the famed "broadcasting boom," a few dozen department stores built their own radio stations. These stations were not as numerous as those operated by newspapers or universities, though they warrant a close examination. Radio, as a new technology, could have developed in a number of ways, though department stores promoted the idea that it should be used to deliver non-offensive entertainment, mixed with advertisements. The success of their stations helped to pave the way for the advertising-supported, commercial system of broadcasting that would eventually dominate the American radio industry.

The fact that department stores were early adopters of radio is not surprising given their prior uses of electric lighting, elevators, and telephones. Many individuals in the late 19th century first encountered these technologies inside the stores. These retailers also had a history of developing new forms of promotion, such as full-page, illustrated newspaper advertisements. Stores also organized elaborate promotional events, fashion shows, musical concerts, and parades to impress their customers. When Horne's department store in Pittsburgh promoted Frank Conrad's experimental broadcasts in an advertisement, it was not trying to inspire a national phenomenon. It was simply doing what department stores had done all along.

For their radio programming, stores favored opera, classical, and conservatory music. In an attempt to support the least offensive kinds of content, they avoided radical political views as well as jazz, which was considered vulgar by some elite members of society at the time. Their radio advertisements were not overt, though whenever the announcer identified the station, he would always mention the name of the store (and sometimes the address). In order to maximize the publicity value, the stores presented lectures based on specific types of merchandise, such as shoes or women's clothing. It was hoped that a listener would associate the store with this particular item, an association that might result in a sale.

The balance between commercial advertisements and editorial content is a delicate issue for all forms of media, though many store stations were praised for the high quality of their programming. Most listeners did not object to the indirect advertising, and some of the stations, such as WOR in Newark and WIP in Philadelphia, established national reputations. In the second half of the 1920s, resistance to advertising decreased, and more stations adopted this practice. The number of store stations decreased at this time, as retailers discovered that it was easier to buy airtime on other stations than to establish their own.

Department stores also made a deliberate effort to bring women into the radio audience. The majority of listeners in the early 1920s were male, many of whom had built their own receivers from spare parts. The stores, which catered to female shoppers, sold attractively designed, factory-built receivers intended for the living room. In the midmorning hours, when presumably all the men were at work, the store stations aired cooking, sewing, or fashion programs to entertain housewives. The hosts of these programs were women, while announcers for other kinds of shows were almost exclusively men.

This brief history illustrates a critical/cultural approach to media in that it does not take a dominant system—in this case, commercial broadcasting—to be natural or logical. The goal rather is to explain how this particular system came to be and how it was promoted by specific institutions, such as department stores. The groups that supported the commercial system of broadcasting did not simply impose their vision on a passive public. Listeners enjoyed the programming from the first commercial stations and accepted the indirect approach to advertising. The success of these stations, including the ones from department stores, encouraged other broadcasters to mix advertisements with content. In this regard the commercialization of American radio broadcasting should be understood as a hegemonic process in which coercion mingled with consent.

The ways in which women were incorporated into the radio audience also illustrate a critical/cultural perspective. It may seem a positive development that the early radio industry sought to appeal to women, though we must consider the narrow range of identities offered to women. They could cook, mend clothing, and look beautiful for their husbands. Similarly, when women presented lectures on the radio, the topics had to be suitably "feminine." This restrictive vision of what it meant to be a woman reveals the patriarchal view that was dominant in the 1920s, a view that is still evident in many contemporary radio and television programs.

(*Note:* Adapted from "Department Stores and the Origins of American Broadcasting, 1910–1931," Ph.D. dissertation, University of Georgia, 2007.)

The first network was the National Broadcasting Company (NBC), a subsidiary of RCA, set up in 1926. NBC actually started two networks. One consisted of stations originally owned by RCA, and another was made up of stations acquired from AT&T when the phone company decided to get out of the broadcasting business. NBC got a competitor when the Columbia Broadcasting System (CBS) went on the air the next year. William S. Paley, whose career with CBS would last into the 1980s, headed the new network.

The two networks grew quickly. By 1937 NBC had 111 affiliated stations, while CBS had 105. Advertisers were spending more than $27 million annually on network radio. It was obvious that the network-affiliate arrangement would persist for some time to come.

Radio receivers in the 1930s no longer required a knowledge of electronics to operate. A family could simply sit back and listen.

Revenues from advertising permitted the networks to hire big-name entertainers. Jack Benny, Ed Wynn, and George Burns and Gracie Allen were all well-known vaudeville entertainers who successfully made the transition to radio. The most successful program, however, was *Amos 'n' Andy,* a comedy starring Charles Correll and Freeman Gosden, two white comedians working in blackface. Although considered racist today, it was a top-rated show during the late 1920s and early 1930s, and listening to it became a national habit.

Government Regulation   The early success of radio broadcasting had unanticipated consequences. As more and more stations went on the air during the 1920s, interference became a tremendous problem, and the government lacked the authority to do anything about it.

Congress finally acted to resolve this situation by passing the **Radio Act of 1927.** This act set up the Federal Radio Commission (FRC), a regulatory body that would issue licenses and try to clean up the chaos. The commission defined the AM broadcast band, standardized channel designations, abolished portable stations, and moved to minimize interference. By 1929 the situation had improved, and the new radio medium was prevented from suffocating in its own growth.

Thus, by the end of the 1920s, the framework for modern radio broadcasting was in place. It would be a commercially supported mass medium dominated by networks and regulated by an agency of the federal government.

The Depression Years and World War II

By most standards radio was not hit as hard by the Depression as were other industries. In fact, the amount of money spent on radio advertising tripled from 1930 to 1935. Profits may not have been as high as they would have been in better economic times, but the radio industry was able to weather the Depression with relatively little hardship.

The FCC   The most significant legal development for radio during the Depression years was the formation of the **Federal Communications Commission (FCC).** President Roosevelt wanted to create a government agency that would consolidate the regulatory

"This . . . is London." Edward R. Murrow's famous opening was familiar to millions of Americans who listened to his reports from the British capital during World War II. Murrow went on to a distinguished career in TV journalism.

functions of the communications industry. In response, Congress passed the **Communications Act of 1934,** which consolidated responsibilities for broadcast and wire regulation under a new seven-member FCC. The expanded commission had increased responsibilities, but the fundamental philosophy underlying the original Radio Act of 1927 remained unchanged.

The Birth of FM   In the mid-1930s Edwin Howard Armstrong, a noted inventor, demonstrated frequency-modulated radio, or FM, to his friend

David Sarnoff, head of RCA. At the time, Sarnoff was more interested in promoting the development of television and, despite the technical advantages of FM, was not interested in backing Armstrong's creation. Armstrong tried to develop FM on his own. He set up his own transmitter for demonstrations and by 1940 had sold the rights to manufacture FM receiving sets to several companies. Sarnoff then offered Armstrong $1 million for a license to his invention, but Armstrong, probably still angry over Sarnoff's earlier rejection, refused. FM's further development was interrupted by the start of World War II.

Radio Programs   Depression-era programs reflected a need for diversion and escape. Action-adventure series such as *The Lone Ranger* were popular, as were daytime soap operas. Network radio news grew during the 1930s, and live coverage of special events, such as the abdication speech of Edward VIII of England, drew huge numbers of listeners. Broadcasts from Europe on the eve of World War II kept many listeners glued to their radio sets for the latest bulletins. During the war Edward R. Murrow gained fame through his reports from war-torn London.

World War II   Radio did well during the war. The number of dollars spent on radio ads nearly doubled from 1940 to 1945. Helped by a newsprint shortage and an excess-profits tax that encouraged companies to advertise, radio broadcasting outpaced the newspapers as a national advertising vehicle in 1943.

The shape of modern broadcasting would be significantly altered by a court ruling that came in the middle of the war. In 1943 the Supreme Court ruled that NBC must divest itself of one of its two networks. NBC chose to sell the weaker network to Edward Noble, who had made his fortune selling Life Savers candy. Noble renamed his network the American Broadcasting Company (ABC), and by the end of the war, ABC had 195 affiliates and was a full-fledged competitor for the older networks.

Innovation and Change: 1945–1954

The nine-year period following World War II was marked by great changes in both the radio and recording industries, changes that ultimately drove them closer together. The development of television delayed the growth of FM radio, altered the nature of network radio, and forced the radio industry to rely on records as the most important part of a new programming strategy.

The Growth of FM   Despite the fact that FM sounded better than AM, was static free, and could reproduce a wider range of sound frequencies, AM broadcasting had started first, and FM struggled to catch up. FM had the misfortune of beginning its development at the same time as TV. In addition, because of technical considerations, both FM radio and TV are suited for about the same place in the electromagnetic spectrum, and in 1945 the FCC decided to give the rapidly expanding TV service the space formerly occupied by FM. The commission moved FM "upstairs" to the 88- to 108-MHz band (where it is today), thus rendering obsolete about half a million FM radios.

The Emergence of Television   Of course, the biggest change in radio's fortunes came about because of the emergence of television. (Chapter 11 has more to say about the development of TV.) By 1948 it was apparent that TV would take over the mass entertainment function served by network radio. The emergence of TV meant changes in the content, economics, and functions of radio. Although many individuals believe that television cut into the revenues of the radio industry, no such thing happened. In fact, radio revenues rose steadily from 1948 to 1952 and, after a brief drop from 1953 to 1956, continued to rise. The part of the industry upon which TV did have a drastic effect was network radio. The percentage of local stations with network affiliations dropped from 97 percent in 1947 to only 50 percent by 1955. Network revenue dropped by 60 percent in approximately the same period. Faced with this loss, stations relied more heavily on revenue from ads for local businesses. In short, they redistributed the makeup of their revenue dollar. As TV became the new mass medium, local stations cut back on their budgets, relied more

media *Payola*
Probe

In the 1950s the DJ became an important figure in radio programming. In fact, many became stars in their own right. DJs sent out glossy pictures of themselves to their fans; they appeared at supermarket openings and record hops; they were the emcees at personal appearances by rock-and-roll groups. As the DJs became more influential, they also began to program their own shows. They picked the records that they would play during their shifts.

Record promoters also recognized the tremendous importance of airplay in the marketing of a hit. The more a record was played on the radio, the more copies it sold. Naturally, record promoters and DJs began to develop close ties. In the beginning the relationship was innocent enough. Promoters would make sure that DJs got the latest releases their companies were offering, and they also put in a good word or two about their companies' products. Competition grew intense, however, and by 1959 about 250 new records were being released every week. Some unscrupulous promoters resorted to more than words to advance their records. At first, they would send DJs an elaborate Christmas gift. If that did not work, some even "hired" the DJ as "creative consultant" and paid him or her a fee every month. Others would cut the DJ in on the action and offer to pay a penny to the DJ for every record sold in the market. Eventually, most promoters stopped these charades and simply passed the DJ an envelope filled with cash in return for airplay of their company's songs. In 1958 and 1959, record distributors reportedly spent more than a quarter-million dollars in the larger markets on payola.

The news of this illicit business practice did nothing to help the image of rock and roll or of broadcasting. Section 508 was added to the 1934 Communications Act to stop this practice, but it was not altogether successful.

New payola scandals broke out in the early 1970s. At least one record company was accused of offering drugs to station personnel in return for increased airplay, and some concert promoters were accused of offering monetary bribes. Payola resurfaced in 2000 when 80 program directors at Spanish-language stations were investigated for allegedly taking bribes from Fonovisa Records.

The most recent twist in the payola saga involves independent promoters who charge music labels a fee to promote their records and pay money to radio stations for access to their programmers and playlists. The money involved can be substantial. In large markets the promoters might funnel as much as $300,000 to the stations. Record labels consider this just another promotional cost in getting their songs on radio. This arrangement is perfectly legal since no covert money flows directly from the labels to the stations. Despite its legitimacy the practice has drawn criticism from several sources. *Rolling Stone* labeled it "legal payola," and congressional leaders found the practice troubling. In response Clear Channel and other radio group owners announced in 2003 that they were cutting their ties with independent promoters. But in 2005 Sony BMG was involved in yet another payola scandal.

Shortly there after, the nation's four largest radio companies agreed to a $10 million deal in payments and other considerations to settle a yearlong FCC investigation into claims that stations owned by the companies accepted cash and other gifts from music companies in return for playing their releases. Part of the money in the 2007 agreement would go to a fund to be used in training stations to avoid payola.

The training was not entirely successful. In 2010, the Univision Music Group was implicated in a payola controversy involving payoffs to radio stations that played Latin music. Payola seems to be one problem that will not disappear.

heavily on music, talk, and news, and began searching for a formula that would allow them to coexist with television.

Specialized Formats   By 1956 it was obvious that the radio networks would no longer be the potent programming source they had been in the past. In that year radio networks were carrying only about 35 hours of sponsored evening programs each week. Finally, by 1960 all the once-popular evening programs and daytime serials had come to an end. Radio network service was limited primarily to news and short features, usually amounting to no more than 2 or 3 hours a day.

Local stations soon adapted to this change. Now that they no longer were tied to the networks for the bulk of their programming, they were free to develop their own personalities. Most did so by adopting a specialized format, a sound that had distinctive appeal to a certain segment of the audience. The most successful experiment occurred in the Midwest, where a station began monitoring the sales of records and sheet music and playing those tunes that were selling the most. Hence, the Top 40 format was born. Featuring a bright, continuous, and upbeat sound, the format was ruled by the **clock hour**, which specified every element of programming. The success of the Top 40 sound encouraged radio stations to experiment with other specialized formats. By 1964 at least a dozen different formats, ranging from country to rock to classical, had sprung up.

Growth and Stabilization: 1955–1990

The number of radio stations continued to grow during these years, from 3,343 in 1955 to more than 7,000 in 1970. More and more stations adopted the Top 40 format, and it very quickly became the format of choice among young listeners—who, as it happened, had a good deal of money to spend on the records they heard played by their favorite disc jockey, or DJ. Since at this time the DJ had control of what songs were played on the air, he or she became the focus of promotional efforts by record companies to gain airplay for their new songs. All too soon this arrangement led to the growth of **payola** (see "Media Probe: Payola").

The most significant development in radio during the 1970s and 1980s was the emergence of FM. By the early 1960s AM station licences were becoming harder to obtain; it was easier to get an FM license. The FCC passed the **nonduplication rule**, which precluded an AM-FM combination from duplicating its AM content on its FM station for more than 50 percent of the time. Faced with this ruling, FM stations developed their own kind of sound (many went to a rock format) that capitalized on FM's better technical qualities. As a result the number of FM stations tripled between 1960 and 1970, and profits began to increase. By 1990 FM accounted for about 70 percent of listening time. Many AM stations switched to a news/talk format to stop the audience erosion (see Figure 8-1).

A noncommercial radio network, **National Public Radio (NPR)**, went on the air in the early 1970s with an 80-station network. Over the next few years its number of affiliates doubled, and by 1980 it was reaching a cumulative audience of more than 5 million people per week. Its most successful programs were its daily news programs *Morning Edition* and *All Things Considered.*

Contemporary Radio

The pivotal event for radio in the 1990s was the passage of the **Telecommunications Act of 1996**. The act was concerned primarily with encouraging competition in the new communication technologies, but the radio industry, through skillful lobbying, was able to include itself in the bill. Only a few sentences in the final version of the act concern radio, but those few sentences had an impact out of proportion to their length. A key provision completely erased the cap on the number of stations a company could own and increased to eight the number of stations a company could own in a single market.

The new law caused an avalanche of buying and selling of radio properties; some stations were sold several times in a single year. In a typical year before the act, about $2 billion was spent on radio acquisitions and mergers. In 1996 the number hit $14.4 billion. That figure was eclipsed the next year when $15.3 billion was spent. New radio giants sprang up almost overnight. The radio industry became even more consolidated as a few large group owners dominated the industry.

On the programming front, talk became the hottest format on AM radio, thanks to the success of such performers as Rush Limbaugh, Dr. Laura Schlessinger, Tom Joyner, and Sean Hannity. The trend toward format specialization continued on FM as stations recognized that attracting as little as 2–3 percent of the audience was enough to keep them profitable.

The first decade of the new century saw several important developments. Two satellite radio companies, XM and Sirius, began operation, transmitting digital signals to subscribers

figure 8-1

Division of AM and FM Audiences

28%   72%   1972

30%   70%   1984

20%   80%   2010

▨ AM   ▨ FM

and offering dozens of talk and commercial-free music channels. The two companies struggled financially and finally merged in 2008.

The recession at the end of the decade slowed the trend toward consolidation in the radio industry. Clear Channel, owner of more than 1,200 radio stations, was acquired by a group of private investors in 2008 and sold off more than 400 of its stations. Other radio station groups were also up for sale, but the bad economy scuttled potential deals. The radio industry also saw its advertising revenue decrease.

The radio industry introduced HD radio, a high-quality digital signal, but the innovation was slow to catch on. Even though more than 1,700 stations were broadcasting HD by 2010, HD radio set sales were minuscule and many consumers were unaware that HD radio even existed.

Thousands of Internet-only radio stations were in operation, and many terrestrial broadcasters expanded their offerings on the Web. The economic future of online radio is closely tied to the amount of copyright fees that stations must pay to play music. Recent legislation called for rates to be negotiated by Web stations, and by 2009 some stations had worked out arrangements with copyright organizations.

Radio stations—satellite, terrestrial, and online—have faced increased competition from iPhones, iPods, and other devices that let people listen to their favorite music on MP3 players rather than on the radio. To stay competitive, radio stations have created apps for mobile media (recall the Pandora example at the beginning of the chapter). Nonetheless, this increased competition is one of the factors that has caused the average time a person spends listening to radio to decline steadily since 1994.

As of 2011, the terrestrial radio business was involved in a legal dispute with the recording industry. Radio stations have always paid royalties to authors and composers for playing their music on the air, but terrestrial stations have not paid royalties to performers or their record labels. Legislation introduced in 2009 would change that situation and require stations to pay performance fees. Despite lengthy negotiations, this issue has yet to be settled.

Despite these difficulties, the radio industry is still a significant advertising medium. More than 240 million Americans listen to terrestrial and satellite radio every day, and many more tune in online. Radio gives advertisers a chance to reach potential customers in their cars and at work. Radio stations are learning how best to use the Web to increase their audiences and their income. In short, radio, in some form, will be around for many more years.

radio in the digital age

Transition

Terrestrial radio stations were slow to enter the digital age, but there are now signs that they are catching up. Early radio station Web sites simply streamed the audio from the station's analog broadcast and posted their playlists and maybe the bios of the DJs. All in all, they were seen as adjuncts to the over-the-air service.

The increased competition from online radio and declining ad revenues prompted terrestrial radio stations to come up with new Web strategies. The result was that traditional radio moved online in a big way.

Terrestrial Stations on the Web

CBS Radio, owner of about 150 terrestrial stations, acquired Web broadcaster Last FM, where listeners can create and share their own playlists with others. CBS then made a deal with AOL Music that put CBS in charge of AOL's Internet radio service. A visitor to the AOL music site can select from about 150 CBS stations or from the 200 or so channels offered by AOL. CBS Radio also made a similar arrangement with Yahoo!'s Music Launchcast Radio, making CBS, one of the first terrestrial broadcasters, a major player online.

Clear Channel Radio took a more local approach and expanded the online versions of eight of its large-market stations. Citadel Broadcasting launched Right Now Radio in 2006, a site

Radio talk show host Sean Hannity. His syndicated program reaches about 12 million people.

that has links to the streaming audio of about 180 Citadel stations and interviews with music industry performers. Other group owners also expanded their online operations.

Internet Radio

There are thousands of **Internet-only radio stations** (or, as they are called in the business, pure-play Internet stations) on the Web. Some are one-person operations run out of a bedroom or garage, such as Blablaradionet. Many offer formats that would never be heard on traditional radio. One Internet station, for example, plays only accordion music; another broadcasts air traffic control transmissions. Others, like Pandora or slacker.com, are music services where users create their radio stations by generating playlists based on their favorite artists or songs. Slacker has about 2 million songs in its database. Other popular online radio sites are Live 365 and Radio Tower.

The biggest problem facing online radio is a financial one. Web stations must pay royalty fees to music performers, songwriters, composers, and record labels. (As of mid-2011, terrestrial radio does not pay fees to performers or labels. As noted previously, however, the recording companies were lobbying to change this situation.) In 2007, the Copyright Royalty Board significantly increased the rates paid by Internet stations. For 2008, for example, Internet stations were scheduled to pay $0.0011 cent per song per listener. This may not sound like much, but the numbers quickly add up. One calculation found that AOL Music would wind up paying more than $1 million a month under the new arrangement. Smaller Web stations would be hard-pressed to stay in business. In 2008 Congress gave Internet stations additional time to negotiate rates with the Recording Industry Association of America, the group representing performers.

The situation is complicated because some Internet-only radio services would prefer to pay a flat percentage of their revenues, while others that have additional revenue streams prefer a per song/per listener system. Most Web radio services owned by terrestrial stations have negotiated their own per song arrangements. In July 2009, an agreement was reached that called for large commercial Webcasters to pay a reduced fee per song/per listener while smaller Web stations would pay a fee based on a percentage of their revenues or a percentage of their expenses.

HD Radio

RadioTower.com lists 6,000 Internet radio stations.

HD radio is a digital service that greatly improves the signal qualities of terrestrial radio stations. With HD radio an FM station sounds as good as a CD, while AM stations sound as good as current FM stations and are static free. Moreover, digital signals can be compressed so that a single station can broadcast several programs at once. For example, a station might play Top 40 music on its main analog and digital signal while broadcasting jazz or classical on its digital-only subchannels.

decision
makers

Catherine Hughes

Catherine Hughes, head of Radio One, the nation's largest radio group targeting black listeners, is the first African American woman to head a publicly traded company. Her path to the top was not an easy one.

Hughes started in radio by working in the sales department at Howard University's radio station. Eventually, she became the station manager. She decided to start her own radio station in 1980 by buying WOL-AM in Washington, D.C. At the time she was a single mother with limited financial resources. Bank after bank rejected her loan application. She finally found one bank willing to lend her part of the money she needed, and she secured additional backing from a consortium of financiers who specialized in funding black business enterprises.

The station nearly failed. Hughes had her house and car repossessed and even sold some family heirlooms to pay the bills. She actually moved into the station, sleeping in a sleeping bag and cooking on a hot plate. She saved programming costs by doing her own talk show. Trying desperately to get advertising, she went door-to-door persuading small retailers to spend $10 for a minute of commercial time. Seven years later, the station finally turned a profit.

Hughes next decided that the time was right for expansion. She noted that African American family income was growing along with its buying power. Taking advantage of relaxed federal ownership regulations, Hughes acquired another 11 stations over the next 6 years. When she took her company public in 1999, Radio One's stock price nearly doubled in the first 3 months.

In 2008 Radio One was the 10th largest radio broadcaster in the United States based on its revenue of more than $300 million. The company owns 52 stations in 16 cities.

By 2010, however, the recession that hurt all of the radio industry also had an impact on Hughes's stations. Advertising dollars that were once targeted to African American audiences dried up. Increased competition from Internet radio and music download sites further eroded the black audience. Hughes's company had to lay off 400 employees. Some African American station owners sold their stations to white-owned corporations. As of 2010, of the more than 11,000 terrestrial commercial radio stations in the United States, African Americans owned only 239 (about 2 percent).

Still, Hughes was somewhat optimistic. In a 2011 interview published in *Ebony*, she said, "Although we are going through some dangerous times, . . . I think there's always going to be a form of communication that's going to be commercially viable in the African American community."

Consumers have to buy a special receiving set to receive the HD signals. Sets used to cost several hundred dollars, but many are now available for $80. Some automakers offer HD radio as an option in their new models. Many new HD radio receivers have an option called tagging that lets listeners press a button to tag a song that they heard on the radio. The tagged song is stored in an iPod that is cradled in the HD receiver. The next time the consumer synchs his or her iPod, he or she is given the option to purchase the song.

HD radio is still struggling in the marketplace. About 3 million HD sets had been sold by 2010, but that's only about 1 percent of all radio sets in use. One of the problems is that HD radio hasn't broken any new ground. It simply offers more of the same with better sound quality.

Satellite Radio

Sirius XM is the name of the new satellite company formed by the merger of Sirius and XM satellite radio services in 2008. About 21 million people subscribe to the combined service. For about $13 a month, subscribers can listen to more than 70 music channels along with more than 30 talk channels. Listeners can also tune in over the Internet.

Commuters are the primary market for satellite radio. Sirius XM has introduced local traffic and weather channels in major cities that broadcast continuous updates. The company has also expanded beyond the automobile by offering portable receivers that can be used in the home.

Financial difficulties continue to plague satellite radio. Both XM and Sirius spent hundreds of millions of dollars attracting talent such as Howard Stern and Oprah Winfrey to their service as well as spending large sums for the rights to professional sports games. As a result, Sirius XM was struggling to reach profitability. The company was also hurt by the downturn in new car sales. Much of the company's growth was due to factory-installed satellite radio as an option for new car buyers.

Apps and Mobile Radio

As noted below, mobility or portability has always been a defining feature of traditional radio. What is different today is that terrestrial, Internet, and satellite radio are available on multiple mobile platforms such as smartphones, iPods, and iPads. Or, to put it another way, listeners are accessing radio less through the browsers on their home computers and laptops and more through mobile applications. As with other media, all forms of radio are betting that specialized apps will bring them more listeners and more money.

The opening of this chapter pointed out how Internet radio station Pandora was helped by the popularity of its iPhone app. Other Internet radio services have also launched apps, such as Slacker Radio and Live 365 Radio. Tune-In Radio, one of the most popular apps in Apple's App Store, lets users choose from 40,000 AM/FM and Internet stations.

Traditional over-the-air radio companies have embraced apps. Clear Channel has had great success with its IHeartRadio app that lets users listen to 750 digital stations in 150 cities. The app also lets listeners share stations via Facebook and Twitter and watch a slide show of artists as their songs play. The AOL radio app (run by CBS Radio) features more than 350 stations. National Public Radio also has an app for the iPad that has been downloaded more than a million times. Individual stations, such as WWWQ in Atlanta and KLIF in Dallas, are also into apps. Not to be outdone, Sirius XM satellite radio also has apps for the iPod, iPhone, and iPad.

User-Generated Content

The most obvious example of user-generated content is podcasting—recording an audio program and making it available for downloading from a Web site. Many traditional radio broadcasters, such as NPR and the BBC, produce hundreds of podcasts per year, but audience members can also get into the act. Podcast.net lists thousands of available programs ranging from personal rants to teen fashions. A public radio station in Chicago, called Vocalo, depends on user-generated content for almost all of its programming.

Social Media

Radio stations, both terrestrial and online, are embracing social media, but some are better at using them than others. It's fairly common for radio stations in large and small markets to have Facebook pages and Twitter accounts. Many pages, however, are impersonal pages or accounts put together by an anonymous station employee and lack the personal touch that social media can provide. WSTR, an adult contemporary station in Atlanta, had only 16,000 fans on its Facebook page and 4,000 followers on Twitter out of a metro population of 4.5 million people. Contrast that to Pandora's 825,000 Facebook fans and 64,000 Twitter followers.

Some traditional stations are stressing social media on their mobile apps. Both Clear Channel's IHeartRadio app and AOL's radio app feature options to share music and messages via Facebook and Twitter. A new experiment combining traditional radio with social media was launched in 2011 by Jelli.com. Started in Las Vegas, Jelli puts listeners in charge of what is being played on select broadcast radio stations. Listeners can vote for songs using Jelli's mobile app or via the station's Web site and share songs and comments via Twitter and Facebook.

Sirius XM satellite radio revamped its Web site and online player in 2011 to put more emphasis on social media. The online player has links to Twitter and Facebook and the company is using the sites to respond to subscriber questions or complaints. Sirius XM also started its own YouTube channel.

In sum, social media will become a more significant part of the strategy used by terrestrial, online, and satellite radio services to attract and keep an audience.

defining features of radio

Radio is portable. Some radio sets, like Sony's Armband Radio, are small and personal. Others, like the boom box, are big and public. No matter their size, radio sets are easily transported and go everywhere—the beach, sporting events, jogging trails, the workplace. Car radios provide news and entertainment to commuters on their way to and from work. In fact, it is hard to find a place where radio cannot go.

Radio is supplemental. Most radio listening occurs while we are doing something else—driving, working, studying, falling asleep, waking up, cleaning, and so on. Radio rarely is the prime focus of our attention; it provides an audio background for our activities.

Radio is universal. Virtually every household has at least one working radio. In fact, the average house has about six. Almost every car is equipped with a radio. In an average day about 70 percent of Americans listen to radio.

Radio is selective. Much like the magazine industry (see Chapter 6), the radio industry has become a niche medium. Radio stations choose formats that attract a small, narrowly defined audience that is attractive to advertisers. If a radio broadcaster can find a formula that attracts just 2–3 percent of the audience, odds are that the station will turn a profit.

organization of the terrestrial radio industry

There are more than a half-billion working radio sets in the United States. That works out to about two radios per person. There are about 14,420 radio stations in operation. Thanks in part to an FCC philosophy that encouraged competition, the number of stations increased 100 percent from 1970 to 2010. To understand how this rapidly growing business is organized, we will examine it from several perspectives: programming, technology, and format.

Local Stations, Nets, and Syndicators

Local radio stations operate in cities, towns, and villages across the country. Big cities have many stations. New York City has about 90; Los Angeles, about 60. Smaller towns may have only one or two. Whitefish, Montana, for example (population 4,000), has four stations. Programming for these stations is provided by networks (nets), program syndication companies, and locally produced music and talk. Technically, the distinction between a net and a syndication service is that all stations on a network carry the net program at the same time, while syndicated programming is carried at different times by different stations. In practice, however, much syndicated radio programming is satellite-delivered and carried simultaneously, and many network affiliates record net programming and broadcast it later. To make things even more complicated, the traditional networks also offer syndicated programs. Consequently, the distinction between the two services may no longer be meaningful.

Some of the most popular syndicators and networks are the Premiere Networks, operated by Clear Channel, which carries, among others, Glenn Beck and Sean Hannity; Dial Global Networks, home of Clark Howard and Ed Schultz; and the Westwood One Networks, home of Charles Osgood and Dennis Miller. The syndicated shows of Rush Limbaugh and Tom Joyner continue to be popular. Many radio stations also subscribe to syndicated shows in specialized areas. The Motor Racing Network, for example, supplies coverage of major NASCAR races to more than 700 stations.

AM and FM Stations

Broadcast radio stations are either AM or FM. **AM** stands for *amplitude modulation,* and **FM** stands for *frequency modulation.* As we saw earlier in the chapter, since about 1975 the fortunes of FM radio have been increasing while those of AM stations are on the decline. In 2010, about 80 percent of listenership went to the FM stations. Keep in mind, however, that some AM stations, particularly those in large markets, are doing quite well. In 2011, AMs were the top-rated stations in Chicago (WBBM) and Cincinnati (WLW).

The WYNK Humvee on a remote in Baton Rouge, Louisiana. Remotes are an important part of promotion for a local radio station.

All physical factors being equal, radio signals sent by AM travel farther, especially at night, than signals sent by FM. The AM dial on a typical radio set illustrates the precise frequencies in the electromagnetic spectrum where the AM station operates. AM stations are further classified by channels. There are three possible channels: clear, regional, and local. A clear channel is one with a single dominant station that is designed to provide service over a wide area. Typically, these dominant stations have a strong signal because they broadcast with 50,000 watts of power. For example, the 720 spot on the AM dial is a clear channel with WGN, Chicago, the dominant station, operating at 50,000 watts. The 770 position is also a clear channel with WABC, New York, dominant. A regional channel is one shared by many stations that serve fairly large areas. A local channel is designed to be shared by a large number of stations that broadcast only to their local communities.

FM signals do not travel as far as AM, but FM has the advantage of being able to produce better sound qualities than AM. FM radio is also less likely to be affected by outside interference such as thunderstorms. Similar to AM, FM stations are organized in classes. Class C FM stations are the most powerful, operating at 100,000 watts. Class B and Class A stations are less powerful. A glance at the FM radio dial reveals that FM stations operate in a different part of the electromagnetic spectrum than does AM. Figure 8-2 is a simplified diagram of the spectrum showing where AM, FM, and television signals are located.

Much of a radio station's operation is automated. A computer sequences when songs play, when commercials run, and when the DJ talks. Modern radio broadcasting equipment has become so compact that a radio station could easily fit inside the average dorm room (except for the antenna tower).

When radio stations broadcast a digital signal, the old analog transmission is replaced by a series of 0s and 1s that represent various sound frequencies. The digital receiver translates these numbers back into sound waves. Obviously, the analog AM and FM distinctions do not apply to digital radio.

Station Formats

figure 8-2

Simplified Diagram of the Electromagnetic Spectrum

Perhaps the most meaningful way we can organize radio stations is according to their **format**, a type of consistent programming designed to appeal to a certain segment of the audience. A format gives a station a distinctive personality and attracts a certain kind of audience that advertisers find desirable. In fact, the development of radio after 1960 is

Hits by artists such as Lil Wayne are a mainstay on the playlists of urban contemporary stations.

marked by the fine-tuning of existing formats and the creation of new ones that appeal to people in distinct demographic and lifestyle categories. Most modern stations can offer an amazingly precise description of the kind of listener they want their format to attract. An adult contemporary station, for example, might set its sights on men and women, ages 25–45, with college educations, making more than $80,000 a year, who read *Rolling Stone*, drive either a BMW or a Volvo, and go to the mall at least twice a week. In our discussion we will cover three basic categories of radio formats: music, ethnic, and news/talk.

The Music Format   The music format is the largest category and includes many subdivisions and variations. In 2010 the two most listened-to formats were adult contemporary (AC) with about 14 percent of the audience and contemporary hit radio (CHR) with about 11 percent. The main appeal of the AC format is to 25- to 49-year-old females. AC stations play the "hits of the '80s, '90s, and today" with a blend of about 80 percent oldies and 20 percent current tunes. Coldplay, Taylor Swift, and Nickelback are artists who are likely to be heard on AC stations.

CHR (also called Top 40) features a small playlist of hits in a fast rotation. The format does best with the 16–24 age group. Artists whose songs were frequently played on CHR stations in 2011 included Katy Perry, Lady GaGa, and The Black-Eyed Peas.

Other top formats are urban and country. The urban format showcases a large number of African American artists and plays rap, hip-hop, and dance music. The format is aimed at city dwellers but has attracted listeners in rural areas as well. As of 2011, some prominent urban artists were Ne-Yo, Kanye West, and Jay-Z.

Country stations, as the name suggests, play hit country-and-western singles and employ DJs who are down-home, friendly, and knowledgeable about country music. The country format has two main divisions: (1) traditional country stations that play mainstream classic, twangy country music and (2) contemporary country stations that play more current artists who might use synthesizers and other modern sounds. A country station's audience still mainly comprises adults ages 35–55.

Format Homogenization   Radio stations sound pretty much alike no matter where you are. Almost all the major music formats are represented in the large and medium markets, and it seems that every market has its morning "zoo crew"; an AC station that specializes in "the classic hits" of the 1980s, 1990s, and today; a modern rock station that calls itself "Power" or "Z" or "Q" something or other; an easy-listening station with a "warm" format that dedicates love songs at night; and maybe even an AM station that specializes in "golden oldies." Even the DJs sound pretty much the same.

There are several reasons for this trend toward homogenization. The most important is the increasing consolidation in the industry. Big radio companies own stations in all the big markets. What works in one market is likely to work in another. In addition, it is cheaper to program the same music from market to market. Finally, radio has become so competitive that programming decisions are based on the recommendations of program consultants and on surveys and focus groups. Since the same records are generally tested in all markets and usually score high, the recommendations about what to play are the same from market to market. Not surprisingly, many stations prefer to adopt a "safe" format, one that has worked in other markets, rather than risking a sizable amount of money on a new and untested format.

ethical issues
Voice Tracking in Radio: Is Anybody There?

It's 11 P.M. Do you know where your radio DJ is?

Thanks to an innovation called **voice tracking**, he or she might be a recorded voice from Los Angeles, Tampa, Norfolk, or Dallas. The concept behind voice tracking is simple enough: A DJ somewhere else records chatter, music introductions, and music recaps. The music itself can be added later. At the local station this recorded content is mixed together with local weather, traffic updates, promotions, and commercials. Thanks to computers and satellite distribution, the whole process sounds seamless, and most listeners cannot tell the difference.

The reason for the growing popularity of voice tracking is also simple: It saves money. Rather than pay six DJs salaries and benefits, a company can pay one DJ to voice track for six shows in six different markets at a substantially lower cost. Since most of a DJ's shift consists of music, one DJ can voice track a 4-hour shift in about 30 minutes.

The consolidation of the radio industry has added extra impetus to the voice-tracking phenomenon. Clear Channel, the largest owner of radio stations, has used voice tracking in every one of its 255 markets except New York, where union rules make it too expensive. Currently, most voice-tracked programs occur overnight, at midday, and in the evening; most drive-time shows are still live and local.

Executives at Clear Channel and other companies have defended the practice as a way of bringing more professional-sounding programming to local markets. From a purely technical perspective, most would agree that the DJs who do voice tracks are smoother and sound more skilled than most

local DJs. The production itself is professional and usually error-free. The companies also tout the greater efficiency and savings of the technique.

Opponents cite the fact that voice tracking has put many local DJs out of work. They also note that the philosophy of localism has always been at the heart of the radio industry. Starting in the 1920s, radio stations were licensed to serve the public interest in a local community. Voice tracking is undesirable because it eliminates local talent and severs ties to the local community.

Perhaps a more pertinent ethical argument against voice tracking is that it is based on deception. The audience is not told that its local DJ taped his or her show in some distant city. In fact, voice-tracking DJs go to great pains to make people believe that they are in fact local. They read local newspapers and Internet sites to learn about local events and drop local references into their chatter ("Don't forget the big rock concert at [insert local name here] on Saturday"); they learn about local traffic hot spots to make their traffic intros sound credible ("How's traffic looking on [insert local name here]? Let's get an updated traffic report"); and they might act as if they had attended a local event ("Wasn't that a great game at [insert local sports venue here]? The crowd was something else").

What do listeners think? Surveys have shown that some feel cheated once they learn that they have been listening to voice tracking and not a live DJ. Others do not seem to care. Many report they listen to hear music and never pay attention to the DJ.

Black and Ethnic Formats These formats aim for special audiences that are defined primarily by race and nationality. There are about 175 stations that program for the black audience, and about 260 stations that serve the Hispanic audience. Many of the black and Hispanic stations feature urban contemporary music and run news, features, and special programs of interest to their audiences. In addition, about 60 stations have formats aimed at other ethnic groups: Polish, German, Italian, French, Irish, and Greek.

News/Talk Format This format is becoming more and more popular on the AM band and accounts for 17 percent of all radio listening time. Some stations emphasize the news part of the news/talk format. National, regional, and local news reports are broadcast periodically throughout the day. Sports, traffic, weather, editorials, public affairs programs, and an occasional feature round out the programming day. News stations appeal primarily to a male audience in the 25- to 54-year-old age category.

The talk format attracts listeners in about the same age group. Common types of programs that appear on stations using the talk format are call-in shows, usually hosted by an opinionated and maybe even abrasive host; interview shows; advice shows; and round-table discussions. News, weather, traffic reports, and other feature material are blended in with these programs. Unlike the music formats, which do not demand their listeners' close attention, the talk format requires that its audience concentrate on the program in order to follow what is being said.

Noncommercial Radio

Many of the early radio stations that went on the air during the 1920s were founded by educational institutions. As the commercial broadcasting system became firmly established, many educational stations were bought by commercial broadcasters, and the fortunes of

Ira Glass is producer and host of NPR's *This American Life.*

noncommercial radio dwindled. In 1945, with the coming of FM broadcasting, the FCC set aside several frequencies for educational broadcasting. This action sparked a rebirth of interest in this kind of broadcasting, so that by 2010 there were about 2,400 noncommercial radio stations on the air.

Most noncommercial radio stations are owned by educational institutions or private foundations. Noncommercial radio gets its support from the institutions that own the stations. Ultimately, some of this support comes from tax revenue since taxes support most public educational institutions. Other sources of support are endowments (gifts), grants from foundations or the federal government, and listener donations.

Noncommercial stations are served by National Public Radio (NPR). Founded in 1970, NPR provides program services to about 850 affiliates around the country. Member stations pay a fee based on audience reach and annual budget and receive in return about 50 hours of programming per week. Many of these shows are produced at NPR headquarters; others are produced at NPR stations and distributed by NPR. Probably the best-known NPR programs are *All Things Considered* and *Morning Edition.* About 33 million people listen to NPR every week.

The public radio stations that help support NPR receive financial support from the Corporation for Public Broadcasting (CPB), a private, nonprofit organization funded by Congress. Member stations receive money from the CPB, and those that decide to affiliate with NPR pay some of this money to the network as a fee. NPR also receives grants directly from the CPB. Congress, however, has threatened to cut the CPB's budget, which, in turn, would lead to less money for stations and for NPR. Consequently, many public radio stations have resorted to underwriting, a practice in which the station accepts money from a person or an organization in return for an acknowledgment on the air. In some cases these acknowledgments sound suspiciously like commercials. In contrast, NPR for the most part has resisted the pressure to air these minicommercials. In 1995, however, NPR relented a bit and allowed underwriters to broadcast brief slogans. NPR's financial fortunes were helped in 2003 when Joan Kroc, widow of McDonald's founder Ray Kroc, donated $200 million to the network.

Unlike commercial radio networks, NPR has found a way to generate significant revenue from the digital revolution: The network is one of the biggest podcasters in the world. Apple's iTunes lists more than 50 NPR shows in its menu, with more than 300 titles available to download. NPR sells sponsorship of these podcasts to advertisers who wish to reach the network's relatively affluent listeners. Podcasts sponsored by the automaker Acura, for example, have been downloaded more than 25 million times. The success of NPR's podcasts has caused some controversy, however. Local NPR affiliates worry that people will download the podcasts and not listen to the local station, thus hurting the local station's chances to raise money during on-air fund drives.

NPR became a center of controversy in 2010–2011 when it abruptly fired a conservative commentator and when one of its executives was caught on a hidden camera saying unflattering things about conservatives.

The other noncommercial radio network is Public Radio International (PRI), formerly known as American Public Radio. The Minneapolis-based organization acquires and distributes programming from station-based, independent, and international producers. Unlike NPR, PRI does not produce any of its programming, but it does finance program production at member stations. A noncommercial station can be an affiliate of both NPR and PRI.

organization of online radio

Unlike terrestrial broadcasting, online radio is streamed directly to a computer or to a smartphone or other portable device. After a brief lag time, the signal starts to play. Anybody who has access to content and the appropriate hardware and software can start an Internet radio station. This fact makes it difficult to construct a comprehensive organizational arrangement. Nevertheless, there are three major types of stations:

1. *Online stations that are affiliated with a terrestrial station.* Many of these simply simulcast what is currently playing on the terrestrial station; others may simulcast part of the time and depart from the terrestrial station's format part of the time.
2. *Choice-based stations,* such as Pandora and Last FM, that let listeners choose their favorite artists and types of music to create their own playlists. In effect, listeners program their own unique radio station.
3. *Format-specific Internet-only stations.* These are stations that play narrowly focused genres of music, such as dr-love.com, specializing in rap and rhythm and blues, and Pluto Radio, specializing in alternative rock. There are hundreds of these stations on the Internet; some are one-person operations; others are part of larger organizations.

Most online stations depend on advertising for support. Others may run ads but also ask for listener contributions. To get some idea about the diversity of radio stations on the Internet, visit www.radiotower.com for a list of more than 5,000 stations.

ownership in the radio industry

As mentioned earlier, the 1996 Telecommunications Act drastically changed the landscape of the radio industry by producing a wave of consolidation that left the industry controlled by a few big media companies. Clear Channel, for example, managed to acquire more than 1,200 radio stations. As of 2010, the trend toward consolidation in terrestrial radio had stopped, at least for the moment, as Clear Channel sold hundreds of its radio stations after being bought by a group of independent investors. Nonetheless, the radio industry was still dominated by big companies. In addition to Clear Channel, other big owners were Cumulus (more than 500 stations) and CBS (more than 150 stations).

The trend for satellite radio was in the other direction as Sirius and XM merged into a single company. The merger was not an easy one, requiring two years to gain approval by the Federal Communications Commission and the Justice Department.

producing radio programs

Departments and Staff

The departmental structure of a terrestrial radio station varies according to its size. Obviously, a small station with five or six employees has a departmental setup different from that of a large station with a 100-person staff.

The two top management positions are the general manager and the program director. The manager has the responsibility for planning and carrying out station policy, maintaining contact with the community, and monitoring program content, audience ratings, and sales information. The program director is responsible for the station's sound. He or she supervises the music or other program material that the station broadcasts and also hires and fires announcers and DJs. Other staff members take responsibility for maintaining the online operation.

The sales department consists of the sales manager and the station's sales force. The news department is responsible for compiling the station's local newscasts and rewriting the wire service reports of national and regional news. The engineering department, under the supervision of the chief engineer, is staffed with technicians responsible for keeping the station on the air and maintaining the equipment.

Putting Together a Program

This section will concentrate on how traditional radio programs are produced for the music, talk, and news formats.

Music Format   When the staff of a local station puts together their program, the first step is generally to lay out a **format wheel** (also called a *format clock*), a pie chart of an hour divided into segments representing different program elements. Figure 8-3 is a simplified version of a wheel for a contemporary rock station. (Note that Figure 8-3 is a visual aid, not something you would find at a radio station. All of the sequencing and scheduling represented in Figure 8-3 is handled by computers.)

Note that the music is structured to flow from one segment to another. Album cuts and hits from the past are spread around the wheel. Additional wheels would be constructed for the various parts of the broadcast day (that is, one wheel for morning drive time, another for 10 A.M.–4 P.M., another for evening drive time, and another for 7 P.M.–midnight).

Talk Format   Most of the content of the talk format is produced by the local station. As is the case with the music format, the makeup of the audience is taken into account. During drive time, talk segments should be relatively short and liberally interspersed with news, weather, and traffic reports. The audience for the 10 A.M.–4 P.M. segment tends to be primarily female, and therefore, topics for discussion reflect the interests of that group. The early-evening audience is generally younger and contains more males.

Producing a talk show requires more equipment than does producing a simple DJ program. Speaker telephones and extra telephone lines are needed, as is a delay system. This device gives the talk-show moderator a 7- to 30-second delay period during which he or she can censor what is said by the caller. Another important part of the talk show is the telephone screener. The screener ranks the waiting calls by importance, letting the most interesting callers go first, and filters out crank calls or calls from regulars who contact the station too frequently.

All-News Format   The all-news station also works with a programming wheel, similar to that of the music format. Instead of music, however, the news wheel shows the spacing between headlines, weather, news, sports, business reports, and commercials. It also illustrates the **cycle**, the amount of time that elapses before the program order is repeated.

figure 8-3

Format Wheel for a
Contemporary Rock Station

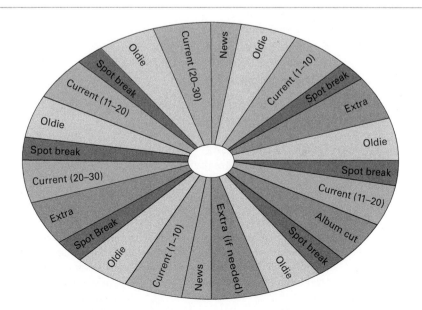

The all-news format is the most difficult to produce. A large staff, consisting of anchorpersons, a managing editor, local reporters, editors, rewrite people, a traffic reporter, and stringers (freelance reporters who are paid per story), is needed. The list of necessary equipment and facilities is also long: radio wire services, sports wire, weather wire, mobile units, police- and fire-frequency scanners, short-wave receivers, and perhaps even a helicopter.

the economics of radio

Radio was affected by the economic recession at the end of the decade. Total revenue in 2010 was $17.3 billion, down about 11 percent from 2008. Further, radio's share of the total amount spent on advertising in the United States also declined during the same period. In short, money that used to be spent on radio ads is now being spent in other media.

On the bright side, terrestrial radio still reaches about 235 million people a week and its drive-time audience is growing, thanks to longer commuting times. Another 13.5 million per week listen online. Radio also attracts targeted audiences, something that appeals to advertisers. Music programming is cheap because much of it comes free courtesy of the recording companies. (The recording industry is trying to change this. See "Social Issues: Should Radio Pay More?")

Sources of Revenue

Radio stations earn their money by selling advertising time. The amount that a radio station charges for time is included in its rate card. A typical radio commercial costs several hundred dollars in large cities. The same commercial in a small town might cost only a few dollars.

The radio industry has five sources of income from the sale of commercial time. The first is the sale of time on network programs to national advertisers trying to reach a broad market. The second is the sale of time on local stations to advertisers who wish to reach a specific region (such as the Northeast) or a specific type of market (such as rural areas). This is called *national spot advertising*. The third source is advertising purchased by local establishments that want their commercials to be heard only in the immediate community. The fourth is off-air income, mainly revenue generated by advertising on the station's Web site and merchandising. The fifth is income from digital radio. In 2010, each of these sources represented the following amounts of each dollar of radio revenue:

- Local: 68 cents
- National spot: 14 cents
- Off-air: 8 cents
- Network: 6 cents
- Digital: 4 cents

As the numbers indicate, the overwhelming amount of revenue in radio comes from local commercials.

General Expenses

Expenses in radio are divided into five areas: (1) technical, (2) programming, (3) sales, (4) general administration, and (5) news. Technical expenses include the payroll for the engineering staff and the cost of maintaining and replacing equipment. Program costs cover salaries paid to talent, outlays for downloads and CDs, and music fees paid to the music licensing organizations. Sales costs are made up of the salaries of the sales staff and all the other expenses that go with selling. General administrative expenses include the salaries of all management, secretarial, and clerical personnel; the depreciation of physical facilities; the cost of office supplies; and any interest that is due on loans to the station. News expenses consist of the costs involved in covering local and national stories.

social issues

Should Radio Pay More?

For about the last 80 years terrestrial radio stations have paid royalties to songwriters, publishers, and composers, but they have never paid royalties to performers or record labels. In 1995 the U.S. Copyright Office authorized a recording industry organization called SoundExchange to collect and distribute performance royalties for artists and labels when their recordings are played on satellite radio, the Internet, and cable and satellite television. Terrestrial radio was exempt from this ruling.

The rationale behind this arrangement is that radio stations are giving performers and labels free advertising and promotion by playing their songs. When listeners buy songs after hearing them on the radio, part of the purchase price goes to the performer and label. The radio industry argument is this: The more radio exposure, the more sales and the more money earned by the artist and label. We're already helping the artists and labels make money, so why should we pay more?

This deal worked fine as long as both the radio and recording industries were making money, but times are different now, especially for the record companies who have seen their revenues drop because of file sharing and a shift away from profitable CDs to less profitable single-track downloads.

The recording industry argues that radio air play is not that important anymore when it comes to promoting sales. There are plenty of places where consumers can hear music—Internet stations, satellite radio, Facebook pages, and so on. Radio is no longer the only engine for driving sales, so the exemption for terrestrial radio no longer makes sense.

Terrestrial broadcasters respond that if they have to start paying more fees to play music, many stations will no longer be able to make a profit and will shut down or shift to formats that don't require payments. Some in the broadcasting industry also point out that there are still quite a few rich recording artists who have done quite well without being paid performance royalties.

The recording industry took its case to Congress in 2007 and again in 2009 as bills to end terrestrial radio's exemption from paying performance royalties were introduced in both the House and Senate. The recording industry has tried this tactic in previous years but has not been successful. The broadcasting industry has a strong lobby and is likely to vigorously oppose this proposed legislation. In any case, the next few years will be pivotal.

As of 2010, general administration expenses ranked first, accounting for about 40 percent of all expenses. Programming came next, making up about 20 percent of the expense dollar, followed closely by costs associated with sales. News and technical expenses taken together accounted for about 15 percent.

global radio

International radio stations broadcast programs deliberately aimed at other countries. These services are usually government run or at least government supervised, such as the Voice of America. Note that these stations are different from foreign stations, whose programming is designed for audiences within the station's native country but whose signals are widely available on the Internet, such as Air FM in Dublin, Ireland.

The first international broadcasting stations were started during the 1920s and 1930s in Europe. The purpose of these early stations was to bring news of their homeland to Europeans living in Africa and Asia. These stations soon began to attract an audience of listeners who were native citizens of the countries receiving the broadcasts. This paved the way for propaganda broadcasts from one nation to another for the purpose of political persuasion. Propaganda broadcasts increased during World War II with Great Britain, Germany, Japan, the Soviet Union, and the United States as the most active broadcasters. Although the shooting war ended in 1945, the subsequent "Cold War" made propaganda even more prevalent on the international airwaves. The end of the Cold War in the late 1980s and early 1990s caused a fundamental shift in the structure and philosophy of international broadcasting. Politically oriented material decreased and was replaced by more public affairs, news, entertainment, and cultural programming. Today's international services still reflect this trend although some services, such as Radio Marti, a U.S.-based service targeting Cuba, have definite political undertones.

Until about 20 years ago, most international radio stations broadcast in the shortwave part of the electromagnetic spectrum. Shortwave signals are reflected by the ionosphere

critical ⊕ cultural issues

Radio and the Local Community

The philosophy that guided the development of radio in the United States was based on localism. Radio stations were licensed to serve the public interest of those who could hear their signals. Stations were expected to be integral parts of their local communities and responsive to the needs of local residents. The Federal Radio Commission set aside a number of AM channels that were dedicated to lower-power stations serving a particular town. Over the years other regulations were enacted that favored localism. To encourage the development of roots in the community, owners were required to hold onto stations for three years before they could be sold. Stations had to survey their listeners and ascertain the needs of their community, and then provide programs to address those needs. Caps were placed on the number of stations one company could own to discourage large corporations from becoming out-of-town station owners with few or no ties to the community. In an effort to ensure access for many voices, there were further caps on the number of stations that could be owned in one market.

As pointed out by Charles Fairchild in his article "Deterritorializing Radio: Deregulation and the Continued Triumph of the Corporatist Perspective in the USA," which appeared in a 1999 issue of *Media, Culture and Society*, this localist philosophy is not much with us today. His analysis of changes in the radio industry in recent decades is a good example of a critical/cultural investigation that focuses on ideology and power relationships in society.

In essence, Fairchild argues that recent changes have removed the connection between a radio station and its local community. He suggests that two dominant ideologies compete as definitions of the *public interest*. One, the statist position, conceives of government as the protector of the public interest and an agency that ensures that the broadest number of people benefit from the medium. The other, the corporatist view, holds that the market is the best determiner of the public interest. The most economically successful service is that which succeeds best in the marketplace. In other words, the public interest is what interests the public.

Fairchild notes that the corporatist view has been the dominant model in recent radio operations. Due in part to an active industry lobby and the economic power wielded by large communications corporations, recent changes have almost erased the notion of local service. Following are just a few of those changes: The three-year ownership rule has been dropped; the requirements for ascertaining the needs of the community have been minimized; and, perhaps most important, the cap on the total number of stations that can be owned has been removed and the limit on the number of stations that can be owned in a market has been raised to eight.

What are the effects of this change in ideology? The radio industry has become consolidated, with big corporations controlling hundreds of stations. Locally owned stations that had deep roots in the community have been gobbled up by big companies whose headquarters are in some faraway city and whose main interest is the bottom line. Consequently, local programming has been reduced in favor of standardized entertainment and news fed from some central location nowhere near the local community. Programming decisions are left to consultants and syndicators who have no local ties whatsoever. Hence, as Fairchild suggests, radio has become "deterritorialized," detached from a community connection.

Fairchild concludes that the corporatist ideology has triumphed: "local radio stations are the objects of unaccountable control from outside local communities and neither the government nor the public have any levers of power with which they can influence broadcasters to provide access to those voices which cannot gain any serious measure of volume elsewhere."

and with the right conditions of power and atmospheric conditions they can travel thousands of miles, particularly at night. Thus it is not uncommon for a listener in North America to be able to pick up signals from Europe and Africa. On the downside, a listener needs a special radio set to pick up a shortwave broadcast and the signals are subject to fading and interference. More recently, international stations have started sending their signals over the Internet or by satellite or by AM and FM relays, making them more accessible to the general population. Nonetheless, a large portion of the audience for international broadcasts still picks them up via shortwave.

The rest of this section looks at the top three international broadcasters: the VOA, the BBC, and China Radio International.

Now in its seventh decade of operation, the Voice of America is the official international broadcasting service of the United States government. The VOA broadcasts news, editorials, features, and music in more than 40 languages through a satellite-fed system of more than 100 transmitters and 27 radio broadcast studios. The service transmits about 1,500 hours of programs per week to an audience of about 125 million. It also operates

VOAnews.com, a popular Internet site that serves as a portal to the home pages of all the languages broadcast by the VOA.

The VOA's parent organization is the Broadcasting Board of Governors, an agency that is also responsible for Radio Free Europe/Radio Liberty, Radio Free Asia, Radio and TV Marti, aimed at Cuba, and the Middle Eastern Broadcasting Networks—Radio Sawa, an Arabic language service, and Alhurra TV, an Arabic TV channel serving the Mideast.

Some popular VOA programs include *American Mosaic,* which features U.S. popular music and culture; *American Stories,* short stories rewritten in simple language to help listeners learn English; *People in America,* about influential people in American history; and *In the News,* current events coverage of U.S. and world news.

The World Service of the British Broadcasting Corporation (BBC) broadcasts about 1,120 hours of programming per week in more than 30 languages to more than 160 million listeners. About 30 million people visit its Web site every month. The BBC has transmitters in England, Singapore, the Persian Gulf, and Ascension Island in the mid-Atlantic and leases time over Canadian transmitters in North America. It is also carried by Sirius XM satellite radio. As a result, few areas of the world are out of the BBC's range.

Unlike the VOA, the BBC service is free of government ownership. The service operates under a Royal Charter that recognizes its editorial independence and spells out its goals. It is funded by a direct grant from the British Parliament.

In addition to its highly respected news programs, the BBC World Service broadcasts many entertainment programs including *The Strand,* a program about the arts; *Sportsworld,* which features soccer coverage; *World Drama,* featuring radio plays from around the world; and *The World Book Club,* where best-selling authors discuss their works.

China Radio International (CRI) carried anti-American propaganda until the 1970s, when improving relations between the United States and China led to a more mellow tone and an increase in nonpolitical content. The station transmits about 1,400 hours of weekly programming in more than 40 languages. In addition, CRI is carried on several AM stations in the United States and is available via satellite and online.

Many of CRI's programs are devoted to cultural information about China, news, analysis, and music. CRI also produces *The Biz China,* a program designed for Western businesses interested in the China market, and *China Drive,* about everyday life in China.

the radio audience

Sources of Feedback

For the last several decades **Arbitron** has provided measurement of the radio audience. Arbitron surveyed approximately 280 radio markets and reported its results to stations, networks, syndication companies, and advertisers.

Individuals who were chosen at random from telephone listings were mailed pocket-size diaries and asked to record their in-home and out-of-home listening. Arbitron mailed out 3,000 to 4,000 diaries in a given market, and despite several reminders, usually less than 40 percent of the diaries were returned in usable form. The returned diaries underwent about three to four weeks of analysis before the data were sent to stations and other customers.

Arbitron changed its method in 2007 by introducing the **portable people meter (PPM)**. The new device is similar to that used to compile television ratings (see Chapter 11). The PPM is clipped to an individual's clothes while the person goes about his or her daily routine. Participating radio stations encode an inaudible unique signal as part of their broadcasts. The PPM "hears" the signal and records the station and the time spent listening. At the end of the day, a person slides the PPM into a docking device and the data are transmitted to a central computer where they are analyzed. Such a device requires far less effort than filling out a diary. Arbitron will have PPMs in all of the top 50 markets by the end of 2011. Smaller markets will still be measured by the paper diary.

When the first PPM ratings reports appeared in late 2007 and early 2008, they contained some surprises for radio broadcasters. Compared to the old diary method, the PPMs indicated that more people were listening to radio but were spending less time with individual stations. Morning drive time did not draw as big an audience as previously thought, but more people were listening on weekends. Moreover, some stations saw their ratings plummet while others improved. In New York, for example, the number-one station as determined by the diary method dropped to 12th place after the PPMs were introduced, and the number-16 station jumped to number 8.

Many radio stations claimed that Arbitron's PPM sample underrepresented key demographic and ethnic groups. Under pressure from local broadcasters, attorneys general in New Jersey and New York sued Arbitron to prevent it from making its data commercially available. After lengthy negotiations, Arbitron agreed to change its sampling methods and the controversy ended.

Ratings and Shares

Measurements of radio and television audiences gathered by the diary or PPM method are usually expressed in terms of two related concepts: (1) ratings and (2) share of the audience. A **rating** is simply the ratio of listeners of a particular station to all people in the market. Suppose that in a market with 100,000 people, 20,000 listen to radio station KYYY from 9:00 A.M. to 9:15 A.M. The rating of KYYY would be 20,000/100,000, or 20 percent. A **share of the audience** is the ratio of listeners of a particular station to the total number of radio listeners in the market. For example, again suppose that 20,000 people are listening to KYYY from 9:00 A.M. to 9:15 A.M. and that in the total market 80,000 people are listening to the radio during the same period. KYYY's share of the audience would be 20,000/80,000, or 25 percent. Shares of the audience divide the listening audience among all stations in the market. When they are summed, shares should total 100 percent. Ratings are important to stations because they are used to establish the rates that stations charge advertisers.

Audiences

There are almost twice as many radio sets in the United States as there are people. As of January 2009, there were more than 575 million radio receivers scattered around the country, with car radios accounting for about one-third of this number. On a typical day at least three-fourths of all adults will listen to radio, and the average person will listen, or at least have the radio on, for about 3 hours. Most people listen to radio in the early morning when they are getting ready for and driving to work and in the late afternoon when they are driving home. These two "day parts," consisting roughly from 6 A.M. to 10 A.M. and 4 P.M. to 7 P.M., are called *drive time.*

The precise audience makeup for a given station depends on that station's format. Top 40 stations draw an audience composed primarily of 12- to 24-year-olds, with females outnumbering males by about 3 to 2. Modern rock attracts 18- to 34-year-olds, in about equal proportions of men and women. Jazz, classical, country, and all-news formats generally attract an older crowd, with most of their audience coming from the 45-and-over age group. Country music stations seem to have an across-the-board appeal to those over 25. As a person gets older, he or she tends to evolve out of the audience for one format and move on to another.

Although the situation is changing rapidly, as of 2010 traditional AM and FM terrestrial stations accounted for about 44 percent of the time spent listening to radio. Listening to Internet stations was next at 27 percent, followed by satellite radio at 19 percent and smartphones and other mobile devices at 10 percent.

the radio industry

The poor economy at decade's end has made the career outlook in radio somewhat pessimistic. The total number of employees in the traditional radio industry dropped by about 12 percent from 2000 to 2010. Much of this drop was caused by consolidation,

media *Mscore*
Probe

New technologies give radio programmers more information about the music they play on their stations. One new technology is Mscore, a measure that combines data from Arbitron's portable people meter (PPM) ratings and actual monitoring of a station's programming. Mscore tracks the amount of station switching that occurs when a certain song is played. A positive Mscore indicates that the song prompted less than the average amount of switching while a negative score signifies that more than the average number of listeners went searching for another station. If a certain song prompts a large number of people to tune out, then the station may consider removing the song from its playlist.

Record labels are not pleased with this new measure. They say Mscore stands for "murder score," because a negative Mscore can kill a new

song's chances for success. Listeners generally prefer established songs and it takes a while before a new release develops fans. They argue that Mscores should not become the most important metric of a song's success. Other measurable factors such as sales, downloads, and requests should also be considered before a song is dropped from the air.

For their part, radio programmers are proceeding carefully in their use of Mscores. The service is not cheap (it costs about $25,000 a year) and some programmers wonder if the sample size is large enough to get a valid reading on a song. Nonetheless, Mscores have already revealed some interesting facts about radio formats. Lady Gaga's "Paparazzi," for example, got positive Mscores on Top 40 stations but negative scores on stations with other formats.

the decline of radio news, and voice tracking. The outlook for radio news jobs and DJs is not bright. Careers in the sales department have somewhat better prospects. Online radio also seems to be a growth area, albeit a modest one. Students who combine a knowledge of radio with Internet and social media skills will have better luck finding a job.

The career outlook in the various media industries changes quickly. For a more current description of conditions in the radio industry and a more detailed look at career options, please consult the book's Web site: www.mhhe.com/dominick12e.

main points

- Radio started out as point-to-point communication, much like the telephone and telegraph. The notion of broadcasting did not come about until the 1920s.

- The decade of the 1920s was an important one in radio. Big business took control of the industry, receivers improved, commercials were started, networks were formed, and the FRC was set up to regulate radio.

- The coming of TV forced local stations to adopt formats, such as Top 40 or country.

- FM became the dominant form of radio in the 1970s and 1980s. Sparked by a loosening of ownership rules, a wave of consolidation took place in the industry during the 1990s.

- Radio is moving slowly into the digital age. Satellite radio and Internet radio are two digital services that will compete with traditional radio. Radio stations are introducing HD radio and promoting themselves via social media.

- Radio programming is provided by local stations, networks, and syndication companies.

- Stations have refined their formats to reach an identifiable audience segment.

- Most radio revenue comes from local advertising. Big companies now dominate large-market radio.

- Radio advertising revenue has recently declined.

- National Public Radio is the best-known public broadcaster.

- Radio audiences are measured by Arbitron using a diary method or the personal people meter. The demographic characteristics of the radio listener vary greatly by station format.

questions for review

1. What were the key developments during the 1920s that helped shape modern radio?

2. What impact did the Telecommunications Act of 1996 have on the radio industry?

3. What are the defining features of radio?

4. What is the function of a format wheel?

5. How is radio listening measured?

6. How do Internet stations differ from terrestrial stations?

questions for critical thinking

1. What might have happened if radio had developed during the 1930s—the Depression years—instead of the Roaring Twenties?

2. What formats might radio stations have developed if rock and roll had not come along?

3. The radio industry is highly concentrated. Consolidation may have helped radio's bottom line, but is the listener better served? Why or why not?

4. Listen to the radio stations in your market. Are there audience segments in the market that are not being served?

5. Read "Critical/Cultural Issues: Radio and the Local Community" on page 198, and consider the following: What effect might the Internet have on the amount of local news, information, and other services in a given community? Will the Internet allow access to "those voices which cannot gain any serious measure of volume elsewhere"? Who owns the radio stations in your hometown? How do the locally owned stations compare with those that are corporate owned?

6. Compare traditional radio listening with listening to a station via a mobile app. How are they different?

key terms

network (p. 179)
Radio Act of 1927 (p. 181)
Federal Communications
    Commission (FCC) (p. 181)
Communications Act of 1934 (p. 181)
clock hour (p. 183)
payola (p. 184)

nonduplication rule (p. 184)
National Public Radio (NPR) (p. 184)
Telecommunications Act of 1996 (p. 184)
Internet-only radio stations (p. 186)
AM (p. 189)
FM (p. 189)
format (p. 190)

voice tracking (p. 192)
format wheel (p. 195)
cycle (p. 195)
Arbitron (p. 199)
portable people meter (PPM) (p. 199)
rating (p. 200)
share of the audience (p. 200)

internet resources

Online Learning Center

On the Online Learning Center home page, www.mhhe.com/dominick12e, *select* Student Center *and then* Chapter 8.

1. Use the Learning Objectives, Chapter Outline, and Main Points sections to review this chapter.

2. Test your knowledge of the chapter using the multiple choice and flashcard features of the site.

3. Expand your knowledge of concepts and topics discussed in the chapter with additional Questions for Critical Thinking and Internet Exercises.

surfing the internet

Web sites devoted to radio are about as changeable as the medium itself. With luck these will still be functioning.

www.otr.com
A site devoted to radio's Golden Age. Listen to clips from kids' after-school serials, radio dramas, and classic comedy shows.

http://pandora.com
Program your own radio station.

www.entercom.com
Entercom Communications Corporation home page. Click on "radio stations" to locate all of Entercom's holdings.

www.kisw.com
KISW-FM, a Seattle rock station. Includes streaming media, links to video, and stuff you can buy.

www.npr.org
The home of National Public Radio. Note the links to podcasts.

www.rab.com
Home page of the Radio Advertising Bureau. Filled with useful statistics and facts about radio.

Justin Bieber got his start when a record producer saw his YouTube video.

Chapter**9**

sound
recording

This chapter will prepare you to:

- understand the development of the recording process
- explain the impact of the Depression and World War II on the industry
- recognize the significance of the recording technology
- discuss the impact of file sharing
- explain how the digital age is affecting the recording industry
- describe the departments that make up the recording industry
- understand the current economic problems of the industry

Justin Bieber was born in 1994 in Ontario, Canada, and became interested in music at an early age. He played guitar, sang for his friends and relatives, and sometimes performed on the street for spare change. When he was 12, he entered a local talent competition based on the *American Idol* format. Since many of Justin's friends and relatives could not attend the show, his Internet-savvy mother posted a video of his performance on YouTube. In the months that followed, Justin and his mother continued to post videos of the youngster covering R&B songs by Usher, Justin Timberlake, and others. Soon his videos were getting hundreds of views.

Then he got a lucky break. Recording executive Scooter Braun was searching YouTube when he accidentally clicked one of Justin's videos. Impressed by his performance, Braun introduced the youngster to Usher and, with Usher's support, Justin was signed to a recording contract with Island Records in 2008.

You probably know the rest of the story. Within five months, the video for his hit *Baby* was viewed more than 170 million times, the third-most-watched video of all time on YouTube. With the release of his album *My World 2.0*, Justin became the youngest male singer ever to top *Billboard* magazine's Top 200. By mid-2011, the album had sold more than 2 million units. His 3-D movie, *Never*

Say Never, grossed more than $72 million at the U.S. box office. In short, Justin Bieber became a huge pop star in a short time.

Justin is the most successful of several recording artists who have been discovered via YouTube: Esmee Denters, Marie Digby, Arnel Pineda, to name a few. Of course, for every performer who succeeds, there are probably hundreds of others whose YouTube videos are seen only by family and friends and never make it big. Nevertheless, a couple of things are clear. Aspiring music stars no longer have to travel to Los Angeles or Nashville to be discovered. Recording industry talent scouts now routinely scan YouTube to look for the next Justin Bieber. Second, it's not just the established recording companies that are cultivating new talent. In 2010, talk show host Ellen DeGeneres started her own music label. The first artist she signed was 12-year-old Greyson Chance. Where did she discover Greyson? On YouTube.

Of all the media discussed in this book, the recording industry was the first to be drastically affected by the shift from tangible atoms (such as CDs) to intangible bits of information (such as MP3 files). The recording industry was blindsided by the digital revolution and is now trying to cope with an innovation that has transformed its distribution system, its economic base, and its traditional business model. This chapter will examine the history, structure, organization, and economics of this rapidly changing industry.

a brief history

Early Technologies

Thomas Edison recited "Mary Had a Little Lamb" into a primitive recording machine consisting of a tinfoil-wrapped cylinder, needle, microphone, and crank. It is interesting to speculate what might have happened if Edison had sung the nursery rhyme rather than recited it. Perhaps innovators would have been more aware of the music potential of this new medium, and the history of the recording industry might have been different. As it was, Edison and others thought his **phonograph**, the name he gave his 1877 invention, might best be suited to recording the spoken word. He eventually tried to sell it to the business community as an aid to dictation. At the time, the idea of using the phonograph to bring musical entertainment into the home was too wild to imagine.

Edison's phonograph faced new competition when Chichester Bell and Charles Tainter patented a device called the **graphophone**, in which Edison's foil was replaced by a wax cylinder. In 1887 more competition emerged when Emile Berliner patented a system that used a disk instead of a cylinder. He called his new invention a **gramophone**.

By 1890 three machines that recorded and played back sound were on the market. At about this time big business entered the picture as Jesse Lippincott, who had made a fortune in the glass tumbler business, purchased the business rights to both the phonograph and the graphophone, thus ending a bitter patent fight between the respective inventors. Lippincott had dreams of controlling the office dictating market, but stenographers rebelled against the new device and the talking-machine business fell upon hard times. Strangely enough, relief appeared quickly and financial solvency returned, a nickel at a time, thanks to a new idea: using the phonograph to record music instead of the spoken voice.

One of Lippincott's local managers hit upon the idea of putting coin-operated phonographs in the many penny arcades and amusement centers that were springing up all over America. For a nickel you could listen through a pair of stethoscope-like earphones to a cylinder whose 2-minute musical recording had a technical quality that could only be described as awful. Still, these **nickelodeons** were immensely popular, and the demand for "entertainment" cylinders grew. Companies quickly scrambled for a share in the new recording production business.

media
Probe   *Recording Pioneer Emile Berliner*

The 100th anniversary of phonograph recording on a flat disk was 1988. This technology was created by Emile Berliner, an immigrant from Germany, who worked as a stock clerk in a clothing store while investigating the intriguing new world of sound amplification and recording. Berliner quickly noted that the cylinders used by Edison had too many disadvantages to be practical. He perfected a way to encode sound on a flat disk that could be easily duplicated by using a master mold, much like pressing waffles in a waffle iron.

His invention was slow to catch on in the United States because of competition from Edison, but it was a success in Europe. Eventually,

Berliner introduced to the American market the phonautograph, which he renamed the gramophone. This eventually replaced the cylinder.

In one area Berliner clearly saw the future. He predicted that prominent singers and performers would collect royalties from the sale of his disks. He was wrong on another count, however. He thought that musicians and artists who were unable to appear at a concert would simply send a record to be played on stage instead.

Berliner also developed the prototype of the modern microphone, and both his inventions—the disk and the microphone—came together when electronic recording was perfected during the 1920s. Even the modern CD owes him a debt. Like his original invention, the CD stores information in a spiral on a flat, rotating surface.

Rivalry and Growth

The two decades spanning the turn of the 20th century were a time of intense business rivalry in the recording industry. While the two major companies, the Columbia Phonograph Company and Edison's North American Phonograph Company, fought one another, Berliner's United States Gramophone Company perfected the process of recording on flat disks. Ultimately, Columbia recognized the superiority of the disk and attempted to break into the market by selling the zonophone, its own version of the disk player. As for Berliner, along with machinist Eldridge Johnson, he formed the Victor Talking Machine Company, which had as its trademark a picture of a dog peering into the bell of a gramophone and the slogan "His Master's Voice." Thanks to aggressive marketing, this new company was highly successful and in 1906 introduced the Victrola, the first disk player designed to look like a piece of furniture. By 1912 the supremacy of the disk over the cylinder had been established.

On the eve of World War I, record players were commonplace throughout America. A dance craze in 1913 sent profits soaring, a trend that was to continue throughout the war. In 1914, 27 million records were manufactured; 107 million were produced in 1919 following the end of the war. The record industry had entered a boom period.

The boom continued when the years after World War I ushered in the Jazz Age, a period named after the spirited, popular music of the Roaring Twenties. **Jazz**, which emerged from the roots of the black experience in America, was spontaneous, individualistic, and sensual. Because of its disdain for convention, jazz was widely denounced as degenerate during its early years (about 30 years later, another spontaneous and sensual musical innovation, rock and roll, would also be denounced).

The good times, however, did not last. In the beginning no one in the record industry regarded radio as a serious threat. Record company executives were sure that the static-filled, raucous noise emanating from radios would never compete with the quality of their recordings. They were wrong.

The phonograph is just one of Thomas Edison's inventions. His 1877 model was hand-cranked, and the sound waves were preserved as scratches in tinfoil.

During the 1940s the local record shop was the place to hang out with friends and listen to the latest releases.

The Impact of Radio on the Recording Industry

Radio gained popularity in the 1920s, and the recording industry felt the effects. By the end of 1924, the combined sales of players and records had dropped 50 percent from those of the previous year. In the midst of this economic downturn, the recording companies quietly introduced electronic recording, using technology borrowed from their bitter rival, radio. The sound quality of records improved tremendously. But despite this improvement, radio continued to be thought of as the medium for "live" music, and records were dismissed as the medium of "canned" music.

In 1926 the record industry began to market radio-phonograph combinations, an obvious testament to the belief that the two media would coexist. This attitude was also prevalent at the corporate level. In 1927 rumors were flying that the Victor Company would soon merge with the Radio Corporation of America (RCA). Frightened by this prospect, Columbia, Victor's biggest rival, tried to get a head start by merging with the new (and financially troubled) radio network United Independent Broadcasters. All too soon, however, the record company became disillusioned and dissolved the deal. The much-discussed RCA and Victor merger came about in 1929, with the new company dominated by the radio operation.

The Depression Years

The Great Depression of the 1930s dealt a severe economic blow to sound recording. Thomas Edison's record manufacturing company went out of business in 1930. Record sales dropped from $46 million in 1930 to $5.5 million in 1933, and several smaller labels folded. The entire industry was reeling.

In the midst of all this gloom, the recording industry was saved once again by the nickel. Coin-operated record players, called *jukeboxes* (the origin of this term is obscure), began appearing in the thousands of bars and cocktail lounges that sprang up after the repeal of Prohibition in 1933. These jukeboxes were immensely popular and quickly spread to diners, drugstores, and restaurants. Starting in 1934, total record sales began to inch upward; by 1939 sales had increased by more than 500 percent.

World War II and After

The record industry did not do well during the war. First, the U.S. government declared shellac—a key ingredient of disks—vital to the national defense, and supplies available for making records dropped drastically. Second, the American Federation of Musicians, fearful of losing jobs because of canned music, went on strike. The strike lasted from 1942 to 1944, and as a result, record sales increased slowly during the war years. However, it was also during the war that Capitol Records embarked on a novel approach to record promotion. The company mailed free records to radio stations, hoping for airplay. This action marked formal recognition of a new industry attitude: Radio could help sell records. This new philosophy would revolutionize the recording industry.

In 1948 Columbia introduced the 33⅓-rpm long-playing record (LP). The new disks could play for 25 minutes a side and were virtually unbreakable. Rather than adopt the Columbia system, RCA Victor introduced its own innovation, the 45-rpm extended-play record. The next few years were described as the "battle of the speeds," as the record-buying public was confronted by a choice among 33⅓, 45, and 78 records. From 1947

Elvis Aaron Presley sold more than 250 million records, starred in 33 movies, and forever changed American popular music.

to 1949, record sales dropped 25 percent as people waited to see which speed would win. In 1950 RCA conceded and began issuing 33⅓ records. Columbia won only a partial victory, however. The 45 would become the preferred disk for single pop recordings, and the 33⅓ would dominate album sales. The 78 became obsolete. There were also changes in record players. High-fidelity sets came on the market in 1954, followed four years later by stereophonic record players. Record sales more than doubled during this period.

The mushrooming popularity of television during the 1950s had an impact on both radio and the recording industry. Television took away the big national stars from radio and forced local stations to experiment with new formats in an attempt to keep their audiences. One of the most popular radio formats that emerged was Top 40, relying on a set playlist based on record sales. The emergence of rock and roll helped the new Top 40 format become popular with a young audience. As we saw in Chapter 8, this young audience had a lot of money to spend on the records they heard played by their favorite DJs.

The Coming of Rock and Roll

Rock had its roots in black rhythm and blues, commercial white popular music, country and western, and jazz. In July 1955, Bill Haley and the Comets moved into the number-one spot on the charts with "Rock Around the Clock." Less than a year later, another performer who would enjoy a far more substantial career came on the scene. "Heartbreak Hotel," recorded by a then relatively unknown Elvis Presley, would stay at the number-one position for seven straight weeks. It was with Elvis that rock and roll first blossomed. Combining a country-and-western style with the beat and energy of black rhythm-and-blues music, Elvis's records sold millions. He appeared on Ed Sullivan's network TV show (from the waist up—Sullivan thought Elvis's pelvic gyrations too suggestive). Through Elvis rock and roll gained wide recognition, if not respectability.

Presley's success inspired other performers from the country-and-western tradition. Jerry Lee Lewis combined Mississippi boogie-woogie with country music to produce a unique and driving style. His "Whole Lotta Shakin' Going On" sold 6 million copies from 1957 to 1958.

Several rock pioneers came from traditional black rhythm-and-blues music. Perhaps the most exciting (certainly the most energetic) was Richard Penniman, or, as he called himself, Little Richard. Except for a period of three months, Little Richard had a record in the Top 100 at all times from 1956 to 1957 (best known are "Long Tall Sally" and "Tutti Frutti"). About the same time, on the South Side of Chicago, Chuck Berry was singing blues in small nightclubs. Discovered by the owner of a Chicago-based record company, Berry was the first artist who paid more than passing attention to the lyrics of rock and roll. His style would later influence many musical groups, including the Beatles.

The Commercialization of Rock

By 1959, through a combination of bizarre events, all the pioneers of rock had disappeared. Elvis had enlisted in the Army. Jerry Lee Lewis had married a 13-year-old girl said to be his cousin and dropped from sight. Little Richard was in the seminary. And Chuck Berry was incarcerated in federal prison. Thus, the way was open for a whole new crop of stars. Economics dictated what this new crop would look and sound like.

Record companies recognized that huge amounts of money could be made from the rock-and-roll phenomenon if it was promoted correctly. Unfortunately, rock and roll had an image problem. In 1959 the record industry was shaken by the payola scandals

decision makers

Berry Gordy Jr.

Berry Gordy began as an assembly-line worker in Detroit but ended up as the head of one of the largest black-owned businesses in America. Along the way he introduced black performers to a wider audience and permanently shaped the evolution of American popular music.

In 1957 Gordy wrote a hit song for R&B artist Jackie Wilson. While Gordy and Wilson were in the studio working on other projects, a group called the Matadors auditioned for Wilson. Although Wilson was unimpressed with their songs, Gordy noticed the potential of their lead singer, a young man named Smokey Robinson.

Over the next few years, Gordy continued to write and produce songs for a number of black artists. Dissatisfied with the way his songs were handled by the major record labels, Gordy decided to start his own. He took an $800 loan from his family and in 1959 opened what would later become Motown Records. The company released its first single in 1959 and had its first number-one hit two years later with the Marvelettes' "Please Mr. Postman."

In its early years Motown appealed primarily to black audiences, but Gordy's strategy was to appeal to both whites and blacks. Motown's advertising slogan was "The Sound of Young America." During the mid-1960s Gordy's company pioneered the Motown sound, which revolutionized the music industry. Artists such as Stevie Wonder, Marvin Gaye, Smokey Robinson, and Diana Ross and the Supremes became popular with both black and white record buyers. A few years later Gordy introduced the Jackson Five, featuring a young Michael Jackson as lead singer.

In 1988 Berry Gordy was inducted into the Rock and Roll Hall of Fame along with the Supremes, Bob Dylan, and the Beatles. That same year, Gordy sold Motown Records to MCA for more than $60 million. He continued, however, to head Motown's record publishing division and its film and television sections. The sound Gordy created will continue to influence the musical tastes of future generations.

Motown star Diana Ross and Berry Gordy Jr.

(see Chapter 8) that, arriving on top of years of bad publicity and criticism of rock and roll as responsible for most of society's ills, threatened rock's profitability. Since rock and roll had too much moneymaking potential to be abandoned, the record companies decided to clean up rock's image.

As the 1960s opened, the new look in rock was characterized by middle-class, white, clean-cut, wholesome performers. Rock stars were young men and women you would not hesitate to bring home and introduce to your parents. On the male side Ricky Nelson, Bobby Vee, Bobby Vinton, Fabian, Paul Anka, Frankie Avalon, and the Four Seasons were popular. There were fewer examples on the female side. Those who had hits included Annette Funicello, Connie Francis, Brenda Lee, and Lesley Gore. All fit the new image of rock and roll. Consequently, the early 1960s saw few musical innovations. In 1963, however, the music changed again.

The British Invasion

Their name was inspired by Buddy Holly and the Crickets, but instead of choosing the entomologically correct "Beetles," the group decided to spell their name "Beatles" (which incorporated the word *beat*). In early 1964 they took the United States by storm.

The Beatles have more gold albums—47—than any other group in the history of sound recording. The Beatles were on top of the charts again in 2009 thanks to the release of the video game *The Beatles: Rock Band.*

The 1960s was a decade of change in American music. Compare early-1960s recording star Annette Funicello (shown in her Mouseketeer costume) with late-1960s star Janis Joplin.

Musically, the Beatles were everything that American rock and roll was not. They were innovative, especially in vocal harmony, and introduced the harmonica as a rock instrument. Ultimately, they would change the shape of the music business and American popular culture. The Beatles had seven number-one records in 1964; they held down the top position for 20 of the 52 weeks that year.

Their success paved the way for a veritable British invasion. Most British rock at this time resembled American rock: cheery, commercial, and white. Not surprisingly, some of the first groups that followed the Beatles represented this school (Herman's Hermits, Freddie and the Dreamers, the Dave Clark Five, and Peter and Gordon, to name a few). There was another style of British rock, however, far less cheery, as represented by the Rolling Stones and the Animals. This style was blues-based, rough-hewn, slightly aggressive, and certainly not bouncy and carefree.

American artists were not silent during this influx of British talent. Folk music, as performed by Bob Dylan and Joan Baez, was also popular. It was only a matter of time before folk merged with rock to produce folk rock. Soul music, as recorded on the Motown label, also made its mark during the 1960s.

Transitions

The late 1960s was a time of cultural transition. Freedom, experimentation, and innovation were encouraged in almost all walks of life, and popular music was no exception. Sparked by the release of the Beatles' *Sgt. Pepper* album, a fractionalization of rock began. Several trends of this period are notable. In 1968 Blood, Sweat and Tears successfully blended jazz, rock, and at times even classical music. The Band introduced country rock. The Who recorded a rock opera, *Tommy*. In the midst of all this experimentation, commercial formula music was also healthy. The Monkees, a group put together by ads in the newspaper, sold millions of records. Bubblegum rockers the Archies kept "Sugar, Sugar" at the top of the charts for a month in 1969 (it replaced a song by the Rolling Stones, "Honky Tonk Woman").

Toward the end of the 1960s and the beginning of the 1970s, rock music became part of the counterculture; in many instances it went out of its way to

media talk

TV Phenom *American Idol*

Clip 8: 6 minutes 25 seconds

You can watch Clip 8 *on the Online Learning Center home page,* www.mhhe.com/dominick12e. *Select* Student Center *and then* Chapter 9.

This clip describes *American Idol*'s effect on the music industry. Note how this is another example of media symbiosis. Have you ever voted for someone on *American Idol*? Do you think that *American Idol* has hurt or helped the music industry? Have you ever bought or downloaded any of the songs by an *American Idol* contestant? When was the last time you went to the store and bought a CD? How do you get the music you want to listen to?

media *Probe*   *Morbidity and Rock and Roll*

One of the strangest trends in the evolution of popular rock-and-roll music has been a small but persistent genre of records that can only be classified under the somewhat macabre title of "morbid rock." Although its roots probably go back further, it became especially notable in the 1960s. Among the first songs to become a hit was "Teen Angel," the tale of an unfortunate couple whose car stalled on the railroad tracks. Although the young man of the song is smart enough to run like crazy, the young woman goes back to the car to retrieve her sweetheart's high school ring. The train arrives at the same time. End of romance.

Another early example was J. Frank Wilson's "Last Kiss," a tragic tale of a guy and girl out on a date who plow into a disabled car. He survives. She doesn't. End of romance. "Tell Laura I Love Her" told the teary story of a young man who needs money to continue his romance with his girlfriend and so resorts to stock car racing to provide extra income. He totals his car

and himself. End of romance. "Patches" concerned the romance between a young woman from the wrong side of the tracks and a middle-class young man. Despondent, the young woman drowns herself in the river. At the end of the song, the young man is contemplating the same thing. Even wholesome Pat Boone got into the act with "Moody River," a song that also told the story of two people who throw themselves into the river and drown.

The trend was less noticeable in the early 1970s, but a song titled "Billy, Don't Be a Hero" enjoyed wide popularity. This song was about a boy who goes off to war, against the wishes of his girlfriend, and gets killed. End of romance. (For those who are true fans of this genre, Rhino Records has collected 10 teen tragedy songs ranging from "Last Kiss" to the little-known but nonetheless moving "The Homecoming Queen's Got a Gun." Incidentally, the back cover of the LP doubles as a tissue dispenser.)

The trend hasn't resurfaced since 1999 when Pearl Jam's remake of "Last Kiss" went to number two on the charts. Perhaps it's . . . dead.

break with the establishment. Musically, many of the songs of this era were characterized by the **heavy metal** sound; amplifiers and electronic equipment began to dominate the stage. The artists also broke sharply with tradition. The pioneers in this style of rock were all vaguely threatening, a trifle unsavory, and definitely not the type you would bring home to the folks.

Industry Trends: 1970s–1990s

The recording industry enjoyed a boom period during the mid-1970s, resulting in large measure from the popularity of disco. A downturn during the early 1980s reversed itself during the second half of that decade thanks to Michael Jackson's *Thriller* album and a few popular movie soundtracks. The 1990s saw the CD replace tape as the preferred playback medium. Record companies were happy about this because the profit margins on CDs were greater than for tape. As a result, recording industry revenues showed some fluctuation but generally increased during the 1990s.

The Contemporary Sound Recording Industry

As we shall see, the contemporary sound recording industry is moving away from selling shiny discs (atoms) to selling digital music (bits). Illegal file sharing is still a problem, but the closing of peer-to-peer network Limewire in 2010 has resulted in a decline in pirated music. Industry statistics suggest that the number of illegal downloaders dropped by 45 percent from 2007 to 2010.

On the business side, Citigroup took over EMI Music when EMI ran into financial trouble. In late 2011 Citigroup sold EMI's music publishing division to Sony

Despite best-selling albums by performers such as Taylor Swift, recording industry revenues are still declining because of illegal downloading.

social issues   *A Music Tax?*

As the recording industry continues to search for a solution to illegal file sharing that would also help its bottom line, one idea keeps popping up: a surcharge, maybe around $5, on a consumer's monthly Internet bill that would cover the cost of pirated music.

There are several variations to this plan. In one version, the surcharge would allow consumers to download all the music they wanted from the recording companies' catalogues. The charge would be mandatory; everybody would pay a little extra whether they downloaded music or not. The money would be collected by an industry organization and doled out to labels and artists by some predetermined formula. The model for this would be the radio industry, where stations pay a compulsory license fee to the industry in return for the right to play music. The Internet Service Provider (ISP) would assume the role of the radio station and collect and pay the fee. ISPs might be persuaded to go along with the plan because they are afraid that they could be sued by the recording industry and eventually be held liable for copyright infringements on their networks.

The plan is strongly opposed by consumer groups. Why should someone who doesn't download music have to pay a surcharge? That seems to violate the basic principle of fairness. In response, the recording industry notes that Americans pay for public broadcasting whether they watch it or not. And what about all those cable channels that people never watch? Consumers still pay for them on their monthly bill. But what about people who legally download music from places such as iTunes? Do they pay twice? Would this system put iTunes out of business?

Another potential problem is that a music surcharge would create guaranteed income for the record labels. This might remove any incentive for innovation or to spend money on the development of new artists. Why take risks when the reward is guaranteed?

And if ISPs collect a surcharge for the music industry, shouldn't they also collect a fee for the movie industry to cover the cost of pirated movies? Or how about another fee tacked on to ISP bills to compensate for illegally shared computer software?

Despite all the problems, the recording industry is still willing to put its support behind this idea. This shows how far the industry will go to shore up its faltering business model.

and its music entertainment division to Universal Music Group. Additionally, the Warner Music Group was acquired by Access Industries for $3.3 billion. The sound recording industry remains highly concentrated, with the four biggest firms controlling about 85 percent of the market. Many critics have blamed concentration for the decline in music sales, arguing that big companies are unlikely to develop new and compelling musical styles.

sound recording in the digital age

Transition

Throughout most of its history, sound recording used the analog technique. Sound waves were first etched into grooves of a vinyl disk or into rearranged particles on a magnetic tape. In both cases the recording industry manufactured and distributed the products (disks or tapes) that consumers purchased. The digital technique changed that by encoding music as pure information, a string of binary numbers, from which music could be recovered. As a result, consumers no longer needed to buy the product from the record companies. All they needed were the numbers and their hard drives or blank CDs. This development would not have been a problem for the industry as long as there was no efficient way of getting those numbers to the consumer. The development of the personal computer and the Internet, however, made it easy for consumers to download digital information to their home computers and other portable devices.

The recording industry was thrust into the digital age before it was fully prepared for the consequences. At first, music executives dismissed downloading from the Internet as something only a few geeks would be interested in.

sound byte

You'll Get a Charge out of This

What's the one thing that's missing from your iPod, Zune, or other MP3 player? A taser, obviously.

At a recent Consumer Electronics Show, Taser International unveiled the Taser MPH—a combination music player and high-voltage, dart-firing, electroshock weapon. The MPH, which can hold about 150 songs, comes with a holster that slips onto a person's belt.

You can probably imagine some songs that would be on the MPH's playlist: "Electric Avenue," "Shock to the System," "Currents"—you get the idea.

ethical issues
The Ethics of File Sharing: Is It Really Stealing?

Recording industry profits slipped steadily from 2000 to 2010. Most experts concede that part of this decrease (some would say most of it) was due to downloading free music. With only a few exceptions, almost everybody in the recording industry considers downloading songs from file-sharing sites such as Pirate Bay and eDonkey to be stealing (or "pirating" as the industry calls it). On the other hand, with few exceptions, people who download music feel quite the opposite.

In that connection, I often asked my students the following question: Would you go to a store and walk out with a CD without paying for it? Aside from a couple of sarcastic replies, almost all students answered in the negative and conceded that taking a CD without paying for it is stealing. I next asked them this: Would you download music from the Internet and share it online without paying for it? Almost everybody answered this in the positive. I then asked them what the difference is between the two situations. Their answers reveal a lot of the complexities involved in developing an ethical stance about file-sharing programs.

Their rationales for their behavior generally fall into these broad categories:

- It's okay to download and share music because the record companies have been overcharging us for CDs and have been exploiting performers for years (just listen to Courtney Love), and the companies deserve it. File sharing is a righteous protest, just another way to "stick it to the Man," a philosophy that was popular during the 1960s.

- It's okay to download and share music because on the Internet all information should be free.

- It's okay to download and share music because I only download stuff that I wouldn't buy anyway, so I'm not really hurting anybody.

Let's look in turn at each of these arguments from an ethical point of view.

Taken to its logical extreme, the first argument suggests that it's okay to steal from any individual company that you think charges too much for its goods or services or somehow mistreats its workers. Would you steal a Buick because you think GM has been pricing its cars too high? Even assuming the premise about exploiting performers is correct (and it should be noted that many of these "exploited" performers have a rather impressive lifestyle), is it okay to steal from companies whose conduct you disapprove of? Suppose some clothing company pays its workers in Thailand only a couple of dollars an hour. Should you steal its goods? Would that make it become less exploitive? This sounds like endorsing the policy that two wrongs actually do make a right. One well-known ethical principle is Kant's Categorical Imperative (see Chapter 17), which states that you should act in the same way that you want others to act toward you. If you ran a business, would you want people who decide they disapprove of your business to steal from you?

The argument that "information should be free" is a common one. At its core is the belief in some sort of entitlement to information, that somehow the existence of the Internet means we have a right to share freely the works of others. In the first place, information doesn't simply appear; somebody has to create it. It would seem more reasonable to argue that the individual who created the information (music, movies, or video) should be the one to decide if it's free. If members of a musical group think that free exposure on the Internet will help them charge more for their concert appearances, they should be able to post their music on file-sharing systems. (Many groups have done this.) On the other hand, if a group decides that it wants people to pay to hear its music, it should have that right. This is the notion behind the legal doctrine of intellectual property. Take an example: Suppose you create a clever new video game and share the software with some friends. Suppose further that Microsoft hears about it and offers you a large sum of money to market the game. In the meantime, however, suppose one of your friends, a strong believer in the idea that information should be free, posts your game on the Web, and it becomes so popular that Microsoft decides the market is already saturated and withdraws the offer. Shouldn't you have the right to decide what to do with your creation?

The argument about downloading only stuff that otherwise wouldn't be bought raises an interesting question. In the first place, if you share files, other people who might have otherwise bought the record might download it and not buy it. This would seem to hurt those who created the music. Second, your decision not to buy might have been influenced by the presence of the music for free on the Internet. Who's to say that you might have a different attitude toward the music if it weren't freely available on the Net? Maybe you would buy it after all.

Putting aside the various legal arguments about downloading, it would appear that all the common arguments justifying downloads from file-sharing systems don't stand up to an ethical analysis. Indeed, now that legal downloading services are available as an alternative, the common rationalizations seem even weaker. Nonetheless, many students appear to be unfazed and continue to download. They apparently don't believe it's stealing.

Why the ethical disconnect between walking out of a store without paying for a CD and downloading a CD without paying? Part of the explanation is the gap between action and consequence. Taking a CD from a store has an immediate and clear effect: The retailer loses the money that he or she paid for the CD. There is a visible victim. Downloading music from the amorphous and impersonal Web separates the act from its harmful consequence. There is no apparent victim. The record companies and the artists who are harmed by downloading are removed and abstract. Would downloading be as popular if the downloader had a clear idea about how his or her act directly affected the artist?

Then came Napster, Kazaa, and their progeny, and the business was forever changed. Never had so much music been available to so many for free. All of a sudden, as recording industry expert John Kennedy put it, the recording industry had to figure out a way to make music easier to buy than to steal.

media *Probe*

Promoting an Album or Single

Not too many years ago promoting a recording was fairly simple: Get the song played as often as possible on big-city radio stations and have MTV feature the song's music video. Today, however, the task has become increasingly complicated as more and more promotion tools are available. A recent edition of *Billboard* magazine listed the top 100 ways to promote a record, based on a survey of industry experts and sales data. Here are the top 10. Note that both traditional and new media make the list.

1. A performance at the Grammy Awards. (After Pink performed at the 2010 Grammies, sales of her *Funhouse* album increased 170 percent.)
2. Appearing in a TV ad for Apple. (Sales of Feist's "1234" skyrocketed after it was played during an iPod Nano ad.)
3. Performing on *The Oprah Winfrey Show*. (Adam Lambert saw sales for his album jump 60 percent after he sang on her show. With Oprah moving to cable, it's hard to predict what her future influence might be.)
4. Being the free single of the week on iTunes. (After "Trinity" was an iTunes free selection, the Paper Tongues' first album debuted in the top 200 on *Billboard*'s album charts.)
5. Wal-Mart endcap display. (An endcap is the hub at the end of an aisle. A customer has an easier time seeing and buying products displayed on an endcap.)
6. Song performed on *Glee*. (After a medley of Journey songs in one *Glee* episode, sales of the band's greatest-hits album increased almost 60 percent.)
7. Album appears as Amazon's MP3 Daily Deal. (Amazon.com now accounts for nearly 10 percent of all U.S. music sales.)
8. Performance on *Saturday Night Live*. (Regina Spektor's album doubled its sales the week after she appeared.)
9. Appearing in the iTunes charts. (People like to buy what's popular.)
10. A successful tour. (Lady Gaga is the best example.)

The biggest developments of the past two decades have been the emergence of portable MP3 players such as Apple's iPod, the smartphone with built-in MP3 capability, and Apple's online iTunes store. Together these three innovations have totally reshaped the industry.

First, the single song has replaced the album as the preferred method of buying music. Consumers no longer want to pay $12–15 for a CD with only a couple of songs that they like; they would rather buy individual songs for a dollar or so and download them to their MP3 players. The digital revolution put more power in the hands of consumers, who could now buy and download only those songs that they liked. Needless to say, consumers began abandoning the album format. Thus, there has been a steady decline in the number of CDs purchased, a 55 percent decrease from 2007 to 2010. On the other hand, downloads of single songs increased 44 percent over the same period. Unfortunately for the record companies, the increased revenue from downloading singles is not enough to offset the losses from the decrease in CD album sales.

Second, Americans now consume a significant portion of their music via a portable device. The hi-fi or the stereo system in the living room or den has given way to MP3 players that can go anywhere. Apple has sold more than 110 million iPods and Microsoft has sold another 2 million Zunes. In addition, there are millions of MP3 smartphones in operation.

The MP3 player created a new cottage industry. More than 200 accessories can be purchased for the device, including a remote control, a nylon carrying case, and external speakers. The iPhone also has a wide range of available accessories.

Third, traditional brick-and-mortar record stores are disappearing as more Americans turn to digital downloading to receive their music. Sales of physical CDs accounted for 80 percent of all music sales in 2007; today that percentage is about 60. Tower Records and Musicland filed for bankruptcy in the mid-2000s. Mass-market retailers such as Target and Best Buy have reduced the number of CDs they keep in stock. Meanwhile, downloading music has seen remarkable growth, increasing 80 percent from 2007 to 2010. Apple's iTunes has sold more than 10 billion songs.

All of these factors have shown the recording industry that its old business model no longer works. Consequently, recording companies and recording artists have sought new ways to make money. Record companies now license songs to video games, sell short snippets of music as ringtones, and sell music video DVDs.

Mobile Music

The Sony Walkman was the first device that enabled consumers to take their recorded music with them. The iPod, iPhone, and related devices, such as the Nokia XpressMusic Phone and the Samsung i450, continue this tradition. Mobile music can be accessed in two ways. Consumers can purchase tunes from an online source, download the songs to their computer, and then sideload the songs to a digital player. The second method is direct downloading to a smartphone such as the iPhone or Google's Android. The iPhone dominates this market, accounting for more than 80 percent of downloads.

In 2011, Apple introduced the iCloud, a service that changes the way consumers access their music. At present, if a person downloads a song to an iPod, the song is stored on that device. The person can't play the song on an iPad or iPhone without first syncing the devices on his or her computer. With iCloud, the song is stored on a server connected to the Internet and a person can access it from an iPhone, iPad, laptop or desk top computer, home entertainment system, Internet-connected TV, and some car audio systems. iCloud could benefit record labels as well. Apple will store 5 gigabytes of music bought from iTunes for free in the cloud. However, most of the music on the average person's MP3 player was not bought via iTunes; the songs were ripped from CDs or obtained from other sources. Apple will charge a fee to store these tunes in iCloud and the record labels will get a cut of this revenue. Amazon has a similar service.

Recording companies are using apps to promote their products. Warner Music Group has about a dozen, including the Rhino Musical Aptitude Test and the Rob Thomas Fanbase. Sony Music has more than 25, many featuring their recording stars. The Pink app lets fans listen to her songs, play her latest videos, and communicate with other Pink fans. Using music recognition technology, the Shazam app "hears" a short segment of music, identifies the song and the artist, and has a link that lets the listener buy the song.

User-Generated Content

Two types of user-generated content are relevant to the music industry. The first involves artists and record labels that make their content available for others to incorporate into their homemade productions. Universal Music Group and Warner Music Group have agreements with YouTube to let users include their music in user-created videos that are then posted on the site. Some performers, including Nine Inch Nails, post raw recording tracks online and allow fans to remix them.

The second type of content includes all of the user-generated videos that are posted on YouTube and other video-sharing sites, the ones that made Justin Bieber and Rebecca Black famous. It's difficult to know how much of this content exists, but a search of YouTube using the term "new bands 2010" returned about 795,000 results.

Social Media

For many years, the music industry viewed the Internet as the enemy because it made possible the illegal sharing of music files. The development of social media, however, has forced the industry to reevaluate its attitude.

Most major artists and labels make use of Facebook and Twitter to promote their new songs, announce tour dates, and generally keep in touch with fans. As of this writing, Lady Gaga has 10 million followers on Twitter, 10 million Facebook fans, and 37 million "likes." Her Facebook page contains notes to fans, photos, and music videos of her latest releases. Jay-Z and Kanye West produced a Facebook page for their album *Watch the Throne*. Any fan who clicked the "like" icon could receive a free download of a single from the album directly from the Facebook site. Artists are also exploring ways to sell their songs directly through Facebook. Twitter has a service called Titurm that allows artists to post music directly on the site while Twt.fm allows fans to listen to songs without having to download them.

Moreover, social media have become the preferred way for new acts to promote themselves. Fledgling artists, like Justin Bieber, produce their own videos for sites such as YouTube and MySpace (although MySpace has declined in popularity with the ascent of

Facebook, it is still a site where many new bands post their music) in the hope of generating buzz and attracting the attention of a big record label.

Finally, fans use social media to communicate among themselves about the songs and artists that they like. Word of mouth has always been an important factor in the success of recordings, and social media have made it even more vital. Apple, for example, has created Ping, a social network for music, where members can "Follow your favorite artists and friends to discover the music they're talking about, listening to, and downloading."

defining features of sound recording

Sound recording is a cultural force. Its products help characterize social groups and define movements and trends in American society. Recorded music has been at the center of a great deal of cultural and social controversy. Sound recording helped usher in the Jazz Age during the Roaring Twenties. This new style of music was condemned as corrupting the nation's morals. The same criticisms were heard during the 1950s when rock-and-roll music became the rallying point for a new youth culture. During the 1960s recorded music joined the counterculture, and big record companies (benefiting from the status quo) earned huge profits from selling albums that challenged the status quo. In the 1990s rap music recordings introduced the hip-hop culture to the rest of America. All in all, the sound recording industry has played a major role in shaping modern culture.

Sound recording is also an international enterprise, with recording artists selling their music worldwide. For instance, Ricky Martin's eponymous album sold 14 million copies worldwide and 7 million in the United States. Celine Dion's greatest-hits album sold 5 million in the United States and 9 million internationally. Recording artists also tour all around the globe.

The recording business is a unique blend of business and talent. Recording companies are continually searching for new artists and new sounds that will succeed in the marketplace. The singers and musicians may be the stars, but the recording companies are the star makers. Most hit recordings owe much of their success to the marketing and promotion efforts of their record labels. Justin Bieber may have gotten a lot of YouTube views, but his career did not take off until he signed with Island Records.

organization of the recording industry

The recording industry consists of the various creative talent and business enterprises that originate, produce, and distribute records to consumers. Rock music accounts for more than 45 percent of the total sales of the recording industry; rhythm and blues and hip-hop account for another 22 percent; country, about 17 percent; Latin, about 5 percent; and jazz, classical, and gospel make up the rest. Although this chapter concentrates on rock, remember that the other music styles are also part of the industry. For our purposes we will divide the business into four major segments: (1) talent, (2) production, (3) distribution, and (4) retail.

Eminem's *Recovery* album sold more than 3 million copies.

Talent

The talent segment of the industry consists of all the singers, musicians, songwriters, arrangers, and lyricists who hope to make money by recording and selling their songs. The phrase "hope to make money"

media *Probe* Turning Music into Gold

In the music business, a relatively few performers make the big bucks while most other performers scrape by. But if you are among the lucky ones, the rewards can be great. *Billboard* magazine, the Bible of the industry, publishes an annual list of the top 40 moneymakers in the music biz. (*Billboard* uses a complicated formula that takes into account the artist's share of money from CD and digital sales, touring revenue, publishing and songwriting royalties, streaming, and ringtones.) Here are the top five moneymakers from 2010 with their approximate net earnings:

1.	Lady Gaga	$31,000,000
2.	Bon Jovi	30,000,000
3.	Roger Waters	25,000,000
4.	Dave Matthews Band	24,000,000
5.	Justin Bieber	22,000,000

is important because far more performers are laboring in virtual obscurity in and around Detroit, Seattle, Nashville, New York, and Los Angeles than are cashing royalty checks from their recordings. Exactly how many people are "out there" hoping to make it big is impossible to pinpoint.

Performers start out as a beginning act. The initial motivation may be simply personal pleasure. Many begin performing during high school. For example, Bob Dylan (then known as Bob Zimmerman) started out with a high school band in Hibbing, Minnesota.

In years past the next step for the novice musician or musical group was to form a traveling act that played anywhere and everywhere to gain experience, a little money, and recognition. Weezer, for example, kicked around southern California for several years, playing in places with names such as Club Dump and Bob's Frolic Room before finding commercial success. Although some bands and artists still go this route, many others, such as Marié Digby, turn to the Internet and post videos on YouTube, Facebook, or MySpace. If the act is good (and lucky), it may be noticed by a talent scout or producer from a major recording label (the record companies keep an eye on the Web and regularly check out anybody who has created an Internet "buzz"). If things go well, the act is signed to a recording contract.

Production

The recording company brings the act to a recording studio, where a large number of songs are recorded. Audio engineers and elaborate sound-mixing facilities are used to get exactly the right sound. Eventually, a single or an album is put together. The company also supplies publicity, advertising, merchandising, and packaging expertise. Promotion—which in the recording industry consists primarily of getting the record played on influential radio stations and prominently displayed on iTunes and social media sites, and getting the music video on YouTube and other video outlets—is also the responsibility of the company. There are dozens of record companies, but as of late 2011 three dominate the business: Warner, Sony, and Universal.

Distribution

There are six main outlets for music distribution: (1) direct retail, (2) rack jobbers, (3) one-stops, (4) direct consumer sales, (5) online sales, and (6) direct download (see Figure 9-1). Of these six outlets, direct retail, online sales, and direct download are most important, accounting for more than 70 percent of all sales.

Direct retail refers to stores that specialize in the sale of CDs and related products. Many retail stores are chain operations with several outlets in different parts of the country.

Rack jobbers service the CD racks in variety or large department stores. Wal-Mart, for example, has its CD shelves serviced by rack jobbers. The rack jobber chooses the CDs that are sold in these locations, thus relieving store management of the task of keeping up with

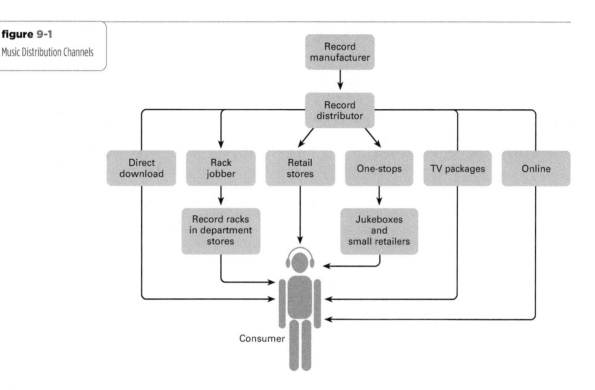

figure 9-1

Music Distribution Channels

the latest Eminem release, as well as other tasks such as reordering titles and returning unused merchandise. The decline in CD sales has made rack jobbers less influential.

One-stops purchase CDs from recording companies and resell them to retail stores. For example, a small, independently owned retail store might not qualify for credit from the recording companies and so might purchase its CDs from a one-stop.

TV packagers sell directly to the consumer. You have probably seen TV ads for collections of music (*The Best of Heavy Metal, Connie Francis's Greatest Hits, Zamfir and the Pan Flute*).

Online distribution is direct: The consumer deals directly with an online retailer, such as Amazon.com, and the product is delivered to his or her door.

The mechanics of digital downloading are also relatively simple: A consumer visits one of the many sites that offer downloads for sale, such as iTunes, MSN Music, or Wal-Mart, and selects a single track or album that he or she wishes to download. Most sites now offer a single download for about $1.29. The price to download an album varies depending on how many songs are available to download.

Retail

The times are not good for traditional music stores. Competition from online music sites and mass-market stores such as Wal-Mart has made it difficult for many retailers to survive. Wherehouse Music filed for bankruptcy in 2003 followed by Tower Records in 2004. Big retailer HMV closed dozens of stores. Transworld Entertainment (TWE), which operates nearly a thousand FYE, Coconuts, and Strawberries stores, has seen its revenue plummet. And Tower eventually folded in 2006, as did Musicland.

While the importance of the traditional music stores declined, the importance of mass marketers such as Target and Wal-Mart increased. In 1992, according to the Recording Association of America, 25 percent of all CDs and tapes were purchased at mass merchandise stores. In 2010 that figure rose to 33 percent. Over that same period the percentage sold in traditional music retail stores dropped from 53 to less than 10 percent. iTunes is the biggest music retailer, accounting for nearly 28 percent of the market. Wal-Mart is in second place.

Retailers are aware that if online downloading becomes the preferred way of delivering music to consumers, there will be little need for brick-and-mortar retail stores. Some retailers now stock DVDs, video games, magazines, and electronic equipment as well as gift cards that let people download from iTunes and other sources. In some retail outfits music accounts for less than half of all sales. Moreover, some electronics retailers, including Wal-Mart, have gotten into the music-downloading business.

ownership in the recording industry

The recording industry is one of the most concentrated of all media industries. As shown in Table 9-1, big companies dominate the business, accounting for more than 85 percent of the market. The three companies that dominate the industry are (1) Universal Music Group, owned by the French conglomerate Vivendi; (2) Sony, a large Japanese conglomerate; and (3) Warner Music, formerly part of the Time Warner empire but now owned by Access Industries, a U.S. -based industrial conglomerate.

producing records

Departments and Staff

There are seven departments within a typical recording company:

1. *Artists and Repertoire (A&R):* This department serves as the talent scout for the industry. A&R personnel monitor influential Internet music Web sites and keep an eye on local markets to see who's hot. Once in a while, they might also venture out on the road to check out acts (called *garage bands* in the trade) in the hope of finding the next superstar.

2. *Sales and Distribution:* As the name suggests, this department sells the company's products and then makes sure the CDs get to the stores and digital tracks get to downloading sites where consumers can buy them.

3. *Advertising and Merchandising:* This division is responsible for planning media ad campaigns and point-of-purchase displays in sales outlets. The efforts of this department are coordinated with those of the promotion department.

4. *Promotion:* This department helps market and promote the company's artists. Although getting a song played on an influential radio station is still an important part of the promotion process, other strategies are effective as well. A song played during a hit TV show such as *Glee* can significantly boost sales. Having a presence on social media is also a necessity.

5. *Business:* This department includes lawyers, accountants, market researchers, financial analysts, and secretarial and clerical staffers. It functions in the recording industry the same as in any other business or industry.

6. *Publicity:* This department attempts to get press coverage for new performers and new releases and also has the job of getting new acts and albums reviewed by influential publications such as *Rolling Stone* and *Billboard* and by influential bloggers.

table 9-1	Company	Major Labels	Top Stars
Top Recording Companies, 2011 (before the sale of EMI)	Universal Music Group	Geffen, Island Def Jam, Motown	Kanye West, Lady Gaga, Gwen Stefani
	Warner Music	Atlantic, Warner Bros., Maverick	James Blunt, Rob Thomas, Green Day
	Sony	Arista, Epic, Jive	Beyoncé, Britney Spears, Shakira
	EMI	Virgin, Capitol, Blue Note	ColdPlay, Keith Urban, Katy Perry

7. *Artist Development:* The duties of this department include coordinating tour dates, making sure the act has a well-produced concert show, and arranging for TV appearances.

Making a Recording

For a performer or a group to win a recording contract, they first must convince someone in a recording company that they have a sound that will sell. Some artists produce a **demo**, a disc that provides a sample of their sound. Others post videos on the Internet and hope that they catch on. Still others bombard the A&R department with e-mails and MP3 attachments or links to music Web sites. These initial efforts don't have to be professional grade, but they do have to highlight the strengths of the performer or group.

If things work out, the performer or group is signed to a contract to produce an album or perhaps just one or two tracks. At that point the act moves into a recording studio to make a master recording.

Resembling something you might see at NASA's mission control center, with banks of modern equipment, blinking lights, and digital readouts, the modern recording studio has machines capable of recording up to 48 different tracks. This means that different instruments and vocals can be recorded on different sections of a disc. Thus, a piano might be recorded on one track, drums on another, bass on another, lead vocals on another, background vocals on yet another, and so on. So that one track does not leak onto another, the studio is set up with careful placement of microphones and wooden baffles—soundproof barriers that keep the sound of one instrument from spilling over into the mikes recording the other instruments. Once the session starts, the producer makes most of the creative decisions. The producer decides when the performers take a break, when the tune has to be played over because of a bad note, when the music should be played back so the group can hear itself and perhaps make changes in the arrangement, and so on.

The advent of multiple-track recording has revamped the music-making process. Currently, it is not even necessary for band members to record together. The instrumentalists can come in one at a time and "lay down" their tracks, the lead singer or singers can add the vocals later, and everything can be put together at the mixing console.

After the recording session the next step is the mix down, the technically exacting job of mixing down the multiple tracks onto a two-track stereo master. In the mix down each track is equalized; echo, overdubbing, or other special effects are added; and certain passages are scheduled for rerecording. If an album is being produced, each track has to be precisely placed on the stereo spectrum. A track can be placed in the left or right speaker or in the center, where it is heard equally in both speakers. Mixing a 16- or 24-track tape down to 2 tracks can take several days. The job has been made somewhat easier in recent years thanks to computerized mixing boards. After the mix is completed, the master is stored on a disc in digital form for possible manufacturing and distribution. At the same time, the promotion department is given a preview of the new release, and the advertising and publicity departments begin their efforts.

A sophisticated mixing board such as this one handles as many as 48 separate sound tracks that contain recordings of instruments and vocals. Note the computer monitors. Computer programs remember previous mixing setups, making the process faster and easier.

the economics of sound recording

We will approach the topic of economics at two levels. First, we will examine the economic structure of the industry as a whole. Next, we will investigate the financial ups and downs of a typical musical group trying to make it in the recording business.

table 9-2 Where the Money Goes	**Typical CD** **(price = $16)**		**Downloaded Track** **(price = $1.29)**	
	Destination	**Amount**	**Destination**	**Amount**
	Record label overhead and profit	$7.04	Record label	$0.65
	Retailer overhead and profit	4.64	Service provider	0.18
	Artist royalty	1.60	Artist royalty	0.14
	Distributor/Manufacturer	1.76	Distributor	0.12
	Publisher	0.80	Publisher	0.10
	Miscellaneous	0.15	Miscellaneous	0.10

Source: Compiled by author from industry trade publications.

Economic Trends

As can be seen from Figure 9-2, the economic outlook for the recording industry is not encouraging. After peaking in 2000, revenues have steadily declined. From 2000 to 2010, revenues fell by more than 50 percent. (Industry experts are quick to point out that 2000 was the year that Napster and other file-sharing services became popular.)

Digital downloading is the only bright spot in this gloomy picture. According to Nielsen SoundScan (see below), there were more than 1 billion digital tracks sold in 2010 and another 83 million digital albums, both up significantly from 2007. In the meantime, sales of CDs continued to fall, dropping 55 percent from 2007. As is the case with other media, the increased revenue from digital sales does not totally offset the loss from the decline of CD sales because the record labels make more from a CD sale (see Table 9-2).

New Business Models

Faced with declining revenues, the recording industry is exploring other ways to make money. One new arrangement is called a 360 deal, in which a company agrees to make a large cash payment to a performer and in return gets a percentage of all revenue generated by the performer, including income from record sales, touring, merchandise, endorsement deals, and any other activity that takes in money. The theory behind this contract is that although consumers are unwilling to pay for CDs, they will buy concert tickets, T-shirts,

figure 9-2
Recording Industry
Revenues, 1980–2010

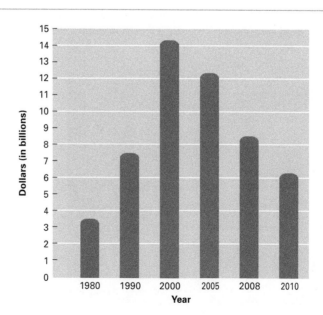

signature clothing, and other items. For example, Madonna signed a 360 deal with concert promoter Live Nation for a reported $120 million.

The industry has also capitalized on the success of video games such as Guitar Hero, Rock Band, and related games. Record labels license their songs to the games in return for a fee. These games have also given some performers new life. Aerosmith reportedly made more money from Guitar Hero: Aerosmith than from any of their albums. Vivendi, the conglomerate that includes Universal Music, showed its confidence in the future earning potential of these games by acquiring Activision, the company that makes Guitar Hero, Call of Duty, and other video games.

Rock Performers: The Bottom Line

Until a few years ago, rock stars made most of their money from the sale of CDs and downloads of albums and singles. At the risk of oversimplifying, the typical artist received a royalty rate of about 10–15 percent of the retail price of a CD. At an average retail price of $14, that works out to about $1.75 per CD sold. That same typical artist received about $0.11 per download of a single priced at 99 cents. As this example illustrates, the bulk of an artist's income came from CD sales.

Fast-forward to today. CD sales have fallen by more than 50 percent and retailers are slashing prices in some cases to under $10. Although digital downloads have increased and most songs are now retailing for $1.29, the dip in CD sales has had a major negative impact on the rock performer's bottom line. Consequently, rock stars are looking for other sources of revenue.

For many performers, touring has become a significant source of income. According to estimates by *Billboard* magazine, nearly all of the 2010 earnings of the Dave Matthews Band and Bon Jovi came from touring. Big stars generate huge touring revenue. Justin Bieber's My World tour grossed about $40 million and Carrie Underwood's tour grossed about $33 million. There were signs, however, that the touring business was leveling off. Gross revenue was down by 20 percent and some big acts canceled tour dates. Part of the reason for the decline was soaring ticket prices, averaging more than $60.

Many performers have turned to corporate sponsorship to buoy up the bottom line (see "Media Probe: Sponsoring Rock"). Others have relied on merchandising, product endorsements, and promotional deals. Go to Justin Bieber's online store and you can buy T-shirts, jewelry, hoodies, tote bags, and lunch boxes. Spend $50 and receive a free wall calendar.

Lady Gaga, Justin Bieber, Carrie Underwood, the Black-Eyed Peas, and other top line performers, however, are the exceptions. The truth is that relatively few acts are able to command the big paydays. The riches in the recording industry are disproportionately divided, with a small number of acts making most of the money. According to the Recording Industry Association of America, out of all the recordings released every year, only about 10 percent are profitable.

the sound recording audience

Sources of Feedback

Every week disk jockeys, program directors, and record company executives scan the *Billboard* charts, the most important channel of feedback in the sound recording industry (see Figure 9-3).

How is the *Billboard* chart put together? In general, the *Billboard* charts are based on two components: (1) exposure and (2) sales. To measure sales, *Billboard* relies on Nielsen SoundScan, a data-reporting system that keeps track of sales and digital downloads in the United States and Canada. Sales data are collected weekly from about 14,000 retail stores, mass merchandisers, and online outlets.

To measure exposure, *Billboard* uses data from Nielsen Broadcast Data Systems (NBDS). This organization monitors airplay on more than 1,600 radio stations in the

media *Probe*   Sponsoring Rock

During the 1960s, many young people rebelled against the prevailing norms of society, forming what sociologist called the "counterculture." Among other things, members of the counterculture opposed the Vietnam War, racial inequality, big corporations, and authority figures (such as the police, the government, the army, the corporate establishment—all subsumed under a generic term, "The Man"). The unifying factor of the counterculture was its rock music. A famous tagline from a 1968 ad in *Rolling Stone* magazine summed it up: "The Man Can't Bust Our Music." Any musical performer or group who wanted to make it big in the music business of the 1960s stayed far away from anything associated with "The Man," particularly big corporations. Rock music and big companies just didn't mix. (Ironically, "The Man Can't Bust Our Music" tagline was actually part of a marketing campaign by Columbia Records, a big corporation trying to profit from the counterculture sentiment.)

Jump to 2012 and things have really changed. These days if a performer or group wants to make money in the music business, corporate backing is a must. Case in point: the Black Eyed Peas, a group that the *Wall Street Journal* labeled "the most corporate band in America." The band was one of the first to realize that declining CD sales meant that performers would have to find new revenue streams and that one of the most promising ways to bring in money was an alliance with corporate America. An industry expert estimated that corporate sponsorship of music groups and music events amounted to about $1 billion in 2010.

The Peas involvement with big business goes back to 2003 when one of their songs was included in Apple's iTunes ad campaign that featured

the dancing silhouette. Since that time the band has made deals with Best Buy, Victoria's Secret, the National Basketball Association (their song "Let's Get It Started" was played before the NBA's 2004 playoff games), PepsiCo, Target, Honda, and Verizon, to name a few. The Peas have also played at numerous private corporate events. In 2010, the Peas performed a concert in Times Square to help launch Samsung's 3-D televisions. During their 2011 tour, group member will.i.am (William Adams) performed a rap number inspired by text messages sent by audience members. The text messages were displayed on two huge screens picturing BlackBerries. The primary sponsor of the tour: RIM, the company that makes the BlackBerry. Big companies have picked up the tabs for the group's tours, video budgets, marketing, and other expenses. The result of these corporate alliances: a bigger bottom line. The Black Eyed Peas made more than $16 million in 2010. It looks like 2011 will also be a good year. Their performance at Super Bowl XLV got mixed reviews but was seen by more than 110 million viewers in the United States. That kind of exposure usually translates into increased sales and more corporate deals.

Of course, the Peas are not the only performers who have gone commercial and endorsed products. U2 performed in Apple ads and a U2 tour was sponsored by BlackBerry. A Sting music video was used by Jaguar. Tim McGraw's 2009 tour was sponsored by Outback Steakhouse. The usually antiestablishment Pearl Jam made a marketing deal with Target. Even Bob Dylan, the hero of the counterculture, appeared in an ad for Victoria's Secret. These days, when it comes to "The Man," rock music is singing a different tune.

United States, Canada, and Puerto Rico that play a variety of formats. NBDS reports that it detects more than 100 million songs every year. For some of its charts—the Hot 100, for example—*Billboard* combines the two measures and winds up with a single index number for each song and rank-orders it accordingly.

Note that another mass medium, radio, plays an important part in the feedback mechanism for sound recording. Radio stations with a music format rely on the *Billboard* charts to determine what songs they should play. Thus, sound recording also functions as a feedback mechanism for radio.

Audiences

Information regarding the audience for sound recording (CDs and music downloads) is somewhat difficult to uncover, partially because the recording industry is supported by audience purchases and not by advertising. This means that recording companies concentrate on compiling overall sales figures and typically do not seek detailed demographic information about the audience. True, some recording companies have sponsored market research to find out more about their audiences, but the results of these studies are usually not made available to the general public. It has been estimated that more than 90 percent of all households in the country have some means of playing a CD or a downloaded music track.

In general, those people who have a sound system have paid about $500–800 for their equipment. They listen to discs and downloads about an hour a day.

Music buying is related to age. Older consumers are accounting for more of the industry revenue. In 2006, according to data from the Recording Industry Association of America,

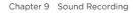

figure 9-3

Excerpt from a *Billboard* Chart

people over 30 accounted for about 55 percent of the total dollar value spent on recorded music. In 2008, the last year for which data are available, the corresponding figure was about 64 percent, a 16 percent increase. At the same time, consumer spending by those younger than 20 decreased, from 21 percent to 18 percent. One reason for this trend is that older people buy more higher-priced CDs than do young people, who are more apt to buy cheaper digital downloads.

Music downloading varies by age, with teens and 20- to 29-year-olds the most active downloaders. Minorities download more music than whites, and men download music slightly more than women.

the recording industry

These are difficult times for the recording industry, and the outlook for the near future at least is not good. All of the major recording labels have cut jobs and downsized some departments. Employment chances might be better with companies that offer digital music downloads, such as Apple and Amazon, or with companies that sponsor tours and concerts.

The career outlook in the various media industries changes quickly. For a more current description of conditions in the recording industry and a more detailed look at career options, please consult the book's Web site: www.mhhe.com/dominick12e.

main points

- Thomas Edison pioneered the development of the phonograph, which was first used as a device to record voice. Emile Berliner perfected the modern technique of recording music in a spiral pattern on a disk. By the end of World War I, record players were found in most American homes.

- The coming of radio and the Depression hurt the development of the recording industry, but the business was able to survive because of the popularity of jukeboxes.

- After World War II the industry grew quickly because of the development of magnetic tape recording and the LP record and, most of all, because radio stations began to play recorded music as part of their formats.

- Rock-and-roll music helped spur record sales and made young people an important part of the market for recorded music.

- Digital downloading is transforming the way the music industry conducts business.

- There are four segments in the recording industry: talent, production, distribution, and retail.

- Four big companies dominate the record business.

- *Billboard* magazine's charts are the most important form of audience feedback for the industry.

- After several years of growth, the recording industry's revenue has declined, due in part to the declining popularity of the CD format.

questions for review

1. Trace the various media that have been used to record sound, from Edison's time to the present.

2. How does cloud storage of music differ from traditional downloading?

3. Trace the distribution arrangement in the sound recording business. How many of the distribution channels have you personally used?

4. If the chance of financial success is so small, why do so many people still try to make it in the recording industry?

questions for critical thinking

1. Why did it take the recording industry so long to figure out that radio airplay helped record sales?

2. What are the implications of large corporate ownership in the record business? Are big companies less likely to promote new acts and risky musical styles?

3. What are the ethical implications of downloading and sharing music from file-sharing services? If you have ever downloaded music illegally, did you feel guilty doing it? Why or why not?

4. What will be the future of the retail record store in the digital era? If you can download music directly to your computer or mobile device, why go to a store? Do people go to music stores for purposes other than simply buying an album?

key terms

phonograph (p. 206)	jazz (p. 207)	demo (p. 221)
graphophone (p. 206)	heavy metal (p. 212)	*Billboard* (p. 223)
gramophone (p. 206)	rack jobbers (p. 218)	
nickelodeons (p. 206)	one-stops (p. 219)	

internet resources

Online Learning Center

On the Online Learning Center home page, www.mhhe.com/dominick12e, *select* Student Center *and then* Chapter 9.

1. Use the Learning Objectives, Chapter Outline, and Main Points sections to review this chapter.

2. Test your knowledge of the chapter using the multiple choice and flashcard features of the site.

3. Expand your knowledge of concepts and topics discussed in the chapter with additional Questions for Critical Thinking and Internet Exercises.

surfing the internet

Web sites for the recording industry are just as evanescent as the industry itself. The following were current as this book went to press.

www.billboard.com
Billboard magazine's online version. Contains the latest news about the industry plus recent charts.

www.sonymusic.com
Home page of Sony Music. Lists all top artists and has links to the company's various labels.

www.apple.com/itunes
You probably already know about this one.

www.recording-history.org
A comprehensive look at the evolution of recording technology.

www.riaa.org
Site of the Recording Industry Association of America. Contains industry data, the latest news, and legal information.

The movies have made the transition from big screen to small screen, such as the Apple iPod.

Chapter**10**

motion
pictures

This chapter will prepare you to:

- explain how the motion picture industry developed
- describe how the studios dominated the industry
- discuss how television affected the film industry and its audience
- understand the implications that digital moviemaking holds for the industry
- explain how the digital age is affecting film
- describe the components of the movie industry and how a motion picture is produced

In order to understand the present situation of the motion picture industry, it helps to look at the past. Here's a table that sums it up.

Decade(s)	Options to See a Movie	Viewing Screen
1920s, 1930s, 1940s	Go out to a theater	Movie screen
1950s 1960s	Go out to a theater Watch movies at home on broadcast television	Movie screen TV screen
1970s 1980s	Go out to a theater Watch movies at home on broadcast television Watch movies at home on basic cable TV Watch movies at home on a premium cable channel such as HBO Watch pay-per-view movies at home Rent or buy a movie videocassette at video store and play it back at home	Movie screen TV screen
1990s	Go out to a theater Watch movies at home on broadcast television Watch movies at home on basic cable TV Watch movies at home on a premium cable channel such as HBO Watch pay-per-view movies at home Rent or buy a movie DVD at a video store and play it back at home Rent or buy a movie over the Internet and have it delivered via mail (e.g., Netflix) and watch on your TV or computer	Movie screen TV screen Computer screen

(continued)

(*continued*)

Decade(s)	Options to See a Movie	Viewing Screen
2000s, 2010s	Go out to a theater	Movie screen
	Watch movies at home on broadcast television	TV screen
	Watch movies at home on basic cable TV	Computer screen
	Watch movies at home on a premium cable channel such as HBO	Portable media player screen
	Watch pay-per-view movies at home	Tablet computer screen
	Rent or buy a movie DVD at a video store and play it back at home	Smartphone screen
	Rent or buy a movie DVD over the Internet and have it delivered via mail (e.g., Netflix) and watch on your TV or computer	
	Watch a movie on video-on-demand from cable TV or satellite company	
	Watch a movie downloaded to a portable media player (such as the iPod or PSP)	
	Download a movie to a tablet computer or smartphone	
	Stream a movie over the Internet from Netflix, Google, and others	
	Stream a movie from Facebook	

As is obvious, there are more ways for people to acquire and view movies. As this chapter will demonstrate, this development has had major consequences for the movie industry. But we're getting ahead of the story. Let's start off by taking a look at how the motion picture industry got started.

a brief history

Motion pictures and television are possible because of two quirks of the human perceptual system: the phi phenomenon and persistence of vision. The **phi phenomenon** refers to what happens when we see one light source go out while another one close to the original is illuminated. To our eyes it looks like the light moves from one place to another. In **persistence of vision**, our eyes continue to see an image for a split second after the image has disappeared from view. In the early 19th century, a host of toys that depended on this principle were created in Europe. Bearing fanciful names (the Thaumatrope, the Praxinoscope), these devices made a series of hand-drawn pictures appear to move.

Early American Cinema
The Edison Lab   Before long, some key inventors realized that a series of still photographs on celluloid film could be used with these devices instead of hand drawings. In 1878 a colorful Englishman (later turned American), Edward Muybridge, attempted to settle a $25,000 bet over whether the four feet of a galloping horse ever simultaneously left the ground. He arranged a series of 24 cameras alongside a racetrack to photograph a running horse. Rapidly viewing the series of pictures produced an effect much like that of a motion picture. Muybridge's technique not only settled the bet (the feet did leave the ground simultaneously in certain instances) but also demonstrated, in a backward way, the idea behind motion picture photography. Instead of 24 cameras taking one picture each, what was needed was one camera that would take 24 pictures in rapid order. It was Thomas Edison and his assistant, William Dickson, who finally developed what might have been the first practical motion picture camera and viewing device. Using flexible film, Dickson solved the vexing problem of how to move the film rapidly through the camera by perforating its edge with tiny holes and pulling it along by means of sprockets. In 1889 Dickson perfected a machine called the **Kinetoscope** and even starred in a brief film demonstrating how it worked.

An early version of the Praxinoscope. Later models would be able to project a moving image onto a large screen for many people to view at once.

These early efforts in the Edison lab were not directed at projecting movies to large crowds. Edison thought the device could make money by showing brief films to one person at a time for a penny a look. He built a special studio to produce films for this new invention, and by 1894 Kinetoscope parlors were springing up in major cities. However, the long-range commercial potential of this invention was lost on Edison. He reasoned that the real money would be made by selling his peep-show machine. If a large number of people were shown the film at the same time, fewer machines would be needed, so he was not interested in adapting the machine for larger audiences.

Developments in Europe proved Edison wrong as inventors there devised large-screen projection devices. Faced with competition, Edison perfected a projector called the *Vitascope* and unveiled it in New York City in 1896.

Early movies were simple snippets of action—acrobats tumbling, horses running, jugglers juggling, and so on. Eventually, the novelty wore off, and films became less of an attraction.

The Nickelodeons   Public interest was soon rekindled when early filmmakers discovered that movies could be used to tell a story. In France, Alice Guy Blache produced *The Cabbage Fairy*, a 1-minute film about a fairy who produces children in a cabbage patch, and exhibited it at the Paris International Exhibition in 1886. Blache went on to found her own studio in America. Better known is the work of a fellow French filmmaker and magician, Georges Méliès. In 1902 Méliès produced a science fiction film that was the great-great-grandfather of *Star Wars* and *Star Trek*; it was called *A Trip to the Moon*. Méliès, however, did not fully explore the storytelling freedom afforded by film. His films were basically extravagant stage plays photographed by a stationary camera. It was an American, Edwin S. Porter, who in his *Great Train Robbery* first discovered the artistic potential of editing and camera placement. This and other new narrative films were extraordinarily popular with audiences and proved to be financially successful. Almost overnight, 50- to 90-seat theaters, called *nickelettes* or *nickelodeons* because of the 5-cent admission price, sprang up in converted stores throughout the nation.

Nickelodeons depended on audience turnover for their profits. Keeping the audience returning required that films be changed often—sometimes daily—to attract repeat customers. This policy created a tremendous demand for motion pictures, and new production companies were quickly formed. (In these early days films were regarded as just another mass-produced product; hence, early film studios were called *film factories*.) New York and New Jersey served as the bases for these early film companies.

media *Probe*   *Birth of a Controversy*

D. W. Griffith's *Birth of a Nation* was made to commemorate the 50th anniversary of the end of the Civil War. The film was based on a novel titled *The Clansman*. In 1906 a stage play based on the novel had caused disturbances in Philadelphia when it opened, but Griffith chose to go ahead with his plans to turn the work into a movie.

The story paints the prewar South as a happy and idyllic place whose serenity is disrupted by the war. At the war's conclusion, Southern whites are shown being victimized by renegade African Americans, northern carpetbaggers, and corrupt politicians. In response, whites form the Ku Klux Klan, which exacts vengeance on black people and restores the prewar utopia.

The NAACP objected to the film when it opened on the West Coast. About 40,000 African Americans demonstrated in California. In response

the San Francisco city censor (several big cities had film censorship boards in this era) ordered a couple of the film's more controversial scenes cut out. A delegation called on the mayor of New York City to stop the premiere but was rebuffed. When the movie opened in Boston, several brawls broke out outside the theater. Unrest was averted in Chicago when the mayor agreed to seat a black man on the city's film censorship board. Griffith, for his part, never understood the feelings of black people toward the film. He responded to these actions by issuing a pamphlet about free speech.

Birth of a Nation is rarely screened today, although it did air on Turner Classic Movies in 2011. Modern audiences find the racial depictions unacceptable. The film is remembered not so much for its content as for its technical achievements and because it served notice that motion pictures could exert a political and social force.

Adolph Zukor and D. W. Griffith   Adolph Zukor decided to copy European filmmakers who were making longer, more expensive films aimed at a middle-class audience. He acquired the four-reel French film *Queen Elizabeth*, starring Sarah Bernhardt, the most famous actress of the period, and distributed it in the United States at the then-exorbitant price of a dollar a ticket. His experiment was successful, proving that American audiences would pay more and sit still for longer films. Nevertheless, *Queen Elizabeth* remained essentially the filming of a stage play.

It was an American, D. W. Griffith, who eventually took full advantage of the film medium and established film as its own art form. Although controversial and racist in its depictions (see "Media Probe: Birth of a Controversy"), his brilliant Civil War drama, *Birth of a Nation*, released in 1915, was the most expensive American film produced to date ($110,000). The 3-hour movie, which was shot without a script, introduced history as a film topic. Griffith went on to top *Nation*'s figures with an even bigger epic, *Intolerance*, comprising four scenarios dealing with life's injustices. The movie was completed in 1916 at a cost of about $2 million (the same film made in the 2000s would easily cost $90–110 million).

In response to the controversy generated by *Birth of a Nation*, two African American brothers, George and Noble Johnson, made films that presented a more realistic and accurate view of African Americans. The first of these, *The Realization of a Negro's Ambition*, demonstrated that there was an African American audience that would support films that spoke to their community. The Johnsons' company, Lincoln Motion Pictures, stayed in operation until the early 1920s, when a lack of capital and an inability to secure bookings at white theaters forced it out of business.

Birth of the MPPC   Events in moviemaking during the decade 1908–1918 had far-reaching effects on the future shape of the film industry. As the basic economic structure of the film industry developed, the center of filmmaking moved to the West Coast, and independent film producers, having survived attempts by the major studios to stamp them out, became an important force in the industry. The tremendous demand for new pictures brought enormous competition into the field. Small film companies cut corners by using bootlegged equipment (for which they paid no royalty fees) and started making films. Competition quickly reached the cutthroat level; lawsuits were filed with alarming frequency. In an effort to bring order to the business (and to cut down on legal expenses), the leading manufacturers of films and film equipment banded together, pooled their patents, and formed the **Motion Picture Patents Company (MPPC)** to restrict moviemaking to the nine companies that made up the MPPC. Film exhibitors were brought into line by a $2-per-week tax, which entitled the theaters to use projection equipment patented by the MPPC. Failure to pay this tax meant that the theater owners would no longer be supplied with MPPC-approved films. Eventually, to accommodate the growing industry, a new role, that of film distributor, was created. The film distributor served the function of a wholesaler, acquiring films from the manufacturers and renting them to exhibitors. This three-level structure—production, distribution, and exhibition—is still with us today. The MPPC was quick to take control of film distribution as well.

Instead of squelching competition, the MPPC actually fueled it. Annoyed by the repressive regulations, independent producers began offering films to exhibitors at cheaper rates than MPPC members. Full-length feature films, several reels in length, were imported from Europe. In response the MPPC declared war. "Outlaw" studios were raided and equipment smashed. In an effort to escape the harassment of the MPPC, independent producers fled New York and New Jersey. They were looking for a location with good weather, interesting geography, low business costs, and proximity to a national border so that the independents could avoid the MPPC's subpoenas. Florida proved to be too humid; Cuba was too inconvenient; Texas was too flat. Finally, they found the perfect environment—a rather sleepy suburb of Los Angeles called Hollywood. By 1913 this new home had so encouraged independent filmmaking that the MPPC could no longer contain its growth. By 1917, for all practical purposes, the patents organization had lost its power.

The Star System   The aura of glamour surrounding Hollywood and its stars might not have emerged if the MPPC had not been so stubborn. Whereas the patents company refused to publicize its performers, the independents quickly recognized that fan interest in film actors and actresses could be used to draw crowds away from the movies offered by the MPPC. Carl Laemmle, an independent producer, shrewdly publicized one of his actresses with a poetic name—Florence Lawrence—until she became what we might call the first movie star. As Florence's fame grew, her pictures brought in more money, spurring other independents to create their own stars to keep pace. The two artists who best exemplified the growth of the star system were Mary Pickford and Charlie Chaplin. In 1913 Chaplin was working in movies for $150 a week, a good salary in those days. Just four years later he was paid a million dollars for making eight pictures. Mary Pickford, nicknamed "America's Sweetheart," was paid $1,000 per week in 1913. By 1918 she was making $15,000–20,000 per week in addition to earning a cut of up to 50 percent of her films' profits.

In 1919 the star system reached its natural conclusion. Chaplin and Pickford joined with other actors and filmmakers to start their own production company—United Artists. The employees now owned the shop.

The star system had other, subtler effects. Once stars became popular, the public demanded to see them in longer movies. However, feature-length films that ran 1–2 hours were more expensive to make. Further, audiences could not be expected to sit for several hours on the wooden benches found in many of the nickelodeons. A need had been created for large, comfortable theaters that could accommodate thousands of patrons and, at the same time, justify higher admission costs. In 1914 the Strand opened in New York. With seats for more than 3,000 people, it occupied a whole city block and had space for an entire symphony orchestra. On the West Coast, Sid Grauman opened his Egyptian Theater (across from the Chinese Theater) in 1922 at a cost of almost a million dollars. His ushers were dressed in Cleopatra costumes. Clearly, the nickel was no longer the symbol of the movies.

Consolidation and Growth   The increased cost of filmmaking made it imperative for producers to make sure that a company's movies were booked into enough big, new theaters to turn a profit. Under this economic pressure the film industry moved in the direction of consolidation. Adolph Zukor, whose company would ultimately become

Charlie Chaplin, one of the first movie superstars created by the Hollywood star system, delighted film audiences throughout the world. This scene is from one of his earlier works, a 1916 short called *One A.M.*

Paramount Pictures, combined the production and distribution functions into one corporate structure. Paramount and its chief rival, Fox, began building their own theaters, and Marcus Loew, owner of a large chain of theaters, purchased his own studio (later to become MGM). Studio owners could exert control over independent exhibitors through another policy known as **block booking**. To receive two or three topflight films from a studio, the theater owner had to agree to show five or six other films of lower quality. Although this policy was not very advantageous to exhibitors, it assured the production companies of steady revenue for their films.

All this was taking place as World War I devastated Europe. When the war ended in 1918, the American film industry was the dominant film force in the world, accounting for upwards of 80 percent of the worldwide market. By the beginning of the 1920s, the major production companies were comfortable and prosperous and enjoyed as firm a lock on the film business as had the old MPPC, which they had replaced only a few years earlier.

The Roaring Twenties

The prosperity boom that followed the war exploded in Hollywood with more force than in other business sectors. Profits were up, and extravagance was the watchword as filmmakers endorsed the principle that the only way to make money was to spend money. Between 1914 and 1924, the cost of a feature film increased 1,500 percent. Salaries, sets, costumes, props, and rights to best-sellers all contributed to the mushrooming costs. Even the lawyer for United Artists was paid $100,000 a year. By 1927 the average film cost about $200,000, and many films easily topped that. *Ben Hur* (1925) was made for a reported $6 million.

Huge salaries created a boomtown atmosphere in Hollywood, and many people—some still quite young—were unprepared to deal with the temptations that came with sudden wealth. Before long, newspapers were reporting stories about orgiastic parties, prostitution, studio call girls, bootleg whiskey, and drugs. Hollywood was dubbed "Sin City." In 1922, within a few short months, comedian Fatty Arbuckle was involved in a rape case, two female stars were implicated in the murder of a prominent director, and popular actor Wallace Reid died while trying to kick his drug addiction. Public reaction to these revelations was predictable: indignation and outrage. By the end of the year, politicians in

Al Jolson in *The Jazz Singer*. This film convinced the industry that audiences wanted to see "talkies," or films with sound, thus ushering in a new era in Hollywood.

36 states had introduced bills to set up censorship boards for films. The motion picture companies hired a well-respected former postmaster general, Will Hays, to head a new self-regulatory body for the industry. Called the Motion Picture Producers and Distributors Association, this organization was successful in heading off government control, and the basic standards it laid down would remain in force for almost four decades.

The Coming of Sound: The Late 1920s

Since optical recording of sound on film had been feasible since 1918, why did Hollywood wait until the late 1920s to introduce sound films? Money.

Business was good during the 1920s, and the major studios did not want to get into costly experimentation with new techniques. Warner Brothers, however, was not as financially sound as the other studios. Since Warner did not own movie theaters in the big cities and could not exhibit all its pictures in the most lucrative markets, the company was willing to try anything to get its films into theaters. In 1927 Warner released *The Jazz Singer,* in which Al Jolson not only sang but spoke from the screen. Within two years the silent film, for all practical purposes, was dead.

The novelty of sound gave a boost to the film industry, despite the devastating economic effects of the Depression. In 1929 average weekly movie attendance was 80 million; by 1930 it had reached 90 million—a fact that led many to regard filmmaking as a Depression-proof industry. They were quickly proved wrong as attendance dropped in 1931 and again in 1932. The industry generated several innovations to attract audiences. *Becky Sharp* was filmed in the new Technicolor process in 1935. Theaters also began the practice of showing double features, two feature films on the same bill. Animated cartoons began to draw sizable audiences. All this new activity called for Hollywood to produce even more films—almost 400 per year during the 1930s—to meet the demands of the market. This high production volume was a boon to major studios since they could churn out larger numbers of films more economically. Moreover, the tremendous amount of money needed to convert to sound and the poor financial conditions created by the Depression forced many small companies out of business, leaving eight major studios with a lock on the industry.

The Studio Years: 1930–1950

The 20 years from 1930 to 1950 were the studio years, with MGM, 20th Century Fox, RKO, Warner Brothers, Paramount, Universal, Columbia, and United Artists dominating the industry. These studios created hundreds of acres of back-lot movie sets, constructed elaborate soundstages, and built up showy stables of creative talent, carefully groomed for stardom. Audiences adored and emulated their favorite screen idols, who were presented as larger-than-life gods and goddesses inhabiting a glamorous fantasyland.

Individual studios left their imprint on the films of the period as each studio's products took on a distinct personality. For example, during this period Warner Brothers became best known for its gangster films, 20th Century Fox for its historical and adventure films, and MGM for its lavish, star-studded musicals.

Orson Welles in a scene from the 1941 film *Citizen Kane*. Welles was 25 when he directed, produced, and starred in this film, considered by many critics the best American movie ever made.

The most significant period for motion picture achievement were the years from 1939 to 1941. *Gone with the Wind,* which showcased the new Technicolor film process, was released in 1939. In that same year two other soon-to-become-classics, *The Wizard of Oz* and *Stagecoach* (starring John Wayne in his first major role), were released. Just two years later, Orson Welles directed and starred in *Citizen Kane,* which some critics consider the best American film ever made.

The financial backing and diverse holdings of the studio system helped the film industry survive the Depression. Attendance and profits began climbing in 1934 and held steady throughout World War II. During the 1940s going to a movie was just as much a part of American life as watching television is today. In fact, the all-time peak for film-going was 1946, when average weekly attendance reached over 90 million. By 1948, however, all this was to change.

Back in 1938, the Justice Department had filed suit against Paramount and the other major film companies, charging that the industry's vertical control of production, distribution, and exhibition constituted restraint of trade and monopolistic practices. The case had been set aside during the war, but by 1948 the courts had ordered the major studios to get rid of at least one of their holdings in these three areas. Most chose to divest themselves of their theater chains. The court also eliminated the block booking system and thus deprived the studios of guaranteed exhibition for all their films. As a result the studios had to cut back on film production and reduce costs.

The Reaction of the Film Industry to TV

When television began building a sizable audience during the late 1940s, it cut into the motion picture industry's profits. The first reaction of the film industry was to fight back. Studios stubbornly refused to advertise their films on TV, and they would not release old films for showing on the newer medium. Many studios wrote clauses into the contracts of their major stars forbidding them to appear on TV. None of their efforts had an appreciable effect on television's growing popularity; more and more Americans bought TV sets, while film attendance slipped.

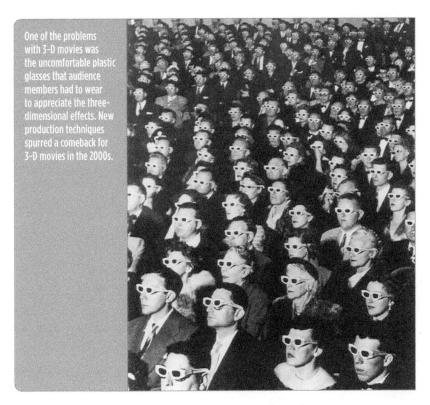

One of the problems with 3-D movies was the uncomfortable plastic glasses that audience members had to wear to appreciate the three-dimensional effects. New production techniques spurred a comeback for 3-D movies in the 2000s.

Hollywood looked for ways to recapture some of its audience from TV. By the early 1950s the film industry thought it had found the answer—technical wizardry. The first technical gimmick was 3-D (three-dimensional film). The audience wore special polarized glasses to perceive the effect and were treated to the illusion of spears, trains, arrows, knives, birds, and even Jane Russell jumping out at them from the film screen. Unfortunately, the glasses gave some people headaches, the equipment was too expensive for most theater owners to install, and audiences quickly became bored with the novelty. It was soon apparent that 3-D was not the answer. The second technical gimmick concerned screen size. Cinerama, which involved the use of three projectors and curved screens, surrounded the audience with film. Less expensive techniques that enlarged screen size, such as Cinemascope, Panavision, and Vistavision, were ultimately adopted by the industry but did little to stem Hollywood's loss of money.

The attitude of the movie companies toward TV during those early years was a clear example of shortsightedness. What the film companies failed to see was that they could have played a dominant role in TV's evolution. Because the major networks were not eager to supply early TV shows, film companies would have been logical sources for programming. Somewhat belatedly, Hollywood recognized that it was in its best interest to cooperate with television. In the late 1950s, the studios began to release their pre-1948 films to TV and to supply programs to the networks. In 1960, post-1948 theatrical films were made available to the smaller TV screens.

By the 1950s, when it became clear that TV would be a formidable competitor, the film industry cast about for new ways to draw audiences back to the theaters. It tried big-budget, spectacle movies, such as *Cleopatra*, as well as films that addressed more adult subjects, such as adultery and homosexuality, that could not be shown on TV.

Realignments: The Film Industry from 1960 to 1990

The 1960s were marked by the waning power of the major studios and by a closer affiliation with their old competitor, television. The continued rise of the independent producer led to a concomitant loss of power by the studios. As major production houses cut back operations, they released many actors, writers, and directors who, naturally enough, formed small, independent production companies. Using the big studios for financing and distribution, these independents and the artists they employed frequently took small salaries in exchange for a percentage of a film's profits. By the mid-1960s roughly 80 percent of all American films were independent productions.

The poor economic climate brought about other changes. Large studios, faced with ever-worsening financial conditions, were absorbed by larger conglomerates. In the early 1970s both the MGM and 20th Century Fox studios were sold to make room for real estate developers.

The late 1960s also saw a change in the regulatory climate that surrounded films. The Supreme Court issued several decisions that loosened controls on content, and filmmakers were quick to take advantage of their new freedom. In 1968 the Motion Picture Association of America (MPAA) liberalized its attitudes toward self-regulation. Whereas the old production code attempted to regulate content, the new system attempted to regulate audiences by instituting a G-PG-R-X labeling system.

The relationship between film and television became even closer in the 1960s, as movies made expressly for TV appeared in the middle of the decade. In 1974 about 180 of these TV movies were shown on network television. In that same year the major film companies distributed only 109 films to theaters.

Film history from 1970 to 1990 was marked by several trends: Revenue went up, as did the budgets of many feature films, and several motion pictures racked up astonishing gross receipts. Foremost among the trends was a reversal of the slump in box office receipts that began in 1946 and finally bottomed out in 1971. With the exception of temporary declines in 1973 and 1976, the general trend has been upward. In 1977 the total box office gross came to about $2.4 billion; by 1981 it had risen to nearly $3 billion, although some of this increase could be attributed to inflation.

With more cash flowing into the box office, more money became available for the budgets of feature films. In fact, films of the late 1970s and early 1980s were reminiscent of the extravaganzas of the 1920s. Perhaps the most interesting film phenomenon of the era was the rise of the blockbuster. From 1900 to 1970 only two films (*Gone with the Wind* and *The Sound of Music*) managed to surpass $50 million in film rentals; between 1970 and 1980, 17 films exceeded this mark. By now at least 10 films have exceeded the $400 million mark (see Table 10-1).

On another front, in 1985 the MPAA instituted a new rating category—PG-13. This category was designed for those films for which parental guidance for children under 13 was recommended. Yet another new category, NC-17, replaced the X rating in 1990.

New Technologies: 1990–2010

These two decades saw motion pictures moving increasingly from the big screen at the theater to smaller screens outside the home. By 1990, first-run movies were widely available on the home TV screen thanks to the popularity of the VCR (videocassette recorder). VCRs were in about 90 percent of homes in 1990. Many businesses, such as Blockbuster, took advantage of the VCR's popularity and rented or sold videocassettes of movies direct to consumers. Starting in the late 1980s, Hollywood made more money from the sale and rental of videocassettes than it did at the box office.

In the 1990s, the **DVD (digital videodisc)** replaced the VCR as the preferred medium for movies. DVD players quickly became popular and by 2006 were in about 80 percent of U.S. households. A short time later DVDs found themselves competing against another new technology. Taking advantage of the fact that more and more households were equipped with fast broadband Internet connections, Apple started a service that let consumers download movies to their computers or other portable devices. In addition, Netflix and other companies began streaming movies direct to TV sets, smartphones, and tablet computers. As illustrated in the table at the beginning of the chapter, options for movie viewing are now more plentiful than ever.

sound byte

Watching Movies Can Be a Pain

About 10 percent of Americans suffer from minor eye problems such as lazy eye, a muscle imbalance, or depth perception problems. When people who have these conditions watch a 3-D movie, their brain and eyes have to work harder and that can result in leaving the theater with a real headache.

Contemporary Trends

The motion picture industry continues to be concerned about piracy and illegal file sharing. Movie executives saw what the original Napster did to the music industry and do not want their industry to share the same fate. The problem is even more pressing now that file-sharing programs such as BitTorrent speed up the process so

table 10-1	Rank	Title	Year	Rental Income (millions)
All-Time Box Office Leaders, 2011	1	*Avatar*	2009	$760
	2	*Titanic*	1997	601
The figures are based on film rentals—that is, the money received by film distributors from motion picture theaters. This figure is not the same as box office receipts, nor does it include DVD or videocassette rentals and sales. The table includes only data from the United States and Canada.	3	*The Dark Knight*	2008	533
	4	*Star Wars*	1977	461
	5	*Shrek 2*	2004	441
	6	*E.T.*	1982	435
	7	*Star Wars—Phantom Menace*	1999	432
	8	*Pirates of the Caribbean—Dead Man's Chest*	2006	423
	9	*Toy Story 3*	2010	414
	10	*Spiderman*	2002	403

that even large movie files can be downloaded in a relatively short time. A visit to the MPAA Web site reveals that much of it is devoted to stopping piracy.

DVD sales still make up most of the income for the film industry, but total revenue from DVD sales and rentals dropped 12 percent from 2007 to 2010. Income from sales and rentals of Blu-ray discs and from video-on-demand increased but was not enough to offset the drop in DVD income. Rather than buying or renting DVDs, it appears many consumers prefer streaming video or digital downloads.

Theatrical box office revenue rose 15 percent from 2007 to 2010. Much of this increase came from higher ticket prices, particularly for 3-D movies, as the number of tickets sold remained constant or declined slightly. Hollywood was not immune to the economic slowdown at the end of the decade. Studios trimmed costs and cut the number of films scheduled for release.

The motion picture industry remains dominated by six big companies: Sony/MGM, NBC Universal, Disney, Fox, Warner Brothers, and Paramount. These firms finance, produce, and distribute motion pictures and typically control about 80 percent of the market.

Modern film content is highly varied. Four of the top 10 films of 2010 were animated. Others in the top 10 leaned heavily on special effects (*Avatar, Iron Man 2, Alice in Wonderland, Inception*) and one was about vampires (*The Twilight Saga: Eclipse*).

motion pictures in the digital age

Transition

Most films are still produced the analog way by capturing images on film. Nonetheless, the digital revolution is affecting the production, distribution, and exhibition of motion pictures.

Making Digital Movies

Digital moviemaking is already a reality. In fact, anybody who shoots video with a digital camera and edits on a computer is making a digital movie. Many big-budget Hollywood movies, such as *The Three Musketeers,* were shot with digital cameras. Animated films, such as *Toy Story 3,* were created entirely by digital effects. A new technology, called motion capture, makes it possible to record the movement of human actors in order to animate digital human characters. Films such as *Rango* relied heavily on this technology.

Digital Distribution to Theaters

The current system of distributing films hasn't changed much in the last 90 years. Hundreds of copies of a celluloid film are printed, checked for quality, put into big metal cans, and shipped to theaters across the country. Each of these copies can cost more than $2,000.

Digital distribution is much cheaper. Movies can be copied to a hard drive and shipped to theaters or transmitted electronically by satellite, optical fiber, or the Internet. Experts calculate that digital distribution might save the industry as much as $1 billion annually. Moreover, digital distribution eliminates the scratches, dust, and "gate jitter" that often occur with traditional film.

Digital Projection

Once a digital movie is sent to a theater, it has to be shown on a special digital projector. The industry has been slow to change to digital because of the cost—about $100,000 per screen. For a 16-screen megaplex theater, that's a lot of money. Theater owners argued that film distributors should pay part of the cost; film distributors were reluctant to chip in, citing increased costs during the transition period when they would have to supply both analog and digital versions of movies. In late 2008, however, theater owners and five major studios worked out a deal in which the studios would help defray the cost of the changeover. Currently, about 15,000 out of 40,000 movie screens in the United States and Canada are equipped with digital projection equipment.

3-D Movies

Digital projection revived an old movie idea—three-dimensional (3-D) films. Studio executives and theater owners quickly embraced 3-D as a potential new revenue stream. In 2010, Hollywood released 25 3-D movies, twice as many as in the previous year. At the same time, the number of theaters capable of showing 3-D movies increased by 122 percent.

Theater owners were happy with 3-D movies because they could charge $3–5 extra for them. In 2010, an adult ticket to a 3-D movie in New York was $17.50. The same ticket cost $15 in Atlanta and $14 in Miami. Studios were happy because they split the revenue from the higher prices with the theater owners. More than one in three people in the United States and Canada saw a 3-D film.

Box office revenue from 3-D films in 2010 was $2.2 billion, double the total of 2009. Some 3-D films, such as *Avatar* and *Alice in Wonderland,* saw their box office revenue increased by one-third thanks to 3-D.

The summer of 2010, however, demonstrated that 3-D was not a surefire road to success. Some big 3-D movies, such as *Cats and Dogs,* bombed at the box office while many of the summer's biggest hits, including *Inception* and *Iron Man 2,* were filmed in traditional 2-D. Early results from 2011 suggested that 3-D revenue was dropping. Industry experts think

Many of today's hit movies, such as *Inception,* rely heavily on digital special effects.

that the novelty effect of 3-D is wearing off and that the weak economy has prompted consumers to cut back on expensive movie ticket purchases.

Digital Distribution to the Home

Buying or renting a DVD from Blockbuster or Netflix is one form of digital distribution, but the method that has attracted the most recent attention is digital downloading. Apple TV, for example, lets consumers download a movie to their computer and wirelessly sends the film to a TV set. Blockbuster offers a service that enables consumers to rent or buy a movie that is then downloaded to a computer. Thanks to a process called buffering, viewers can start watching the beginning of a movie while the rest of it continues to download. In addition, both Blockbuster and Netflix offer real-time streaming movies over the Internet that can be played on big-screen TV sets. Note that this is another example of the transition from atoms (tangible DVDs) to bits (intangible digital bits of information).

Mobile Movies

Movies seem the least portable of all media. They were designed to be viewed in a large hall on a large screen. Nonetheless, the digital age has opened new possibilities. Portable DVD players that weigh less than 2 pounds and are not much bigger than this book are becoming popular. Many SUVs and vans have video screens installed so that passengers in the back can watch DVDs during a trip. And, as we have already mentioned, there are many services that give subscribers the ability to download movies onto their laptops.

Mobile movies keep getting smaller—in screen size, that is. Owners of an iPhone, iPad, iPod Video or iPod Touch, and other devices can download and view movies on a 3.5-inch screen. Sprint offers a pay-per-view service that streams full-length movies to consumers' cell phones for about $4–5 each. There are even services that offer porn films delivered to a cell phone.

User-Generated Content

Given the nature of film production, user-generated content is not yet a significant factor in the movie industry. Nonetheless, there are some examples. During the production of the cult classic *Snakes on a Plane,* New Line Cinema reshot some scenes incorporating suggestions from fans across the Internet. In early 2009, an independent film, *Perkins 14,* premiered at a national horror film festival. The film was created on Massify, an online collaboration site for filmmakers, and users were involved in making all decisions, from scripting to postproduction.

Social Media

The movie industry was one of the first to appreciate the marketing power of social media. Back in 1999, the makers of *The Blair Witch Project* used the Internet to promote their movie using viral marketing techniques. Information about the movie spread quickly through chat rooms and bulletin boards. The movie *Paranormal Activity* used many of the same techniques in 2009.

There are numerous other examples. Twentieth Century Fox promoted an "*Avatar* Day," featuring previews of the movie, through Facebook and Twitter and tickets sold out in a few hours. Paramount generated interest in *Super 8* by premiering its first full-length trailer on Twitter. *The Hangover* sponsored a contest on Facebook where fans could post their funniest party photos. The person who posted the funniest picture won a trip to Las Vegas (where else?). Social media have given filmmakers new channels to promote their projects directly to the audience.

defining features of motion pictures

The most noticeable characteristic of motion pictures is their potential cost. Many big-budget Hollywood movies have production expenses that top the $100-million mark. Tack on another $20 million or so for marketing and distribution, and you're talking real money. No

media *Probe*   *More Than You Ever Wanted to Know About Trailers*

Trailers are those snippets of scenes from an upcoming movie that are shown before the main feature. Trailers date back to 1913 and have always been a key part in the marketing of a soon-to-be-released film. In years past, the only place you could see a trailer was at a local movie theater or maybe on a cable network. Now the Internet has provided a potent new channel for movie promotion.

Trailers are routinely placed on MySpace, YouTube, Facebook, Yahoo!, iTunes, and a film's Web site. The trailer for the vampire hit *Twilight* got 55 million views online. Movie studios also like the fact that on the Internet they can show "red band" trailers, the ones that contain content a bit too edgy for the theater venue.

The growing importance of the Internet does not mean that film studios are overlooking the traditional in-theater trailer. In fact, trailers are more important than ever. Short "teaser trailers" are released to movie theaters about six months before a film is due to be released. The main trailer is ready to hit theaters three months later. Studios try to aim their trailers at the film's target audience. Thus, a raunchy comedy usually contains a trailer for another raunchy comedy.

The Motion Picture Association of America's guidelines suggest that trailers should run no longer that 2½ minutes. Theaters usually run about four to six trailers before the feature and limit the total time allotted to trailers to about 10–11 minutes.

There's even an awards show: The Golden Trailer Awards. In 2010, the best trailer of the year was the one for the documentary *The Cove*.

other media product—book, magazine, TV series, CD—costs as much as a motion picture. (Of course, filmmakers sometimes put together films for much less and sometimes make big money—*Paranormal Activity*, for example—but these tend to be rare events.)

Partly because commercial moviemaking is so expensive, the industry has become dominated by big conglomerates. As noted earlier, six major companies now control most of the market. These companies have the financial resources to risk $100 million or so on a few dozen films each year in hopes of finding a blockbuster. Making motion pictures tends to be only one of many media interests in which these conglomerates are involved. Some have holdings in TV and the Internet; others own publishing companies and recording companies.

Film has a strong aesthetic dimension. Of all the media discussed in this book, film is the one most often discussed as an art form. My university library lists 110 entries under the heading "motion picture aesthetics." This characteristic introduces a tension in the field because most big-studio films are produced to make a profit rather than to showcase their artistic merit. Many independent filmmakers, however, make films not because of the bottom line but because they find their efforts artistically satisfying. Although this chapter discusses primarily mainstream Hollywood moviemaking, keep in mind that thousands of freelance filmmakers work outside the established corporate structure and produce films of varying length on a myriad of topics.

Going to the movies continues to be a social experience. It is the only medium that facilitates audiences gathering in large groups to be exposed to the same message. And, of course, moviegoing is still a popular dating activity. In fact, the social dimension of moviegoing might be the most important one.

organization of the film industry

Although film is an art form, the film industry is in business to make a profit. If an occasional moneymaking film also turns out to have artistic merit, so much the better, but the artistic merit is usually a by-product rather than the main focus. Our analysis of the film industry divides its structure into three areas: (1) production, (2) distribution, and (3) exhibition.

Production

Films are produced by a variety of organizations and individuals. For many years the major studios controlled virtually all production, but independent producers have recently become prevalent. The major studios now finance and distribute many films made by independent companies.

decision

makers

James Cameron: Two Billion Dollar Man

James Cameron grew up in Canada but moved to southern California when he was 17. After attending community college, Cameron took a job as a truck driver but began reading about motion picture special effects in his spare time. Impressed by the 1968 Stanley Kubrick film *2001: A Space Odyssey* and the original *Star Wars* film in 1977, Cameron and a few of his friends wrote, produced, and directed their own 10-minute science fiction film.

When a position for a miniature model maker opened up at a local studio that made low-budget films, Cameron was lucky enough to land the job. In the next few years, he worked as an art director for the 1980 film *Battle Beyond the Stars* and did special effects on a film directed by John Carpenter, *Escape from New York*. He got his first big break when the director of *Piranha II: The Spawning* quit the project and Cameron took over. (Although Cameron got the screen credit as director, the film's producer did most of the editing.)

While filming *Piranha II,* Cameron came up with a story idea about a robot from the future that travels back in time to kill a young woman and change the future. Cameron wrote the script, called *The Terminator,* and shopped it around to major production companies with the condition that he be allowed to direct the movie. All were unwilling to trust the project to a rookie director. Finally, Cameron found a relatively small company, Hemdale Pictures, willing to take a chance and Cameron got his first job as director of a big-budget movie. *The Terminator* went on to gross more than $38 million in the United States and made Cameron a sought-after director.

In 1986, Cameron directed *Aliens,* the sequel to the famous 1979 film directed by Ridley Scott, *Alien*. The film was another box office success and won two Oscars for special effects. Cameron followed up *Aliens* with other box office winners: *The Abyss* (1989), about underwater creatures;

Terminator 2 (1991), the sequel to the original which became the biggest box office success of the year; and *True Lies* (1994).

During the next few years, Cameron worked on a script about the sinking of the *Titanic*. As part of his research, he made 12 deep-sea dives to the ship's resting place deep in the Atlantic and filmed the actual wreck. (Much of this footage was incorporated into the final film.) In order to make the film, Cameron erected a $20 million studio in Mexico, a huge tank that held 17 million gallons of water, and a 750-foot-long replica of the real *Titanic*. Postproduction work using the latest in computer-generated special effects added even more to the budget. When the three-hour film was finally ready to be released, total production cost was about $200 million, the most expensive movie ever made at the time.

As everybody knows, *Titanic* was a huge success, netting 11 Oscars, including a Best Director award for Cameron, and taking in more than $1.8 billion at the box office. Cameron followed up *Titanic* with *Avatar,* a 3-D science fiction movie that grossed more than $1 billion worldwide in less than three weeks. The film also helped popularize the huge screen format known as IMAX. *Avatar* is the biggest IMAX movie to date and IMAX admissions, which may cost twice as much as a regular ticket, are a significant part of a film's profit. As of mid-2011, *Avatar* had taken in more than $2.7 billion, giving James Cameron the distinction of directing the top two all-time box office leaders.

Cameron has also produced and directed several documentaries about the undersea world. He is one of the biggest advocates of 3-D moviemaking and an expert in computer-generated special effects. He was one of the founders of Digital Domain, a visual effects and animation company. His next projects include *Avatar 2* and *Avatar 3.* We'll see if he becomes Hollywood's first Three Billion Dollar Man.

Film studios differ in their arrangements, but a typical setup involves four main departments: (1) film production, (2) distribution, (3) TV production, and (4) administration. The film production department handles all those elements that actually go into the making of a film, including story development, casting, art, makeup, and sets. The distribution department handles sales and contracts for domestic and worldwide duplication and delivery of films to theaters and to home video. As its name suggests, the TV division develops and produces movies and series for first-run and syndicated television. Sales, financial deals, and legal arrangements are the provinces of the administration department.

Distribution

The distribution arm of the industry is responsible for supplying prints of films to the thousands of theaters located across the United States and around the globe. In recent years distribution companies have also supplied films to TV networks and to makers of DVDs. Distribution companies maintain close contact with theater owners all over the world and also provide a transportation and delivery system that ensures that a film will arrive at a theater before its scheduled play date. In addition to booking the film at local movie houses, the distribution company is responsible for making the multiple prints of a film that are necessary when the film goes into general release. They also take care of advertising and promotion for the film. Most of the distribution of motion pictures is handled by the large studios, which are firmly entrenched in both the production and distribution aspects of the business.

The nature of film distribution ensures that the large companies will control a large portion of the business. First, it is too expensive for an independent producer or a small

media
Probe

Food and Flicks

In the past, a typical date often included dinner and then a trip to a movie theater. If some movie theater owners are correct, in the near future a typical date will consist of dinner in a movie theater. Attendance at movie theaters has been falling the last few years and theater owners are searching for ways to get more people into their seats. One option involves turning a movie theater into a dine-in restaurant.

Called "in-theater" dining, audiences at these new theaters can choose from such entrees as lemon shrimp, calamari, chicken Caesar salad, and lobster rolls, as well as the more traditional fare such as cheeseburgers and pizza. Some theaters offer beer and wine. There about 350 "dine-ins" in the United States, only 5 percent of the total number of theaters, but experts suggest that the number will probably double in the next five years.

Seats are arranged in pairs with wide aisles so that waiters can serve food during the movie without blocking the screen. Patrons place their orders by pressing buttons on an electronic menu next to their seat. Some seats have folding trays that swing out from their armrests while others have tables in front of the seats. A few theaters even offer moist towelettes and free chocolate mints after the meal.

All of this luxury, of course, comes with a price. A cheeseburger will set you back about $10; a shrimp entree goes for around $15. In addition, there is usually a surcharge on top of the regular ticket price, so dinner and a movie can get rather pricey.

In-theater dining presents a new set of problems for theater owners. Seats have to be farther apart so patrons aren't bothered by the sounds of others chewing and swallowing. China plates can't be used because they are too noisy. Drippy foods that are hard to eat in the dark are kept off the menu. Finally, dine-in theaters have to be careful about what films they show. Most people don't like to eat during movies that feature blood and gore.

distribution company to contact theaters and theater chains spread all over the globe. The big studios already have this communication network set up and can afford to maintain it. Second, the large studios can offer theater owners a steady stream of films that consistently feature big-name stars. A small company could not withstand that competition for long.

Distribution companies also serve as a source of financing for independent producers. These companies lend money to a film's producer to cover all or most of the estimated cost of a film. In this way the major studios acquire an interest in films that they did not directly produce. This arrangement will be discussed further in the section on film economics.

Exhibition

In 2010 there were about 40,000 movie screens in the United States, an all-time high. Multiplex theaters, featuring 12 or 18 screens clustered around a central concession stand, are still the rule. Most new theaters seat 200–400 patrons. The massive movie palaces of the 1920s and 1930s have not reemerged, but there are noticeable changes inside the motion picture theater as exhibitors go after a slightly older demographic. Soundproofing to prevent spill from adjoining theaters is now common, and concession stands are putting real butter on popcorn, with a few even offering mineral water, cappuccino, and valet parking (see "Media Probe: Food and Flicks").

ownership in the film industry

Big conglomerates, many of them mentioned in earlier chapters, dominate the film industry. As of 2011 the top six were as follows:

1. *The Walt Disney Company:* Headquartered in California, Disney has two movie enterprises: Touchstone, for mature-audience films, and Buena Vista, for general films. Disney has holdings in television, cable, and publishing in addition to its interests in theme parks, hotels, music, real estate, golf courses, and cruise ships. Disney also makes money licensing Disney characters for use by other companies.

2. *Time Warner:* Warner Brothers is the motion picture arm of this huge conglomerate, which has interests in the Internet, magazine publishing, movie theaters, and cable TV, among other media.

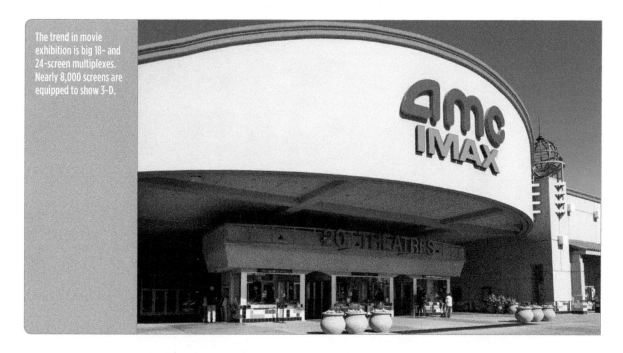

The trend in movie exhibition is big 18- and 24-screen multiplexes. Nearly 8,000 screens are equipped to show 3-D.

3. *Paramount (Viacom):* In addition to owning and making motion pictures, Viacom owns cable TV networks, movie theaters, and music publishing companies.

4. *Sony/MGM:* In 2004 Sony added MGM to its list of properties that include movie theaters, TV production facilities, consumer electronics, and video games.

5. *NBC Universal:* The company is jointly owned by cable giant Comcast and the General Electric Corporation.

6. *News Corporation:* Rupert Murdoch's Australian-based company owns 20th Century Fox. The company is also involved in satellite broadcasting and publishing and owns a TV network and a cable news channel.

producing motion pictures

Preproduction

How does a film get to be a film? The three distinct phases in moviemaking are (1) preproduction, (2) production, and (3) postproduction.

All films begin with an idea. The idea can be sketchy, such as a two-paragraph outline of the plot, or detailed, such as a novel or a Broadway play.

The next step of the preproduction process is writing the screenplay. In general, the route to a finished motion picture script consists of several steps:

- *Step 1. Treatment:* This is a narrative statement of the plot and descriptions of the main characters and locations; it might even contain sample dialogue.
- *Step 2. First-draft script:* This version contains all the dialogue and camera setups and a description of action sequences.
- *Step 3. Revised script:* This incorporates changes suggested by the producer, director, actors, and others.
- *Step 4. Script polish:* This process involves adding or subtracting scenes, revising dialogue, and making other minor changes.

While all this is going on, the producer tries to find actors (in the film industry, people who act in films are described by the generic term "talent," whether they have any or not) who will appear in the film. The contracts and deals that are worked out vary from

The budget for *Pirates of the Caribbean: At World's End* was reportedly in excess of $300 million.

astronomical to modest. One common arrangement is for the actor to receive a flat fee. These fees have been rising in the past few years and are one of the reasons films cost so much to produce. For example, Jim Carrey gets around $20 million per picture, and Reese Witherspoon receives about $15 million. At the other end of the scale, the Screen Actors Guild has a contract that spells out the minimum salary that must be paid to talent in minor roles and walk-on parts.

Meanwhile, the producer is also trying to secure financial backing for the picture. We will say more about these monetary arrangements in the section on economics. For now, it is important to remember that the financial arrangements have to be worked out early in the preproduction process.

At the same time, the producer is busy lining up skilled personnel to work behind the camera. Of these people the film's director is central. When all the elements have been put together, the director will determine what scenes get photographed from what angle and how they will be assembled in the final picture. Working closely with the director are the cinematographer (the person responsible for the lighting and filming of the scenes) and the film editor (the person who will cut the film and assemble the scenes in the proper order). A movie crew contains dozens of other skilled people: set designers, makeup specialists, electricians, audio engineers, crane operators, painters, plumbers, carpenters, property masters, set dressers, caterers, first-aid people, and many others.

Shortly after the director has been signed for the project, he or she and the producer scout possible locations for shooting the film. Some sequences may be shot in the sound studio, but others may need the authenticity that only location shooting can provide. As soon as the locations have been chosen, the producer makes the necessary arrangements to secure these sites for filming. Sometimes this entails renting the studios of a major motion picture production company or obtaining permits to shoot in city streets or other locales. The producer must also draw up plans to make sure that the filming equipment, talent, and technical crew are all at the same place at the same time.

Production

Once all these items have been attended to, the film moves into the actual production phase. Cast and crew assemble at the chosen location, and each scene is shot and reshot until the director is satisfied. The actors and crew then move to another location, and

media *Probe*

All-Time Box Office Leaders—Another Look

Most of the top 10 films listed on page 239 are from the past couple of decades. This is because tickets have become more expensive over the years. The following list is adjusted for inflation.

Film	Year	Adjusted Box Office (billions)
Gone with the Wind	1939	$1.61
Star Wars IV: A New Hope	1977	1.43
The Sound of Music	1965	1.14
E.T.: The Extraterrestrial	1982	1.13
The Ten Commandments	1956	1.05
Titanic	1997	1.03
Jaws	1975	1.03
Doctor Zhivago	1965	0.99
The Exorcist	1973	0.88
Snow White	1937	0.87

the process starts all over again. Overriding the entire production is the knowledge that all this is costing a great deal of money. Shooting even a moderate-budget film can cost $400,000–500,000 *per day.* Therefore, the director tries to plan everything so that each dollar is used efficiently.

The average shooting schedule for the typical film is about 70 days. Each day's shooting (and some days can be 16 hours long) results in an average of fewer than 2 minutes of usable film.

Postproduction

The postproduction phase begins after the filming has been completed. A film editor, working with the director, decides where close-ups should be placed, what angles scenes should be shown from, and how long each scene should last. The elaborate special effects that some films require are also added during postproduction. Once the scenes have been edited into an acceptable form, postproduction sound can be added. This might include narration, music, sound effects, and original dialogue that, for one reason or another, has to be redone. (About 10–15 percent of outside dialogue has to be rerecorded because of interfering noises.) Finally, the edited film, complete with final sound track and special effects, is sent to the laboratory where a release print of the film is made.

the economics of motion pictures

There are several revenue streams for the motion picture industry: (1) money taken in at the U.S. box office, (2) revenue from the international box office, (3) sales and rentals of DVDs, and (4) miscellaneous video sources such as pay-per-view, streaming video, and video-on-demand.

As far as the U.S. box office is concerned, film revenue tied an all-time high in 2010 at $10.6 billion. The international box office was also at a record high. On a less optimistic note, movie attendance actually declined slightly from 2007 to 2010. Also troubling to the industry is the fact that revenue from DVD sales and rentals dropped for the first time from 2007 to 2010, from $21 billion to about $19 billion. (Note that DVD income far exceeds box office revenue.) Movie executives are hoping that revenue from streaming movies over such services as Netflix will help offset some of the losses in DVD sales.

In short, Hollywood is not yet in need of a bailout, but its future fortunes remain hard to predict. Many studios have cut back on the number of films they are releasing and are no longer giving movie stars the generous paydays of years past.

Movies are an expensive medium. In 2010 the cost of producing and marketing the typical film was nearly $110 million, up about 30 percent from 2002. And some films cost much more. *Pirates of the Caribbean: At World's End* and *Spiderman 3* both topped the $250-million mark. If you've been to the movies lately, you're also aware that movies are getting expensive for consumers. The average ticket price in 2010 was $7.89, and in many cities a ticket to an evening performance costs more than $10. Add in another $5 for a medium popcorn (about 90 percent of that is profit for the movie theater) and $4 for a soft drink, and a night at the movies can be an expensive proposition—but still less expensive than attending a professional sporting event or going to a theme park.

Financing a Film

Where do producers get the enormous sums of money necessary to make a film? Let us take a look at some common financing methods. If a producer has a good track record and a film looks promising, the distributor might lend the producer the entire amount needed to make the film. In return the distributor gains distribution rights to the film. Moreover, if the distributor also has studio facilities, the producer might agree to rent those facilities from the distributor.

A second method is to arrange for a **pickup**. Under this arrangement a distributor agrees to "pick up" the cost of a finished picture at a later date for a set price. Although this agreement does a producer little immediate good, he or she can take the pickup to a bank to help secure a loan for the cost of the film.

A third method is a **limited partnership**, an arrangement whereby the film is financed by outside investors. Each limited partner puts up a set amount, and his or her personal liability is limited to the amount invested; that is, a partner cannot lose any more money than he or she put up even if the film goes over budget.

A fourth method is a **joint venture**. Under this setup several companies involved in film production and distribution pool their resources and agree to finance and distribute one or more films. Given the increasing cost of motion pictures, this arrangement is becoming more common as several companies share the risk and potential rewards of a movie. *Ironman,* for example, was financed by a joint venture between Paramount and Marvel Entertainment.

The producer and distributor also agree on how to divide the distributor's gross receipts from the film (the money the distributor gets from the theater owners, TV networks, pay-TV operations, and DVD revenues). Since the distributor takes the greater risk in the venture, the distributor is the first to be paid from the receipts of the film. Distribution companies charge a distribution fee for their efforts. In addition, there are distribution expenses (cost of making multiple prints of the film, advertising, taxes, insurance). Lastly, the actual production cost of the film must be repaid. If the distributor or a bank lent the producer $50 million to make the film, that loan has to be paid off (plus interest). Because of all these expenses, it is estimated that a film must earn two and one-half to three times its production cost before it starts to show a profit for the producers. Hollywood accounting tends to be complicated, however, and sometimes it is hard to determine when a film is profitable.

Dealing with the Exhibitor

The distributor is also involved in other financial dealings, specifically with the exhibitors. An exhibition license sets the terms under which the showing of the film will occur. The license specifies the run of the film (the number of weeks the theater must agree to play the picture), holdover rights, the date the picture will be available for showing, and the clearance (the amount of time that must elapse before the film can be shown at a competing theater).

The license also contains the financial terms for the film's showing. There are several common arrangements. The simplest involves a specified percentage split of the money

ethical issues

History and The Social Network

The Social Network, the story of Mark Zuckerberg and the founding of Facebook, was a financial and critical success. Grossing more than $100 million at the box office, the film also won three Oscars.

Despite its achievements, the film generated some controversy over its accuracy. The screenplay was adapted from a book, *The Accidental Billionaire,* that was criticized for its emphasis on the frivolous and lack of supporting sources. Zuckerberg refused to cooperate with the filmmakers and later called the movie misleading and a work of fiction.

Like many other movies that deal with living or historical figures, the movie raises the question of how much leeway screenwriters and directors have when dealing with history, both recent and past. One could argue that moviemakers have a greater ethical responsibility to be accurate and truthful when dealing with a living person. It's one thing to fictionalize Abraham Lincoln as a vampire hunter because the outlandish premise will probably not harm anybody, but it's another case entirely when portraying a 26-year-old as arrogant, overly ambitious, untrustworthy, and as someone who would betray his best friend. If such a characterization is inaccurate, yet becomes permanently attached to the young man, then it seems that harm has been done.

Aaron Sorkin, the Oscar-winning screenwriter of *The Social Network,* made the following comments about this issue in a *New York* magazine article. "[T]hat's always a question that you're wrestling with, especially when you're writing about people who are still alive. On one hand, you don't want to screw around with people's lives, you never want to say anything that isn't true, and you don't want to mess with history. On the other hand, this isn't a documentary. Art isn't about what happened, and the properties of people and the properties of 'characters' are two completely different things." He later told Reuters: "This movie is absolutely a true story, but with the catch that people disagree about what the truth was and the movie takes no position on what the truth is. It presents everybody's story."

Some might argue with that last assertion since the movie seems to be told from the perspective of Eduardo Saverin, who was also a consultant on *The Accidental Billionaire.* If Zuckerberg didn't cooperate in the making of the film, it's hard to argue that the movie actually represented his perspective. For example, the movie suggests that Zuckerberg created the site to impress the elite clubs at Harvard and to win back an old girlfriend. That concept makes a great storyline but it's probably not how Zuckerberg would tell it.

taken in at the box office. The exhibitor agrees to split the money with the distributor according to an agreed-upon formula—perhaps 50/50 the first week, 60/40 the second, 70/30 the third, and so on—with the exhibitor keeping more money the longer the run of the film. Another alternative is the **sliding scale**. Under this setup, as the box office revenue increases, so does the amount of money the exhibitor must pay the distributor. For example, if a week's revenue was more than $30,000, the exhibitor would pay the distributor 60 percent; if the revenue was between $25,000 and $29,999, the distributor would receive 50 percent; and so on. Another common approach is the 90/10 deal. Under this method the movie theater owner first deducts the house allowance (called the *nut*) from the box office take. The house allowance includes all the operating expenses of the theater (heating, cooling, water, lights, salaries, maintenance, and so on), plus a sum that is pure profit for the theater (this sum is called *air*). From the revenues (if any) that remain, the distributor gets 90 percent and the house 10 percent.

As suggested earlier, concession stand sales are a significant source of income for movie theater owners. If the average moviegoer spends $20 on popcorn, candy, soft drinks, nachos, and other munchies, and a billion or so tickets are sold every year, that works out to about $20 billion in annual revenue.

Movie theaters now have an additional revenue stream from on-screen advertising. Theaters love this because the cost to them is minimal. In order to clear time to show in-theater commercials, however, the exhibitor often cuts back on the time devoted to showing movie previews, a move that doesn't sit well with the studios.

global movies

Although American films still do well overseas, they are becoming less dominant as locally produced films grow in popularity. Nevertheless, they still contribute mightily to Hollywood's bottom line. In 2010, foreign box office revenue was double the domestic total.

media Probe
Scream 4, Toy Story 3, Hangover 2

Keeping score of movies is getting difficult as sequels have recently become more numerous. In addition to the three mentioned above, there's *Fast [and Furious] 5*, *Saw VI* (it's unclear why the *Saw* series uses Roman numerals), *Kung Fu Panda 2*, *Spy Kids 4*, *Final Destination 5*, and several others with numbers in their titles. Then there are the sequels that don't identify themselves by number such as *Alvin and the Chipmunks: Chipwrecked* (the third in the series), *Mission Impossible: Ghost Protocol* (the fourth in the series), and *X-Men: First Class* (the fifth in the series). All in all, the 27 sequels released in 2011 were an all-time record.

Why so many sequels? The answer is money. Sequels of successful films have a ready-made audience and since most people are already aware of the series, advertising and marketing costs are less. However, the primary reason is that a hit series of films can bring in more money in merchandising and other ancillary sales (toys, clothing, DVDs, etc.). For instance, as of 2011, *Toy Story 3* had generated more than $9.8 billion in DVD sales, toys, clothing, and attractions at Disneyland and Disney World. So don't be surprised if there's a *Toy Story 4* in the future.

Some films do much better overseas than they do in the United States. *Alice in Wonderland* grossed nearly $700 million overseas compared to $330 million domestically. The fastest growing overseas markets for U.S. films are the BRIC countries (Brazil, Russia, India, and China). In China, film revenue grew 64 percent from 2009 to 2010; in Russia, revenue jumped 56 percent.

the motion picture audience

Sources of Feedback

Feedback in the movie industry revolves around the weekly box office figures compiled and reported in various trade publications including *Variety*. Each week *Variety* reports the top-grossing films in the American and foreign markets. An example of this listing is reproduced in Figure 10-1.

To compile these data, *Variety*, in cooperation with Nielsen Entertainment Data Incorporated, collects box office results from 50,000 movie screens in 14 countries, including the United States, Canada, Mexico, and several countries in South America, Europe, and Asia. Most of the column headings in *Variety*'s chart are self-explanatory. Each film's title is listed, followed by the distributor. The remaining columns show box office revenue, number of screens showing the picture, average revenue per screen, and domestic and foreign revenue estimates. Note that this chart reports only a film's gross earnings; it does not show how much profit, if any, a film has made.

The economic feedback contained in *Variety* is extremely important in the movie industry. One or two blockbuster films can improve the financial position of an entire company. In addition, a film successful at the box office is apt to inspire one or more sequels and several imitators.

Market Research

Audience research has become more influential in the movie business because of the tremendous cost of motion pictures. At most studios the first step is concept testing to find promising plotlines. The next step is an analysis of the script. If the script seems promising, the studio will go ahead and film it and make a rough cut. The rough cut is then used by movie researchers in a series of test screenings. In addition, **focus group** sessions are held. A focus group is a small sample (usually about 10–15 people) of the target audience that is asked detailed questions about what the viewers liked and did not like. With this information the studio can add or drop a scene, modify the ending, change the musical score, or make other alterations. Once these changes are completed, the movie is released for a sneak preview. The big studios now use social media to recruit audiences for sneak

figure 10-1

Variety Box Office Revenue Chart

previews. Audience members fill out preview cards that summarize their reactions to a film, its characters, and its stars. It is possible for the director to make limited changes in the film in response to this feedback, but it is usually too late to make wholesale changes.

Audiences

Average weekly attendance had been slowly rising from 1980 to 2000, but admissions fell slightly from 2000 to 2010. As shown in Figure 10-2, attendance is nowhere near the levels of the 1930s and 1940s when film was in its heyday.

The movie audience tends to be young. About 60 percent of filmgoers are under 40. Frequent moviegoers (those who see at least 12 films a year) account for about three-quarters of all film admissions. They tend to be young, single (going to movies continues to be a popular dating activity), from middle-class families, and from urban areas. The average person in the United States attends about six films a year.

The audience for movies is largest in July and August and smallest in May. The worst two weeks of the year for moviegoing are the first two weeks in December, when attendance drops 30–50 percent.

movies at home

sound byte

Suppose They Made a Movie and Nobody Came . . .

Zyzzyx Road, a film starring Tom Sizemore and Katherine Heigl (from *Grey's Anatomy*), made a whopping $30 at U.S. theaters.

Despite the decline in DVD sales and rentals, home video is still a major contributor to Hollywood's bottom line. The home video business, however, has changed dramatically in the last few years thanks to Netflix and other movie-streaming services. In years past, consumers would go to the local video store and buy or rent a DVD for home viewing. Then along came Netflix with its DVD-by-mail arrangement. It wasn't long before traditional brick-and-mortar stores were in trouble. Blockbuster and Movie Gallery filed for bankruptcy in 2009–2010. Netflix then got

figure 10-2

Average Weekly Film Attendance in the United States

Source: Motion Picture Association of America. Used by permission.

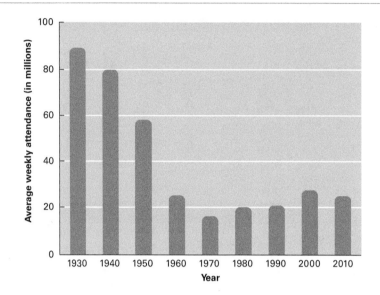

into the movie-streaming business, letting users instantly watch a movie through their Internet-connected TV or Blu-ray player, Xbox 360, PS 3, Wii, or other device. Consumers flocked to Netflix and the service boasted a subscription list of more than 20 million. In a few short years, Netflix moved from being the biggest user of the U.S. Postal Service to being the biggest source of Internet broadband traffic. (Another example of the shift from atoms to bits.)

Hollywood studios are moving cautiously in their dealings with Netflix. On the one hand, the studios sell about $250 million worth of DVDs to the service each year. On the other hand, the studios are leery of letting Netflix stream films that are more recent. Currently, Netflix streams films that are at least a year old, but ongoing negotiations with the studio could result in newer titles being offered. Hollywood fears that Netflix availability will further erode DVD sales and make films less attractive to cable networks, premium services such as HBO, pay-per-view, and broadcast networks. The final arrangements between the movie studios and Netflix and Amazon, which recently started a similar downloading service, will have a major impact on the future of home video.

The home video market, like the theatrical market is driven by big hits. Movies that were popular on the big screen are almost invariably popular on the home screen. For example, *Toy Story 3* grossed about $415 million at the U.S. box office and another $162 million from DVD sales.

Pay-per-view (PPV) and **video-on-demand (VOD)** television provides another revenue stream for movie companies. More than 50 million homes are equipped for PPV or VOD, and the number is growing steadily. In addition, the number of channels available on cable and satellite systems is increasing, and many of these new channels are devoted to PPV. Finally, Hollywood gets income from licensing its movies to premium cable channels, such as HBO and Showtime, in addition to

DirectTV was the first pay TV service to offer premium VOD. *Just Go With It* was offered to subscribers for $29.99.

media *Premium VOD*
Probe

Would you be willing to pay $30 to rent a recently released movie? That's the idea behind Premium VOD, a service that would allow subscribers to see movies on their home TV only eight weeks after they premiere. In the traditional system, theater owners get an exclusive period, usually four months, to offer new films. After that time, the movies are available for about $4.95 on video-on-demand. Since much of the revenue from VOD goes to the studio, Hollywood sees premium VOD as a way to make up for the drop in DVD sales and rentals.

Premium VOD does not sit well with theater owners because it will hurt their business. Two movie chains, Regal and AMC, have threatened to not show or promote any movies that will be shown via Premium VOD. Regal has also announced it will reduce the number of trailers it shows from the studios that have signed onto the Premium deal. These drastic steps indicate how seriously theater owners fear the coming of this service.

receiving money from selling the rights to movies to traditional over-the-air broadcasters. Given these numerous video aftermarkets, it is no surprise that TV generates more revenue for the movie industry than does the box office. Chapter 11 contains more information on home video.

the film industry

Job prospects in the film industry are highly volatile, but most college students who are interested in a career in film are not discouraged by the difficulty involved in becoming successful. Film students tend to be dedicated and passionate about their interest in film and will try to succeed no matter what the employment forecast.

Taking college courses in film is great preparation for a career because it provides students an opportunity to become familiar with the hardware and software used in the industry. In addition, purchasing a good digital camera, investing in professional editing software, and making a couple of films on your own can build a good foundation for later efforts.

The career outlook in the various media industries changes quickly. For a more current description of conditions in the film industry and a more detailed look at career options, please consult the book's Web site: www.mhhe.com/dominick12e.

main points

- The motion picture developed in the late 19th century. After being a main attraction in nickelodeons, films moved into bigger theaters, and movie stars quickly became the most important part of the new industry. Sound came to the movies in the mid-1920s.

- Big movie studios dominated the industry until the late 1940s, when a court decision weakened their power. Television captured much of the film audience in the 1950s. By the end of the 1960s, however, Hollywood had dapted to television and was an active producer of TV shows. A major trend in modern movies is the rise of big-budget movies.

- The transition to digital moviemaking may transform the film industry.

- The movie industry consists of production, distribution, and exhibition facets. Large conglomerates control the business. Producing a motion picture starts from a concept, proceeds to the production stage, and ends with the postproduction stage.

- Movie revenues have shown small but steady growth over the past 10 years. DVD sales and rentals and foreign box office receipts are important sources of movie income.

- Movie audiences are getting older, but a significant part of the audience is still the 30-and-under age group.

- Streaming is becoming a popular way to view movies at home.

questions for review

1. What are the defining features of motion pictures?
2. What caused the rise and fall of the Motion Picture Patents Company?
3. How did the film industry react to TV?
4. What are the three main segments of the motion picture industry?
5. What are the various ways films are financed?

questions for critical thinking

1. Suppose the movie industry had never moved to Hollywood, staying instead on the East Coast. How might films be different?
2. What are the potential advantages and disadvantages of big corporations controlling motion picture production?
3. Do filmmakers have an obligation to be socially responsible for what they present on the screen? Why or why not?
4. Will movie theaters still exist in 20 years? Or will people watch movies in their homes on big HDTVs?
5. Someone once said that Hollywood producers don't make films; they make deals. Comment on the validity of this statement and its implications.

key terms

phi phenomenon (p. 230)
persistence of vision (p. 230)
Kinetoscope (p. 230)
Motion Picture Patents Company (MPPC) (p. 233)

block booking (p. 234)
DVD (digital videodisc) (p. 239)
pickup (p. 248)
limited partnership (p. 248)
joint venture (p. 248)

sliding scale (p. 249)
Variety (p. 250)
focus group (p. 250)
pay-per-view (PPV) (p. 252)
video-on-demand (VOD) (p. 252)

internet resources

Online Learning Center

On the Online Learning Center home page, www.mhhe.com/dominick12e, *select* Student Center *and then* Chapter 10.

1. Use the Learning Objectives, Chapter Outline, and Main Points sections to review this chapter.
2. Test your knowledge of the chapter using the multiple choice and flashcard features of the site.
3. Expand your knowledge of concepts and topics discussed in the chapter with additional Questions for Critical Thinking and Internet Exercises.

surfing the internet

These represent a variety of movie theme sites.

www.filmsite.org/filmh.html
A history of motion pictures arranged by decades.

www.imdb.com
The Internet Movie Database. Contains everything you ever wanted to know about movies. Has information about stars, cast, plot, and box office performance for just about every movie.

www.mpaa.org
The official Web site of the Motion Picture Association of America. Contains industry statistics and the latest news releases. Has an extensive section that deals with copyright issues.

www.mrcranky.com
An offbeat review page featuring a reviewer who has high standards and a caustic style. Mr. Cranky rates movies by assigning a number of bombs. For example, four bombs means "As good as a poke in the eye with a sharp stick."

www.variety.com
The Web site of the trade paper that is the bible of the entertainment industry. Includes the latest industry news, global box office charts, film reviews, and profiles of production companies.

www.Warnerbros.com
The Warner Brothers Web site. Check out new releases, view movie trailers, and see which Warner products are available on DVD.

The audience for broadcast television is getting older. The average age of a viewer of a prime-time network series in 2010 was about 50. The average viewer of *Dancing with the Stars* was over 60.

Chapter**11**

broadcast
television

This chapter will prepare you to:

- trace the development of television

- describe the evolution of the networks

- explain the impact of the Telecommunications Act of 1996

- detail the implications of the digital age for broadcast television

- explain how television ratings are formulated

- describe the departments of the television industry and how programs are produced

Let's start off this chapter with a quiz. How many of these TV shows did you or do you usually watch? *CBS Evening News? Dancing with the Stars? The Good Wife? NCIS? Two and a Half Men?* If you answered "no" to most of these choices, you are not alone.

Broadcast network TV audiences are not as young as they used to be. In 1991, the median age (the age at which half the viewers are younger and half older) for Fox was 29, ABC's median age was 37, while NBC's was 42. CBS, which has traditionally had the oldest audience, was 45.

Flash forward 20 years. Median age for Fox: 44. For ABC: 51. For NBC: 49. CBS: 55. The median audience age for specific shows tells the same tale. The median age for viewers of network news programs is 61; *Dancing with the Stars* median audience age is 60; *The Good Wife* is 58; and *NCIS* is 57 while Two and Half Men is 50. Fox's *Glee* looks like it robs the cradle with a median audience age of 38.

In contrast, look at the average ages of the audiences of some cable networks: MTV, median age 23; Comedy Central, median age 31; E!, median age 34; TBS, median age 35; Bravo and Oxygen, median age 42.

There are several reasons why the broadcast TV audience is aging. First, the general population is getting older as more Baby

Boomers mature. Second, young people spend more time playing video games or logging on to social network sites on the Internet and less time with broadcast TV. Third, when young people do watch TV, they tend to gravitate to niche cable programs such as *Jersey Shore, Pawn Stars, Keeping Up with the Kardashians,* and *Teen Mom.*

Why is this trend significant for broadcast TV? First, the prime audience for advertisers is 18- to 49-year-olds. The fewer members of this age group who watch broadcast TV, the harder it will be for the networks to pull in advertising revenue. To be sure, the networks have nothing to worry about, at least for now, because the broadcast TV networks still attract large audiences and many advertisers are willing to purchase commercials on net shows despite the fact that many in the audience are not their prime demographic target. In other words, enough young people still watch *Grey's Anatomy* (median average audience age around 50) to make it worthwhile to buy commercials during the program. If the aging trend continues, however, there may come a time when broadcasters may have to rethink their programming or convince advertisers that the senior citizen demographic is one they should aim for. Second, taking the long view, it's hard to be optimistic about the future of broadcast TV when most of its core audience will be dead in 30 to 40 years. In sum, broadcast TV faces an uncertain and challenging future.

This chapter will examine broadcast TV, and the next chapter will look at other forms of television: cable, satellite, and Internet. (This is not a totally neat division because broadcast stations are also carried via cable and satellite, and stations and networks both have a Web presence.) Although the distinction between traditional broadcast TV and the newer forms doesn't concern most people, there are some areas where the distribution channel does make a difference. In addition to variations in programming strategies, broadcast TV is regulated differently from the other forms of TV while cable, satellite, and Internet TV have different revenue sources than broadcast TV. Most important, broadcast, cable, satellite, and Internet TV are all coping differently with the digital revolution.

a brief history

The two men who developed television in the United States could not have been more different. At the age of 16, Philo Farnsworth diagrammed his idea for a television system on the chalkboard in front of his somewhat amazed high school teacher. Farnsworth, an individualistic and lone-wolf inventor, worked at developing his new device, which he called an *image dissector,* and eventually patented it in 1930. In contrast, Vladimir Zworykin was an organization man, working first for Westinghouse and then for RCA. By 1928 he had perfected a primitive camera tube, the iconoscope.

Picture quality of the early television systems was poor, but technical developments during the 1930s improved performance. RCA, with Zworykin's help and with a patent arrangement that permitted it to use Farnsworth's invention, set out to develop TV's commercial potential. NBC, owned by RCA, gave the first public demonstration of broadcast commercial television at the 1939 World's Fair.[1]

The initial public response to TV was lukewarm. Sets were expensive, and there were not many programs for people to watch. Even early TV actors were somewhat skeptical about the future of the new medium. They had to wear green makeup to look normal for the TV camera and swallow salt tablets because the intense heat of the lights necessary for TV made them perspire constantly.

---

[1]In fairness to Farnsworth, the inventor demonstrated his system in 1934 using what today would be called a *closed-circuit telecast.*

World War II interrupted TV's development. When peace returned in 1945, new technology that had been perfected during the war greatly improved both TV reception and working conditions for the performers. New TV cameras required much less light. TV screens were bigger. There were more programs available, and stations were being linked into networks. All the signs pointed to big things for TV. In 1945 there were only eight TV stations and 8,000 homes with TV in the entire United States. Ten years later, there were nearly 100 stations, and 35 million households (about 67 percent of the country) had TV.

TV's rapid success caught the industry and the Federal Communications Commission (FCC) off guard. Unless technical standards were worked out, the TV spectrum was in danger of becoming overcrowded and riddled with interference, just as had happened with radio 30 years earlier. To guard against this possibility, the FCC imposed a freeze on all new applications for TV stations. The freeze, which went into effect in 1948, would last for 4 years while the FCC gathered information from engineers and technical experts. When the freeze was lifted in 1952, the FCC had established that 12 VHF and 70 UHF channels (see page 269) were to be devoted to TV. In addition, the commission drew up a list that allocated television channels to the various communities in the United States and specified other rules to minimize interference. Also, thanks largely to the efforts of Frieda Hennock, the first woman to serve on the commission, TV channels were set aside for educational use.

The 1950s: Television Takes Off

Networks, Tape, UHF, and Color   The early television industry was modeled after radio. Local stations served their communities and, in turn, might be affiliated with networks. There were four TV networks during this period: CBS, NBC, ABC, and DuMont, a smaller network that went out of business in 1956. Also much like early radio networks, TV networks quickly became the primary programming sources for their affiliates. NBC and CBS were usually the most popular networks, with ABC trailing behind. Most early network programs were game shows, sports events, and interviews, with a few comedies and dramas interspersed throughout the schedule.

In the early days of TV, most network prime-time programs were produced by advertising agencies that retained control over their content. The agencies also decided on the length and placement of the commercials. After the 1959 scandal that followed the discovery that some quiz shows had been "fixed," the networks reasserted their control over programming. Most programs were produced by independent production companies, with much of the financing provided by the networks, an arrangement that would remain in place for the next several decades.

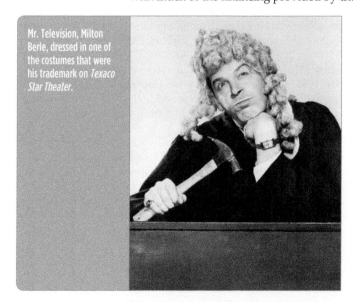

Mr. Television, Milton Berle, dressed in one of the costumes that were his trademark on *Texaco Star Theater*.

Most programs were broadcast live from New York or were filmed in California. Live programs, of course, could not be repeated and often had to be performed again for the West Coast. In 1956 the Ampex Corporation developed videotape, a cheap and efficient way of storing TV programs. By the beginning of the 1960s, most of TV's live programming had switched to tape.

After the FCC-imposed freeze ended, TV stations and TV sets multiplied rapidly. The new UHF channels, however, did not do so well. Few sets equipped with UHF receivers were made during the 1950s. The UHF stations had smaller coverage areas than the VHF stations, and most advertising dollars went to VHF stations. As a result, UHF TV, much like FM radio, started off at a disadvantage.

The Beverly Hillbillies was the most popular of the "bucolic" situation comedies. It was the number-one show during the 1961–1962 TV season and spent 9 years on the air.

Color television was introduced during the 1950s. Led by NBC (RCA, the parent company, was manufacturing color TV sets), the networks were broadcasting 2–3 hours of color programming per day by 1960.

The Golden Age of Television Many broadcast historians refer to the 1950s as the golden age of TV. Many shows that aired during the decade became extremely popular. *Toast of the Town,* hosted by Ed Sullivan, is still regarded as the exemplar of the variety series. *Texaco Star Theater,* starring ex-vaudevillian Milton Berle, prompted many people to buy TV sets just to see what wacky stunts Berle would pull off on his next program.

Live prestige dramas were also run in prime time. Programs such as *Studio One* featured plays by Rod Serling, Gore Vidal, and Reginald Rose. Broadway stars such as Rex Harrison and Tallulah Bankhead performed in live TV drama. The growing popularity of videotape, however, put an end to these live productions.

By the end of the 1950s, a new genre, the adult Western, in which character and motivation overshadowed gunfights, dominated TV. By 1959, there were 26 Westerns in prime time, including *Gunsmoke, The Life and Legend of Wyatt Earp,* and *Wagon Train.*

Coming of Age: Television in the 1960s

By the early 1960s TV had lost its novelty and become just another part of everyday life. The number of TV stations continued to increase, and by the close of the decade, more than 95 percent of all American households owned at least one TV.

Television journalism came of age during the 1960s. NBC and CBS expanded their nightly newscasts from 15 to 30 minutes in 1963, and ABC followed suit shortly thereafter. In November of that year, TV journalism earned praise for its professionalism during its coverage of the assassination and funeral of President John F. Kennedy. The networks also covered the civil rights movement and the growing social unrest across the country. Perhaps the most exciting moment for television news came in 1969 with its live coverage of Neil Armstrong's historic walk on the moon.

Noncommercial broadcasting also evolved during the 1960s. About 69 educational stations were broadcasting by 1965. A report issued by the Carnegie Commission proposed that Congress establish a Corporation for Public Broadcasting. The commission's recommendations were incorporated into the **Public Broadcasting Act of 1967,** which set up the Public Broadcasting Service.

Another segment of the video industry was also experiencing growth during this time period—cable television. We will discuss the history of cable TV in the next chapter.

Television programs popular in the early 1960s included a number of rural comedies, such as *The Beverly Hillbillies* and *Green Acres.* After the Kennedy assassination, however, fantasy and escapist programs dominated prime time. In 1964, for example, some of the shows that premiered included *Bewitched* (about a friendly witch), *My Favorite Martian* (about a friendly Martian), and *My Mother the Car* (self-explanatory).

The 1970s: Growing Public Concern

As the 1970s began, public concern over the impact of television programming was growing. A panel of scientists set up by the Surgeon General's office to investigate the impact of exposure to TV violence suggested that TV violence was related in a modest

media *Probe*

The More Things Change . . .

Drive through Anytown, U.S.A., in the 1960s and you would see a veritable forest of TV antennas moored to the rooftops of houses. Sitting atop masts up to 30 feet tall, these metal gadgets were often connected to a rotor that moved the antenna around until it picked up the strongest broadcast signal. When cable TV became popular, the rooftop antennas became as rare as the hula hoop, bell-bottoms, and other phenomena of the 1960s.

Now, in another illustration of history repeating itself, they're back. As it happens, those same old rooftop antennas that used to pick up broadcast analog TV can also pick up digital HDTV. Better yet, with an antenna you don't need cable or satellite, and there's no monthly fee for the improved picture. (Of course, the antennas pick up only broadcast stations;

if you want ESPN or the Food Network in high definition, you'll have to pay a monthly fee.)

Even more interesting is the fact that HDTV looks better when it is received by an antenna than when it comes through a cable or via satellite. The broadcast signal is crisper and sharper because it is not compressed and then expanded as happens with cable or satellite transmission.

Don't expect, however, to see those rooftop antenna forests reappearing. Modern antennas are smaller and more powerful than the 1960s versions. For aesthetic reasons most homeowners install them in their attics. Viewers who live near their local TV stations' digital transmitters have found that they can get a great picture with small set-top antennas that cost as little as $25.

way to aggressive behavior in some young children. We'll explore this topic further in Chapter 18.

The early 1970s were also characterized by the growth of citizen group involvement in FCC decisions. Groups such as Action for Children's Television and the Office of Communication of the United Church of Christ and coalitions of minority groups became influential in shaping broadcasting policy.

The three networks continued to dominate the industry during the early to mid-1970s, but by the end of the decade, they were beginning to feel the competition from the growing cable industry. Friction between the traditional over-the-air broadcasters and the cable companies continues today.

The biggest trend in television programming during the early 1970s was the growth of law-and-order programs, such as *The FBI*, *Charlie's Angels*, and *Mannix*. By the middle of the decade, these shows were replaced by a number of adult situation comedies,

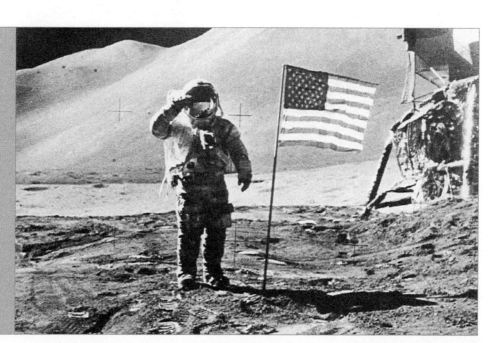

Live TV coverage of the first man landing on the moon in 1969 reached hundreds of millions of viewers.

shows that dealt with more mature themes. *All in the Family*, *M**A*S* *H*, and *Sanford and Son* typified this trend. By the end of the decade, prime-time soap operas such as *Dallas* and *Dynasty* topped the ratings.

The 1980s and 1990s: Increased Competition

The biggest trends in the TV industry in the 1980s and 1990s were the continuing erosion of the three big networks' audiences and the increased competition from new networks and cable channels. In the early 1970s the three networks routinely pulled down about 90 percent of the prime-time audience. By the late 1990s their share had dropped to less than 60 percent. In addition, a fourth network, the Fox Broadcasting Company, owned by Rupert Murdoch's News Corporation, started broadcasting in 1987. In the early 1990s two other networks started up: the United Paramount Network (UPN) and the Warner Broadcasting Network (the WB). Both began with limited schedules but had plans to expand their offerings. (In 2006, the WB and UPN would merge to form a single network, CW.)

In 1995 the world of network broadcasting was shaken by two megadeals. First, the Walt Disney Company acquired CapCities/ABC for $19 billion. Then, with the ink barely dry on that deal, Westinghouse disclosed that it was buying CBS for $5.4 billion and eventually changed its name to CBS Corporation.

Cable's Continued Growth

Cable reached more than 68 percent of the population by 2000. As cable systems increased their capacity, new cable programming services rushed to fill the new channels. By 2000 there were six national pay-per-view services; six premium services, including HBO and Showtime; and more than 75 cable networks, including the Sci Fi Channel, Animal Planet, and the Outdoor Channel. Many cable systems were providing more than 100 channels of television to their subscribers. Some new cable networks were having trouble because there was no room left on local systems to carry them. The growing popularity of cable channels further eroded the audiences of the traditional TV networks.

Advertising revenue also grew, topping the $11-billion mark in 1999. By the turn of the century, it was obvious that the cable industry was a full-fledged competitor of traditional broadcasting.

New Technologies

A development that had a significant impact on both traditional TV and the cable industry was the spectacular growth of videocassette recorders (VCRs). Fewer than 5 percent of households had VCRs in 1982. By 2000 that figure was 90 percent. In fact, the VCR was adopted faster than any other appliance except television. The effects of the VCR were many.

First, the renting of movies on cassettes became a multibillion-dollar business, with motion picture studios depending on cassettes for a large part of their revenue.

Second, the VCR encouraged **time shifting**, playing back programs at times other than when they aired. Although this increased total audience by allowing people who might not otherwise have viewed a program to do so, it caused some new problems for advertisers because viewers fast-forwarded through commercials.

Finally, the proliferation of the handheld remote-control device has also caused problems for advertisers and programmers. Remote units have encouraged the tendency toward *grazing*, rapidly scanning all the channels during a commercial or dull spot in a program in search of greener pastures.

After a slow start, direct broadcast by satellite (DBS) got a big boost in 1994 when two companies, DirecTV and United States Satellite Broadcasting (USSB), offered subscribers about 150 channels of programming beamed directly to their homes via a small (18-inch diameter) receiver.

On the legal side the biggest development was the Telecommunications Act of 1996 (discussed in Chapter 16), which introduced program ratings and the V-chip while encouraging competition between cable and phone companies and easing ownership restrictions on TV stations.

decision makers

Ted Turner

R. E. "Ted" Turner inherited his family's outdoor advertising company in 1963, when he was 24. The Atlanta-based business was in poor economic shape, but the young Turner managed to turn it around. Six years later, Turner learned that a financially troubled UHF television station was for sale. Disregarding the fact that the station's signal was so weak that he could not pick it up on his own TV set, Turner bought the station, renamed it WTCG, and began to advertise it on his unused billboards around Atlanta. With a skillful programming mix of TV reruns and old movies, the station eventually became one of the few UHF stations in the country at the time to turn a profit. Turner, however, was not content with merely turning the station around. He had much bigger plans for it.

One day in 1976, at a meeting of the station's managers, Turner placed a beat-up model of the RCA Satcom I satellite on the table and proclaimed that WTCG would soon be competing with CBS, NBC, and ABC. Turner had decided that he would use the new communication satellites to beam WTCG to cable systems all over the country, making it a national network. Not surprisingly, his managers were incredulous. Almost everybody dismissed Turner's idea as totally impractical.

There were many reasons to think this bold move would not work. First, cable TV had not yet caught on; it was available in only 16 percent of the country, mostly in rural areas. Second, cable systems relied on terrestrial microwave signals; not many were equipped to receive satellite feeds. Third, the FCC had a rule against leapfrogging that prohibited cable systems from importing signals from distant cities unless they also took the signals of stations closer to their market. Additionally, FCC regulations permitted cable systems to use only expensive 10-meter satellite dishes, which most systems could not afford. Undaunted, Turner pitched his idea to big cable operators. They were not impressed.

As fate would have it, however, two weeks later, the FCC dropped its leapfrogging rules and permitted stations to use smaller and cheaper satellite dishes. All of a sudden, Turner's idea did not seem so far-fetched. In December, Turner renamed his station WTBS and started distributing it by satellite, thus creating the first superstation.

WTBS caught on slowly. When it first went on the satellite, the station was received by a grand total of four cable systems. Turner helped its fortunes by purchasing the Atlanta Braves baseball team and making

their games available on WTBS. The new superstation continued to grow in popularity, eventually reaching 74 million homes. The success of WTBS inspired the creation of other cable networks and totally changed the cable TV industry. Turner proved that people would subscribe to cable not just to get good reception but also to get programming.

Turner had other ideas. He had encouraged cable systems to carry WTBS by promising them that he would also provide them with additional cable networks. In 1980 he launched the first of those networks—CNN. Cable operators were lukewarm toward the new project. Most refused to provide money to cover start-up costs. Turner invested $21 million in the new venture, which was immediately derided by competitors for its bargain-basement approach to news. Critics labeled CNN the *Chicken Noodle Network*.

CNN started off losing money, but Turner kept the network alive with the profits from WTBS. Finally, CNN went into the black in 1985. Six years later, during the Gulf War, CNN scooped the other networks by having reporters on the scene in Baghdad when the war broke out. CNN's success spawned several 24-hour news service competitors, including MSNBC and Fox News Channel.

Several other Turner decisions have also paid off. In 1986 he paid more than $1 billion for the MGM/United Artists film library. Turner used the films to help launch two other cable networks—Turner Network Television and Turner Classic Movies. Turner also bought the Hanna-Barbera animation studio and started the Cartoon Network.

However, some of Turner's ventures did not work out so well. After Time Warner merged with AOL, Turner became a vice chair of the new company. The merger was a disappointment, and AOL Time Warner stock suffered a huge drop in value. Turner lost millions as a result. In 2003 he resigned his position with the company.

Turner also has an interest in philanthropy. His United Nations Foundation grants money to organizations that are interested in population control and the environment. His Turner Foundation concentrates on improving life in the United States. The decline in AOL Time Warner stock, unfortunately, has meant a cutback in funding for both organizations.

Turner has made some good decisions and some that have not been successful. Regardless, his decisions have had an enormous impact on television and have been key contributors to the design of the modern TV industry landscape.

contemporary broadcast television

Broadcast television is in a state of change. Network and local station audiences continue to shrink, and advertising dollars are finding their way to the Web. The big four networks—ABC, CBS, NBC, and Fox—have made programming available on the Internet. NBC Universal and Fox launched hulu.com where viewers could watch clips and full-length programs (more on Hulu in Chapter 12). ABC.com offers streaming versions of its hit programs a few hours after they are broadcast. Viewers can watch episodes of CBS shows on its Web site and on TV.com.

Digital video recorders (DVRs) such as Tivo have changed the way Americans watch TV. The DVR makes it easy for viewers to record programs and watch them at more

The Disappearing Soap

TThe soap opera *One Life to Live* premiered on the ABC television network in 1968, followed two years later by *All My Children*. ABC's daytime slogan from 1975 to 1985 was "Love in the Afternoon," and both programs featured lots of hot actors and actresses in romantic situations and provocative costumes. The programs had story lines that dealt with social issues such as abortion, homosexuality, AIDS, and teenage alcoholism long before such topics cropped up in prime-time shows. Together the two shows gave ABC a powerful afternoon lineup, and both were consistently among the top-rated daytime programs during the next the next three decades.

In 2011, however, ABC announced it was canceling both shows and replacing them with two talk shows that focus on food and lifestyle. Over the years, the daytime audience had changed as many more women joined the workforce and left the daytime TV audience. Competition from cable networks aimed at women, such as Lifetime and Oxygen, siphoned off more potential viewers. Soaps had trouble attracting younger viewers, who preferred to spend time with the Internet and social media. Finally, soap operas were expensive to produce. They required a large cast of actors, writers, producers, crewmembers, and several sound stages. Experts estimated that a soap opera cost about $50 million per year to produce; a talk show costs about 30 percent less. ABC is not the only network moving away from soaps. CBS canceled two of its long-running soaps, *Guiding Light* and *As the World Turns*, in 2009.

The decline of the soap opera genre is another consequence of the changing world of broadcast television.

convenient times and to fast-forward through commercials, a development that advertisers find troubling. More than 40 percent of U.S. households were equipped with DVRs in 2011, and that number is expected to climb in the future.

Also on the technology front, the DVD player has replaced the VCR as the preferred playback medium for home video. As of 2011, nine out of ten households were equipped with a DVD player. And those DVD players are increasingly connected to big-screen TV sets capable of receiving **high-definition television (HDTV)**, an innovation that offers far better picture and sound quality than ordinary standard-definition TV. About 65 percent of households had HDTV in 2011.

Network audience erosion continued as viewers migrated to cable channels, the Web, and video games. The four major networks' share of the TV viewing audience in 2011 was down to less than 40 percent. Network advertising revenue dropped from 2009 to 2010. As revenue dropped, costs increased, resulting in significant profit declines. Local stations' ratings also dropped, as did ad revenue.

The drop in ad revenue and the bad economic climate prompted the networks to economize. They cut back on program development and looked for ways to trim the production costs of their series. In that connection, all the networks were relying more on lower-cost reality series, such as *American Idol, The Biggest Loser*, and *Dancing with the Stars*, and less on scripted programs. In 2010–2011, the four major networks scheduled nearly 20 hours of nonscripted programs per week.

On a more positive note, even though their audiences are declining, broadcast networks and local stations are still the best means for advertisers to reach a large audience in a hurry. Some hit TV shows, such as *American Idol*, can reach more than 25 million viewers. In addition, online ad revenue has been increasing.

television in the digital age

Transition

Broadcast television is now fully digital. As of June 19, 2009, all television stations were broadcasting **digital television (DTV)**. DTV offers many advantages over analog TV. Digital pictures are clearer and sound quality is better. DTV makes possible high-definition television, plus the DTV picture has an aspect ratio more like that of a motion picture screen. Finally, since digital signals can be compressed and take up less space in the electromagnetic spectrum, broadcasters can subdivide the digital channel and offer several

media *Probe*   *Getting into College Thanks to Reality TV*

Who could guess that all of those hours teens spend watching reality TV shows such as *Jersey Shore, Teen Mom, Project Runway,* and *Keeping Up with the Kardashians* could actually help them get into college?

All college students are familiar with the Scholastic Aptitude Test (SAT) that many colleges use as a tool in deciding admissions. The essay portion of one version of the 2011 SAT asked high schoolers to compose an essay about reality TV. Part of the actual assignment: *Do people benefit from forms of entertainment that show so-called reality, or are such forms of entertainment harmful?"*

Many SAT takers and their parents complained that they were at a disadvantage because the question assumes that students (1) watch TV and (2) watch enough reality TV to provide a meaningful response to the question. One father noted that he was proud that his child studied too much to watch TV and thought the question was unfair. A teen who took the test complained that kids who watched "crap TV" probably did better than he did.

SAT officials defended the question, arguing that the explanatory statement that preceded it *(These shows depict ordinary people competing in everything from singing and dancing to losing weight, or just living their everyday lives.)* should have been enough for students to write the essay. Or as one executive from the College Board put it: "Questions raised about a recent SAT essay [assignment] miss [the] basic point and confuse the literal topic with the task of writing the essay. If presented with a topic about balancing the risk of climbing a mountain with the reward of reaching the summit, for example, a good writer could compose a strong essay without ever having reached the summit of Mount Everest." Well, maybe, but it would certainly help if the good writer actually saw a mountain before assessing the risks of climbing one.

Some students who did not watch reality TV had to stretch in order to compose their essay. One wrote about 19th-century social critic Jacob Riis and the absence of an objective reality. That's a long way from Snooki and The Situation.

different programs in the same space. For example, a station might broadcast a network program on its main channel, a local newscast on a digital subchannel, and weather on another subchannel. As of 2011, most local stations were still looking for ways to make a profit from their subchannels.

3-D TV

After the success of *Avatar* in 3-D, the TV industry hoped that 3-D TV would also become popular. In 2010, TV set manufacturers shipped 4 million 3-D capable sets to vendors. Big retailers such as Best Buy set up special displays to demonstrate the new technology. Consumers, however, were not impressed. The sets carried a big price tag (averaging nearly $3,000), required bulky glasses to view, and suffered from a shortage of 3-D content to watch. Even after price cuts, sales did not pick up. Industry experts, such as director James Cameron, think that once technology perfects 3-D TV without glasses the process will become more popular. For the time being, however, 3-D TV has not lived up to expectations.

Broadcasters and the Web

Broadcast networks are putting more effort into making their Web sites attractive to visitors. In addition to full episodes of ABC programs, ABC.com runs promotional videos and presents additional background material, such as games and quizzes based on its popular programs. CBS.com offers an HDTV player, full episodes of CBS programs, previews, and special features. Although these efforts increase the viewership of network programs, they may hurt a network affiliate. A local affiliate understands that if people watch net programs on hulu.com or a net Web site, they probably won't be tuning in to a local station.

Local stations were slow to realize the importance of a Web presence. Many stations simply used their Web sites to promote the on-air operation. As a result, local-market newspaper Web sites generated significantly more revenue than TV station sites. In response, local stations have improved their Web sites, adding breaking news stories, more video clips, and social media. Rather than an adjunct to the broadcast station, the Web sites have become stand-alone sites with content and features not available over the air. The Pew Research Center reported that local TV stations' Web sites generated $1.34 billion in revenue in 2010, up 8 percent over 2009.

Broadcasters and Broadband

A high-speed broadband connection, such as with a cable modem or DSL, makes it possible for networks and local stations to create their own specialized shows that are distributed only through the Web site. Disney-ABC, for example, operates ESPN 360, an online sports channel available through certain Internet service providers that streams live coverage of sporting events. CBS.com has *Heckle U*, a Web series about a slacker who excels at heckling during basketball games.

Broadband series, however, have yet to generate a profit for broadcasters, and the networks do not invest a lot of money in their development. Nonetheless, they do represent a place where the networks (and maybe a few local stations) can experiment with new programming forms and new creative personnel without risking a lot of money. Occasionally a Web series makes it to broadcast TV. *Quarterlife*, for example, started out as a Web series and was picked up by NBC in 2008. The show was canceled after one episode. In the 2009 season, ABC premiered *In the Motherhood*, a series that started on MSN.com.

Mobile TV: Apps

Telecommunications companies such as MobiTV and Qualcomm pioneered early efforts in mobile TV viewing, but the recent trend has been for content providers to offer access to their programming through apps. ABC's app for the iPad, for example, allows users to watch full episodes of selected ABC series with limited commercials. NBC Live provides a similar service. ABC news has its own app that displays current news stories; CBS News has a similar app. Many TV shows, including *60 Minutes, CBS Sunday Morning*, and *Grey's Anatomy* have their own apps. Many local TV stations have also created applications that feature local news coverage. In addition, MLB.com offers subscribers access to video of major league baseball games.

User-Generated Content

Broadcasters were the first to realize the potential of user-generated content. *America's Funniest Home Videos* premiered in 1989 and as of this writing was still on the air. Aside from that program, however, with the exception of the occasional cell phone video of a news event, network broadcasters use little user-generated content. Local stations are more likely to employ user-generated material. One study found that 50 percent of stations accepted content from the audience, most of it consisting of photos and video of weather-related events.

Social Media

Broadcasters understand the importance of social media and use them for various purposes. The first and most obvious is to promote their shows. When *Glee* went off for the summer after its first season, interest in the show was kept alive by contests on Twitter and Facebook. Many TV series have their own Facebook pages where they keep in touch with fans and advertise upcoming episodes. *Modern Family*'s page had nearly 4 million "likes." Stars of TV series help promote their series by interacting with fans. Nathan Fillion, star of *Castle*, tweets to his almost 900,000 followers on Twitter.

Second, broadcasters, both network and local, use social media to build communities of fans. The Web site for the CBS series *The Big Bang Theory* has a community link where viewers can comment on the series' story line, vote for their favorite character, and get exclusive tweets. NBC features MyNBC, with message boards for favorite shows, blogs, and community games. At the local level, WSB-TV in Atlanta encourages viewers to get involved in their public service Family 2 Family program.

Finally, broadcasters have discovered that many people like to tweet during the live broadcast of a program. During Super Bowl XLV, there were more than 4,000 tweets per second near the end of the game. Broadcasters are using social media to encourage this trend. Advertisers like the idea because it means people can't fast-forward through their commercials as might happen if the program was recorded on a DVR. CBS, for example, created TweetWeek, a week when stars of CBS series such as *NCIS* tweeted during the live broadcast of the show. The CW network introduced an online game called Bwingo that viewers can play while watching a live broadcast of a CW show. A company called

Shopkick developed an app that works with retailers. If a viewer opens the app during a retailer's commercial in a live program, the viewer can receive special discounts from that business.

Social media can also cause problems for broadcasters. When a Connecticut TV station failed to renew the contract of its longtime meteorologist, upset fans created a Facebook page with more than 10,000 members urging the station to reverse itself, causing a public relations problem for management.

defining features of broadcast television

Like radio, TV is a universal medium. About 99 percent of the homes in the United States have at least one working TV set. In fact, most homes have more than one. Tablet computers and smartphones make it possible to take TV anywhere.

Television has become the dominant medium for news and entertainment for Americans. Surveys have consistently revealed that most people choose television as their main source of news. In addition, in the average American household, the TV set is on for about 8 hours every day. Prime-time television series may draw an audience of 15 million households. In short, TV has become an important part of our society.

Further, TV, especially network television, is an expensive business. It costs the production company more than $3 million to produce one episode of a typical one-hour scripted prime-time series. Most series produce about 20–22 original episodes a year. A little math reveals that the total cost for one season of one prime-time hour for one network is about $60 million. Some more math discloses that the total tab for prime-time programming for the four major networks is more than $2 billion. Added to that is the cost of daytime programs and newscasts. TV advertising is also costly, averaging more than $200,000 for a 30-second spot in network prime time.

Finally, over the past several decades, the broadcast television industry has watched its audience fragment. Back in 1970, the major networks' share of the audience was about 90 percent. Today, the increase in cable networks, DVD usage, video games, and home video has cut that share to less than 30 percent.

organization of the broadcast television industry

The **commercial television** system consists of all those local stations whose income is derived from selling time on their facilities to advertisers. **Noncommercial television** consists of those stations whose income is derived from sources other than the sale of advertising time.

A local TV station is licensed by the FCC to provide TV service to a particular community. In the industry these communities are customarily referred to as *markets*. There are 210 markets in the United States, ranging from the number-one market, New York City, with about 7.4 million homes, to number 210, Glendive, Montana, with about 4,000 homes. Some of these local TV stations enter into contractual agreements with TV networks. As of 2011, six commercial networks in the United States supplied programs to local stations: the American Broadcasting Company (ABC), the Columbia Broadcasting System (CBS), the National Broadcasting Company (NBC), the Fox Broadcasting Company (FBC), the CW, and My Network TV. The Public Broadcasting Service (PBS) serves as a network for noncommercial stations. A local station that signs a contract with one of the networks is an **affiliate**. ABC, CBS, and NBC have about 200 affiliates scattered across the country; Fox has slightly fewer; and the CW and My Network TV have still fewer. Local stations that do not have network affiliation are **independents**.

Much like the film industry, the TV industry is divided into three segments: (1) production, (2) distribution, and (3) exhibition. The production element is responsible for providing the programming that is ultimately viewed by the TV audience. The distribution function is handled by the TV networks and cable and syndication companies. The exhibition of television programs—the element in the system that most people are most familiar with—is the responsibility of local TV stations.

A local TV news program. News is the most common form of production at a local station and also produces the most revenue.

Production

Pretend for a moment that you are the manager of a local TV station in your hometown. Your station must provide 24 hours of programming every day, or approximately 8,800 hours of programming each year. Where does one get all this programming? There are three basic sources: (1) local production, (2) syndicated programming, and (3) for most stations, network programs.

Local production consists of those programs that are produced in the local station's own studio or on location with the use of the station's equipment. The most common local productions are the station's daily newscasts, typically broadcast in the early morning, at noon, in the early evening, and in the late evening. These newscasts attract large audiences, which in turn attract advertisers. As a result the local news accounts for a major proportion of the ad revenue that is generated by a local station. Not surprisingly, local stations devote a major share of their production budgets to their news shows. Other locally produced programming might consist of local sporting events, early-morning interview programs, and public affairs discussion shows. It would be difficult, however, for a local station to fill its entire schedule with locally produced programming. As a result most stations turn to programming produced by other sources.

If the station is affiliated with a network (and most stations are), much of its programming problem is solved. Networks typically supply about 60–65 percent of the programming carried by their affiliates. Many of the programs supplied by the networks are produced by the networks themselves. News, sports, early-morning talk shows, and an increasing number of prime-time dramas and sitcoms are network productions. Independent production companies or the TV divisions of major motion picture studios supply other programs. Table 11-1 lists some programs and their production companies.

Many independent production companies sell their shows to syndication firms. For instance, King World Productions handles *Wheel of Fortune, Jeopardy,* and *Inside Edition.* Programs that have already played on the networks (called *off-net series*) are also distributed by syndication companies. These programs usually air during the late afternoon or early evening, not in prime time. In addition, packages of movies, made up from some of the 30,000 films that have been released for TV, can be leased from syndication companies.

Distribution

The three main elements in the distribution segment of television are the broadcast networks, cable and satellite networks, and syndication companies. The network distributes programs to its affiliates by transmitting them via satellite. The station then transmits them to its viewers as they are received, or it records them and airs them at a later time.

table 11-1	Production Company	Programs
Examples of Production Companies and Their Programs for the 2010–2011 Season	Networks	
	ABC	*20/20, Grey's Anatomy*
	CBS	*60 Minutes, Hawaii 5-0*
	NBC	*The Office*
	Fox	*Cops*
	Independents	
	Mark Burnett Prods.	*Survivor, Celebrity Apprentice*
	Endemol	*Big Brother, Extreme Makeover, Home Edition*
	TV Divisions of Film Companies	
	Warner Bros.	*Two and a Half Men, Chuck*
	20th Century Fox	*Raising Hope, Glee*

The affiliation contract between a local station and the network is a complicated document that specifies the terms under which the station agrees to carry the network's programs.

For many years, the networks compensated the stations for turning over their airtime so that the networks could air network commercials, but that model is now changing. As network revenue declined and the networks found that they could effectively distribute their programs via the Web, the networks asked for "reverse compensation," charging the local stations a fee to carry net programs. As of 2011, Fox, the CW, and NBC have adopted this system and it's likely the other networks will follow suit. This is not a positive development for local stations since it increases their costs when many are struggling to stay profitable.

Syndication companies provide another kind of program distribution. These organizations lease taped or filmed programs to local television stations in each local market. Sometimes, as mentioned, the syndication company also produces the program, but more often it distributes programs produced by other firms. Local stations that purchase a syndicated program receive exclusive rights to show that program in their market (a situation complicated by cable TV systems that bring in distant stations). Usually, a station buys a package of programs—perhaps as many as 120 episodes or more—and the contract specifies how many times each program can be repeated.

Syndication companies try to sell their shows in as many TV markets as possible. The greater the coverage of the show, the more appealing it is to national advertisers. Top-rated syndicated shows, such as *Wheel of Fortune* and *Jeopardy,* are seen in nearly all TV markets.

Syndication functions as an important aftermarket for prime-time TV shows. In fact, some prime-time series are produced at a deficit, sometimes $200,000 or more for each one-hour episode. Production companies gamble that they can make back this money in the syndication market. It is a risk, but if a show hits it big in syndication, it might earn half a billion dollars or more. To be attractive in the syndication market, however, a prime-time show must have enough back episodes stockpiled so that stations can run episodes for a long time without showing repeats. Since 100 seems to be the magic number, series usually have a big party to commemorate the production of their 100th episode. Since only 22 or 24 new shows are produced each season, it is obvious that those series that last four or five years are the best bets for syndication success.

Exhibition

In June 2009 all U.S. broadcast stations switched from analog to digital transmission. Before the transition, analog stations were divided into two types: **VHF** stations, broadcasting on channels 2–13, and **UHF** stations, broadcasting on channels 14–69. The digital transition, however, has scrambled things a bit because all of the existing VHF and UHF stations were assigned new digital channel numbers, and some old VHF stations got UHF channels and vice versa. Luckily, the new digital arrangement includes a feature that changes the new digital channel back into the old channel number that everybody is

Inside a TV control room. The director scans the bank of monitors before deciding what to put on the air.

used to. So viewers in Madison, Wisconsin, used to watching analog Channel 3, the CBS affiliate, still see their station identified as Channel 3 even though the new digital channel is actually Channel 50.

As suggested earlier, another important difference among stations concerns their affiliation with national networks. As of 2010, more than 90 percent of all commercial stations were affiliated with CBS, NBC, ABC, or Fox. Of the remaining 10 percent, many are affiliates of the CW or My Network TV.

Those stations not affiliated with networks are called independents. For many years independents were hampered because most were UHF stations and had less coverage area than VHFs. The emergence of cable, however, gave UHF independents more of a competitive advantage because, unlike the situation with over-the-air signals, with cable both UHF and VHF stations have the same audience reach. Recently, most independent stations signed on with either the CW or My Network TV. "Pure" independents are now hard to find.

ownership in the television industry

As of 2011, all the major networks were under the control of large conglomerates:

- NBC Universal was acquired by cable giant Comcast in 2011. In addition to its holdings in cable, the new company owns motion picture companies, TV stations, a TV production company, and theme parks.
- ABC is owned by the Walt Disney Company, which also owns theme parks, a cruise line, retail stores, and media holdings that include magazines, film production companies, radio networks, record companies, cable networks, and TV stations.
- Fox is controlled by Rupert Murdoch's News Corporation, which owns a major film and TV production company, more than 20 TV stations, cable networks, satellite networks, a record company, newspapers, magazines, and a book publishing company.
- CBS is part of CBS Corporation, a company that was spun off from media conglomerate Viacom in 2005. In addition to the network, the CBS Corporation includes the CBS-owned TV and radio stations, a TV production company, and book publisher Simon & Schuster.

The two newest networks, the CW and My Network TV, are also part of large organizations. The CW is a joint venture between the CBS Corporation and media giant Time Warner. My Network TV is owned by the News Corporation, parent of Fox.

At the station level the Telecommunications Act of 1996 (see Chapter 16) allowed a person or organization to own an unlimited number of TV stations as long as the combined reach of the stations did not exceed 35 percent of the U.S. population (later amended to 39 percent). By the end of 2010, big groups controlled most of the TV stations in the top 100 markets. The top five groups were CBS Corporation, Fox, NBC Universal, Univision (a Spanish-language service), and Ion Media (a network of primarily smaller UHF stations).

producing television programs

Departments and Staff

There are many different staffing arrangements in television stations. Some big-city stations employ 300–400 people and may be divided into a dozen different departments. Small-town stations may have 20–30 employees and only a few departments.

In one common arrangement, a station manager is ultimately responsible for all station activities. The rest of the station is organized into five departments:

1. *Sales:* Is responsible for selling time to local and national advertisers, scheduling ads, and billing clients.
2. *Engineering:* Maintains technical equipment.
3. *Production/Programming:* Puts together locally produced programming; also acquires programming from outside sources and is responsible for scheduling.
4. *News:* Is in charge of producing the station's regularly scheduled news programs.
5. *Administration:* Consists of clerical, accounting, and personnel segments that help in the day-to-day running of the station.

At the network level the divisions are somewhat more complicated. Although the major networks differ in their setups, all seem to have departments that perform the following functions:

1. *Sales:* Handles the sale of network commercials and works with advertising agencies.
2. *Entertainment:* Works with producers to develop new programs for the network.
3. *Owned and operated stations:* Administers those stations owned by the networks.
4. *Affiliate relations:* Supervises all contracts with stations affiliated with the network (and generally tries to keep the affiliates happy).
5. *News:* Is responsible for all network news and public affairs programs.
6. *Sports:* Is responsible for all sports programming.
7. *Standards:* Checks all network programs to make sure they do not violate the law or the network's own guidelines for appropriate content.
8. *Operations:* Handles the technical aspects of actually sending programs to affiliates.

Digital operations (maintaining the Web site, developing apps, managing social media) may be done internally by a special department or the station/network may hire an outside firm to perform these functions.

Getting TV Programs on the Air

At the local level the biggest effort at a TV station goes into the newscast. Almost every station has a studio that contains a set for one or two anchorpeople, a weather forecaster, and a sportscaster. The station's news director assigns stories to reporters and camera crews, who travel to the scene of a story and videotape a report. Back at the station, the newscast producer and news director are planning what stories to air and allotting time to each. In the meantime the camera crews and reporters return; the reporters write copy and editors prepare video segments. When the final script is finished (this may be only a few minutes before airtime), it is given to a director, who is responsible for pulling everything together and putting the newscast on the air.

ethical issues *Sending a Message*

Some television shows do more than entertain; they try, in a subtle way, to encourage people to do things. The tactic is called "behavior placement" and it's a lot harder to spot than product placement. The purpose of behavior placement is to persuade viewers to copy behaviors they see on their favorite shows.

A good example is NBC's "green week" campaign, when producers of network series inserted a message into their programs that encouraged good environmental habits. Sometimes the messages were hard to spot. On *30 Rock*, for example, Tina Fey's character got rid of her mini-fridge to lessen her carbon footprint, and a character on *Law and Order* used energy-efficient lightbulbs. Other times they were a bit more noticeable, such as chefs on *Top Chef* using organically grown foods in their recipes or Dwight of *The Office* becoming obsessed with recycling. The network has so far limited its message to noncontroversial topics such as saving the environment or eating right.

Advertisers like the idea of behavior placement because it allows them to be associated with a socially aware show. Companies that make

environmentally friendly products also buy commercials on these shows in the belief that consumers will take the message to heart and buy green products.

Critics suggest that all of this sounds suspiciously like brainwashing and that NBC is exploiting environmentalism to attract advertising. The actions encouraged by behavior placement are actions that would benefit certain industries. If banks were interested in spending money on NBC ads, would NBC programs show characters opening savings accounts? Still others think that NBC has no business telling people what they should or shouldn't do. Do viewers need a TV network telling them how to run their lives? Additionally, the persuasion is masked. The viewer is not told that these episodes have been designed to incorporate a specific message.

Finally, there is irony in the idea that NBC thinks these subtle portrayals will influence people's behavior. For years, the TV networks have argued that explicit and frequent portrayals of violence on their shows have little or no impact on society.

In addition to the news, the local station might produce one or two interview programs. Some stations also produce a "magazine" program consisting of segments videotaped on location and later edited into final form. Aside from these kinds of shows, most local stations do little other production.

Because they are responsible for filling the hours when the biggest audience is watching (called *prime time,* 8–11 P.M., Eastern Time), the networks must pay special attention to cultivating new shows. For the moment we will concentrate on how a prime-time series is produced.

Everything starts with an idea. Network executives receive hundreds of ideas every year; some come from independent producers, some from TV departments of motion picture companies, some from network employees, and a good many from amateurs hoping for a break. From this mass of ideas, the networks select perhaps 50–75, usually submitted by established producers or companies, for further attention. After examining plot outlines and background sketches of the leading characters for these 50–75 potential series, the networks trim the list once again. For those ideas that survive, the networks request a sample script and a list of possible stories that could be turned into scripts. If the idea still looks promising, the network and producer enter into a contract for a **pilot**, the first episode of a series. In a typical year perhaps 25 pilots are ordered by each network. If the pilot show gains a respectable audience, the network may order five or six episodes produced and may place the program on its fall schedule. From the hundreds of ideas that are sent to the network, only a few ever make it to prime time.

The process does not stop with the fall season. If a program does well in the ratings, the network will order enough episodes for the rest of the season. If the show does not do well, it will be canceled and replaced with another show. Meanwhile, network executives are sifting through the hundreds of program ideas for the next season, and the cycle begins once again.

the economics of broadcast television

The television industry has been profitable since 1950, and its total income has increased every year since 1971. In 2010, according to the Television Bureau of Advertising, television advertising revenue amounted to about $45 billion. The changing structure of the television industry, however, has had a significant economic impact on both local stations and the networks. We will explore more about this after we look at the traditional sources of television advertising revenue.

Commercial Time

Where did the $45 billion in revenue come from? It came from the sale of commercial time by networks and local stations to advertisers. A station or network makes available a specified number of minutes per hour that will be offered for sale to advertisers. There are three different types of advertisers who buy time on TV: (1) national advertisers, (2) national spot advertisers, and (3) local advertisers.

National advertisers are those that sell general-consumption items: soda pop, automobiles, deodorant, hair spray, and so on. These advertisers try to reach the biggest possible audience for their messages and usually purchase commercial time on broadcast network programs or syndicated shows.

In contrast, other advertisers have products that are used mainly in one region or locale. For example, a manufacturer of snowmobiles would gain little by having his or her ad seen in Miami or New Orleans. Likewise, a manufacturer of farm equipment would probably not find many customers in New York City. These companies turn to national spot buying. The snowmobile manufacturer would buy spots in several northern markets, such as Minneapolis, Minnesota; Fargo, North Dakota; and Butte, Montana. The farm equipment company would place ads in primarily rural markets.

Finally, many local businesses buy advertising time from TV stations. They purchase time on one or more TV stations located in a single market. Network spots (national advertising) account for 50 percent of the total amount of advertising dollars, and the remainder is divided about equally between national spot and local advertising.

Revenues depend on the amount of money a station charges for its commercial time. The larger the audience, the more money a station can charge. The prices for 30- and 60-second commercials are listed on the station's rate card. The cost of an ad will vary tremendously from station to station. A 30-second ad might cost only $100–200 in a small market, but the same ad would cost thousands in a major market. The same general pricing principles apply at the network level. Shows with high ratings have higher advertising charges than shows with low ratings. For example, in 2010, the average network 30-second spot in prime time cost about $200,000. On top-rated shows, spots were going for about $250,000; on lower-rated shows, the cost was about $100,000. To gain some perspective on how expensive it can get, consider that for the 2010 Super Bowl, a 30-second spot was going for about $3 million.

Some television shows are finding novel ways to generate income. Product placement in TV shows, for example, has become a big business, with companies sometimes paying millions of dollars to get their product prominently displayed. In the first three months of 2008, there were more than 100,000 instances of product placement on prime-time TV. NBC's *The Biggest Loser* led the way with nearly 4,000 instances, followed by *American Idol*.

Broadcasters also receive payments from cable systems in return for retransmitting broadcast programs.

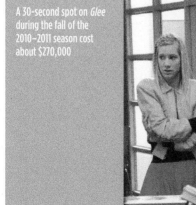
A 30-second spot on *Glee* during the fall of the 2010–2011 season cost about $270,000

Where Did the Money Go?

At the network level, one of the biggest expenses is programming. For example, a typical half-hour sitcom costs about $1.5 million. Hit shows cost much more. An hour-long show might have a price tag approaching $3 million. Game and reality shows are much cheaper to produce, and it's not a surprise to find that networks are relying on them more and more.

social issues   *Diversity in Television*

Kweisi Mfume, president of the NAACP, speaking at his organization's national convention, criticized the four major TV networks for the lack of diversity in the new shows planned for the 1999–2000 season. He noted that none of the 26 series had a minority person in a leading or starring role. Mfume's criticism marked another chapter in the continuing controversy over the portrayals of minorities in prime time.

During the early years of TV, African American performers were difficult to find. And when they did appear, it was usually in a menial or subservient role. In 1965, however, a young Bill Cosby costarred with Robert Culp in *I Spy* and paved the way for more substantial roles for African American performers. By the 1970s several shows that featured black casts appeared in prime time—most were situation comedies, such as *The Jeffersons*. The number of African American performers increased slowly but steadily during the 1980s. For most of the 1990s, the proportion of black characters seen in prime-time TV was about the same as the percentage of African Americans in the general population. This increase, however, was due in part to the emergence of UPN and WB, two networks that targeted several of their series to African American viewers.

The apparent lack of diversity in the 1999–2000 season was especially troubling to Mfume. The NAACP noted that minorities were hard to find behind the camera as well. Of all the writers who worked on TV sitcoms and dramas, only 6 percent were black. FCC data show that minorities own about 2.8 percent of all broadcast stations.

Mfume threatened a boycott of the networks and their sponsors unless something was done. The networks responded by adding some minority characters to the casts of existing shows. CBS aired *City of Angels*, a drama set in an inner-city hospital, that featured a predominantly black cast and creative team. The networks also planned to increase minority hiring and to appoint executives in charge of their diversity efforts. These moves apparently satisfied Mfume, who called off plans for the boycott.

The 2000–2001 TV season did not spark similar protests. In addition to *City of Angels*, there were several new series with African Americans in major roles, such as *Boston Public*. The situation behind the camera and in minority ownership, however, was unchanged. Things improved a bit in the 2002 season when there were 43 series featuring multiethnic characters. Back in 1995, there were only 13 such shows on the air.

The diversity issues surfaced again in 2003, but this time the focus was on cable. Members of the Congressional Black Caucus sent a letter to the cable TV industry asking for more minority-themed programs and more minority-owned cable networks. It resurfaced when the NAACP noted that none of the situation comedies scheduled by the major networks for the 2006 season starred an African American actor or actress. A 2008 report compiled by the NAACP showed that the number of minority actors had actually decreased from 2006 to 2007.

Why should the networks present a diverse view of society? Many would argue that the networks have a social obligation to present an accurate view of society so that members of minority groups do not feel marginalized or disenfranchised from society. Others would suggest that TV should present role models for all groups. These high-minded reasons aside, it also makes economic sense for the networks to present a diverse menu of programs. The 2000 census showed that minorities constitute more than 35 percent of the U.S. population, and their buying power is increasing each year. Presenting shows that appeal to these groups is simply good business.

Further, some critics suggest that paying large amounts of attention to the way the broadcast networks portray minorities overlooks the gains minorities have made in cable. For instance, Black Entertainment Television draws a significant audience. Two Spanish-language networks, Galavision and Univision, are aimed at Hispanics.

Finally, consider the opinion of commentator Earl Ofari Hutchinson, who suggests that prime-time TV is not worth fighting for. He charges that the networks have oversaturated the airways with silly sitcoms and action shows designed to appeal to young, affluent whites. These types of programs, he argues, have no relevance for African Americans, who should focus their attention elsewhere. In a similar vein Cynthia Tucker, the African American former editor of the editorial page of the *Atlanta Journal-Constitution*, suggests that the NAACP is misplacing its efforts by concentrating on network TV programs. Instead, she argues, the organization should encourage young African Americans to stop watching TV. "Let prime-time TV keep its bland cast of characters," says Tucker. "There are plenty of good books in which black youngsters can find themselves reflected."[1]

---

[1]Quoted in Richard Breyer, "Color TV," *Word and I*, March 2000, 84.

At the local level, the costs are broken down differently, but the heavy cost of programming is evident there as well. Programming costs account for about 35–40 percent of the local station expense dollar, followed by administrative costs and expenses for news.

public broadcasting

A Brief History

Public broadcasting in the United States has been in existence for more than 40 years. Over that time its achievements have been considerable, but its evolution has been hampered by political infighting, a lack of a clear purpose, and, most of all, insufficient funding.

Until 1967 noncommercial TV was known as educational television. In 1967, following the recommendations of the Carnegie Commission, Congress passed the Public Broadcasting Act, which authorized money for the construction of new facilities and established the Corporation for Public Broadcasting (CPB) to oversee noncommercial TV and distribute funds for programs. The government also created the Public Broadcasting Service (PBS), whose duties resemble those of commercial networks. Although this arrangement seemed to work well at first, internal disputes soon surfaced concerning which of these two organizations had final control over programming.

In addition, several cable channels began to offer programs that competed for public TV's audience. Many experts thought that much of the traditional programming on public TV would eventually move to cable or to videocassette. On top of this came further reductions in federal funds for public broadcasting.

Then things started to change. Somewhat surprisingly, cable turned out to be more of a friend than a foe to public TV. Since two-thirds of all public stations are in the UHF band, carriage by local cable systems increased their coverage area and helped public TV double its audience from 1980 to 1984. Public TV wound up as the primary cultural channel in the nation, with 90 million viewers every week.

In the mid-1980s, however, the Reagan administration cut funds for public broadcasting and proposed to freeze future funding at current levels. Congress restored some of the cuts, but in 1987 the system was struggling to get along on about the same amount of money it had in 1982. PBS funding became a major political issue again in the early 1990s. Faced with this financial uncertainty, public TV looked to other sources for funding: corporate underwriting, auctions, viewer donations, and sales of program guides.

Public television's problems continued into the new century. PBS's average prime-time ratings are down 37 percent over the past 10 years. (PBS has about the same level of viewing as the Cartoon Network cable channel.) To make matters worse, PBS's loyal audience is getting older (the average viewer is in his or her mid-50s), and younger viewers are not flocking to public TV. Any attempt to attract younger viewers risks alienating public TV's core audience of mature Americans.

Money is still a problem as well. Public stations have moved to digital transmission, a conversion that cost millions. Dwindling revenues have meant layoffs at local stations and at the network level. Congressional funding continues to be tight. The 2010 budget for the Corporation for Public Broadcasting totaled $422 million. That is about what ESPN collects every two months in subscriber fees. In short, public TV faces significant challenges if it is to remain a viable alternative for television viewers.

Programming and Financing

In 1990 PBS presented an 11-hour documentary titled *The Civil War*, which became the highest-rated program in the history of PBS. Although it might be a bit of an exaggeration, much of the history of PBS programming can be described as a civil war between the local public stations and the centralized PBS organization. Each side has scored significant victories in this fray over the years, but most recently, the tide has turned in favor of the centralized authority. Let us quickly review how the system used to work and how it has changed.

Prior to 1990 PBS used a mechanism called the Station Program Cooperative (SPC) to determine which programs were carried by its member stations. The SPC system represented a decentralized decision-making process. Member stations were given a ballot that contained the descriptions of possible programs, and they voted for those they wished to broadcast. After several rounds the initial list was pared down and stations voted again, but this time each station had to promise that it would help pay for the programs it voted for.

This system encouraged the broadcast of programs that already had some funding or series that could be acquired cheaply. Innovative or daring series that were expensive and had no prior funding commitments were seldom produced. The system also leaned heavily on a few big public TV stations that did the bulk of the production work. Finally, PBS had no cohesive national scheduling system.

social issues   *Do We Need the Public Broadcasting Service?*

The debate about PBS has been going on since the growth of cable television in the 1980s and 1990s. Many of the new channels featured content that was previously the province of PBS. The History Channel, the Discovery Channel, Animal Planet, Nickelodeon, the Hallmark Channel, and others fragmented the audience for PBS programs. PBS ratings have been declining (along with the ratings of many other networks) for the past decade. From 2000 to 2010, PBS's ratings dropped 37 percent.

What should be the role of PBS in a 500-channel television universe? A mission statement adopted by PBS stations in 2004 says in part that "public television is more essential than ever in the cluttered media landscape." It goes on to point out that in an age of conglomerate media ownership, PBS stations may be the only locally owned stations in the community and are better suited to responding to local needs. The document goes on to state:

Public television . . . strives for impact and measures its success by the extent of its ability to educate and inform, to enlighten and entertain. In short, public television strives to:

- *Challenge the American mind.*
- *Inspire the American spirit.*
- *Preserve the American memory.*
- *Enhance the American dialogue.*
- *Promote global understanding.*

Those are lofty goals. Does the programming on PBS stations fulfill them? Critics suggest that PBS programs have grown musty with age. *Nova*, *Masterpiece*, and *NewsHour* have all been on the air for 30 to 40 years. The American version of *Antiques Roadshow* has been around for more than a decade. (The U.S. program was based on a British series that premiered in 1979.) Typical prime-time programming includes reruns of old British sitcoms such as *Keeping Up Appearances* and *Are You Being Served?* Critics also suggest looking at the schedule of the local PBS affiliate. How much local programming is aired during the typical week?

The programmers at PBS, however, face a dilemma. If their shows venture too far away from mainstream, such as programs that examine gay and lesbian lifestyles or global warming, PBS is criticized as being too liberal. If their shows stick with the familiar, they are branded as obsolete or redundant with those of the commercial networks.

A second issue concerns the drift of public television toward its commercial counterparts. That 2004 mission statement proclaims the goal of commercial television is to attract as many viewers as possible and expose them to advertising but suggests that PBS is different. In the past decade, however, PBS has opened up its programs to an expanded program of underwriting, whereby a sponsor donates money to a station or PBS in return for a 30-second message at the beginning of the program. Many of these messages look exactly like ads playing on commercial TV. In addition, underwriters would rather reach a large audience than a small one. This means that public TV, if it wants to continue to attract underwriting revenue, will try to air programs that attract a large audience, much like commercial TV.

The transition to digital makes the questions about the role of PBS even more complicated. Does PBS really need a Facebook fan page or a YouTube channel? Check out the PBS Twitter feed. Does it fulfill the goals of the mission statement? This is a debate not likely to end soon.

In 1990, faced with declining funds and viewers, PBS suspended the SPC and moved toward more centralized programming. An executive vice president for national programming was appointed with the power to develop and schedule new programs. By any measure the first PBS season under the new centralized system was a success, exemplified by the fact that the *Civil War* series was watched by millions.

Successive seasons, however, were not as successful. For the entire decade of the 1990s, despite being one of the most established TV networks, PBS got an average prime-time rating of 2.0 (of all the TV homes in America, about 2 percent watched PBS in prime time). PBS's average rating dropped even further during the new decade. In addition, PBS occasionally lands in political hot water. In the late 1990s, Congress grilled PBS executives when it was learned that PBS stations, which are supposed to be politically neutral, were providing Democratic and Republican groups with their donor lists. Political parties could then use these lists to solicit donations. After a controversy involving National Public Radio (see Chapter 8) in 2010–2011, members of Congress introduced bills to "defund" public broadcasting, but none passed.

Along with its political problems, PBS was having problems with its affiliates. Local public broadcasting stations that belong to PBS pay dues to PBS to carry net programs. In 2010, KCET, the PBS flagship station in Los Angeles, announced that it was leaving PBS because it could no longer afford its dues, about $6.8 million a year. A few weeks later, the primary PBS station in Orlando, Florida, also left the network. WTTW in Chicago also considered leaving but decided to stay. In response, PBS reworked its complicated

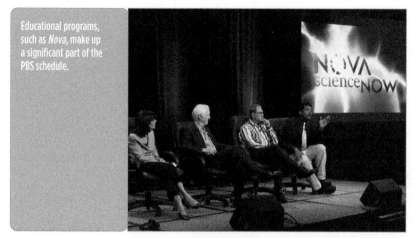

Educational programs, such as *Nova*, make up a significant part of the PBS schedule.

dues formula in order to prevent more stations from leaving and considered interrupting programs to promote its corporate underwriters.

PBS programs have earned numerous awards and substantial praise from critics. *Sesame Street* revolutionized children's TV by presenting educational content in an entertaining format. *Nova* and *Cosmos* introduced millions to the wonders of science. However, PBS programs have also come in for their share of criticism. Many critics have charged that PBS displays a liberal bias, and they have complained about the size of the salaries PBS pays to some of its performers.

Like commercial stations, public TV stations receive licenses from the FCC. As of 2011, there were more than 350 PBS stations operated by 168 licensees. About half of these licensees are community organizations, another one-third are colleges and universities, about 12 percent are state-operated networks, and the remainder belong to local educational or municipal authorities.

In 2010, more than a third of the homes in America watched public TV at least once a week. Viewing times, however, are far lower than those for commercial TV. Average household daily viewing time for public TV is about 25 minutes, compared with more than 4 hours for commercial TV.

Unlike commercial TV, public television is funded by a number of sources. About one-third of the support for public television comes from federal, state, and local governments; about one-fourth comes from member contributions; another 15 percent comes from corporations; and the rest comes from foundation grants, auctions, and other miscellaneous sources.

Public broadcasting has moved into the digital age. Previews of upcoming programs are streamed from the PBS site, which also contains blogs and links to PBS's Facebook page. PBS also makes portions of its popular *NewsHour* available on iTunes, and the network recently started a video-on-demand service.

home video

The home video industry came into existence because of the tremendous growth of VCR sales. By 2005 about 92 percent of homes in the United States were equipped with the device. The VCR gave way to DVD (digital videodisc) players. DVD offers better pictures and sound than videotape; can contain additional video material, such as outtakes and interviews with a director; and can feature multiple-language soundtracks. Sales of DVD players have skyrocketed; it is estimated that there are now more than 85 million in U.S. homes.

DVD players are used to play back prerecorded discs that can be purchased or rented from video stores such as NetFlix. There are more than 50,000 prerecorded titles on the market, and many more are introduced each month.

Another entry in the home video market is the **digital video recorder (DVR)**, such as TiVo, which allows viewers to record television programs on a hard drive. About 40 percent of U.S. households have DVRs.

Like most other businesses, home video can be divided into three segments: production, distribution, and retail. The production side of the industry consists of those companies that produce prerecorded discs. Since much of the home video market consists of movies, many of the large motion picture studios also dominate the DVD business.

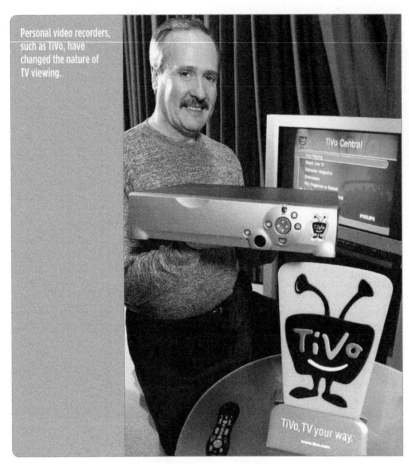

Personal video recorders, such as TiVo, have changed the nature of TV viewing.

These companies sell to distributors, who form the bridge between production and retail. Currently, some 90 distributors in the United States handle DVDs. Major companies include Disney, Fox, Columbia, and Paramount.

The DVD has opened up a new aftermarket for television. Boxed sets of an entire season of such contemporary series as *Sex in the City, The Simpsons,* and *24* have generated increased revenue for production companies. Moreover, classic TV series also do well. *I Love Lucy: The Complete First Season* and *The Dick Van Dyke Show: Season One* were best sellers. Even shows that didn't do all that well when they first aired, such as *Sports Night* and *The Family Guy,* have found new life on DVDs.

Netflix has also contributed to the aftermarket for TV series. The company pays a fee to broadcasters so that subscribers can stream past episodes from series such as *Lost* and *30 Rock.* Netflix reported that more than half of its 20 million subscribers are streaming movies and TV shows via the Internet.

As noted in Chapter 10, DVD sales have been declining as more consumers move to video-on-demand or live streaming as their first choice for home video. Nonetheless, there will always be some individuals who prefer to have a hard copy of a movie or TV show to store in their video library.

global tv

Thanks to the Internet and improved satellite distribution, international video is currently more popular than ever. Global video traffic consists of TV signals sent by satellite or over the Internet designed to cross international borders and discs or films that are physically shipped from one country to another.

International video involves both public and private broadcasters. On the public side, the Voice of America operates VOA-TV, transmitting programs in more than 20 languages to Europe and other parts of the world via satellite and the Internet. The BBC operates BBC America, an ad-supported network available on most U.S. cable and satellite systems. The German international service Deutsche Welle has channels in German, English, Arabic, and Spanish. Its English-language programming is available via cable and satellite systems. China Central TV offers a similar service.

sound byte

How Many in Your House?

The average home in the United States has more television sets than people. According to Nielsen, the average home has 2.73 sets and 2.55 people. More than half of American homes have more than three TVs.

On the private side, international news, sports, and entertainment channels are growing more numerous. CNN was a pioneer in this area, and its news channels are seen in more than 170 million households and thousands of hotel rooms worldwide. CNN International, started in 1990, is available on all continents except Antarctica. CNBC offers business news to 70 countries. Russia Today, a 24-hour news channel, began broadcasting in 2005.

Sports network ESPN International is seen in more than 140 countries. Fox Sports International specializes in soccer coverage. The News Corporation operates a satellite service that beams sports to subscribers in Europe and Asia. In entertainment, MTV reaches more than 400 million households and the Cartoon Network, Nickelodeon, the Discovery Networks, and TNT are popular all over the globe.

Moreover, foreign domestic TV networks are widely available both via cable/satellite and online. DirecTV offers channels from Brazil, Greece, Russia, and Vietnam, among others. Comcast has programs from Korea, China, Japan, and Greece. JumpTV.com has a selection of more than 250 channels from 70 countries. Video-sharing site YouTube features video clips from across the globe.

U.S. TV series are still popular throughout the world, but the economic downturn has prompted many countries to produce cheaper local programs rather than buy expensive imports. In many countries, prime time is dominated by local productions and U.S. shows are seen in the daytime or late at night.

The lack of new hit series has also weakened the U.S. position. Currently, international buyers of TV programs are more interested in buying scripts or formats of U.S. shows and turning them into local dramas, comedies, and game shows. There are dozens of foreign versions of *Jeopardy* and *Wheel of Fortune*. There are Spanish-language versions of *Desperate Housewives* and a French version of *Without a Trace*. Twentieth Century Fox TV recently sold 40 episodes of *How I Met Your Mother* to Russian TV for a local remake. (Of course, this arrangement works both ways as the U.S. has imported formats from overseas and turned them into domestic series, such as *American Idol* and *Survivor*.)

American-made films often show up on foreign TV systems. Local versions of HBO are available in more than a dozen countries. Turner Classic Movies is carried by Scottish TV and is available in many other countries. MGM sold all of its *Rocky* films to Spanish TV and the *Batman* series of films are shown frequently on French TV.

the broadcast television audience

Sources of Feedback

Let us examine how the ratings for both network programs and local stations are determined.

Network Ratings Nielsen Media Research, serving the United States and Canada, provides the networks with audience data through its Nielsen Television Index (NTI). To compile these ratings, Nielsen uses a device called a *people meter*, introduced in the late 1980s. The people meter consists of an apparatus about the size of a clock radio that sits on top of a TV set and a handheld device that resembles a TV remote-control unit. Demographic data are gathered from each household member, and then each is assigned a number. While watching TV, each family member is supposed to periodically punch in his or her number on the handheld device to indicate viewing. People meters can be used to tabulate all viewing—network, syndicated shows, and cable—and can even tabulate DVD or DVR playbacks. There are more than 12,000 households in the Nielsen people meter sample (the sample size will increase to 37,000 by 2012), and usable data are obtained from more than 90 percent of the meters. The sample is replaced every two years. The people meter service is not cheap. Networks pay millions of dollars annually for the service.

Nielsen is also testing other systems. The **portable people meter (PPM)** is a device about the size of a pager that detects inaudible signals that are encoded into radio and television programs. It requires little effort on the part of the respondent (a person simply clips the PPM to an article of clothing), and there are no buttons to push. The PPM can measure viewing or listening both in and out of the home. Preliminary tests of the device are being carried out in several U.S. cities.

Local-Market TV Ratings   Nielsen surveys more than 200 markets in the United States at least four times a year, using a combination of diary and electronic meter techniques. A computer selects phone numbers at random from all telephone directories in the area. The households selected into the sample are asked to keep a diary record of their television viewing.

Households that agree to participate receive one diary for every working TV in the household. The diary provides a space for entering the viewing of the head of the household as well as that of other family members or visitors. Participants are asked to record their viewing every quarter-hour. In addition, the respondents are asked to record the sex and age of all those who are watching. At the back of the diary are questions concerning how big the family is, where the household is located, and whether the family subscribes to cable. Diaries are kept for seven days and then returned to the ratings company. Nielsen reports that it is able to use approximately 40–50 percent of all the diaries it sends out.

Nielsen uses two kinds of electronic devices to measure local TV viewing. Set meters record any time a sample household TV is turned on and what channel is being viewed. The meters also record DVR usage. Meter data are supplemented by information from diaries.

In the 50 largest markets, Nielsen has introduced the local people meter, the same device used with its national sample, but in the local-market situation the sample is drawn only from the local viewing area.

Nielsen's long-term plans call for the phasing out of paper diaries. The company will use local people meters in the top 50 markets while the remaining markets will use electronic meters or Internet diaries. Nielsen's ultimate goal is to measure media usage on all media platforms: MP3 players, cell phones, and Internet video.

The popularity of DVRs has made Nielsen's job more complicated. The company provides three measures of viewing: (1) live viewing, (2) live plus same day DVR viewing, and (3) live plus seven days of DVR viewing. Nielsen also reports viewership of commercial minutes that interrupt the programs. The **C3** rating is the rating of the average commercial minute including live viewing and DVR playback within three days. Advertisers buy time based on the C3 numbers.

Ratings Reporting

Television viewing data are reported essentially the same way as for radio. The following formula is used to calculate the **rating** for a TV program in a local market:

$$\text{Rating} = \frac{\text{Number of households watching a program}}{\text{Number of TV HH}}$$

where "TV HH" equals the number of households in a given market equipped with television.

Similarly, the **share of the audience** is found by using the following formula:

$$\text{Share of audience} = \frac{\text{Number of households watching a program}}{\text{Number of HUT}}$$

where "HUT" equals the number of households using (watching) television at a particular time.

Four times every year (February, May, July, and November), Nielsen conducts a "sweep" period during which every local television market in the entire country is measured. Local stations rely on these ratings to set their advertising rates. As Nielsen moves away from diaries to local-market people meters, demographic audience data will be available year-round, thus making the traditional sweep periods less meaningful.

Determining the Accuracy of Ratings   Because the numbers in the rating reports are the basis for spending vast amounts of money, it is important that they be as accurate and reliable as possible. During the early 1960s, in the wake of quiz show and payola scandals, Congress took a close look at the broadcasting industry. In response to one congressional committee's criticism of audience measurement techniques, advertising and broadcasting leaders founded the Electronic Media Ratings Council, subsequently renamed the Media Ratings Council (MRC). The task of the MRC is threefold: It monitors, audits, and accredits broadcast measurement services. The council monitors performance of ratings companies by making sure that reported results meet the minimum standards of performance set by the MRC. Audits are performed on a continuing basis. If the ratings company passes the audit, it is accredited and is allowed to display the MRC's seal of approval on its ratings reports.

Despite the MRC's work, broadcast ratings are still subject to widespread criticism. One common complaint, voiced by many who evidently do not understand the statistical theory that underlies sampling, is directed at Nielsen's national survey. How can a sample of only 37,000 homes, these critics ask, accurately reflect the viewing of more than 100 million television households? In actuality, this sample size will generate tolerably accurate results within a specified margin of error. Other criticisms, however, deserve closer attention.

First, it is possible that the type of person who agrees to participate may have viewing habits different from those of the viewer who declines to participate. Second, in the case of the Nielsen reports (based on about 55 percent of the diaries sent out), it is possible that "returners" behave differently from "nonreturners." Third, people who know that their viewing is being measured may change their behavior. Fourth, ratings companies admit that they have a problem measuring the viewing of certain groups. For example, minorities—particularly blacks and Hispanics—may be underrepresented in the ratings companies' samples. Finally, the stations that are being measured can distort the measurement process by engaging in contests and special promotions or by running unusual or sensational programs in an attempt to "hype" the ratings. The distinction between hype and legitimate programming, however, is somewhat fuzzy. Clearly, the ratings are not perfect. Nonetheless, despite all their flaws, they present useful information at an affordable price to advertisers and to the television industry. As long as the United States has a commercial broadcasting system, some form of the ratings will be around.

Audiences

The TV set has become firmly entrenched in the life of Americans. As of 2011, some 99 percent of all homes in the country had at least one working television set. About 75 percent had more than one.

The set in the average household is on for about 8 hours a day, with each individual watching an average of more than 3 hours daily. The TV audience changes throughout the day, steadily growing from 7 A.M. until it reaches a peak from 8 to 11 P.M., Eastern Time. After 11 P.M., the audience drops off dramatically. Figure 11-1 details this pattern of audience viewing.

Not surprisingly, the television audience is largest during the winter months and smallest during July and August, when people spend more time outdoors. The composition of the television audience changes during the day. Preschool and female viewers tend to predominate during the daytime hours from Monday to Friday. Prime time is dominated by those in the 18- to 49-year-old age group.

Various demographic factors, such as age, sex, social class, and education, affect viewership. For example, teenagers watch the least. People in low-income homes generally watch more television than their middle-income counterparts. People with more education tend to watch less, and women watch more often than men.

critical cultural issues

The Bachelor

One of the interesting things about the critical/cultural approach is the range of items that can serve as texts for analysis. From popular mail-order catalogues to mass-marketed toys, critical/cultural scholars have mined all sources for insights on our society. Popular TV shows have also come under scrutiny. For example, a doctoral dissertation by Dr. Amanda Hall about ABC's *The Bachelor* illustrates how audiences use this program to construct meaning.

Hall looked at both the program and its audience. She performed a textual analysis of the program. She interviewed viewers about their impressions of the program and what it meant to them, and she observed groups of viewers as they watched the programs.

What did she discover about the program? She argued that *The Bachelor* is a modern fairy tale. The man is Prince Charming. The competition itself, with the lavish trimmings and carefree lifestyle, is the Big Ball. All of the women are vying to be Cinderella. Moreover, like many fairy tales, there is an element of melodrama (a melodrama has a simplified plot, stereotypical characters, exaggerated emotion, and a happy ending) in *The Bachelor*.

The audience apparently recognized and embraced both the fairy tale and melodramatic dimensions of the program. Hall's research revealed that viewers vicariously helped Prince Charming by participating in discussions with other viewers about whom the bachelor should choose.

She also found evidence of patriarchy in the program. The man was active and dominant and had a voice. The women were passive and subservient and were given a voice only when they were talking about the bachelor and their chances to be the chosen one. Further, the whole program was told from the masculine point of view. The words of the bachelor gave direction and a story line to the program.

The patriarchy was evident on other levels as well. The bachelor was controlled and rational. The women were portrayed as emotional and frequently teary. The competition among them became fierce and resulted in catfights and "bitchy" behavior. As Hall concluded, the program "sends a strong patriarchal message about heterosexual relationships—a woman's place is to serve in a subordinate (and emotional) position to her husband."

Finally, the theme of domestication was vividly present. The ideal wife, the choice of Prince Charming, had to be a mate and potential mother who knew how to behave. Women who did not fit this characterization were often removed early in the competition. Women who understood this requirement and acted accordingly generally lasted longer.

Young women who viewed *The Bachelor* used the program as an aid in understanding themselves and their own relationships. Messages from the program serve to illustrate socially prescribed expectations of gender roles. Viewers enjoyed the show even while recognizing the patriarchal elements. Indeed, many seemed to reject the dominant theme of the program and instead chose to focus on ways that they could reject the patriarchal interpretations and substitute more liberating ones of their own.

In sum, Hall's research underscored a key point in the critical/cultural approach. As she concluded, "A central argument for this study is that text and audience are both powerful—one does not overpower the other. As such, it is necessary to study both in order to effectively engage with issues of consumption and representation."

figure 11-1

Household Viewing of Television at Various Times of the Day

the broadcast television industry

 >>

Career prospects in the broadcast media were not bright, but improving, in 2011. About 120,000 people were employed in the industry in 2010, down from about 129,000 in 2005. Job opportunities seem to be a bit better at the local level than at the networks. Those interested in production jobs should consider looking at companies that specialize in non-scripted reality programs. Individuals with digital media production skills will have more opportunities in the future.

The career outlook in the various media industries changes quickly. For a more current description of conditions in the broadcast television industry and a more detailed look at career options, please consult the book's Web site: www.mhhe.com/dominick12e.

main points

- Electronic television developed during the 1930s. After World War II it quickly grew in popularity and replaced radio as the main information and entertainment medium.

- Three networks—NBC, CBS, and ABC—dominated early TV. Live drama, variety, and quiz and game shows were popular during the 1950s.

- Television matured in the 1960s, and its content became more professional. The public television network began in 1967. Cable TV grew slowly during this decade.

- The 1970s saw TV programs criticized for excessive violence.

- In the 1980s and 1990s, the three traditional TV networks lost viewers to cable and to VCRs. The Fox network became a major competitor.

- The Telecommunications Act of 1996 had a significant impact on TV station ownership and also introduced program content ratings. Rules for the eventual conversion to digital TV were announced in 1997.

- TV broadcasting has switched from analog to digital broadcasting. TV stations may use the digital signal to broadcast high-definition television or lower-definition programs among which viewers may choose. HDTV sets are in more than 50 percent of U.S. homes.

- TV is universal, dominant, and expensive. Its audience is currently fragmenting into smaller segments.

- The broadcast TV industry consists of program suppliers, distributors, and local stations.

- Big conglomerates own the major TV networks, and large group owners control most of the stations in large markets.

- Public broadcasting relies less on tax revenues and more on private sources of funding.

- The Nielsen Company compiles both network and local-station television ratings.

questions for review

1. What are the defining features of the TV medium?
2. What are some of the advantages of being an affiliate of a major TV network?
3. Who owns the TV networks?
4. Trace the evolution of U.S. noncommercial TV programming.
5. How has the DVR affected TV viewing?

questions for critical thinking

1. What should be the goal of public television? Should the government support public broadcasting?

2. Large companies control the broadcast television industry. What are some of the good points and bad points of large corporate ownership?

3. The major broadcast networks have been losing viewers for the past two decades or so. Will they still be around 10–15 years from now? Why or why not?

4. What will be the impact of social media on broadcast television?

5. Review "Critical/Cultural Issues: *The Bachelor*," on page 282. Next, consider the following. *The Bachelor* has a female counterpart in *The Bachelorette*. Ratings for *The Bachelorette* have not been as good. Can you think of any reasons why? Are there other reality programs that utilize a fairy tale theme?

key terms

Public Broadcasting Act of 1967 (p. 260)
time shifting (p. 262)
high-definition television (HDTV) (p. 264)
digital television (DTV) (p. 264)
commercial television (p. 267)

noncommercial television (p. 267)
affiliate (p. 267)
independents (p. 267)
VHF (p. 269)
UHF (p. 269)
pilot (p. 272)

digital video recorder (DVR) (p. 277)
portable people meter (PPM) (p. 280)
C3 (p. 280)
rating (p. 280)
share of the audience (p. 2580

internet resources

Online Learning Center

At the Online Learning Center home page, www.mhhe.com/dominick12e, *select* Student Center *and then* Chapter 11.

1. Use the Learning Objectives, Chapter Outline, and Main Points sections to review this chapter.

2. Test your knowledge of the chapter using the multiple choice and flashcard features of the site.

3. Expand your knowledge of concepts and topics discussed in the chapter with additional Questions for Critical Thinking and Internet Exercises.

surfing the internet

www.abc.com
Watch hit ABC shows in full screen and high
resolution—along with a few commercials.

www.museum.tv
Home page of the Museum of Broadcast Communication.
Site contains clips from old TV programs.

www.nbcnewyork.com
The Web site of the local NBC affiliate in New York City.
Note the large number of choices for the user, ranging
from news headlines to traffic information.

www.turnoffyourtv.com
If you do not like TV, this is the site for you. Includes a
page that suggests things to do instead of watching TV.

www.nielsenmedia.com
Information about Nielsen Media Research, the firm that
rates TV programs. Check out the Measurement link for a
basic description of how the TV audience is measured.

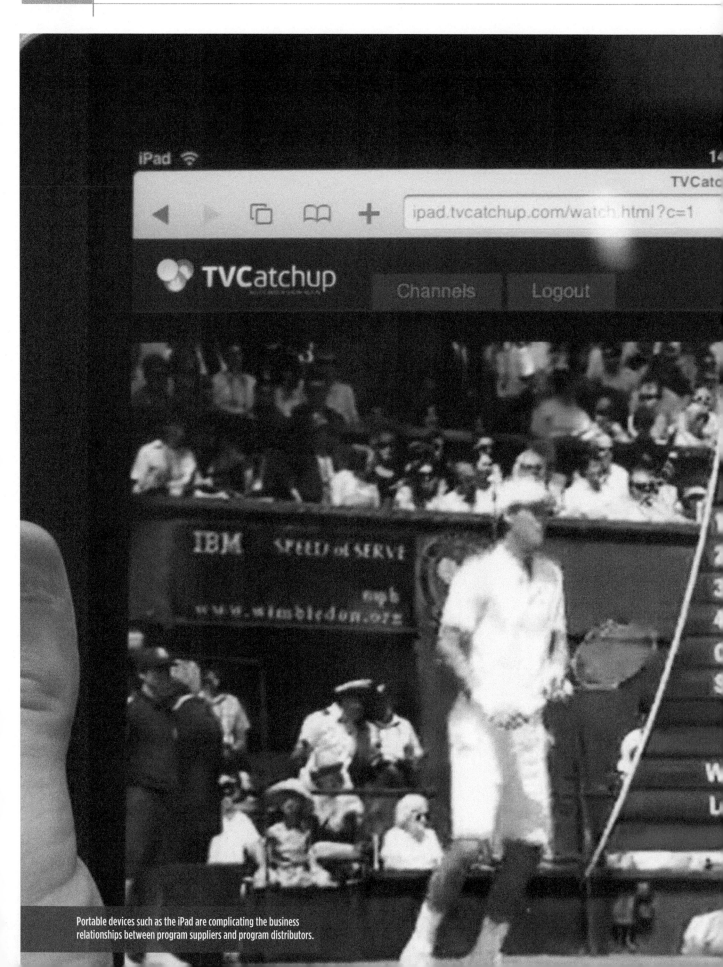

Portable devices such as the iPad are complicating the business relationships between program suppliers and program distributors.

Chapter**12**

cable,
satellite, and
internet television

This chapter will prepare you to:

- trace the development of cable, satellite, and Internet television
- describe the implications of the digital age for these media
- understand the structure, content, and finances of cable, satellite, and Internet TV
- appreciate the potential of Internet TV
- explain the audience measurement techniques used for these media

When is a TV set not a TV set? The answer to that question will be the centerpiece of an interesting debate between television program providers (such as Viacom, the company that produces MTV and other programs) and companies that distribute programs to subscribers (such as Time Warner Cable). The problem exists because program suppliers and cable companies have old contract agreements signed before tablet computers such as the iPad existed.

The dispute started in early 2011 when Time Warner Cable announced that it was offering an application that would allow customers to stream 32 live TV channels to their iPads, turning every room in the house into a potential TV room and every iPad into a TV set. While Dad watches sports on the big screen TV, Junior could be tuning in to the Cartoon Network in the kitchen and Mom could be catching up on the news while out on the deck.

There were some limitations. Subscribers could only view the shows in their homes and they had to be connected to a Time Warner Internet provider. Nonetheless, the app was extremely popular and was downloaded more than 360,000 times in the first few days it was available. (The app crashed on its first day because of high demand.)

Other companies have more ambitious plans. Comcast has an app that lets its subscribers stream video-on-demand TV shows to their iPad. Cablevision is planning an app that will make every existing cable network as well as its video-on-demand service available on the iPad.

The success of the Time Warner application did not escape the notice of program providers, who argued that their existing contracts with Time Warner did not cover streaming programs to portable devices and that Time Warner should pay extra for that privilege (an extra cost that could eventually be passed on to subscribers). Time Warner responded by pointing out that the contract didn't specify what constituted a viewing device because technology is moving so quickly. As one Time Warner executive phrased it, "I don't know what a TV [set] is anymore. It's kind of an anachronistic term." Nonetheless, under pressure from program providers, Time Warner removed more than a dozen channels from its app, including MTV and Comedy Central.

The courts may eventually decide if the iPad is just another TV set. Time Warner and Viacom filed lawsuits against each other in April 2011. The media company argued that Time Warner should pay it more money to stream its content on devices other than TV sets. In reply, Time Warner contended that its original contract allows customers to watch TV on as many screens as they wish.

Whatever the final decision, this issue has major implications for cable, satellite, and Internet TV because it will set a precedent for digital viewing. For example, what happens when a company offers to stream video to iPads outside the home? People could watch live TV virtually anywhere. Will that require an additional contract and fee? Or how about a service that streams a full lineup of cable/satellite networks directly to a smartphone or a portable gaming device? Or to some other portable device that's yet to be invented? All in all, it seems likely that people will be watching more streaming video on portable devices. Less clear is how they will get it and how they will pay for it. Will they watch on an app provided by a cable company (such as Time Warner), or an individual channel app (such as MLB.com), or an app from a paid service (such as Netflix or Amazon)? The next few years will determine how all of this plays out.

The last chapter examined traditional broadcast TV. This chapter will examine the history, economics, structure, and potential of the newer forms of television—cable, satellite, Internet—as they face the challenges posed by the digital age. We'll start with a look at how they came to be.

a brief history

Cable TV began modestly in the 1950s as a device used to bring conventional television signals to areas that could not otherwise receive them. As cable grew, some systems imported signals from distant stations into markets that were already served by one or two local stations. The local stations, as you might imagine, were not pleased, because their audiences were being siphoned off by the imported signals. This situation caused some political maneuverings as stations affected by cable appealed to the FCC and to Congress for help. The FCC vacillated over the question of cable regulation before issuing, in 1965, a set of rules that retarded the growth of cable in large markets. In 1972 the FCC enacted a new set of less restrictive rules for cable. By 1980, in a move toward deregulation, the FCC had dropped virtually all rules governing cable.

This deregulation move helped systems grow as cable companies scrambled to acquire exclusive franchises in communities across the nation (see Figure 12-1). Some companies made extravagant promises to win these contracts: a hundred or more channels, local-access channels, community channels, shopping and banking at home, two-way services—and all at bargain prices. After the smoke cleared, the industry recognized the economic reality dictating that its performance would fall short of promises.

figure 12-1

Growth Within the U.S. Cable TV Industry

Cable subscribers have been declining lately as people switch to satellite services or to Internet TV sites.

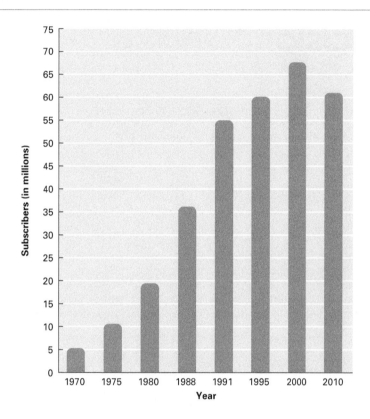

figure 12-1

Growth Within the U.S. Cable TV Industry

Cable subscribers have been declining lately as people switch to satellite services or to Internet TV sites.

While all this was going on, the United States and the Soviet Union were competing in the "space race" that culminated with the lunar landing in 1969. One of the by-products of the space race was the development of rockets that could launch communication satellites into Earth orbit. The first satellite TV transmission occurred in 1962 using *Telstar I* (this satellite has the distinction of being the only satellite commemorated by a rock song). In the early 1970s more communication satellites circled the Earth.

Satellite TV transmission came of age in 1976 when a little-known pay-TV cable service, HBO, used a satellite to transmit the "Thrilla in Manilla" heavyweight championship fight between Muhammad Ali and Joe Frazier to cable systems across the United States. That same year, media entrepreneur Ted Turner started transmitting "superstation" WTBS to cable systems. Other satellite-distributed channels quickly followed, and cable subscribers could now receive a host of new programming, including CNN, MTV, and ESPN. This gave people in urban and suburban areas a compelling new reason to subscribe to cable, and the industry grew quickly during the 1970s and 1980s. For example, the percentage of homes with cable increased from about 14 percent in 1975 to more than 50 percent in 1987. By the end of the 1980s, the cable industry was dominated by large **multiple system operators (MSOs)** such as TCI. Locally owned cable systems were quickly disappearing.

As of 1991, some 7,500 cable systems served about 55 million households. Keep in mind that this growth occurred despite the fact that cable companies generally avoided expensive urban installations. The growth rate slowed somewhat during the mid-1990s, and declined slightly in the 2000s, but by 2010 about 61 million households subscribed to cable.

Cable also scored several programming coups. ESPN signed a contract with the National Football League to carry prime-time pro football games. CNN's coverage of the Gulf War, the O. J. Simpson trial, and 9/11 attacks demonstrated that it could be a formidable competitor to network news. Big-ticket network series bypassed the traditional syndication route and premiered first on cable.

Cable got a competitor in the mid-1990s thanks to the development of high-powered **direct-broadcast satellites (DBS)** that could send a signal directly to a small home satellite

decision makers   *Judy McGrath*

For many of you reading this, Judy McGrath would seem to have the ultimate dream job: As president of the MTV Networks Music Group, she was responsible for MTV, MTV2, VH1, CMT, and all of the company's digital media services. Under her direction MTV has grown from a small niche cable network to an international brand that symbolizes a unique attitude and lifestyle.

Always a music fan, McGrath first tried to get a job writing for *Rolling Stone*. When her efforts proved unsuccessful, she turned to writing advertising copy and then went to work for *Mademoiselle* and *Glamour*. In 1981 she heard about a new cable channel launched by Warner Entertainment that would be devoted to rock music. Despite the fact that she could not even get the channel on her home TV, McGrath joined the newly created MTV as a copywriter and on-air promotion person. (She was one of the ones responsible for using all the space film footage to promote the channel.) To the surprise of many people, MTV was successful in attracting 16- to 24-year-olds, an audience coveted by advertisers. MTV became part of the huge Viacom conglomerate, and McGrath quickly moved up the ranks to creative director, executive vice president, and eventually chair and chief executive at MTV Networks. Under her direction MTV expanded all over the world.

When the music video novelty began to wear off in the mid-1980s and ratings started to sag, McGrath introduced programs that became popular culture icons: *Beavis and Butt-Head, The Real World, The MTV Music Awards, MTV Unplugged,* and *Total Request Live.* She also introduced political coverage to MTV and was instrumental in the development of the 1992 *Choose or Lose* get-out-the-vote campaign. More recently, McGrath has led MTV into other media: movies, books, and the Internet.

What does she see in MTV's future? Since a high proportion of MTV viewers are also Web surfers and spend a good deal of time on MTV.com, look for more integration of the music on MTV and MTV2 with the Web site. MTV.com will be used to highlight some of the artists or genres featured on the cable channels. In addition, plans are under way for more international expansion, particularly in Asia. Her plans will have to be carried out by someone else. McGrath stepped down from her position in 2011.

dish, bypassing the cable system altogether. Two companies, Echo Star (Dish Network) and DirecTV, eventually dominated the industry. The number of households subscribing to satellite companies increased from about 2 million in 1995 to more than 30 million in 2011.

On the economic side, cable advertising revenues exceeded $2 billion in 1990 and rose to about 27 billion by 2010. Although still small in comparison with the ad revenues generated by traditional television, the 2010 figure represents an increase of almost 50 percent over that of 2004.

The most significant developments in the cable industry in the past three decades have been legal ones. In 1984 Congress deregulated the rates cable systems could charge consumers. Eight years later, in response to subscriber complaints, Congress reregulated the industry by passing the Cable Television Consumer Protection and Competition Act, which caused about a 17 percent reduction in rates and mandated that broadcasters choose between *must carry* (the local cable system had to carry the station's signal) and *retransmission consent* (the local station had the right to negotiate compensation for carriage of its signal). Most broadcasters opted for consent and were compensated with promotional time on the system or were granted space for their own existing or planned cable networks. But this situation changed in the mid-2000s when broadcasters, facing declining ad revenues and looking for new sources of revenue, began demanding payment from cable companies in order to carry their programs. Satellite systems and phone companies that offer video already pay a fee to the broadcasters. Cable will eventually follow suit, a move that could mean increased monthly bills for subscribers.

The next major piece of legislation was the Telecommunications Act of 1996 (discussed in more detail in Chapter 16). The new law gave telephone companies the right to enter the cable business and gave cable companies the right to provide telephone services. In addition, both telephone and cable companies could own competing systems in the same community. Finally, the act allowed most cable companies to once again set their own rates. Significant competition between phone companies and cable companies did not materialize for several years, but by the middle of the decade, the situation was changing. Thanks to a new technology, **Voice over Internet Protocol (VoIP)**, cable companies were able to offer an alternative to the traditional phone lines. For their part the telephone companies are moving into the television business. Verizon offers TV programming over its fiber optic system (FiOS). As of mid-2011, FiOS subscribers could receive 348 digital

critical ● cultural issues

Who's That in the Kitchen?

Cooking has often been associated with "women's work." There are signs, however, that the roles of men and women in the domestic arena, particularly in the kitchen, are shifting. One of the factors influencing this transition may be television. In an article published in the March 2009 issue of *Critical Studies in Media Communication,* Rebecca Swenson takes a close look at how one cable channel, the Food Network, might be contributing to a change in the ideologies associated with men, women, food, and cooking.

Ms. Swenson notes that the way cooking tasks are divided within the home and portrayed on television is important because our ideas of "who does what" often reflect deeply held beliefs about significant social categories such as "man" and "woman." If men are doing more in the kitchen, our cultural notions about what is traditionally women's work might also be changing. Is the Food Network reflecting any change in long-established male and female roles in the kitchen?

In order to answer this question, the researcher examined Food Network series during 2006 and 2008, focusing on themes, narratives, and social cues contained in the programs. Her results indicate that the programs are structured to show that men can cook and still retain their masculinity. Ms. Swenson identified several ways in which male cooks are portrayed differently than female cooks that help to maintain a more masculine image.

In the first place, men are more likely to be portrayed as professional cooks who prepare complicated dishes and educate their audiences about food-related topics, whereas women are portrayed as approachable, domestic cooks who prepare food for friends and family members. Male hosts often make references to their formal training or business experiences; female hosts, although equal in expertise and experience, rarely make such statements. Male cooks usually appear wearing the traditional chef's white jacket. Female cooks are often casually dressed and wearing an apron. Other male hosts preserve their masculinity by appearing as more than cooks. Alton Brown, for example, takes on the roles of historian, food scientist, and anthropologist during his program.

Second, when males cook on the Food Network, it is generally for leisurely entertainment. When males enter the kitchen, it's usually for some special event, such as Sunday dinner, holiday entertaining, or some kind of festive occasion. For example, on *Guy's Big Bite*, the host usually is cooking food for his "posse" in preparation for some upcoming party. In contrast, female cooks are typically shown preparing weekday family meals.

A third theme is to portray cooking as a journey. Although both male and female hosts go on the road during this type of program, female hosts are more likely to act as practical, budget-conscious trip advisors (such as Rachel Ray's *$40 a Day*) while male hosts are searching for "real" American food to satisfy their manly appetites. In short, males seem more like adventurers, females more like thrifty homemakers.

A final theme portrays cooking as a competitive contest. In programs such as *Iron Chef America* and *ThrowDown with Bobby Flay*, male chefs are no longer cooks: They take on the traditional male role of athlete as they compete against others and against the clock. Portraying cooking as an activity that depends on speed, cunning, power, and stamina runs counter to the traditional feminine model, in which cooking is nurturing, democratic, and family centered. Ms. Swenson does acknowledge, however, that both male and female contestants compete in these programs, a fact that suggests a more nongendered division of labor.

In sum, the author concludes: "The Food Network does construct food preparation as gendered work, and cooking is negotiated in ways that protect traditional understandings of masculinity and femininity. . . . To protect the concept of masculinity, men enter the kitchen as scientists, chefs, athletes and entertainers."

channels, including 100 in high-definition, along with high-speed Internet access. AT&T offers U-verse, a similar service.

Cable was experiencing problems resulting from its own growth. There were more cable networks around than available space on local systems. In addition, like the broadcast networks, cable TV was becoming a victim of audience fragmentation.

Despite these difficulties, the long-range outlook seems positive. Cable continues to draw viewers away from the broadcast TV networks. In addition, thanks to their existing coaxial cable and fiber optic cables, cable companies can offer subscribers high-speed Internet connections.

The late 1990s saw the development of a different way to distribute TV signals: **Internet TV** or Webcasting. The key to this process was an innovation called *streaming,* in which a computer stores video signals—a process known as **buffering**—and plays them back while at the same time storing new, incoming signals. In short, the head end of the video is playing while the tail is being extended.

Video on the Web grew slowly, primarily because most people had slow, dial-up connections, and it took a long time to play even a short clip. But the increasing popularity of high-speed broadband connections and the ease with which video could be uploaded on the Web helped fuel an explosion of user-generated content. By mid-decade, sites such as YouTube, where audience members upload and share their videos, became the hip places to visit. More than half of the video content on the Web is user-generated. The broadcast networks and cable companies started their own broadband channels, as did many private companies and individual entrepreneurs.

The huge success of Apple's iPod sparked another channel for Web video—the **podcast**. A podcast is a media program that is downloaded from a Web site and played back at an individual's convenience over a computer or an MP3 player such as an iPod. By 2010 thousands of video podcasts were available on the Internet.

cable, satellite, and internet tv in the digital age

Transition

All three of these delivery systems are firmly established in the digital age. Cable and satellite systems now use digital techniques to distribute their programming. Internet TV has always been digital.

For cable and satellite systems, digital signals make possible video-on-demand, interactive program guides, high-definition TV, and digital video recorders (DVRs). Digital signals create sharper and crisper video and can be compressed, increasing the number of channels that can be transmitted over a single system.

In addition to television programs, cable systems use digital technology to provide telephone service to their customers as well as Internet access. Telephone companies are doing the same. This makes it possible for telephone and cable companies to offer a "bundle" of services—Internet, TV, phone—for a lower price. Satellite systems have trouble matching this feature.

Mobile Media and Apps

Similar to broadcast TV, cable/satellite networks have embraced mobile media. As noted earlier, Time Warner has an app for the iPad and other mobile media. Comcast offers an Xfinity app for the iPhone and iPad that lets subscribers view TV shows and movies. Satellite broadcasters Dish and DirecTV have similar apps for the iPad. Cable channels also offer apps. HBO has HBO GO, an app that makes it possible for subscribers to view HBO shows on their iPad. Fans of *Pawn Stars* can watch full episodes with the History Channel app. Of course, the problems between content providers and cable companies, as detailed in the opening to this chapter, still must be resolved.

User-Generated Content

Like the broadcast industry, networks carried by cable and satellite are increasingly turning to user-generated video. CNN has a feature called I-Report that lets individuals send video to the news channel, where it might make it on the air. Cell phone videos of the tornadoes that devasted the Southeast in 2011 were played on CNN dozens of times. MSNBC features FirstPerson, where users can submit news video. ESPN has something similar called Sports Center Home Video.

The biggest place, of course, to find user-generated video is the Internet. Thanks to the success of YouTube (see "Media Probe: The Guys Behind YouTube"), user-generated content has exploded on the Web. There were at least 150 video-sharing sites on the Web in 2010. YouTube, the most popular, with more than 120 million videos, streams about 125 petabytes of data per month (a petabyte is a "1" followed by 15 zeros). YouTube also has what media gurus call "stickiness," the amount of time a person spends visiting a site. Visitors to the video-sharing site spend an average of nearly 15 minutes per session. Most sites are lucky if their stickiness number gets above 5 minutes.

YouTube has become so popular that it is used by politicians, advertisers, recording hopefuls (remember Justin Bieber from Chapter 9), aspiring actresses (lonelygirl15), comedians, and others hoping for their 15 minutes of fame.

Not all the news about user-generated content was positive. Current TV announced that it was moving away from user-generated features to more professional programming.

media *Probe*   *The Guys Behind YouTube*

Talk about striking it rich. In the digital age one good idea can be worth money—an awful lot of money.

Chad Hurley was raised in Birdsboro, Pennsylvania. He attended Indiana University of Pennsylvania where he first majored in computer science and later switched to graphic design. After graduating in 1999, he took a job with a new company based in California called PayPal. Steve Chen was born in Taiwan but moved to the United States when he was 15. He majored in computer science at the University of Illinois, Urbana-Champaign. He too wound up working at PayPal in the late 1990s. Jawed Karim also attended the University of Illinois but dropped out to move to Silicon Valley where he too took a job at PayPal.

At a dinner party one night in 2004, the three were talking about how easy it was to share photographs on the Internet but how hard it was to share video clips. They decided to work on that problem and started meeting at Karim's apartment and in Hurley's garage. Karim was impressed by a site called HotorNot.com that let users post pictures of potential dates and rate them on a 1–10 scale. This site was unique because up to this point only the people who owned the site could post content whereas with HotorNot anybody could post photos for everybody else to see.

The three young men managed to cobble together a simple routine that allowed users to post their own videos in any format and play them back using any Web browser. In addition, they built in a search function and allowed people to rate and tag other people's videos. They also incorporated a feature that let people insert a video directly into a Web page. They came up with a name for the site—YouTube—and a slogan—"Broadcast Yourself."

As is sometimes the case with breakthrough technologies, the creators had no idea about the ultimate use of their invention. They thought that people would use it to illustrate items for sale on eBay or to show travel videos. What happened next was totally unexpected: The audience took over the site. They posted karaoke sessions, snowboarding wipeouts, amateur stand-up comedy routines, stupid pet tricks, and introspective soliloquies. Some posted news footage, such as the aftermath of Hurricane Katrina and rocket attacks in Afghanistan. Others lifted clips from *The Daily Show* and the Cartoon Network and posted them (raising an issue with copyright holders that would become a continuing problem for YouTube). A couple of clips—one featuring Diet Coke and Mentos and another a skit from *Saturday Night Live*—were viewed by millions. Many used YouTube to post videos on their MySpace pages. Less than a year after it was launched, YouTube became a media phenomenon.

YouTube was lucky to capitalize on two developments that fed on each other. The first was the revolution in digital video made possible by cheap cameras and simple editing software. The second was the rise of the Internet as an interactive social network where users generated and shared information. It was not coincidental that YouTube grew at the same time as Wikipedia, Facebook, MySpace, Flickr, and other similar sites.

What about the three guys who made YouTube happen? They're a lot richer now. In 2006 Google bought YouTube for $1.65 billion.

Social Media

Cable/satellite network Web sites, like their broadcast counterparts, are making extensive use of social media. All of the major channels have Facebook pages, Twitter accounts, and Linkedin profiles. Comedy Central has 1.5 million fans on Facebook. The Web site of the Travel Channel includes a travel community link where visitors can share their top restaurant picks and favorite destinations. Sports fans can join ESPN's SportsNation to discuss questions such as what pro team did best in the draft or what baseball team is likely to win the pennant.

CNN is heavily involved with Twitter. In 2009, the cable network joined a competition with celebrity Ashton Kutcher to see who could be the first to amass 1 million followers (Kutcher won but it was close). TNT relied heavily on Facebook and Twitter to promote its coverage of the 2010 NBA playoffs. Dish Network and DirecTV have teams that monitor their Twitter accounts.

defining features of cable, satellite, and internet tv

Obviously, a person needs at least one extra piece of equipment in order to receive video from these sources. Cable subscribers rent set-top boxes or use cable "smart cards" to receive their programs. Satellite viewers need a receiver and a satellite dish. Internet TV viewers have to have a computer and a modem.

A second obvious feature is that the consumer has to pay extra to receive these services. Unlike broadcast TV, where a rabbit-ears antenna connected to the set is enough to bring in their programs, cable and satellite subscribers must pay a monthly fee to receive their programs. On the Internet, viewers can watch some programs for free but must pay to receive others (such as the $1.99 on iTunes). All, however, have to pay extra for Internet access.

A third feature is that these services carry many channels that appeal to niche or highly differentiated audiences. Unlike broadcasters, who still try to aggregate the biggest possible general audience, cable/satellite systems carry such specialized channels as the History Channel, the Weather Channel, and the Documentary Channel. And even the niche audiences are being divided up. There are two cable networks devoted to health programming, for example, and five devoted to home and lifestyle topics.

organization of the cable and satellite industries

We'll first focus on the organization of the cable and satellite industries and then take a look at Internet television.

Structure: Cable TV

Cable systems are structured differently than those of conventional TV. There are three main components in a cable system: (1) the head end, (2) the distribution system, and (3) the house drop (see Figure 12-2).

The **head end** consists of the antenna and related equipment that receive signals from distant TV stations or other programming services and process these signals so that they may be sent to subscribers' homes. Some cable systems also originate their own programming, ranging from local newscasts to weather radar, and their studios may also be located at the head end.

The **distribution system** consists of the actual cables that deliver the signals to subscribers. The cables can be buried or hung on telephone poles. In most systems the main cable (called the *trunk*) has several feeder cables, which travel down side streets or to other outlying areas. Finally, special amplifiers installed along the distribution system boost the strength of the signal as it comes from the head end.

The **house drop** is that section of the cable that connects the feeder cable to the subscriber's TV set. Drops can be one-way (the signal travels in only one direction—from the head end to the house) or two-way (the signal can also be sent back to the head end by the subscriber). Fiber optic cables make it possible to carry 500 or more channels.

Programming and Financing: Cable TV

We will examine these topics from two perspectives: (1) that of a local cable system operator and (2) that of a national cable network.

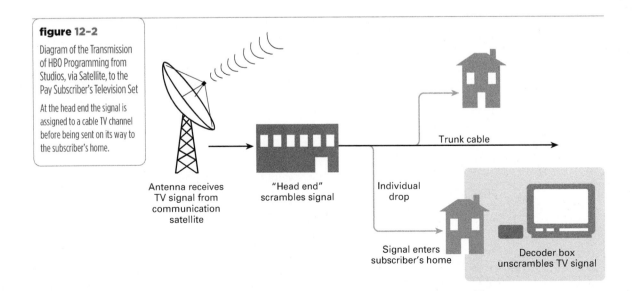

figure 12-2

Diagram of the Transmission of HBO Programming from Studios, via Satellite, to the Pay Subscriber's Television Set

At the head end the signal is assigned to a cable TV channel before being sent on its way to the subscriber's home.

Antenna receives
TV signal from
communication
satellite

"Head end"
scrambles signal

Trunk cable

Individual
drop

Signal enters
subscriber's home

Decoder box
unscrambles TV signal

Local Operators   There are six basic sources of programming for a local system:

1. *Local origination:* This programming might include local news, high school football, and discussions. A local government channel may carry city council meetings or zoning board hearings. Some systems have set aside public access channels that anyone can use for a modest fee.

2. *Local broadcast television stations:* Some cable systems carry signals from nearby cities in addition to local channels.

3. *Superstations:* These are local stations whose signals are carried by many systems nationwide. Major superstations include WGN, Chicago; KTLA, Los Angeles; and WPIX and WWOR, New York. The original superstation, WTBS, Atlanta, changed its status in 1998 to that of a cable network.

4. *Special cable networks:* These are services distributed by satellite to cable systems. Most of these networks are advertiser supported. Examples include MTV, the Weather Channel, USA Network, Black Entertainment Television, and the noncommercial C-SPAN (which covers Congress).

5. *Pay services:* These are commercial-free channels that typically provide theatrical movies and original programming. HBO, Showtime, the Movie Channel, and Cinemax are examples.

6. *Pay-per-view and video-on-demand:* These are channels set aside for the showing of recently released theatrical films and special sports and entertainment events. Subscribers receive the programs for a specified price. Movies, for example, might cost $4.95; special events, such as Wrestlemania, might run $20–30.

A local cable system has two basic sources of income: (1) subscription fees from consumers and (2) local advertising. Most systems charge a fee for local stations, superstations, and special cable networks. In addition, consumers might pay an additional fee to receive one or more pay channels. Cable is a capital-intensive industry: It takes a lot of money to start a system. The operating costs of a typical system are more reasonable. A good part of the basic cable monthly subscription fee goes to cover construction and maintenance costs.

Cable systems must also pay for their programming. In the case of pay services, the consumer fee is split between the cable system and the cable network. There has been a recent shift in the composition of cable system revenue. Pay-cable, video-on-demand, and pay-per-view receipts now account for more than half of cable operators' income. Local advertising on cable represents another source of income for operators. This sum is growing, but it still represents less than 20 percent of total income for local systems. In addition, cable systems that carry home shopping networks generally receive a percentage of the sales revenue generated in their market. Figure 12-3 illustrates the growth in cable TV revenue.

figure 12-3

Cable Industry Revenue, 1996–2010 (millions of dollars)

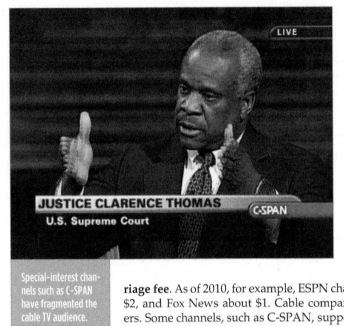

Special-interest channels such as C-SPAN have fragmented the cable TV audience.

National Operators At the national level cable networks draw upon three major sources for their programming: (1) original production, (2) movies, and (3) syndicated programs. The all-news channel CNN relies on original production for virtually all of its content. Most of ESPN's programming is also original, as is C-SPAN's. Movies make up most of the content on HBO and Showtime. Superstations program a mix of all three sources, while channels such as USA Network and Lifetime depend heavily on syndicated programs.

There are three main revenue sources for national cable services: (1) advertising, (2) carriage fees, and (3) subscription fees. Pay-TV channels such as Showtime and HBO make their money from subscription fees paid by consumers. Some cable networks, such as MTV and ESPN, charge local operators a **carriage fee**. As of 2010, for example, ESPN charged about $4 per subscriber, Fox Sports about $2, and Fox News about $1. Cable companies pass these charges along to their customers. Some channels, such as C-SPAN, support themselves entirely from this money. Other networks sell advertising in addition to the carriage fee, and still others support themselves almost entirely through ads. As mentioned earlier, advertising revenues for cable are growing, but cable still accounts for only a small percentage of the total TV ad dollars. Table 12-1 lists the top cable channels.

Pay-per-View (PPV)

PPV makes most of its money from sporting events (mainly high-profile boxing matches), movies, concerts, and adult content. Subscribers pay fees ranging from $5 to $50 to see these events. After racking up impressive revenue figures during the late 1990s, PPV has fallen on difficult times. Increasing competition from video-on-demand and digital cable channels has forced many cable system operators to reexamine the long-range future of this service. Still, the potential for big money exists. The Oscar de la Hoya–Floyd Mayweather boxing match brought in $134 million and was the biggest moneymaker in PPV history.

Video-on-Demand (VOD)

VOD works like this: A cable or satellite company stores movies or TV shows on a huge server. A searchable index contains a list of everything that is available. A subscriber scans the list and selects the program that he or she wants to watch; the selection is sent immediately to the person's TV set. A special set-top box lets the viewer pause, fast-forward, or rewind. In short, you get to watch whatever you want to watch whenever you want to watch it. Most cable/satellite services offer a per-program fee.

table 12–1

Top Cable Services, 2010

Network	Number of Subscriber Households (in millions)
TBS	102.1
Discovery	102.0
ESPN	101.4
CNN	101.3
USA	101.3

VOD has been around for a number of years but was slow to catch on because of a lack of content and a complicated user interface. Its fortunes have improved a bit recently as cable/satellite companies have simplified the ordering process and added more movies and TV shows to VOD libraries. Movies are still popular, but TV show episodes are the fastest-growing genre.

Structure: Satellite TV

A satellite system consists of five elements (see Figure 12-4):

1. Content providers, such as ESPN, Nickelodeon, or local broadcast stations, who send their signals to
2. A broadcast center, which takes the programming and transmits it to
3. Geosynchronous communication satellites (a **geosynchronous satellite** is one whose orbit keeps it over the same spot on Earth), which receive the programs from the broadcast center and send them back down to
4. A small satellite receiving dish, which picks up the signal and transmits it to
5. A satellite receiver, which transforms the signal so that it can be viewed on a conventional TV set.

Satellite signals are compressed in order to allow a greater number of channels to be transmitted to and from an orbiting satellite. To prevent people from receiving the signals without a subscription, the signals are **encrypted** (scrambled so that only those with a proper decoder can view them). The satellite receiver decrypts the signals and distributes them to one or more TV sets.

Programming and Financing: Satellite TV

The same programming carried by the major cable companies is also distributed by satellite, including local broadcast stations; superstations; nonbroadcast networks such as MTV, USA, and CNN; pay services such as HBO; and pay-per-view. Unlike cable, satellite networks are national in focus; there is no local origination of programs.

Similar to cable, the biggest source of revenue for satellite companies is the monthly subscription fees paid by their customers. In addition, DirecTV and Dish charge extra for

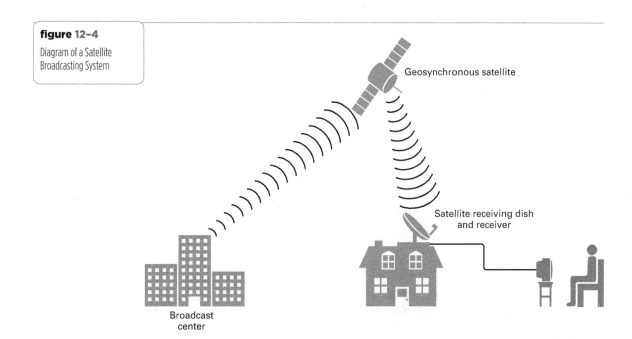

figure 12-4

Diagram of a Satellite Broadcasting System

Geosynchronous satellite

Satellite receiving dish and receiver

Broadcast center

DVRs, HDTV, and additional receivers. Unlike cable, local advertising is not a significant revenue stream.

Also similar to cable, satellite providers' biggest expenses are related to hardware. It costs a lot of money to launch, maintain, and eventually replace a communication satellite. Installing, servicing, and replacing dishes and receivers constitute another significant expense. DirecTV and Dish also pay content producers for the right to carry their programs.

As mentioned above, DirecTV and the Dish Network are having trouble competing against the cable industry's ability to bundle voice, video, and high-speed Internet access. In response, the satellite providers have explored alliances with phone companies.

Ownership of Cable and Satellite TV

The ownership trend in cable, as in other media, has been toward consolidation. Comcast acquired the assets of AT&T Broadband in 2002 to become the nation's largest cable provider. Comcast and number-two Time Warner serve more than half of all cable customers. The five largest cable companies are listed in Table 12-2.

Two major companies dominate the U.S. satellite TV market: DirecTV and Dish Network. DirecTV, with about 19 million subscribers, is controlled by Rupert Murdoch's News Corporation. The Dish Network is owned by EchoStar and has about 14 million customers.

internet video

Not too many years ago, video on the Internet was difficult to find. Connection speeds were slow, video software was complicated, and there were few content providers. As a result, even short video clips were hard to find. And even if a person found one, it would take a long time to load.

Just a few years later there has been an explosion of video on the Web. Faster connections and easy-to-use software have made Internet video the norm rather than the exception. Today it's hard to find a Web site of a major corporation, organization, or business that doesn't include video. About 183 million people watched online video in 2011 and advertisers spent more than $4 billion advertising on Internet video. By 2015, experts estimate that there will be 500 billion hours of video on the Internet.

Many TV sets and Blu-ray disc players are connected to the Web, making it easy to watch Web video on a big-screen TV. Full-length movies and TV shows are easily available. Advertisers rely on Web video as key parts of their campaigns. Social media have made it simple for members to embed and share videos on their pages. Some people in the United States are "cutting the cord," canceling their subscriptions to cable and satellite companies and watching all their television on the Web (see "Media Probe: Cutting the Cord?").

Compared to starting a cable or satellite TV channel, starting an Internet TV channel is relatively easy. No expensive studios and pricey equipment are needed. All it takes is a camera, a computer, some software, and a Web site, and you're in business. It's no wonder that this is a hot area.

table 12-2	Company	Number of Subscribers (in millions)
Five Largest Cable System Operators, 2010	Comcast	22.9
	Time Warner	12.6
	Cox Communications	4.9
	Charter Communications	4.6
	Cablevision Systems	3.0

media *Probe*   *Cutting the Cord?*

Cable and satellite TV companies are worried that subscribers might drop their services and watch TV programs on Web sites such as Hulu or from a streaming service such as Netflix. A 2011 survey of 1,000 respondents suggests that so far their worries are premature. The survey found that about 5 percent had actually canceled their cable or satellite service. Moreover, of those who "cut the cord," about half did it for budgetary reasons and not because they preferred other ways to get their TV shows. The survey also contained other good news. More subscribers were upgrading their existing service by purchasing a more expensive tier of channels, buying a premium service (such as HBO), or adding HD channels. Much of TV viewing might eventually migrate to the Web, but for now it appears that most consumers are still happy with their cable/satellite providers.

Further, the explosion of video on the Internet in recent years is another indication that the convergence between television set and computer is well on its way. Of course, an explosion is a difficult thing to analyze. Internet video is still expanding, and its final configuration is up in the air. This section will try to make some sense out of this rapidly changing area by examining its structure and finances.

Structure: Sources and Content

One way to analyze Web video is to classify it first by source—professional or amateur, or as they say in the business, "pro or Joe" (as in the average Joe)—and then by its content—original or repurposed. Let's first look at professionally produced content.

Professionally Produced Content This has been a huge growth area. Today it's unusual to find a major company or organization that does not have video available on its Web site or through its app. Professional video sources include the following:

- Commercial media companies, such as broadcasting and cable/satellite networks, local stations, and movie studios. Examples include abc.com, cbs.com, and usanetwork.com.
- Content aggregators that make available video content from a number of sources. Examples would be hulu.com, tv.com, and Netflix.
- Public relations, marketing, and advertising firms, such as leoburnett.com and edelman.com.
- Companies that sell products and services, such as amazon.com and delta.com.
- Political figures, such as Newt Gingrich (www.newt.org) and Nancy Pelosi (http://pelosi.house.gov).
- Service organizations, such as the USO and Rotary International.
- Government agencies, such as Social Security and the Food and Drug Administration.

These organizations typically have their own in-house production facilities or hire an outside production company to put together their video.

Professional content can be repurposed or original. Current or past television programs available at network Web sites or at video sites such as Hulu and Joost are examples of repurposed content. These programs reach (or reached) the majority of their viewers through traditional television, and the Internet provides a supplemental channel that attracts additional viewers. An episode of ABC's *Grey's Anatomy,* for example, draws about 10 million viewers when it is broadcast over-the-air and close to another million online.

There are abundant examples of professionally produced original online series. Here are just a few. Sony's Crackle.com has a slate of several original series produced for the Web site. Original episodes of *High Drama,* a dramatic series (what else?), are available on thewb.com.

Advertisers and marketers are another source of professionally produced original video. Ford, along with many other companies, has a YouTube channel, where you can follow the company's latest efforts at achieving fuel economy. Coca-Cola includes several short video features on its Web site, as does Wrigley's Gum. French Maid TV offers "how to" instructions on various topics (geared to the needs of marketers) that feature a trio of French maids (who else?).

The candidates in the 2008 presidential campaign made heavy use of Internet video. Hillary Clinton announced her candidacy with a video posted on her Web site. Eventual winner Barack Obama's site included BarackTV, complete with clips of speeches and campaign rallies. After the election, video of President Obama's weekly address was regularly posted on the White House's official Web site.

The White House is not the only branch of government producing original Web content. In mid-2009, Patty Duke was starring in an original video on the Web site of the Social Security Administration urging people to apply for benefits online. The U.S. Census Bureau and the National Oceanic and Atmospheric Administration have started YouTube channels.

Amateur-Produced Content   Some amateur-produced content is repurposed, such as posting a homemade wedding or birthday party video on YouTube, but most "Joe-produced" content is original. One study indicated that more than half of all online videos are amateur productions. The subject matter of these amateur clips is so diverse that it defies categorization. A quick scan of some of the more popular video-sharing sites reveals clips that range from serious to funny, from mundane to bizarre, and from intriguing to absolutely boring. In addition, they are almost always short clips, seldom more than 5 minutes long—"bite-size entertainment," as suggested by a recent issue of *Wired*.

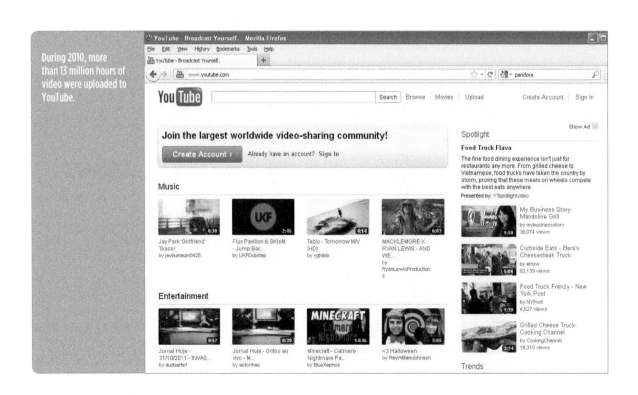

During 2010, more than 13 million hours of video were uploaded to YouTube.

media *probe*   *The Uploaders*

Who are the people who are uploading all those videos to YouTube and Facebook? Thanks to the research done by the Pew Center, we have some basic information. About 15 percent of teens have posted a video online, compared to 19 percent of 18- to 29- year-olds and 17 percent of 30- to 49- year-olds. Of those in the 50-plus age category, 10 percent reported posting a video. Among adults, women were as likely as men to post a video.

Uploaders were about as likely to post a video on Facebook (52 percent did this) as they were on YouTube (49 percent). Home videos are the most popular content to post, followed by travel videos. The uploaders are happy to share their creations. Half of them report they never restrict access to their videos.

Homemade video, of course, is the ultimate example of user-generated content, and it has spawned a whole new Web industry—video sharing. Why is video sharing so popular? Three possible reasons are (1) we are inherently nosy and want to find out what's happening in other people's lives, (2) we have lots of free time, and (3) we all want our 15 minutes of fame.

YouTube, of course, is the best example of what can be done with user-generated content. The statistics surrounding YouTube are staggering: About 2 billion videos are viewed per day, more than 700 billion in 2010. Thirty-five hours of content are uploaded every minute. ABC, NBC, and CBS would have to broadcast 24 hours a day, 7 days a week, for more than 100 years to equal the amount of video uploaded to YouTube in 60 days. The most popular video on YouTube has been viewed more than 185 million times (Lady Gaga's "Bad Romance"). Although the site does contain movies and episodes of professionally produced TV shows, most of the videos on the site are amateur productions.

YouTube and other video-sharing sites have created a new set of problems for the video age. Some users illegally post copyrighted material or make unauthorized use of copyrighted material, causing legal problems for YouTube's parent company, Google. Invasion of privacy is another problem. Since cell phone video is easily posted to YouTube, many people upload video to YouTube without the permission of those who have been recorded. YouTube has instituted a process that helps people who feel their privacy has been invaded to request that the offending video be removed, but this occurs only after the video has been posted and potentially seen by many people.

Internet video can also be used for microcasting.

Microcasting

When the Brookwood High School Marching Bronco Band of Snellville, Georgia, spent a few days at band camp in South Carolina, parents back in Georgia could check up on their progress thanks to a Web cam that sent video of their practices over the Internet. People who board their dogs at Camp BowWow can see how their pooches are doing via Web cam. As its name suggests, HighSchoolPlaybook.com aggregates amateur videos of high school sports. Relatives can't get to the wedding? Vowcast offers a live Webcast. Relatives can't get to the funeral? Around 60 funeral parlors offer live (?) Webcasts.

The word *broadcasting*, as first used with early radio and then TV, meant sending a message to a large, heterogeneous group of people. When format radio and cable TV networks came into being, the word *narrowcasting* was coined for targeting your message to appeal to a small, well-defined subsegment of the total audience. Top 40 radio stations, for example, narrowcast to 12- to 22-year-olds; ESPN, primarily to male sports fans; and C-SPAN, to aficionados of politics. Video sent over the Internet takes this process one step further by making possible **microcasting**, sending a message to a small group of interested people. This is another example of the "few-to-few" model of communication mentioned in Chapter 1.

Internet video is in the peculiar position of moving in two directions at once. At one end of the spectrum, it is becoming more like a traditional mass media channel as people turn

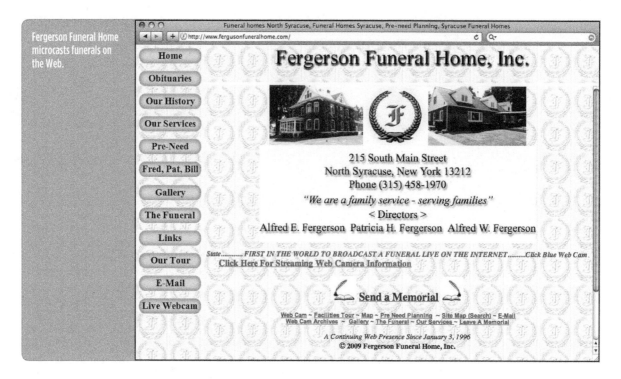

Fergerson Funeral Home microcasts funerals on the Web.

to it to watch TV shows and Hollywood movies. But the Internet is moving in the other direction as well. The most successful applications on the Web are examples of improved forms of machine-assisted interpersonal communication: e-mail, social media such as Facebook and Twitter, auction sites, peer-to-peer file sharing. Interestingly, these applications were created by end users and not by big mass media companies. Microcasting is yet another example of this trend.

Internet-capable cell phones with video cameras open new possibilities for Web microcasts. Dad could microcast Scott's and Buffy's soccer games or band recitals to the grandparents in another state. High schools could microcast the prom to interested parents. How about video of the local Little League games? Microcasting, of course, will raise all sorts of questions about privacy that will have to be resolved in the near future.

Economics of Online Video

There are several ways that an online video site can make money: (1) subscription fees, (2) merchandising, (3) advertising, and (4) some combination of the above.

The subscription model is the simplest. A viewer pays a fee and in return is allowed to see a program or movie. This is the model used by Netflix, MLB.TV, and a large number of porn video sites. Merchandising consists of selling items related to the video site. YouTube sells notebooks, T-shirts, Frisbees, and many other items in its YouTube store. Posters, coffee mugs, and iPhone cases are for sale at abc.com.

Making a profit by selling advertising is a difficult task for online video sites. Despite the fact that watching online video has become a popular activity and average time spent watching online video has increased, this popularity has not translated into a bonanza of ad revenue. Hulu has turned a relatively modest profit over the last two years, primarily because the networks or production companies bear the cost of producing the programs Hulu makes available. In any case, to increase revenue, Hulu has instituted a subscription service and increased the number of commercials it airs during playback.

Google closely guards profit and loss information about YouTube. Since acquiring the service, some experts suggest that Google has lost hundreds of millions of dollars on YouTube. Recently, however, YouTube has become more sophisticated about courting

The Ethics of Cell Phone Video

The 1969 film *Medium Cool* deals with the ethical obligations of reporters. In the opening scene, a photographer and his soundman come upon an auto accident that apparently happened only a few minutes before. One of the victims of the accident is hanging out of an open window on the side of the vehicle and is audibly moaning. The photographer films the scene from several angles and the soundman makes sure to record the victim's groans. After they return to their news vehicle, they discuss whether they should call an ambulance. This disturbing scene raises the fundamental ethical question: When does the ethical obligation of helping another human being in pain override the professional obligations of reporting the news?

It's been said that in the age when most people carry video-capable cell phones, we have all become reporters. There are numerous examples of ordinary citizens recording news events on their cell phones and sharing them with news organizations. Cell phone video of the 2009 protests of the elections in Iran, the 2010–2011 demonstrations in North Africa and the Middle East, the earthquake and Tsunami in Japan, have all been viewed by millions.

But other recent cell phone videos reveal a disturbing trend. Here are just a few examples (there are many more): In Florida, one middle school student attacked and injured another student while a bystander recorded the beating and posted the video online. The father of the injured student found out about the attack while browsing YouTube. In Indianapolis, a fight broke out in the school cafeteria. None of the dozens of bystanders intervened, but several shot cell phone video of the fight and posted it online. One video had generated more than 2,000 views before it was taken down. Finally, in Maryland, two teenagers in a McDonald's restaurant viciously beat a young woman until she had a seizure. A McDonald's employee recorded the attack on a cell phone but did not intervene. Instead, he posted the video on YouTube.

These and similar incidents raise disturbing questions. What ethical obligations, if any, do people have if they find themselves witnessing a brutal attack? Is it ethical to do nothing but record such an attack on a cell phone? Is it ethical to record such an upsetting event? Is it ethical to post the video online for all to see?

Let's see if we can find some preliminary answers. If you are a bystander, do you have an ethical obligation to intervene in an attack? If we accept the Categorical Imperative, the answer is yes. If you were being beaten, you would want someone to intercede for you. Ethicists would probably agree that there is a human obligation to help others avoid harm. An exception to this obligation might occur if the bystander feared that intervening would bring him or her physical injury or raise questions of subsequent liability for harm. In that case, alerting the authorities might be the more prudent thing to do.

Is it ethical to record such an event? One justification might be that a video record might be helpful to authorities if subsequent legal action ensues. This approach raises the question of how much of the event should be recorded before the obligation to intervene kicks in. Note that in this situation it is assumed that the video is shared only with the proper authorities and doesn't appear on some Web site.

Is it ethical to post the video of such an event online? It seems difficult to justify this decision. Any beneficial aspect of sharing the video (such as demonstrating to society how violent we have become) seems outweighed by the negative effects (humiliating the victim, encouraging others to be violent). Posting the video also exploits another person's misery for personal gain (such as the right to brag that your video got 10,000 views on YouTube). It also seems to violate the Categorical Imperative (you probably wouldn't someone to post a video of your getting beaten up).

In any case, the surveillance culture encouraged by cell phone cameras may be doing society a disservice. When many people see violence occurring, their first response is less "I've got to help" and more "I've got to record this for YouTube."

advertisers, and the company is optimistic about turning a profit in 2011. To make the site more appealing to advertisers, YouTube has reorganized itself around a set of channels, including music, sports, and entertainment, and will increase the amount of professionally produced content on those channels. Advertisers are more comfortable placing their ads in professional rather than amateur videos.

the cable, satellite, and internet tv audience

Sources of Feedback

Networks distributed by cable and satellite are measured by Nielsen Media Research. The techniques are the same as reported for broadcast TV in Chapter 11. A national sample using people meters provides viewing data that are reported in terms of ratings and shares. Ratings for cable/satellite-distributed networks tend to be smaller than for broadcast networks. Nielsen also publishes a *Cable Network Audiences Composition Report* that provides more detailed information about audience demographics.

Gathering feedback on Internet video is a new and difficult area. The Nielsen company reports video viewing using its VideoCensus service, which combines panel data with usage data. Clients tag each of their videos with a sort of electronic watermark that allows Nielsen to track viewings. A second firm, comScore, tracks video viewing using a sample of about 2 million people worldwide who agree to install tracking software on their computers. The numbers from the two services sometimes differ widely.

Audiences

More than 85 percent of American households get their television from either a cable or a satellite provider. Those who subscribe tend to be younger, have more children, and be more affluent than those who are not subscribers. Cable/satellite networks are more specialized than over-the-air networks, and their demographic makeup varies according to their target market. ESPN, for example, attracts a male audience; Oxygen, a female one. Nickelodeon aims for youngsters while CNN and MSNBC try for a more mature audience.

Some preliminary data about the audience for online video are available from Nielsen and comScore. About 150 million Americans watch online video. Men are more likely than women to be viewers, and men tend to watch short, amateur-produced videos while women watch more full, professionally produced episodes. Young people are more likely to watch than older people, with 18- to 24-year-olds watching the most. The two most preferred places to watch Web video are YouTube and the networks' Web sites. Although the time spent with online video is increasing, about 70 percent of all television viewing time is spent in front of a traditional TV set. Finally, the average time spent watching online video is about 10–20 minutes a day. (Compare this figure to the 4-hours-a-day average time spent watching conventional TV.)

cable, satellite, and internet tv industries

The cable and satellite industry is smaller than the broadcast TV industry, employing about 90,000 people. The number working in Internet television is difficult to determine. The job prospects in this area, particularly Internet video, seem more positive than in the other media we have discussed. Specialized cable/satellite channels continue to premiere, and they will need people in production, sales, marketing, performance, and public relations. And, as the chapter indicates, Internet TV is a big growth area.

The career outlook in the various media industries changes quickly. For a more current description of conditions in the cable/satellite Internet business and a more detailed look at career options, please consult the book's Web site: www.mhhe.com/dominick12e.

main points

- Cable TV began in the 1950s as a way of bringing TV signals to places that could not otherwise receive them.

- Cable TV reached maturity by the turn of the century and was facing competition from DBS satellite systems.

- The Telecommunications Act of 1996 permitted cable and telephone companies to compete with one another.

- Internet TV developed in the late 1990s and became more popular with the growth of broadband.

- Cable and satellite systems are structured differently from those of conventional TV.

- Cable television is dominated by large multiple system operators. Two companies, DirecTV and the Dish Network, are the leading DBS providers.

- Internet video can be categorized by source (professional or amateur) and content (original or repurposed).

- User-generated videos, such as those on YouTube, have become extremely popular.

- Internet video sites make money by charging a fee for their content or by selling advertising.

- Nielsen provides rating data for cable/satellite networks. Ratings for online video-sharing sites are provided by companies that measure Internet usage.

questions for review

1. What are the defining features of cable/satellite TV? Of Internet TV?
2. Who are the major owners of cable and DBS systems?
3. How does cable/satellite programming compare to traditional broadcast network programming?
4. Trace the structure of a cable system from head end to home.
5. How can online video sites make money?

questions for critical thinking

1. How, if at all, will VOD change the cable TV industry?
2. Have you ever posted a video online? Why? Have you ever looked at online videos? Why?
3. Google paid $1.65 billion for YouTube. Do you think Google will get its money back?
4. Will everybody eventually watch TV over the Internet? If so, what happens to cable and satellite companies?

key terms

multiple system operators (MSOs) (p. 289)
direct-broadcast satellites (DBS) (p. 289)
Voice over Internet Protocol (VoIP) (p. 290)

Internet TV (p. 291)
buffering (p. 291)
podcast (p. 292)
head end (p. 294)
distribution system (p. 294)

house drop (p. 294)
carriage fee (p. 296)
geosynchronous satellite (p. 297)
encrypted (p. 297)
microcasting (p. 301)

internet resources

Online Learning Center

On the Online Learning Center home page, www.mhhe.com/dominick12e, *select* Student Center *and then* Chapter 12.

1. Use the Learning Objectives, Chapter Outline, and Main Points sections to review this chapter.
2. Test your knowledge of the chapter using the multiple choice and flashcard features of the site.
3. Expand your knowledge of concepts and topics discussed in the chapter with additional Questions for Critical Thinking and Internet Exercises.

surfing the internet

www.historychannel.com
Has more about history than it does about the cable network, but contains good examples of streaming video and interactivity.

www.ovguide.com
The ultimate source for online video.

www.multichannel.com
Multichannel News is the leading trade publication covering cable, satellite, and wireless companies.

www.ncta.com
Web site of the National Cable Television Association. Contains information about the latest issues facing the industry.

www.vivalasvegasweddings.com
Watch live weddings from Las Vegas.

Specific Media Professions

Part III

Specific Media Professions

Despite strong ratings for Fox News, the total audience for television network news programs continues to decline.

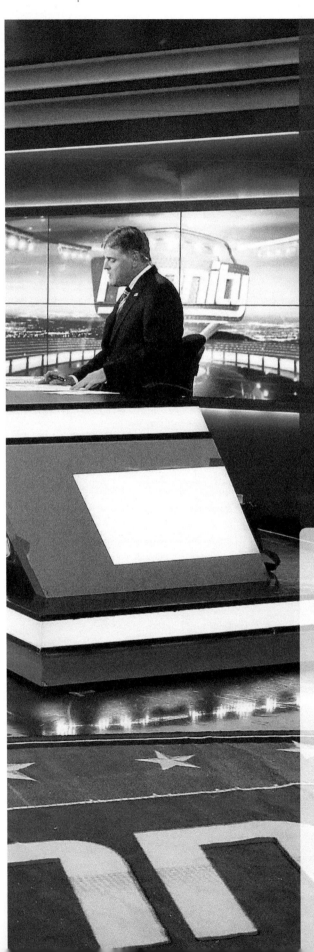

Chapter13

news
gathering and reporting

This chapter will prepare you to:

- understand the most important theories of the press
- describe the qualities that characterize news
- identify the three main types of news stories
- understand how the digital revolution has affected news gathering, reporting, and the news business
- discuss the similarities of broadcast, print, and online journalism
- describe the changes in the news audience over the past several years

As in past editions, we will begin this section by examining the most recent report from the Project for Excellence in Journalism sponsored by the prestigious Pew Research Center, a highly respected authoritative organization whose conclusions are not taken lightly. Its latest report, "The State of the News Media 2011," suggests that there may be a reason for optimism after several years of discouraging findings. Here are some excerpts from the report:

By several measures, the state of American news media improved in 2010.

After two dreadful years, most sectors of the industry saw revenue begin to recover. With some notable exceptions, cutbacks in newsrooms eased. And while still more talk than action, some experiments with new revenue models began to show signs of blossoming. . . .

Beneath all this, however, a more fundamental challenge to journalism became clearer in the last year. The biggest issue ahead may not be lack of audience or even lack of new revenue experiments. It may be that in the digital realm the news industry is no longer in control of its own future. . . .

In the digital space, the organizations that produce the news increasingly rely on independent networks to sell their ads. They depend on aggregators (such as Google) and social networks (such as Facebook) to bring them a substantial portion of their audience. And now, as news consumption becomes more mobile, news companies must follow the rules of device makers (such as Apple) and software developers (Google again) to deliver their content.

Although the model and method of delivery may change, Americans still have an appetite for the news, and they now have more control than ever over what information they consume and how and where they consume it. This chapter will take a look at how the digital revolution has transformed the basic principles of journalism, the technology of news gathering, and the way stories are reported.

theories of the press

Before we begin our examination of news gathering, let's step back and take a look at some fundamental issues concerning the relationship between the government and those who report the news.

Since the 16th century, scholars and philosophers have attempted to describe the relationship between the government and the media and its implications with regard to freedom and control. Over the years, as political, economic, and social conditions have changed, various theories of the press have developed to articulate and explain this relationship. All theories, however, fall somewhere between two "isms" that reflect polar opposites in the amount of control the government exerts over the media—authoritarianism and libertarianism. Current theories of the press represent modifications of these two fundamental principles. Let us look at each of them.

The **authoritarian theory** arose in 16th-century England, at about the same time as the introduction of the printing press in that country. Under the authoritarian system the prevailing belief was that the ruling elite should guide the masses, whose intellectual ability was held in low esteem. Public dissent and criticism were considered harmful to both the government and the people and were not tolerated. Authoritarians used various devices to force compliance of the press, including licensing, censorship of material before publication, the granting of exclusive printing rights to favored elements of the press, and the swift, harsh punishment of government critics. Iran and Syria are two countries that still endorse the authoritarian theory.

The **libertarian theory** is directly opposed to authoritarianism. Libertarians assume that human beings are rational and capable of making their own decisions and that governments exist to serve the individual. Libertarians believe that the common citizen has a right to hear all sides of an issue to distinguish truth from falsehood. Since any government restriction on the expression of ideas infringes on the rights of the citizen, the government can best serve the people by not interfering with the media. In short, the press must be free from all government regulation.

The libertarian theory fit well with the freewheeling political climate and rugged individualism of early America. By the mid-20th century, however, two world wars and a depression had changed world politics, media industries had become big business, and broadcasting had made it possible to reach millions of people instantaneously. As a result, new theories of the press emerged. In 1956 a book titled *Four Theories of the Press* reexamined the libertarian and authoritarian philosophies and described two more modern approaches. The **social responsibility theory** (also referred to as the *Western concept*) incorporates part of the original libertarian approach but introduces some new elements as well. This approach holds that the press has a right to criticize government and other institutions, but it also has a responsibility to preserve democracy by properly informing the

President Barack Obama meets the press.

public and by responding to society's needs and interests. The press does not have the freedom to do whatever it pleases; it has certain obligations to society. The government may involve itself in media operations by issuing regulations if the public interest is not being adequately served. The regulation of broadcasting by the Federal Communications Commission is a good example. The United States, Japan, Britain, and many other European countries subscribe to this theory.

The other theory spelled out in *Four Theories of the Press* is the **communist theory**. This theory is a variant on the authoritarian scheme. The media are "owned" by the people as represented by the state. Their purpose is to support the Marxist system and to achieve the goals of the state as expressed through the Communist Party. Recent history has shown that the communist approach to the press works best in a closed society in which information is tightly controlled by the government. Once information is available from competing sources, people give little credibility to the official media.

The communist theory of the press has few proponents today. China, Cuba, and North Korea are about the only places where it can be found, and even in those countries the official theory often bears little resemblance to the actual practices of the media. In short, the communist theory has been rendered obsolete by history. All in all, the growth of democracy and the growing popularity of free-market economics have resulted in more countries endorsing the social responsibility model.

Now let's take a look at some specifics of news gathering.

deciding what is news

Deciding what is newsworthy is not an exact science. News values are formed by tradition, organizational policy, and economics, and, more recently, by the digital revolution. Nonetheless, most journalists still agree that there are five core elements that characterize newsworthy events.

1. **Timeliness:** Put glibly, news is new. Yesterday's news is old news. A consumer who picks up the evening paper or turns on the afternoon news or visits a news Web site expects to be told what happened earlier that same day. News is perishable, and stale news is not interesting. The digital revolution has put an additional premium on timeliness. With Web sites that operate 24/7 and bloggers and Twitterers who provide firsthand information about an event minutes after it happens, news no longer has to wait for the morning edition or the evening newscast. As a result, the "shelf life" of news has become shorter.

2. **Proximity:** News happens close by. Readers and viewers want to learn about their neighborhood, town, or country. A train derailment in France, for example, is less likely to be reported than a similar derailment in the local train yard. News media are placing additional emphasis on this factor as they examine the potential of hyperlocal news (see below). Proximity, however, means more than a simple measure of distance. Psychological proximity is also important. Subway riders in San Francisco might show interest in a story about rising vigilantism on the New York subways, even though the story is happening 3,000 miles away. Social media sites have given a new dimension to psychological proximity. A member of Twitter or Facebook can receive news feeds from a specific network of friends. In other words, a person can define those

media
talk

The Dumbing
of America

Clip 3: 4 minutes 39 seconds
You can watch Clip 3 *on the Online Learning Center home page,* www.mhhe.com/dominick12e. *Select* Student Center *and then* Chapter 13.

In this clip, authors Noah Oppenheim and Susan Jacoby discuss whether Americans are indeed dumber than in previous years and whether the current pop culture says it is okay to be clueless about current events. Do you feel that the media have made Americans dumber? If so, in what ways? Has increased technology use distracted you from picking up a book and reading? Do you think that most Americans feel it is cool to be clueless about current events? Does pop culture promote ignorance of current events?

WWW

individuals with whom he or she feels a psychological proximity. Traditional news media cannot offer this degree of precision.

3. **Prominence:** The more important a person, the more valuable he or she is as a news source. Thus, activities of the president, other heads of state, and sports and entertainment figures attract tremendous media attention. Americans apparently love celebrities and seldom tire of news about them. Even the infamous have news value. The past lives and recent exploits of many criminals are frequently given media coverage.

4. **Consequence:** Events that affect a great many people have built-in news value. The reason an increase in the price of gas is a big story is that it affects nearly everybody in the country. The Internet has given audience members more influence in determining the consequence of certain news items. News media monitor the "clickstream" to see what stories audience members are choosing to read on their Web sites. Stories that rank high are apparently of importance to a great many people and assume added consequence. The negative aspect of this is that some stories that generate lots of clicks tend to be about the bizarre, the sensational, and the unusual rather than the serious and wind up with more coverage than they might otherwise have received. (How much news coverage did Charlie Sheen get?)

5. **Human interest:** These are stories that arouse some emotion in the audience—stories that are ironic, bizarre, uplifting, or dramatic. Typically, these items concern ordinary people who find themselves in circumstances with which the audience can identify. Thus, when a poor young mother finds a $10 bill and uses the money to buy a $1-million-winning lottery ticket, the story becomes newsworthy.

In addition to these five traditional elements of news value, economics plays a large role. First, some stories cost more to cover than others. It is cheaper to send a reporter or a camera crew to the city council meeting than to assign a team of reporters to investigate city council corruption. Some news operations might not be willing to pay the price for such a story. Conversely, after spending a large sum of money pursuing a story, the news organization might run it, even if it has little traditional news value, simply to justify its cost to management.

By the same token, the cost of new technology is reflected in the types of stories that are covered. When TV stations went to electronic news gathering (ENG), stories that could be covered live became more important. In fact, many organizations, conscious of the scheduling of TV news programs, planned their meetings and/or demonstrations during newscasts to enhance their chances of receiving TV coverage. Further, after helicopters became an expensive investment at many large TV stations, traffic jams, fires, beautiful sunsets, and other stories that lent themselves to airborne journalism suddenly became newsworthy.

the news business

The business model that has historically supported the news media is a simple one: Advertising pays for most of the cost of gathering and distributing news. There is, however, no necessary connection between advertisers and news. Why should Target, AT&T, and other advertisers pay for a reporter to cover the Supreme Court? Note that this business model works as long as the news media draw the audiences that advertisers want to reach. For almost two centuries the model worked fine, but then the Internet came along. Advertisers discovered that they had other, more efficient ways to reach an audience, and the revenue started to flow away from the news media to the Web. This is what the 2009 "State of the News Media" report referred to as the "decoupling" of advertising from news. The revenue declines were considerable: Newspaper income was down 23 percent in two years; newsmagazines were folding or cutting back; even local TV

social issues   *Journalism and the Financial Crisis*

As we saw in Chapter 2, surveillance is one of the functions performed by the mass media. The media alert us to threats, both short-term and long-term. It seems, however, that the media do a better job alerting the public to more immediate threats, such as an approaching hurricane, than to ones that take longer to unfold.

The financial crisis of 2007–2009 is a case in point. The sudden collapse of the housing market, the failure of huge financial institutions, and the worldwide plunge in stock prices seemed to catch Americans by surprise. Did the media, particularly the business media, fail in their watchdog role?

There are three main viewpoints when it comes to explaining the performance of the media during the recent crisis:

1. The media not only failed to report on the impending crisis, they also made it worse.

2. The media failed to report on the impending crisis, but the causes of the problem were so complex that no journalist should be expected to understand them, let alone report intelligently about them.

3. The media sounded the alert, but nobody listened to them.

Let's take a look at each of these assertions.

The media failed to alert us and made things worse. Critics charge that business coverage has too often taken on a probusiness spin. Newspapers and TV stations make money from advertising, and advertisers don't like bad publicity. Consequently, the pressure was on to report only the good and to ignore the bad. To take a specific example, real estate advertising contributes to a newspaper's bottom line (although not as much as it used to), and most Sunday editions have special real estate sections or pages. Not surprisingly, there were more stories written about the handsome profits made by people who were "flipping" houses and how real estate values kept skyrocketing than there were about what might happen if the bubble were to burst.

Second, the focus of business reporting has changed from consumers to investors. Stories about the positive earnings reports for the financial sector and glowing personality portraits of leading financial figures replaced investigative stories. A flattering profile of Merrill Lynch's CEO concluded that Merrill Lynch couldn't be luckier to have him. In 2007, the CEO was ousted and Merrill Lynch was saved from bankruptcy when it was acquired by Bank of America.

The media failed to alert us, but the problems were too complicated to understand. There is no doubt that the problems underlying the financial crisis were complicated. Intricate financial dealings and arcane investment instruments were certainly part of the predicament. Should we have expected journalists to unravel them for us? Proponents of this view note that federal regulatory bodies failed to predict the collapse. If economic experts couldn't figure out what was going on, why expect journalists,

who, as a rule, have little formal training in economics, to figure it out? Further, the economic crisis came at a time when newspapers were cutting back on staff and resources. Covering the financial sector is a huge job and requires a commitment of time and money. Cutbacks in the newsroom may have reduced the number of veteran business journalists, making it harder for those who remained to make sense of the broader picture.

The media sounded the alert, but nobody listened. Several journalists would argue that media did an adequate job of surveillance. An article in the December 2008/January 2009 issue of the *American Journalism Review* summarizes this view: "Well before this year's economic collapse, business journalists shined a spotlight on serious problems in the U.S. economy. But regulators and members of the public didn't pay much attention." The article cites examples of stories in *Fortune* magazine, the *Wall Street Journal*, and the *New York Times* that warned of problems with derivatives, the precarious situation of mortgage lenders, and the housing bubble. But, says the article, no one wanted to hear negative news, particularly when the stock market was climbing and housing values were steadily increasing.

Don't blame the journalists for missing the problem. Blame the financial experts, the regulators, and the public for not listening. The article concludes that business journalists must better educate the public so that when journalists sound the danger signal for the next economic crisis they won't be ignored.

Did the media fail us? The issue is a complex one, and parts of all three perspectives expressed above are valid. There is little doubt that the media did not function as effectively as they might have. A poll of financial journalists found that two-thirds faulted the media for failing to recognize the magnitude of the problem. Too many stories focused on how people were making a quick buck.

Granted that the causes of the crisis were numerous and not easy to understand and explain. Granted also that journalists are not economics experts, but journalists are trained to find experts and to ask the right questions. Reporters should know enough about a topic to be able to dig beneath the surface and make sense of what they find. It's the fundamental responsibility of journalists to understand what they are covering.

Journalism education is also partly to blame. I know from experience that economics and finance courses are not popular among journalism students. Perhaps such specialized training should be required of more of our graduates.

Finally, it is true that many stories were written and aired that did warn of the crisis. But these alarms were probably lost in the far greater number of optimistic articles and glowing CEO portraits that also appeared. Moreover, it is not enough for the media to report two or three stories on an impending problem and then move on. To get the attention of policy makers and the general public, journalists must be persistent.

All in all, one would hope that the media learned lessons from the economic crisis that will help them better report the next one.

news, a usually reliable income generator, saw revenue drop by 7 percent. Only the cable news networks were able to stay in the black, thanks to the 2008 elections. The traditional news media cut costs, reduced staff, and were able to shore up some of their losses from their online operations, but it was clear that revenue from their Internet properties would never cover the shortfall.

media *Probe*   *The Erosion of Trust*

Gallup poll data show a troubling trend: Americans are losing confidence in the trustworthiness of their news media. As the following table illustrates, the percentage of survey respondents who reported having little or no trust has nearly doubled in the last 40 years.

The question: "In general how much trust do you have in the mass media . . . when it comes to reporting the news fully, accurately and fairly?"

Year	1972	2000	2010
Percentage saying they have a "fair" amount of trust or a "great deal" of trust	68	51	43
Percentage saying they have "not much" or no trust	30	49	57

If that wasn't bad enough, the news media took another hit when the economy went into a recession. As the 2010 "State of the News Media" report put it: "Imagine someone about to begin physical therapy following a stroke, suddenly contracting a debilitating secondary illness." In the wake of all of this, the news media were looking for other sources of income and other business models. As we saw in Chapter 5, newspapers were investigating micropayments for access to some of their content. Both television and print media were exploring charging for content downloaded to portable devices such as cell phones and Amazon's Kindle e-book reader.

What does the future hold for the news business? The 2011 "State of the News Media" report suggests that things may have turned around a bit. Advertising revenue was up for all media except newspapers, fewer people were losing their jobs, and news organizations were making investments in additional resources. Nonetheless, the Internet and the economic climate have irrevocably changed the news business. The report concludes:

> Traditional newsrooms, meanwhile, are different places than they were before the recession. They are smaller, their aspirations have narrowed and their journalists are stretched thinner. But their leaders also say they are more adaptive, younger and more engaged in multimedia presentation, aggregation, blogging and user content. In some ways, new media and old, slowly and sometimes grudgingly, are coming to resemble each other.
>
> The result is a news ecology full of experimentation and excitement, but also one that is uneven, has uncertain financial underpinning and some clear holes in coverage.

news reporting in the digital age

To say that the digital revolution has prompted significant changes in news reporting is an understatement. We will discuss six: (1) increasing number of news sources, (2) blogs, (3) citizen journalism, (4) hyperlocal news, (5) converged journalists, and (6) new reporting tools.

More Sources of News

The Internet has increased the number of available news sources. Audience members can examine (1) general news sites, such as CNN.com or usatoday.com, that offer video, text, and pictures in broad topic areas like world news, national news, technology, entertainment, and politics; (2) news aggregators, such as Google News, Drudge Report, and the Huffington Post, that offer a digest of news from other sources; (3) specialized news sites that offer content with a tight focus, such as ESPN for sports news and the *Wall Street Journal's* Web site for financial news; and (4) blogs.

Blogs

As mentioned above, first and foremost, blogs represent another source of news, one that is free from economic, corporate, political, or advertising considerations. Morsels of news of interest to a small number of people that would otherwise go unreported go into blogs. There are blogs devoted to political news, technology news, entertainment news, and countless other topics. In countries where the government exercises tight control over the media, blogs offer an alternative version of events.

Second, blogs have an agenda-setting effect. They can concentrate the attention of the traditional media on selected events and keep those events in the news cycle. CNN has a special reporter who monitors blogs to see what current issues are being discussed.

Third, blogs provide a check on the traditional media. For example, during the 2004 election campaign, bloggers called into question documents that CBS had publicized in a story about President George W. Bush's National Guard service. CBS ultimately admitted that it could not authenticate the documents. The established media are not used to this level of scrutiny (particularly from people the media regard as amateurs), and this generates a certain amount of friction between bloggers and traditional journalists.

Fourth, blogs represent an additional outlet for reporters to explain why they reported a story the way they did. Why did the reporter frame a story in a certain way? Why were some sources quoted and not others? Why did the reporter use an anonymous source? As Bill Kovach and Tim Rosenstiel, the authors of *The Elements of Journalism,* put it, the audience should be "given a chance to judge the principles by which journalists do their work." Some reporters have started blogs as a first step in this direction. CNN's Anderson Cooper, for example, authors the 360 blog, where he provides background about stories he is working on.

Finally, blogs have made it possible for everybody to be a newsperson and have opened the way for what's being labeled *citizen journalism.*

Citizen Journalism

As mentioned earlier, the first news about the death of Osama Bin Laden appeared on someone's Twitter account. Demonstrators in North Africa and the Middle East captured scenes of violence on their cell phones and uploaded the video to YouTube and Facebook. TV news networks replayed many of these videos on their nightly newscasts.

This trend was made possible by the development of easy-to-use digital and cell phone video cameras and high-speed Internet access. Its potential was first demonstrated in 2005 when cell phone images of the London Underground bombings and the Asian tsunami were prominently featured on television and in newspapers.

Citizen journalism is a trend that is actively encouraged by the traditional news media. CNN has iReport, Fox News has uReport, CBS has EyeMobile, and MSNBC has Citizen Journalists. The *New York Times* recently launched several local-community citizen efforts. According to the Knight Citizen News Network, there are nearly 800 citizen media sites in the United States.

Of course, one of the reasons citizen journalism is popular among the mainstream news media is that it is free. In an industry faced with declining audiences and shrinking revenues, citizen input can be a way to cut costs and perhaps eliminate some personnel. Professional journalists, not surprisingly, look upon this trend with some concern. Some argue that these citizen reporters are not journalists at all, but merely witnesses who happen to be in the right place when news breaks out. Legitimate journalism requires balance, fairness, and a sense of ethics, traits that are not necessarily present in amateur reporters.

On the other hand, citizen journalism does empower the audience. News organizations no longer have a monopoly on what gets reported or how it's reported. For example, the official version of the execution of Saddam Hussein was contradicted by a cell phone video shot by someone on the scene.

Citizen journalists often report on news items of interest to a relatively small number of people, a trend labeled *hyperlocal news*.

Hyperlocal News

There's an old maxim in journalism that says "all news is local," but these days it might better be rephrased as "a lot of news is hyperlocal." **Hyperlocal** is another one of those emerging terms that has a wide range of use. Generally, hyperlocal coverage concentrates on the stories, no matter how small, of a particular community or zip code or interest group in a defined geographic area. Most, but not all, hyperlocal coverage can be found on Web sites.

In Naples, Florida, for example, the Web site of the local paper carries detailed news about local real estate prices, restaurant critiques, and extensive information on high school athletics. Other sites might contain coverage of the neighborhood's Little League or soccer teams, rezoning proposals, business start-ups, local crime statistics, and yard sales. The publishers of hyperlocal news hope that the focus on topics that the traditional news media ignore will help them attract the audience that generally does not consume news. MySpace and Facebook are probably the ultimate examples of hyperlocal news. Visitors to these sites can find out news that is of interest to them and their friends.

Patch.com is the latest entrant in the hyperlocal arena. Acquired by AOL in 2009, Patch now has sites in more than 500 communities in 22 states and the District of Columbia. In Georgia, for example, Patch covers 42 neighborhoods with populations generally ranging from 5,000 to 30,000. AOL committed $50 million to the Patch project in 2010 and it was one of the few news organizations that was expanding its reporting staff.

Making money from hyperlocal coverage presents a challenge. Most Web sites obtain revenue by selling inexpensive ads to local merchants and entrepreneurs who can't afford to buy newspaper space or TV and radio time. A brief tour of some hyperlocal sites revealed ads for neighborhood kids who will work as pet sitters, after-school gymnastics programs, and magicians who perform at local birthday parties. Obviously, these ads may not represent a huge revenue stream, but the cost of hyperlocal news coverage tends to be small. Web sites are simple, without a lot of costly graphics, and much of the content on the site is generated by users.

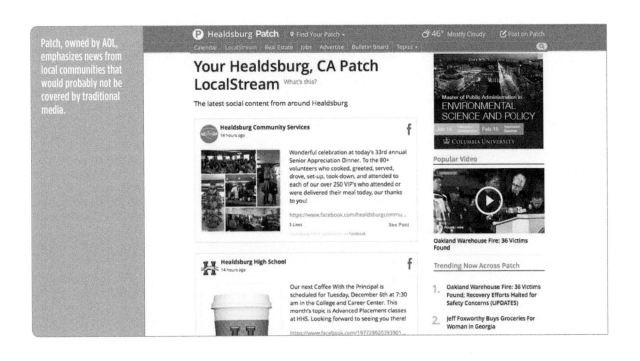

Patch, owned by AOL, emphasizes news from local communities that would probably not be covered by traditional media.

media Probe   *Top Sites for News*

Note the variety among the top 10 general news sites in 2011. Four were news aggregators, three were maintained by television networks, and three were newspaper sites.

Site	Unique Visitors/Month (approx.)
1. Yahoo News	110 million
2. CNN	74
3. MSNBC	73
4. Google News	65
5. NY Times.com	59
6. Huffington Post	54
7. Fox News	32
8. Digg	25
9. Washington Post	25
10. LA Times	25

The journalists who report hyperlocal news have to be skilled in several areas: writing, video, audio, and photography. In short, they provide yet another example of convergence.

The Converged Journalist

As mentioned in Chapter 5, the converged reporter is one who can write stories for a print medium or a Web site, shoot and post photos online, and do video reports as well. In short, the print journalist and the video journalist have converged to produce the 21st-century version of the news correspondent. In fact, a couple of new terms have been coined to describe this new type of reporter. The **backpack journalist** is a "do-it-all" reporter who carries around a small digital camera, a laptop, and a satellite phone (presumably in a backpack) that enables her or him to produce stories for print, television, and online media. Next-generation reporters who eschew backpacks in favor of the automobile are called **mobile journalists**, or **mojos.** These are staff reporters or freelancers who work out of their cars, covering local news that is usually posted to a Web site or appears in a newspaper print edition.

Whether a traditional reporter or a mojo, journalists in the digital age have a powerful new tool in the Internet.

New Tools

As pointed out by Randy Reddick and Elliot King in *The Online Journ@list,* in the past elite media organizations would send reporters to power centers and other locations where news usually happened to cover events. Today's reporter can sit at his or her desk and instantly access documents, databases, government records, and expert sources. In short, journalists can now bring to their desks information they previously went out to look for.

In order to make the most efficient use of this new tool, however, reporters must learn new skills. The 21st-century journalist must be able to perform Web searches, download data files and analyze them with spreadsheets, set up listservs, and use geographic mapping software. These skills are generally lumped under the term **computer-assisted reporting**.

Although the changes brought about by the move to digital media are extensive, there are still some constants, and we will examine them next.

social issues *Where the Boys Aren't*

When TV news first started it was a male-dominated profession. Female reporters were rare, and female anchors even rarer. All that has changed. Starting in the 1980s, the number of female anchors steadily increased. By the 1990s the number of female anchors equaled the number of male anchors. In 2008 female anchors outnumbered male anchors 60 to 40 percent. The male-female pairing is the typical coanchor arrangement, but female-female teams are more common, as are solo female anchors. What is rare these days is what was typical a few decades ago: a male-male anchor team or a solo male. (Remember Ron Burgundy in *Anchorman*?)

Women have become more numerous in other positions as well. About 60 percent of all field reporters are female. Behind the camera more than half of newscast producers and writers are female. And the trend looks like it will continue into the future. A recent survey conducted by the University of Georgia noted that about two-thirds of bachelor's degrees in journalism and mass communication were granted to women.

Several reasons are behind this shift. Equal opportunity employment laws and the journalism profession's promotion of diversity have certainly helped. Additionally, news directors realized that half their potential audience was female and might welcome a woman's perspective on news events.

Some observers find the dwindling percentage of males in video journalism a disturbing trend that might lead to the "feminization" of TV news and the alienation of the male viewers in the audience. Others note that today's male audience is more accustomed to seeing females in powerful roles (senators, secretaries of state, CEOs of large corporations), and the growing journalistic gender disparity should be of little consequence. At any rate, it's highly probable that the TV newsroom will continue to be a place populated by a majority of females.

categories of news and reporting

Generally, news can be broken down into three broad categories: (1) hard news, (2) features, or soft news, and (3) investigative reports.

Hard News

Hard news stories make up the bulk of news reporting. They typically embody the first four of the five traditional news values discussed. Hard news consists of basic facts: who, what, when, where, how. It is news of important public events, such as government actions, international happenings, social conditions, the economy, crime, the environment, and science. Hard news has significance for large numbers of people. The front sections of a newspaper or newsmagazine and the lead stories of a radio or TV newscast are usually filled with hard news.

Print Media   There is a standard technique used to report hard news. In the print media it is the traditional inverted pyramid form. The main facts of the story are delivered in the first sentence (called the *lead*) in an unvarnished, no-nonsense style. Less important facts come next, with the least important and most expendable facts at the end. This structure aids the reporter (who uses it to compose facts quickly), the editor (who can lop off the last few paragraphs of a story to make it fit the page without doing wholesale damage to the sense of the story), and the reader (who can tell at a glance if he or she is interested in all, some, or none of the story). This format has been criticized for being predictable and old-fashioned. More literary writing styles have been suggested as alternatives, but the inverted pyramid has survived.

Broadcast/Cable Media   In the broadcast/cable media, with the added considerations of limited time, sound, and video, broadcast reporting follows a square format. The information level stays about the same throughout the story. There is usually no time for the less important facts that would come in the last paragraphs of a newspaper story. TV and radio news stories use either a "hard" or a "soft" lead. A hard lead contains the most important information, the basic facts of the story—for example,

"The city council has rejected a plan to build the Fifth Street overpass." A soft lead is used to get the viewers' attention; it may not convey much information: "That proposed Fifth Street overpass is in the news again." The lead is then supported by the body of the story, which introduces new information and amplifies the lead. The summation, the final few sentences in the report, can be used to personalize the main point ("This means that the price you pay for gasoline is likely to go up"), introduce another fact, or discuss future developments.

The writing style of broadcast news is completely different from that of print news: It is more informal, conversational, and simple. In addition, it is designed to complement sound bites (recorded comments of the newsmaker) or videotape segments.

Online Media   The writing style for online media is highly variable. Some newspaper sites may simply post the print version of the story with minor editing. Other sites might post the headline and a couple of sentences highlighting the main points of the story with a link that will take readers to the rest of the story. The newspaper inverted-pyramid style is generally used, and photos and video are integrated into the text. Links to other sites that contain supplemental information are often included. Television network and local station Web sites generally have shorter stories written in the broadcast news style, with video clips that are related to the story.

Soft News

Soft news, or features, covers a wide territory. The one thing that all soft news has in common is that it interests the audience. Features typically rely on human interest for their news value. They appeal to people's curiosity, sympathy, skepticism, or amazement. They can be about places, people, animals, topics, events, or products. Some stories that would be classified as soft news are the birth of a kangaroo at the local zoo, a personality sketch of a local resident who has a small part in an upcoming movie, a cook who moonlights as a stand-up comedian, and a teenager who mistakenly gets a tax refund check for $400,000 instead of $40.

Features are entertaining, and the audience likes them. Many television and print vehicles are based primarily on soft content (*Entertainment Tonight; E!*, the cable entertainment network; *People; Us* magazine; the "Life" section of *USA Today*). Even prime-time newsmagazines such as *60 Minutes* and *20/20* have substantial amounts of soft news. Likewise, the fiercely competitive early-morning network TV shows are turning more to soft news.

The techniques for reporting features are as varied as the features themselves. In the print media, features seldom follow the inverted-pyramid pattern. The main point of the feature is often withheld until the end, much like the punch line to a joke. Some features are written in chronological order. Others start with a shocking statement, such as "Your secrets just might kill you," and then proceed with an explanation: "If you have a medical problem, you should wear a Medic-Alert bracelet." Still other features are structured in the question-and-answer format.

TV features are more common than radio features. In some large TV markets, one or more reporters cover nothing but features. Almost all stations have a feature file where story ideas are catalogued. If a local station does not have the resources to produce local features, it can look to syndication companies that provide general-interest features for a fee. Broadcast features also use a variety of formats. Using humorous leads and delaying the main point until the end sometimes work well, a technique often used by Andy Rooney in his features for *60 Minutes*. Other times a simple narrative structure, used in everyday storytelling, is quite effective. The interview format is also popular, particularly when the feature is about a well-known personality.

There are dozens of Web sites, such as *Entertainment Weekly* and *E!* online, that specialize in soft news, particularly celebrity news. Other Web sites may concentrate on a specific topic, such as food (www.food411.com), fashion (www.zoozoom.com), or pets (www.dogster.com).

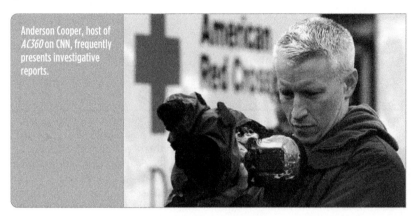

Anderson Cooper, host of *AC360* on CNN, frequently presents investigative reports.

Investigative Reports

Investigative reports unearth significant information about matters of public importance through the use of nonroutine information-gathering methods. Since the Watergate affair was uncovered by a pair of Washington, D.C., newspaper reporters, investigative reporting has been perceived as primarily concerned with exposing corruption in high places. This connotation is somewhat unfortunate for at least two reasons. In the first place, it encouraged a few short-sighted reporters to look upon themselves as self-appointed guardians of the public good and to indiscriminately pursue all public officials, sometimes using questionable techniques in the hope of uncovering some indiscretion. Much of this investigative journalism turned out to be insignificant. In the second place, this emphasis on exposing political corruption distracted attention from the fact that investigative reporting can concentrate on other topics and perform a valuable public service.

Investigative reports require a good deal of time and money. Because of this heavy investment, they are generally longer than the typical print or broadcast news item. Broadcast investigative reports are usually packaged in documentaries, or in 10- to 15-minute segments of a newsmagazine program (such as *Dateline NBC* or *60 Minutes*). Print investigative pieces are usually run as a series of articles.

Bloggers have also entered the realm of investigative journalism. Some of the top investigative blogs are the Center for Investigative Reporting, The Blotter, and Washington Post Investigations.

Examples of noteworthy investigative reports include a 2010 Peabody Award–winning story by WFAA-TV, Dallas, about problems with government-funded technical schools and a Pulitzer Prize–winning report by the Sarasota, Florida, *Herald-Tribune* concerning weaknesses in the state's property insurance program.

the news flow

As mentioned in Chapter 1, one of the characteristics of traditional mass communication is the presence of a large number of gatekeepers. This fact is seen in the gathering and reporting of news for conventional print and broadcast media. Reporting is a team effort, and quite a few members of the team serve as gatekeepers. Online reporting, in contrast, may have only one or a few gatekeepers. This section will first examine the news flow in the traditional print and broadcast media and then look at online media.

Print Media

There are two main sources of news for a newspaper: staff reports and the wire services. Other, less important sources include feature syndicates and handouts and releases from various sources.

Let us first examine how news is gathered by newspaper personnel. The city editor is the captain of the news-reporting team. He or she assigns stories to reporters and supervises their work. There are two types of reporters: (1) beat reporters, who cover some topics on a regular basis, such as the police beat or the city hall beat; and (2) general-assignment reporters, who cover whatever assignments come up. A typical day for the general-assignment reporter might include covering an auto accident, a speech by a visiting politician, and a rock concert. Stories from the reporters are passed along to the city editor, where they are approved and sent to the copy desk for further editing. The managing editor and assistant managing editor are also part of the news team. They are responsible for the overall daily preparation of the paper.

Broadcast/Cable Media

The sources of news for the broadcast media are similar to those for the newspaper. Special wire services cater to TV and radio stations, and local reporters are assigned to cover nearby events. In addition, many broadcast newsrooms subscribe to syndicated news services or, if affiliated with a network, have access to the network's news feeds.

The broadcast newsroom is organized along different lines from its print counterpart. At the local station the news director is in charge of the overall news operation. In large stations most news directors spend their time on administrative work—personnel, budgets, equipment, and so on. In smaller stations most news directors perform other functions (such as being the anchorperson) as well. Next in command is the executive producer. This person supervises all the producers in the newsroom. Typically, producers are assigned to the early-morning, noon, evening, or late-night newscasts. In addition to looking after the other producers, the executive producer might produce the evening news, typically the station's most important program. Here are some of the things that an executive producer does:

1. Decide which stories are covered, who covers them, and how they are covered.
2. Decide the order in which stories appear in the newscast.
3. Determine the amount of time each story is given.
4. Write copy for some stories.
5. Integrate live reports into the newscasts.

The assignment editor, who assigns and monitors the activities of reporters, camera crews, and other people in the field, works closely with the news producer. Since speed is important in broadcast news, there is great pressure on the assignment editor to get the crews to the story in the shortest amount of time.

Then, of course, there are the "glamour" jobs—on-air reporters and anchors. Most reporters in broadcast news function as general-assignment reporters, although the large-market stations might have one or two regularly assigned to a beat, such as the entertainment scene. In many stations anchors occasionally do field reports, but most of the time they perform their work in the studio, preparing for the upcoming newscast. In addition to the people seen on camera, there are quite a few workers whom no one ever sees or hears. Photographers accompany reporters to shoot the video. Editors trim the footage into segments that fit within the time allotted to the story. Big stations also have newswriters and production assistants who pull slides and arrange other visuals needed during the newscast.

Online Media

The news flow in an online news department is similar to that in the traditional media. Top executives decide how the site will be structured and how many specialty areas (such as sports, finance, weather, and entertainment) it will contain. Editors decide what content will be used on the Web site, which stories will have additional audio and video files, where the stories will be placed, and how often they will be updated. Reporters revise and update their stories when appropriate. Online news departments that are affiliated with a broadcast or cable network, such as CNN or MSNBC, will use the audio and video that appeared on the parent network but may edit it differently. Other stories may be rewritten from wire copy or from copy that has appeared in print or on the air. Not all online news, however, is recycled. Some online news staffs also employ reporters who do original reporting for the Web site.

ethical issues   *The Innocence Project*

The Medill School of Journalism at Northwestern University is one of the most prestigious J-schools in the United States. In 1999, the school began the Medill Innocence Project, an investigative journalism project conducted by students in a class taught by Professor David Protess. The project reexamined murder cases in Illinois to see if anyone had been wrongly convicted. Over the years, Medill's Innocence Project has helped free nearly a dozen innocent men and has been widely praised in the media.

In 2008–2009, with help from students working with the Innocence Project, attorneys for a convicted murderer asked the court to reconsider its guilty decision. In response, prosecutors argued that Protess and the students who worked on the case had violated ethical boundaries and requested information from Protess and the university concerning unpublished course materials, student grades, and e-mails. The request started a complicated legal battle between the county attorney and lawyers for Protess and Northwestern.

The legal controversy called attention to the ethics of those involved in the project. An article in the *Daily Northwestern* revealed that students investigating cases used methods that were ethically questionable. Students apparently routinely misrepresented themselves. One student posed as a utility worker in an attempt to gain information about a witness involved in the case. Another posed as a census worker. Others downplayed their status by saying they were "just students," hoping that people might be more forthcoming with information if they thought what they said would have little impact on the legal process. Some students even partied with witnesses in an attempt to get closer to them and gain information. Another technique involved students' showing witnesses mug shots of six men, five of whom looked similar to the convicted man. If the witness

picked the wrong man, students would later ask if the witness was willing to recant his or her testimony.

Although the stated aim of the project was to find the truth, some students wondered if the real goal was to overturn the conviction. The information obtained during an Innocence Project investigation was shared freely with defense attorneys but not with the prosecution. People familiar with the project suggested that the students functioned more as defense investigators than journalists.

The controversy about the Innocence Project underscores a familiar ethical dilemma: Does the end justify the means? The project has apparently done great social good—releasing individuals who were wrongly convicted—but were journalistic norms violated in the process? Some experts would argue that they were. The Code of Ethics of the Society of Professional Journalism discourages deception and surreptitious means of gathering information except as a last resort. It appears that the deception used by the students who posed as utility workers or census workers was not used as a last resort. Medill's own Integrity Code states that students should not misrepresent themselves. Moreover, one of the fundamental ethical responsibilities of a journalist is to be objective and not favor one side over another. Sharing information only with the defense seems to violate this principle.

In the course of the legal battle with the state over subpoenaed student records, Northwestern removed Protess from his position as instructor of the investigative reporting class, claiming that he misrepresented his behavior to the university administration and to its lawyers. Protess denied the charges and retired from the university in June 2011.

the associated press

The next time you read your local newspaper, notice how many stories have the initials AP in the dateline. *AP* stands for Associated Press, a wire service that provides you with much of the news about what is going on outside your local community.

In simplified form, here is how a wire service works: A correspondent covers a local news event, such as a fire. He or she reports the event to the bureau chief of the local wire service. If the bureau chief thinks the story is newsworthy enough, the chief will send it on to the state bureau to go out on the state or regional wire. The state bureau chief then decides whether to send it on for inclusion on the national wire. All in all, the wire services are the eyes and ears for local papers and broadcasting stations that cannot afford to have people stationed all over the country.

The AP has about 240 bureaus around the world. Members of the association pay for this service according to their size and circulation. A large paper, such as the *New York Times,* will pay more than a small-town paper.

In 2010 the AP had about 16,000 customers worldwide, including about 1,700 member newspapers. It serves about 5,000 radio and TV stations, plus more than 500 international broadcasters. The AP offers a wide range of services to its clients, encompassing a weather wire, a sports wire, and a financial wire along with a broadcast wire used by TV and radio stations.

The Associated Press has shifted its focus in recent years to supplying more content to cable TV and to the Web, including those sites that are in direct competition with newspapers, such as Yahoo! and Google. In fact, broadcasters and digital media have replaced newspapers as the source of most of AP's income.

The AP is not without competition. Major newspapers, such as the *New York Times*, the *Los Angeles Times*, and the *Washington Post*, offer supplemental news stories generally not covered by other services. Some newspaper groups, such as Gannett, have their own wire services. There is competition overseas as well. The British-based Reuters agency has about 30 bureaus in North America. Agence-France-Press is another formidable world-wide service.

media differences and similarities in news coverage

For many years, people argued about what type of journalism is better, print or broadcast. Proponents of print journalism contended that broadcast news was shallow and rarely scratched the service while print could handle in-depth and lengthy reports. Advocates of broadcast journalism pointed out that print media lacked the visual dimension and that print journalism was old-fashioned, slow, and dull.

This debate has subsided now that both newspapers and television emphasize their online versions. A quick glance at a newspaper Web site and a television Web site will reveal that they look pretty much alike. They both have headlines, story summaries, links to full stories, photos, and video. Consequently, it is probably more useful to concentrate on the similarities that cross media lines.

To begin, all professional journalists share the same basic values and journalistic principles.

Honesty in news reporting is crucial for television, online, and newspaper reporters. Stories must be as truthful as possible. The print or online journalist should not invent fictional characters or make up quotations and attribute them to news makers. Broadcast journalists should not stage news events or rearrange the questions and answers in a taped interview.

Another shared value is accuracy. Checking facts takes time, but it is something that a professional reporter must do for every story.

A third common value is balance. Every story has two or more sides. All journalists must make sure that they do not publicize or promote just one of them. Information should be offered on all sides of a story.

Print, online, and broadcast reporters also share the value of objectivity. Objectivity means that the reporter tries to transmit the news untainted by conscious bias and without personal comment or coloration. Of course, complete and total objectivity is not possible because the process of reporting itself requires countless judgments, each influenced in some way by the reporter's value system. Nonetheless, journalists have traditionally respected the truth, refused to distort facts deliberately, and consciously detached themselves as much as possible from what they were reporting.

Finally, online, print, and broadcast reporters must maintain credibility with their audiences. The news media periodically undergo crises of confidence, during which people begin to doubt the integrity of journalists. Sometimes these crises occur because of excesses in reporting, or they may arise following disclosure of violations of journalistic values. Whenever public opinion polls reveal that the news media have slipped another notch or two in credibility, journalists try to regain the lost confidence. After much soul-searching, the crisis usually passes. Credibility,

sound byte

We Needed a Study to Tell Us That?

According to an experiment done by the European Society of Psychoanalysis and Psychodynamics, male viewers have trouble paying attention to the news when a pretty female anchor is on the screen. About 75 percent of the men couldn't remember a thing that was said during the first minute of the newscast because they were paying more attention to the anchor's good looks.

ethical
issues
Naming Names

There's nothing illegal about reporting the name of a juvenile who has been charged with a crime, but the news media have generally followed a policy of not revealing the suspect's name. The Code of Ethics of the Society of Professional Journalists urges that news media be cautious about naming juvenile suspects. The reasoning behind this policy is that juveniles lack the maturity of adults and often don't realize the consequences of their actions. Identifying youthful suspects may result in stigmatizing them for the rest of their lives. In short, the media give the juvenile a chance to go straight without carrying the baggage associated with an arrest.

Recently, however, there has been a trend toward naming juveniles, particularly if they have been involved in serious crimes. The decision to publish or not publish the name varies from newsroom to newsroom and illustrates an ethical philosophy called *situational ethics.* Situational ethics suggests that each individual problem or situation is unique and calls for a unique solution. There is no universal ethical principle that yields an unswerving path of action. For example, some media outlets will name the juvenile suspect if he or she has been charged as an adult. Others will take the age of the person arrested into consideration. They may report the names of 16- or 17-year-olds but refrain from identifying younger individuals. Still others look at the severity of the crime; the more severe, the more likely they are to reveal the name of the suspect. The problem with this approach is that it sometimes leads to inconsistent results. A teen in one story may be named while a teen in another story is not identified.

The most extreme position argues that the name of anybody arrested for a crime should be reported. Not naming the suspect leaves a hole in the story. Somebody committed a crime. Somebody was arrested. Who? It makes no difference to the person whose car was carjacked if it was taken by a teen or an adult. The car is still gone. Suspects have the entire criminal justice system protecting them while the victims have no one to advocate for them. Finally, the proponents of this position argue that naming juvenile offenders might even encourage them to go straight and prevent future crimes.

however, is not something that should be examined only during journalistic crises. If a reader or a viewer loses trust or stops believing what is being reported, the fundamental contract between audience and reporter is undermined, and the news organization cannot survive. It matters little if the news organization is a newspaper, magazine, radio, online site, or TV station; its credibility is paramount to its viability.

Keep in mind that the above discussion refers to professional journalists. One of the problems with online citizen journalists is that a person is never sure if they subscribe to the same values as do professional reporters. Do citizen journalists check their facts and cross-validate sources? Do they provide the objective stance of a professional, or do they slant their reports because they are trying to promote a personal agenda? Are they aware of the ethics of the profession that prohibit doctored photographs and rearranged quotes? Citizen journalists are a valuable source of news but one that should be treated with caution.

BP spent more than $3 billion in connection with the damage resulting from its oil leak in the Gulf of Mexico. Some images are replayed so often that it's difficult to forget them.

readership and viewership

Table 13-1 does not paint a positive picture for the news media. The audience for network news, newspapers, and

table **13-1** News Audiences, 1980–2008	Year	Network Evening News (total ratings of ABC, NBC, CBS)	Newspapers' Total Weekday Circulation (millions)	Total Readership of Three Major Newsmagazines (millions)
	1980	42	62	10.1
	1990	30	62	9.8
	2000	24	56	9.3
	2010	15	45	4.8

table **13-2** Sources of News, 2005 and 2010	Site	2005	2010
	Television	73%	66%
	Newspapers	36	31
	Internet	20	41
	Radio	16	16

Source: Excerpted from Pew Research Center. Numbers in table are percentage of respondents naming the source.

newsmagazines has been shrinking for the past 30 years. The same trend holds true for local TV news. The audience for cable news fluctuates significantly depending on the occurrence of major news events, but, on average, it too has declined. Further, the audience is getting older. The average age of the typical TV newscast viewer is around 60.

Where is the audience going? Some have dropped out entirely; many people report no interest in following the news. Others go online: On a typical day about 30 percent report visiting a traditional online news site such as MSNBC. Quite a few are looking for news on nontraditional sites, such as YouTube. Still others may get their news via cell phone.

The smaller the audience, of course, the smaller the revenue received from advertising and the smaller the bottom line. This trend has already had great impact on those who report the news. Newspapers and TV networks have cut personnel, closed bureaus, and cut back news-gathering costs.

Table 13-2 contains data from two recent Gallup polls about how Americans get their news. An examination of this table reinforces and extends the conclusions of Table 13-1: Only the Internet has shown an increase, due in part to the rapid growth of reading news on smartphones and tablet computers.

The audience is also becoming less likely to trust the news media. Surveys done by the Pew Research Center for the People and the Press revealed that credibility ratings for local TV news, broadcast news, and cable news had all declined from 2000 to 2010. The same trend showed up for local newspapers, national newspapers, and newsmagazines. All in all, the above data are not encouraging to those in the news-reporting profession.

news gathering and reporting

Job prospects for aspiring journalists are fairly bleak. Many news organizations are cutting back staff and reducing hiring. There are a couple of bright spots. Specialized news sources such as Bloomberg News have increased their number of employees in the last few years. Likewise, online journalism may be somewhat of a growth area.

The career outlook in the various media industries changes quickly. For a more current description of conditions in news gathering and reporting and a more detailed look at career options, please consult the book's Web site: www.mhhe.com/dominick12e.

main points

- The qualities that characterize news are timeliness, proximity, prominence, consequence, and human interest. Economics is also important.

- News media are searching for new business models.

- There are three main types of news stories: hard, soft, and investigative.

- The digital revolution has increased the number of available news sources, encouraged the growth of blogs, contributed to the rise of citizen journalism and hyperlocal news, and supplied new tools to reporters.

- The Associated Press is a wire service that provides stories to print and broadcast journalists.

- Print, broadcast, and online journalism have their unique strengths and weaknesses.

- All forms of news media strive for credibility.

- Online news enables audience members to select from more news sources and customize their news.

- The audience for news has been declining across all media.

questions for review

1. What are the characteristics that determine newsworthiness? Should others be added to the list?

2. What is the difference between hard and soft news? Is it possible to do a hard-news report on a soft-news topic, such as entertainment?

3. How does blogging differ from traditional print and broadcast reporting?

4. How is blogging similar to traditional print and broadcast reporting?

5. What is hyperlocal news?

questions for critical thinking

1. Should news be what the audience wants to know or what the audience needs to know? Who should decide?

2. Where do you get most of your news about what is going on in the world? Why?

3. What news medium is most believable? Print? TV? Online? Why?

4. Why is the audience for news getting smaller?

key terms

authoritarian theory (p. 310)
libertarian theory (p. 310)
social responsibility theory (p. 310)
communist theory (p. 311)
timeliness (p. 311)
proximity (p. 311)

prominence (p. 312)
consequence (p. 312)
human interest (p. 312)
hyperlocal (p. 316)
backpack journalist (p. 317)
mobile journalist (mojo) (p. 317)

computer-assisted reporting (p. 317)
hard news (p. 318)
soft news (p. 319)
investigative reports (p. 320)

internet resources

Online Learning Center

On the Online Learning Center home page, www.mhhe.com/dominick12e, *select* Student Center *and then* Chapter 13.

1. Use the Learning Objectives, Chapter Outline, and Main Points sections to review this chapter.

2. Test your knowledge of the chapter using the multiple choice and flashcard features of the site.

3. Expand your knowledge of concepts and topics discussed in the chapter with additional Questions for Critical Thinking and Internet Exercises.

surfing the internet

There are hundreds of sites that have a connection to journalism. Only a few are listed here.

www.aim.org
Site of the media watchdog group Accuracy in Media, which critiques the operation of the news media.

www.backfence.com
An example of a hyperlocal news site. Check out what's going on in 50 different communities.

www.cnn.com
CNN Interactive's site. A good example of an online news service. Contains international and national spot news plus links for political, scientific, health, travel, financial, and entertainment news.

www.freedomforum.org
The Freedom Forum is an organization dedicated to exploring and improving journalism.

www.newslink.org
Has links to other media sources as well as research tools.

www.ojr.org
Home of the *Online Journalism Review,* at the Annenberg School of Communications at the University of Southern California. The single best resource for information concerning online journalism.

www.powerlineblog.com
One of the better-known political blogs.

www.stateofthemedia.org/2011/
Read the entire report: "State of the News Media 2011."

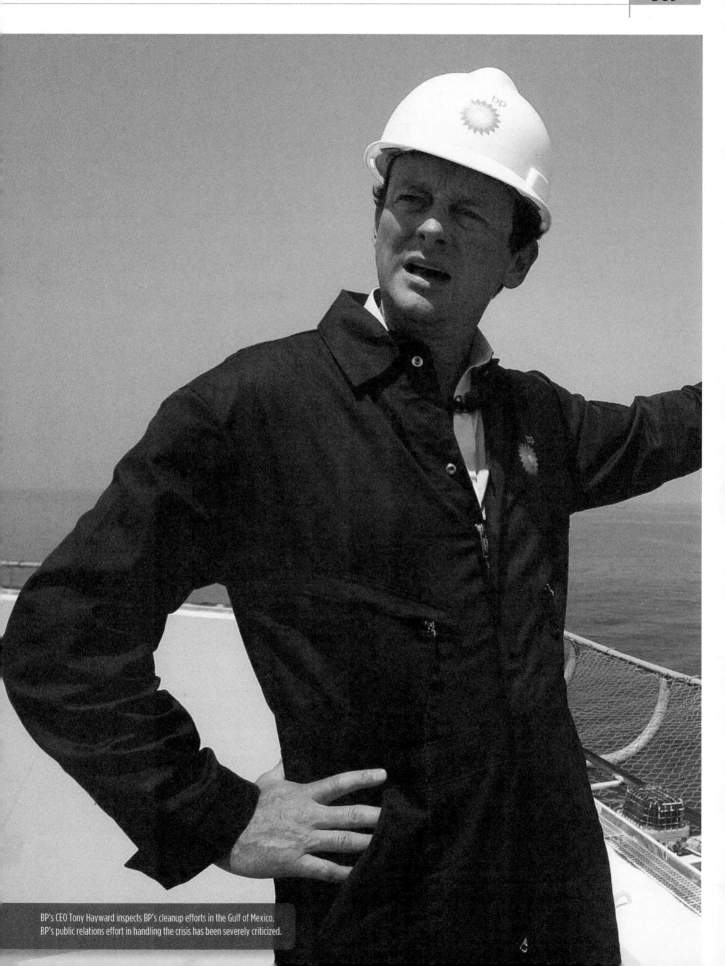

BP's CEO Tony Hayward inspects BP's cleanup efforts in the Gulf of Mexico. BP's public relations effort in handling the crisis has been severely criticized.

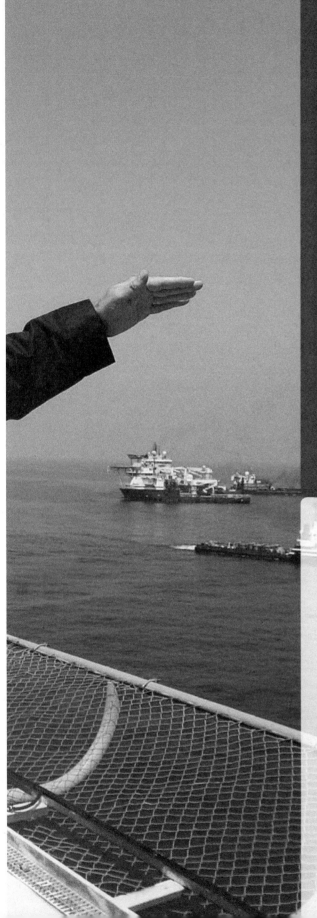

Chapter14

public
relations

This chapter will prepare you to:

- distinguish among *public relations, publicity, press agentry,* and *advertising*
- understand the background of modern public relations
- recognize the impact of the Internet on public relations
- discuss the major areas in which public relations is practiced
- explain the steps involved in developing a public relations campaign

At approximately 11 P.M. on April 20, 2010, an explosion occurred on the Deepwater Horizon oil rig, a drilling platform in the Gulf of Mexico owned by BP, a global oil and natural gas company based in Britain. The explosion killed 11 crewmembers, set off a massive oil leak that would last for months, and caused a colossal public relations problem for BP.

Although an entire chapter could be devoted to the way BP mishandled the crisis, this introduction will focus on a few key mistakes that illustrate several lessons about public relations in the digital age. First, in the age of Twitter when news and bloggers are on the job 24/7, a company the size of BP should have a comprehensive and up-to-date crisis strategy in place before a calamity occurs. BP's engineering plan was lacking. It overestimated the company's level of preparedness, designated a dead scientist as one of its wildlife experts, and listed an out-of-business Japanese home-shopping network as one of its equipment suppliers. Parts of the plan reportedly were written in pencil. The company's public relations plan was equally lacking.

Second, in the age of the sound bite, company leaders should be circumspect in what they say. In an interview with Britain's Sky News, Tony Hayward, the CEO of BP, made the following statement about the environmental impact of the spill: "It is impossible to say, and we will mount, as part of the aftermath, a very detailed environmental assessment, but everything we can see at the moment suggests that the overall environmental impact will be very, very modest." Many news organizations and bloggers chose not to use the entire quote but to lift the last nine words and use them. Hayward also committed other gaffes. When speaking to reporters in Louisiana, he said, "We're sorry for the massive disruption it's caused their [Gulf residents'] lives. There's no one who wants this over more than I do. I would like my life back." The insensitive "I would like my life back" sound bite would come to haunt him many times over.

Third, companies need to be transparent and honest when it comes to describing the extent of the crisis. Two days after the explosion, BP announced that no oil was leaking. Two days later BP reversed itself and said about 1,000 barrels per day was leaking. A week later, the company raised its estimate to 5,000 barrels per day. A congressional committee looking into the spill, frustrated with BP's response, pressured the company to release live video of the spill taken by BP's undersea robotic cameras. When the live feed, dubbed "spillcam," was posted on the committee's Web site, the number of people accessing the site was so great that it crashed the House of Representatives Web system. Shots from spillcam showing mud, gas, and oil erupting from the sea bottom were shown repeatedly on cable and broadcast TV news shows and viewed by millions on the Internet. The moral of this story is simple: In the Internet age, it's difficult to keep anything private, even if it's 5,000 feet beneath the sea.

Finally, BP was lax in its use of social media. BP never had much of a presence on social network sites. Before the spill, the company (which employs about 100,000 people) had about 25,000 fans on Facebook and about 14,000 followers on Twitter, a relatively small number. (By comparison, Starbucks has about 1.4 million Twitter followers.) As the spill progressed, a parody BP Twitter account surfaced and quickly amassed about 200,000 followers. As you might imagine, tweets on the parody account were caustic. One reported that BP was offering a deal on "blackened shrimp" at its gas stations; another said, "Black sand beaches are trendy in some places." A YouTube video showing Tony Hayward apologizing for the spill came across as slick and insincere. BP eventually launched a $50 million advertising and public relations campaign to help restore its image. As part of the campaign, BP bought the rights to advertise on Google and Yahoo! when people searched for "oil spill" and related terms. The ads popped up and directed people to BP's own sites. Critics blamed BP for trying to steer searchers away from bad news about the company and for spending money on public relations that might have been better spent cleaning up beaches.

More than a year after the spill, BP had set up a $20 billion fund to compensate victims. Its stock, which had plummeted from $60 a share to about $28 a share during the crisis, has rebounded somewhat. The company was involved in lawsuits seeking to establish liability for the disaster, and the long-term environmental impact is still unknown, but it appears to be less than what some had predicted. It's also safe to assume that BP has learned a lesson about public relations during a crisis.

Luckily BP's problems are not typical of those faced by public relations firms and corporate public relations departments, but they do indicate the tremendous importance that public relations can play in the corporate arena, especially in times of crisis. The rest of this chapter examines the history, structure, and economics of public relations as it is transformed by the age of digital and social media.

defining public relations

Before we investigate what public relations is, it may be helpful to compare it with other facets of mass communication. There are, for example, similarities between advertising and public relations. Both are attempts at persuasion, and both involve using the mass media. Public relations, however, is a management function; advertising is a marketing function. Another difference is that advertising uses the mass media and machine-assisted communication settings; unlike PR it does not involve interpersonal communications. A third difference is that advertising is normally sponsored. Public relations messages appear as features, news stories, or editorials, and the space or time involved is not paid for. In many instances, advertising, particularly corporate advertising, is used to help further a public relations program. As we shall see in the next chapter, however, the line between advertising and public relations is becoming blurred as advertisers turn to nontraditional ways of getting their messages to consumers and more businesses adapt the integrated marketing communications perspective. (See "Social Issues: IMC: Integrated Marketing Communications" on page 334.)

A concept that is sometimes confused with public relations is promotion. Promotion involves staging events or planning enterprises that attract media or public attention to a person, product, organization, or cause. Although promotion is useful in some PR campaigns, public relations encompasses a much broader area and involves more than just attracting attention.

Another concept that is sometimes confused with public relations is **publicity**, the placing of stories in the mass media. Publicity is a tool in the public relations process, but it is not equivalent to PR. For example, it is perfectly possible for a firm to have extensive publicity and bad public relations. Further, publicity is primarily one-way communication; public relations is two-way.

Having examined what public relations is *not*, we may now turn to what it *is*. The term *public relations* has many interpretations and meanings. One PR veteran has compiled 500 different ones, ranging from the concise "PR is doing good and getting credit for it" to the 100-word definition in the *Encyclopaedia Britannica*. Most of the leading textbooks on PR usually lead off with a chapter that attempts to define exactly what public relations is or is not. Rather than catalogue these many definitions, we may find it more useful to define PR by examining what PR people do:

1. *Public relations involves working with public opinion.* PR professionals attempt to influence public opinion in a way that is positive to the client. For example, after the 2010 oil spill was capped, BP launched an extensive public relations campaign to restore its image.

sound byte

Telling Them Apart

The difference between advertising, promotion, publicity, and public relations is illustrated by the following classic example that first appeared some years ago in the *Reader's Digest*: "If the circus is coming to town and you paint a sign saying 'Circus Coming to the Fairground Saturday,' that's advertising. If you put the sign on the back of an elephant and walk it into town, that's promotion. If the elephant walks through the mayor's flower bed and the newspaper reports it, that's publicity. And if you get the mayor to laugh about it and forgive you, that's public relations."

2. *Public relations is concerned with communication.* Most people are interested in what a given organization is doing to meet their concerns and interests. It is the function of the public relations professional to explain the organization's actions to various **publics** involved with the organization. As noted previously, public relations communication is two-way communication. The PR professional also pays close attention to the thoughts and feelings of the organization's publics. Some experts refer to public relations as a two-way conduit between an organization and its publics.

Note that the word *publics* in the preceding section is plural. This is because an organization typically deals with many different publics in its day-to-day operations. Several PR scholars divide these groups into internal and external publics. *Internal* publics include employees, managers, labor unions,

ethical issues
Public Relations Ethics: What Would You Do?

Imagine that your PR firm has been offered a sizable fee to represent Seven-Eleven Limited, a big conglomerate that owns gambling casinos in several states. A state referendum legalizing casino gambling is planned in your state. The casino group wants you to organize a grassroots citizens' group called Citizens for Economic Growth that will campaign in favor of legalizing casino gambling. Seven-Eleven Limited has conducted economic studies that have indeed shown that your state's treasury would benefit from legal gambling. They have ample funds available to set up and finance the operations of the citizens' group. There is one condition, however. The casino group does not want to be connected with Citizens for Economic Growth. They think that revealing the connection would hurt their chances in the referendum. Do you accept the assignment? Is it ethical to conceal information that might have an impact on the results of a public relations campaign?

On the one hand, there would be positive results if your firm took the assignment. Your firm would make a profit, and employees would be happy. Moreover, as the research suggests, casino gambling might in fact benefit the residents of your state. More jobs would be created and more tax revenue generated.

On the other hand, a deception is involved. If a reporter subsequently discovered the casino group's involvement in the campaign, it would hurt the credibility of your firm and maybe hurt the overall credibility of the public relations profession. In addition, the public would be voting on an issue without having all of the relevant facts before them.

The deception may never be uncovered, and the deception might serve a good cause. Is it worth doing?

The Code of Ethics of the Public Relations Association of America offers some guidance. It states, in part, that open communication is necessary for informed decision making. All information that might influence a decision should be revealed: "Be accurate and honest in all communications. . . . Avoid deceptive practices."

and stockholders. *External* publics consist of consumers, the government, dealers, suppliers, community members, and the mass media. Public relations serves as the link for all these publics.

3. *Public relations is a management function.* It is designed to help a company set its goals and adapt to a changing environment. Public relations practitioners regularly counsel top management. Inherent in the specification of public relations is a planned activity. It is organized and directed toward specific goals and objectives.

Of course, public relations involves much more than just the three functions mentioned. Perhaps it would be easier, for our purposes, to use the following definition approved by the World Assembly of Public Relations:

> *Public relations is the art and social science of analyzing trends, predicting their consequences, counseling organization leaders, and implementing planned programs of action that serve both the organization's and the public's interest.*

a brief history

If the term *public relations* is interpreted broadly enough, its practice can be traced back to ancient times. The military reports and commentaries prepared by Julius Caesar can be viewed as a triumph in personal and political public relations. During medieval times both the church and the guilds practiced rudimentary forms of public relations.

It was not until the American Revolution that more recognizable public relations activities became evident. The early patriots were aware that public opinion would play an important role in the struggle with England, and they planned their activities accordingly. For example, they staged events, such as the Boston Tea Party, to gain public attention. They also used symbols, such as the Liberty Tree and the Minutemen, that were easily recognized and helped portray their cause in a positive light. Skillful writers such as Samuel Adams, Thomas Paine, Abigail Adams, and Benjamin Franklin used political propaganda to swing public opinion to their side. As a case in point, note that the altercation between an angry mob and British soldiers became known as the "Boston Massacre," an interpretation well suited to the rebel cause.

The Boston Tea Party was a PR move calculated to gain support for the colonists' cause. Such an event today would be done in daylight so that TV news crews would have an easier time covering it.

Later, the Industrial Revolution and the resulting growth of mass production and mass consumption led to the emergence of big business. Giant monopolies were formed in the railroad, steel, and oil businesses. Many big corporations tended to disregard the interests of the consumer in their quest for more profits. In fact, many executives felt that the less the public knew about their practices and operations, the better. Around the turn of the 20th century, however, public hostility was aroused against unscrupulous business practices. Muckrakers (see Chapter 6) filled the nation's magazines with exposés of industrial corruption and ruthless business tactics. In response, corporations hired communications experts, many of them former newspaper writers, to counteract the effect of these stories. These specialists tried to combat negative publicity by making sure the industry's side of the issue was also presented. These practitioners were the prototypes of what we might call *press agents* or *publicists*.

The debut of modern public relations techniques dates back to the first decade of the 1900s. Most historians agree that the first real public relations pioneer was a man named Ivy Lee. In 1903 Lee and George Parker opened a publicity office. A few years later, Lee became the press representative for the anthracite coal operators and the Pennsylvania Railroad. When these industries were confronted with a strike in the coal industry, Lee issued a "Declaration of Principles." This statement endorsed the concepts of openness and honesty in dealing with the public; it also marked the shift from 19th-century press agentry to 20th-century public relations. Lee went on to have a successful career counseling people such as John D. Rockefeller Jr. Among other achievements Lee is credited with humanizing business and demonstrating that public relations is most effective when it affects employees, customers, and community members. Moreover, Lee would not carry out a public relations program unless it was endorsed and supported by top management.

The government got involved in public relations during World War I when President Woodrow Wilson set up the Creel Committee (named for its chair, journalist George Creel). Creel enlisted the top figures in the public relations field to mount a campaign that persuaded newspapers and magazines to donate space for ads that urged Americans to save food and to buy war bonds. Creel advised Wilson on communication strategies and was instrumental in publicizing Wilson's war goal "to make the world safe for democracy." The work of the Creel Committee was significant because it demonstrated the power of a well-planned and well-executed public relations campaign. In addition, it helped legitimize the field of public relations.

Public relations pioneer Ivy Lee.

Following World War I, two more public relations pioneers, Carl Byoir and Edward L. Bernays, appeared on the scene. Bernays is credited with writing the first book on public relations, *Crystallizing Public Opinion*, published in 1923. In 1930 Byoir organized a public relations firm that became one of the world's largest.

The Depression caused many Americans to look upon business with suspicion and distrust. In an attempt to regain public favor, many large corporations established their own public relations departments. The federal government, in its attempt to cope with the bad

social issues   *IMC: Integrated Marketing Communications*

Where does PR fit in the organization? Traditional thinking, as mentioned in the chapter, treats PR as a management function. Another philosophy (which emerged during the mid-1990s), called *integrated marketing communications*, or *IMC*, argues that PR should really be part of the marketing function. This distinction involves more than just an organizational war for turf; it holds significant implications for the future of the field. If PR is subsumed within marketing, it loses much of its management component.

Those who advocate IMC point out that, in addition to product and price, public and social issues influence marketing. An integrated approach ensures that a company responds to all these concerns with a single voice. Additionally, proponents of IMC note that clients want their advertising, PR, and marketing activities coordinated and unified. Further, IMC saves a company money since a single IMC department can operate more efficiently than separate departments of advertising, marketing, and PR. Finally, proponents argue that everything that a PR department does—employee communication, crisis management, promotion—boils down to marketing functions.

Opponents of IMC argue that the credibility of PR efforts will be hurt if they are seen as simply another marketing tool. It is already difficult for PR practitioners to maintain perceptions of honesty and believability on the part of the audience, and lumping the PR department with marketing will make the problem even worse. Another argument suggests that IMC hurts the diversity of opinion available to management. A separate PR department makes it more likely that different suggestions and alternative courses of action will be advanced. Finally, opponents argue that PR involves two-way communication that takes into account the needs of various publics, whereas IMC treats everybody as a customer and places top priority on sales.

One of the struggles for the industry in the years to come will be the development of a structure that recognizes the unique contributions of each of the departments that make up the modern organization.

economic climate, also used good public relations practices to its advantage. President Franklin Roosevelt introduced his New Deal reform program complete with promotional campaigns to win public acceptance. Roosevelt also recognized the tremendous potential of radio in shaping public opinion, and his radio-broadcasted fireside chats were memorable examples of personal public relations. The government intensified its public relations efforts during World War II with the creation of the Office of War Information.

During the second half of the 20th century, changes in American society created an atmosphere in which public relations grew tremendously in importance. What are some of the reasons behind the recent surge in this area?

- Many corporations recognized that they had a social responsibility to serve the public. Finding the means of fulfilling this responsibility was the task of the public relations department.

- A growing tide of consumerism caused many corporations and government agencies to be more responsive to and communicative with their customers or clients, a function served by the public relations department.

- The growing complexity of modern corporations and government agencies made it difficult for them to get their messages to the public without a department that was specifically assigned that task.

- Increasing population growth along with more specialization and job mobility made it necessary for companies to employ communication specialists whose task it was to interpret the needs of the audience for the organization.

All these trends have combined to make the past 50 or so years the "era of public relations." The profession grew from about 19,000 members in 1950 to more than 200,000 in the United States and 300,000 worldwide in 2011. Along with this growth has come increased professionalization among public relations practitioners. The Public Relations Society of America, founded in 1947, adopted a code of standards in 1954. Public relations education has also made great strides. Recent estimates suggest that about 400 colleges across the country offer courses in public relations. In 1967 the Public Relations Student Society of America was founded. It now has 300 chapters and 10,000 members.

The past decade has seen public relations become even more important. Spin doctors, specialists in political public relations, have assumed prominence in political campaigns and government activities. The Bush administration used public relations extensively to gather public support for Operation Iraqi Freedom in 2003. One facet of this program was the "embedding" of more than 500 journalists with military units to provide firsthand accounts of the action. In the business sector the accounting scandals at major corporations such as Enron, Global Crossing, and Arthur Andersen increased the need for better public relations in order to restore confidence in a company's financial reports and to make top executives more responsible to their employees and shareholders.

The recession at the end of the 2000s caused some firms to cut the amount they spent on general public relations activities, but overall the public relations industry was in fairly good financial shape by 2011. Competition for jobs in public relations increased but there were still opportunities to be found.

The beginning of the new decade highlighted several developments in the field. One was the increasing importance of public relations during a crisis. In addition to BP, Toyota and golfer Tiger Woods had to deal with unfavorable publicity and attempt to remake their images. Second, public relations firms adopted social media as a new channel for clients to build relationships with their publics. It was rare to find an agency or a PR campaign that did not emphasize social media as part of its strategy. Third, tablet computers and other mobile devices are becoming more important and public relations practitioners are searching for ways to use them effectively. There are apps that are helpful to public relations professionals, such as Instapaper and Dragon Dictation. Further, brands such as Nike, Pampers, and Purina have developed apps that engage the consumer and offer new ways to connect with their brand.

public relations in the digital age

The Internet has added several new dimensions to public relations. It has opened up new channels of communication between organizations and the public and between public relations practitioners and the media. It has also become a major channel of feedback for organizations interested in their public image.

Communicating with the Audience: Web Sites, Podcasts, and Blogs

Public relations practitioners use a number of Web tools to help clients communicate with their publics.

Corporate Web sites have evolved from sites that were primarily designed to sell a product and have become a significant channel of communications for brands and their consumers and shareholders. In mid-2011, the Levi Strauss Web site, for example, had a section on how Levi's was striving to improve the living standards of garment workers across the globe and a sustainability division that detailed the company's efforts to preserve the environment.

Public relations firms are counseling their clients to build in more interactive features and video to their sites. The Mercedes Benz Web site opens with a video montage and the rest of the site is built around the theme "What Drives Us." Visitors can then click on a variety of options that show animations of the car's innovative design and fuel efficiency. Many corporations use podcasts as a public relations tool. BMW has 100 video podcasts available for free on iTunes. Other corporations rely on company blogs. Dairy Queen uses its blog to offer deals on products and has a section where DQ fans can post comments, stories, and other information. Even customer gripes are attended to. A recent post grumbled that the new DQ TV ads weren't funny; the company responded by trying to point that the main purpose of the ads was not humor but to show that Dairy Queen products were ri"DQ"ulously good.

Communicating with the Audience: Social Media

In 2010–2011 it seemed that every public relations trade magazine or blog had an article about how public relations professionals should use social media. This development indicates two things. First, companies and organizations are turning more and more to social media rather than Web sites and blogs to get across their messages. Big companies such as General Motors or the neighborhood restaurant down the street all have Facebook pages and Twitter accounts. Politicians have also adopted social media. Local and national representatives use social media to stay in touch with voters. The election of Barack Obama in 2008 was due in part to his campaign's use of social media. The White House has its own blog, Facebook page, and is on Twitter. Second, the responsibility for planning and executing social media strategies has largely fallen to the public relations department or agency rather than the marketing department, making public relations an even more important function for organizations.

It's not surprising that organizations have embraced social media. They represent a direct link to the consumer and encourage two-way communication. Traditional media, such as newspapers and TV, were one-way channels. Marketers sent the messages and the consumer received them. Feedback was slow and minimal. Social media allow immediate interaction between an organization and its publics. If a company's public relations efforts are misfiring, comments on the various social media sites will let the company know about it, as was illustrated by the BP example in the opening of the chapter.

There are several ways that social media can be helpful in public relations:

- They can serve as an early warning system. Monitoring social media can give a company information about potential problems with its product or service. For example, problems with the diabetes drug Avandia first surfaced on social media sites before medical studies confirmed the risk.
- They can provide information about the launch of new products or services. When Verizon introduced the Verizon wireless iPhone, it examined mentions of the new phone on Twitter, Facebook, YouTube, Flickr, and blogs. The company found that the most discussed issues concerned pricing and whether it made economic sense to switch from AT&T to Verizon. Subsequent public relations and marketing efforts were directed toward responding to these issues.
- They can help deal with complaints. Delta Airlines monitors its Twitter account to address customers' problems, from changing flights to tracing lost luggage.
- They can provide new connections between a company and its customers. H&R Block's Facebook page and Twitter feed answer tax questions, explain changes in tax law, and provide general financial information. The company also has an app for the Android and iPhone. Old Navy describes its Facebook page as "an online hangout for the Old Navy community. Learn about upcoming sales, new styles, contests, promotions and more. If you feel so inclined, leave us a comment or ask a question on our wall." The company also uses the site to offer special deals and coupons.

Of course, every innovation has advantages and disadvantages, and the same holds true when using social media for public relations. First, public relations firms must devote extra time and energy to monitoring social media sites and responding to questions and problems. This is not an easy task. Imagine how hard it would be to monitor every time the name of a company or an organization popped up on Facebook, Twitter, or Linkedin, was mentioned in a blog, or was the subject of a YouTube video. In addition, just counting mentions doesn't give a complete picture. For this feedback to be truly useful, the company would need to know specific information about each mention, such as the context and whether the mention was favorable, unfavorable, or neutral. There are professional monitoring firms that will provide such an analysis, but their services are not cheap.

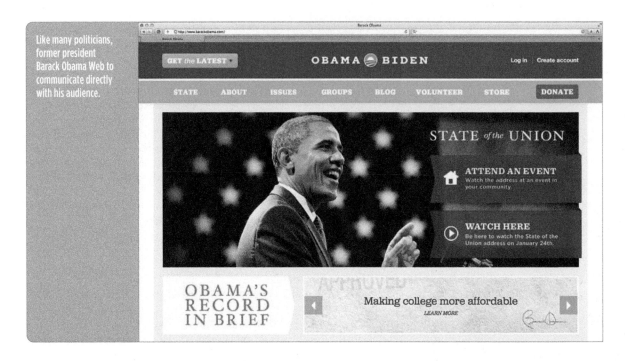

Like many politicians, former president Barack Obama Web to communicate directly with his audience.

Second, it's easy to overestimate the impact of social media. Measuring their effectiveness is a difficult task, and having a lot of Facebook fans and Twitter followers does not necessarily translate into more sales or better public relations for a company or organization. Social media are obviously helpful, but they should be employed intelligently as part of the overall public relations plan.

Third, companies must draw up new policies regarding the use of social media. In order to comply with federal regulations, when public relations professionals respond to comments or take part in discussions on behalf of their clients, they must identify whom they represent. For example, "My name is John and I work for AT&T." In addition, companies need policies for their own employees' use of social media. A thoughtless "tweet" sent over a company account can come back to haunt those involved, as happened when a Chrysler employee mistakenly sent out an obscene tweet over a company account.

Fourth, a bad corporate mistake can explode in a hurry and create big public relations problems for a company, as was the case mentioned above involving Chrysler. Thanks to Twitter and Facebook, one corporate miscue can quickly snowball into a public relations disaster and companies and their public relations firms have to be prepared to respond quickly to any problem.

Communicating with the Media

It didn't take long for public relations practitioners to start using the Internet to streamline their media efforts. E-mail and Facebook press releases have replaced the traditional paper-mail releases, and e-mail and Twitter rather than the telephone have become the preferred means of communication between journalists and public relations professionals. Further, the Web has become an important channel in distributing information to the media. PR Newswire's Web site, for example, collects information from agencies and public relations departments and makes this information available to newsrooms across the country. A PR Newswire app for the iPhone and iPad allows press releases to be distributed via mobile media. Practitioners can also distribute photos and video clips via the Internet.

The Internet has made it easier for professionals to target their story proposals and press releases to the appropriate sources. A search engine makes it simple to research a given journalist's recent articles to see what kinds of topics he or she might be interested

media *Full Disclosure?*
Probe

The word *pundit* is derived from a Hindu word that means "learned." Today a pundit is an expert who offers analysis and commentary on a particular area to some mass media outlet, frequently a cable news channel. Ideally, pundits should offer their objective opinions and analysis. But what does the audience know about these pundits? Most are introduced as former leaders of industry or the military or simply identified as a Republican or Democratic strategist. But do they have other ties that might lead them to tilt their views toward a particular policy or course of action?

An analysis done by *The Nation* magazine in 2010 found that since 2007 at least 75 lobbyists, public relations representatives, and corporate offices had given their views on cable news channels. These pundits were being paid by corporations, trade groups, and other organizations to promote their image and interests but none of this was disclosed by the cable news networks. For example, during the scandal over the high bonuses paid to executives at insurance company AIG, several individuals who were lobbyists paid by the insurance industry or worked for PR firms that represented insurance companies appeared on cable news programs to discuss the financial crisis that rocked AIG.

In response to the revelations, Fairness and Accuracy in Reporting, a group that specializes in media criticism, circulated a petition urging cable news networks to disclose fully the corporate ties of the pundits who appear on their programs. Although some cable nets have established guidelines concerning full disclosure, they have not always been followed.

The next time you watch a program on Fox, CNN, MSNBC, CNBC, or other channels that feature pundits, check to see if their ties to industry are revealed.

in. Some online Web sites track journalists' job movements. A reporter just starting a new assignment might be particularly interested in story ideas. Finally, database software and e-mail merge programs make it possible for practitioners to efficiently target possible outlets for stories.

New social media tools have added new ways for practitioners to communicate with the media and with themselves. For example, helpareporter.com and its Facebook page let reporters submit questions to PR professionals. The Public Relations Society of America lets its members communicate with one another on its Facebook page, Twitter feed, and Linkedin account.

organization of the public relations industry

Public relations activities are generally handled in two ways. Many organizations have their own public relations departments that work with the managers of all other departments. About 85 percent of the 1,500 largest U.S. companies have such departments. In many companies these departments are part of top management, and the PR director is responsible to the president of the company. For example, General Motors and General Electric both employ about 100 people in their U.S. PR departments. Other organizations hire an external public relations counsel to give advice on press, government, and consumer relations. In business and industry, about one-third of the PR activity is handled by outside counseling firms. Many major corporations retain an outside agency in addition to their own internal public relations department.

Each of these arrangements has its particular advantages and disadvantages. An in-house department can be at work on short notice and has in-depth knowledge about the company; in addition, its operations tend to be less costly. On the other hand, it is hard for a corporate PR team to take an objective view of the company. Further, internal PR departments tend to have trouble coming up with fresh ideas unless

Many organizations have their own public relations departments that have in-depth knowledge about the company.

new personnel are added frequently. An outside agency offers more services to its clients than does an internal department. Additionally, external counselors have the advantage of being objective observers, and many firms like the prestige associated with being a client of a respected PR firm. On the other side of the coin, outside agencies are expensive, it takes time for them to learn the inner workings of their client's operations, and their involvement may cause resentment and morale problems among the staff of the client's organization.

Internal or external, public relations professionals perform a wide range of services. These include counseling management, preparing annual reports, handling news releases and other forms of media coverage, supervising employee and other internal communications, managing promotions and special events, fund-raising, lobbying, handling community relations, publishing blogs, creating Web sites, administering social media sites, and writing speeches.

Public relations is practiced in a variety of settings. Although the general principles are the same, the actual duties of the PR practitioner will vary according to the setting. Following are brief descriptions of a "baker's dozen" areas in which public relations is practiced:

1. *Business:* Public relations helps the marketing process by instilling in consumers a positive attitude toward the company. Public relations also helps promote healthy employee-management relations and serves as a major liaison between the firm and government regulators. Further, all businesses have to be located somewhere, and the PR department makes sure the company is a good citizen in its community.

2. *Government:* Many government agencies hire PR specialists to help them explain their activities to citizens and to assist the news media in their coverage of the different agencies. These same specialists also communicate the opinions of the public back to the agency. Government PR is big business; its total expenditures on public information rival the budgets of the four major TV networks. The Department of Defense, for instance, produces thousands of films and TV programs every year. The Department of Agriculture sends out thousands of news releases annually. Members of the Senate and the House make extensive use of public relations, particularly social media channels.

3. *Education:* PR personnel work in both elementary and higher education. The most visible area of practice in elementary and high school concerns facilitating communication between educators and parents. Other tasks, however, are no less important. In many school systems the PR person also handles relations with the school board, local and state legislative bodies, and the news media. Public relations at the college and university level, although less concerned with parental relations, has its own set of tasks. Fund-raising, legislative relations, community relations, and internal relations with faculty and students would be concerns of most college PR departments.

4. *Hospitals:* The rising cost of health care and greater public expectations of the medical profession have given increased visibility to the PR departments in our nation's hospitals. Some of the publics that hospital PR staffs have to deal with are patients, patients' families, consumers, state insurance commissions, physicians, nurses, and other staff members. Despite the increasing importance of hospital public relations, many hospitals do not have a full-time PR staff. Consequently, this is another area that should see significant growth in the future.

5. *Nonprofit organizations:* The United Way, the Girl Scouts, the American Red Cross, and the Salvation Army are just a few of the organizations that need PR professionals. Probably the biggest PR goal in organizations such as these is fund-raising. Other objectives include encouraging volunteer participation, informing contributors how their money is spent, and working with the individuals served by an organization.

6. *Professional associations:* Organizations such as the American Medical Association, the American Dairy Association, and the American Bar Association employ PR

practitioners. In addition to providing news and information to the association's members, other duties of the PR staff are recruiting new members, planning national conferences, influencing government decisions, and working with the news media.

7. *Entertainment and sports:* A significant number of PR experts work for established and would-be celebrities in the entertainment and sports worlds. A practitioner handling this type of client has two major responsibilities: Get the client favorable media coverage, and protect the client from bad publicity. Additionally, many sports and entertainment events (such as the Super Bowl, or a motion picture premiere) have PR campaigns associated with them.

8. *International PR:* Corporations with branches throughout the world, global news media such as CNN, an interrelated world economy, the shifting political scene in Europe—all these factors have combined to make this area one of the fastest growing in public relations. International PR specialists help businesses operating in other countries with local customs, language problems, cultural difficulties, and legal dilemmas.

9. *Investor relations:* This area (called *IR* for convenience) entails building a favorable image for a company and keeping shareholders happy. A public company needs to communicate information, both positive and negative, that might have an impact on its stock price to the financial community in general and shareholders in particular. To do this effectively, IR professionals must know the workings of the financial press and the various channels used to communicate with shareholders, such as annual reports, quarterly reports, and annual meetings. As more and more Americans invest in the stock and bond markets and as financial markets become more global, the importance of IR will surely increase.

10. *Politics:* The importance of PR in political campaigns increases with every election. Building the right personal image, putting the proper spin on the interpretation of events, and responding to the charges of other candidates are all part of the job of a political PR specialist. Many PR firms specialize in political campaigns.

11. *Environment:* Global warming, water conservation, recycling, energy conservation, and other environmental issues have made this area extremely visible in recent years. Practitioners represent both advocacy groups and industries.

12. *Crisis management:* Probably the ultimate test for the PR practitioner is dealing with a crisis. Such crises arise infrequently, but poor handling of a crisis can have long-term negative effects that might cripple a company and/or ruin the reputation of a PR firm. In a crisis the public seeks more information, and the organization involved in the crisis is subjected to increased scrutiny by both the media and the public. Experts in crisis management PR generally counsel their clients to accomplish three goals: terminate the crisis, limit damage, and restore credibility.

13. *Digital public relations:* This is a fast-growing field in which PR professionals manage the digital presence of their clients, including preparing e-mail newsletters, handling social media, writing blogs, and preparing podcasts. Several public relations agencies, such as Weber Shandwick and Coyne PR, specialize in this area.

As this list suggests, the profession requires PR specialists as well as generalists. In the next section, we will see how the PR function is typically organized and what jobs PR professionals perform.

pr departments and staff

At the outset, remember that no two companies have the same exact departmental structure. In one common arrangement for an internal corporate PR department, the director of public relations reports directly to the president of the company. Since PR affects every department, its supervision by the person who runs the entire organization makes sense. Nonetheless, some organizations endorse integrated marketing communications, which puts the PR department in the marketing division. A recent survey noted that about 40 percent of PR departments report to the CEO while 32 percent report to the head of the marketing department. The PR department is further subdivided into three main divisions that are designed to communicate with both internal and external publics: (1) corporate communications, (2) community relations, and (3) press relations. The corporate communications division handles communication with internal publics (workers, shareholders, unions), and the community relations division deals with external publics (community residents, customers, the government). As its name suggests, the press relations division deals with the news media.

The organization of an external PR agency is more complex. One possible arrangement consists of five departments:

1. *Creative services:* Is responsible for ideas and the production of press releases and audio/video media.
2. *Research:* Supervises survey research, focus groups, and data collection.
3. *Publicity and marketing:* Takes charge of merchandising and sales promotions.
4. *Accounts:* Oversees and coordinates relations with clients.
5. *Administration:* Is responsible for the day-to-day personnel, clerical, legal, and financial tasks that keep a business running.

The personnel at a public relations firm include a president and several vice presidents. To succeed in public relations it is necessary for a firm to continually seek out new business or increase the amount of business it does with current clients. The top executives at a PR firm usually spend a good deal of time meeting with prospective clients, preparing proposals, and making presentations.

Account supervisors manage one large account or a number of smaller ones. They are responsible for budgeting, quality control, and managing the workload of project teams. An account executive is responsible for the day-to-day operations involved in dealing with a client. Assistant account executives handle routine work such as writing press releases and conducting basic research.

Firms usually put together account teams to handle large-scale public relations campaigns. Teams may include creative personnel, graphic artists, market researchers, social media designers, and experts in setting up media tours and special events.

the public relations program

Imagine that you are the public relations director for a leading automaker. The company is entering into an agreement with a foreign car manufacturer to produce a foreign model in the United States. Unfortunately, to increase efficiency and centralize its operations, the company will have to close one of its plants located in a midwestern city. About 1,000 employees will have to be transferred or find new jobs, and the community will face a significant economic blow. It will be the job of the public relations department to communicate this decision to the community.

The thorny problem just outlined is a typical one for the public relations professional. Handling it requires a planned, organized, and efficient public relations program. This section will trace the four main steps involved in developing a typical PR campaign: (1) information gathering, (2) planning, (3) communication, and (4) evaluation.

Information Gathering
The information-gathering stage is an important one because what is learned from it will influence the remaining stages. **Information gathering** can be achieved through several means. Organizational records, trade journals, public records, and reference books serve as valuable sources of data. Personal contacts, mail to the company, advisory committees,

media *Probe*   *How Ethical Are Public Relations Professionals?*

That was the question asked by a couple of communication researchers who were interested in seeing how public relations practitioners stacked up against other groups of people when it came to ethical decision making.[1] The researchers administered the Defining Issues Test (DIT) to a sample of 118 professionals employed at leading public relations agencies. The DIT is a standardized test that has been administered to thousands of people over

[1]Renita Coleman and Lee Wilkins, "The Moral Development of Public Relations Practitioners: A Comparison With Other Professions and Influences on Higher Quality Ethical Reasoning," *Journal of Public Relations Research*, Vol. 21, No. 3, pp. 318–340 (2009).

the last four decades. The test presents respondents with ethical dilemmas and asks them to rank 12 statements according to the statements' importance in the respondents' decision making. The 12 statements reflect varying levels of ethical development. The scores are then tabulated and compared to the scores of other groups.

Overall, public relations professionals scored pretty well. Their average DIT score was 46 compared to a score of 40 for the general adult population. Seminarians and philosophers ranked highest on the test (not much of a surprise) with a score of 65. Medical students and practicing physicians ranked next, followed by journalists and dental students. Undergraduate students came in with a score of 43, just ahead of business professionals and sailors. The group that scored the lowest: junior high school students.

and personnel reports represent other sources of information. If more formal research methods are required, they might be carried out by the PR department or by an outside agency that specializes in public opinion polling or survey research. Return to our example. The PR director at the auto company will need to gather a great deal of information. How much will the company save by its reorganization? Exactly how many workers will be transferred? Will the company help find new jobs for the workers who will be unemployed? What will be the precise economic impact on the community? What will become of the empty buildings that will be left behind? Will the employees believe what the company tells them? What do people expect from the company? Will the company's image be hurt in other areas of the United States?

Planning

Phase 2 is the planning stage. There are two general types of planning: **strategic** and **tactical**. Strategic plans involve long-range, general goals that the organization wishes to achieve. Top management usually formulates an organization's strategic plans. Tactical plans are more specific. They detail the tasks that must be accomplished by every department in the organization to achieve the strategic goals. Some plans that are drawn up might be used only once; others might serve as standing plans that set general organizational policy.

Planning is a vital part of the PR program. Some of the items involved in a PR campaign are framing the objectives, considering the alternatives, assessing the risks and benefits involved in each alternative, deciding on a course of action, figuring out the budget, and securing the necessary approvals from within the organization. In recent years many PR practitioners have endorsed a technique known as **management by objectives (MBO)**. Simply put, MBO means that the organization sets observable and measurable goals for itself and allocates its resources to meet those objectives. For example, a corporation might set as a goal increasing sales by 25 percent over the next 2 years. When the time had elapsed, it would be easy to see if the goal had been achieved. This approach is becoming more popular in PR because top management typically thinks in these terms, and if PR practitioners speak the same language as chief executives, they can communicate more effectively with them. It also keeps the department on target in solving PR problems, and it provides concrete feedback about the efficiency of the PR process. In our hypothetical example, some objectives might be informing more than 50 percent of the community about the reasons for the move and making sure community and national attitudes about the company are not adversely affected.

Communication

Phase 3 is the communication phase. After gathering facts and making plans, the organization assumes the role of the source of communication. Several key decisions are made at this stage concerning the nature of the messages and the types of media to be used. Because mass communication media are usually important channels in a PR program, it is necessary for public relations practitioners to have a thorough knowledge of the various media and their strengths and weaknesses. Moreover, PR professionals should know the various production techniques for the print and broadcast media. Some common ways of publicizing a message through the mass media are press releases, video news releases, press kits, photographs, paid advertising, films, videotapes, press conferences, and interviews.

Public relations also makes use of other channels to get messages to its publics. These include both the interpersonal and the machine-assisted settings. House publications, brochures, faxes, letters, bulletins, posters, Web sites, blogs, social media, e-mail, billboards, and bulletin boards are communication channels used by a company to reach its own employees. Social media such as Twitter and Facebook could be used to disseminate daily updates and answer questions. A video posted on the company Web site and/or YouTube might also help explain the situation. On a more personal level, public meetings, speeches, demonstrations, staged events, open houses, and tours are other possibilities.

In our hypothetical example, the PR director would probably use a variety of messages and media. News conferences, ads, press releases, social media, and public meetings would be appropriate vehicles for explaining the company's position to its external public. Meanwhile, house publications, bulletin boards, speeches, and letters could be used to reach its internal public.

Evaluation

The last phase concerns **evaluation** of the PR program. How well did it work? The importance of evaluation in public relations is increasing through the use of MBO techniques. If a measurable goal was proposed for the PR program, then an evaluation

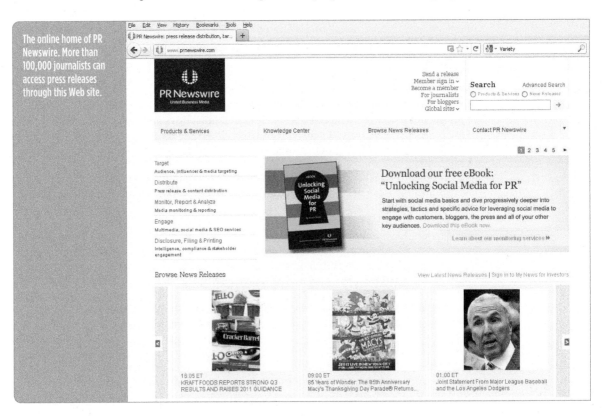

The online home of PR Newswire. More than 100,000 journalists can access press releases through this Web site.

ethical issues   *Negative Public Relations*

Is it ethical for a public relations firm to promote negative stories about one of its client's competitors? Google and Facebook are fierce rivals as both battle for Internet supremacy and the increased revenue that goes with it. In 2011, Facebook hired well-known public relations firm Burson-Marsteller to pitch stories to leading newspapers, including the *Washington Post* and *USA Today,* and to influential bloggers about Google's privacy policies.

Burson-Marsteller representatives offered information and assistance to columnists and bloggers to help them write stories about Google's Social Circle (Google's attempt to compete with Facebook). The main point of the proposed story was that Social Circle was secretly collecting data about its users that would be provided to advertisers and marketers. When asked if they were pitching the story for a specific client, the Burson-Martseller representatives refused to disclose the client's identity.

The full story came to light when an influential blogger released a series of his e-mails to the public relations company questioning the identity of their client. Facebook later admitted that it had hired Burson-Marsteller to pitch the negative story and had asked the public relations firm not to identify Facebook as its client.

This episode raises several ethical issues. First, is it ethical for a public relations firm to promote negative stories about a rival? If the information is publicly available, easily accessed, and independently verified, then there appears to be no ethical problem. But what if the information in the proposed story is exaggerated or blown out of proportion? This was one of the problems in the Facebook episode. The story was slanted in such a way that the real danger of privacy invasion was overstated. In fact, the hyped nature of the story led news outlets to suspect that Facebook was behind the campaign. Public relations organizations have an obligation to be truthful and fair when pitching story ideas to the media. Finally, the biggest ethical issue raised in this case was keeping the client secret. This was ultimately the reason that Burson-Marsteller canceled the deal with Facebook. As a Burson-Marsteller representative put it, "When talking to the media, we need to adhere to strict standards of transparency about clients and this incidence underscores the absolute importance of that principle."

technique should be able to measure success in reaching that goal. Several different aspects might be measured. One easy method is simply to gauge the volume of coverage that the campaign generated. The number of press releases sent out, letters mailed, speeches made, and so on are simple to compute. In like manner, press clippings and mentions in TV and radio news can be tabulated. It is important to remember, however, that volume does not equal results. A million press clippings mean nothing if they are not read by the audience. Measuring the impact of a campaign on the audience requires more sophisticated techniques of analysis. Some common techniques are questionnaires distributed to random samples of the audience, telephone and Web surveys, panels, reader-interest studies, and experimental campaigns. It is likely that our hypothetical PR director would use many of these techniques.

Before closing, we should note that we have been talking about these four steps as though they were distinct stages. In actuality the PR program is a continuous process, with one phase blending into the next. The results learned in the evaluation stage, for example, are also part of the information-gathering phase of the next cycle of the PR program. In our car company example, the PR department would use the results of surveys and focus groups to determine whether the company's image had suffered, how much credibility the company had with consumers, and if there were any change in customer loyalty. These findings would help in planning the goals of the next PR campaign.

the economics of public relations

The total amount of money spent on corporate public relations activity is hard to measure, but some information is available about the revenues of PR agencies. In 2010 the top 50 independent PR firms in the United States collected about $1.46 billion, up 4 percent from 2008.

The industry is dominated by giant PR firms owned by ad agencies. As of 2011, the biggest PR firms with ad agency parent companies were Porter-Novelli and Fleischman-Hillard (part of the Omnicom Group) and Hill & Knowlton and Burson-Marsteller (part of the WPP Group). The two largest independent PR firms were Edelman and Ruder Finn.

The PR business can be volatile, especially for smaller agencies, whose fee income might vary by 40–80 percent from year to year.

PR agencies earn their fees in a variety of ways. Some perform specific projects for specific fees. An annual report, for example, might cost $10,000. Some charge their clients a retainer every month, which might range from a few hundred dollars to considerably more. Other firms keep track of time spent on various projects and charge clients an hourly rate. Still others bill for time plus for extra services and materials.

public relations

 CAREER >>
OUTLOOK

Job prospects in public relations will continue to improve as the economy recovers. Industry statistics show that jobs at public relations firms increased from 2006 to 2010. The Bureau of Labor Statistics predicts that the upward trend should continue well into 2018.

The career outlook in the various media industries changes quickly. For a more current description of conditions in the public relations industry and a more detailed look at career options, please consult the book's Web site: www.mhhe.com/dominick12e.

main points

- *Public relations* is difficult to define, but most practitioners agree that PR involves counseling management about communication strategies that can improve public opinion about an organization.

- Modern public relations began around the turn of the 20th century and has steadily increased in importance.

- The Internet is an important part of PR. It is used to provide information to the public and to obtain background information for PR professionals.

- Social media have become more important in public relations.

- PR is practiced in numerous settings, including business, government, and the nonprofit sector.

- A PR campaign consists of the following stages: information gathering, planning, communication, and evaluation.

questions for review

1. Define *public relations*.
2. What are some of the major areas that make use of public relations?

3. What are the stages in a public relations campaign?
4. How have social media changed the practice of public relations?

questions for critical thinking

1. Can you think of any examples of your using PR in your personal life (like putting the best spin on a bad grade in a course)?
2. Why is the term *public relations* so hard to define? Is it important to have a definition that everybody agrees on?

3. How much faith does the public have in the credibility of PR professionals?
4. Many journalists look with disfavor on the field of public relations. What might account for this attitude?

key terms

publicity (p. 331)   strategic (planning) (p. 342)   evaluation (p. 343)

publics (p. 331)   tactical (planning) (p. 342)

information gathering (p. 341)   management by objectives (MBO) (p. 342)

internet resources

Online Learning Center

On the Online Learning Center home page, www.mhhe.com/dominick12e, *select* Student Center *and then* Chapter 14.

1. Use the Learning Objectives, Chapter Outline, and Main Points sections to review this chapter.

2. Test your knowledge of the chapter using the multiple choice and flashcard features of the site.

3. Expand your knowledge of concepts and topics discussed in the chapter with additional Questions for Critical Thinking and Internet Exercises.

surfing the internet

Some of these sites are mentioned in the text. Others appear first on this list. Remember that the Web is always changing. Some sites move, some change their focus, and others simply evaporate.

http://ewatch.prnewswire.com
A site that tracks what the media, investors, consumers, and the competition are saying about an organization.

www.ketchum.com
The home page of Ketchum Public Relations Worldwide. Includes a description of the company, and links to its blogs and Facebook page.

http://aboutpublicrelations.net
A how-to-do-it site for those interested in public relations.

www.prmuseum.com
A museum of public relations. Contains extensive information on the pioneers of PR.

www.prsa.org
The home page of the Public Relations Society of America. Includes general information about the society, a list of relevant publications, and a link to the PR student society. A recently added feature enables members to post their résumés in cyberspace.

www.prssa.org
The site of the Public Relations Student Society of America. A good site for information on jobs and internships.

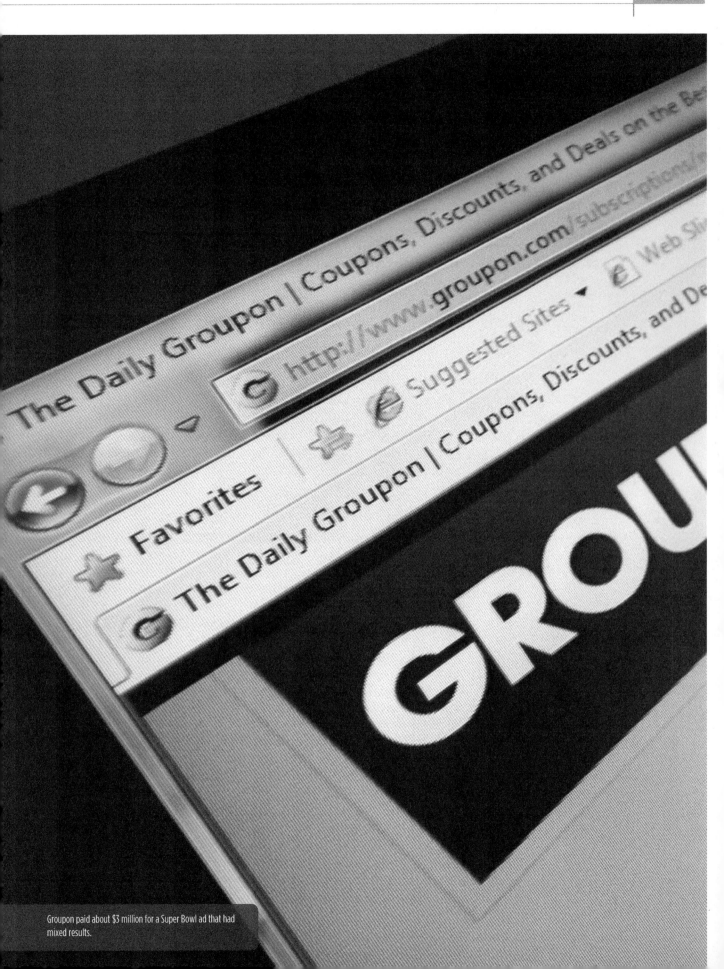

Groupon paid about $3 million for a Super Bowl ad that had mixed results.

Chapter**15**

advertising

This chapter will prepare you to:

- define *advertising* and explain how it is classified
- explain how advertising developed
- recognize the impact the Internet has had on advertising
- distinguish among the three main components of the advertising industry
- discuss the components of an advertising campaign

Groupon, a social shopping Web site that offers daily deals and discounts, was launched in 2008 and quickly became a huge success. By 2010, it had amassed 35 million members across the globe. Most of Groupon's early advertising efforts relied on online ads, but in 2011 it decided to go into television advertising in a big way by launching a TV ad campaign on Super Bowl Sunday. Groupon hired Crispin, Porter & Bogusky (CP&B), an agency known for its edgy commercials, to create ads for the campaign. (Crispin, Porter & Bogusky was the agency that put together Burger King's "Whopper Virgins" campaign, which featured a taste test with people who had never tasted a Whopper, such as poor villagers in Thailand and Transylvanian farmers. CP&B also created the Domino's campaign in which a Domino's executive admitted his pizzas had historically been terrible.)

CP&B came up with an equally edgy idea for Groupon. The agency produced three ads that satirized the use of celebrity spokespeople in ads for humanitarian causes. One ad featured Cuba Gooding Jr. bemoaning the fate of the whales and then touting a discount on a whale-watching boat ride. In another, Elizabeth Hurley talked about the deforestation of the Brazilian rain forest and then quickly touted a 50 percent discount on a Brazilian wax in New York City. Probably the most controversial ad that aired during the game (at a cost of about $3 million) starred Timothy Hutton warning that the people of Tibet are in trouble and are losing their culture. He then abruptly shifted tone and mentioned a great deal on Tibetan food at a Chicago restaurant.

The reaction to the ads probably surprised Groupon. Postings on Twitter and Facebook accused the company of trivializing tragedy and exploiting charitable causes. Critics started a Facebook group called "Shame on You Groupon." Many Twitter users tweeted false ads making fun of the company. A survey on viewer reaction to Super Bowl ads found that audience sentiment was negative and many subscribers felt like canceling their membership.

Groupon initially defended its efforts, saying that the messages were benevolent and meant in jest. The company also noted that it was planning to make donations to related charitable groups. That wasn't enough for most people, and the negative buzz on social media continued for a week until finally Groupon pulled the ads off the air. The chief executive at Groupon apologized and announced it was not renewing its contract with CP&B.

What can we learn from this episode about today's advertising industry? Obviously, a client shouldn't take the risk of creating an edgy campaign if it is not ready for the criticism that is likely to result. Second, in today's social media environment, negative reaction to an ad can be swift and self-perpetuating.

This chapter examines the history, structure, operation, and social impact of the ever-changing world of advertising.

defining advertising

Simply defined, *advertising* is any form of nonpersonal presentation and promotion of ideas, goods, and services, usually paid for by an identified sponsor. Note three key terms in this definition. First, advertising is "nonpersonal"; it is directed toward a large group of anonymous people. Even direct-mail advertising, which may be addressed to a specific person, is prepared by a computer and signed by a machine. Second, advertising typically is "paid for." This fact differentiates advertising from publicity, which is not usually purchased. Sponsors such as Coke and Delta pay for the time and the space they use to get their message across. (Nonprofit organizations, such as the Red Cross and the United Way, advertise but do not pay for time or space. Broadcast stations, newspapers, and magazines run these ads free as a public service.) Third, for obvious reasons, the sponsor of the ad is "identified." In fact, in most instances, identifying the sponsor is the prime purpose behind the ad—otherwise, why advertise? Perhaps the only type of advertising in which the identity of the advertiser may not be self-evident is political advertising. Because of this, broadcasters and publishers will not accept a political ad without a statement identifying those responsible for it.

Before we leave this topic, it should be noted that in the 21st century this definition of advertising has gotten a little blurry around the edges. Many practitioners consider advertising part of the overall marketing mix, along with promotion, branding, word of mouth, and public relations. (Note how this approach is consistent with the integrated marketing communication, or IMC, philosophy mentioned in the previous chapter.) Taking that view, differentiating advertising from other forms of marketing is not particularly useful.

Functions of Advertising

Advertising fulfills five basic functions in society. First, it serves a marketing function by helping companies that provide products or services sell their products. Personal selling, sales promotions, and advertising work together to help market the product. Second, advertising is educational. People learn about new products and services, or improvements to existing ones, through advertising. Third, advertising plays an economic role. The ability to advertise

An example of a primary demand ad. The "got milk?" campaign was designed to promote milk drinking, not the purchase of a particular brand of milk.

enables new competitors to enter the business arena. Competition, in turn, encourages product improvements and can lead to lower prices. Fourth, advertising reaches a mass audience, thus greatly reducing the cost of personal selling and distribution. Finally, advertising performs a definite social function. By vividly displaying the material and cultural opportunities available in a free-enterprise society, advertising helps increase productivity and raise the standard of living.

Types of Advertising

Advertising can be classified in several ways. One useful approach is to identify the **target audience**—the specific segment of the population to which the product or service has a definite appeal. Many target audiences can be defined; the most general are consumers and businesses. **Consumer advertising**, as the name suggests, is targeted at the people who buy goods and services for personal use. For example, Campbell's (known for its soups) uses consumer advertising to direct its ads to the adults and children most likely to buy soup at the grocery store. Most of the advertising that people are exposed to falls into this category. **Business-to-business advertising** is aimed at people who buy products for business use. Industrial, trade, and professional—as well as agricultural—advertising are all part of this category. Consumer advertising is the focus of most of this chapter, but we will also take a brief look at business-to-business advertising.

Geographic focus is another way to classify advertising. International advertising is employed for products and services that are used all over the globe. Coca-Cola and McDonald's, for example, advertise in dozens of countries and in many different languages. National advertising is advertising in many different regions of the same country. Delta, Wal-Mart, and Sprint, for example, run ads on TV networks and in national magazines to reach customers in many different markets across the United States. International advertisers, of course, also use national ads. Retail or local advertising is done within one specific market. The neighborhood restaurant or car dealership typically relies on local ads.

Yet a third way to categorize advertising is by purpose. Some ads are for specific products or services, such as frozen pizzas or muffler repairs, while others try to improve a company's image or influence public opinion on an issue, such as the ads run by oil companies describing their efforts to keep down fuel costs. Another distinction involves primary demand and selective demand ads. A **primary demand ad** has as its purpose the promotion of a particular product category rather than a specific brand. The campaign to encourage milk drinking that shows various celebrities with milk moustaches is an example of this type. A **selective demand ad** is used by an individual company to sell its particular brand, such as a certain brand of milk. Finally, ads can be classified as direct action and indirect action. A **direct action ad** usually contains a toll-free number, coupon, e-mail or Web address, or some similar device to enable the advertiser to see results quickly. In contrast, an **indirect action ad** works over the long run to build a company's image and increase consumer awareness.

a brief history

Advertising's beginnings are impossible to pinpoint, but several examples date back thousands of years. Clay tablets traced to ancient Babylon have been found with messages that touted an ointment dealer and a shoemaker. The town crier was an important advertising medium throughout England and other countries in Europe during the medieval period.

In more recent times, the history of advertising is inextricably entwined with changing social conditions and advances in media technology. For instance, Gutenberg's invention of printing using movable type made possible several new advertising media: posters, handbills, and newspaper ads. The first printed advertisement in English, produced about 1480, was a handbill that announced a prayer book for sale. Its author, evidently wise in the ways of outdoor advertising, tacked his ad to church doors all over England. By the late 1600s, ads were common sights in London newspapers.

Advertising made its way to the American colonies along with the early settlers from England. Ben Franklin, a pioneer of early advertising, made his ads more attractive by using large headlines and considerable white space. From Franklin's time to the early 19th century, newspaper ads resembled what today are called *classified ads.*

The Industrial Revolution caused major changes in American society and in American advertising. Manufacturers, with the aid of newly invented machines, were able to mass-produce their products. Mass production, however, also required mass consumption and a mass market. Advertising was a tremendous aid in reaching this new mass audience.

The impact of increasing industrialization was most apparent in the period from the end of the Civil War to the beginning of the 20th century. In little more than three decades, the following occurred:

An ad from the 1900s for Coca-Cola.

The Year-Round Drink

- The railroad linked all parts of the country, making it possible for Eastern manufacturers to distribute their goods to the growing Western markets.

- The population of the United States doubled. More people meant larger markets for manufacturers.

- The invention of new communication media—telephone, typewriter, high-speed printing press, phonograph, motion pictures, photography, rural mail delivery—made it easier for people to communicate with one another.

- Economic production increased dramatically, and people had more disposable income to spend on new products.

This improved economic and communication climate helped advertising thrive. Magazines were distributed from coast to coast and made possible truly national advertising. The development of the halftone method for reproducing photographs meant that magazine advertisers could portray their products more vividly. By

social Issues   *Advertising: Good or Bad?*

The most outspoken critics of advertising charge that it stimulates greed, envy, and avarice—three of the seven deadly sins—a claim that can be made by no other industry. Specifically, foes of advertising claim that it causes people to buy things that they otherwise would not. Flashy ads for new-model cars prompt people to trade in perfectly good older models simply for the prestige and status of owning new ones. Even though the old DVD player works fine, run out and buy the latest version with new bells and whistles. Still wearing last year's clothes? Shame on you. Go out and buy the latest fashions as seen in print and TV ads. In short, advertising *creates* needs and makes people buy things they do not *really* need or want.

In reply to this criticism, advertising practitioners point out that humans have a variety of needs; some are biological (the need for food) and basic (the need for a safe place to live). Others are more complicated (the need for self-esteem and self-actualization). Advertising, say its supporters, caters to a wide variety of needs, not just basic ones. There is nothing wrong with buying a new car every year if it helps a person's self-esteem. Buying the latest fashions can help a person on a quest for self-actualization. Advertising is directed at many forms of need fulfillment, some of them subtle and personal. It is presumptuous of critics to tell consumers what they need or do not need. In this argument advertising is pictured as catering to a variety of needs that are already present in consumers; it does little to create new ones. As further support for this argument, advertisers point out that many heavily advertised products fail, and there is no evidence to suggest that advertising compels people to purchase things they do not want.

A second line of criticism holds that advertising promotes materialistic values and lifestyles. Advertising persuades us to evaluate others not by who they are but by what they possess. Material objects are portrayed as desirable goals. The people whom advertising presents as models to be emulated are not those who possess admirable personal qualities. Instead, consumers are urged to emulate people who drive fancy or powerful cars, wear expensive jewelry, write with the best pen, wear the trendiest clothes, or watch TV on the biggest set. Advertising encourages people to spend and acquire and makes consumption the most important activity in life. Critics go on to point out that this aspect of advertising is particularly disruptive for those with low incomes who do not have the means to attain the material goals portrayed in ads.

In response to this argument, supporters of advertising point out that advertising did not create the emphasis on materialism in American life. Writings about rampant materialism in American culture were present as early as 1830. Major holidays in the United States celebrate consumption and materialism. Christmas, for example, encourages gift giving; Thanksgiving, eating. Our basic economic system of capitalism stresses the production and consumption of goods. Advertising simply reflects the larger values of U.S. society and should not be blamed for portraying them.

Finally, advertising is criticized for its intrusiveness. The typical American is the most advertised-to person in the world. U.S. companies spend more than $500 per person on advertising, more than companies in any other country. According to *BusinessWeek*, we are exposed to about 3,000 commercial messages a day. In addition to the ubiquitous commercials on radio, on TV, on the Internet, and in print, advertising is now piped into supermarkets, airports, and doctors' offices; plastered on bathroom walls; splashed on the sides of race cars; snuck into the plots of feature films; displayed on blimps; and printed on the sides of hot dogs. Plans are even in the works to put ads in outer space. The avalanche of ads has made it difficult for advertisers to get consumers to notice their ads, let alone remember them. This leads to additional pressure to find new channels and new attention-getting techniques and results in even more intrusiveness.

Even advertising's supporters agree that advertising is hard to avoid. But they point out that this is a small price to pay for the social and economic benefits that it provides for society. Without advertising, television and radio would not be free, and magazines and newspapers would cost at least twice as much. Advertising that appears on the sides of buses helps keep fares down. The uniforms worn by Little League teams are often given for free in return for plastering the advertiser's name on the back. Would you mind seeing ads for Coke in this textbook if it meant the price was $10 cheaper?

Obviously, these are complicated issues, made even more difficult because there is no simple way to sort out the effects of advertising from the effects of all the other factors in modern life. Nonetheless, because of its high visibility and its role in the well-being of consumers, advertising will continue to be subjected to intense social scrutiny.

1900 it was not unusual for the leading magazines of the period (*Harper's, Cosmopolitan, McClure's*) to run 75–100 pages of ads in a typical issue.

It is not surprising that the increased importance of advertising in the marketing process led to the birth of the **advertising agency**, an organization that specializes in providing advertising services to its clients. The roots of the modern-day agency can be traced to Volney B. Palmer of Philadelphia. In 1842 Palmer bought large amounts of space in various newspapers at a discount and then resold the space at higher rates to advertisers. The actual ad—the copy, layout, and artwork—was still prepared by the company wishing to advertise; in effect, Palmer was a space broker. That situation changed in the late 19th century when the advertising agency of N. W. Ayer & Son was founded. Ayer & Son offered to plan, create, and execute complete advertising campaigns for its customers. By 1900 the advertising agency had become the focal point of creative planning, and advertising was firmly established as a profession.

critical ⊕ cultural issues

Cultural Meaning and Trade Characters

Tony the Tiger, Mr. Clean, the Maytag repairman, Ronald McDonald, the Jolly Green Giant, Betty Crocker, the Keebler Elves—these are examples of trade characters, fictional beings, played by actors or animated, created to help sell a product, service, or idea. Like slogans, trade characters are popular because they are an effective way of linking the product and its advertising so that consumers can easily remember the message. But trade characters do more than slogans; they give a product personality, style, and depth by creating an image with a clear cultural meaning with which the audience can identify.

An article by Barbara Phillips in a 1996 issue of the *Journal of Popular Culture* examines the role of trade characters in American culture. Phillips notes that mass-produced products have little

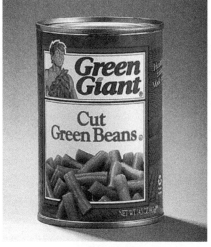
■ Created by the Leo Burnett Agency, the Jolly Green Giant has been ho-ho-ho-ing for more than 50 years.

cultural meaning. A Duracell battery is hard to distinguish from an Eveready battery, and neither is likely to arouse any emotional response. Trade characters, however, give meaning and significance to otherwise indistinguishable products by linking a product to an image that has a cultural meaning. One way that trade characters create this meaning is by employing commonly accepted mythical symbols—images that convey cultural meaning. Take the Jolly Green Giant, for example. The giant is a common mythical figure whose size connotes strength, power, and authority. His green color is associated with freshness, while his hearty "ho-ho-ho" imparts warmth and humor. The giant's image on a can of peas makes the product less remote and more friendly.

The use of mythical symbols gives trade characters another quality: They communicate messages without having to state them explicitly. Mr. Clean, for example, immaculate in his all-white costume, symbolizes cleanliness and purity. His image suggests that using his product will produce these results, but he never actually says so. In contrast, an ad that proclaims, "Our cleaner will leave your countertop spotless and pure," might be met with some degree of doubt. Since trade characters do not directly state that a product has specific attributes, their "claims" are less likely to be rejected.

There are, of course, some drawbacks to the use of trade characters. Cultural meanings shift over time, and advertisers must be careful to monitor changing attitudes in society. Perhaps the best example of this potential is Aunt Jemima. The Quaker Oats Company started using this trade character in 1889. Over the years, however, the image became an unacceptable stereotype. In 1968, during the civil rights movement, her image changed: She lost 100 pounds and became younger; her red bandana was replaced by a headband. In 1990 she was made over again into an image that was the black equivalent of Betty Crocker, an image the company hoped was more positive. Some trade characters may be entirely inappropriate. Joe Camel, for example, was the subject of much criticism because the cartoon character seemed designed to encourage children to smoke. Camel eventually phased him out.

Trade characters have become an established part of American culture. Their ranks will undoubtedly increase in the future.

The 1920s saw the beginning of radio as an advertising medium (see Chapter 8). Network broadcasting made radio an attractive vehicle for national advertisers; by 1930 about $27 million was being spent annually on network advertising, and many of the most popular shows of the day were produced by advertising agencies. However, the stock market crash of 1929 had a disastrous effect on the U.S. economy, and total dollars spent on advertising dropped from $2.8 billion in 1929 to $1.7 billion in 1935. It would take a decade for the industry to recover. During World War II many civilian firms cut back on their advertising budgets. Others simply changed the content of their ads and, instead of selling their products, instructed consumers on how to make their products last until after the war.

World War II was followed by the Cold War, when Americans were concerned about the rise of communism. Despite growth in mass consumption and economic prosperity, the prevailing mood of the country was one of apprehension as many people were afraid that communists were secretly taking over the government and subverting the American way of life. This mood also had an impact on public opinion about advertising. After the Korean War many stories surfaced about brainwashing and mind control of American prisoners. It was not long before advertising was indicted as a form of mind control that seduced people by subtle appeals to subconscious urges. A best-seller called *The Hidden Persuaders* explained how advertisers used psychological research and motivational analysis to sell consumers things they really did not need or want. It was during this time that the concept of subliminal advertising was introduced, which further deepened the suspicions about the advertising industry.

This paranoia gradually subsided during the 1960s, which were characterized by the growth of the creative side of advertising as art directors, copywriters, and TV directors had more input into the way advertising was presented. This trend weakened during the 1970s when a bad economic climate prompted a return to a more direct selling technique and a focus on efficient media planning.

The 1980s and 1990s saw the social and media environment for advertising change dramatically. Cable television opened up dozens of new and specialized channels that siphoned advertising dollars away from the major TV networks. New video forms of marketing emerged, such as the infomercial and home shopping. Moreover, improved transportation and communication gave birth to the mega–ad agency with branches throughout the world. Political changes in Europe created new opportunities for global marketing. Changes in society also had an impact. Advertisers were facing a more culturally diverse marketplace that required

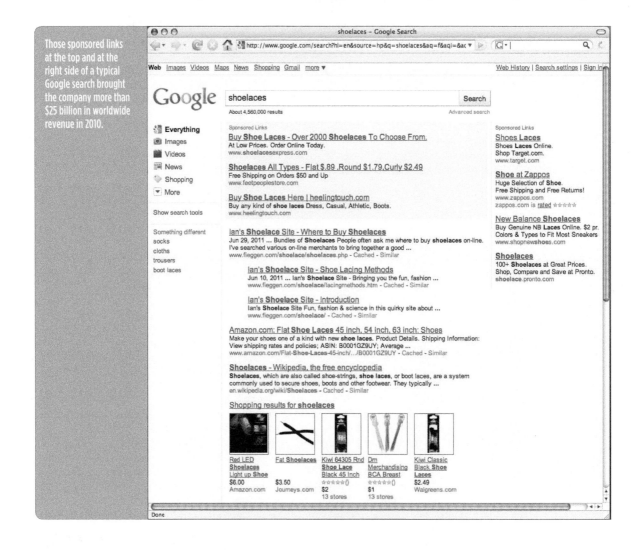

Those sponsored links at the top and at the right side of a typical Google search brought the company more than $25 billion in worldwide revenue in 2010.

356   Part III   Specific Media Professions

sound byte

Do You Watch the Commercials?

Here are some of the results of a recent survey about what people do during TV commercials:

- 53 percent get annoyed at the number of commercials.
- 52 percent talk to others and don't pay attention.
- 50 percent get up and do something else.
- 43 percent switch to another channel.
- 27 percent mute the sound.
- 13 percent sit and watch the commercial.

more selective ads. Consumer attitudes toward products were changing, and new regulations promised to forever alter tobacco advertising. Liquor ads also drew criticism.

Contemporary advertising finds itself coping with technological and social change. As mentioned in Chapter 1, consumers are taking more and more control over their media choices. The Internet, TiVo, the iPod, smartphones, iPads, and other technologies have given consumers the power to choose when, where, and how they look for news and entertainment. The traditional advertising model, whereby advertisers interrupt a program or place ads around print articles in the hope that someone sees them, is becoming harder to justify. Couple that trend with the fact that many young people are no longer getting their news and entertainment from traditional media, and it's easy to understand why a lot of advertising money is shifting from the established media to more nontraditional forms, such as text message ads on cell phones, ads on NASCAR race cars, and Internet advertising.

Speaking of Internet advertising, the industry is exploring ways to use this new medium effectively. When it first appeared in the early 1990s, Internet advertising was hailed as the next great advance in advertising reach. As it turned out, however, these hopes were exaggerated. Banner advertising on Internet sites generated little traffic, pop-up blockers screened out pop-up ads, and spam filters quarantined much of e-mail advertising. As a result, advertising professionals had to rethink their Internet strategies. Contemporary Internet advertising is more targeted. Google, for example, lets advertisers buy space on a Web page that displays the results of an individual's Web search. Second, Web ads are becoming more interactive and more engaging. Procter & Gamble's Club Olay Web site encourages women to sign up for special offers and free samples and to receive monthly e-mail from the company.

The advertising industry is finally recovering from the recession at the end of the decade. Ad revenue dropped 9 percent from 2008 to 2009 but rebounded from 2009 to 2010, increasing by nearly 6 percent. Most of the traditional media showed revenue gains, with television leading the way. Moreover, 2010 marked the first time that online ad revenue topped that of the newspaper industry. The biggest advertisers in 2010 were Procter & Gamble, Verizon, AT&T, and General Motors.

advertising in the digital age

Online advertising began in 1994 when HotWired, the digital counterpart to the hip *Wired* magazine, started a Web site with about a dozen sponsors who paid to have advertising banners embedded throughout the site. Since that time, advertising as well as the Internet have undergone a number of changes.

Audience Control

As far as advertising is concerned, consumers are increasingly making media choices that involve avoiding advertising. In a recent survey about half the respondents said that ads spoil their reading or viewing experience. About 18 million people have opted for commercial-free music on satellite radio. Digital video recorders, such as TiVo, are in about half of U.S. homes, and the number is increasing daily. As you might expect, about two-thirds of DVR owners fast-forward through the ads. Thousands of commercial-free episodes of TV shows have been downloaded from iTunes. Most people have ad- and spam-blocking software installed on their computers.

These developments have forced advertisers to look for other means to reach the audience. Product placement has become common in movies, TV shows, and even video games. **Viral advertising**, a technique by which companies try to create messages that are so compelling, interesting, funny, or suggestive that consumers willingly and spontaneously

sound byte

Typosquatting

Ever make a mistake typing in the name of a popular website? Maybe typing "goigle.com" instead of "google.com"? If so, you may be the victim of "typosquatting," a method that unscrupulous individuals use to get you to visit an alternative Web site where you may be bombarded with spam and unwanted ads or your computer infected with spyware or a virus. Many big companies register the common misspellings of their brands or Web site addresses, but typosquatting still occurs. The best defense is to make sure you have arrived at the site you were looking for and bookmark it. The fewer times you type in a URL address, the less likely it is that you will make a mistake and be rerouted to a bogus page.

share them with others, usually via e-mail, social networking sites, or cell phones, is a hot area. If the technique is successful, word spreads rapidly to a large number of people, much like a virus. For instance, Dove Evolution, a short film posted on YouTube, got more than 1.7 million views thanks to good consumer reaction.

Targeted search advertising, paying for links to a product or service on search results pages, accounted for more than $30 billion in revenue in 2010. Finally, some advertisers have turned to "buzz marketing," a technique that pays consumers to talk about products and services.

New Channels

The digital revolution has opened up additional avenues for advertising. Bloggers represent a segment of the population that wields significant influence. Advertisers can use networks such as Blogads to target specific blogs whose readers would be likely customers for their product or service.

Podcasts are another emerging channel. Podtrac, for example, offers advertisers access to 1,500 podcasts, ranging from "This Week in Tech" to "Mugglecast" for Harry Potter fans. Advertisers select the demographics and interests of their target market, and Podtrac selects the most appropriate podcasts. Companies typically sponsor an entire podcast and pay on the basis of how many times the podcast is downloaded.

Advertisers are also relying heavily on social media, such as Facebook and YouTube. Every major ad campaign during the past few years has included a social media dimension.

Mobile Media: Apps and Advertising

Businesses are aware that more people are using their mobile devices—smartphones and tablet computers—to access the Internet. As a result, companies are turning to special mobile applications to reach their customers. Unlike traditional ads that interrupt programs, obscure Web page content, or clutter up the pages that people are reading, apps give the user control over the process. The consumer has to elect to download the app and decide when to use it.

Apps have many advantages. They connect with the consumer at home, at work, or on the go. They keep a brand in the consumer's consciousness because the consumer may see the app every time he or she uses the phone. They offer a gateway to a brand's several services and special offers, such as coupons.

Most apps offer entertainment or information along with the opportunity to purchase the product. Benjamin Moore Paints, for example, has an app that enables users to snap a picture of something and matches its color with a shade in the company's color library. If the user wants to buy the paint, the app provides directions to the nearest retailer. People who have downloaded the Starbucks app can use it to find the nearest outlet, scan the menu, and build their own customized drink.

Apps have the potential to be a major advertising channel. The average smartphone owner has downloaded more than 50 apps. Cumulative app sales at the App Store will soon total more than downloads of music and video from iTunes. Experts predict that revenue from mobile apps will top $40 billion by 2015.

User-Generated Content

User-generated content has obvious benefits for advertisers. Amateur ads cost almost nothing and create a word-of-mouth buzz. Nonetheless, user-generated content is not as popular with advertisers as it was a few years ago. Doritos and Pepsi Max sponsored a contest that allowed consumers to make their own commercials for the product. The winning ads were shown during the Super Bowl. Web host GoDaddy.com ran a contest with a top prize of $100, for homemade ads touting the Web site's services. Many companies, however, have been steering away from user-generated content.

Decoupling

Finally, mass marketers are no longer as dependent on the mass media as they were 30 years ago, a trend that has serious implications for the media. Back then, if Sony wanted to introduce a new-model TV set, it would advertise in newspapers and magazines and on various television programs or networks. The company realized that much of its advertising would reach people who had absolutely no interest in buying a TV, but Sony would tolerate that inefficiency in order to reach those few who were interested. As department store mogul John Wanamaker once said, "I know half my advertising is wasted but I don't know which half." With the Internet, however, advertisers may be able to figure out how to drastically cut waste.

The Internet lets advertisers target ads at the people most likely to buy the product or service. Search engine ads are the most obvious example. Rather than spending huge amounts of money on TV ads, Sony could pay Google to have an ad displayed next to the search results whenever anybody searched for "television set" or a similar term. To use another example, sites such as Amazon, eBay, and Netflix keep track of what a person buys or rents so that when the person returns to their site, he or she gets a list of recommended items based on his or her search and/or purchasing behavior as well as on the behavior of other people who bought or rented similar items.

Moreover, the Internet makes it easier for advertisers to collect huge amounts of data from large groups of people. Data processing software lets them mine the data for associations that would otherwise seem counterintuitive. One data-mining exercise found that the number-one online activity of people who bought big-screen TVs was visiting military Web sites. Shopping online for TVs ranked 18th. As a result, TV set manufacturers are likely to devote part of their budget to advertising on military Web sites, something they would probably have never done before the age of data mining.

Further, advertisers are putting more of their budgets into nonmedia sources, such as viral marketing, sponsorship of special events, and public relations efforts. For example, check out the number of advertisers on a typical NASCAR vehicle. Point-of-purchase or in-store advertising is gaining in popularity and attracts more than $10 billion annually.

All of this leads to the **"decoupling"** of advertising from mass media. There is no compelling reason why advertisers should pay the salaries of TV stars and radio DJs. As companies and organizations find more efficient ways to market their goods and services, there will be a further migration of revenue from the media to other forms of advertising and marketing. This will obviously not happen overnight, but the pattern is clear. The old advertising model is losing more and more of its foundation, and one of these days it may collapse altogether. Traditional ad-supported media are looking for ways to survive the transition.

organization of the consumer advertising industry

There are three main components of the advertising industry: (1) advertisers, (2) advertising agencies, and (3) the media. We will discuss each of these in turn.

Advertisers

Advertising is an important part of the overall marketing plan of almost every organization that provides a product or a service to the public. Advertisers can range from the small bicycle shop on the corner that spends $4 on an ad in the local weekly paper to huge international corporations such as AT&T, which spends about $3 billion annually for ads.

At a basic level we can distinguish two different types of advertisers: national and retail. **National advertisers** sell their product or service to customers all across the country. The emphasis in national advertising is on the product or service and not so much on the place where the product or service is sold. For example, the Coca-Cola Company is interested in selling soft drinks. It does not matter to the company if you buy its product at the local supermarket,

The boss as spokesperson: Papa John's founder, John Schnatter, frequently appears in his company's commercials.

at a small convenience store, or from a vending machine. **Retail advertisers** (also called *local advertisers*) are companies such as local restaurants, car dealerships, TV repair shops, and other merchants and service organizations that have customers in only one city or trading area. The retail advertiser wants to attract customers to a specific store or place of business. Some companies are both national and local advertisers. Sears and Target, for example, advertise all over the country, but their individual stores use local advertising to highlight their specific sales and promotions. Franchises, such as McDonald's and Burger King, keep up their national image by advertising on network TV, while their local outlets put ads in the paper to attract customers from the local community.

Naturally, the way organizations handle their advertising depends on their size. Some companies have their own advertising departments; a small retail store might have one person who is responsible for advertising and marketing and who may also have other job functions. Whether large or small, all advertisers must attend to several basic functions. These include planning the ads and deciding where they will appear, setting aside a certain amount of money for the advertising budget, coordinating the advertising with other departments in the organization, and, if necessary, supervising the work of an outside agency or company that produces the ad. In addition, some large advertisers have departments that can create and prepare all the advertising materials, purchase the space and airtime for the ads, and check to see if the ads were effective in achieving their goals.

media talk

Food for Thought: Advertising to Kids

Clip 4: 6 minutes 26 seconds

You can watch Clip 4 *on the Online Learning Center home page*, www .mhhe.com/dominick12e. *Select* Student Center *and then* Chapter 15.

This clip discusses how most American children can identify the McDonald's brand. It also describes how a majority of children prefer foods wrapped in a McDonald's wrapper to the identical food not wrapped in a McDonald's wrapper. Can you remember any McDonald's commercials from your childhood? Do you think that McDonald's unfairly targets children who are too young to know about commercials? Should McDonald's stop advertising aimed toward children?

WWW

Agencies

According to the American Association of Advertising Agencies, an **agency** is an independent business organization composed of creative people and businesspeople who develop, prepare, and place advertising for sellers seeking to find customers for their goods and services. In the past, advertising agencies were located in a few big cities, such as New York, Chicago, and Los Angeles. That trend has changed, however, and many of the more memorable ad campaigns of recent years have been put together by agencies located far from Madison Avenue. When it comes to total income, however, the big-city agencies still dominate.

The past few years in the agency business have seen the spawning of super-agencies, or mega-agencies, resulting from the merger and consolidation of several large ad agencies. In addition, the business has been globalized, since these new mega-agencies have branches all over the world. The five mega-agencies listed in Table 15-1 dominated the industry at the close of 2009.

The global reach of advertising is apparent in the agency business as in many other media. Three of the megagroups in Table 15-1 are foreign-owned.

Agencies can be classified by the range of services they offer. In general terms there are three main types: (1) full-service agencies, (2) media buying services, and (3) creative boutiques.

As the name implies, a **full-service agency** handles all phases of the advertising process for its clients; it plans, creates, produces, and places ads. In addition, it might provide other marketing services, such as sales promotions, trade show exhibits, newsletters, and annual reports. In theory, at least, there is no need for the client to deal with any other company for help promoting its product.

table 15-1	Company	Headquarters	2010 Revenue (in billion U.S. dollars)
Top Five Advertising Agencies, 2010	WPP Group	Dublin	$14.4
	Omnicom	New York	12.5
	Publicis	Paris	7.2
	Interpublic	New York	6.5
	Dentsu	Tokyo	2.6

A **media buying service** specializes in buying radio and TV time and reselling it to advertisers and advertising agencies. The service sells time to the advertiser, orders the spots on the various stations, and monitors the stations to see if the ads actually run.

A **creative boutique** (the name was coined during the 1960s and has hung on to the present) is an organization that specializes in the actual creation of ads. In general, boutiques create imaginative and distinctive advertising themes and produce innovative and original ads. A company that uses a creative boutique would have to employ another agency to perform the planning, buying, and administrative functions connected with advertising.

What does a full-service ad agency do for a client? To begin with, the agency studies the product or service and determines what its marketable characteristics are and how it relates to the competition. At the same time, the agency studies the potential market, possible distribution plans, and likely advertising media. The agency then makes a formal presentation to the client detailing its findings and its recommended advertising strategy. If the client agrees, the agency launches the execution phase. This phase entails writing and producing the ads, buying space and time in various media, delivering the ads to the appropriate media, and verifying that all ads actually appear. Finally, the agency works closely with the client's salespeople to make sure they get the greatest possible benefit from the ads.

As advertising continues to move online, several new advertising agencies specializing in creating and delivering ads to Web sites have emerged. These digital ad agencies work with ad networks, organizations that buy Web space from different sites and resell it to advertisers. Once the Web sites have been lined up by the ad network, the ads themselves are distributed by ad-serving firms, such as DoubleClick.

Media

The final part of the advertising industry consists of the mass media. The media serve as the connection between a company and its customers. The media that are available for advertising include some obvious ones—radio, TV, newspapers, magazines, the Internet—and others that are not so obvious, such as direct mail, billboards, transit cards (bus and car cards), stadium scoreboard ads, point-of-purchase ads, e-mail, chat rooms, and even iPods. Chapters 5, 6, 8, and 10–12 presented an overview of the mainstream mass media and discussed their dependence on various kinds of advertising. This section examines these media from the perspective of an advertiser.

Even the slickest and most imaginative advertising message will fail if it is delivered to the wrong people. To make sure that this does not happen, advertisers employ highly skilled media planners to help them place and schedule their ads.

Advertising specialists evaluate media along four dimensions:

1. *Reach:* How many people can get the message?
2. *Frequency:* How often will the message be received?
3. *Selectivity:* Does the medium actually reach potential customers?
4. *Efficiency:* How much does it cost to reach a certain number of people? (This is usually expressed as cost per thousand people.)

social Issues *Scraping*

Ever wonder about those squiggly, distorted letters and numbers that some Web sites require you to type before you can enter the site? They're called "captchas" and they separate real-live humans from computers that may be "scraping" the site to gather personal information on its users.

Given all the information that is present on the Web, it is no wonder that many companies are interested in using it to promote their businesses. Scraping gathers large amounts of information from thousands or even millions of Web sites. If a business lacks the resources or the time to do its own scraping, it can hire an outside firm to do the work. A quick Google search for "Web site scraping" will reveal many firms that specialize in this activity. The Web site of one company, aptly named "Web Site Scraping," promises that it can scrape anything on the Web, including images, files, and data. The company further states, "We guarantee we will get your data, even if the site blocks."

Some scrapers specialize in scraping commercial data: information about competitors' products, prices, and marketing strategies. Others are more personal in scope. One scraping company offers individuals information about a potential date for $14.95. Another company has developed scraping software that will match people's real names with the fake names they might use on their blogs and social networking Web sites. The biggest scraping company, Nielsen Buzz Metrics, is part of the Nielsen Company, the same organization that reports the ratings of TV shows. Buzz Metrics collects data from 130 million blogs, 8,000 message boards, Twitter, and other social networks. If someone is saying something bad about a company, Buzz Metrics will report it using a service it calls "Threat Tracker." The big scraping companies might charge $10,000 per job. If you can't afford that, you can find free do-it-yourself scraping software on the Web.

Of course, there is a lot of public information on the Web that is readily available to scrapers. On Spokeo.com., for example, a free search can reveal a person's age, marital status, address, home purchase price, and the number of people living in the household. All of this information could be found in public records, but it's much easier to collect thanks to all of the publicly available databases on the Web. For an additional price, Spokeo .com and similar firms can report personal information about hobbies, estimated income, and home phone number and can scrape social network sites for data about friends, photos, and videos. It's important to note that there is no guarantee that the information scraped from a site is accurate or up-to-date.

Although many companies don't object to having their sites scraped, Web scraping raises several ethical and legal issues including invasion of privacy, theft of intellectual property, and unauthorized access to computers. In one case, a real estate firm was scraping all of the for-sale listings from its competitors and posting the information on its own Web site. In another case, a company scraped information from Facebook and published it on the company's Web site. The most notable case involved the Nielsen Company and a Web site called PatientsLikeMe.com, a site where patients share comments about their conditions and the medicines they take. The site requires a person to have an account with a unique log-in name to participate. Nielsen's scraping program was creating false member accounts and copying all the messages on the site's online forums (information that might be of great interest to big drug companies). PatientsLikeMe.com eventually discovered what was happening and Nielsen promised not to scrape sites that require a log-in.

Web sites have several methods they can use to protect against unwanted scraping. Using the captchas mentioned at the beginning of this discussion is one method. Other sites use software that flags suspicious activity, such as viewing lots of posts in a short period. All agree on one recommendation: A person should read and understand each site's privacy policy before posting comments.

Table 15-2 summarizes how the various media rate on these dimensions.

In addition to considering these factors, advertisers have to take into account many others before deciding on which medium to use. An important part of any decision involves considering the creative limitations imposed by the physical properties of each medium. Television, for example, enables the advertiser to show the product in action. On the other hand, TV ads are short and cannot be used to present a great deal of technical information.

table 15–2 Characteristics of Various Media	CHARACTERISTICS	MEDIUM						
		Newspapers	Magazines	Radio	TV	Outdoor	Direct Mail	Internet
	Reach	High	Low	High	High	High	High	Medium
	Frequency	High	Low	High	High	High	Medium	Medium
	Selectivity	Low	High	High	Medium	Low	High	High
	Efficiency	Medium	Medium	Low	High	High	High	Medium

YouTube advertising videos can be any length, but they may get lost in the plethora of other videos on the site. A magazine ad can be in full color and can present a large amount of data, but it might not have the same impact as a TV ad. Ads on Facebook are relatively cheap, but they reach an audience that is less engaged with advertising in general. All in all, choosing which media to use in the final advertising mix is a difficult decision.

producing advertising

Departments and Staff

There are typically four major departments in a big advertising agency: (1) creative services, (2) account services, (3) marketing services, and (4) administration.

The creative department, as the name implies, actually produces the ad. The people in this department write the advertising **copy** (the headline and message of the ad), choose

One of the tasks of the creative department of an ad agency is to come up with attention-getting print ad layouts such as this one.

the illustrations, prepare artwork, and/or supervise the scripting and production of radio, TV, and Web ads.

The account services department is responsible for the relationship between the agency and the client. Because the advertising agency is an organization outside the firm doing the advertising, it is necessary to appoint someone, usually called an *account executive* (AE), to promote communication and understanding between client and agency. The AE must represent the viewpoint of the agency to the client but at the same time keep abreast of the needs of the advertiser. Since the AE tends to be the person in the middle, his or her job is obviously an important one in the agency.

The marketing services department is responsible for advising the client as to what media to use for his or her messages. Typically, this department makes extensive use of the data collected by the Audit Bureau of Circulations, Arbitron, Nielsen, comScore, and the other audience research services mentioned in earlier chapters. This department is also in charge of any sales promotions that are done in connection with the advertising. These may include such things as coupons, premiums, and other aids to dealers.

Finally, like any other business, the advertising agency needs a department to take care of the day-to-day administration of the agency. This department is in charge of office management, clerical functions, accounting, personnel, and the training of new employees.

The Advertising Campaign

The best way to illustrate how ads get produced is to present a general discussion of an advertising campaign for a national product. A **campaign** consists of a large number of advertisements, all stressing the same major theme or appeal, that appear in a number of media over a specified time. Following is a discussion, greatly simplified, of the six phases of a typical campaign:

1. Choosing the marketing strategy
2. Selecting the main appeal or theme
3. Translating the theme into the various media
4. Producing the ads
5. Buying space and time
6. Executing and evaluating the campaign

Many advertisers like to use well-known celebrities in their ad campaigns. Christina Aguilera, for example, appears in TV commercials for Pepsi and other products.

In the first phase, a great deal of research is done to determine the target audience, the marketing objective, the appropriate price for the product or service, and the advertising budget. It is during this phase that the word **positioning** is often heard. Positioning has many interpretations, but in general it means fitting a product or service to one or more segments of the broad market in such a way as to set it apart from the competition without making any change in the product.

Panera Bread, for example, tried to differentiate itself from other sandwich shops by emphasizing that dining at Panera was a better experience. The slogan for the campaign was "Make today better" and the ads pointed out that Panera uses professional bakers for its bread and gives customers real silverware.

Old Navy's research revealed that the commonly accepted assumption that women buy men's clothes was faulty. Men often shop for themselves and frequently purchase items in bulk. Consequently, Old Navy launched a campaign whose goal was to position the company as a store that catered to both men

media
Probe

Is That a Smile I See?

That billboard you just passed may be smarter than you think. Advertisers are developing electronic billboards and other devices that can recognize human facial expressions and gestures. Why are advertisers interested in doing this? Imagine the possibilities. New facial recognition software has become so sophisticated it can detect something as subtle as a raised eyebrow. If the billboard detects a smile, it can display more information about the product. If it detects a frown, it may change to a different view. Billboards might also be able to tailor their message depending on the sex of the viewer.

Those who have played the Xbox's Kinect game system have firsthand experience with the new technology. Kinect lets players play video games by recognizing their bodily movements. No controller or wand is required. The device also uses facial recognition technology to match players with their stored profiles or avatars. Needless to say, advertisers are looking for ways to use this information to target ads to specific game players.

Like many of the new technologies, facial and gesture recognition raises questions about privacy. As soon as Buffy walks in the door, an in-store billboard could recognize her face, associate it with her name, and check the Internet for information about her. How much do you want your department store to know about you?

and women. The company placed its ads on You Tube, on Facebook, and in magazines, and developed its own app for mobile media.

After the product or service has been positioned, an overall theme for the campaign is developed and the theme is translated into print, broadcast, and online ads. In 2010, for example, AT&T launched a campaign based on the theme "Rethink Possible," whose goal was to make consumers more aware of AT&T's globe logo. Featuring the song "Pure Imagination" from the Willy Wonka film, the campaign used TV commercials, print, and social media to display the globe in different colors and styles.

The actual production of the ad is done in much the same way that other media content is produced. In the print media the copy, the headline, subheads, any accompanying illustrations, and the layout are first prepared in rough form. The initial step is usually just a thumbnail sketch that can be used to experiment with different arrangements within the ad. The headline might be moved down, the copy moved from right to left, and so on. Next, a **rough layout**—a drawing that is the actual size of the ad—is constructed. Usually, several layouts are prepared, and the best are used to produce the **comprehensive layout**, the one that will be used to produce the ad. Many agencies use outside art studios and printers to help them put together print ads and billboards.

Radio commercials are written and created in much the same way that early radio drama shows were produced. A script is prepared in which dialogue, sound effects, and music are combined to produce whatever effect is desired. The commercial is then either produced in the sound studio or recorded live on location. In either case postproduction editing adds any desired special effects, and eventually a master disc is prepared for duplication and distribution.

The beginning step in the preparation of a television commercial is a **storyboard**, a series of drawings depicting the key scenes of the planned ad. Storyboards are usually shown to the client before production begins. If the client has any objections or suggestions, changes can be made to the script before production. Once the storyboards are approved, the commercial is ready to go into production. Most TV commercials are shot on film (although some are now switching to videotape). Television commercials are the most expensive ads to produce. A 30-second spot can easily cost $350,000. Special effects, particularly animation, can drive the costs even higher. In an effort to keep costs down, much of the time spent producing TV commercials consists of planning and rehearsing. As with the print media, many agencies hire outside production specialists to produce their commercials.

While all this is going on, other members of the creative team are preparing Web ads and ads for social and mobile media. Banner ads, pop-ups, and pop-unders are still the most common types of online ads, but other configurations are becoming popular. Splash pages are Web pages that appear before a Web page loads and then disappear a short time later. Skyscraper ads are elongated vertical banners that border one or both sides of a Web page. Floating ads move up, down, or across a page as the user scrolls through a Web site.

ethical issues   *Do They Really Mean It?*

There are many blogs across the Web that specialize in writing about travel. People consult them to find out information about airlines, hotels, and tourist attractions. They assume that the blog writer is giving his or her honest and unbiased assessment of a product or service. If the blogger raves about the accommodations at a particular hotel, the reader assumes the blogger is telling the truth.

Well, maybe yes and maybe no. In many instances, advertisers are funneling money to bloggers in return for favorable mentions. Most of the time, the reader is unaware that a payment has been made. The practice is gaining in popularity thanks to the poor economy, as more bloggers look for ways to increase their income. For their part, some bloggers are posting messages on their sites indicating that they accept compensation but that it has no effect on their opinions. Even those bloggers who do not disclose that they are compensated argue that payments have no influence on their opinions.

Of course, many traditional media outlets also take gifts from potential advertisers, but there are ethical guidelines about what they can accept. Advertising professionals also have ethics codes that offer guidance about full disclosure in ads. The code of the Word of Mouth Marketing Association states in part: "We stand against marketing practices whereby the consumer is paid cash by the manufacturer, supplier, or one of their representatives to make recommendations, reviews, or endorsements."

The ethical issues raised here are similar to those with regard to "buzz marketing." The situation is a little different with bloggers because they operate in a different forum. Consumers are probably more skeptical of claims made by a relatively unknown blogger than they would be of claims made by an acquaintance. Nonetheless, if a blogger refuses to acknowledge that he or she accepted a payment from the manufacturer of a product being reviewed, then deception is involved. It matters little if the blogger claims that payments do not affect the stated opinions. Deception is still involved, and ethical experts agree that deception is seldom the proper way to act.

What about the ethics of acknowledging a payment but claiming that it didn't affect a review? Ethically speaking, that position is more defensible, but the blogger owes his or her readers some proof of that claim. Showing examples of payments for products that eventually received poor reviews might be one way to substantiate the claim of objectivity.

As sometimes happens in a situation where the law and ethics are ambiguous, the government fills in the blanks. In late 2009, the Federal Trade Commission proposed rules to regulate what bloggers and people on social media sites can claim about products. One section of the proposed rules states that if someone is compensated to review a product and then makes false claims about the product, that person could be sued for false representation. If, for example, a medical firm paid a blogger to review a new foot care product and the blogger incorrectly claimed that the product cured athlete's foot, then the FTC could sue the blogger as well as the medical firm.

In any case, like everything else on the Internet, readers should be skeptical of blogs that review products until they can assess the blogger's credibility.

A wallpaper ad changes the background of the page being viewed. Shorter or longer versions of a TV ad might also be prepared to run on the advertiser's Web site or posted on YouTube.

While the creative department is putting together print, Web, and broadcast ads, the marketing department is buying time in those media judged to be appropriate for the campaign. If the product is seasonal (suntan lotion, snowmobiles), the ads are scheduled to reflect the calendar, appearing slightly before and during the time people might begin buying such items. Other products and services might call for a program of steady advertising throughout the year.

The last phase of the campaign consists of the running of the ads. Testing is done during and after this phase to see if consumers saw and remembered the ads. In addition, sales data are carefully monitored to determine if the campaign had the desired effect on sales.

Advertising Research

Advertising research, which takes place during all phases of the campaign, helps agencies and their clients make informed decisions about their strategy and tactics. **Formative research** is done before the campaign begins to help guide the creative effort. It can take several forms. One is audience definition—identifying the target market, such as "females 18–34" or "all adults." After this is accomplished, audience profiling is done to discover as much as possible about how the target market lives—what they think, what their attitudes are, and how they decide to buy.

The next phase, **message research**, involves pretesting the messages that have been developed for the campaign. At its most basic level, pretesting determines if the audience can actually understand the ads. This type of testing guards against possible double meanings or overlooked sexual connotations that might have eluded the creative staff. In

Advertising and Social Media: New Risks

For the past several years comedian Gilbert Gottfried has been the voice of the duck in commercials for the Aflac insurance company. Those who have heard Gottfried's stand-up routine will probably agree that his jokes sometimes border on the insensitive and tasteless. Like most comedians, Gottfried also has a Twitter account where he posts the occasional joke or two.

After the earthquake and tsunami in Japan, Gottfried posted several jokes about the disaster that were, to put it mildly, in questionable taste. Had Gottfried merely told those jokes during one of his stand-up performances, a few people might have been offended but the matter would have probably stopped there. Once something is on the Internet, however, it can spread rapidly and might be seen by millions of people. Such was the case with Gottfried's Twitter one-liners.

Aflac is the largest insurance agency in Japan and gets about 75 percent of its revenue from the Japanese market. When the company learned of Gottfried's jokes, they immediately fired him. The comedian removed the jokes from his Twitter account and posted an apology, but Aflac announced that it was going to find a new voice for the duck.

Around the same time, an employee of the ad agency that was handling the Twitter marketing account for Chrysler posted the following: "I find it ironic that Detroit is known as the motor city and yet no one here knows how to [bleeping] drive." Apparently, the tweet was intended for the employee's personal Twitter account but was posted instead on the Chrysler brand account. The ad agency quickly removed the message and dismissed the employee. This unfortunate incident came in the midst of a Chrysler ad campaign that was committed to praising Detroit and its hardworking residents. To no one's surprise, Chrysler announced it would not renew the ad agency's contract.

These two episodes raise some novel issues for advertisers and employees as social media marketing becomes more popular. First, advertisers need to establish a policy that addresses what their employees or spokespersons can post on social media sites. Did Aflac expect Gottfried to refrain from making jokes on his Twitter posts? Humor is one way that people cope with tragedy and comedians have historically pushed the envelope on what is socially acceptable. One can argue that Gottfreid was fired for simply doing what comedians do: making jokes. In any case, there needs to be a clear understanding that when a spokesperson is being paid to do a job, the boundary between the spokesperson's public and personal utterances is porous and the spokesperson should think before he or she speaks—or tweets.

Second, advertisers such as Aflac can't be shocked and sanctimonious when a spokesperson with a track record such as Gottfried's exceeds the bounds of good taste. He told jokes about the Kennedy assassination and the *Challenger* disaster. If Aflac was concerned about social niceties, they could have hired someone else.

Finally, the Chrysler incident raises questions about what measures are appropriate for employees who transgress via social media. The Detroit comment was posted by mistake. Is making such a mistake a firing offense? Was it serious enough to justify terminating a contract? (Chrysler's reaction is even more puzzling because their spokesperson in the campaign that stressed the company's Detroit roots is rapper Eminem whose songs contain frequent repetitions of the word that so offended the auto company.) In any case, advertisers and their agencies would benefit from explicit guidelines to handle situations such as this.

a second type of pretest, researchers show mock-ups of magazines that contain the prototype of the print ad and rough cuts of TV ads to test audiences. Consumers are tested to see whether they recall the main points of the ad and whether their attitude toward the product has shown any change. Some advertising campaigns go through pilot tests in actual markets. A split-cable transmission can show one version of an ad to one group of people and a second version to another group. The ads are compared to see which did a better job. A split-run of a magazine uses the same strategy.

Tracking studies examine how the ads perform during or after the actual campaign. Samples of consumers are studied to see if they recall the ads, if their attitudes about the product have changed, and if they have bought the product or used the service advertised.

the economics of advertising

In this section we will examine the economics of advertising on two levels. First, we will look at the total industry and trace expenditures in various media. Second, we will narrow our focus and examine how an advertising agency makes money.

Advertising Volume in Various Media

Global advertising spending totaled $390 billion in 2010. Figure 15-1 shows how this money was divided among the various media. Since 1980, newspapers have seen a decrease in their relative share of advertising volumes, as have magazines. Television has shown a

media *Probe* Price Comparisons

Advertisers use a measure called cost-per-thousand (abbreviated CPM, where M is the Roman numeral for 1,000) to help them compare ad buys across media. CPM is calculated by dividing the cost of the ad by the audience reached by the ad (expressed in thousands). Thus, an ad that reaches 200,000 people and costs $400 would have a CPM of $2 (400/200 = 2).

As of 2010, here are some typical CPMs for selected media:

Broadcast TV	$10.25	Radio	$4.54
Magazines	6.98	Online	2.43
Cable TV	5.99	Social media	0.56
Newspapers	5.50		

The online and social media CPMs are so cheap because of the tremendous amount of space on the Web available for advertising and, as any Econ 101 student knows, with no change in demand, as supply goes up, prices generally come down.

figure 15-1

Global Advertising Expenditures in Various Media, 2010

(Dollar figures are in billions.)

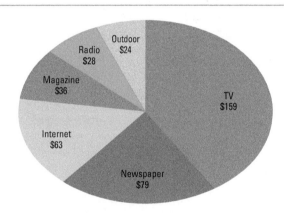

significant increase, while outdoor advertising has shown modest growth. The Internet will probably account for more of the pie in the future.

Agency Compensation

Historically, the major mass media have allowed advertising agencies a 15 percent commission on the time and space they purchase. Recently, however, the commission system has been declining in popularity. Many advertisers have struck pay-for-performance deals with ad agencies. Payments to ad agencies are based on sales or some other measure of performance. If sales go up, the ad agency gets more money. Other companies pay agencies a fixed fee, and still others use a combination of a flat fee plus performance-based incentives.

business-to-business advertising

As its name suggests, business-to-business advertising is designed to sell products and services not to general consumers but to other businesses, typically via specialized trade publications, direct mail, e-mail, Web sites, professional journals, and display advertising at trade shows. There are four main categories of business-to-business advertising:

1. *Trade:* Advertising goods and services to wholesalers and retailers who, in turn, resell these items to a more general audience.
2. *Industrial:* Advertising those items that are used in the further production of goods and services, such as copy machines, forklifts, and drill presses.

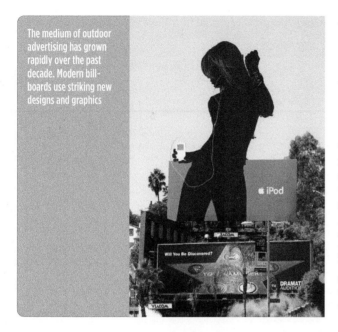

The medium of outdoor advertising has grown rapidly over the past decade. Modern billboards use striking new designs and graphics

3. *Professional:* Advertising aimed at doctors, lawyers, architects, nurses, and others who might influence the buying process or use the product in their profession.

4. *Agricultural:* Advertising aimed at farmers and possibly including products such as feed, fertilizer, seed, and chemicals.

Although its visibility might not be high, business-to-business advertising is a multibillion-dollar industry. Some people overlook the potential for a career in business-to-business advertising because they feel it is not as glamorous as consumer advertising. There may be some truth to this: Ads for a chemical solvent, bench-top fermenter, or blast furnace usually are not as flashy as campaigns for sleek new sports cars. In its own way, though, business advertising poses greater creative challenges. Coming up with a theme to sell the sports car is probably much easier than coming up with a winning idea for the chemical solvent.

Consumer Versus Business-to-Business Advertising

There are some obvious differences between advertising directed at consumers and business advertising. In this section we will consider four.

First, the target audience in business advertising is much smaller. In some industries the audience may number in the hundreds. Companies that manufacture storage tanks for petroleum products, for example, have determined that there are only 400 people in the United States authorized to purchase their product. In other areas, the audience may be in the thousands. This means, of course, that the media used to reach the target market must be selected carefully. In the nuclear reactor business, for instance, everyone in the market may read one or two publications.

Second, most of the products that are advertised tend to be technical, complicated, and high-priced. For the advertiser this means that the ads will probably contain a great deal of technical information and will stress accuracy.

Third, the buyers are professionals—purchasing agents whose only job is to acquire products and services for their company. Generally, the decisions of the purchasing agent are based on reason and research. An error of a penny or two on a large purchase might cost a company thousands of dollars. Consequently, business advertising typically uses the rational approach. Additionally, it is important for advertisers to know exactly who makes buying decisions, since most purchases in large business are generally made in consultation with others in a company.

Fourth, personal selling plays a greater role in the business arena, and advertising is frequently used to support the sales staff in the field. As a result, ad budgets in the business sector may not be as high as those of their consumer counterparts.

Media

The media mix for business advertising is also different from that of consumer advertising. Since the target audience tends to be small, personalized media are best. Business publications tend to be the mainstay of campaigns. One study suggested that about 60 percent of industrial advertising dollars went to business and trade publications. Trade publications can be horizontal, dealing with a job function without regard to industry (such as *Purchasing*), or vertical, covering all job types in an entire industry (such as *LP/Gas*).

ethical issues   *Advertising and Kids*

There is no doubt that advertisers have zeroed in on the child audience. The last several years have seen the growth of kid-specific media: Nickelodeon, Web sites, kid-oriented magazines, movie tie-ins, and even hamburger wrappers. In 2008, about $2 billion was spent on advertising aimed at children.

Part of the reason behind this increase is the fact that kids have become important factors in family buying decisions. First, they have more money to spend. The under-14 set gets allowances, earns money, and receives gifts to the tune of about $20 billion per year. In addition, kids probably influence another $200 billion worth of shopping decisions. Second, the increase in single-parent families and dual-career families means that kids are now making some of the purchasing decisions that were once left to Mom and Dad.

It is not surprising, then, to find that companies are intensifying their efforts to reach this market segment. And it is not just traditional toymakers, cereal companies, and fast-food restaurants that are in the mix. General Motors, for example, placed ads for its new minivan in *Sports Illustrated for Kids* and sent prototype vans to shopping malls where they showed previews of Disney's *Hercules* on a VCR inside the van. GM does not expect many 6-year-olds to go out and buy a van, but the company knows through its research that kids can play an influential role in the decision about which van to buy. In that connection United Airlines kept its younger travelers happy by serving McDonald's Happy Meals.

Market research that examines children's psychology has been used to help sell goods. Researchers know that 7- and 8-year-olds like to collect things. This urge used to be satisfied by bottle caps, seashells, and baseball cards. More recently, the maker of Beanie Babies cashed in on this urge by creating a large number of different animals to collect, limiting production and discontinuing models to create artificial scarcity.

The marketing even extends into schools. Companies donate money, equipment, and educational materials to schools in return for the opportunity to advertise their products. It all started with Channel One, a news program for students. In return for a donation of electronic equipment, schools agreed to show a newscast that contained commercials. Other companies did not take long to follow Channel One. Nike, for example, mailed out shoe assembly kits to schools. Teachers were supposed to help kids make the sneakers while teaching a lesson on environmentally safe manufacturing (presumably by companies like Nike). McDonald's sponsored a seven-week curriculum on how to build a McDonald's restaurant and how to interview for a job there. Some school districts, hard up for cash, have sold advertising space on the sides of school buses and in school hallways.

There are many who feel that all this selling to children is not right. They argue that children are an unsophisticated audience and are vulnerable to the flashy, persuasive techniques of the advertising industry. Not many parents would allow a salesperson to come into their home and talk to their kids; why, then, should they allow TV to target their children? Additionally, critics contend that advertising teaches values that are undesirable. Advertising focuses on the superficial and the material, and it glorifies consumption. Finally, critics contend that advertising creates conflicts between parents and children by encouraging kids to pester their parents for all the products they see advertised. Parents must continually say no and run the risk of possible strife. There is some evidence to support these positions. Even without this support, however, many people feel that advertising to kids is just plain wrong.

The advertisers reply that these critics do not give kids enough credit. They argue that kids are more sophisticated consumers than people realize and learn very quickly to see through the hype and manipulation that may be found in some ads. Additionally, the marketing community points out that kids are going to live in a world saturated by advertising. Coming into contact with it at an early age may help them learn how to deal with it when they become adults. Finally, they argue that kids get valuable information about new products and services from advertising, information that improves their lives.

The issue, of course, has legal as well as ethical overtones. To date, the government has weighed in on the side of kids. The Children's Television Act limits the number of commercial minutes in TV shows that can be directed at children. The government and the tobacco industry worked out an agreement that prohibited the Camel cigarette company from using the cartoon character Joe Camel in its ads because the character appealed to children. There have been proposals to ban or limit beer, wine, and liquor advertising. Despite these efforts, it is clear that parents will be the ones to confront this issue head-on.

Direct mail and e-mail are valuable business advertising tools. Highly differentiated mailing lists can be prepared and ads sent to the most likely prospects. Research has shown that mail is perhaps more effective among businesspeople than among consumers. Whereas a large percentage of direct-mail material is thrown out unopened by the general public, most businesspeople read or at least scan their e-mail and direct-mail ads.

Advertising in trade catalogues is particularly important to companies that sell through distributors rather than via their own sales staff. Since a catalogue is a direct reflection of a company, extra care is taken to make sure it is up-to-date, accurate, and visually appealing.

Business-to-business advertising in the mass media used to be rare, but some large companies, such as FedEx, UPS, and Xerox, have used it to great effect. FedEx, for example,

Exceeding Your Expectations

▶ ▶ ▶ ▶ **Cat® 315/315 L:**
The New Size in Power
and Efficiency

To get the highest return on your
machine investment you need an
excavator that will do the job efficiently
and move on to the next job site quickly.
The new Cat 315 is designed to do just
that. With all the performance features
of the Cat 300 Family and a design
which allows it to be hauled on a tag-
along trailer, the new 315 can increase
your productivity. Here are some of
the benefits:

• 300 Family advanced hydraulics with
three Power Mode Settings, three Work
Mode Settings, Automatic Engine Control
and self-diagnostic capabilities for
improved productivity, increased fuel
efficiency and lower maintenance costs.

© 1994 Caterpillar

• 99 FWHP, turbocharged Cat 3046
Engine designed for more efficient,
responsive power and fuel efficiency,
plus reduced sound levels.

• Two undercarriage options, standard
and long (L), both with a maximum
shipping width of less than 9'0" for
hassle-free movement from job to job.

• Three stick options to match your
job needs: 10'2"   8'6"   7'5"

• Standard auxiliary hydraulic valve for
attachment flexibility to do a wider range
of jobs more efficiently.

• New control features, including light-
touch joysticks...automatic low-to-high-
speed travel selection...and winged foot
pedals for easier operation.

• Comfortable, efficient cab with
large windows for excellent visibility...
fully adjustable seat...and sliding
joystick consoles.

All these 300 Family advantages...along
with your Cat Dealer's unsurpassed
service, support and industry-leading
parts network...work together to Exceed
Your Expectations in every way. Stop
in and see the new Cat 315 today!

	315/315 L
Power:	99 FWHP
Operating Weight Up To:	36,000 lb
Ground Level Reach:	30'0"
Maximum Digging Depth:	21'6"
Bucket Capacity Range:	0.68 - 0.97 yd³
Shipping Width, **24" Shoes:**	8'6"

CATERPILLAR®

An example of business-to-business advertising. This ad for Caterpillar industrial equipment contains far more technical information than would be found in a consumer ad.

found that its business increased more than 40 percent after it started to advertise in consumer media. Purchasing time and space in the mass media must be done skillfully because of the expense and the chance of wasted coverage if the right decision makers are not in the audience. Specialized cable channels have made it possible for many business-to-business advertisers to use more general media with reduced chances of wasted coverage. CNN's *MoneyLine* and several shows on CNBC, for example, attract an audience that contains many business decision makers. General newsmagazines, such as *Time* and *Newsweek,* along with *Forbes, BusinessWeek,* and *Fortune,* are rather obvious choices for this type of advertising.

Business advertisers have also increased their use of the Internet. Business-to-business sites can include large amounts of technical data, product descriptions, search engines that allow customers to find the exact product they are interested in, and other information useful to potential purchasers.

Appeals

Close attention is paid to the copy in business-to-business advertising. Many consumer ads depend on impression and style to carry their messages. The copy tends to be brief and can cater to the emotions. Business copy tends to be longer, more detailed, and more factual. A premium is placed on accuracy and completeness. If the ad contains technical inaccuracies or exaggerations, the credibility of the product is compromised. Some of the most-used formats in business advertising are testimonials, case histories, new-product news, and demonstrations.

This is not to say, however, that all industrial ads must be stodgy and dull. In recent years several ad agencies specializing in business ads have introduced warmth, humor, and creativity into their messages. The philosophy behind this movement is that businesspeople are also consumers and that they respond as consumers to business and trade ads.

advertising

After a couple of dismal years, advertising industry employment is rebounding slowly. Ad agencies hired about 2,500 new employees in 2010, reversing a two-year decline. Nationwide, about 700,000 people worked in advertising or marketing services in 2010, down nearly 10 percent from 2007. Individuals with digital production skills and a knowledge of social media were the ones with the best chances of landing a job.

The career outlook in the various media industries changes quickly. For a more current description of conditions in the advertising industry and a more detailed look at career options, please consult the book's Web site: www.mhhe.com/dominick12e.

main points

- Advertising is any form of nonpersonal presentation and promotion of ideas, goods, and services paid for by an identified sponsor.

- Advertising can be classified by target audience, geographic focus, and purpose.

- Modern advertising began in the late 19th century and grew during the early 20th century as magazines and radio became mass advertising media.

- After World War II, advertising grew at a fast rate, particularly when TV came on the scene.

- The past two decades have seen the start of new channels for advertising, including cable TV and the

Internet. Online advertising has grown in the past few years.

- The three main components of the advertising industry are advertisers, agencies, and the media.

- Advertising agencies put together large-scale campaigns for clients, consisting of a market strategy, theme, ads, media time/space, and evaluation.

- Although not as visible as consumer advertising, business-to-business advertising makes up a significant portion of the industry.

questions for review

1. What are the three defining characteristics of advertising?

2. Briefly describe the three main components of the advertising industry.

3. What is meant by "decoupling"?

4. What is positioning? Why is it important to advertisers?

5. How does consumer advertising differ from business-to-business advertising?

questions for critical thinking

1. What would society be like without advertising?

2. Is it right to advertise to children? If you think it is appropriate to advertise to children, what special considerations, if any, should be applied to such ads?

3. Check the national media for ongoing advertising campaigns. What are some themes that are currently running?

4. How can you tell if an advertising campaign has been effective?

5. Will "viral marketing" be around five years from now? Why or why not?

6. Review "Critical/Cultural Issues: Cultural Meaning and Trade Characters on page 354" and then consider the following. Why do marketers want us to have emotional connections to mass-produced products? Does the Aflac duck make you feel more positive toward insurance? In addition to the Aunt Jemima example, how are expectations for and stereotypes of race and gender reflected in trade characters?

key terms

target audience (p. 351)

consumer advertising (p. 351)

business-to-business advertising
  (p. 351)

primary demand ad (p. 351)

selective demand ad (p. 351)

direct action ad (p. 351)

indirect action ad (p. 351)

advertising agency (p. 353)

viral advertising (p. 356)

decoupling (p. 358)

national advertisers (p. 358)

retail advertisers (p. 359)

agency (p. 359)

full-service agency (p. 359)

media buying service (p. 360)

creative boutique (p. 360)

copy (p. 362)

campaign (p. 363)

positioning (p. 363)

rough layout (p. 364)

comprehensive layout (p. 364)

storyboard (p. 364)

formative research (p. 365)

message research (p. 365)

tracking studies (p. 366)

internet resources

Online Learning Center

On the Online Learning Center home page, www.mhhe.com/dominick12e, *select* Student Center *and then* Chapter 15.

1. Use the Learning Objectives, Chapter Outline, and Main Points sections to review this chapter.

2. Test your knowledge of the chapter using the multiple choice and flashcard features of the site.

3. Expand your knowledge of concepts and topics discussed in the chapter with additional Questions for Critical Thinking and Internet Exercises.

surfing the internet

The following sites represent just a small sample of the hundreds and hundreds of sites that are relevant to this chapter. All were current as of late 2011. Keep in mind, however, that ad sites change rapidly.

www.aaaa.org
Home of the American Association of Advertising Agencies. Contains agency news, career information, and awards programs.

www.adage.com
Advertising Age is the leading trade publication for the industry. Its Web page has current news, useful statistics, and critiques of Web site advertising.

www.ddb.com
DDB is an ad agency that handles McDonald's and Volkswagen. A sampling of the agency's current and past award-winning work is available.

www.clioawards.com
The Clios are advertising's counterparts to the Oscars. This site has a listing of winners and a searchable archive.

www.womma.com
Learn more about viral advertising at the site of the Word-of-Mouth Marketing Association.

Regulation of the Mass Media

Part **IV**

Regulation
of the Mass Media

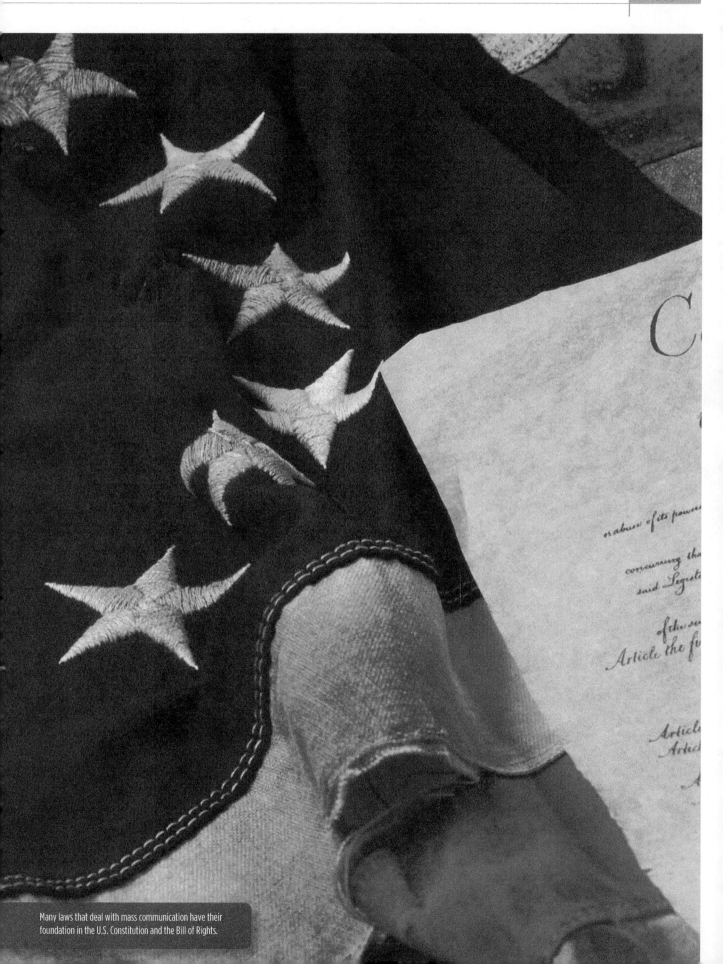

Many laws that deal with mass communication have their
foundation in the U.S. Constitution and the Bill of Rights.

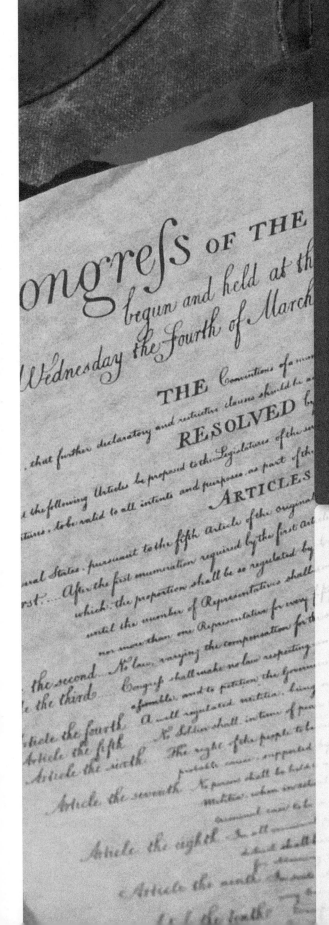

Chapter**16**

formal controls: laws, rules, regulations

This chapter will prepare you to:

- define *prior restraint*
- understand the special protective privileges of reporters
- distinguish among *libel, slander, libel per se,* and *libel per quod*
- explain how invasion of privacy can occur
- describe copyright law
- recognize the impact of media regulation of the Internet

et's suppose you wrote a book about how to commit the perfect murder. Your book detailed how to stalk your victim, when to strike, what weapons to use, and how to dispose of the body. Now let's suppose that somebody got a copy of your book and followed your instructions to actually commit a murder. Let's also suppose that relatives of the victim claim that you and your book bear some responsibility for the crime and sue you and your publisher for millions in damages. You have nothing to worry about, right? The First Amendment protects your right to free speech. Even though what you wrote might be objectionable, unpopular, and even repugnant to some, you're still protected.

It might not be that simple. The publisher of *Hit Man: A Technical Manual for Independent Contractors* found itself in the situation described above in 1998 when someone followed the directions in the book to murder three people. Relatives brought a wrongful death suit against the publisher. A federal court ruled that the book was protected by the First Amendment, but an appeals court reversed the decision and ruled that the book merited no First Amendment protection. The Supreme Court declined to hear an appeal and allowed the case to go to trial. Experts predicted that whatever the trial outcome, the case would probably find its way back to the

Supreme Court and raise significant First Amendment issues. The case never got back to the Court; the publisher and the relatives reached a settlement before the trial. The vexing issue of what speech falls outside the protection of the law continues to concern those in the mass media. As is clear by now, this chapter is concerned with media law and other regulations dealing with the media.

For purposes of this chapter, formal controls over the media include laws, court decisions that refine those laws, and rules and regulations administered by government agencies. We will examine six areas in which these controls are important: (1) the controversy over a free system of mass communication, (2) copyright, (3) restrictions on obscenity and pornography, (4) regulation of broadcast media, (5) regulation of the Internet, and (6) commercial speech.

Many students have the idea that the field of mass communication law is dull and boring. Nothing could be further from the truth. In what other academic field could you read about raunchy magazines, the CIA, celebrities uttering four-letter words on TV, mass murderers, women in men's locker rooms, juicy divorces, and a man who owned a submarine?

the press, the law, and the courts

A Free Press

As noted in Chapter 5, the idea of a free press did not catch on at first in America. The early colonial papers had problems if they were not "published by authority"—that is, if they were not open to censorship by the Crown. Through the Stamp Act the British government attempted to suppress dissent by taxing printed matter. Recognizing these dangers to a free press, the framers of the Constitution added an amendment (the **First Amendment**) that stated in part that "Congress shall make no law . . . abridging the freedom of speech, or of the press." The precise meaning and interpretation of these words, however, have been open to some debate. Let us examine some key instances in which press and government have come into conflict.

Prior Restraint

When the government censors the press by restraining it from publishing or broadcasting material, that act is called **prior restraint**. Attempts at prior restraint have been relatively rare. Nonetheless, this area does illustrate that the provisions in the First Amendment are not absolute. The Supreme Court has ruled that under certain circumstances prior restraint or censorship of the press is permitted, but the government faces a difficult task in proving that the restraint is justified. There are some obvious examples of legal censorship. During wartime a newspaper could be prevented from publishing the sailing schedules of troop transports, and a radio station could be prohibited from broadcasting the location and numbers of soldiers on the front lines. Other attempts at prior restraint have not been particularly successful; the Supreme Court has generally upheld the right of freedom of the press. Two seminal cases in this area are worth examining. One is not widely known; the other made the front pages.

The Near Case   During the 1920s the Minnesota legislature passed a law under which newspapers that were considered public nuisances could be curtailed by means of an **injunction** (an order from a court that requires somebody to do something or refrain from doing something). The motives behind this law may have been praiseworthy because it appears to have been designed to prevent abusive attacks on minority groups. Using this public nuisance law, a county attorney sought an injunction against the *Saturday Press* and the paper's manager, J. M. Near, on the grounds that the paper had printed malicious statements about city officials in connection with gangland activities allegedly controlled

media *Probe* *The Broad Reach of the First Amendment*

Two recent Supreme Court decisions demonstrate how the First Amendment protects free speech. In the first, the Court ruled that laws that banned so-called "animal cruelty" videos were unconstitutional. Despite the fact that most people found the videos repugnant, the Court stated that the First Amendment protects even distasteful expression. The Court concluded: "Our Constitution forecloses any attempt to revise that judgment simply on the basis that some speech is not worth it."

A second case involved a California law that prohibited the sale or rental of violent video games to minors. The Court found that the law was overly broad and infringed upon the free speech rights of minors. As the Court explained: "Video games qualify for First Amendment protection. . . . Like protected books, plays and movies, they communicate ideas through familiar literary devices and features distinctive to the medium."

by minority groups. In 1931 the Supreme Court ruled that the Minnesota law was unconstitutional. Said the Court,

> *The fact that for approximately 150 years there has been almost an entire absence of attempts to impose previous restraints upon publications relating to the malfeasance of public officers is significant of the deep-seated conviction that such restraints would violate constitutional rights.*

This issue would not be raised again for 40 years.

The Pentagon Papers   U.S. Attorney General John Mitchell was eager to see the Sunday, June 13, 1971, edition of the *New York Times*. Mitchell had attended the wedding of President Richard Nixon's daughter Tricia the day before, and he wanted to see how the *Times* had covered it. On the left side of page 1, Mitchell saw a flattering picture of the president with his daughter on his arm. Next to the wedding picture, another story caught Mitchell's eye: "Vietnam Archive: Pentagon Study Traces 3 Decades of Growing U.S. Involvement." As Mitchell read further, he realized that the *Times* article was sure to cause problems.

The basis for the story in the *Times* began three years earlier when Secretary of Defense Robert McNamara became disillusioned with the Vietnam War and ordered a massive study of its origins. This study, known eventually as the Pentagon Papers, was put together by 36 different people and ran to more than 7,000 pages. The final report was classified "Top Secret—Sensitive." During April 1971, one of the Pentagon staff members who had compiled the report leaked a copy to a reporter for the *New York Times*. After much study and secrecy, the paper was ready to publish the story in nine installments. The U.S. Justice Department, under John Mitchell's direction, asked a U.S. district court judge to halt publication of the stories on the grounds that they would "cause irreparable injury to the defense interests of the United States." The order was granted, and for the first time in history, a U.S. paper was ordered by the courts to suppress a specific story. By then, however, other newspapers had obtained copies of some or all of the Pentagon documents and started publishing them. The Justice Department sought more restraining orders, but as soon as one paper was ordered to stop publishing, another newspaper in another part of the country would pick up the series. It was obvious that the Supreme Court would eventually have to intervene.

The Court did intervene and with uncharacteristic haste. On June 30, 1971, only 17 days after the story first appeared and only 4 days after hearing oral arguments on the case, the Court decided in favor of the newspapers' right to publish the information. Naturally, the staff at the *New York Times* was delighted. The paper called the decision a "ringing victory for freedom under law." Upon closer examination, however, the victory was not quite as ringing as it was made out to be. The Court did not state that prior restraint could never be invoked against the press. Instead, it pointed out that the government "carries

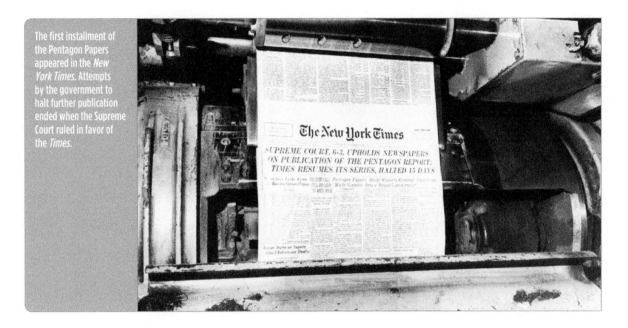

The first installment of the Pentagon Papers appeared in the *New York Times.* Attempts by the government to halt further publication ended when the Supreme Court ruled in favor of the *Times.*

a heavy burden of showing justification" for imposing restraint. The government, in the opinion of the Court, had not shown sufficient grounds for doing this. The government was free, if it wished, to bring other prior restraint cases to the courts to establish exactly how much justification it needed to stifle publication. In addition, each of the nine judges wrote a separate opinion that highlighted the ambiguities and complexities surrounding this topic.

More Recent Cases   After the release of the Pentagon Papers, the prior restraint issue cropped up several times in cases involving ex–CIA agents. In one case the CIA was successful in having portions of a book deleted because they revealed classified information.

In 1999 a ruling by a district court judge held that the prohibition against prior restraint also included Web sites. The creator of a Web site devoted to news about the Ford Motor Company had posted documents obtained from Ford employees. The company had obtained a ruling that prevented the documents from being posted, but the ruling by the district court judge overturned that prohibition.

In 2004, an Alabama district court turned down a government request for prior restraint against a Web site that published the names of investigators for the Drug Enforcement Agency. The court ruled that although the site might make some people uncomfortable, it did not present a threat so serious as to justify prior restraint. In 2008, a U.S. Circuit Court of Appeals held that journalists have a right of access to jurors' identities and that a federal judge was wrong to try to empanel an anonymous jury. The court acknowledged that although the press might publish stories about the background of the jurors that could make some less willing to serve, that possibility did not outweigh the judicial system's interest in openness.

In 2010, WikiLeaks, an organization that publishes private, secret, and classified information supplied by anonymous news sources and whistle-blowers, published on its Web site classified documents about the war in Iraq and Afghanistan. The *New York Times* published many of the leaked documents (see Chapter 17). Observers were quick to point out the similarities between the WikiLeaks case and the Pentagon Papers. Keep in mind, however, that in the WikiLeaks case, the government made no effort at prior restraint—that is, they did not try to stop the *Times* from publishing. Nonetheless, there may be similarities between the two cases concerning what happened after the information was published. In the 1970s, the government convened a grand jury to investigate the *New York Times* for conspiracy to commit espionage, but the grand jury did not return

media Probe
Prior Restraint and the High School and College Press

In 1983 a principal in Hazelwood, Missouri, deleted from a high school paper an article that dealt with teenage pregnancy and another article about divorce, on the grounds that they were inappropriate. Three student journalists, with the help of the American Civil Liberties Union, filed suit claiming that their First Amendment rights had been violated. The Supreme Court eventually decided the case in favor of the school system. The Court held that since the paper was part of the high school's journalism curriculum and used school supplies and its staff was restricted to journalism students, it was not a public forum and not entitled to First Amendment protection.

Until recently, it appeared that the college press merited more protection. In the fall of 2002, the dean of student affairs and services at

Governors State University in Illinois informed the printer of the college's newspaper that prior approval by a university official was required before the paper was printed. The student editors of the paper filed a lawsuit and won a victory when a three-judge panel ruled that the decision in the Hazelwood case did not apply to college newspapers. In 2005, however, the U.S. Court of Appeals reversed that decision declaring that since the newspaper was subsidized by funds from the university, it did not qualify as a public forum. The Supreme Court refused to grant an appeal in the case. Although some states have passed laws providing some degree of protection to student journalists, it appears that high school and college press is entitled to less than the full protection of the First Amendment.

an indictment. In 2011, a grand jury was also investigating Julian Assange, WikiLeaks editor-in-chief, for a possible indictment on espionage charges.

In sum, there is a strong constitutional case against prior restraint, but gray areas exist in which censorship might be legal. These areas will probably remain ambiguous until further court cases help define the limits of government authority. It is likely, however, that the barriers against prior restraint will remain formidable.

protecting news sources

Before we begin an examination of this topic, it is important to consider that the issues are fairly complicated. Conflicting interests are involved. Reporters argue that if they are forced to disclose confidential sources, those sources will dry up and the public's right to know will be adversely affected. Government arguments cite the need for the administration of justice and the rights of an individual to a fair trial.

Perhaps a hypothetical example will help bring these issues into focus. Suppose you are a reporter for a campus newspaper. One of your sources calls you late one night and informs you that several students are running a drug ring that has monopolized the sale of illegal drugs on campus. To check the accuracy of this report, you call another one of your sources, one who in the past has given you reliable information on campus drug dealing. This second source confirms what your caller told you and adds more details. For obvious reasons both of your sources ask not to be identified, and you agree. On the basis of these reports and some additional research, you publish a lengthy article in the campus newspaper about the drug ring. A few days later you are summoned before a grand jury that is investigating criminal drug dealings. You are asked to reveal your sources. If you refuse, you will be charged with contempt and possibly fined or sent to jail. What do you do?

The Reporter's Privilege

Other reporters have found themselves in the same fix. One was Paul Branzburg. In 1969 Branzburg wrote a story for the *Louisville Courier-Journal* in which he described how two local residents were synthesizing hashish from marijuana. His article stated that he had promised not to reveal their identities. Shortly thereafter, Branzburg was subpoenaed (ordered to appear) by the county grand jury. He refused to answer questions about his sources, claiming, in part, that to do so would violate the First Amendment provision for freedom of the press. The case ultimately reached the Supreme Court, which ruled that the First Amendment did not protect reporters from the obligation to testify before grand juries to answer questions concerning a criminal investigation.

Initially, this ruling was viewed as a setback for reporters' rights. However, the Court did suggest some situations in which the reporter's claim to privilege would be valid. These included harassment of news reporters, instances in which grand juries do not operate in good faith, and situations in which there is only a remote connection between the investigation and the information sought. Additionally, the Court suggested that Congress and the states could further define the rights of a reporter to protect sources by enacting legislation (called **shield laws**) to that effect.

After the Branzburg decision, state courts were somewhat inconsistent in their rulings. On the one hand, several cases upheld the reporter's right to keep her or his sources secret. In Florida, Lucy Ware Morgan, a reporter for the *St. Petersburg Times,* refused to disclose her source for a story about a grand jury report on corruption in city government. She was promptly convicted of contempt of court and received a 90-day jail sentence. In 1976, however, the Florida Supreme Court overturned the conviction. Using the Branzburg decision as a guideline, the court concluded that the name of her source was not relevant to the investigation of a crime and that the contempt charge was designed to harass her.

Other decisions have narrowly defined the test of relevancy between the case at hand and the reporter's sources. In Virginia a newspaper reporter refused to identify a source during testimony at a 1978 murder trial. The lawyer for the accused argued that the source was needed to question the credibility of a prosecution witness. The Virginia Supreme Court ruled in favor of the reporter and stated that a reporter's privilege must yield only when the defendant's need for the information is essential. To be essential, said the court, the information had to (1) relate directly to the defendant's guilt or innocence, (2) bear on the reduction of an offense, or (3) concern the mitigation of a sentence.

Just because these cases are taken from the 1970s, do not get the idea that reporters no longer go to jail or get fined. From 1999 to 2000, three reporters in California, a state with what many experts consider the strongest shield law in the country, got into legal trouble when they failed to reveal confidential sources of information. One journalist went to jail for five days, and another was fined $1,000 a day for every day he refused to testify. Fortunately for the reporters, either the sanctions were overturned on appeal or the original requests were dropped. Finally, there is the complicated case of Judith Miller of the *New York Times* and Matthew Cooper of *Time.* The two were subpoenaed and ordered to reveal their confidential sources during an investigation by the Justice Department probing who leaked the name of a covert CIA operative to a newspaper columnist. The reporters declined to cooperate and turned to the legal system for protection. Two federal courts ruled against them, and in mid-2005 the Supreme Court declined to review the case, raising the possibility that the two could serve up to 18 months in prison. In the wake of the Court's action, Cooper's source released him from his promise of confidentiality. Miller, however, began serving a jail term. Miller was eventually released from jail when she was satisfied that her source had granted permission to reveal his name.

Reporters for the *San Francisco Chronicle* published information leaked from grand jury testimony during investigations concerning the use of performance-enhancing drugs by athletes. In 2006 a new grand jury ordered the reporters to reveal their sources. The reporters appealed the order, but a district court judge ruled that they had to comply with the grand jury's instructions or face a lengthy jail term. The source of the story eventually came forward, and the matter came to a close.

In 2008, a reporter for *USA Today* was ordered to reveal her sources in connection with stories she wrote in a libel case concerning the government's investigation into the 2001 anthrax attacks. The reporter refused, was charged with contempt, and was fined $5,000 a day. The fines were put on hold while the reporter appealed the ruling. The contempt charge was eventually dropped when the original libel case was settled. In another case that same year, an appeals court ruled that the author of a book about Donald Trump was protected by New York's shield law and did not have to reveal his sources. This ruling is interesting in that it appears to extend the protection of the shield law to authors of entertainment books.

media *Probe*   *Who Carries the Shield?*

Shield laws are designed to protect reporters' materials, including the names of sources. It sounds simple in theory, but in practice the Internet has forever complicated matters. At issue are the more than 100 million people who publish blogs on the Internet. Are they reporters who qualify for protection under the various states' shield laws?

Various states define journalists and reporters differently. In Illinois, a reporter is "any person regularly engaged in the business of collecting, writing or editing news for publication through a news medium on a full-time or part-time basis." A "news medium," in turn, is "any newspaper or other periodical issued at regular intervals whether in print or electronic format and having a general circulation" as well as broadcast media such as radio and television stations. Would a blogger be covered by this statute? Illinois has yet to have a test case.

California's law is different. Its shield law protects a "publisher, editor, reporter, or other person connected with or employed upon a newspaper, magazine, or other periodical publication, or by a press association or wire service, or any person who has been so connected or employed" or "a radio or television news reporter or other person connected with or employed by a radio or television station, or any person who has been so connected or employed." Does this definition include a blogger? A California court ruled that bloggers were covered if they were "gathering news for public knowledge."

The shield law in Kentucky is straightforward. It covers "newspaper, radio or television broadcasting station personnel." This would seem to rule out bloggers, but again no test case has come forward.

In short, bloggers should be aware of the limits of the shield laws in the various states and act accordingly. A state-by-state listing of shield laws is available at http://www.poynterextra.org/shieldlaw/states.

These examples suggest that the nation's courts are taking a more skeptical view of the media's claim to privilege when it comes to revealing sources. In that connection media organizations are counseling reporters to be careful when making promises of confidentiality.

As of 2011, 39 states and the District of Columbia had shield laws. Journalists generally recognize these laws as helpful, but most realize that they are not the powerful protectors of the press that many had hoped for. In addition, the laws themselves represent a bewildering collection of provisions, qualifications, and exceptions. Some states protect only confidential material; some protect the reporter from revealing the name of a source but do not protect the information obtained from sources. Other state laws confer less protection if the reporter is involved in a libel case. In some states shield laws do not apply to reporters subpoenaed by a grand jury. Further, many courts are interpreting the shield laws on a case-by-case basis and ignoring or limiting the interpretation of judgments contained in the law. There have been several attempts to establish a federal shield law, most recently in 2011, but none has succeeded.

Search and Seizure

Finally, there is the troublesome question of protecting notes and other records that might disclose sources or other information relevant to an investigation. In this regard the courts have offered little protection. Three particular cases have disturbed the news media.

In the first case, in 1971, four police officers entered the offices of the *Stanford Daily*, the campus newspaper of Stanford University, and produced a warrant authorizing them to search for photographs of a clash between demonstrators and police that the *Daily* had covered the day before. The newspaper brought suit against the authorities, charging that its First Amendment rights had been violated. In 1978 the Supreme Court ruled that the search was legal. (In 1980, however, Congress extended some protection to newsrooms by passing the Privacy Protection Act, which requires the government to secure a subpoena to obtain records held by reporters. The scope of a subpoena is somewhat more limited than that of a search warrant. In addition, a subpoena can be challenged.)

In the second case, the U.S. Court of Appeals in the District of Columbia issued a decision that further eroded reporters' rights to protect sources. In 1974 the Reporters Committee for Freedom of the Press filed suit against AT&T because the company would not pledge to keep records of reporters' toll calls safe from government scrutiny. (An analysis of these calls might help locate a reporter's source of information.) The court of appeals

ruled that it was legal for the government to examine such records without a reporter's knowledge or consent. Another court of appeals ruling in 2006 reinforced this viewpoint when it ruled that the phone records of two *New York Times* reporters who refused to cooperate with a grand jury investigation were not protected by privilege. The court declared that the government's need for the records took precedence over First Amendment concerns.

The third case involved *New York Times* reporter Myron Farber. During 1976 Farber had been reporting on an investigation into mysterious deaths at a New Jersey hospital. The stories led to the indictment of a prominent physician on charges of poisoning five patients. Defense lawyers ultimately subpoenaed notes and documents pertaining to the case that were held by Farber and the *Times*. Both Farber and the paper refused to provide the documents, and both were convicted of contempt of court. Farber was sentenced to 6 months in jail and a $1,000 fine; the *Times* was slapped with a $100,000 fine and was ordered to pay $5,000 every day until it complied with the court's order. The *Times* ultimately turned over its files, but a judge ruled that the paper had "sanitized" them by removing some relevant material, so it reinstated the fine. Farber, meanwhile, had spent 27 days in jail. Eventually, Farber wound up spending 40 days in jail, and the *Times* paid $285,000 in fines. All penalties finally ended with the jury's verdict that the physician was innocent.

In 2005 a freelance journalist/blogger was ordered by a grand jury to turn over to authorities outtakes from videos that he had shot of a violent demonstration in which a police officer was injured. The blogger refused and eventually served 7½ months in federal prison before his lawyer worked out a compromise with prosecutors.

The privacy of computer-stored messages and e-mail received protection from the Electronic Communication Privacy Act, which requires the government to obtain a search warrant before examining online or stored messages intended to be private.

Perhaps the safest conclusion that we can draw is that a reporter's privilege in protecting sources and notes is not absolute. Even those decisions that have favored journalists have been qualified. It also appears that further developments in this area will be put together on a piece-by-piece basis by lower courts unless the Supreme Court issues a precise decision or Congress passes a comprehensive law. As for reporters, they must carefully consider these issues when they promise confidentiality to a news source.

covering the courts

On the one hand, the Sixth Amendment guarantees a defendant the right to a trial before an impartial jury; on the other, the First Amendment guarantees freedom of the press. Trial judges are responsible for the administration of justice; reporters are responsible for informing the public about the workings of the legal system. Sometimes these responsibilities clash.

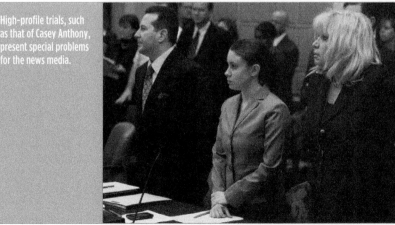

High-profile trials, such as that of Casey Anthony, present special problems for the news media.

Publicity Before and During a Trial

If a potential jury member has read, seen, or heard stories in the news media about a defendant that appear to indicate that person's guilt, it is possible that the defendant will not receive a fair trial. Although research has not produced definitive evidence linking pretrial publicity to prejudice, this concern has been at the heart of several court decisions that have castigated the news media for trying cases in the newspaper or on television instead of in the courtroom.

The 1960s saw a flurry of cases suggesting that the Supreme Court was taking a close look at pretrial publicity. In 1961 the Court for the first time reversed a criminal conviction entirely because pretrial publicity had made it impossible to select an impartial jury. The case concerned Leslie Irvin, a rather unsavory character who was arrested and charged with six murders. Newspapers carried police-issued press releases that said "Mad Dog" Irvin had confessed to all six killings. The local media seized upon this story with a vengeance, and many stories referred to Irvin as the "confessed slayer of six." Of the 430 potential jurors examined by attorneys, 90 percent had formed opinions about Irvin's guilt—opinions that ranged from suspicion to absolute certainty that he was guilty. Irvin was convicted—hardly a surprise—and sentenced to death. After six years of complicated legal maneuvers, made even more complicated by Irvin's escape from prison, the case went before the Supreme Court. The Court ruled that the pretrial publicity had ruined the defendant's chances for a fair trial and sent the case back to be retried. (Irvin, who had been recaptured, was again found guilty, but this time was sentenced to life imprisonment.)

Perhaps the most famous case of pretrial publicity concerned an Ohio physician. On July 4, 1954, the wife of Cleveland-area osteopath Dr. Sam Sheppard was found slain in the couple's home. Sheppard became a prime suspect, and the news media, especially the Cleveland newspapers, were impatient for his arrest. "Why Isn't Sam Sheppard in Jail?" and "Why Don't Police Quiz Top Suspect?" were headlines that appeared over page-one editorials. News reports carried the results of alleged scientific tests that cast doubt on Sheppard's version of the crime (these tests were never brought up at the trial). Articles stressed Sheppard's extramarital affairs as a possible motive for the crime. After his arrest the news stories and editorials continued. There were enough of them with headlines such as "Dr. Sam Faces Quiz at Jail on Marilyn's Fear of Him" and "Blood Is Found in Garage" to fill five scrapbooks. Every juror but one admitted to reading about the story in the newspapers. The sensationalized coverage continued during the trial itself, which produced a guilty verdict. Twelve years later the Supreme Court reversed Sheppard's conviction because of the extremely prejudicial publicity. This case assumed added importance because the Court listed six safeguards that judges might invoke to prevent undue influence from publicity. These safeguards included sequestering the jury (that is, moving them into seclusion), moving the case to another county, and placing restrictions on statements made by lawyers, witnesses, or others who might have damaging information.

In a high-profile case, former Enron executive Jeffrey Skilling argued that he did not receive a fair trial in his fraud case because it was impossible to seat an impartial jury in Houston, Enron's home base, where so many people had been hurt by the Enron collapse. In 2010, the Supreme Court ruled against Skilling, stating that heavy pretrial publicity did not necessarily create a presumption of juror bias.

Gag Rules

Some judges have issued restrictive orders, or **gag rules**, that restrain the participants in a trial (attorneys, witnesses, defendants) from giving information to the media or that limit media coverage of events that occur in court. For example, a superior court judge in a Washington murder trial ordered reporters to report only on events that occurred in front of a jury. Two reporters violated this rule by writing about events that took place in the courtroom while the jury was not present; they were subsequently charged with contempt. The Washington State Supreme Court refused to review this ruling.

The whole question of gag rules reached the Supreme Court in 1976. A Nebraska judge had prohibited reporters from revealing certain information about a mass murder case. The Nebraska Press Association appealed the order to the Supreme Court. The Court ruled on the side of the association and held that reporting of judicial proceedings in open court cannot be prohibited. Once again, upon first examination, this rule appeared to be a significant victory for the press. As time passed, however, it became apparent that the Nebraska decision had left the way open for court-ordered restrictions on what the trial participants could say to the press. It seemed to indicate that some legal proceedings, primarily those that take place before the actual trial begins, might be legitimately closed to the public. By the early 1980s this was exactly what was happening. Although the press was left free to report what it chose, its news sources were muzzled by judicial order. During the late 1970s judges began holding pretrial hearings in private to limit pretrial publicity. A 1979 Supreme Court decision held this practice to be constitutional. In 1980 the Court went on record as stating that the press did, in fact, have a constitutional right to attend criminal trials. *Pretrial* events, however, might still be closed. Because many criminal cases are settled out of court, these pretrial hearings are often the only public hearings held.

In the 1980s the press gained wider access to court proceedings. In 1984 the Supreme Court ruled that the jury selection process should be open to the press except in extreme circumstances, and it established standards that judges must meet before they can close a pretrial hearing. A 1986 Supreme Court decision, however, gave the press a major victory in its efforts to secure access to pretrial proceedings. The Court held that preliminary trial proceedings must be open to the press unless the judge could demonstrate a "substantial probability that the defendant's right to a fair trial would be violated." Additionally, lower courts have held that the First Amendment right of access to trials extends to documents used as evidence. Also in 1986, the Supreme Court ruled that the jury selection process, as well as the trial itself, must ordinarily be open to the public. The Court provided a set of strict guidelines that would justify a private selection of a jury.

In summary, Supreme Court decisions do not give the press an absolute right of access to all court proceedings. Some parts of trials and pretrial hearings may still be closed if the judge can fulfill the Court's guidelines regarding closure. Further, these decisions have not changed the legal status surrounding the privacy of grand jury hearings—they continue to have the right to secrecy. All in all, it might be safe to conclude that the press has been given a green light to report on matters that occur in open court with little fear of reprisal. But gag orders on news sources and the closing of various legal proceedings threaten to be areas of tension between the press and the judiciary for some time to come.

Cameras and Microphones in the Courtroom

For many years the legal profession looked with disfavor on the idea of cameras and microphones in the courtroom. There was a time when this attitude may have been entirely justified. The whole problem seems to have begun in 1935 when Bruno Hauptmann was put on trial for the kidnapping and murder of the son of national hero Charles Lindbergh. Remember that news photography and radio journalism were still young in 1935, and this fact may have contributed to some of the abuses that occurred during this trial. After the trial the American Bar Association added Canon 35 to its Canons of Professional Ethics. This provision stated that the taking of photographs in the courtroom and the broadcasting (later amended to include telecasting) of court proceedings should not be permitted. Although Canon 35 was not law, its language or some variation of it was adopted as law by every state except Colorado and Texas.

In 1965 the Supreme Court entered the picture when it ruled on the Billie Sol Estes case. Estes was on trial in Texas for allegedly swindling several farmers. The trial judge, over Estes's objections, had allowed the televising of the trial. Estes was found guilty, but he soon appealed that decision to the Supreme Court on the grounds that the presence of television had deprived him of a fair trial. The high court agreed with Estes and argued for the prohibition of television cameras in the courtroom. The Court said that broadcasting a trial would have a prejudicial impact on jurors, would distract witnesses, and would burden the trial judge with new responsibilities. However, the Court went on, there might come a day when broadcast technology would become portable and unobtrusive and television coverage so commonplace that trials might be broadcast. Thus, the decision in the Estes case was not a blanket provision against the televising of trials.

Since 1965 the trend has been toward a general relaxation of the tension between the legal profession and the electronic press. In 1972 the American Bar Association adopted a new code of professional responsibility. Canon 3A(7) of this document superseded the old Canon 35. Canon 3A(7) maintained the ban on taking photographs and broadcasting in the courtroom, but it did allow the judge the discretion to permit televising a trial to a pressroom or to another courtroom to accommodate an overflow crowd. In 1981 the Supreme Court ruled that broadcast coverage of a criminal trial is not inherently prejudicial, thereby clearing the way for the presence of radio and TV in the courtroom. The Court left it up to the states to devise their own systems for implementing such coverage.

As of 2011, all 50 states allowed some form of coverage. The rules for coverage vary state by state. In Georgia, for example, the judge may permit one television camera in the courtroom. In Ohio trial courts, coverage of nonconsenting victims and witnesses is prohibited. Although the situation may change, as of late 2010 cameras are not allowed in federal district courts or at Supreme Court proceedings.

reporters' access to information

Government Information

Reporting the doings of the government can be a frustrating task if the government insists that information about its activities be kept secret. After World War II many members of the press complained that government secrecy was becoming a major problem. Reporters were being restricted from meetings, and access to many government documents was difficult to obtain. Under continuing pressure from journalists and consumer groups, Congress passed the **Freedom of Information Act (FOIA)** in 1966. This law gave the public the right to discover what the federal government was up to—with certain exceptions. The law states that every federal executive-branch agency must publish instructions on what methods a member of the public should follow to get information. If information is improperly withheld, a court can force the agency to disclose what is sought. There are nine areas of exemptions covering material that does not have to be made public, including trade secrets, files of law enforcement investigations, and maps of oil wells. In 2007 a bill was introduced in Congress to streamline the FOIA and make it easier for the public to access government records. Moreover, a 2010 Supreme Court decision made it easier to obtain information when it narrowed the scope of one of the exemptions to the FOIA.

In 2009 President Barack Obama ordered the government to disclose more information under the FOIA. A memo from the Justice Department informed federal agencies that they should disclose information unless there was a legal ban or foreseeable harm in doing so. The agencies were instructed to cooperate with the Office of Government Information Service, an organization established in 2007 to mediate disputes between agencies and those requesting information. In sum, it appears that the media will have an easier time accessing government materials.

In 1996 the Electronic Freedom of Information Act (EFOIA) was passed to make more information available on the Internet. Currently, many government agency Web sites contain a variety of information, ranging from statistics to press releases, that can be accessed online rather than through an FOIA request. Nonetheless, many agencies have been slow to fully implement the requirements of the EFOIA.

A "Sunshine Act" ensures that regular meetings of approximately 50 federal government agencies will be open to the public. There are, however, 10 different situations that might permit an agency to meet behind closed doors, so the right of access to meetings is far from absolute. In addition, many states have their own versions of laws pertaining to information access and open meetings. The degree of compliance with these laws varies widely from state to state.

In the aftermath of the September 11 terrorist attacks, concerns about safety and security came into conflict with guarantees of press freedom. The **USA Patriot Act**, passed in October 2001, gave the government more power to access e-mail and telephone records. This increased monitoring power can be used not only to track terrorists but also to eavesdrop on journalists. In addition, the new law makes it easier for the government to restrict access to official records, and another provision prevents the press from finding out about FBI searches of books bought in bookstores or borrowed from libraries by those suspected of terrorist activities. In 2011, President Obama signed into law a four-year renewal of the Patriot Act.

Access to News Scenes

We have already examined the issue of access in our discussion of the right of the press to attend certain judicial proceedings. But what about the reporters' right of access to news settings outside the courtroom? The law here appears to be in the developmental stage. In the few decisions that have been handed down, the courts have given little support to the notion that the First Amendment guarantees a right of access. In separate rulings the courts have declared that journalists may be sued for invasion of privacy, for trespassing on private property, and for disobeying a police officer's legitimate command to clear the way at the scene of a serious automobile accident. Most recently, in 2009 a reporter for a Michigan newspaper was convicted of a felony for obstructing police officers at an accident scene. Officers testified that the reporter violated police orders when she crossed a police line in order to take photographs of victims of the accident. Three of the most relevant Supreme Court opinions have focused on the question of access to prisons and prisoners. In these cases the courts have ruled that reporters do not have the right to visit specific parts of a prison, to speak to specific prisoners, or to bring cameras inside. In general, the Court seems to be saying that the access rights of the press are not different from the access rights of the general public. When the public is not admitted, neither is the press.

Some rulings, however, have recognized a limited right of access. A Florida court said that journalists who are customarily invited by police onto private property to view a news scene cannot be prosecuted for trespassing. The courts have also allowed access to news settings in order to halt discrimination among journalists. For example, in one case it was ruled that a female journalist could not be barred from entering a baseball team's locker room if male reporters had been admitted. In sum, the final words on this topic have yet to be written by the courts. A case as influential as the Branzburg or Estes decision has yet to be adjudicated in the area of press access. It is a good bet, however, that such a test will not be long in surfacing.

defamation

As the preceding discussion makes clear, in its news-gathering activities the press often collides with the government. In addition, the right of free speech and the rights of a free press sometimes come into conflict with the right of an individual to protect his or her reputation. Protection for a person's reputation is found under the laws that deal with **defamation**.

To understand this somewhat complicated area, let us start with some general definitions:

- **Libel:** Libel is written defamation that tends to injure a person's reputation or good name or that diminishes the esteem, respect, or goodwill due a person.
- **Slander:** This is spoken defamation. (In many states, if a defamatory statement is broadcast, it is considered libel even though technically the words are not written. Libel is considered more harmful and usually carries more serious penalties than does slander.)
- **Libel per se:** Some words are always libelous. False written accusations, such as labeling a person a "thief" or a "swindler," automatically constitute libel.
- **Libel per quod:** Words that seem perfectly innocent in themselves can become libelous under certain circumstances. For instance, erroneously reporting that Joe Smith was seen eating a steak dinner last night may seem harmless unless Smith happens to be the president of the Worldwide Vegetarian Society.

For someone to win a libel suit brought against the media, that person must prove five things: (1) that he or she has actually been defamed and harmed by the statements,

sound byte

Handle with Care

Here are some red-flag words and expressions that may be libelous per se. Extreme care should be exercised in using these words in news reports:

bankrupt	corrupt	blockhead
intemperate	dishonest	rascal
unprofessional	amoral	scoundrel
communistic	disreputable	sneak
incompetent	illegitimate	deadhead
morally delinquent	hypocritical	fool
smooth and tricky	dishonorable	slacker
profiteering	cheating	skunk
sharp-dealing	unprincipled	poltroon
unethical	sneaky	ignoramus

(This list is also a handy reference guide for insults. Simply choose one word from the left list, one from the center, and one from the right: "You profiteering, amoral poltroon," or "You incompetent, corrupt deadhead." Just make sure that you do not put it in writing and that no third party is listening. Otherwise, you may get hit with a defamation suit.)

(2) that he or she has been identified (although not necessarily by name), (3) that the defamatory statements have been published, (4) that the media were at fault, and (5) in most instances, that what was published or broadcast was false.

Not every mistake that finds its way into publication is libelous. To report that James Arthur will lead the Fourth of July parade when in fact Arthur James will lead it is probably not libelous because it is improbable that leading a parade will cause harm to a person's reputation. (Courts have even ruled that it is not necessarily libelous to report incorrectly that a person died. Death, said the courts, is no disgrace.) Actual harm might be substantiated by showing that defamatory remarks led to physical discomfort (such as sleepless nights) or loss of income or increased difficulty in performing a job.

Identification need not be by name. If a paper erroneously reported that the professor who teaches Psych 101 at 10 A.M. in Quadrangle Hall is taking bribes from his students, that would be sufficient.

Publication, for our purposes, pertains to a statement's appearance in a mass medium and is self-explanatory.

Fault is a little more complicated. To win a libel suit, some degree of fault or carelessness on the part of the media organization must be shown. As we shall see, the degree of fault that must be established depends on several things: (1) the person who is suing, (2) the subject matter of the suit, and (3) the particular state's laws that are being applied.

A 1986 Supreme Court decision held that private persons (as opposed to public figures) suing for libel must prove that the statements at issue are false, at least when the statements involve matters of public concern. For all practical purposes, however, proving that the media were at fault also involves proving the falsity of what was broadcast or published, so that virtually everyone who brings a libel suit must show the wrongfulness of what was published.

It should be emphasized that a mass medium is responsible for what it carries. It usually cannot hide behind the fact that it only repeated what someone else said. For example, in most situations a magazine could not defend itself against a libel suit by claiming that it simply quoted a hospital worker who said a colleague was stealing drugs. If, in fact, the hospital worker's colleague was not stealing drugs, the magazine would have to look to some other defense against libel. A 2004 decision by the Pennsylvania Supreme Court further clarified this situation when it ruled that the First Amendment does not create a "neutral report privilege" for media when they report newsworthy statements made by one public official about another that might be defamatory. The case stemmed from a story in a local newspaper that quoted one city official calling two other city officials "child molesters." The Pennsylvania court ruled that even though the newspaper reported the story accurately, it could still be sued for defamation if the plaintiff could establish that the paper acted with actual malice.

Defenses Against Libel Suits

What are some of the defenses that can be used? There are three.

The first is truth. If what was reported is proved to be true, there is no libel. This defense, however, is rarely used since it is extremely difficult to prove the truth of a statement. In addition, since the Supreme Court's decision placed the burden of proving the falsity of a statement on the person bringing the libel suit, the truth defense has become even less attractive.

media Probe   *What Is Actual Malice?*

Many people are confused by the meaning of the phrase *actual malice* as it applies to defamation. Some individuals mistakenly think that a person who is defamed has to prove evil motives, spite, or ill will on the part of the person or medium that allegedly committed the defamation. Not so. In the famous *New York Times* v. *Sullivan* case, the Supreme Court defined *actual malice* as (1) publishing something that is known to be false ("I know what I'm publishing is not true but I'm going to publish it anyway") or (2) publishing something with reckless disregard for whether it is true or not ("I have good reason to doubt that what I'm publishing is true, but I'm going to publish it anyway").

A libel case involving CBS, Inc., and Walter Jacobson, a news anchor and commentator at WBBM-TV (the CBS affiliate) in Chicago, illustrates this definition. The Brown & Williamson Tobacco Corporation (maker of Viceroy cigarettes) claimed that Jacobson libeled its company when he charged during a TV commentary that Viceroy was using an ad campaign to persuade children to smoke. Viceroy, said Jacobson, was equating cigarette smoking with "wine, beer, shaving, or wearing a bra . . . a declaration of independence and striving for self-identity . . . a basic symbol of the growing-up process." The commentary cited as evidence a Federal Trade Commission report that claimed the company had been advised by

its advertising agency to launch such a campaign. Brown & Williamson, forced to prove actual malice on the part of Jacobson because of the company's position as a public figure, denied ever having launched such a campaign. In fact, company lawyers argued that Brown & Williamson was so outraged by its ad agency's advice that it fired the advertising firm. Further, Brown & Williamson argued that Jacobson knew this fact before he broadcast his commentary. In court one of the officials for the tobacco company testified that a researcher for Jacobson had been told that the ad agency had been fired and that the campaign was not used. During the trial Jacobson said that he had rejected a suggestion from this researcher that a disclaimer should be included in the commentary stating that Brown & Williamson had not used the campaign. Evidently, this fact was enough to convince the jury that Jacobson knew that what he was saying was false—thus establishing actual malice. The jury found in favor of the tobacco company and awarded Brown & Williamson more than $5 million in damages.

For their part Jacobson and CBS maintain that the commentary was an accurate summary of the FTC report and that Brown & Williamson had a strategy directed toward children, even if the company did not fully implement it. In late 1985, CBS announced plans to appeal the decision. The appeal was decided in 1988 in favor of the tobacco company. CBS was ordered to pay $3.05 million in damages.

A second defense is privilege. There are certain situations in which the courts have held that the public's right to know comes before a person's right to preserve a reputation. Judicial proceedings, arrest warrants, grand jury indictments, legislative proceedings, and city council sessions are examples of situations that are generally acknowledged to be privileged. If a reporter gives a fair and accurate report of these events, no lawsuits can result, even if what is reported contains a libelous statement.

The third defense is fair comment and criticism. Any person who thrusts him- or herself into the public eye or is at the center of public attention is open to fair criticism. This means that public officials, professional sports figures, cartoonists, artists, columnists, playwrights, and all those who invite public attention are fair game for comment. This defense applies only to opinion and criticism, not to misrepresentations of fact. You can report that a certain director's new movie stank to high heaven without fear of a lawsuit, but you could not report falsely that the director embezzled funds from the company and expect protection under fair criticism. However, criticism can be quite severe and caustic and still be protected from lawsuit. In 1990 the Supreme Court ruled that expressions of opinion are not automatically exempt from charges of libel. Opinions that contain an assertion of fact that can be proved false might trigger a defamation suit.

In 1964 the Supreme Court, in the *New York Times* v. *Sullivan* case, significantly expanded the opportunity for comments on the actions of public officials and also changed the nature of the law governing defamation. The case involved the *Times* and an official of the Montgomery, Alabama, police department, L. B. Sullivan, and took place during the civil rights struggle of the early 1960s. A civil rights group published an ad in the *Times* concerning a protest in Montgomery that Sullivan claimed libeled him. Testimony in the case revealed that, indeed, several statements in the ad were false. An Alabama court awarded Sullivan $500,000, but the *Times* appealed the case to the Supreme Court.

The Court reversed the Alabama decision and enumerated three major principles that would affect future decisions concerning defamation:

1. Editorial advertising is protected by the First Amendment.
2. Even statements that are false might qualify for First Amendment protection if they concern the public conduct of public officials.
3. To win a libel suit, public officials must prove that false and defamatory statements were made with actual malice.

The Court also clarified what is meant by *actual malice*—publishing a statement with the knowledge that it is false or publishing a statement in "reckless disregard" of whether it is true or not. A few years later, the Court expanded this protection to include statements made about public figures as well as public officials. In 1971 it appeared that the Supreme Court would even require private individuals who become involved in events of public concern to prove actual malice before collecting for a libel suit. Three years later, the Court seemed to retreat a little from this position when it held that a lawyer involved in a civil lawsuit was not a public figure, that he was not involved in an event of public interest, and that he did not have to prove actual malice.

Even more protection was extended to the private citizen in 1976 in a case concerning the divorce of Mary Alice Firestone and tire heir Russell Firestone Jr. The trial lasted 17 months and received large amounts of media coverage. Ms. Firestone even called several press conferences while the trial was taking place. When *Time* magazine erroneously reported that the divorce had been granted on the grounds of extreme cruelty and adultery, Ms. Firestone sued for libel. (Her husband had charged her with adultery, but adultery was not cited as grounds for the divorce.) *Time* argued that she was a public figure and contended that she had to show not only that the magazine was inaccurate but also that it acted with malice. The Supreme Court ruled that she was not a public figure, despite all the attendant press coverage, and drew a distinction between legitimate public controversies and those controversies that merely interest the public. The latter, said the Court, are not protected, and actual malice need not be proved.

The Court affirmed this distinction in 1979 by noting that the fact that someone is involved in a "newsworthy" event does not make the person a public figure. When a U.S. senator presented a scientist with a satirical award used to denote wasteful spending of government funds, the scientist sued for defamation. The Court ruled that even though the scientist became the subject of media attention, his public prominence before receiving the satirical award did not merit labeling him a public figure. Therefore, he did not have to meet the actual malice standard. Private citizens, however, do have to show some degree of fault or negligence by the media. In many states this means showing that the media did not exercise ordinary care in publishing a story. Establishing this allows a private citizen to collect compensation for any actual damages that stem from the libel. The big bucks, however, come from punitive damages assessed against the media. These awards are designed to punish the media for their past transgressions and serve as a reminder not to misbehave again. To collect punitive damages, even private citizens must show actual malice.

The amount of money that juries award to the winners of libel cases can be substantial. Awards of $1 million or more have become common. Singer Wayne Newton, for example, received a $20-million judgment against NBC. On the other hand, most libel cases are appealed, and about 75 percent either are reversed or have the monetary awards substantially reduced. For example, the Wayne Newton verdict was eventually reversed.

The difficulty that public figures face in successfully bringing a libel suit against the media has prompted some news subjects to look for other remedies. In the past decade several subjects of news stories have sued the news media for the way they gathered the news rather than the content of the story. Lawsuits concerning trespass and invasion of privacy by the media have become more common.

media *Probe*   *Is This Fair Comment?*

One of the most famous cases in the law of libel occurred in 1901 when a newspaper printed a review of a less-than-sensational vaudeville act performed by "The Cherry Sisters," Effie, Jessie, and Addie. Here is part of the review:

Effie is an old jade of fifty summers, Jessie is a frisky filly of forty, and Addie, the flower of the family, a capering monstrosity of thirty-five. Their long, skinny arms, equipped with talons on the extremities, swung mechanically. . . . The mouths of their rancid features opened like caverns and sounds like the wailing of damned souls issued therefrom.

Effie is spavined [afflicted with a disease that typically attacks horses' legs], Addie is springhalt [afflicted with a nerve disorder common to horses], and Jessie, the only one who showed her stockings, has legs as classic in their outlines as the curves of a broom handle.

The Cherry Sisters sued the paper for libel; the paper claimed fair comment as a defense. Legend has it that the judge asked the three sisters to perform their act in court. After seeing it, the judge ruled in favor of the paper.

Interestingly enough, according to the Media Law Resource Center, the number of libel cases in the United States has dropped significantly in recent years, from 266 during the 1980s to 124 during the 2000s. Factors contributing to this decline include the difficulty, particularly for a public figure, to win a libel case and the fact that the Internet lets media post corrections or retractions quickly. In addition, those who were defamed have access to blogs and social media where they can present their side of the story.

Defamation and the Internet

The Internet has created new problems with regard to defamation. One problem involves who can be sued for defamation. Suppose you post a defamatory message on an AOL message board. Can someone sue both you and AOL? Congress addressed this issue in the Communications Decency Act of 1996. The law states that Internet service providers such as AOL are not liable for the content that they carry unless they (the providers) are the actual authors of the content. A 2006 decision by a Pennsylvania court seemed to broaden this protection. The court ruled that a person who republished on a Web site a potentially defamatory story written by someone else was also entitled to protection under the act.

Recent court decisions have extended protection to anonymous online speech. In 2009 a Maryland appeals court invalidated a subpoena that sought to identify the authors of online comments. The court went on to enumerate a multipart test that should be applied in future cases. The test included a stipulation to balance the anonymous poster's First Amendment rights against the rights of the person bringing a defamation suit. In a related case, a Tennessee court refused to force the disclosure of the identity of an anonymous blogger, noting that the request for disclosure would have to pass the test articulated in the Maryland case.

A second vexing question involves jurisdiction. Since the online versions of newspapers, magazines, and newsletters are available all over the world at the click of the mouse, where should a lawsuit be filed? This is an important question because laws governing defamation vary by state. In one recent case, online newspapers in Connecticut published a story about prison conditions in Virginia. A court ruled that the warden of a Virginia prison could sue the newspapers for libel in Virginia because the publications were accessible in that state. This decision, however, was reversed by the court of appeals on the grounds that the newspaper's Web site was not aimed at a Virginia audience. The international situation is muddier. A court in Australia ruled that the Dow Jones Company, based in New Jersey, could be sued for defamation in Australia because the online version of one of its magazines was available for downloading in Australia. Dow Jones eventually lost the case and had to pay out about a

media *Probe* What Is Negligence?

For a private citizen to prevail in a defamation case, he or she must prove some degree of negligence on the part of the media. The standards for determining what constitutes negligence vary from state to state, and as with the actual malice standard, negligence is determined on a case-by-case basis. Nonetheless, some general statements can be made.

A common legal definition of *negligence* states that it is conduct that creates an unreasonable risk of harm. The standard of conduct that the possible negligence is measured against is whether a reasonable person under the same circumstances would behave in the same way. As far as the media are concerned, employees are to be judged against the appropriate practices and customs for their profession. Thus, in many cases the issue of negligence boils down to whether the reporter or editor exercised reasonable care and followed the accepted practices of the profession in determining whether a story was true or false.

Some specific factors might also be taken into account. First, was the story prepared under deadline? If sufficient time and opportunity were available, then reasonable care might require more checking of facts. Second, what was the interest being promoted by the story? Stories covering heated political debates have greater merit than gossip, but gossip can be extremely harmful. Hence, greater care should be exercised in the latter situation.

A concrete example might help illustrate negligence and show how it differs from actual malice. In a 1975 case in Massachusetts, a rookie reporter had been covering a drug trial. The reporter was unaware that a table in the front of the courtroom was reserved for the press. Consequently, he sat in the back, where he had trouble hearing the testimony. One of the defendants was the 20-year-old son of a man named John Stone, who ran the lunchrooms in a public school. When the prosecutor asked a marshal the question of who had the drugs, the reporter thought he heard the marshal say, "Mr. Stone" and assumed he meant John Stone, the only "Mr. Stone" the reporter was aware of. He wrote in his story that John Stone had possession of the drugs. When questioned by his editor, who knew John Stone personally and had a hard time believing that he could have possessed illegal drugs, the reporter said he had heard the name in court. In fact, the marshal was talking about Jeffrey Stone, the son of John Stone. John Stone, naturally enough, sued for libel.

The court found that the reporter was guilty of negligence because he did not sit where he could properly hear and did not check with another source to confirm who the "Mr. Stone" was—two practices that were in keeping with the accepted procedures of journalism. However, the reporter's conduct did not constitute actual malice since he was new in town and did not have reason to doubt that the Stone mentioned in court was the only Stone he knew.

But what about the editor, who knew Mr. Stone personally and had trouble believing the story? The editor had reason to doubt the story but did not even make a phone call to check its accuracy. The court ruled that he had acted with reckless disregard for the truth of the report, which was enough to constitute actual malice.

half-million dollars in damages. On the other hand, a British appeals court ruled that a Dow Jones publication that was available online could not be sued in England when it was shown that only five people had clicked on the Web site. The court said that there had to be evidence of substantial publication in England before a publication could be sued there.

In that connection, the state of New York passed the Libel Terrorism Protection Act in 2008. The law prevents the enforcement of libel judgments in the state unless a New York court finds that the foreign jurisdiction issuing the ruling has the same free speech protections as guaranteed under U.S. law. In addition, the law allows a citizen of New York to petition a state court to render the foreign verdict unenforceable in New York. A similar law on the federal level was passed in 2010.

invasion of privacy

The Right to Privacy

Closely related to libel is the issue of privacy. In fact, a single publication will often prompt both types of suits. The big difference between the two is that libel protects a person's reputation, but the right to privacy protects a person's peace of mind and feelings. A second difference is that libel involves the publication of false information; invasion of privacy might be triggered by disclosing the truth.

There are four different ways that the mass media can invade someone's right to privacy.

Intrusion upon Solitude   The first is intruding upon a person's solitude or seclusion. This generally occurs when reporters wrongfully use microphones, surveillance cameras, and other forms of eavesdropping to record someone's private activities. A TV news crew hiding in a van outside your room and secretly taping your activities while you are inside would probably constitute intrusion.

The use of tiny, hidden cameras and microphones by reporters in their quest for news has raised special problems in this area. In a 1999 decision the California Supreme Court ruled that an ABC reporter committed an invasion of privacy when she went to work for a psychic hot line and secretly videotaped a conversation with a coworker. Even though the conversation took place in an open office and was overheard by others, the court ruled that the coworker had a reasonable expectation that a reporter would not secretly video-tape his conversations. This decision suggests that reporters should give extra thought to the use of hidden recordings in their news-gathering activities.

Unauthorized Release of Private Information   The second occasion is the unau-thorized release of private information. A newspaper's publishing private medical records that reveal that a person has a dread disease is an example in this area. The courts allowed a suit claiming invasion of privacy to be filed when a newspaper published information about a person's sex-change operation without the person's consent.

The Internet has raised new concerns about privacy. In 2008, a federal judge ordered Google to provide information about videos watched on YouTube. The order came in the midst of a copyright suit brought by Viacom against the Internet search company. Viacom wanted access to the data to determine how many times its copyrighted videos were watched on the video-sharing site. Google had resisted providing the information because it might allow Viacom to determine the viewing and video-uploading activity of YouTube users.

Creation of a False Impression   A third method is publicizing people in a false light or creating a false impression of them. This invasion is most closely related to libel because falsity is also involved. Some TV stations get into trouble in this area through the practice of putting new narration over some stock tape footage, which sometimes creates a false impression. For example, a Chicago TV station was sued when it ran stock footage taken three years earlier of a doctor performing a gynecological exam with a story describing how another doctor allegedly used an AIDS-infected swab during a similar exam. The face of the doctor in the stock footage was readily identifiable, and she sued the station, claiming the story made it appear that she had performed the allegedly negligent procedure. (The station settled the suit out of court and paid the doctor an undisclosed amount of money.)

The decision in a 2008 false-light suit in Florida may have implications for invasion-of-privacy laws in other states. The Florida Supreme Court ruled that under Florida law false light was not a legitimate reason to bring a lawsuit. The ruling added, however, that Florida law does recognize defamation by implication, whereby a true statement is reported in such a way as to create a false impression. In short, those bringing cases in Florida for the creation of a false impression will have to show some harm to their repu-tation; claiming that their feelings have been hurt or that their peace of mind has been harmed will not be enough.

Appropriation of Identity   The last means of invading privacy is through appropria-tion of a person's name or likeness for commercial purposes. This commonly involves stars and celebrities who find their names or images used without their permission in some business or promotional activity. Model Christie Brinkley, for example, success-fully filed suit to stop poster stores from selling her picture without her permission. The not-so-famous are also protected against appropriation. One man sued because he found that a camera company had used his picture without permission in its instruction manual.

media *Probe*   *Facebook in the Court*

Those readers who have been called for jury duty know that one part of the process is called the *voir dire*, when opposing attorneys question prospective jurors about their experiences, beliefs, and backgrounds. Now, in addition to the *voir dire*, lawyers have new tools to aid them in jury selection: Facebook, Twitter, blogs, and other social media.

Since lawyers have only limited time to ask questions during the *voir dire*, it is becoming common for both prosecuting and defense attorneys to scour social media sites to see what information they can glean about potential jurors. For example, a lawyer for the prosecution would

probably reject a person who blogged about his bad experiences with law enforcement officers. Persons whose Facebook pages reveals that they are big fans of TV crime programs might think police are more efficient in solving crime than they actually are. A potential juror whose hobbies include kickboxing and the martial arts might be more sympathetic to someone accused of assault. A person's Facebook page might also reveal that he or she has friends with links to the case. People who post numerous messages on Twitter might also tweet about the trial and jury deliberations. In sum, the courtroom is yet another arena where social media have had an impact.

Trespass

Trespass, defined as unauthorized entry into someone else's territory, is a concept that is closely related to invasion of privacy. The close of the 20th century saw a significant increase in the number of trespass cases brought against the news media. These cases highlighted a fundamental question for news reporting: Do journalists have a special First Amendment privilege to break the law in pursuit of a legitimate news story that will advance the public interest? Several recent court decisions suggest that the answer to this question is no.

In one case a Wisconsin court found that a TV photojournalist who had entered private property with the permission of a police officer responding to a call was guilty of trespassing. Similarly, a 1999 circuit court ruling found that journalists who enter a private home with law enforcement officers but without consent of the homeowner could be sued for trespass. In another case reporters who followed antinuclear demonstrators through a fence onto the property of a utility company were found guilty of trespassing. A related 1999 Supreme Court case found that law enforcement officers who permitted the news media to accompany them across the threshold of a home when serving a search warrant were violating the Fourth Amendment's provisions against unreasonable searches.

Finally, consider the 1996 case of *Food Lion* v. *ABC*. Reporters for the newsmagazine *Prime Time Live* faked résumés to get jobs at a Food Lion supermarket and used hidden cameras to shoot video to document their story. After the program aired, Food Lion brought suit against the network not for defamation, but for fraud and trespass. Outside the courtroom, lawyers for Food Lion explained that they thought the story was libelous, but they thought they had a better chance of winning on the basis of the trespass and fraud charges. A jury found in favor of Food Lion and awarded the supermarket chain a whopping $5.5 million in damages. A district court judge reduced this amount to $350,000. Eventually, the circuit court of appeals dismissed most of the case, but it did uphold the trespass decision. The original jury awarded Food Lion only $1 in damages for the trespass, but now that the precedent has been set, it is possible that future lawsuits will seek far greater sums for trespass violations.

copyright

Copyright protects an author against unfair appropriation of his or her work. Although its roots go back to English common law, the basic copyright law of the United States was first enacted in 1909. In 1976, faced with copyright problems raised by the new communications technologies, Congress passed legislation covering literary, dramatic, and musical works, as well as motion pictures, television programs, and sound recordings. The law also states what is not covered. For example, an idea cannot be copyrighted, nor can a news event, a discovery, or a procedure.

For works created on or after January 1, 1978, copyright protection lasts for the life of the author plus 70 years. Works published before that date are eligible for copyright protection for a total of 95 years. To obtain full copyright protection, it is necessary to send a special form, copies of the work, and a small fee to the Register of Copyrights. The owner of a copyrighted work can then reproduce, sell, display, or perform the property.

It is important to note that copyright protection extends only to copying the work in question. If a person independently creates a similar work, there is no copyright violation. As a result, one of the things that a person who brings a copyright suit must prove is that the other person had access to the work under consideration. Thus, if you contend that a hit Hollywood movie was actually based on a pirated script that you had submitted to the company, you must show that the people responsible for the movie had access to your work. (To guard against copyright suits, most production companies will not open the envelopes of what look like unsolicited scripts.) Note, however, that you do not have to prove that someone intentionally or even consciously copied your work.

In addition, the law provides that people can make fair use of copyrighted materials without violating the provisions of the Copyright Act. *Fair use* means that copies of a protected work can be made for such legitimate activities as teaching, research, news reporting, and criticism without penalty. Four factors are taken into consideration in determining fair use:

1.   The purpose of the use (whether for profit or for nonprofit education)
2.   The nature of the copyrighted work
3.   The amount reproduced in proportion to the copyrighted work as a whole
4.   The effect of the use on the potential market value of the copyrighted work

Thus, a teacher who reproduces a passage from a long novel to illustrate writing style to an English class will probably not have to worry about copyright. On the other hand, if a commercial magazine reproduces verbatim a series of articles published in a not-for-profit magazine, it is likely that the copyright statute will be determined to have been violated.

The "fair use" provision in copyright law was in the spotlight in 2008 when J. K. Rowling, the author of the Harry Potter novels, brought suit against a company that planned to publish a *Harry Potter Lexicon.* The judge ruled in Rowling's favor, noting that the proposed book reproduced too much of Rowling's original work and added little that was new or transformative.

Recent cases involving copyright law have dealt with the new communication media. In what is popularly known as the "Betamax case," the Supreme Court ruled in 1984 that viewers who owned videocassette recorders could copy programs off the air for later personal viewing without violating the Copyright Act. Such taping, ruled the Court, was a fair use of the material. In 1991 a federal court ruled that commercial copying companies, such as Kinko's, had to get permission from the publishers before copying and selling copyrighted articles and book excerpts used for college courses.

The 1998 Digital Millennium Copyright Act (DMCA) makes it unlawful to create services that are used to circumvent measures that control access to copyrighted works. In general, service providers, search engines, and Web hosts are immune from copyright infringement liability for simply transmitting information over the Internet. This provision was included to protect companies from having to monitor the activities of everybody who uses the Internet, a practical impossibility. Service providers, search engines, and Web sites do have a responsibility to remove material that appears to constitute copyright infringement when such an infringement is brought to their attention. When that occurs, companies must "expeditiously" remove or block access to the material. However, the DMCA does not provide guidelines on what constitutes an "expeditious" reaction.

The Napster case vividly highlighted some of the copyright problems caused by the Internet. In 1999 the recording industry filed suit against the file-sharing service. Napster argued that its activities were protected by the "fair use" provision of copyright law: Making copies of a song for noncommercial, personal use was the same as videotaping a TV program for personal use. The recording industry argued that Napster was knowingly facilitating the illegal distribution of copyrighted material.

The courts sided with the recording industry and ordered that Napster remove all copyrighted material from its system. The decision spelled the end for Napster, and the service filed for bankruptcy in 2002. Napster's demise, however, did not put an end to file sharing. New, harder-to-shut-down services, such as Kazaa and Grokster, took its place. By 2004 more people were downloading and sharing music than during Napster's heyday.

The recording industry responded in two ways. First, it filed copyright infringement suits against several hundred individuals for sharing music files on the Internet. Those targeted first were those who had more than 1,000 songs stored on their hard drives. Some of those who were sued wound up settling their cases by paying thousands of dollars to the recording companies. As noted in Chapter 9, the recording industry dropped this tactic in 2009. Second, the recording industry sued the file-sharing services that made illegal file sharing possible. The courts found in favor of the recording industry in cases involving peer-to-peer networks Grokster and LimeWire. (LimeWire agreed to pay the record labels $105 million to settle the lawsuit.) Although the long-term effects of these legal victories are yet to be seen, illegal file sharing has decreased slightly since the LimeWire decision.

Video-sharing sites also raise copyright issues. In 2007 Viacom and NBC sued YouTube for $1 billion, claiming that the site hosted videos that infringed upon Viacom's and NBC's

> After a copyright expires, a work enters the public domain and may be freely used by anyone. This is one of the reasons that Amazon can sell the collected works of Jane Austen for only 99 cents.

copyrights. Google, YouTube's parent company, argued that YouTube had complied with the provisions of the DMCA. NBC and Viacom countered that the site should be more proactive about removing copyrighted material and not shift the burden of enforcement to the victims of infringement. They also argued that YouTube had not done enough to stop copyright infringements and that YouTube's lack of zeal in this area actually promoted copyright violations. In mid-2010 a judge ruled in favor of Google, but this legal battle may continue since Viacom was considering an appeal.

The most recent controversy over copyright issues involves newspapers and news aggregator sites such as Google News. News aggregators condense news stories from other sources or reproduce the first few paragraphs of a story and generally include a link back to the original story. They generally do not pay anything to the source of the news item. Newspapers, in particular, have objected to this practice, claiming that the news aggregators are using their content without permission. Although some news organizations have filed suits against news aggregators, most of these suits have been settled out of court and a definitive case that sets the legal limits of aggregators has yet to occur. Legal experts, however, suggest that under current copyright law, the activities of news aggregators generally fall under the "fair use" provision.

obscenity and pornography

Obscenity is not protected by the First Amendment; that much is clear. Unfortunately, nobody has yet come up with a definition of *obscenity* that satisfies everybody. Let us take a brief look at how the definition of this term has changed over the years. (If, when we are done, you are a little confused about this whole issue, do not feel bad. You are not alone.)

For many years the test of whether something was obscene was the **Hicklin Rule**, a standard that judged a book (or any other item) by whether isolated passages had a tendency to deprave or corrupt the mind of the most susceptible person. Thus, if one paragraph of a 500-page book tended to deprave or corrupt the mind of the most susceptible person (a 12-year-old child, a dirty old man), then the entire book was obscene. The standard was written in the 1860s and widely used for the next 80 years.

In a 1957 case, *Roth* v. *United States,* the Supreme Court tried its hand at writing a new definition. The new test for detecting obscenity would be the following: whether to the average person, applying contemporary standards, the dominant theme of the material taken as a whole appealed to prurient interests. (*Prurient* means "lewd" or "tending to incite lust.") The Roth test differed from the earlier rule in two significant ways. Not only did the entire work, rather than a single passage, have to be taken into consideration, but the material had to offend the average person, not simply anyone who saw it. Obviously, this standard was less restrictive than the Hicklin Rule, but gray areas remained. Should the community standards be local or national? How exactly would prurient interest be measured?

The next few years produced more obscenity cases to plague the high court. According to other decisions the material had to be "patently offensive" and "utterly without redeeming social value" to be obscene. During the 1960s the Supreme Court began considering the conduct of the seller or distributor in addition to the character of the material in question. For example, even if material was not considered hard-core pornography, it could be banned if sold to minors, thrust upon an unwilling audience, or advertised as erotic to titillate customers. A 1969 ruling introduced the concept of "variable obscenity" when it stated that certain magazines were obscene when sold to minors but not obscene when sold to adults.

By 1973 so many legal problems were cropping up under the *Roth* guidelines that something had to be done. Consequently, the Supreme Court attempted to close up loopholes in the case of *Miller* v. *California.* This decision did away with the "utterly without redeeming social value" test and stated that the "community standards" used in defining obscenity could be local standards, which, presumably, would be determined by local juries. The new test of obscenity included three principles:

1. Whether the average person, applying contemporary community standards, would find that the work as a whole appealed to prurient interests

2. Whether the work depicted or described in a patently offensive way certain sexual conduct that was specifically spelled out by a state law
3. Whether the whole work lacked serious literary, artistic, political, or scientific value

Despite this new attempt, problems were not long in coming. The language of the decision appeared to permit a certain amount of local discretion in determining what was obscene. The question of how far a local community can go in setting standards continues to be troublesome. The Supreme Court has since ruled that the motion picture *Carnal Knowledge* is not obscene, even though a state court said that it was. The Court has also said that *Screw* magazine and the *Illustrated Presidential Report of the Commission on Obscenity and Pornography* are obscene no matter what community's standards are invoked. The Court further clarified the third of the *Miller* guidelines in a 1987 case when it ruled that judges and juries must assess the literary, artistic, political, or scientific value of allegedly obscene material from the viewpoint of a "reasonable person" rather than applying community standards. These issues could be decided with the help of experts who would testify about the value of a work. The first two guidelines, however, would still be decided with reference to contemporary community standards.

Over the years the Court has taken a somewhat more lenient view as to what constitutes obscenity. The Miller case suggested that the Court was encouraging the states to deal with the problem at the local level. Given the long history of controversy that surrounded this topic, however, it was unlikely that this predicament would end soon. In fact, the whole issue surfaced again in 1986 when the Justice Department released a report on pornography. The report, which had strong political overtones, called for more stringent laws concerning pornography. One such law, the Child Protection and Obscenity Enforcement Act, took effect in 1988.

More recent problems have concerned the Internet. Child pornography is illegal on the Internet just as it is in other media. The 1988 act specifically mentions computers as one of the channels through which this illegal material might be circulated. Sexual "stalking" over the Net is also prohibited. In an effort to keep pornographic material from children, Congress passed the Communications Decency Act in 1996. Part of the act made it illegal to use a computer to create, solicit, or transmit any obscene, lewd, lascivious, filthy, or indecent communication. The Supreme Court eventually found the act to be unconstitutional and ruled that the Internet should be given the highest level of First Amendment protection, similar to that given to books and newspapers, rather than the more limited rights of broadcasting and cable, where regulation is more common. The Court noted that even though the government has a legitimate interest in trying to protect children from harmful content, this interest does not justify broad suppression of materials directed at adults.

A second attempt at protecting children from pornography also ran into legal difficulty. The Child Online Protection Act required commercial Web sites to demand proof of age before delivering material that might be harmful to minors. In 2000 an appeals court upheld an injunction that blocked implementation of the act, ruling that the act raised serious First Amendment problems. As a result, the act has never been enforced. The law was effectively killed in 2009 when the Supreme Court refused to hear an appeal of the lower court's ruling.

A similar measure, the Children's Internet Protection Act, required libraries that receive federal funds to use filters to block access to pornographic images on their computers. The American Library Association challenged the act, but in 2003 the Supreme Court ruled that the act was constitutional.

What about pornography on cable TV and the Internet? Although they don't publicize it much, cable and satellite operators offer explicit X-rated movies on pay-per-view or video-on-demand channels. Family Safe Media estimated that there are more than 240 million pages of porn on the Internet. Don't these items meet the criteria for obscenity described in the Miller decision? They might, but society has become more tolerant of sexually explicit material and more reluctant to interfere with what people do in the privacy of their homes. So far no test case has reached the Supreme Court.

As is probably apparent by now, the Internet brings new challenges along with its benefits.

regulating broadcasting

The formal controls surrounding broadcasting represent a special case. Not only are broadcasters affected by the laws and rulings previously discussed, but they are also subject to additional controls because of broadcasting's unique position and character. When broadcasting was first developed in the early 20th century, it became clear that more people wanted to operate a broadcasting station than there were suitable frequencies available. As a result, the early broadcasters asked the U.S. Congress to step into the picture. Congress passed the Radio Act of 1927, which held that the airwaves belonged to the public and that broadcasters who wished to use this resource had to be licensed to serve in the public interest. A regulatory body, called the Federal Radio Commission (later known as the Federal Communications Commission), was set up to determine who should get a license and whether those who had a license should keep it. Because of this licensing provision, radio and television are subject to more regulations than are newspapers, magazines, films, and sound recordings.

The Federal Communications Commission

The Federal Communications Commission (FCC) does not make law; it interprets the law. One of its big jobs is to interpret the meaning of the phrase "public interest." For example, the FCC may write rules and regulations to implement the Communications Act of 1934 if these rules serve the public interest. Moreover, the FCC awards and renews licenses if the award or renewal is in the public interest. Over the years several significant FCC rulings have shed some light on this rather ambiguous concept. One of the first things the commission established was that it would examine programming and determine whether the public interest was being served. It was not enough for a station to adhere to the technical operating requirements of its license. It would also have to provide a

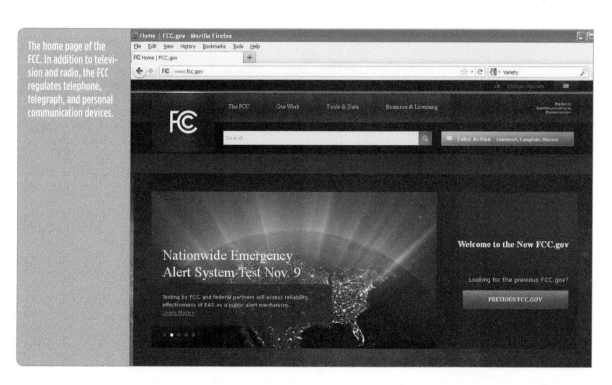

The home page of the FCC. In addition to television and radio, the FCC regulates telephone, telegraph, and personal communication devices.

"well-rounded" program structure. In its 1929 Great Lakes decision, the commission also put broadcasters on notice that the broadcasting of programs that tended to injure the public—fraudulent advertising, attacks on ethnic groups, attacks on religions—would not be in the public interest.

What can the FCC do to stations that do not operate in the public interest? It can take several official actions. At the mildest level, it can fine a station up to $325,000. The next level of severity is to renew a station's license only for a probationary period (usually a year). This action typically puts the station on notice that it has to improve its performance or face even more serious consequences. The most severe form of official action is the revoking or nonrenewal of a license. Revocation/nonrenewal is more of a threat, however, than a reality. From 1934 to 1978, the FCC took away the licenses of only 142 stations. This figure should be weighed against the thousands of renewals that the commission granted in each of those years. In fact, it has been calculated that 99.8 percent of all licenses are renewed. Nonetheless, the threat of revocation is a potent one that is universally feared among broadcasters.

During the 1980s, as was the case in many industries, the prevailing philosophy that governed broadcasting was one of deregulation. The FCC and Congress eliminated literally dozens of rules and regulations, including the controversial Fairness Doctrine (see the section devoted specifically to this doctrine). The rush to deregulation slowed during the 1990s as the FCC and Congress established new rules and regulations for broadcasting and cable.

For instance, Congress passed the Children's Television Act, which required that TV stations present programs designed to meet the educational and informational needs of young persons through the age of 16. The bill also created a $2-million endowment to fund children's educational programs. Additionally, the act limited the amount of commercial time during children's programming to 10½ minutes per hour on weekends and 12 minutes per hour on weekdays, a limit that applies to both broadcasters and cable operators. Stations and systems that violate these standards could be subject to a fine. In response to a provision in the law that instructed the FCC to encourage children's programming, the commission mandated that stations devote 3 hours per week to informational and educational programs for children.

The FCC is also involved in policy making through its Office of Strategic Planning and Policy Analysis. This office acts as economic, business, and market consultant to the FCC in order to identify trends and recommend future courses of action. In 2011, for example the FCC issued a report on the changing media landscape in the age of broadband.

The FCC has no regulatory control over the Internet or over Internet service providers. The commission does have some indirect influence, however, because it has some regulatory power over telephone and cable companies and can thus affect how you connect to the Internet. In 2005 the FCC issued a policy statement endorsing **Internet neutrality**—a provision that would block Internet service providers from favoring one Web company over another. How much jurisdiction the FCC has over this topic, however, is still open to debate. In 2008, for example, the FCC voted to punish Comcast Corporation for limiting Internet traffic to its consumers in apparent violation of the FCC's network neutrality principles. Comcast admitted to preventing some subscribers from swapping video files over services such as BitTorrent. The FCC didn't fine the company but did require it to stop blocking traffic and disclose more information about its practices to consumers. Comcast argued that the FCC could enforce specific rules but not general principles and appealed the decision. In 2010, an appeals court said that the FCC had overstepped its authority and ruled in favor of Comcast, dealing a setback to network neutrality. In response, the FCC reclassified broadband as a transmission service, reversing its earlier position that broadband was an information service. Reclassifying the service gave the FCC more power to regulate broadband and allowed it to implement a network neutrality policy. This decision will probably start a legal battle with Internet service providers such as Comcast and AT&T on one side and Internet companies such as Google and Amazon on the other.

media talk

Yahoo! Caught in the Web

Clip 10: 2 minutes 8 seconds
You can watch Clip 10 *on the Online Learning Center home page,* www .mhhe.com/dominick12e. *Select* Student Center *and then* Chapter 16.
   This clip talks about search engine Yahoo! giving personal information about a Chinese user to the Chinese government that led to his arrest. Do you think Yahoo! was right in giving the Chinese government the name of the Chinese user? Should any government be able to access personal information about any user on the Internet? What kinds of restrictions do you think should be placed on government's capability of finding out information on Internet users? Should there be a universal law governing the Internet?

WWW

Indecent Content

When it comes to regulating indecent content, the FCC finds itself caught between the wishes of Congress and the rulings of the federal court system. A 1978 Supreme Court ruling gave the FCC the right to regulate indecency because the pervasive presence of broadcasting made it easily accessible to children. In the late 1980s, after many radio stations began to air raunchy content, Congress passed legislation that instructed the FCC to ban indecent programming 24 hours a day. A federal court declared that this ban was unconstitutional and ordered the FCC to establish a "safe harbor," a time when indecent material could be aired without much chance of reaching children. The FCC responded by banning indecent content between the hours of 6 A.M. and 8 P.M. This did not satisfy Congress (there is some political benefit to be derived from being against indecency), which passed a law banning indecency before midnight. This law was ruled unconstitutional, and finally, a law that banned indecent content between 6 A.M. and 10 P.M. was approved. As should be clear by now, trying to protect children from indecency while protecting the First Amendment rights of adults is an exasperating task.

Indecent content became a hot topic in 2004 thanks in part to Janet Jackson's wardrobe malfunction during the Super Bowl halftime show that revealed more of Janet than many people felt was appropriate. The incident sparked renewed regulatory fervor at the FCC and Congress. The FCC issued more than $3.6 million in fines for indecency in 2004, the most ever recorded. The biggest fine, of more than $1 million, was issued to Fox Broadcasting for airing *Married by America,* in which bachelors licked whipped cream off of strippers. Fox also got hit with a $550,000 fine for the Super Bowl overexposure. The fine was later tossed out by an appeals court, but a Supreme Court decision ordered the lower court to reexamine its ruling. Moreover, Congress passed stiffer regulations covering indecency. The maximum amount that a station could be fined for airing indecency was raised to $325,000, 10 times the previous maximum amount.

The FCC continued its crackdown on indecency in 2006. The commission fined CBS and its affiliates more than $3 million for an episode of *Without a Trace* that the FCC ruled obscene. The FCC also changed its policy regarding what it calls "fleeting expletives," such as four-letter words that slip out during a live broadcast. For many years the commission had declined to fine stations for such slips. But in response to a couple of celebrities who used what the FCC termed "the f-word" during awards programs, the commission reversed course and declared that any use of forbidden words, fleeting or not, would invite a fine. The new policy, however, was short-lived. A federal appeals court ruled that the new regulations were arbitrary and declared them null and void. The FCC appealed to the Supreme Court. In a 2009 decision, the Court ruled that the FCC's change in policy was not arbitrary but did not decide if the policy was a violation of broadcasters' First Amendment rights. The Court sent the case back to a lower court for an examination of the free speech issue. In 2010, a Court of Appeals struck down the FCC policy on fleeting expletives, labeling it "unconstitutionally vague."

The Equal Opportunities Rule

The **Equal Opportunities Rule** is contained in Section 315 of the Communications Act and is thus federal law. Section 315 deals with the ability of bona fide candidates for public office to gain access to a broadcast medium during political campaigns. In simple terms, this section states that if a station permits one candidate for a specific office to appear on the air, it must offer the same opportunity to all other candidates for that office. If a station gives a free minute to one candidate, all other legally qualified candidates for that office are also entitled to a free minute. If a station sells a candidate a minute for $100, it must make the same offer to all other candidates. Congress has made some exceptions to

social issues

How Fair Is the Fairness Doctrine?

Everybody would probably agree that fairness is a good idea. We should strive to be equitable and evenhanded in our dealings with others. It's the "doctrine" part that raises issues.

The Fairness Doctrine was first articulated in 1949 when most communities had one or two TV stations and maybe a few AM radio stations. The rationale behind the doctrine was that because of the limited number of broadcast frequencies available, a radio or TV station should not become an advocate of one particular point of view. The public interest was better served if the stations allowed a reasonable opportunity for discussion of contrasting points of view on controversial issues of public importance.

Broadcasters (the rule does not apply to print media) never liked the Fairness Doctrine, arguing that it interfered with their First Amendment rights. A test of the constitutionality of the doctrine came in 1969, and the Supreme Court ruled in favor of the doctrine. The Court held that the First Amendment right of the viewers and listeners to be exposed to different points of view was paramount and overrode the right of the broadcasters. The Court added, however, that if it could be shown at some later date that the doctrine actually restrained free speech, then its constitutionality might be reconsidered.

In the years that followed, broadcasters argued that the doctrine did exactly what the Court feared in restraining free speech. Rather than go to the trouble and expense of seeking out other points of view on controversial issues, broadcasters simply ignored them. Moreover, as more and more radio and TV stations went on the air and cable TV networks were available to more Americans, the scarcity principle underlying the doctrine no longer seemed valid. Conflicting points of view were widely available to the public.

Sentiment at the FCC also turned against the doctrine. The commission found itself spending time and effort evaluating hundreds of complaints that required it to determine what exactly a controversial issue was and what was meant by a reasonable opportunity for discussion. Finally, in the spirit of deregulation during the 1980s, the FCC decided to scrap the doctrine.

Nonetheless, efforts to reinstate the doctrine in one form or another have repeatedly cropped up. Attempts during the administrations of Presidents Reagan and George H. W. Bush both failed. Another attempt in 2005 failed to come to a vote. In 2009, with the Democratic Party in control of the White House and Congress, the Fairness Doctrine was again under consideration. Several members of Congress, including Senator John Kerry and Speaker of the House Nancy Pelosi, have come out in favor of resurrecting the doctrine in some form, but as of 2011 no legislation had been enacted.

The subtext in this recent debate concerns conservative talk radio. Talk radio blossomed after the demise of the Fairness Doctrine when stations could present partisan programs without fear of being reported to the FCC. Commentators such as Rush Limbaugh and Sean Hannity argued that bringing back the Fairness Doctrine was an effort to curb their influence and limit exposure to a conservative point of view.

Opposition to any reinstatement of the Fairness Doctrine has also come from libertarians, who warn against government regulation of free speech. Other critics point out that the Internet provides ample sources for people who are looking for opposing points of view. In addition, opponents point out that a revived Fairness Doctrine cuts both ways. Conservative talk radio would not be the only medium that would be affected. Stations carrying a liberal talk show would also be subject to the doctrine. Public broadcasting, sometimes charged with being liberal, would also be governed by the doctrine and find its programming open to challenge from conservatives. Even some politically oriented skits on *Saturday Night Live* might trigger a Fairness Doctrine challenge. If, as some propose, the doctrine should be expanded to cover cable TV, then both Fox News and MSNBC would be affected.

Keep in mind that the doctrine deals with controversial issues, those that have already sparked extreme emotions. What seems like balanced coverage to station management might seem biased and unfair to a zealous supporter of a particular issue who would be more than happy to file a Fairness Doctrine complaint. It's not surprising that both broadcasters and the FCC were not fond of the doctrine while it existed.

Although the FCC abolished the Fairness Doctrine in 1987 and no longer enforced it, the rules were still part of the Code of Federal Regulations until 2011, when the FCC finally got around to formally deleting the Fairness Doctrine from the Code. Getting the policy off the books may finally settle the issue, but the Fairness Doctrine has a strange way of resurrecting itself as the political climate changes.

this law, the most notable of which are legitimate newscasts and on-the-scene coverage of authentic news events.

The Fairness Doctrine

The **Fairness Doctrine** no longer exists. The FCC repealed it in 1987, and subsequent attempts to revive it have not been successful. (See "Social Issues: How Fair Is the Fairness Doctrine?")

When it was still in force, the Fairness Doctrine provided that broadcasters had to seek out and present contrasting viewpoints on controversial matters of public importance. On any issue broadcasters had to make a good-faith effort to cover all the opposing viewpoints. This did not have to take place in one program, but the broadcaster was expected to achieve balance over time. Note that the Fairness Doctrine never said that opposing views were entitled to equal time. It simply mandated that some reasonable amount of time be granted.

regulating cable tv

The regulatory philosophy of the FCC and Congress toward cable has shown wide variation over the years. In the 1950s the FCC ruled that it had no jurisdiction over cable. This notion changed in the 1960s when the commission exerted control over the new medium and wrote a series of regulations governing its growth. By 1972 a comprehensive set of rules governing cable was on the FCC's books. The growth of cable during the 1970s led to successful lobbying efforts by the industry to ease many of these restrictions. In the 1980s, in line with the deregulatory philosophy of the Reagan administration, almost all the FCC rules concerning cable were dropped. In 1984, Congress passed the Cable Communications Policy Act, which gave cable operators great freedom in setting rates and deciding what channels they would carry on their systems. The law also allowed state and local governments the right to grant cable **franchises** (a franchise is an exclusive right to operate in a given territory).

Unlike broadcast stations, cable systems were not licensed by the FCC. Instead, under the 1984 law, the local franchise authority, should it wish to do so, had the power to terminate a franchise at the end of the franchise period. In addition, cable companies were free to set their own rates.

In the years following the passage of this act, many consumers complained that their cable system raised rates and was insensitive to the needs of its customers. Consequently, in 1992 Congress passed the Cable TV Act, which gave the FCC the authority to regulate the rates of most cable systems, required that cable systems carry the signals of any broadcast station with significant viewing in their market, and allowed commercial broadcast stations to waive their right to be carried in exchange for appropriate compensation from the cable system.

Two provisions in this law had important consequences. First, most consumers saw their monthly cable bills go down as the FCC instituted rate reductions of about 17 percent. Second, the provision requiring cable systems to carry the signals of broadcast stations was challenged in federal court as a violation of the First Amendment rights of cable operators. In 1994 the Supreme Court ruled that cable operators deserved more First Amendment protection from government regulation than did broadcasters but not as much as newspapers and magazines. Consequently, the Court declared that it was constitutional for Congress to pass laws to guarantee that the free flow of information not be restricted by a private company that controlled the means of transmission.

The issue of the constitutionality of the specific rules regarding which stations must be carried by cable systems was decided in 1997 when the Supreme Court ruled in favor of the "must carry" provision. The must-carry provision resurfaced again in 2007 when the FCC issued its dual-carriage rules. The rules specified that cable system operators had to deliver both the analog and digital signals of must-carry stations after the 2009 transition to digital TV. In a compromise worked out with cable operators, the rules would be phased out after three years. In addition, the rules reaffirmed that cable systems also had to carry the stations' high-definition signal.

In 2006 –2007, Kevin Martin, the FCC chair, proposed that consumers be given an "à la carte" option when it came to subscribing to cable. Instead of the traditional bundle or tiers of channels that cable systems typically offer, subscribers would be able to choose only those channels that they wanted to receive. Martin argued that the à la carte option would enable customers to avoid cable channels that might carry indecent material. With Martin's departure from the FCC in 2009, prospects for the à la carte option were not bright.

In 2010, many cable and satellite subscribers were denied access to their broadcast channels during transmission fee disputes between TV stations and cable and satellite operators. In response, the FCC was examining possible ways to protect consumers from losing their programs during future negotiations.

the telecommunications act of 1996

The **Telecommunications Act of 1996** was the first major overhaul of communication laws in more than 60 years. The act contained provisions that affected traditional broadcasters, cable companies, and telephone companies. The following are among the key provisions of the law:

- It removed limits on the number of radio stations that can be owned by one person or organization. Up to eight stations may be owned in a single market. (See Chapter 8.)
- It removed limits on the number of television stations that can be owned as long as stations do not reach more than 35 percent (later changed to 39 percent) of the nation's TV homes.
- It extended the term of broadcast licenses to eight years.
- It allowed telephone companies to enter the cable TV business.
- It allowed cable TV companies to enter the telephone business.
- It deregulated the rates of many cable systems.
- It mandated that newly manufactured TV sets come with the ability to block unwanted programming based on an electronically encoded rating (popularly called the **V-chip;** see Chapter 17).
- It mandated that the TV industry come up with a voluntary ratings system for violence, sex, and other indecent materials.

Now that the 1996 Telecommunications Act has been in force for several years, we can see evidence of its impact. As mentioned earlier, the removal of the cap on radio station ownership unleashed a wave of consolidation in the industry. The deregulation of cable rates has led to a general increase in cable subscribers' bills. It took a while but competition between phone companies and cable companies has become more vigorous. Phone company AT&T has started U-Verse, a video service with more than 300 channels. Cable giant Comcast offers telephone service, and many companies are bundling phone, TV, and Internet service into one package.

regulating advertising

Deceptive Advertising

The problem of deceptive and potentially harmful advertising has been around a long time. The philosophy of *caveat emptor* (let the buyer beware) was dominant until the early 1900s. Exaggerated claims and outright deception characterized many early advertisements, especially those for patent medicines. Spurred on by the muckrakers (see Chapter 6), the government took steps to deal with the problem when it created the Federal Trade Commission (FTC) in 1914. In the early years of its existence, the commission was concerned with encouraging competition through the regulation of questionable business practices, such as bribery, false advertising, and mislabeling of products; protecting the consumer was not the main focus. The consumer started to receive some protection in 1938 with the Wheeler-Lea Act, which gave the FTC the power to prevent deceptive advertising that harmed the public, whether or not the advertising had any bad effects on the competition.

Like the FCC, the FTC has several enforcement techniques available to it. First of all, it can issue trade regulations that specify guidelines for the industry to follow. In 1965, for example, it ruled that auto ads must contain both the city and highway estimates of gas mileage. The FTC also uses the **consent order**. In a consent order the advertiser agrees to halt a certain advertising practice, but does not admit to any violation of the law; there is only an agreement not to continue. Somewhat stronger is a **cease-and-desist order**. This order follows a hearing by the commission that determines that a certain advertising practice does indeed violate the law. Violation of a consent order or failure to comply with a cease-and-desist order can result in fines being levied against the advertiser.

In the late 1960s and the 1970s, the FTC took a more active role in the regulation of advertising. The rising tide of interest in the rights of the consumer and the emergence of consumer activist groups (such as Ralph Nader's Raiders) led to a flurry of activity. First, the FTC wanted documentation for claims. If Brand Y claimed to be more effective in relieving pain than Brand X, the advertiser was now required to have evidence for that claim. The FTC also ordered "corrective advertising," in which some advertisers were required to clarify some of their past claims.

More recently, the FTC has been concerned about advertising inappropriately directed toward children. In 1997 the FTC issued an unfair advertising complaint against the R. J. Reynolds Tobacco Company. The FTC argued that ads featuring Joe Camel, the company's cartoon character, encouraged children to start smoking. In response, Reynolds announced it would no longer use the controversial camel in its ads.

In 2000 the FTC targeted the film industry for marketing R-rated movies to persons under 17. An FTC report found that marketing plans for 28 R-rated films included strategies for reaching children as young as 10. The report criticized Hollywood for routinely aiming its advertising at children for movies that its own rating system labeled as inappropriate. In response, eight movie studios announced plans to reform their promotional efforts. More recently, the FTC has cracked down on products that make deceptive health claims. In 2005, for example, the commission instructed Tropicana orange juice to stop claiming that the product reduced the risk of heart disease and strokes. The FTC also filed lawsuits against six companies whose advertising claimed that people who used their products would lose weight without dieting or exercise. In 2007 the FTC stated that companies that engage in word-of-mouth or "buzz" marketing must disclose these relationships to consumers.

In 2009 the FTC was looking closely at testimonial ads. Under scrutiny were ads for diets and weight-loss programs in which a person claims to have lost a huge amount of weight using such-and-such a program, followed by a disclaimer such as "Results not typical" or "Your experience may vary." Proposed new FTC guidelines would require that advertisers give some indication of a typical result.

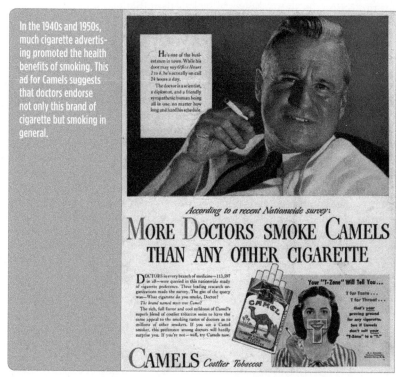

In the 1940s and 1950s, much cigarette advertising promoted the health benefits of smoking. This ad for Camels suggests that doctors endorse not only this brand of cigarette but smoking in general.

Commercial Speech Under the First Amendment

The 1970s marked a change in judicial thinking about the amount of protection that advertising, or *commercial speech*, should receive under the First Amendment. Before the 1970s, advertising had little claim to free-speech protection. In the 1940s F. J. Chrestensen found this out the hard way. Chrestensen owned a former U.S. submarine. There is not much that a private individual can do with a submarine, aside from charging admission to view it. This was Chrestensen's idea, and he wanted to distribute handbills advertising the sub. No way, said the New York City police commissioner. The city's sanitation code did not allow the distribution of advertising matter in the streets. However, handbills of information or of public protest were allowed. Inspired, Chrestensen put his submarine advertising message on one side of the handbill, while the other side was printed with a protest against the City Dock Department. Sorry, said the city, the protest message could be handed out, but the advertising on the other side would have to go. Chrestensen appealed, and two years later the Supreme Court ruled against him, agreeing with the city of New York that advertising merited no First Amendment protection.

Since that time, however, the Supreme Court has retreated from this view. In 1964, in the *New York Times* v. *Sullivan* case, it extended First Amendment protection to ads that dealt with important social matters. Seven years later, the Court further extended this protection when a Virginia newspaper ran an ad for an abortion clinic located in New York and thus violated a Virginia law against such advertising. The Supreme Court ruled that the ad contained material in the public interest and merited constitutional protection. More recent cases suggest that in many instances commercial speech falls under the protection of the First Amendment.

In a 1980 ruling concerning advertising by an electric utility company, commonly called the Central Hudson case, the Supreme Court enunciated a four-part test for determining the constitutional protection of commercial speech. First, commercial speech that involves an unlawful activity or advertising that is false or misleading is not protected. Second, the government must have a substantial interest in regulating the commercial speech. Third, the state's regulation must actually advance the government interest involved. Fourth, the state's regulations may be only as broad as necessary to promote the state's interest.

A 1984 ruling illustrated the use of these principles: The Court upheld a prohibition against posting signs on city property. The Court first noted that, although the advertising was for a lawful activity and not misleading, the government has a substantial interest in reducing "visual blight" and that the ordinance directly advanced that interest and was not overly broad. Further, the Court affirmed that corporations also have the right of free speech and granted lawyers, doctors, and professionals the right to advertise their prices. Although all the questions surrounding this issue have not been answered, it seems safe to conclude that at least some commercial speech is entitled to First Amendment protection. Its status, however, is less than that given to political and other forms of noncommercial expression.

conclusion

The term *half-life* is a useful concept in physics. It refers to the length of time in which one-half of the radioactive atoms present in a substance will decay. We might borrow this term and reshape its meaning so that it is relevant to this book. The half-life of a chapter in this text is the time it takes for half the information contained in the chapter to become obsolete. With that in mind, it is likely that the half-life of this chapter may be among the shortest of any in this book. Laws are constantly changing; new court decisions are handed down frequently, and new rules and regulations are written all the time. All this activity means that what is written in this chapter will need frequent updating. In addition, it means that mass media professionals must continually refresh their understanding of the law. Of course, this also means that there will be a continuing stream of colorful characters, intriguing stories, and high drama as the courts and regulatory agencies further wrestle with the issues and problems involved in mass communication regulation.

main points

- There is a strong constitutional case against prior restraint of the press.

- Reporters have special privileges that protect them in some instances from having to reveal the names of their news sources. These privileges, however, are not absolute.

- Reporters can cover matters that occur in open court with little fear of reprisal. Some pretrial proceedings can still be closed to the press.

- All but two states now allow cameras in the courtroom on a permanent or experimental basis. Cameras and microphones are still barred from federal trial courts and from the Supreme Court.

- Defamation can be either libel or slander. To prevail in a defamation suit, a public figure must show that the published material was false and harmful and that the media acted with actual malice when they published the information. A private citizen must also show that the material was false and harmful but only that the media acted with negligence.

- Invasion of privacy can occur when the media intrude upon a person's solitude, release private information,

create a false impression, or wrongfully appropriate a person's name or likeness.

- Copyright law protects authors from unfair use of their work. There are instances, however, when portions of copyrighted material can be reproduced for legitimate purposes.

- Online file-sharing systems have raised serious questions about copyrights in a digital medium.

- Obscenity is not protected by the First Amendment. To be legally obscene, a work must appeal to prurient interests, depict or describe certain sexual conduct spelled out by state law, and lack serious literary, artistic, political, or scientific value.

- Special laws and regulations apply to broadcasting. The FCC is charged with administering the rules and regulations that deal with cable, TV, and radio. The Telecommunications Act of 1996 had a major impact on the electronic media.

- The FTC oversees advertising. Commercial speech has recently been given more First Amendment protection.

questions for review

1. Whom do shield laws protect?
2. Whom do gag orders gag?
3. What is the Freedom of Information Act? How have reporters used it?
4. What is the difference between libel and slander?
5. What factors determine fair use?

6. Briefly explain the significance of the following court cases:
   a. The Betamax case
   b. The Pentagon Papers case
   c. *New York Times* v. *Sullivan*
   d. *Miller* v. *California*

questions for critical thinking

1. Why should reporters have special privileges when other professionals, such as architects, nurses, and accountants, have none?

2. Libel suits can be long and expensive for both sides. What are some other methods of conflict resolution that might cut down the time and the cost but still provide satisfaction for both sides?

3. Why are broadcasting and cable not entitled to the same degree of First Amendment protection as

newspapers and magazines? Do you agree with this type of differentiation?

4. Should TV stations be punished if they unexpectedly air a "fleeting expletive"?

5. How can children be protected from exposure to adult-oriented content on the Internet?

key terms

First Amendment (p. 376)	defamation (p. 386)	Equal Opportunities Rule (p. 400)
prior restraint (p. 376)	libel (p. 386)	Fairness Doctrine (p. 401)
injunction (p. 376)	slander (p. 386)	franchises (p. 402)
shield laws (p. 380)	libel per se (p. 386)	Telecommunications Act of 1996 (p. 403)
gag rules (p. 383)	libel per quod (p. 386)	V-chip (p. 403)
Freedom of Information Act (FOIA) (p. 385)	trespass (p. 393)	consent order (p. 403)
USA Patriot Act (p. 385)	Hicklin Rule (p. 396)	cease-and-desist order (p. 403)
	Internet neutrality (p. 399)	

internet resources

Online Learning Center

On the Online Learning Center home page, www.mhhe.com/dominick12e, *select* Student Center *and then* Chapter 16.

1. Use the Learning Objectives, Chapter Outline, and Main Points sections to review this chapter.
2. Test your knowledge of the chapter using the multiple choice and flashcard features of the site.
3. Expand your knowledge of concepts and topics discussed in the chapter with additional Questions for Critical Thinking and Internet Exercises.

surfing the internet

Many Web sites deal with legal matters. The ones listed here seem most helpful for students.

www.fcc.gov
The FCC's home page. Contains an archive of recent speeches, a search engine, and consumer information, along with more technical data.

www.freedomforum.org
Contains a summary of recent First Amendment court decisions, relevant law articles, a First Amendment time line, and the full text of relevant Supreme Court rulings.

www.rcfp.org
The Reporters Committee for Freedom of the Press maintains this site, which contains recent court decisions, legal news, and a link to its publication, *The News Media and the Law.*

www.rtnda.org
Home page of the Radio and Television News Directors Association. Contains information about covering the courts, libel, copyright, and other legal issues.

John Stuart Mill (1806–1873) refined the ethical theory
of utilitarianism.

Chapter**17**

ethics
and other informal controls

This chapter will prepare you to:

- distinguish among the types of informal controls on the media
- explain the most important ethical principles
- explain what the standards departments and performance codes are
- discuss the relationship between the media and their advertisers vis-à-vis ethical practices
- understand the pros and cons of pressure groups

Laws and regulations are not the only controls on the mass media. Informal controls, stemming from within the media themselves or shaped by the workings of external forces such as pressure groups, consumers, and advertisers, are also important. The following hypothetical examples illustrate some situations in which these controls might spring up:

- You are the program director for the campus radio station. You get a call one morning from the promotion department of a major record company offering you a free trip to California, a tour of the record company's studios, a ticket to a concert featuring all the company's biggest stars, and an invitation to an exclusive party where you will get to meet all the performers. The company representative explains that this is simply a courtesy to you so that you will better appreciate the quality of her company's products. Do you accept?

- You are a reporter for the local campus newspaper. The star of the football team, who also happens to be the president of the Campus Crusade for Morality, has been involved in a minor traffic accident, and you have been assigned to cover the story. When you get to the accident scene, you examine the football player's car and find a half-dozen pornographic magazines strewn across the backseat. You have a deadline in 30 minutes; what details do you include in your story?

■ You are the editor of the campus newspaper. One of your reporters has just written a series of articles describing apparent health-code violations in a popular off-campus restaurant. This particular restaurant regularly buys full-page ads in your paper. After you run the first story in the series, the restaurant owner calls and threatens to cancel all her ads unless you stop printing the series. What do you do?

■ You are doing your first story for the campus paper. A local businessperson has promised to donate $5 million to your university so that it can buy new equipment for its mass communication and journalism programs. While putting together a background story on this benefactor, you discover that he was convicted of armed robbery at age 18 and avoided prison only by volunteering for military duty during the closing months of the Korean War. In the more than 50 years that have passed since then, his record has been spotless. He refuses to talk about the incident, claims his wife and his closest friends do not know about it, and threatens to withdraw his donation if you print the story. Naturally, university officials are concerned and urge you not to mention this fact. Do you go ahead and include the incident as simply one element in your overall profile? Do you take the position that the arrest information is not pertinent and not use it? Do you wait until the university has the money and then print the story?

We could go on listing examples, but by now the point is probably clear. There are many situations in the everyday operation of the mass media in which thorny questions about what to do or not to do have to be faced. Most of these situations do not involve laws or regulations but instead deal with the tougher questions of what is right or what is proper. Informal controls over the media usually assert themselves in these circumstances. In this chapter we will discuss the following examples of informal controls: personal ethics; performance codes; internal controls, such as organizational policies, self-criticism, and professional self-regulation; and outside pressures.

personal ethics

Ethics are rules of conduct or principles of morality that point us toward the right or best way to act in a situation. Over the years philosophers have developed a number of general ethical principles that serve as guidelines for evaluating our behavior. We will briefly examine five principles that have particular relevance to those working in the mass media professions. Before we begin, however, please note that these principles do not contain magic answers to every ethical dilemma. In fact, different ethical principles often suggest different and conflicting courses of action. There is no perfect answer to every problem. Also, these ethical principles are based on Western thought. Other cultures may have developed totally different systems. Nonetheless, these principles can provide a framework for analyzing what is proper in examining choices and justifying our actions.

Ethical Principles

The Principle of the Golden Mean Moral virtue lies between two extremes. This philosophical position is typically associated with Aristotle, who, as a biologist, noted that too much food as well as too little food spoils health. Moderation is the key. Likewise, in ethical dilemmas the proper way of behaving lies between doing too much and doing too little. For instance, in the restaurant example mentioned earlier, one extreme would be to cancel the story as requested by the restaurant owner. The other extreme would be to run the series as is. Perhaps a compromise between the two would be to run the series but also give the restaurant owner a chance to reply. Or perhaps the story might contain information about how the restaurant has improved conditions or other tempering remarks.

Examples of the **golden mean** are often found in media practices. For example, when news organizations cover civil disorders, they try to exercise moderation. They balance the necessity of informing the public with the need to preserve public safety by not inflaming the audience.

The Categorical Imperative   What is right for one is right for all. German philosopher Immanuel Kant is identified with this ethical guideline. To measure the correctness of our behavior, Kant suggested that we act according to rules that we would want to see universally applied. In Kant's formulation *categorical* means "unconditional"—no extenuating circumstances, no exceptions. Right is right and should be done, no matter what the consequences. The individual's conscience plays a large part in Kant's thinking. A **categorical imperative** is discovered by an examination of conscience; the conscience informs us what is right. If, after performing an act, we feel uneasy or guilty, we have probably violated our conscience. Applied to mass communication, a categorical imperative might be that all forms of deception in news gathering are wrong and must be avoided. No one wants deception to become a universal practice. Therefore, for example, a reporter should not represent him- or herself as anything other than a reporter when gathering information for a story.

The Principle of Utility   **Utility** is defined as the greatest benefit for the greatest number. Modern utilitarian thinking originated with the 19th-century philosophers Jeremy Bentham and John Stuart Mill. The basic tenet in their formulations is that we are to determine what is right or wrong by considering what will yield the best ratio of good to bad for the general society. Utilitarians ask how much good is promoted and how much evil is restrained by different courses of behavior. Utilitarianism provides a clear method for evaluating ethical choices: (1) Calculate all the consequences, both good and bad, that would result from each of our options; then (2) choose the alternative that maximizes value or minimizes loss.

Looking at the mass communication area, we can easily see several examples of utilitarian philosophy. In 1971 the *New York Times* and other papers printed stolen government documents known as the Pentagon Papers (see Chapter 16). Obviously, the newspapers involved thought that the good that would be achieved by printing these papers far outweighed the harm that would be done. (Note that the Kantian perspective would suggest a different course of action. Theft is bad. Newspapers do not want the government stealing their property, so they should not condone or promote the theft of government property.) Or take the case of a small midwestern paper that chose to report the death of a local teenager who had left town, turned to prostitution and drugs, and been murdered. The paper decided that the potential benefits of this story as a warning to other parents outweighed the grief it would cause the murder victim's family.

The Veil of Ignorance   Justice is blind. Philosopher John Rawls argued that justice emerges when everyone is treated without social differentiations. Everybody doing the same job equally well should receive equal pay. Everybody who got an 80 on the test should get the same grade. Rawls advocated that all parties in a problem situation be placed behind an imaginary barrier, the **veil of ignorance**, that conceals roles and social differentiations and that each participant be treated as an equal member of society as a whole. Rawls's veil of ignorance suggests that we structure our actions to protect the most vulnerable members of society. It is easy to see the relevance of this principle to the workings of the mass media. If we applied the veil of ignorance to the problem of hammering out the proper relationship between politicians and journalists, the blatant adversarial relationship so often found between the groups would disappear. Behind the veil all newsmakers would be the same. Inherent cynicism and abrasiveness on the part of the press would disappear, as would mistrust and suspicion on the part of the politicians. On a more specific level, consider the case of a financial reporter who frequently gets tips and inside information on deals and mergers that affect the prices of stocks and passes these tips on to friends who use this information for their own profit. The veil of ignorance suggests that the reporter must treat all audience members the same. Personal friends should not benefit from inside information.

The Principle of Self-Determination   This principle, closely associated with the Judeo-Christian ethic and also discussed by Kant, might be summarized as "Love your neighbor as yourself." Human beings have unconditional value apart from any and all circumstances. Their basic right to **self-determination** should not be violated by using them as simply a means to accomplish a goal. A corollary to this principle is that no one should allow him- or herself to be treated as a means to someone else's ends. Suppose that sources inside a government investigation on political corruption leak to the press the names of some people suspected of taking bribes, and the press, in turn, publishes the allegations and the names of the suspects. The principle of self-determination suggests that the press is being used by those who leaked the story as a means to accomplish their goal. Perhaps those involved in the investigation want to turn public opinion against those named or simply to earn some favorable publicity for their efforts. In any case, the press should resist being used in these circumstances. The rights, values, and decisions of others must always be respected.

A Model for Individual Ethical Decisions

In numerous situations, personal ethical decisions have to be made about what should or should not be included in media content or what should or should not be done. Every day, reporters, editors, station managers, and other media professionals have to make these decisions. Too often, however, these decisions are made haphazardly, without proper analysis of the ethical dimensions involved. This section presents a model that media professionals can use to evaluate and examine their decisions. This model is adapted from the work of Ralph Potter.[1]

$$Definitions \rightarrow Values \rightarrow Principles \rightarrow Loyalties \rightarrow Action$$

In short, the model asks the individual to consider four aspects of the situation before taking action. First, define the situation. What are the pertinent facts? What are the possible actions? Second, determine what values are involved. Which values are more relevant to deciding a course of action? Third, establish what ethical principles apply. We have discussed five that might be involved; there may be others. Fourth, decide where our loyalties lie. To whom do we owe a moral duty? It is possible that we might owe a duty to ourselves, clients, business organizations, the profession, or society in general. To whom is our obligation most important?

Let us examine how this model would work in a real situation. WikiLeaks bills itself as a nonprofit international organization that publishes secret and private communications submitted by anonymous sources. WikiLeaks set up a Web site in 2006 and soon had a database with more than 1 million entries. Even so, relatively few people in the United States

Julian Assange, editor-in-chief of WikiLeaks. The *New York Times* decided to publish confidential documents obtained by the Web site.

---

[1]Ralph Potter, "The Logic of Moral Argument," in *Toward a Discipline of Social Ethics,* P. Deats, ed. (Boston: Boston University Press, 1972).

paid attention to the site until 2010, when WikiLeaks announced it would publish six years' worth of formerly classified documents regarding the war in Afghanistan. (WikiLeaks would also later publish a trove of diplomatic cables.) The site made a deal with the *New York Times*, a British newspaper, and a German magazine that would give those publications an advance look at the material and a chance to publish stories about it when the actual documents went online. (Fortunately, Bill Keller, executive editor of the *Times*, published a long apologia for his decision that will help in this analysis.)

As we saw in the preceding chapter, dealing with the problems presented by publishing classified data was a situation the *Times* had faced before, and once again the *Times* faced a clear ethical dilemma. There were good reasons not to run a story. Publishing a story based on the secret documents might endanger national security and severely restrict diplomatic efforts that depend on confidentiality to succeed. Moreover, publishing the information might endanger the lives of people who were secretly working with the United States and its allies. On the other hand, perhaps publication would further public understanding of the conflict and help people decide if the conflict was necessary. Publication would also let citizens compare what the government was publicly telling them to what the government was saying in private. What would the *Times* decide?

Let's apply the Potter model and see what we can conclude. First, establish the facts. The *Times* was dealing with the putative leader of WikiLeaks, an Australian named Julian Assange, whom Keller likened to a character from a Stieg Larsson thriller. Keller was apprehensive about Assange's motives in providing the information and, at the time, was unclear where WikiLeaks had obtained the documents. Keller assigned a *Times* employee the task of looking over the documents to see if they were genuine and contained anything newsworthy. The employee reported that the documents were authentic and had news value. Further, the *Times*'s lawyers determined that the newspaper would not face legal problems in publishing the information. After due consideration, Keller decided that if the paper published the information, Assange would be treated as a source, rather than a fellow journalist or a partner.

Second, clarify the values. News organizations value openness and the public's right to know. Would the publication of classified documents serve the public good? On the other hand, governments sometimes need secrecy to conduct sensitive negotiations. Of course, news organizations value human life. Would publication endanger sensitive diplomatic relations and ultimately encourage terrorists? Would people be put at risk if their names were revealed to a potential enemy?

Next, state principles. There are at least three ethical principles involved in this situation. The first is utilitarianism. Do the benefits of publishing the story outweigh the harm that might result? The second is the golden mean. At one extreme the *Times* could choose not to publish any of the documents; at the other extreme it could choose to publish them all in their original form. The golden mean would suggest that the best course of action lies between these two poles. Perhaps some of the documents could be published with names and potentially harmful information removed. Finally, there is the principle of self-determination. The *Times* has an ethical obligation not to let itself be exploited or used as a means to an end. Were Assange and WikiLeaks using the *Times* to pursue their own political agenda? Likewise, the *Times* has a similar obligation toward Assange. It should not exploit him for the purpose of breaking a major story.

Fourth, determine loyalties. A journalist's primary loyalty is to fully report the facts of a story to his or her audience. Of course that is not the journalist's only loyalty. The press has a loyalty to society that requires it to be a good citizen in a democracy. Jeopardizing international relations may not be the hallmark of good citizenship. Finally, the *Times* has a loyalty to its own heritage of exposing misdeeds of government officials and agencies. In the Pentagon Papers case mentioned in Chapter 16, the *Times* chose to publish secret documents because they revealed that the government was not being entirely truthful with its citizens about America's involvement in the Vietnam War.

What did the *Times* finally decide? The paper chose to publish many of the secret documents but took care not to reveal the names of any persons whose lives might be put in danger by publishing the documents. The *Times* also redacted any information that might be helpful to the enemy. It appears that the newspaper endorsed the principle of utilitarianism. In an editor's note, the paper stated that publishing the documents served "an important public interest, illuminating the goals, successes, compromises and frustrations of American diplomacy." Experts in media ethics generally praised the way the *Times* handled the situation. The Society of Professional Journalists concluded that the *Times* had acted responsibly by verifying the information and minimizing harm by redacting certain passages and names. The WikiLeaks episode once again demonstrated that no matter what the choice, journalists should be ready to explain and defend their decisions.

performance codes

Many ethical decisions have to be made within hours or even minutes, without the luxury of lengthy philosophical reflection. In this regard media professionals are not very different from other professionals, such as doctors and lawyers. In these professions, codes of conduct or of ethics have been standardized to help individuals make decisions. If a doctor or a lawyer violates one of the tenets of these codes, he or she may be barred from practice by a decision of a panel of colleagues who oversee the profession. Here the similarity with the mass media ends. Media professionals, thoroughly committed to the notion of free speech, have no professional review boards that grant and revoke licenses. Media codes of performance and methods of self-regulation are less precise and less stringent than those of other organizations. But many of the ethical principles discussed are incorporated into these codes.

The Print Media

During the colorful and turbulent age of jazz journalism (see Chapter 5), several journalists, apparently reacting against the excesses of some tabloids, founded the American Society of Newspaper Editors. This group voluntarily adopted the Canons of Journalism in 1923 without any public or governmental pressure. There were seven canons: responsibility, freedom of the press, independence, accuracy, impartiality, fair play, and decency. By and large, the canons are prescriptive (telling what ought to be done) rather than proscriptive (telling what ought to be avoided). Some of the canons are general and vague, with a great deal of room for individual interpretation. Under *responsibility*, for example, it is stated that "the use a newspaper makes of the share of public attention it gains serves to determine its sense of responsibility, which it shares with every member of its staff." This is a noble thought, but it is of little help when it comes to deciding if a newspaper should include the detail about the pornographic magazines in the star football player's car. Other statements seem simplistic. Under *accuracy*, for example, one learns that "headlines should be fully warranted by the contents of the article they surmount." Nevertheless, these canons should not be dismissed as mere platitudes and empty rhetoric. They do represent the first concrete attempt by journalists to strive for professionalism in their field.

When the canons were first released, *Time* magazine held out grandiose hopes for the future of the profession: "The American Society of Newspaper Editors (ASNE) aims to be to journalism what the American Bar Association is to the legal fraternity." *Time* was overly optimistic. The legal fraternity, through its powerful bar associations, has the power to revoke a member's license to practice. Journalists have fiercely resisted any idea that resembles licensing as a restriction on their First Amendment rights.

For this reason, the ASNE has never proposed licensing or certifying journalists. In fact, the ASNE has never expelled a member in its history, even though it has had ample reason to do so.

The Society of Professional Journalists (SPJ; formerly Sigma Delta Chi) adopted its code at about the same time as the ASNE. The code was designed to guide journalists working in all media. The SPJ code remained unchanged for more than 45 years, but as journalistic ethics became more problematic, the code was revised in 1973, 1984, 1987, and again in 1996. The current SPJ code is organized around four main principles:

1. *Seek the truth and report it.* Journalists should be honest, fair, and courageous in reporting the news.
2. *Minimize harm.* Journalists should treat sources, subjects, and colleagues as human beings deserving of respect.
3. *Act independently.* Journalists should be free of obligation to any interest other than the public's right to know.
4. *Be accountable.* Journalists should be accountable to their audience and to each other.

In 1975 the Associated Press Managing Editors (APME) association adopted a code that also discussed responsibility, accuracy, integrity, and independence. Revised in 1995, the APME code covers such issues as plagiarism and diversity. As with the ASNE's canons, adherence to the code is voluntary. Neither the SPJ nor the ASNE association has developed procedures to enforce its codes.

In late 1999 the Gannett Company became the first newspaper chain to spell out ethical principles for its papers. Other newspaper chains have companywide guidelines covering general issues, but individual papers can set policy in their own newsrooms. The Gannett guidelines are the first to be newsroom-specific. The decision to establish guidelines stemmed from a growing public distrust of the media and a desire to reassure readers about the fairness and accuracy of newspaper content. These guidelines forbid, among other things, lying to get a story, fabricating news, and publishing misleading alterations of photographs.

Broadcasting

For many years radio and television broadcasters followed the National Association of Broadcasters (NAB) Code of Good Practice. This code first appeared in 1929 and was revised periodically over the years. It was divided into two parts, one covering advertising and the other covering general program practices. In 1982, however, a court ruled that the code placed undue limitations on advertising, and the NAB suspended the advertising part of its code. The next year, to forestall more legal pressure, the NAB officially dissolved the code in its entirety.

Although the code is gone, its impact lingers. In 1990 the NAB issued voluntary programming principles that addressed four key areas: children's TV, indecency, violence, and drug and substance abuse. The new guidelines were stated in a broad and general way: "Glamorization of drug use and substance abuse should be avoided. . . . Violence . . . should only be portrayed in a responsible manner and should not be used exploitatively." To stay out of trouble with the Justice Department, the NAB declared that there would be no interpretation or enforcement of these provisions and that the standards were not designed to inhibit creativity.

Trying to resurrect a code for broadcasters is a favorite activity among politicians. In 1997 four U.S. senators introduced a bill that would exempt the broadcasting and cable industries from antitrust laws so that they could develop a new code. Other bills that urged broadcasters to develop a voluntary code of conduct were introduced in Congress in 1998 and 1999. Support for a new code cropped up again in 2004 after Janet Jackson's wardrobe malfunction during the Super Bowl's halftime show. The FCC and members of congress suggested that a new code would help limit indecent broadcasts, but nothing came of the effort. There have been no serious attempts to revive the code since 2005.

In the broadcast journalism area, the Radio and Television News Directors Association has an 11-part code that covers everything from cameras in the courtroom to invasion of privacy.

The V-chip and its companion ratings system are an interesting interaction between formal and informal controls. For purposes of this discussion, it is important to point out that the V-chip represents an example of the government's pressuring the video industry to adopt "voluntary" guidelines that categorize programming. If the industry failed to develop its own program ratings to work with the V-chip, Congress left the door open for the FCC to do it for them. The threat of government action has been used before to prod broadcasters into reforms that they were reluctant to make on their own. In fact, scholars who have studied the FCC have even given this phenomenon a name: the "raised eyebrow" technique. The V-chip legislation is a bit stronger than the raised eyebrow, but its end result is the same.

Producers rate program content according to an age-based scale ranging from "TV-G," suitable for a general audience, to "TV-M," for mature audience only. Further, special advisories for specific content are also displayed: "S" for sexual content and "V" for excessive violence. Parents can set the V-chip to block whatever programming they feel is unacceptable for their children. For example, the V-chip can be set to block all "TV-M"-rated shows. Interestingly, in its 2007 report on television violence, the FCC declared that the V-chip, while helpful, was not an effective tool in protecting young people from violent TV content. Despite a public service campaign to educate viewers about the device, a 2007 survey noted that about 90 percent of respondents didn't use it.

Motion Pictures

Codes of conduct in the motion picture industry emerged during the 1920s. Scandals were racking Hollywood at that time (see Chapter 10), and many states had passed or were considering censorship laws that would control the content of movies. In an attempt to save itself from being tarred and feathered, as it were, the industry invited Will Hays, a former postmaster general and elder of the Presbyterian Church, to head a new organization that would clean up films. Hays became the president, chairman of the board, and chairman of the executive committee of a new organization, the Motion Picture Producers and Distributors of America (MPPDA). In 1930 this group adopted the Motion Picture Production Code. The code was mainly proscriptive; it described what should be avoided in order for filmmakers to get their movies past existing censorship boards and listed what topics should be handled carefully so as not to rile existing pressure groups. The 1930 code is remarkable for its specificity; it rambles on for nearly 20 printed pages. The following are some excerpts:

> *The presentation of scenes, episodes, plots, etc. which are deliberately meant to excite [sex and passion] on the part of the audience is always wrong, is subversive to the interest of society, and is a peril to the human race.*
>
> *The more intimate parts of the human body are the male and female organs and the breasts of a woman.*
>
> a. *They should never be uncovered.*
> b. *They should not be covered with transparent or translucent material.*
> c. *They should not be clearly and unmistakably outlined by garments. . . .*
>
> *There must be no display at any time of machine guns, sub-machine guns or other weapons generally classified as illegal weapons. . . .*
>
> *Obscene dances are those which represent sexual actions, whether performed solo or with two or more, which are designed to excite an audience, arouse passion, or cause physical excitement.*

A few years after the Production Code was drafted, a Roman Catholic organization, the Legion of Decency (see "Media Probe: The Legion of Decency"), pressured the industry to put teeth into its code enforcement. The MPPDA ruled that no company belonging to its organization could distribute or release any film unless it bore the Production Code

Administration's seal of approval. In addition, a $25,000 fine could be levied against a firm that violated this rule. Because of the hammerlock that the major studios had on the movie industry at this time, it was virtually impossible for an independent producer to make or exhibit a film without the aid of a member company. As a result, the Production Code turned out to be more restrictive than many of the local censorship laws it was designed to avoid.

The Production Code was a meaningful force in the film industry for about 20 years. During the late 1940s, however, changes that would ultimately alter the basic structure of the motion picture industry also led to the code's being scuttled. In 1948 the Paramount case ended producer-distributor control of theaters, thus allowing independent producers to market a film without the Production Code seal. In addition, economic competition from television prompted films to tackle more mature subjects. The industry responded during the 1950s by liberalizing the code; despite this easing of restrictions, more and more producers began to ignore them. Nonetheless, the code, outdated and unenforceable, persisted into the 1960s. A 1966 revision that tried to keep pace with changing social attitudes proved to be too little too late.

In 1968 the motion picture industry entered into a new phase of self-regulation when the Production Code seal of approval was dropped and a new motion picture rating system was established. Operated under the auspices of the Motion Picture Association of America (successor to the MPPDA), the National Association of Theater Owners, and the Independent Film Importers and Distributors of America, this new system, commonly referred to as the **MPAA rating system**, places films into one of five categories:

G: Suitable for general audiences.

PG: Parental guidance suggested.

PG-13: Some content may be objectionable for children under 13 (a new category added in 1984).

R: Restricted to persons over age 17 unless accompanied by parent or adult guardian.

NC-17: No children under 17 admitted. (This category replaced the X rating in 1990. The MPAA made the change in response to several producers who argued that adult-themed, daring, but nonpornographic films should not be lumped into the same category as porno films.)

Unlike the old Production Code, which regulated film content, the new system leaves producers more or less free to include whatever scenes they like as long as they realize that, by so doing, they may restrict the size of their potential audience. One possible repercussion of this system may be the steady decline in the number of G-rated films released each year. Producers evidently feel that movies in this category will be perceived as children's films and will not be attractive to a more mature audience. During the first 11 years of the rating system's existence, the percentage of films in the G category dropped, while the percentage of films in the R category increased. X-rated or NC-17-rated films have never accounted for more than 10 percent of the total number of films submitted for review (of course, many low-budget, hard-core pornographic films are never submitted for classification).

In order for the MPAA rating system to work, producers, distributors, theater owners, and parents must all cooperate. There is no governmental involvement in the classification system; there are no fines involved. Moviemakers are not required to submit a film for rating.

The Advertising Industry

In the advertising industry several professional organizations have drafted codes of performance. The American Association of Advertising Agencies first adopted its Standards of Practice in 1924. This code, which covers contracts, credit extension, unfair tactics, and the creative side of advertising, contains provisions prohibiting misleading price claims, offensive statements, and the circulation of harmful rumors about a competitor. The Advertising Code

media *Probe*   *The Legion of Decency*

After World War I, during the roaringest part of the Roaring Twenties, the films that grossed the most money had titles like *Red Hot Romance, She Could Not Help It, Her Purchase Price,* and *Plaything of Broadway.* One movie ad of the period boasted breathlessly of "brilliant men, beautiful jazz babies, champagne baths, midnight revels, petting parties in the purple dawn." Before long, public opposition to such sensational movies began to form. The appointment of Will Hays, the creation of the Motion Picture Producers and Distributors of America, and the adoption of the Motion Picture Production Code were designed, in part, to forestall this public criticism.

Much of the code was suggested by a Roman Catholic layman, Martin Quigley, and a Roman Catholic priest, Father Daniel Lord. Despite the existence of the code, however, sensational films still appeared in significant numbers. This trend was disturbing to many segments in society, particularly the Catholic Church. Keep in mind that at this time the United States was in the midst of a severe economic depression. Many individuals, including prominent Catholics, connected the country's economic poverty with the nation's moral bankruptcy as evidenced by the films of the period. Additionally, an Apostolic Delegate from Rome took the film industry to task in a blistering speech before the Catholic Charities Convention in New York.

In April 1934 a committee composed of American bishops responded to the speech and to the general tenor of the period by announcing the organization of a nationwide Legion of Decency, whose members were to fight for better films. The legion threatened to boycott those theaters that exhibited objectionable films, and it sometimes made good on its threats. The Chicago chapter of the legion enrolled a half-million members in a matter of days and was matched by equal enrollment in Brooklyn.

Detroit Catholics affixed "We Demand Clean Movies" bumper stickers to their cars. Other religious groups joined the legion—Jewish clergy in New York, Lutherans in Missouri. Pope Pius XI praised the legion as an "excellent experiment" and called upon bishops all over the world to imitate it.

There were 20 million Catholics in the United States in 1934, and naturally the film industry took this group seriously. The Production Code Administration was set up with the power to slap a $25,000 fine on films released without the administration's seal of approval. The Legion of Decency's boycotts hurt enough at the box office to force many theaters to book only films that the legion approved. In Albuquerque, New Mexico, 17 of 21 theaters agreed not to book a film condemned by the legion. In Albany, New York, Catholics pledged to avoid for six months each theater that had screened the condemned film *Baby Doll.* Producers, frightened by this display of economic power, began meeting with legion members to make sure there were no potentially inflammatory elements in their films.

By the 1960s, however, the Legion of Decency was losing most of its clout. The restructuring of the film industry allowed independent producers to market their films without code approval. Many producers did just that and demonstrated that some films could make money even without legion and Production Code approval. The increasingly permissive mood of the country encouraged an avalanche of more mature and controversial films. Moreover, the legion, renamed the National Catholic Office for Motion Pictures, painted itself into a corner when it condemned such artistically worthwhile films as Bergman's *The Silence* and Antonioni's *Blowup,* and endorsed such films as *Godzilla vs. the Thing* and *Goliath and the Sins of Babylon.* By the 1970s this group had effectively lost all its power; it was essentially disbanded in 1980. Nonetheless, during its prime the Legion of Decency was the single most effective private influence on the film industry.

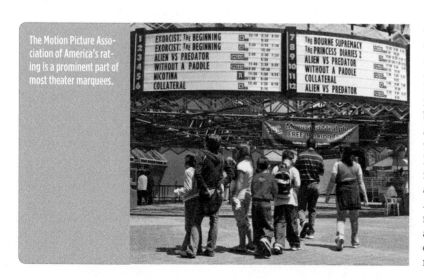

The Motion Picture Association of America's rating is a prominent part of most theater marquees.

of American Business, developed and distributed by the American Advertising Federation and the Association of Better Business Bureaus International, covers much the same ground. Memberships in these organizations and adherence to the codes are voluntary. In public relations the Public Relations Society of America adopted its first code in 1954 and revised it during the 1980s. As with the other codes, enforcement is essentially voluntary, and the society has no control over a practitioner who is not a member.

media *Probe*

Policing YouTube

About 20 hours of video are uploaded to YouTube every minute. Making sure that inappropriate content doesn't appear on the site is obviously a big job. Like many other content-sharing sites, YouTube depends greatly on its users to keep things proper.

First, the site expects users to abide by its Community Guidelines. In addition to the obvious copyright cautions, here are some of the "common-sense rules" that YouTube has established concerning inappropriate content:

■ YouTube is not for pornography or sexually explicit content. If this describes your video, even if it's a video of yourself, don't post it on YouTube. Also, be advised that we work closely with law enforcement and we report child exploitation.

■ Don't post videos showing bad stuff like animal abuse, drug abuse, underage drinking and smoking, or bomb making.

■ Graphic or gratuitous violence is not allowed. If your video shows someone being physically hurt, attacked, or humiliated, don't post it.

■ We encourage free speech and defend everyone's right to express unpopular points of view. But we don't permit hate speech (speech which attacks or demeans a group based on race or ethnic origin, religion, disability, gender, age, veteran status, and sexual orientation/gender identity).

Second, visitors are given the chance to flag offending videos if they think content is in violation of the site's guidelines. YouTube staff members review every flagged video to see if it conforms to its content policy. If it doesn't, it is taken down from the site and a warning is sent to the user. If the violation is extreme or if the user continues to post inappropriate content, the account might be suspended or canceled.

In late 2008, YouTube announced stricter guidelines for users. It expanded its interpretation of sexually suggestive ads and stated that such ads would not be available for viewing by those under 18. In addition, suggestive videos and those with profanity and vulgarity would be banned from the site's Most Viewed and Top Favorites listings. The crackdown comes as YouTube struggles to make a profit. Convincing advertisers that the site has become more respectable is one step toward that goal.

internal controls

Codes established by professional organizations and individual ethics are not the only informal controls on media behavior. Most media organizations have other internal controls that frequently come into play. Written statements of policy can be found in most newspaper, television, radio, and motion picture organizations. In advertising, a professional organization for self-regulation has existed since 1971.

Organizational Policy: Television Networks' Standards and Practices

For many years each major network maintained a large department that was usually labeled "Standards and Practices" or something similar. Staff members in these departments would make literally thousands of decisions each season on the acceptability of dialogue, plotlines, and visual portrayals. During the late 1980s, however, network budget cuts took their toll, and most of these departments were scaled back dramatically. As criticism of television content increased during the 1990s, these departments were enlarged somewhat, but they still have far fewer people working in them than they did in the early 1980s. The departments at Fox, NBC, and ABC review everything their networks air, including commercials. At CBS the standards department reviews children's programs, docudramas, ads, new shows, and about a dozen existing series. The efforts devoted

The reality series *Jersey Shore* raised questions about what was acceptable in prime time.

ethical issues

Ethical Problems Shared by Journalists and College Students

It is unethical for journalists to plagiarize the work of another or to fabricate a story by making up facts and inventing sources. Similarly, when writing research papers, it is unethical for college students to plagiarize and to make up information. What should be the appropriate punishment for such offenses for journalists? For college students? Those were the questions under investigation in an October 2009 article by Mike Conway and Jacob Groshek published in *Communication Education*.

For six semesters, the researchers surveyed students enrolled in journalism classes at the beginning and again at the end of their program of studies, just before graduation. The investigators were able to gather data from 2,925 students, an extremely large sample for a survey. The survey questions asked about how concerned students were about several ethical issues relating to plagiarism and fabrication by both journalists and students.

The results suggested that students were more concerned about ethical lapses among professional journalists than they were about ethical violations committed by students. For example, about 56 percent of the students were quite concerned or very concerned about their fellow students making up quotes, but about 80 percent were quite or very concerned about journalists making up quotes. Similarly, about 46 percent of students were concerned about their peers stealing information from the Internet, but 83 percent were concerned if journalists did the same.

The students were also much more lenient on themselves when it came to punishment. About two-thirds of the students thought that journalists found guilty of plagiarizing or fabricating information should be fired. But what about college students who fabricate or steal or copy from the Internet without attribution? Only 2 percent of the students thought that expulsion was the appropriate penalty for those infractions. The same trend emerged for making up sources. Approximately 61 percent of the students thought that a journalist who makes up sources should be fired, but only 3 percent of the students thought that students who make up sources should be expelled.

As the authors of the article state, "[I]t is quite clear that students are far more concerned about professional journalists behaving badly than they are about students failing to meet fundamental ethical standards." The authors don't speculate on why students are far more sympathetic to their comrades than they are to professionals. That's an issue that would make a separate research project in itself.

By the way, the title of this article pretty well sums it up: "Forgive Me Now, Fire Me Later: Mass Communication Students' Ethics Gap Concerning School and Journalism."

to monitoring standards vary greatly among cable networks. MTV, for example, closely monitors all its programs; the Discovery Channel rarely has problems regarding taste. Pay channels, such as HBO, have more liberal standards.

The broadcast and cable networks are also relying more and more on the judgment of series producers to determine standards of acceptability. Producers, for their part, have a general notion about how far they can go without raising network displeasure. The networks will generally closely monitor the first few episodes of a series that may cause problems. After that they will put more trust in the producers' standards.

It is probably obvious to any casual observer of broadcast television that network standards have become more liberal over the years. For instance, top-rated *CSI* has broadcast episodes dealing with sadomasochism and sexual fetishes. *Modern Family* and *Grey's Anatomy* have gay characters as stars.

There are several reasons behind these changes. First, society has become more open-minded. Subjects that were once taboo, such as male impotence, are now discussed routinely in commercials. Second, the broadcast networks have to compete with the more permissive cable networks, on which shows such as *Sex and the City* have pushed the envelope of acceptability even further. Finally, the sex scandal involving President Bill Clinton and Monica Lewinsky put sexual topics on the evening newscasts and immediately eliminated many taboos.

Despite this liberalization the networks' standards and practices departments still exercise some caution. Offensive stereotypes are not allowed. Networks traditionally have not aired ads for abortion clinics, contraceptives (some local stations have aired contraceptive ads), or massage parlors.

The Internet can provide an outlet for material that the standards and practices department deems inappropriate for broadcast TV. The unedited versions of comedy skits from network shows such as *Saturday Night Live* sometimes make their way onto YouTube or other video-sharing sites.

In addition to the networks, local stations also exercise self-regulation. Occasionally, a local station will decide that a network show is inappropriate for its audience and decline to show it or broadcast it at a later time. For example, a Salt Lake City station refused to carry NBC's 2011 drama *The Playbay Club.*

Local stations also construct a **policy book**. This book typically spells out the station's philosophy and standards of operation and identifies which practices are encouraged or discouraged. For example, most television and radio stations have a policy against newsroom personnel functioning as commercial spokespersons. Radio stations typically have a policy against airing "homemade" tapes and records. Other stations may have rules against playing songs that are drug-oriented or sexually suggestive. Commercials that make extravagant claims or ads for questionable products and services might also be prohibited under local-station policy.

Organizational Policy: Newspapers and Magazines

Newspapers and magazines create policy statements that take two distinct forms. **Operating policies** cover the everyday problems and situations that crop up during the normal functioning of the paper or magazine. **Editorial policies** are guidelines that the newspaper or magazine follows to persuade the public on certain issues or to achieve specific goals.

Operating policies vary from one paper or magazine to another. In general, however, these policies cover such matters as accepting freebies, using deception to gather information, paying newsmakers for a story or exclusive interview (checkbook journalism), taking junkets, conducting electronic surveillance, using stolen documents, accepting advertising for X-rated films, and publishing the names of rape victims. Also covered are outside employment of reporters and editors and conflicts of interest. Here, for example, are excerpts from the Rules and Guidelines used by the *Milwaukee Journal*:

> Free tickets or passes to sports events, movies, theatrical productions, circuses, ice shows, or other entertainment may not be accepted or solicited by staff members.
>
> A gift that exceeds token value should be returned promptly with an explanation that it is against our policy. If it is impractical to return it, the company will donate it to a charity.
>
> Participating in politics at any level is not allowed, either for pay or as a volunteer. Public relations and publicity work in fields outside the Journal should be avoided.

Some newspapers and magazines are liberal; some are conservative. Some support Democratic candidates; others support Republicans. Some are in favor of nuclear energy; others against. These and other attitudes are generally expressed in the editorial pages of the newspaper. Editorial policy is generally clear at most publications. The *Chicago Tribune* has traditionally expressed a conservative point of view. The *New York Times* has a more liberal policy. The editorial policy of a paper will exert a certain amount of control over the material that is printed on its editorial pages. Of course, the paper has a perfect right to do this. There may be times, however, when the editorial policy of the paper spills over onto its news pages, and this might cause a problem for the paper's reputation for objectivity, responsibility, and integrity.

One problem that crops up periodically is called *boosterism,* a procommunity philosophy that sometimes causes not-so-good news to go unreported. In Flint, Michigan, when the local Fisher Body plant closed, TV networks and newspapers across the country announced the bad news that Flint was about to lose 3,600 jobs. The local Flint paper did not mention the job loss until the 11th paragraph on an inside page. "Good news," however, got prominent play: A story about new shrubs being planted at the local Buick facility earned front-page coverage.

Owners and publishers can exert editorial control over news policy in several ways. They can hire only those people who agree with their editorial views. For example, the *New Orleans Times-Picayune* ran an ad in a trade magazine for a business reporter. One of the qualifications was a "probusiness philosophy." They can also fire people who produce stories that the owner does not like, or they can issue orders to downplay some topics while paying large amounts of attention to others.

social issues   *Disappearing Public Editors*

Public editors (the term newspapers use to refer to ombudspeople) are an endangered species. As newspapers trim their staffs to reduce costs, one of the first positions to go is that of public editor. In 2008, about a dozen papers announced that they were laying off public editors or assigning them to different jobs. (A dozen may not sound like a lot, but remember that there were only about 40 papers that employed public editors.)

Will the disappearance of these positions make newspapers less responsive to their readers? Some editors defend the cuts by noting that newspapers must give priority to news gathering, selling advertising, and customer service in order to stay in business. If the newspaper folds, its responsiveness to readers is a moot point. Other editors contend that the public editor is not the only method that ensures that newspapers keep in touch with their readers. A recent article in the trade publication *Editor & Publisher* quotes the editor of the *Orlando Sentinel:* "Papers can distance themselves too much from readers if everything goes to one person." At the *Sentinel*, every editor is directly accountable to readers. Another argument suggests that technology has made public editors irrelevant. Modern newspapers allow comments on stories, editor blogs, and forums that permit discussion about stories.

There is, of course, another side to the argument. The public editor was the one person that people could contact if they had a problem. Public editors gave readers a voice that wasn't lost in the chatter of story comments or forums. Moreover, the public editor could be an advocate for readers inside the newspapers, and a full-time, in-house advocate is more likely to get a response from management than a comment posted at the end of a story. In addition, suggesting that all editors are responsible to readers spreads the responsibility so thin that it may result in nobody being responsible. Further, public editors developed ties within the community that are lost when the position is eliminated. Losing these ties eliminates another channel of reader-newspaper interaction. Finally, the public editor was a symbol who embodied the idea that newspapers were accountable for their mistakes and their operations were open for public inspection. Eliminating the public editor might hurt the credibility of a publication.

Perhaps the unkindest cut of all occurred when, after having a public editor for more than 40 years, the *Louisville Courier-Journal* decided to eliminate the position. The person who last held the job was also the president of the Organization of News Ombudsmen.

What is the significance of these examples for the news-consuming public? For one thing, the sample cases are probably exceptions to the norm rather than the norm itself. Nonetheless, they do illustrate the potential hazards of relying on only one source for news. The intelligent consumer of news and information should rely on several different media to get a more complete picture.

Media Self-Criticism

Some informal control over media content and practices comes from within. Although the amount of internal media criticism has grown in the past few years, it is still small when compared with the amount of investigative reporting and critical analyses that newspapers, magazines, television, and radio conduct about other facets of society. Many newspapers and magazines have media critics and media reporters. The amount of meaningful critical writing done by these journalists, however, is highly variable. Some of the better-known critics in the print media are Ken Auletta of the *New Yorker,* Howard Kurtz of the *Daily Beast,* and Tom Shales of the *Washington Post.*

A few journalism reviews regularly criticize media performance. The *Columbia Journalism Review* is the best known, but its circulation is only about 18,000. Others that are important are the *American Journalism Review* and the *St. Louis Journalism Review.*

The Internet has opened up a new channel for media self-criticism. The Media Channel (www.mediachannel.org), for example, contains news, analysis of issues, and criticism about media across the globe. Journalist Jim Romenesko maintained a similar site at www.poynter.org. The impact of these and similar sites is yet to be determined.

Cable and broadcast television networks usually offer few programs with serious criticism of the media. Newspapers do a bit more in this area; the *Wall Street Journal*

They Obviously Weren't Listening

Thirty-one engineering students enrolled in a course at a Canadian university were recently punished for cheating. The students had downloaded term papers from the Internet and submitted them as original work. What course were they taking? "Introduction to Ethics."

has occasionally run an in-depth study of the problems facing the newspaper industry. In film the industry newspaper *Variety* has sometimes published an article critical of the film industry. *Billboard,* the trade publication of the sound-recording industry, has run analytical, if not critical, pieces on the recording industry.

Some newspapers and other media organizations have tried to incorporate an idea from Scandinavia into their operations to provide some internal criticism. An **ombudsperson** is employed by the company to handle complaints from audience members who feel they have gotten a raw deal. The ombudsperson also criticizes in general the performance of the organization's personnel. Although the number of ombudspersons (sometimes called public editors) in the United States was never large, interest in the position grew because news organizations were worried that they are losing credibility with their audiences. At one point there were about 40 ombudspersons in the United States, just about all at newspapers. Budget cuts, however, have meant that many ombudspersons are no longer on the job (see "Social Issues: Disappearing Public Editors"). The position is almost nonexistent in TV newsrooms.

Professional Self-Regulation in Advertising

In 1971 the leading advertising professional organizations—the Council of Better Business Bureaus, the American Advertising Federation, the American Association of Advertising Industries, and the Association of National Advertisers—formed the National Advertising Review Council. Its objective is to sustain high standards of truth and accuracy in advertising. The council itself is composed of two divisions: the National Advertising Division (NAD) and the National Advertising Review Board (NARB). When a complaint about an ad is made by a consumer or competitor, the complaint goes first to the NAD, which evaluates it. The NAD can dismiss the complaint as unfounded or trivial, or it can contact the advertiser for an explanation or further substantiation. If the NAD is satisfied that the ad in question is accurate, it will dismiss the complaint. If the NAD is not satisfied with the explanation, it can ask the advertiser to change the ad or discontinue the message.

If the advertiser disagrees, the case goes to the NARB, which functions as a court of appeals. Ultimately, if the case does not result in an acceptable solution, the NARB may call it to the attention of the Federal Trade Commission or other appropriate agencies. Sending a case to the FTC happens rarely. In 1993 the board turned over to the FTC the first fraudulent advertising case in the NARB's 22-year history. Most advertisers generally comply with the NAD's wishes. In 2010, for example, the NAD recommended that the Liquid HCG Diet discontinue its weight-loss claims on Facebook and Twitter, pending evidence to support those claims.

Industry groups also exert control over advertising for their products. For example, the Miller Brewing Company and the Anheuser-Busch Company voluntarily agreed to remove their ads from MTV because they did not want to appear to be encouraging underage drinking.

outside influences

The larger context that surrounds a media organization often contains factors that have an influence on media performance. In this section we will discuss three: (1) economics, (2) pressure groups, and (3) education.

Economic Pressures

Money is a potent influence on media gatekeepers. In commercial media the loss of revenue can be an important consideration in controlling what gets filmed, published, or broadcast. Economic controls come in many shapes and forms. Pressure can be brought to bear by advertisers, by the medium's own business policy, by the general economic structure of the industry, and by consumer groups.

Pressure from Advertisers   The recording industry gets its revenue from the purchase of individual tracks and discs. Consequently, it earns virtually no money from advertisers

ethical issues

New Code of Ethics for the Advertising Industry

In March 2011 the Institute for Advertising Ethics (IAE) released a set of ethical principles that it hoped would guide decision making in the world of modern advertising, public relations, and marketing. The principles were developed with help from the American Advertising Federation and the Reynolds Journalism Institute at the University of Missouri. As is the case with most codes of ethics, the eight principles are expressed in general terms and tend to be prescriptive (telling advertisers what to do) rather than proscriptive (telling advertisers what not to do).

Here is a brief summary of the eight principles in the code:

- Advertisers should have high ethical standards.
- Advertisers have an obligation to be ethical when disseminating commercial information to consumers.
- Advertisers should distinguish advertising and public relations content from news and entertainment content, both online and offline.
- Advertisers should reveal all payments or other conditions (such as getting a free product) affecting endorsements in traditional media and social media.
- Advertisers should treat consumers fairly.
- Advertisers should never compromise consumers' personal privacy, and consumers should have a clear option to opt in or opt out when it comes to providing information.

- Advertisers should follow state and local laws dealing with advertising and cooperate with industry self-regulation programs.
- Advertisers should privately discuss potential ethical issues, and members of the team creating the ads should be given a chance to voice ethical concerns.

Some of these principles are easier to abide by than others. For example, suppose someone on Twitter is getting a free night at a hotel in return for tweeting positive messages about the hotel. When does the disclosure occur? Only in the first tweet? In every following tweet? With only 140 characters to work with, how much space is left for a message after providing disclosure? Another example: Suppose a member of the creative team putting together an ad has an ethical concern that is not satisfied by internal discussions. Is it ethical for the employee to make his or her concerns public?

The Institute recognizes that these principles are not immutable and that they might be revised based on feedback and changing conditions. Similar to other codes of ethics, the IAE code depends on voluntary compliance. The Institute hopes that advertising agencies and public relations firms will sponsor seminars and conferences to explain the principles and encourage their employees to sign pledges to adhere to the new code.

and is generally immune to their pressures. The film industry makes most of its money from the sale of individual tickets. Advertisers have some limited influence through what is called *product placement*—an arrangement whereby an advertiser pays a movie studio to include its product in a film. *Super 8,* for example, had several scenes that featured 7-Eleven convenience stores. Nonetheless, in relative terms, advertisers have only modest influence over motion picture content. In the print media, on the other hand, newspapers depend on advertising for about 75 percent of their income, while magazines derive more than 50 percent of their revenues from ads. Radio and television, of course, depend on ads for almost all their income.

The actual amount of control that an advertiser has over media content and behavior is difficult to determine. It is probably fair to say that most news stories and most television and radio programs are put together without much thought as to what advertisers will say about them. Occasionally, however, you may find examples of pressure:

- In 2008, a reporter for a Virginia paper wrote unfavorable stories about a local hospital. The hospital complained and pulled all of its advertising from the paper. The reporter was then assigned to another beat. (The paper claimed that the hospital's actions had nothing to do with the reassignment.)
- Executives at the *Boston Herald* suspended a reporter who wrote columns critical of a merger between two big Boston banks. One of the banks was a big advertiser in the newspaper and held the mortgage on the newspaper's building. (Management eventually relented and reinstated the journalist.)

Business Policies   Economic pressure on media content is sometimes encouraged by the business practices of the media themselves. When the Massachusetts Supreme Court ruled that a creditor could be sued for harassing those who owed money, the Boston newspapers declined to identify the retail store involved in the suit. The store in question was a big newspaper advertiser. In San Francisco a newspaper killed a column that criticized the Nike Company. It so happened that Nike was the sponsor of the paper's popular "Bay to Breakers" race.

Trading news coverage for advertising time or space is a common problem. A TV station in south Florida sent a flyer to its advertisers offering to do a news story on them in return for $5,000. While trying to negotiate a contract to carry live drawings for the New York State Lottery, a TV station promised lottery officials positive news coverage of lottery events. In both instances the stations withdrew the offers when their breach of ethics was revealed.

Then there is the problem of revenue-related reading matter. This issue crops up when a new shopping center or discount store opens in a community and gets heavy news coverage, maybe more than is justified by ordinary journalistic standards, in return for advertising revenue. Recently, in Waco, Texas, the local newspaper devoted half its front page and two inside pages (with seven color photographs) to the opening of a new supermarket. Not surprisingly, supermarkets spend a lot on newspaper ads.

These examples are not meant to criticize or impugn the reputation of any medium or profession. There are probably countless, less-publicized examples of newspapers, magazines, television, and radio stations resisting advertising and economic pressure. What you should learn from this section is the nature of the close relationship that can sometimes exist between advertisers and media and the pressures that can result. Most of the time, this relationship causes few problems. When professional judgment is compromised by dollar signs, however, then perhaps the economic pressures are performing a dysfunction for the media.

Pressure Groups

Various segments of the audience can band together and try to exert control over the operation of mass media organizations. These groups sometimes use the threat of economic pressure (boycotts) or simply rely on the negative effects of bad publicity to achieve their goals. In radio and television, pressure groups (or *citizens' groups*, as they are often called) can resort to applying legal pressure during the license renewal process. Because of broadcasting's unique legal position, it has been the focus of a great deal of pressure group attention. In 1964, for example, a group of black citizens working with the Office of Communication of the United Church of Christ formed a pressure group and attempted to deny the license renewal of a TV station in Jackson, Mississippi, because of alleged discrimination on the part of station management. After a long and complicated legal battle, the citizens' group succeeded in its efforts. This success probably encouraged the formation of other groups. John Banzhaf III headed an organization called ASH (Action for Smoking and Health), for example, which was instrumental in convincing Congress to ban cigarette advertising from radio and television.

At about the same time, perhaps the most influential of all the pressure groups interested in broadcasting was formed: Action for Children's Television (ACT). From a modest start, this group was successful in achieving the following:

- Persuading the networks to appoint a supervisor for children's programming
- Eliminating drug and vitamin ads from kids' shows
- Instituting a ban on the host's selling in children's programs
- Reducing the amount of advertising during Saturday morning programs
- Helping a bill concerning children's TV pass Congress in 1990

ACT disbanded in 1992. In its final press release, the organization said that its major goal had been achieved with the passage of the 1990 Children's Television Act and that people who want better television for kids now "have Congress on their side."

social *Political Pressure: The Blacklist*
Issues

After World War II, during a period generally referred to as the Cold War, tensions between the United States and the Soviet Union ran high. Many in the government feared that communists or communist sympathizers had assumed positions of importance in U.S. society. Anticommunist groups charged that the entertainment industry in particular was home to many communist sympathizers who made films that glorified communism. In 1947, the House Un-American Activities Committee (HUAC), an investigative committee of the House of Representatives, held hearings on supposed communist influences in the motion picture industry. Many well-known Hollywood stars, along with several directors, producers, and writers, were called to testify before the committee. Citing the First Amendment's right to freedom of speech and assembly, ten witnesses (dubbed "The Hollywood Ten") refused to answer the committee's questions about past or current contacts with the Communist Party. All were cited for contempt of Congress.

Their refusals caused the committee to put more pressure on the film industry to take a stand against communism and reaffirm its commitment to American values. Hollywood executives issued an announcement stating that any witness who refused to answer HUAC's questions would not be employed by the motion picture industry until they were cleared of contempt charges and had sworn they were not communists. In effect, the Hollywood Ten and others suspected of communist leanings were put on a blacklist and denied the opportunity to work in the film industry.

In 1950, the blacklist spilled over into broadcasting when a group of three former FBI agents published a newsletter called *Red Channels* that listed 151 people, many in the broadcasting industry, who were allegedly working on behalf of the Communist Party. Although the list was put together using poor and questionable information, broadcasting executives drew up their own informal list of people whose loyalties to the United States were suspect. Anybody on this list had to undergo a demeaning 12-step process of rehabilitation or be barred from working in the industry. Many actors, reporters, writers, and directors had their careers cut short because of this list.

Another self-appointed group dedicated to eliminating what it called the "communist conspiracy," Aware Inc., sprang up in 1953. Performers whose backgrounds were thought to be the least bit questionable were blacklisted by the organization, and many were unable to find work in the industry. Aware Inc.'s methods went to the heart of the commercial broadcasting system. Its founders threatened to boycott the products of advertisers who sponsored shows with suspected communists. Broadcasters took that threat seriously and avoided hiring anyone on the blacklist.

Aware Inc.'s investigation techniques were slipshod and careless. Many innocent performers were put on the blacklist and had their careers permanently damaged. Finally, one performer, John Henry Faulk, sued Aware Inc. for libel. After hearing the evidence during the trial, the jury was so aghast at the tactics and techniques used by Aware Inc. that they awarded Faulk a record $3.5 million in damages. (Faulk was able to collect only a small portion of this sum because the chief defendant died shortly after the trial.)

The period of the blacklist was not the proudest moment for the film and broadcasting industries. For our purposes, the episode illustrates some of the negative consequences that follow when politicians and pressure groups exert unreasonable power over the media industries.

In the mid-1970s other self-interest groups whose primary interest was not broadcasting began to get involved in television programming. The American Medical Association and the National Parent-Teacher Association both criticized TV violence. The National Organization for Women campaigned for more representative portrayals of women in the mass media. The American-Arab Anti-Discrimination Committee protested that Disney's *Aladdin* featured a song whose lyrics contained a slur against Arabs. Protests by gays and lesbians against the 2000 launch of Dr. Laura Schlessinger's TV show prompted many advertisers to back out from sponsoring the show and several stations to drop it altogether. Dr. Laura eventually apologized for some of her antigay remarks.

As the audiences of traditional media have gotten smaller, pressure group activity has declined. There are, however, some recent examples. The Parents Television Council has urged its members to file complaints with the FCC about certain episodes of *Family Guy*, and the Media Research Center has campaigned against what it perceives as liberal bias in TV news. In addition, issues surrounding the Internet have given rise to a new generation of pressure groups. The Center for Digital Democracy has campaigned on behalf of network neutrality, and the Media and Democracy Coalition has spoken out concerning the recent broadband stimulus program.

We can sum up by saying that there are both positive and negative aspects to the activities of these citizens' groups. On the one hand, they probably have made some media organizations more responsive to community needs and more sensitive to the problems of minorities and other disadvantaged groups. Citizen group involvement with media organizations probably has also increased the feedback between audience and the media industry. On the other hand, these groups are self-appointed guardians of special interests. They are not elected by anyone, and their wishes may not be at all representative of those of the larger population. In addition, many of these groups have exerted unreasonable power, and some extremist groups may actually abuse their influence and do more harm than good.

Education

Education also exerts informal control over the media. Ethics and professionalism are topics that are gaining more and more attention at colleges and universities. In fact, there has been a recent upsurge of interest in teaching ethics at many schools of journalism and mass communication. About 40 percent of the schools in the United States offer a special ethics course to their students. More than half of the approximately 40 books specifically devoted to mass media ethics have been published since 1980. Most of the experts in this area agree that instead of teaching specific codes of ethics to students, a systematic way of thinking about ethics should be stressed, so that individuals can consider issues and arrive at decisions rationally.

Even this book can be thought of as a means of informal control. The hope is that, after reading it, you will bring a more advanced level of critical thinking and a more sensitive and informed outlook to your media profession or to your role as a media consumer.

main points

- There are several types of informal controls on the mass media, including ethics, performance codes, organizational policies, self-criticism, and outside pressures.

- The most important ethical principles that provide guidance in this area are the golden mean, the categorical imperative, the principle of utility, the veil of ignorance, and the principle of self-determination.

- All the media have performance codes that guide professional behavior.

- Many media organizations have standards departments that monitor the content that is published or broadcast.

- The National Advertising Review Council is the main organization that supervises self-regulation in advertising.

- Outside pressures from advertisers can sometimes influence media conduct.

- Special-interest groups, such as Action for Children's Television, have been successful in modifying the content and practices of the TV industry.

questions for review

1. What are the main ethical principles discussed in the chapter?

2. Why was the NAB Code of Good Practice discontinued?

3. What is the difference between editorial policies and operating policies?

4. What is an ombudsperson? What does he or she do?

5. What are some ways advertisers can influence news content?

questions for critical thinking

1. How would you handle each of the examples mentioned in the introduction to the chapter?

2. What are some of the advantages and disadvantages of written codes of conduct?

3. Do special-interest groups exert too much power over the media?

4. Do advertisers have too much power over the media?

5. Consider the case of the *New York Times* and Wiki-Leaks discussed at the beginning of the chapter. Did the paper act ethically?

key terms

golden mean (p. 411)

categorical imperative (p. 411)

utility (p. 411)

veil of ignorance (p. 411)

self-determination (p. 412)

MPAA rating system (p. 417)

policy book (p. 421)

operating policies (p. 421)

editorial policies (p. 421)

ombudsperson (p. 423)

internet resources

Online Learning Center

On the Online Learning Center home page, www.mhhe.com/dominick12e, *select* Student Center *and then* Chapter 17.

1. Use the Learning Objectives, Chapter Outline, and Main Points sections to review this chapter.

2. Test your knowledge of the chapter using the multiple choice and flashcard features of the site.

3. Expand your knowledge of concepts and topics discussed in the chapter with additional Questions for Critical Thinking and Internet Exercises.

surfing the internet

There are few Web sites that deal with the topics discussed in this chapter, but the ones listed here are relevant.

www.mediaethicsmagazine.com
Examines practical and theoretical ethical issues in mass media communication.

http://asne.org/AdminTools/Articles/
The American Society of Newspaper Editors has collected codes of ethics from about three dozen media organizations.

www.mpaa.org/ratings
Information about the MPAA movie rating system. The MPAA offers Red Carpet Ratings Service—an e-mail update of the ratings of movies about to be released.

www.poynter.org/category/latest-news/everyday-ethics
The Poynter Institute's ethics page. Good for finding out about the most current ethical issues.

www.spj.org/ethics.asp
The ethics page of the Society of Professional Journalists. Contains the latest ethics news and an "Ethics Hotline" that you can call for advice.

Impact of the Media

Part V

Impact of the Media

THEMES

Why we removed the school shooter mod

We have removed the School Shooter mod from ModDB, read on for ou

Posted by **INtense!** on Mar 19th, 2011

A llow me to begin this post by saying we believe in the freedom of speech, the rig
and be creative. We have enjoyed watching mod developers push the boundaries
amazing content, and shall always do this.

However, recently a mod on the site called School Shooter: North American Tour 2012
bit of mainstream press due to the controversial nature of the content. It seems that p
of the fence on this one. There are those that believe the makers of this mod should h
whatever they want, while there are others that believe it is disgusting and crosses the

We sit on both sides, on one hand we find the content to be deliberately offensive and
the other we also feel people should have the right to be creative and share what they
developer run site, and we shouldn't have the right to dictate what is/isn't allowed.

The challenge faced is we are currently receiving quite a bit of threatening mail as pec
creators, supporters and makers of this content. I want to stress that this absolutely is
never encouraged or made any content, we disagree with the mod but at the same tir
speech and the unique ability modders and indie developers should have to create gam
topics, issues and events considered risky or taboo.

There is also quite a bit of confusion from non-gaming press, who state that games like
why all bad things occur, spreading misinformation and fear. As a result of this confus
moment we feel the best course of action is to remove the mod. We don't want the ha
other mod developers to be threatened by people misunderstanding this one mod/gam
others are like it.

Edit: We did contact the developers with no reply back in August 2010, chances are th
differently if they had replied.

The web hosting company for School Shooter explained its decision to drop the game from its database.

Comments (0 - 50 of 460)

Chapter18

social effects of mass communication

This chapter will prepare you to:

- explain how scientists use surveys and experiments to study the effects of mass communication
- describe how the media can serve as agents of socialization
- discuss the impact of televised violence
- define the *agenda-setting effect* and *agenda building*
- explain how the media can help crystallize a viewer's political choices
- describe how the Internet may affect social involvement

ir explanation.

ht to share information for years and create

has been getting quite a eople sit on two sides ave the right to make e line.

in poor taste, but on want on a community /

ple believe we are the n't the case. We have e believe in freedom of es (good-or-bad) about

this are the reason ion and hate, at the rd work of thousands of e, and assuming all

is would have ended

News

Browse

New

Views

Report Abuse

Related Mods

School Shooter: North American
Tour 2012
Half-Life 2 - S
Shooter

Related Games

This sounds like a really bad idea.

A company called Checkerboarded Studios is developing a game called *School Shooter: North American Tour 2012* that lets players reenact the horrific school shootings at Columbine and Virginia Tech, among other places. If that weren't disturbing enough, the game, a mod (modification) of the popular *Half-Life 2,* even lets people choose the same weapons that were used by the real-life killers. Checkerboarded Web site described the game this way:

[Y]ou play as a disgruntled student fed up with something or other (We're not exactly sure what), who after researching multiple school shooting martyrs, decides to become the best school shooter ever.

The controversy over the game prompted its Web-hosting service to remove the game from its database and the company's domain name expired in August 2011, but the game's creator promised that *School Shooter* would still be released. As of late 2011, however, no sign of the game had appeared.

It should not surprise anyone that legislators, educators, parents, and social scientists are upset about the possible release of such a game. Their concern is based on research that examines the social effects of playing video games. Although the evidence could be stronger, many studies have found that spending a lot of time playing violent video games is related to an increase in real-life violent behavior.

This final chapter examines the social effects of mass media. The first part looks at the impact of the media on people's attitudes, perceptions, and knowledge. The second part looks at how the media affect the way people behave. Before we discuss these effects, however, we need to examine how they have been investigated.

investigating mass communication effects

There are many ways to investigate what is or is not an effect of mass communication. Some people claim that personal observation is the best way to establish proof. As we noted in Chapter 2, the critical/cultural analysts focus on the various meanings that audience members construct from specific texts. Others rely on expert opinions and evaluations; still others point to common sense when they wish to support their views. All these methods are valuable, but this chapter will focus on the results of scientific studies of the media's impact on individuals. Keep in mind, however, that the scientific approach is only one of many ways to examine this topic.

When it comes to gathering information about media effects, scientists have typically used two main methods:

- A **survey** is carried out in the real world. It usually consists of a large group of individuals answering questions put to them via a questionnaire. Although the survey is usually not sufficient proof of cause and effect, it does help establish associations. A special kind of survey, a **panel study,** enables researchers to be more confident about attributing patterns of cause and effect in survey data. The panel study collects data from the same people at two or more points in time. As a result, it is possible, using sophisticated techniques that control the effects of other variables, to determine, for example, if viewing televised violence at an early age is related to aggressive behavior at a later date. Panel studies are expensive and take a long time to complete.
- An **experiment** is performed in a laboratory and usually consists of the controlled manipulation of a single factor to determine its impact on another factor. A special kind of experiment, a **field experiment,** is conducted in a real-life setting. Experiments are useful because they help establish causality.

In the remainder of this chapter, we will focus on scientific findings about the effects of media on knowledge, attitudes, perceptions, and behavior.

effects of mass communication
on knowledge and attitudes

The dividing line between attitudes and behaviors is fuzzy. In many instances we can only infer that an attitude or perception exists by observing relevant behavior. Thus, many of the studies mentioned in this section involve the measurement of *both* behavior and attitudes.

We will examine three topics that have generated the most research interest: (1) the role of the media in socialization, (2) cultivation analysis, and (3) agenda setting.

Media and Socialization

In Chapter 2 we defined *socialization* as the ways in which individuals come to adopt the behavior and values of a group. In this section we will concentrate on the socialization of children. Socialization is a complex process extending over a number of years and involving various people and organizations, called **agencies of socialization,** that contribute in some degree to the socialization process. Figure 18-1 presents a simplified diagram of some of the more common agencies.

figure 18-1

Agencies of Socialization

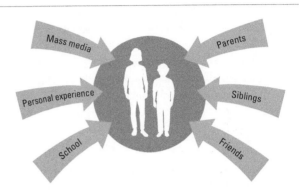

Mass media

Parents

Personal experience

Siblings

School

Friends

In many situations the media's contribution to socialization will be slight. Parents might have greater influence ("Eat your spinach; it's good for you"). So might friends ("Don't be a tattletale"). So might direct experience ("I'd better not take my sister's stuff because the last time I did, she popped me one").

On the other hand, the media, especially television, may play an important role in socialization when it comes to certain topics. Let us now look at evidence pinpointing some of these areas.

The Media as a Primary Source of Information

Learning is an important part of the socialization process, and the media serve as important sources of information for a wide range of topics, especially politics and public affairs. For example, a survey of sixth and seventh graders found that 80 percent named a mass medium as the source of most information about the president and vice president, 60 percent named a mass medium as the primary source of information about Congress, and half named a mass medium as the chief information source about the Supreme Court.

Other research has shown that the media, primarily TV, serve as primary information sources for many age groups about a wide range of topics. More than 90 percent of Americans cited television as their primary source of information about the September 11 terrorist attacks. Television is the source of most information for local and congressional elections. This phenomenon is not limited to political and public affairs information. There is reason to believe that media presentations, including those in entertainment programs, are important sources of information on topics such as occupations, crime, law enforcement, alcohol and drug usage, the environment, and minorities. One recent study of high school students, for example, found that about 1 in 4 listed rock music as an important source of information about moral values and that 1 in 4 specified it as an important source of information about interpersonal relationships. Another survey found that many young people listed Comedy Central's *The Daily Show* as their main source of news.

Could a media celebrity, such as Katy Perry, serve as an agency of socialization for young women? Could she influence what behaviors are appropriate for teens?

media *Probe*   *Untangling the Effects of TV*

New perspectives on the effects of television are coming from a surprising source: economists. The biggest problem in determining the social effects of television is isolating the TV effect from that of parents, peers, social class, ethnicity, and a host of other variables. In the past 30 or 40 years, however, economic researchers have developed new, high-power statistical methods that have made it a little easier to determine what causes what in complex relationships. These new techniques have sparked research into issues not commonly investigated by traditional economists, such as why most drug dealers live with their mothers and how a person's income is influenced by the condition of his or her teeth.

Some economists have used these new statistical methods to take advantage of "natural experiments" to investigate the effects of television viewing. One such test was made possible when the FCC froze the construction of new TV stations from 1948 to 1952, resulting in some cities having TV while others did not. The researchers looked at 1965 test scores from elementary and high school students, and after controlling for numerous

sociological variables, they discovered that children who had more exposure to television had better scores than those with less exposure. This effect was even more pronounced in households where English was not the primary language.

Another economist looked at the impact of Brazilian telenovelas (soap operas) on the fertility rate. There are few children in these programs because it would be difficult for viewers to keep track of shows with large numbers of characters. Because one company has a virtual monopoly on the airing of Brazilian telenovelas, the researchers were able to look at when the broadcasts were shown in various parts of the country. They then looked at changes in the fertility rate, again controlling for numerous other influences. After the broadcasts appeared, the average number of births per woman consistently declined. Interestingly, exposure to a competing TV network that aired Mexican and American shows did not have the same effect.

Scholars interested in the effects of TV can no longer confine their research to the traditional mass communication journals; these days they must scan the economics journals as well.

Shaping Attitudes, Perceptions, and Beliefs

The mass media also play an important role in the transmission of attitudes, perceptions, and beliefs. Several writers have suggested that under certain conditions the media (especially TV) may become important socialization agencies in determining the attitudes of young people. Specifically, TV will be an influential force when the following factors are operative:

- The same ideas, people, or behaviors recur consistently from program to program; that is, they are presented in a stereotyped manner.
- A child is heavily exposed to TV content.
- A child has limited interaction with parents and other socializing agents and lacks an alternative set of beliefs to serve as a standard against which to assess media portrayals.

All this means that under certain conditions TV will be an influential force in shaping what children think about certain topics. Complicated though the task is, some researchers have identified some of the conditions, the topics, and the children to which this theory applies. Moreover, they have specified some of the effects that may result when television does the socializing.

Stereotypes   In the study of media socialization, it is helpful to identify consistent themes or stereotypes present in media content. For instance, consider how television programs typically portray law enforcement and crime. Programs about crime and law enforcement are a staple of prime-time television; 20–35 percent of all program time consists of shows dealing with cops and criminals. However, the large percentage of law enforcement characters portrayed on TV does not accurately reflect the actual percentage employed in this capacity in real life. Further—on television, at least—crime doesn't pay. One study found that some 90 percent of TV crimes were solved; real-life law enforcement agencies are not nearly as effective.

Further, consider how social roles as seen on television are influenced by gender. In one study published in 2008, researchers examined all comedy, drama, and reality programs that aired during prime time on the six broadcast networks. They found that female

media Probe
Reality TV: A Model for Social Media Behavior?

Is there a relationship between watching reality TV and how we behave in real life? This was the question addressed by a trio of researchers in a research study published in the September 2010 issue of the *Journal of Broadcasting & Electronic Media.*

Reality TV programs, such as *Jersey Shore, Big Brother, Survivor, The Amazing Race*, and scores of others, have turned ordinary people into "celebrities" whose every move seems worthy of attention. Although there is wide variation among reality shows, the researchers noted that some common themes stand out. Actors engage in confessional moments, where they disclose their inner thoughts. They form alliances and build entourages. Reality participants carefully manage their on-screen identities.

The interactive tools of the Web, and social media sites in particular, make it possible for anyone to mimic many of these behaviors. Specifically, the researchers wanted to see if there was a connection between reality TV show viewing and the time a person spent on social networks, the number of friends a person reported, the proportion of friends that the person had never met face-to-face, and the number of photographs on the person's site.

The results were consistent. Compared to people who watched only a little reality TV, respondents who watched a lot of reality TV spent more time on social media sites, had more online friends, had more friends that they had never personally met, and were more apt to share photographs.

The authors conclude: "The evidence presented herein suggests that behavior traditionally associated with celebrities is being adopted en masse as people's interpersonal communication increasingly becomes mediated."

characters were significantly more likely than male characters to appear in interpersonal roles that centered on romance, family, and friends. In contrast, male characters were significantly more likely to appear in work-related roles. This gender distinction in social roles had been found by similar research done in the 1970s, 1980s, and 1990s.

In sum, evidence suggests that the TV world often presents images that are at odds with reality. Stereotyping has also characterized, in addition to police dramas and gender-role portrayals, the depiction of occupations, methods of problem solving, portrayals of scientists, the depiction of mental illness, and many other topics.

The Effects of Heavy Viewing   It seems probable that youngsters who are heavy TV viewers would display a pattern of beliefs and perceptions consistent with media portrayals. The earliest research in this area, completed in the 1930s, found that frequent viewing of crime and gangster movies could change attitudes on topics such as capital punishment and prison reform. More recently, other researchers have noted a connection between heavy viewing of violent TV programs and favorable attitudes toward the use of violence in real life. Further, children who are heavy viewers of cops-and-robbers TV programs are likely to believe that police are more successful in apprehending criminals than are children who are not fans of these shows.

Several studies have also linked high levels of television viewing with attitudes favoring traditional gender roles. In other words, children who are heavily exposed to television are more likely to believe, among other things, that men make better doctors and women make better nurses or that raising children is a job for women rather than men.

To be fair, we must again stress that this type of research *assumes* but does not necessarily *prove* that the mass media play a significant part in creating the attitudes held by these youngsters. Surveys can only highlight associations, not prove causality. Although some experimental evidence points to the media as the cause of certain attitudes, we cannot entirely rule out other interpretations. Nevertheless, it is likely that the link between media exposure and certain attitudes demonstrates reciprocal causation. What this

Do TV programs such as *Meet the Browns* represent an important source of information about African American families for white viewers? Mass media researchers have studied how TV shows influence attitudes toward minorities.

means is best shown by an example. Watching violent TV shows might cause a youngster to hold favorable attitudes toward aggression. These favorable attitudes might then prompt him or her to watch more violent TV, which, in turn, might encourage more aggressive attitudes, and so on. The two factors might be said to be mutually causing each other.

The Absence of Alternative Information   Although research evidence is less consistent in this area than in others, it appears that under some circumstances television can affect young people's attitudes about matters for which the environment fails to provide firsthand experience or alternative sources of information. One survey that examined the potential impact of TV on dating behavior found that teenagers are more likely to turn to TV for guidance when they have limited real-life experience with dating.

Where media influence is indirect, it is difficult to pinpoint. This is particularly true when the media operate simultaneously with other agencies of socialization and when interpersonal channels outweigh media channels in forming attitudes and opinions. In the area of politics, for instance, the media probably supply youngsters with information and viewpoints that are subsequently commented on by parents and friends. Political beliefs and attitudes evolve out of this double context. In such cases the socializing impact of parents and other interpersonal sources is more important than that of the media. One study dealing with attitudes toward police found that, although children spend a great deal of time watching TV cop shows, friends and family are the important socializing agents. The point is this: The media play a significant role in socialization. Sometimes this role is easy to detect; sometimes it is indirect and harder to see; at still other times it is apparently slight. Clearly, numerous factors are influential in determining how a child comes to perceive the world. The media (and television, in particular), however, have become important factors in the socialization process.

Cultivation Analysis

Directly related to socialization is an area of research called **cultivation analysis.** Developed by George Gerbner and his colleagues at the University of Pennsylvania, cultivation analysis suggests that heavy TV viewing "cultivates" perceptions of reality consistent with the view of the world presented in television programs. Cultivation analysis concentrates on the long-term effects of exposure—on both adults and children—rather than on the short-term impact on attitudes and opinions.

Methodology   The first stage in cultivation analysis is a careful study of television content to identify predominant themes and messages. Not surprisingly, television portrays a rather idiosyncratic world that is unlike reality along many dimensions. For example, television's world is usually populated by a preponderance of males: Two-thirds to three-quarters of all leading characters are men. Moreover, television over-emphasizes the professions of—and, as previously mentioned, overrepresents the proportion of workers engaged in—law enforcement and the detection of crime. Last, the TV world is a violent one—around 50 percent of all programs contain at least one instance of violence.

The second stage involves examining what, if anything, viewers absorb from heavy exposure to the world of television. Respondents are presented with questions concerning social reality and are asked to check one of two possible answers. One of these answers (the "TV answer") is in line with the way things are portrayed on television; the other (the "real-world answer") resembles actual life. Here is an example:

What percentage of all males who have jobs work in law enforcement and crime detection? Is it _____ 1 percent or _____ 10 percent?

On television about 12 percent of all male characters hold such jobs; thus, 10 percent would be the TV answer. In reality about 1 percent are employed in law enforcement; thus, 1 percent is the real-world answer. The responses of a large sample of heavy TV viewers are then compared with those of light TV viewers. If heavy viewers show a definite tendency to choose TV answers, we would have evidence that a cultivation effect is occurring.

How many doctors are like the acerbic but brilliant Dr. House on the Fox show of the same name? Cultivation analysis suggests that for some heavy viewers, TV portrayals might influence their perceptions of real life.

Research Findings   Is there evidence to suggest such an effect? Most findings suggest that among some people TV cultivates distorted perceptions of the real world. In one survey of approximately 450 New Jersey schoolchildren, 73 percent of heavy viewers compared with 62 percent of light viewers gave the TV answer to a question about the number of people involved in violence in a typical week. Youngsters who were heavy viewers were also more fearful about walking alone at night in a city. They overestimated how many people commit serious crimes, how often police find it necessary to use force, and how frequently police shoot at fleeing suspects.

Other cultivation research has focused specifically on college students. In one study students' exposure to pornography was examined to see if stereotyped perceptions were being cultivated. Among males, those who were heavy users of pornography were more apt to report that they had less confidence in females doing certain jobs (such as mechanic or mayor). They also tended to agree more with stereotypes of sexuality ("Men have stronger sexual urges than women; women say 'no' to sex when they don't really mean it") than did light users. These relationships held even after rigorous statistical controls removed possible influences of other factors. Women showed no such effects from exposure. A 2007 study looked at the cultivation impact of TV's portrayal of mental health. Content analysis revealed that in prime-time programs the mentally ill were 10 times more likely to be violent criminals than those without mental problems. In line with cultivation, a survey disclosed that heavy television viewers were more fearful of having a mental health facility located in their neighborhood and were less likely to support living next to someone who was mentally ill. A 2009 study examined viewers of *Grey's Anatomy* and their perceptions of doctors. Heavy viewers thought the program presented a credible portrayal of doctors. Heavy viewers were also more likely to believe that real-world doctors were courageous and reported more satisfaction with their own real-world doctors than did light viewers.

Although the results of cultivation analysis studies are evocative and fascinating, conclusions are clouded by three problems. First, it is difficult to determine cause and effect. For example, does heavy TV viewing cause people to be fearful of walking alone at night, or does being fearful cause them to stay home and watch more TV?

The second problem is that people differ in ways other than their TV viewing habits. Consequently, factors other than TV watching might affect the differences in perceptions and attitudes between heavy and light viewers. When certain factors that appear relevant to the cause-and-effect relationship (such as age, sex, and education) are statistically controlled, one factor at a time, the association between TV watching and perceptions is evident but somewhat weakened. When two or more factors are controlled simultaneously (such as examining the relationship between TV viewing and anxiety while simultaneously controlling for effects of both sex and age), some overall relationships disappear. We cannot conclude, however, that a relationship does not exist. In fact, recent research indicates that certain subgroups will show a cultivation effect and others will not.

One group of researchers, for example, detected a phenomenon they labeled **mainstreaming,** whereby differences apparently due to cultural and social factors tend to diminish among heavy TV viewers. They have also found evidence for what they call **resonance,** a situation in which the respondent's real-life experiences are congruent with those of the television world, thereby leading to a greater cultivation effect.

Third, technical decisions about the way TV viewing and attitudes are measured can have a significant impact on findings. For example, the precise wording of the questions has been shown to be important. In addition, some researchers argue that exposure to a particular kind of program (such as violent shows) gives a more accurate picture of cultivation than simply measuring overall TV viewing. Others note that deciding on the number of hours of viewing that differentiates heavy and light viewers has a bearing on the magnitude of cultivation.

An essay by Michael Morgan and James Shanahan in the June 2010 issue of the *Journal of Broadcasting & Electronic Media* noted that more than 500 studies directly relevant to cultivation analysis have been published, with 125 appearing since 2000. Examining the future of cultivation research, the authors note that even though television audiences have fragmented, overall television viewing per household has increased and devices such as the DVR and Web sites such as Hulu make it even easier to watch. Therefore, as the authors put it, "Television still dominates the flow of words and information that pass by our eyes and ears each day." Given this situation, it is likely that even more cultivation studies will be added to the research literature.

To sum up and perhaps oversimplify, we can say that, although not all mass communication scholars are totally convinced by the reasoning underlying cultivation analysis, a growing body of evidence suggests that the cultivation effect is indeed real for many people.

Agenda Setting

One influence of mass media that has turned up in many studies of mass communication is the **agenda-setting effect**. (An agenda is a list of things to be considered or acted upon.) When we say that the media have an impact on agenda setting, we mean that they have the ability to choose and emphasize certain topics, thereby causing the public to perceive these issues as important. To paraphrase Bernard Cohen in his book *The Press and Foreign Policy,* we can say that the media may not always be successful in telling people what to think, but they are usually successful in telling people what to think about.

Agenda-setting studies typically concern themselves with information media: newsmagazines, newspapers, television, and radio. Much of the research on agenda setting has been carried out during political campaigns. There are two reasons for this. First, messages generated by political campaigns are usually designed to set agendas (politicians call this tactic "emphasizing the issues"). Second, political campaigns have a clear-cut beginning and end, thus making the time period for study unambiguous.

One typical agenda-setting study was an investigation of the 1968 presidential election. The researchers asked a sample of voters to rank what they believed to be the key issues of the campaign. While this was going on, the researchers examined newsmagazines, newspapers, and television newscasts and ranked the campaign issues according to the time and space the media devoted to each issue. When the media's ranking was compared with the voters' ranking, there was a strikingly high degree of correspondence. In other words, the voters perceived as important those issues that the media judged important, as evidenced by the amount of coverage they received. Similar studies of more recent elections have found similar results. Although such studies strongly suggest a relationship between personal agendas and media agendas, they do not address the question of causation, an issue that we have encountered before.

Some studies indicate that there are situations in which the

TV coverage of news events, such as the social unrest in Greece, can shape the public's agenda.

direction of cause and effect is unclear—or will even depend on the medium under consideration. At least two studies report that newspapers exert a greater agenda-setting effect than does television. In fact, one survey found that during a political campaign television appeared to alter its coverage to conform to voter interest, and newspapers appeared to shape the voters' agendas.

Recent reviews published in scholarly journals noted two new directions of research interest. The first pertains to the notion of **framing,** the general way a news topic is treated by the media. This line of research posits that not only do the media tell us what to think about, they also tell us how to think about it by the way the story is framed. For example, suppose Congress is considering changes in the food stamp program. One way the media might frame this story is by concentrating on both the increased efficiency that might result from the changes and the savings to taxpayers. Alternatively, the media might choose to emphasize the hardships that might be experienced by people who will no longer qualify for the program. The particular choice of frames will affect the salience of the story and our attitudes toward the revised program.

A second direction concerns **agenda building.** Research on this topic examines how the media build their agenda of newsworthy items. Some factors that seem to have an impact are presidential press conferences, congressional hearings, and public relations efforts. One recent study, for example, found that a public relations effort by the Christian Coalition was influential in shaping the media agenda some three months later. Another recent study suggested that a journalist's own personal agenda (the issues that he or she considers important) might also have an impact on the media agenda. A study published in 2005 suggested that entertainment programs that focus on crime and law enforcement are influential in building the audience's personal agenda, which may eventually have an impact on polling data that help shape the media agenda.

Research into the impact of online media on agenda setting is a growing area. There is obvious evidence that bloggers can set the news media agenda, as seen in the controversy over CBS News's airing of questionable documents relating to President George W. Bush's military service during the Vietnam era. Bloggers first raised questions about the authenticity of the documents, and the story was quickly picked up by the mainstream media. Two studies of the 2004 presidential election found that topics frequently mentioned in blogs were related to the media agenda.

How have social media, such as Facebook and Twitter, affected agenda setting? There is little research so far about this question, but it would appear that social media allow an individual to seek out what he or she sees as important rather than what media gatekeepers perceive as important. Many media monitor the hot topics trending on Twitter and adjust their coverage accordingly. This would indicate that social media have some influence on setting the media agenda.

President Franklin D. Roosevelt used radio effectively as a political communications tool during his "fireside chats" with the nation. The increasing importance of radio as a tool prompted several large-scale studies during the 1940s.

media effects on behavior: a short history

The political effects of the mass media, especially radio, prompted much of the early research. Many people feared that a skilled political demagogue might use the new medium of radio to gain political power. As a result, large-scale studies were conducted during the 1940s to gauge the extent of media influence. Somewhat surprisingly, these early surveys found that the media had little direct effect on political decision making. Personal influence was more important, and individuals labeled "opinion leaders" were thought to be more important in transmitting political orientations.

The explosive growth of TV during the 1950s and 1960s shifted the research focus to young people. Early large-scale surveys noted that television could influence children's values and perceptions of the world. In addition, the new medium might adversely affect social relationships and skills necessary for success in school. The impact of media portrayals of violence was of special concern, as evidenced by Senate subcommittee hearings on the topic in 1961 and 1964. In 1967 a national commission concluded that a steady diet of media violence had "an adverse effect on human character and attitudes."

The topic was revisited again in 1970 when the United States Surgeon General issued a report that linked exposure to TV violence with antisocial behavior. A 1982 follow-up study reinforced the conclusions of the original report. Media violence remained the center of attention during the 1990s. As mentioned in previous chapters, the Telecommunications Act of 1996 contained provisions for program ratings and a V-chip that enabled parents to block violent and other unwanted programming from their TVs. Televised violence came under the spotlight again in 1999 after the Columbine shootings and yet again after the Virginia Tech massacre.

We will next examine more closely some of the topics mentioned in the 1970 Surgeon General's report, beginning with the topic that has generated the most research attention: the effects of TV violence.

the impact of televised violence

Does television viewing prompt violent or other antisocial behaviors on the part of the viewer? As we have just seen, this question has been debated for four decades. It is a complicated issue, and the definitive answer has not yet been found. Nonetheless, enough evidence has been gathered that we can begin to point to some preliminary conclusions. To arrive at these conclusions, we must examine research data from surveys and from experiments.

Survey Results

Table 18-1 contains abbreviated and modified questionnaire items taken from surveys designed to analyze the viewing of TV violence and aggressive behavior.

table 18-1

Questionnaire Items

	Almost always	Often	Sometimes	Never
1. About how often do you watch the following TV programs?				
NCIS	_____	_____	_____	_____
Modern Family	_____	_____	_____	_____
Criminal Minds	_____	_____	_____	_____
The Office	_____	_____	_____	_____
CSI	_____	_____	_____	_____
Law & Order: SVU	_____	_____	_____	_____

2. Next, what would you do if these things happened to you?

  a. Pretend somebody you know took something from you and would not give it back. What would you do?

    _____ Hit the other person and take my property back.

    _____ Call the police.

    _____ Ask the person to return it.

    _____ Nothing.

  b. Pretend somebody was telling lies about you. What would you do?

    _____ Hit the person and make the person stop.

    _____ Ask the person to stop telling lies.

    _____ Nothing.

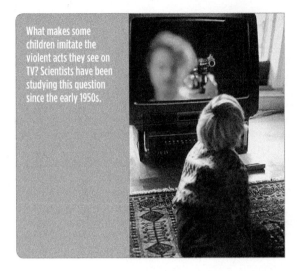

What makes some children imitate the violent acts they see on TV? Scientists have been studying this question since the early 1950s.

As you can see, with measures such as the ones in the table (assuming, of course, a questionnaire that was much longer), it would be possible to index a person's viewing of programs that generally contain violence. It would also be possible to measure that same person's tendency to report his or her willingness to use violence in everyday situations. If viewing violent TV does affect behavior, we would expect to find some relationship between reported heavy viewing of violence and an individual's own self-report of aggressive tendencies. If we do not find such a link, we might assume that exposure to media violence has no impact on subsequent aggressive tendencies. If, however, we do find a connection, we might suspect that media violence actually causes aggression. We could not be sure, however, because survey data alone are not sufficient to establish a cause-and-effect relationship. We must also keep in mind that there are different ways of measuring exposure to TV violence and aggressive tendencies.

Viewed as a whole, surveys compiled over the years are difficult to summarize. Perhaps the most concise generalization is one that appeared in a recent summary of television research findings. After carefully analyzing all survey results, the authors of this summary "conclude that the evidence to date indicates that there is a significant correlation between the viewing of violent television programs and aggressive behavior in day-to-day life."

Nevertheless, as already mentioned, a relationship is not necessarily evidence of cause and effect. Remember, however, that the special survey technique known as a *panel study* gives us a little more confidence in making cause-and-effect statements based on survey data. However, since panel studies cost a lot and sometimes take years to complete, not many exist. Further, the results from those that are available are not as clear as we might like them to be. One panel study whose methods might have been stronger was included in the 1970 Surgeon General's report on television and social behavior. It found evidence that viewing violent TV shows at an early age was a cause of aggression in later life.

Additional survey evidence appeared in 1982 with the publication of *Television and Aggression: A Panel Study*. This book reported the results of a three-year research project sponsored by NBC. Data on aggression, TV viewing, and a large number of sociological variables were collected on six different occasions from children in two midwestern cities. Eventually, about 1,200 boys in grades two through six participated in the main survey.

Lengthy and detailed analysis of the data suggested that there was no relationship between the viewing of TV violence and subsequent aggressive behavior. Later, other researchers were given the opportunity to reanalyze the NBC data. One reexamination did find some partial evidence of a causal relationship between TV violence and aggression, but its impact was tiny. In sum, if a causal relationship was present in the NBC data, it was extremely weak and hard to find.

In 1986 an international team of scientists reported the results of panel studies done in five countries: the United States, Finland, Australia, Israel, and Poland. The U.S. study and the Polish study found that early TV viewing was significantly related to later aggression. The Finnish study reached a similar conclusion for boys but not for girls. In Israel viewing TV violence seemed to be a cause of subsequent aggression among boys and girls who lived in urban areas but not among those who lived in rural areas. The panel study done in Australia was not able to find a causal relationship. Despite these differences the five panels were consistent in at least two findings. First, the relationship between the viewing of violence and aggression tended to be somewhat weak. Second, there was a pattern of circularity in causation. Viewing violent TV caused some children to become more aggressive. Being aggressive, in turn, caused some children to watch more violent TV.

You Can't Tell a Book by Its Cover: Textbooks and Hate

Clip 1: 2 minutes 29 seconds

You can watch Clip 1 *on the Online Learning Center home page,* www .mhhe.com/dominick12e. *Select* Student Center *and then* Chapter 18.

This clip discusses how some Saudi Arabian textbooks teach young Saudis intolerance toward Jews and Christians. When you were in grades K–12, were there any references to Muslims in your textbooks? Do the Saudis criticize their portrayal in American media? How effective are these portrayals at influencing young Saudis' views toward the West? How do you feel these views can be changed?

WWW

The results of an extensive panel survey reported in 2002 found that teens who watched more than one hour of TV a day were more likely to commit violent acts in later years than were teens who watched less. The survey tracked 707 children for more than 17 years. The researchers interviewed the participants several times and also checked arrest records to document violent behavior. The relationship between TV viewing and aggressive acts was still evident after other factors such as low family income and a prior history of violence were controlled statistically. The results of the study were weakened, however, by the fact that the researchers measured the total amount of TV exposure rather than exposure to violent content. It is difficult to explain why general TV exposure, much of it to nonviolent programs, would be related to aggression.

A study published in 2004 found results consistent with past research. More than 400 third, fourth, and fifth graders were surveyed at the beginning and at the end of the school year. The researchers found that children who were exposed early in the school year to media violence in TV, movies, and video games were more likely to see the world as a hostile place and to behave more aggressively at the end of the year. A 2007 panel study done by researchers at the Child Health Institute at the University of Washington found that viewing violent TV at ages 3–5 was associated with increased risk of antisocial behavior for boys but not for girls at ages 7–10.

What are we to make of all these panel studies? On the whole, they seem to suggest that there is a mutual causal connection between watching TV violence and performing aggressive acts. This connection, however, is small and influenced by individual and cultural factors. At this point, we will turn to the results of laboratory studies to aid us further in forming a conclusion about what causes what.

Experimental Results

Imagine that it is a cold winter night. As part of the requirements of Psychology 100, a course in which you are enrolled, you are required to serve as a subject in 3 hours of research. Tonight is your night to fulfill part of your obligation. Thus, you find yourself trudging across campus to the Psychology Building. Upon arriving, you join several dozen other students in a large auditorium. Before long, an individual enters the room, introduces himself as Professor So-and-So, and tells you that you are about to begin your first experiment of the evening.

Professor So-and-So has a new IQ test that he is trying to develop, and he needs your cooperation. The test booklet is passed out, and you are told to begin. As soon as you start the test, you realize that it is unlike any IQ test you have ever seen before. There are questions about advanced calculus, early Greek architecture, and organic chemistry, which you have no idea how to answer. In a few minutes the professor starts making sarcastic comments: "You'll never finish college if this simple test takes you so long"; "It looks as if this group will certainly flunk out"; "High school students have finished this test by now." Finally, with an air of exasperation, the professor says, "There's no hope for you. Hand in the papers. Since most of you won't be in school after this semester's grades, let me say good-bye to you now." With that the professor storms out of the room.

A few minutes go by, and then another individual enters the room and calls out two lists of names. Each group is assigned to another room down the hall. When you report to your assigned room, you find another professor already there. She tells you that this is the second experiment you will participate in tonight. It is a study to see how much people remember from films. You are going to be shown a brief excerpt from a film, and then you will be asked questions about it. The lights go out, and all of a sudden you are watching an 8-minute fight scene from a Kirk Douglas film called *The Champion*. In the movie Douglas, playing a boxer, gets the stuffing beaten out of him as he competes for the title. (Unknown to you, that other group of students is also seeing a film. At the same time you are watching Douglas get battered, they are viewing a scene from the film *Canal Boats in Venice.*) When the film ends, you are asked several questions about its content.

You are then directed to yet another room. Once in this cubicle, you are told that the third and last experiment is to begin. You are seated in front of a rather strange-looking machine with a dial that can be moved from a setting of 1 to 11. You also notice a button and a light connected to something behind the machine. The researcher explains that you are to be part of an experiment designed to investigate memory. In another room, but wired up to this same machine, is a student who is learning a word-association test. Every time this other student makes a mistake, you are to punish him by giving him a shock. The dial on your panel determines the intensity of the shock; when you press the button, it will be administered. You can choose any level you like; you can hold the button down as long as you like. The experimenter then gives you a level-2 shock to show you what it feels like. You jump and wonder why you did not take poly sci instead of psych. Your thoughts are interrupted, however, when the little light on the panel flashes on. The other student has made a mistake. It is your job to administer punishment. Your hand reaches for the dial. . . .

The Catharsis Versus Stimulation Debate

This is an abstracted, simplified, and condensed version of the prototype experimental design used in several key studies to investigate the impact of media violence. The idea behind this experiment is to test two rival theories about the effects of watching violence. The first theory is thousands of years old; it is called the **catharsis theory** and can be traced back to Aristotle. This theory holds that viewing scenes of aggression can actually purge the viewer's own aggressive feelings. Thus, a person who sees a violent television program or movie might end up less likely to commit violence. The other theory, called the **stimulation theory,** argues just the opposite: Seeing scenes of violence will actually stimulate an individual to behave more violently afterward.

As you may have understood, in the hypothetical experiment, everybody was first insulted and presumably angered (this part of the experiment gave you some hostility to be purged); one group saw a violent film, and the other saw a nonviolent film. Both groups were then given a turn at the punishment machine. If catharsis was at work, then the group that saw *The Champion* would have given less intense shocks; if stimulation was at work, then *The Champion* group would have given more intense shocks.

The catharsis versus stimulation debate was one of the earliest to surface in the study of mass media's effects. One early study seemed to point to catharsis, but a series of studies carried out by psychologist Leonard Berkowitz and his colleagues at the University of Wisconsin found strong support for the stimulation hypothesis. Since that time, the bulk of the evidence seems consistent: Watching media violence tends to stimulate aggressive behavior on the part of the viewer. There is little evidence for catharsis.

Field Experiments

In field experiments people are studied in their typical environment, where they probably react more naturally than they do in the lab. At the same time, field experiments are subject to the contaminating influences of outside events.

At least two field experiments done in the early 1970s revealed no link between TV and aggression. On the other hand, five field experiments have yielded data consistent with the survey and lab data. Their main conclusion is that people who watch a steady diet of violent programs tend to exhibit more antisocial or aggressive behavior.

One of the more elaborate field experiments involved a Canadian town that did not receive a TV signal until 1974. Two similar towns were selected for comparison—one could get only Canadian TV, and the other could get Canadian and U.S. channels. The research team gathered data from all three towns in 1974 and again two years later. Children in the town that had recently received access to U.S. TV showed an increase in their rate of aggressive acts that was more than three times higher than that of children living in the other two towns. Taken as a whole, the results from the field experiments tend to support the notion that viewing TV violence fosters aggressive behavior.

What Can We Conclude?

Let us now try to summarize the results of these surveys and experiments. Although no single survey or experiment can provide a conclusive answer, and although every study has certain shortcomings, there appears to be a thread of consistency running throughout these studies. Surveys and panel studies have shown a relationship between the viewing of violent programs and aggressive behavior. Lab and field experiments also have shown that watching violence increases the probability of behaving aggressively. Taken as a whole, these results encourage a tentative acceptance of the proposition that watching violence on television increases aggressiveness on the part of at least some viewers.

However, viewing TV violence is only one of many factors that might prompt a person to behave aggressively, and in relative terms its influence is not particularly strong. But is a weak relationship an inconsequential relationship? Much of the recent debate about TV violence has centered on this question. In statistical terms researchers gauge the strength of any relationship by the amount of variability in one measure that is accounted for by the other. For example, height and weight are two factors that are related. If I know how tall you are, I can make a better guess about your weight than if I do not know your height. I may not get your weight exactly right, but at least I will be closer to the correct figure. Consequently, height "explains" some of the variability associated with weight. If two factors are perfectly related, one explains 100 percent of the variability of the other. If two factors are not related (for example, weight and IQ), one explains 0 percent of the variability of the other. Exposure to TV violence typically explains from about 2–9 percent of the variability of aggression. In other words, about 91–98 percent of the variability in aggression is due to something else. Given these figures, can we conclude that the impact of TV violence is really that important?

The answer to that question is more political and philosophical than scientific, but research does provide some benchmarks for comparison. In psychology the relationship between undergoing psychotherapy and being "cured" of your mental ailment is only slightly stronger than that between TV violence and aggression. Further, the effect size for TV violence's impact on antisocial behavior is only slightly less than that of the effect size between viewing *Sesame Street* and readiness for school. *Sesame Street,* of course, was regarded as a great success. Lastly, the Food and Drug Administration has released for general use several drugs whose therapeutic effect is about the same as or even less than the effect of TV violence on aggression. Thus, although the effect might be small, it is not necessarily trivial.

Video Game Violence

As noted at the beginning of the chapter, violent video games have raised many of the same concerns about violence as have TV programs. The techniques used to study televised violence—surveys, experiments, panel studies—have also been employed to investigate the impact of violent video games. Although there have been some exceptions, the results of these studies generally parallel the results found for TV violence.

The results from lab experiments are complicated because many variables, including the age of the player, the type of game, the time spent playing the game, the player's perspective (first person or third person), the reality level (battling monsters vs. shooting humans), and the presence or absence of bloody graphics can have an impact on the outcome. In general, although there are some exceptions, most experiments found that playing violent video games results in a short-term increase in aggressive actions and aggressive thoughts.

Surveys about the effects of playing violent video games have been done across many cultures and age groups and

sound byte

Good Vibrations?

Video games not realistic enough for you? You might like an invention called the KOR-fx (Kinetic Omnidirectional Resonance Effect). The KOR-fx looks like a small harness that fits over the shoulders and connects to a gaming console. Two transducers turn audio signals into vibrations that the wearer feels through the chest and rib cage. While playing *Halo 3*, firing a weapon causes the player's shoulder to vibrate. In *Jurassic Park*, the dinosaurs' footsteps pulsate in the player's chest. The total effect makes a person feel like he or she is actually in the game.

media *Is Anybody Watching?*
Probe

A recent experiment suggests that several factors influence the performance of prosocial behavior. Subjects were first given a test that measured their "need for approval," a personality trait. At a later date, half of the subjects were directed to go to a room where they thought they were to participate in another experiment. When they got to the room, an experimenter noted the presence of a security camera and casually mentioned that the building was under constant video surveillance. At this point, the experimenter "accidentally" dropped an armful of questionnaires. An observer noted if the subjects helped to collect and sort the questionnaires—this was a measurement of public prosocial behavior. The subjects then filled out a survey that contained an item about how willing the subjects were to donate to a charitable organization—this was a

measure of private prosocial behavior. The other half of the subjects went through the same procedure except that they were taken to a room with no security camera.

What were the results? The subjects in the room with the camera offered more help to the experimenter than subjects in the room with no camera. People with a high need for approval were also more likely to help than those with a low need for approval. The presence of the camera, however, had no effect on the private prosocial behavior. There was no difference between the groups in their willingness to donate to charity, nor did need for approval make a difference. In short, prosocial behavior is a function of a person's desire for approval and the expectation that the prosocial act will be witnessed by others who will reward the person with their approval.

have used various methods to gauge aggressive behavior, including self-reports, official records of crimes and delinquent behaviors, and peer and teacher ratings. Despite the wide range of respondents and measures, survey results have been fairly consistent, suggesting that there is a connection, albeit a weak one, between playing violent video games and increased aggressive behavior and more favorable attitudes toward aggression.

Only a few long-term panel studies have been reported. One examined the effects of playing violent games on teens in Japan and the United States. The researchers gathered data at two points in time separated by several months. The results suggested that in both countries those who spent a lot of time playing video games showed an increased amount of aggression. A recent panel study conducted among Hispanic youth, however, did not find a link between game playing and serious antisocial behavior, such as criminally violent acts.

Research reviews that look at the results of many studies across a variety of samples are another source of information about the effects of violent video games. Unfortunately, two recent reviews of the dozens of studies involving video games reached different conclusions. One suggested that playing violent games led to long-term harmful outcomes; the other argued that the existing research had not provided compelling evidence of a cause-and-effect relationship between game playing and real-life aggression. (See the March 2010 issue of the *Psychological Bulletin* for details.) Both reviews agreed, however, that the impact of video game violence was relatively weak and that other factors, such as belonging to a gang or having abusive parents, were better predictors of future violent behavior.

In sum, researchers are still learning about the potential effects of these games, and it is certain that the amount of research in this area will continue to grow. In the meantime, even though any impact of video games may be relatively small, even a small impact may have serious long-term consequences.

encouraging prosocial behavior

Most early research into the effects of mass communication dealt with the negative or antisocial effects of the media. Toward the end of the 1960s, however, sparked perhaps by the success of public television's *Sesame Street*, researchers recognized that positive behaviors could be promoted by television programs. (These behaviors, generally referred to by the umbrella term **prosocial behavior**, may include actions such as sharing, cooperating, developing self-control, and helping.)

Experiments

Lab experiments have shown that films and TV programs can affect the performance of prosocial behavior, including such things as exercising self-control, cooperating, sharing, and helping. These experiments typically show a brief segment from a television program demonstrating one of these behaviors to one group of children and show a different program or no program at all to another group. After watching the segment, the children are given a chance to exercise self-control (such as by following directions from the experimenter) or to share (such as by winning money in a game and giving some to charity).

Surveys

Surveys measure what TV programs children watch and how often they perform prosocial acts in real life. A wide range of prosocial behaviors have been examined, including altruism, sharing, friendliness, and peaceful conflict resolution. Some surveys ask children how often they have performed the above behaviors while others rely on parents' or teachers' reports of these actions.

Research Results

Do prosocial messages actually influence day-to-day behavior? Generalizing about the results of research in this area is difficult because the term *prosocial behavior* covers so many different areas. The best summary available comes from a 2006 review published in *Media Psychology* that examined the results of 34 studies, both experiments and surveys, conducted between 1970 and 1990. The authors noted that experimental results showed a moderate short-term impact of exposure to prosocial material. Children who were exposed to prosocial programs were slightly more likely to perform prosocial acts in a laboratory setting. Interestingly, surveys that measured voluntary exposure to prosocial programs revealed a moderate positive impact, about as strong as the negative effect that resulted from viewing violent content. The one prosocial behavior that was affected the most by exposure to prosocial media content was altruism, a behavior that was simple and easy to imitate. In sum, as the authors concluded, "Television has the potential to foster positive social interactions . . . and encourage viewers to be more tolerant and helpful."

political behavior effects

Trying to summarize the many studies that have been conducted about the influences of the media on politics would require far more space than we have available. Consequently, we will restrict our discussion to the more central findings. At the core of our current discussion will be an examination of the individual's most important political behavior, the ultimate payoff in any political campaign—namely, voting behavior.

Shows such as *Between the Lions* carry an obvious prosocial message.

Negative Advertising

Recent political campaigns have centered attention on negative political advertising. Although there is no standard definition of this term, most political experts interpret it as a personal attack on the opposing candidate or an attack on what the opposing candidate stands for. There was much speculation that negative advertising would turn off voters, make them distrustful of politics, and make them less inclined to participate in the political process. Both survey and laboratory research suggested that most of these fears were unfounded. When compared with those who did not view negative ads, voters who were exposed to negative ads were just as likely to vote, were just as involved, and showed little difference in the amount of trust they placed in the political system. There was a tendency, however, for negative advertising to be related to more polarized attitudes, but this polarization did not seem to have much impact on political behavior.

More recent surveys indicate that those candidates who use a lot of negative advertising tend to receive a lower proportion of the vote. This does not necessarily mean that negative ads are ineffective; it may be that candidates who are behind in preelection polls turn to negative advertising because they have little to lose. (For a summary of the rather voluminous research literature on negative advertising, see "The Effects of Negative Political Campaigns: A Meta-Analytic Reassessment," *Journal of Politics,* 2007, pp. 1176–1209.)

Mass Media and Voter Choice

A person's decision to vote for a particular candidate is affected not only by the mass media but also by many other factors, both social and psychological. Still, some tentative generalizations can be made.

It would appear that conversion (changing your vote from Republican to Democrat, for example) is unlikely to result from media exposure, because it is difficult for the media to persuade someone whose mind is already made up to change and because most people (roughly two-thirds) have already made up their minds before the campaign begins. Far more common are two effects that have a direct bearing on voter choice: reinforcement and crystallization. **Reinforcement** means the strengthening of support for existing attitudes and opinions. **Crystallization** means the sharpening and elaboration of vaguely held attitudes or predispositions. If a person approaches a campaign undecided or neutral, then crystallization is likely to occur. If the person has already made up his or her mind, then reinforcement will probably take place.

In recent national elections there has been an increase in ticket splitting (supporting one party's candidate for president and another's for governor, for example). This phenomenon may be due to crystallization, which in turn results from exposure to mass media. The flow of information during the campaign evidently crystallizes a voter's vague intention, and in many instances these new choices do not square with party loyalty. On the other hand, when partisan voters are exposed to the media, reinforcement is likely.

These findings do not necessarily mean that the media are not influential. A key factor in winning any election is to keep the party faithful loyal (reinforcement) and to persuade enough of the undecideds to vote for one side or the other (crystallization). Thus, even though widespread conversion is not usually seen, the media are still influential. Even more important, the media may have significant indirect influence on the electorate. By serving as important sources of political news, by structuring "political reality," and by creating an image of candidates and issues, the media may have a potent effect on a person's attitudes toward the political system. Furthermore, our discussion has been mainly concerned with the effects of the media in national elections. Local elections present a somewhat different picture. Most research evidence indicates that the media, especially local newspapers, may be highly influential in affecting voter choice in a city, county, or district election.

Televised Debates

The first series of presidential debates between John Kennedy and Richard Nixon during the 1960 election prompted more than 30 different studies. Most concluded that the main effect of the debates was reinforcement, since most people had made up their minds before the debates. There was also evidence of a crystallization effect as independent voters shifted to the Kennedy camp. Although the crystallization effect was small, the 1960 election was decided by a tenth of a percentage point, suggesting that even small effects can have significant results.

The reinforcement effect was found again during the 1984 and 1988 debates. In 1996 the debates between Bill Clinton and Bob Dole seemed to have little impact on voter choice. Any effect of the debates between Al Gore and George W. Bush in the 2000 election was difficult to detect. The audience for these debates was the smallest ever due to competition from sporting events and entertainment programs. Most surveys done about the 2004 debates between Bush and John Kerry indicated that Kerry was perceived the winner in all of them. Nonetheless, Bush still won reelection, suggesting that winning a debate does not necessarily translate into winning an election. In 2008, surveys consistently found that Barack Obama was perceived as the winner in his debates with John McCain. Obama maintained a clear lead in the polls throughout the campaign and went on to win the election.

Television and the Political Behavior of Politicians

On a general level, it is clear that the emergence of television has affected the political behavior of politicians and political campaigns. A comparison of pre-TV practices with those occurring after TV's adoption reveals the following:

- Nominating conventions are now planned with television in mind. They are designed not so much to select a candidate as to make a favorable impression on the public.
- Television has increased the cost of campaigning.
- Television has become the medium around which most campaigns are organized.
- Campaign staffs now typically include one or more television consultants whose job it is to advise the candidate on his or her television image.
- The Internet has become an important channel of political communication and a new means of fund-raising. Many influential blogs are concerned with politics and candidates make extensive use of social media.

research about the social effects of the internet

For obvious reasons, research concerning the effects of spending time on the Internet is still in a formative stage. Nonetheless, we can already identify two major trends in Net studies: (1) the impact of Internet use on other media and (2) the relationship between Internet use and social involvement.

The Internet seems to have had the most impact on television usage. This is not surprising since much Internet use takes place during the evening—the same time that most TV viewing generally takes place. The time spent viewing TV decreases less than one might think, however, because many people multitask—they watch TV while surfing the Net. Magazine and newspaper reading, radio listening, and moviegoing seem not to have been significantly affected.

As mentioned in Chapter 13, the Internet is becoming more important as a source of news. At the same time, there has been a decline in the number of people who rely on broadcast TV and newspapers as their main sources of news. A 2010 survey found that TV was still the main source for national and international news but that the percentage who named it as their main source had dropped from 82 percent in 2002 to 66 percent in 2010. Meanwhile, the Internet had overtaken the newspaper as the main source of news, with 41 percent naming the Internet and 31 percent citing the newspaper. The percentage relying on the Internet will doubtlessly increase in the next several years.

Early studies that looked at the Internet and social involvement suggested that people who were heavy users of the Internet were also those who reported greater feelings of loneliness and social isolation. More recent surveys, however, have discovered just the opposite. One survey found that Internet use was related to more social involvement in the local community; another found that those who spent a great deal of time on the Internet were more politically involved and had more contacts than those who did not spend time online. Yet another found that Internet users were the ones with the most social contacts. Apparently, both the audiences and the Internet have changed over the past few years, and innovations such as instant messaging encourage greater social contact. Not all demographic groups, however, are benefiting from the expanding Internet. One 2004 study revealed that Internet use had no impact on social involvement or psychological well-being among low-income Americans.

All in all, surveys that have studied people's Internet use support the "rich get richer" model. Extroverted people are the ones who gain the most social contacts through the

media *Probe*   *The Internet and Depression*

A study done in Great Britain found that people who spend a lot of time on the Internet are more likely to show signs of depression. The researchers noted that some fervid fans of the Net develop a syndrome in which they replace real-life communication with social media and chat rooms.

The study collected data from more than 1,300 residents of the United Kingdom between the ages of 16 and 51. Of these, the researchers concluded that slightly more than 1 percent were Internet addicted. The addicts spent more time visiting sexually oriented sites, online gaming sites, and social media networks. They also reported more instances of moderate to severe depression than did people who spent less time surfing the net.

The researchers concluded that excessive Internet use is associated with depression but cautioned that they don't know what causes what. It's possible that depressed people are attracted to the Internet, but it's also possible that Internet causes people to be depressed.

How much time do you spend on the Internet?

Internet. To them, it is just another channel to use to link up with friends. Conversely, introverted people who go online tend to shy away from social contacts.

communication in the future: the social impact

Let us close this chapter (and this book) with an examination of some of the relevant questions about the impact of the new communications technology on society. Advances in media technology usually have an upside and a downside. The telephone, for example, made communication at a distance much more convenient. It also meant that we could be interrupted, awakened, or bothered at any hour of the day or night. Radio and television brought immediate access to information and entertainment but also encouraged the proliferation of couch potatoes. What might the future bring?

Threats to Privacy

Computers have opened up threats to privacy. Some systems enable supervisors to monitor every keystroke of their employees to observe productivity. E-mail, no matter how personal, can be read by anyone with access to the system. Consumers who subscribe to computerized data services run the risk of having their personal files examined by unauthorized persons or, even worse, having their identities stolen.

Some scary examples: In 2008, the Bank of New York Mellon lost a box of computer backup tapes containing names, social security numbers, and bank account numbers of more than 12 million customers. The next year the National Archives lost a hard disk drive that contained sensitive data from the Clinton administration, including social security numbers and Secret Service operating procedures. At the University of California, Berkeley, a database containing personal information on 160,000 present and former students was accessed by hackers. Hackers broke into Sony's Online Entertainment system and gained access to personal information on 25 million users. Unfortunately, there are plenty of other examples (see www.privacyrights.org/data-breach#CP for a detailed list of recent security breaches).

In the past, spying on our personal habits was made difficult simply because information was scattered about in different places. Now computers store huge amounts of information about us in one centralized place, the computer's memory, that is easily accessed from anywhere over phone lines. We willingly provide much of this information when we apply for a credit card, buy a car or a house, take out insurance, file a lawsuit, claim unemployment benefits, and so on. Moreover, many Web sites use tracking technologies, such as cookies, that monitor people's online activities. What many consumers do not know is that much of this information is sold to other organizations for other purposes. This is one of the reasons many of us are hit with barrages of spam from organizations we have never heard of.

sound byte

Technology Improves Relationships

A survey of DVR owners found that 80 percent of married couples claimed that the DVR has actually improved their relationship. Among the survey respondents with children, 81 percent said the DVR has improved their family life. They reported fewer fights about what to watch and more family time gathered to watch TV. Just another example of better living through technology.

Computer scanning systems used at the checkout counters of supermarkets and drug and discount stores now record your every purchase. Such information is invaluable to marketers. For instance, the makers of Mylanta can offer discounts to people who regularly buy Tums to get them to switch to their product. Bumble Bee tuna can send free samples to Chicken of the Sea buyers. Although this is great for marketing purposes, it is troubling for consumers. If you are like the rest of us, there are some purchases you make that you might like to keep private. Do you want everybody to know what kind of birth control method you use?

Fragmentation and Isolation

The mass media are increasingly serving the needs of more specialized audiences. Magazines, radio stations, satellite radio, cable TV networks, and broadband TV channels, with their highly targeted niche audiences, are the best examples of this trend, but the other media are moving in this direction. Technology is increasingly directing individuals toward more selective content exposure, as demonstrated by the iPod, TiVo, and Facebook. If this trend continues, it might result in a generation of consumers fragmented into smaller and smaller interest groups with little in common with the rest of society. If people are overspecialized in their interests, they may run the risk of being ignorant about the rest of the world.

This phenomenon has been labeled the *cocoon effect* by sociologists. From their perspective it refers to the process whereby people surround themselves with only the political and social information that they find comforting, appealing, or acceptable. It is as though people retreat into their informational cocoon to escape some of the uncertainty of modern life and to help reduce the multitude of choices that have to be made in today's society. It seems possible that this cocooning could generalize into cultural and recreational use of knowledge as well, further increasing an individual's isolation from society.

Moreover, as telecommuting becomes more popular, more and more people will stay at home. The computer will enable people to work, bank, shop, and be entertained at home. Books, groceries, flowers, movies, meals, medicines, diapers, and deodorants can be delivered directly to a consumer's door. With worries over personal safety mounting daily, will people decide to just stay home?

Communication Overload

Innovations in communication technology have made us better connected, but that connectivity has come with a price. We now put up with people talking loudly into their cell phones, cell phones going off during movies and plays, people constantly updating their Twitter accounts, people texting while talking, and people ignoring us while they tap and touch their iPhones.

Furthermore, it's becoming increasingly difficult to keep up with the flood of messages that we send or receive daily. E-mailing, texting, IMing, blogging, updating Twitter and Facebook pages, talking on cell phones, and uploading photos and videos now consume a significant portion of our time—perhaps too much. Do we really need 150 million blogs and countless Facebook status updates? Psychiatrists have identified a new ailment called FAD, or Facebook Addiction Disorder, among people who spend inordinate amounts of time on Facebook. Texting while driving has been the cause of numerous automobile accidents. About 80 percent of all e-mail is spam, and the time that employees spend deleting these unwanted messages costs corporations more than $20 billion a year.

The increased availability of these new communication channels has created a tremendous drain on our time. For example, a typical teenager in 2008 spent about 31 hours a week online—that's only 9 hours short of a full workweek. About 9 hours were spent on social media, another 2 hours watching YouTube, about 3 hours doing school-related searches, and the rest on general information and entertainment sites. In addition, the

Will isolation increase as more people interact online and not in person?

average teen sends and receives about 80 text messages every day and spends more than an hour a day talking on the phone. In all, not counting sleep or school, in an average week the typical teen spends about half of his or her time in some form of communication. It's entirely possible that many young people have trouble managing their time in the face of this commitment to communication.

Escape

The issue of escape has been around almost since the mass media were invented. Many parents and educators were worried that young people would prefer to spend their time in the media world instead of the real world. Social critics have painted bleak pictures of mesmerized children attending to various forms of media: radio, movies, TV, video games, and Net surfing. In the future this concern may have more validity because the media realities that are available are becoming more and more like life outside the media. Home theaters that duplicate the theater experience are already on the market. Big-screen 3-D HDTV sets with stereo sound and interactive features are also available. Manufacturers of video games are experimenting with ways to make their displays three-dimensional. And who knows what advances will be made in the virtual reality area? What happens when it is far more fun to be in some media-generated reality than in real life? In fact, virtual reality simulations raise the question "What exactly is 'real' life anyway?" Will large numbers of us abandon socially relevant pursuits for a romp in the media world?

And what happens farther down the road? In William Gibson's 1984 novel *Neuromancer*, people plug computer chips, called *stims*, directly into their brains. Stims provide experiences for all the senses and are usually preprogrammed, but there is also the possibility of becoming a *rider*, traveling through the world computer matrix (which bears an eerie resemblance to the Internet) or even shifting yourself into another person's reality and experiencing the world as the other person experiences it. Could this be the ultimate media experience? Alternate realities hardwired into the cerebral cortex? Will there be an app for that? You decide.

main points

- Surveys and experiments are the two main quantitative techniques used to study the effects of mass communication.

- Media can serve as agencies of socialization when they are the primary sources of information about a topic and that information is presented in a consistent manner.

- Media can cultivate false perceptions of reality among some heavy users.

- The media can set the priority of certain issues for the public.

- TV violence shows a small but persistent correlation with antisocial behavior among heavy viewers.

- Experiments have shown that TV can produce prosocial behavior, and some evidence of this effect has been found in surveys.

- The media can be effective in reinforcing or crystallizing a person's voting choice. TV has had a significant impact on the conduct of politicians and political campaigns.

- The main topics of research concerning the Internet are its effects on the usage of other media and the relationship between social isolation and online media use.

- Other concerns about the effects of mass communications focus on the areas of privacy, isolation, communication overload, and escape.

questions for review

1. What are the two main methods that social scientists use to investigate media effects?

2. What gets cultivated in a cultivation analysis?

3. Summarize the catharsis versus stimulation debate. Which viewpoint does research evidence favor?

4. What is the difference between the public's agenda and the media's agenda?

5. How do the media influence the voting choices of their audience?

questions for critical thinking

1. Why is it difficult to establish the effects of mass communication?

2. Young children are not the only ones who go through a socialization period. College students have to be socialized as well. What were the main socialization agencies that prepared you to fit into college life? How important were the media?

3. How are college students portrayed on prime-time TV? Do these portrayals perpetuate any stereotypes?

4. Why has the debate over media violence gone on so long? Will scientists ever amass enough evidence to satisfy everybody? Why or why not?

5. What sorts of research projects should be developed to study the social impact of the Internet?

key terms

survey (p. 432)
panel study (p. 432)
experiment (p. 432)
field experiment (p. 432)
agencies of socialization (p. 432)
cultivation analysis (p. 436)

mainstreaming (p. 437)
resonance (p. 437)
agenda-setting effect (p. 438)
framing (p. 439)
agenda building (p. 439)
catharsis theory (p. 443)

stimulation theory (p. 443)
prosocial behavior (p. 445)
reinforcement (p. 447)
crystallization (p. 447)

internet resources

Online Learning Center

On the Online Learning Center home page, www.mhhe.com/dominick12e, *select* Student Center *and then* Chapter 18.

1. Use the Learning Objectives, Chapter Outline, and Main Points sections to review this chapter.

2. Test your knowledge of the chapter using the multiple choice and flashcard features of the site.

3. Expand your knowledge of concepts and topics discussed in the chapter with additional Questions for Critical Thinking and Internet Exercises.

surfing the internet

In addition to Web sites, several newsgroups and listservs are useful to those interested in mass media effects. The listings that follow represent only a small sample.

www.aber.ac.uk/media/Documents/short.cultiv.html
Contains a thorough description of the history, techniques, and issues connected to cultivation analysis.

www.surgeongeneral.gov/library/youthviolence/chapter4/sec1.html
Thorough discussion of risk factors for youth violence, including a summary of the research on TV violence.

www.wimmerdominick.com
Contains a discussion of media effects and related readings.

http://allpsych.com/researchmethods/index.html
Good introduction to basic research methods used in the social sciences.

glossary

advertising agency   A company that handles both the creative and the business side of an advertising campaign for its clients.

affiliate   A television or radio station that carries the programming of a certain network.

agencies of socialization   The various people or organizations that contribute to the socialization of an individual.

agency   An organization that handles basic needs of advertisers.

agenda building   The ways the media decide what is newsworthy.

agenda-setting effect   The influence of the mass media created by emphasizing certain topics, thus causing people to perceive those same issues as important.

AM   Amplitude modulation of radio waves.

Arbitron   The professional research organization that measures radio audiences.

Audit Bureau of Circulations (ABC)   An organization formed by advertisers and publishers in 1914 to establish ground rules for counting circulation data.

authoritarian theory   The prevailing belief that a ruling elite should guide the intellectually inferior masses.

backpack journalist   A reporter who can prepare news stories for print, electronic, and online media.

best-seller lists   The ranking of books based on retail sales.

beware surveillance   A media function that occurs when the media inform the public of short-term, long-term, or chronic threats.

Billboard   The sound recording industry trade publication that tabulates record popularity.

block booking   A policy of major film studios that required theater owners to show several of a studio's low-quality films before they could receive the same studio's top-quality films.

blog   A personal journal kept on the Web.

broadband   Increased bandwidth for Internet connections, which speeds up downloads.

browsers   A type of software that enables individuals to search for content on the Web.

buffering   Storing video signals for video transmitted via the Internet.

business-to-business advertising   Advertising directed not at the general public but at other businesses.

C3   The ratings for average commercial minutes in live programming plus three days of DVR playback.

campaign   In advertising, a large number of ads that stress the same theme and appear over a specified length of time.

carriage fee   A fee paid by cable systems to carry a cable network.

categorical imperative   The ethical principle that people should behave as they wish all others would behave.

catharsis   A release of pent-up emotion or energy.

catharsis theory   The theory that viewing aggression will purge the viewer's aggressive feelings.

cease-and-desist order   A Federal Trade Commission order notifying an advertiser that a certain practice violates the law; failure to comply with a cease-and-desist order can result in fines being levied against the advertiser.

channels   Pathways by which a message travels from sender to receiver.

circulation   The total number of copies of a publication delivered to newsstands, vending machines, and subscribers.

clock hour   A radio format that specifies every element of the program.

cloud computing   Applications and services offered over the Internet.

commercial television   Television programs broadcast by local stations whose income is derived from selling time on their facilities to advertisers.

Communications Act of 1934   An act of Congress creating the Federal Communications Commission.

communist theory   The theory of the press that the media should promote the goals of the ruling political party.

comprehensive layout   The finished model of a print ad.

computer-assisted reporting   Skills involved in using the Internet to aid reporting.

concept testing   A type of feedback in which a one- or two-paragraph description of a new series is presented to a sample of viewers for their reactions.

consent order   A Federal Trade Commission order in which the advertiser agrees to halt a certain advertising practice without admitting any violation of the law.

consequence   The importance or weightiness of a news story.

consumer advertising   Advertising directed at the general public.

controlled circulation   A type of circulation in which publications are sent free or distributed to a select readership, such as airline passengers or motel guests.

convergence   The blending of communication technologies, operations, or businesses.

conversational currency   Topic material presented by the media that provides a common ground for social conversations.

copy   The headlines and message in an ad.

corporate convergence   The merging of companies with holdings in one medium with companies that have assets in other media.

creative boutique   An advertising organization that specializes in the creative side of advertising.

credibility   The trust that the audience holds for media that perform surveillance functions.

critical/cultural approach   An analytical technique that examines power relationships in society and focuses on meanings people find in texts.

crystallization   The sharpening and elaboration of a vaguely held attitude or predisposition.

cultivation analysis   An area of research that examines whether television and other media encourage perceptions of reality that are more consistent with media portrayals than with actuality.

culture   Common values, behaviors, attitudes, and beliefs that bind a society together.

custom magazines   Free magazines published by corporations for current and prospective customers.

cyberbullying   Using the Internet or other communication technologies to deliberately harass, threaten, or intimidate someone.

cycle   In all-news radio, the amount of time that elapses before the program order is repeated.

decoding   The activity in the communication process by which physical messages are translated into a form that has eventual meaning for the receiver.

decoupling   A separation of the connection between two entities. In mass communication, it refers to the breaking of the traditional link between advertising support and content.

defamation   The act of harming the reputation of another by publishing false information.

demo   A demonstration disk used to sell a musical performer or group.

device convergence   The tendency for functions once served by separate machines to be merged into a single device.

Digital Millennium Copyright Act   Protects Internet service providers from copyright suits for simply transmitting information provided by others.

digital technology   A system that encodes information—sound, text, data, video—into a series of on and off pulses that are usually denoted as zeros and ones.

digital television (DTV)   Television signals consisting of binary signals that enable improved picture quality.

digital video recorder (DVR)   A device, like TiVo, that records television content on a hard disc.

direct action ad   An ad that contains a direct response item (such as a toll-free number) that enables advertisers to see results quickly.

direct broadcast satellite (DBS)   A system in which a home TV set receives a signal directly from an orbiting satellite.

distribution system   The cables that deliver the signals to subscribers.

double features   The practice started by theaters in the 1930s of showing two feature films on the same bill.

dummy   A rough version of a magazine that is used for planning how the final version will look.

DVD (digital videodisc)   A disc that stores audio, movies, video, and graphics in a digital format that is compatible with DVD players and home computers.

dysfunctions   Consequences that are undesirable from the point of view of the welfare of society.

e-book   A digital version of a book, which can be read by using a computer or a special reader.

editorial policies   Guidelines the print media follow to persuade the public on certain issues or to achieve specific goals.

e-mail   Electronic messages sent from computer to computer.

empirical approach   Method that is based on experiment and observation.

encoding   The activity in the communication process by which thoughts and ideas from the source are translated into a form that can be perceived by the senses.

encryption   Scrambling video signals so that only those with the proper decoding hardware can receive them.

Equal Opportunities rule   Part of the Communications Act of 1934; Section 315 allows bona fide candidates for public office to gain access to a broadcast medium during political campaigns.

e-reader   A device designed to electronically display books, newspapers, and magazines.

evaluation   Research done to measure the effectiveness of an advertising or a public relations campaign.

Evernet   The successor to the Internet; an arrangement by which an individual is constantly connected to the Internet using various information devices.

experiment   A research technique that stresses controlled conditions and manipulates variables.

Fairness Doctrine   A now defunct FCC doctrine that required broadcast stations to provide various points of view on controversial issues.

Federal Communications Commission (FCC)   A regulatory agency, composed of five individuals appointed by the president, whose responsibilities include broadcast and wire regulation.

feedback   The responses of the receiver that shape and alter subsequent messages from the source.

field experiment   An experiment that is conducted in a natural setting as opposed to a laboratory.

First Amendment   The first amendment to the U.S. Constitution, stating that Congress shall make no law abridging the freedom of speech or of the press.

FM   Frequency modulation of radio waves.

focus group   A group of 10–15 people led by a moderator that discusses predetermined topics.

format   Consistent programming designed to appeal to a certain segment of the audience.

format wheel   A visual aid that helps radio programmers plan what events happen during a given time period.

formative research   Advertising research done before developing a campaign.

framing   The general way a news medium treats a topic.

franchises   Exclusive rights to operate a business in a given territory.

Freedom of Information Act (FOIA)   A law stating that every federal executive-branch agency must publish instructions on the methods a member of the public can follow to get information.

full-service agency   An ad agency that handles all phases of advertising for its clients.

functional approach   A methodology that holds that something is best understood by examining how it is used.

gag rules   Judicial orders that restrict trial participants from giving information to the media or that restrain media coverage of events that occur in court.

gatekeepers   Individuals who decide whether a given message will be distributed by a mass medium.

geosynchronous satellite   A satellite whose orbit keeps it over the same spot on Earth.

golden mean   The ethical principle that moderation is the key to virtue.

gramophone   A "talking machine" patented in 1887 by Emile Berliner that utilized a disk instead of a cylinder.

graphophone   A recording device similar to the phonograph but utilizing a wax cylinder rather than tinfoil.

hard news   Timely stories with significance for many people.

head end   The antenna and related equipment of the cable system that receives and processes distant television signals so that they can be sent to subscribers' homes.

heavy metal   A counterculture musical trend of the 1960s–1970s, characterized by a vaguely threatening style and heavy use of amplification and electronic equipment.

hegemony   The dominance of one entity over another.

Hicklin Rule   A long-standing obscenity standard based on whether a book or other item contains isolated passages that might deprave or corrupt the mind of the most susceptible person.

high-definition television (HDTV)   A supersharp television system that delivers about twice the resolution of traditional TV.

house drop   The section of the cable that connects the feeder cable to the subscriber's TV set.

human interest   A news value that emphasizes the emotional, bizarre, offbeat, or uplifting nature of a news story.

hyperlocal   News that concentrates on stories from a small geographic area.

hypertext   A digital navigational tool that links one electronic document to another.

ideology   A particular set of beliefs or ideas.

independents   Radio or TV stations unaffiliated with any network.

indirect action ad   An advertisement that works over the long run to build a company's image.

information gathering   A phase of a public relations campaign in which pertinent data are collected.

injunction   A court order that requires an individual to do something or to stop doing something.

instrumental surveillance   A media function that occurs when the media transmit information that is useful and helpful in everyday life.

Internet neutrality   The idea that Internet service providers cannot favor one company over another.

Internet-only radio stations   Radio stations that exist only online.

Internet TV   Sending video signals over the Internet.

interpersonal communication   A method of communication in which one person (or group) interacts with another person (or group) without the aid of a mechanical device.

investigative reports News reporting that requires extraordinary efforts to gather information about matters of public importance.

jazz A form of popular music that emerged during the Roaring Twenties and was noted for its spontaneity and disdain of convention.

jazz journalism Journalism of the Roaring Twenties that was characterized by a lively style and a richly illustrated tabloid format.

joint venture A method of movie financing in which several companies pool resources to finance films.

Kinetoscope The first practical motion picture camera and viewing device, developed by William Dickson in 1889.

libel Written defamation that tends to injure a person's reputation or good name or that diminishes the esteem, respect, or goodwill due a person.

libel per quod Written material that becomes libelous under certain circumstances.

libel per se Falsely written accusations (such as labeling a person a "thief" or a "swindler") that automatically constitute libel.

libertarian theory The assumption that all human beings are rational decision makers and that governments exist to serve the individual.

limited partnership A method of movie financing in which a number of investors put up a specified amount of money for a film.

linkage The ability of the mass media to join different elements of society that are not directly connected by interpersonal channels.

machine-assisted interpersonal communication A method of communication involving one or more persons and a mechanical device (or devices) with one or more receivers.

macroanalysis A sociological perspective that considers the functions performed by a system (such as mass media) for the entire society.

magazines Printed publications that contain an assortment of materials that appear on a regular basis.

mainstreaming In cultivation analysis the tendency of differences to disappear among heavy-TV-viewing people, apparently because of cultural and social factors.

management by objectives (MBO) A management technique that sets observable, measurable goals for an organization to achieve.

marketing Developing, pricing, distributing, and promoting an idea, a good, or a service.

mass communication The process by which a complex organization, with the aid of one or more machines, produces and transmits public messages that are directed at large, heterogeneous, and scattered audiences.

mass media The channels and the institutions of mass communication.

meaning The interpretation an audience makes of text.

media buying service An organization that specializes in buying media time to resell to advertisers.

Mediamark Research Inc. (MRI) A company that measures magazine readership.

media vehicle A single component of a mass medium, such as a newspaper or TV network.

message The actual physical product in the communication process that the source encodes.

message research Pretesting messages in an ad campaign.

microanalysis A sociological perspective that considers the functions performed by a system (such as mass media) for the individual.

microcasting Sending an audio or video message to a small group of interested people.

mobile journalist (mojo) Reporter who works out of a car covering local community news.

mobile parenting An arrangement by which parents keep track of children by using cell phones and pagers.

Motion Picture Patents Company (MPPC) An organization formed by the nine leading film and film equipment manufacturers in 1908 for the purpose of controlling the motion picture industry.

MPAA rating system The G, PG, PG-13, R, NC-17 rating system for movies administered by the Motion Picture Association of America.

muckrakers A term coined by Theodore Roosevelt to describe the reform movement undertaken by leading magazines in the 1890s to expose corrupt practices of business and government to the general public.

multiple system operators (MSOs) Companies that own cable systems in more than one market.

national advertisers Advertisers who sell a product all across the country.

National Public Radio (NPR) A noncommercial U.S. radio network.

network An organization composed of interconnecting broadcasting stations that cuts costs by airing the same programs.

newshole The amount of space available each day in a newspaper for news.

nickelodeons   The popular name for the many penny arcades and amusement centers that emerged around the beginning of the 20th century and specialized in recordings and film.

noise   In communication, anything that interferes with the delivery of a message.

noncommercial television   Television programs broadcast by stations whose income is derived from sources other than the sale of advertising time.

nonduplication rule   An FCC rule passed in 1965, stating that an AM-FM combination may not duplicate its AM content on its FM channel more than 50 percent of the time.

ombudsperson   An individual in a media organization assigned to handle complaints from audience members.

one-stops   Individuals who sell records to retail stores and jukebox operators who are not in a position to buy directly from the record company.

operating policies   Guidelines that cover the everyday problems and situations that crop up during the operation of a media organization.

operational convergence   A system used in media organizations whereby one staff produces content for two media.

paid circulation   A type of circulation in which the reader must purchase a magazine through a subscription or at a newsstand.

panel study   A research method in which data are collected from the same individuals at different points in time.

paradigm   A model used for analysis.

parasocial relationship   A situation whereby audience members develop a sense of kinship or friendship with media personalities.

pass-along audience   That portion of a magazine's total audience composed of individuals who pick up copies of a magazine while at the doctor's office, at work, while traveling, and so on.

payola   Bribes of gifts and money paid to DJs by record companies in order to gain favorable airplay for their releases.

pay-per-view (PPV)   A system that enables cable TV subscribers to pay a one-time fee to view one specific program or movie.

penny press   The mass-appeal press of the early 19th century.

persistence of vision   The quality of the human eye that enables it to retain an image for a split second after the image has disappeared.

personal digital assistants (PDAs)   Digital devices that keep track of addresses, schedules, and other useful information.

phi phenomenon   The tendency of the human perceptual system to perceive continuous motion between two stationary points of light that blink on and off; the basis for the illusion of motion in motion pictures.

phonograph   A "talking machine" developed by Thomas Edison in the late 1870s; the hand-cranked device preserved sound on a tinfoil-wrapped cylinder.

photojournalism   Journalism in which written text is secondary to photographs in news stories.

pickup   A technique of financing a motion picture.

pilot   The first episode of a projected television series.

pilot testing   A process that involves showing a sample audience an entire episode of a show and recording their reactions.

podcast   A prerecorded program that can be downloaded to an iPod or other MP3 player and played at the listener's convenience.

policy book   At radio and TV stations, a book that spells out philosophy and standards of operation and identifies practices that are encouraged or discouraged.

political press   Newspapers and magazines of the 1790–1820 era that specialized in publishing partisan political articles.

polysemic   Having many meanings.

portable people meter (PPM)   A small device carried by an individual that automatically records radio and television exposure.

portals   The first pages a person sees when opening an Internet browser.

positioning   In advertising, stressing the unique selling point of a product or service to differentiate it from the competition.

primary audience   The portion of a magazine's total audience made up of subscribers or those who buy it at the newsstand.

primary demand ad   An advertisement that promotes a specific product category, such as milk.

printing on demand   One-at-a-time printing of books that exist in a digital database.

prior restraint   An attempt by the government to censor the press by preventing it from publishing or broadcasting material.

prominence   News value that stresses the importance of the person involved in the event.

prosocial behavior   People helping each other with no thought of personal reward.

proximity   News value based on the location of a news event.

Public Broadcasting Act of 1967   A congressional act that established the Public Broadcasting Service.

publicity   The placing of stories in the mass media.

publics   The various audiences served by public relations.

publishers   A segment of the print media industry responsible for the creation of content.

rack jobbers   Individuals who service music racks located in variety and large department stores by choosing the CDs to be sold in each location.

Radio Act of 1927   A congressional act establishing the Federal Radio Commission, a regulatory body that would issue broadcasting licenses and organize operating times and frequencies.

rating   The ratio of listeners to a particular radio station to all people in the market; the ratio of viewers of a particular TV program to the number of households in the market equipped with TV.

receiver   The target of the message in the communication process.

reinforcement   Support of existing attitudes and opinions by certain messages.

resonance   In cultivation analysis, the situation in which a respondent's life experiences are congruent with what is seen on TV, thus reinforcing the effect of TV content.

retail advertisers   Businesses that have customers in only one trading area.

rough layout   An early version of a print ad.

search engine   Software that enables users to search the Internet for specific information.

selective demand ad   An ad that stresses a particular brand.

self-determination   The ethical principle that human beings deserve respect for their decisions.

share of the audience   The ratio of listeners to a particular radio station to the total number of listeners in the market; the ratio of the number of households watching a particular TV program to the number of households watching TV at that time.

shield laws   Legislation that defines the rights of a reporter to protect sources.

slander   Spoken defamation; in many states, if a defamatory statement is broadcast, it is considered libel, even though technically the words are not written; libel is considered more harmful and usually carries more serious penalties than does slander.

sliding scale   An arrangement between a motion picture exhibitor and a distributor that details how much box office revenue will be kept by the movie theater.

social media   A set of Internet tools that encourage content sharing and community relationships.

social responsibility theory   The belief that the press has a responsibility to preserve democracy by properly informing the public and by responding to society's needs.

social utility   The media function that addresses an individual's need to affiliate with family, friends, and others in society.

socialization   The ways an individual comes to adopt the behavior and values of a group.

soft news   Features that rely on human interest for their news value.

source   A person who initiates communication.

spam   The electronic equivalent of junk mail.

stimulation theory   A theory that suggests that viewing violence will stimulate an individual to behave more violently.

storyboard   A series of drawings depicting the key scenes in a TV ad.

strategic planning   A management technique that sets long-range, general goals.

subsidiary rights   Rights given by a publisher to others, allowing them to reproduce certain content.

surveillance   The news and information function of the mass media.

survey   A technique of gathering data that typically uses a questionnaire.

tabloids   Heavily illustrated publications usually half the size of a normal newspaper page.

tactical planning   A management technique that sets short-range, specific goals.

target audience   In advertising, the segment of the population for whom the product or service has an appeal.

technological determinism   The theory that contends technology drives historical change.

Telecommunications Act of 1996   A major revision of U.S. communication laws that affected broadcasting, cable, and telephone industries.

text   The object of analysis in the critical/cultural approach.

timeliness   News value that stresses when an event occurred.

time shifting   Recording programs and playing them back at times other than when they are aired.

time softening   Tendency of cell phone users to treat appointed times with more flexibility.

tracking studies   Studies that examine how ads perform during or after a campaign.

trespass   Illegal entry onto another's property.

UHF   The ultra-high-frequency band of the electromagnetic spectrum; channels 14–69 on the TV set.

underground press   A type of specialized reporting that emerged in the mid-to-late 1960s, with emphasis on politically liberal news and opinion and cultural topics such as music, art, and film.

USA Patriot Act   A law that gave the government increased powers of surveillance.

uses-and-gratifications model   A model proposing that audience members have certain needs or drives that are satisfied by using both nonmedia and media sources.

utility   The ethical principle that stresses the greatest good for the greatest number.

Variety   The entertainment industry trade publication.

V-chip   A device installed in a TV set that restricts the reception of violent or objectionable material.

veil of ignorance   The ethical principle that everyone should be treated equally.

VHF   The very-high-frequency band of the electromagnetic spectrum; channels 2–13 on the TV set.

video-on-demand (VOD)   A system by which a cable TV system can provide movies to customers at times of the customers' choosing.

viral advertising   Technique of creating messages so interesting that consumers spontaneously share them.

Voice over Internet Protocol (VoIP)   Method for sending a phone call over the Internet.

voice tracking   A technique in radio in which a disc jockey prerecords the voice portion of a shift that is later broadcast on several stations.

Web page   A hypertext page contained within a Web site.

Web site   A set of hypertext pages linked to each other that contain information about a common topic.

(wireless fidelity) WiFi   A system by which personal computers and other information devices connect to the Internet without wires.

WiMax   Technology that allows wireless Internet access over a wide area.

World Wide Web (WWW)   A network of information sources that uses hypertext to link one piece of information to another.

yellow journalism   Sensationalized journalism, appearing during the 1890s, noted for its emphasis on sex, murder, popularized medicine, pseudoscience, self-promotion, and human-interest stories.

zoned editions   Newspapers that have special sections for specific geographic areas.

Photo Credits

Chapter 1 Opener: © Dave Thompson/AFP/Getty Images; p. 6: AP Photo/Jeff Christensen; p. 8: Raymond Reuter/Sygma/Getty Images; p. 12: © Walt Disney Pictures/Album/Newscom; p. 16: © ABC/Courtesy Everett Collection. Photo by Danny Feld; **Chapter 2 Opener:** © Mathew Imaging/FilmMagic/Getty Images; p. 24: © Masterfile Royalty-Free; p. 32: © Tony Freeman/PhotoEdit; p. 35: © Michael S. Wirtz/MCT/Newscom; p. 42: © Kevin Winter/American Idol 2011/Getty Images; p. 43: © Lisa Werner/Getty Images; p. 45: Photofest/Walt Disney Pictures; p. 46: Everett Collection; **Chapter 3 Opener:** © Royalty-Free/Corbis; p. 55: © Universal History Archive/UIG/Getty Images; p. 59: © Photos.com/Getty Images; p. 60: © The Granger Collection, New York; p. 61: © Library of Congress Prints and Photographs Division [LC-DIG-ppmsca-19470]; p. 63: The Granger Collection, NYC—All rights reserved.; p. 66: © s76/ZUMA Press/Newscom; p. 72: © Creatas/PunchStock; p. 74: © dolphfyn/Shutterstock.com; p. 82: © Bettmann/Getty Images; p. 87: McGraw-Hill Companies; p. 95: © Justin Sullivan/Getty Images; p. 96: © Mohannad Sabry/Tribune News Service/Getty Images; p. 107: © SuperStock/Getty Images; p. 108 (top): General Research and Reference Division. Schomberg Center for Research in Black Culture. The New York Public Library. Astor, Lenox and Tilden Foundations; p. 108 (bottom): © The Collection of The New York Historical Society #54956; p. 110: © J.E. Purdy/Library of Congress Historical/Getty Images; p. 120: © Cynthia Johnson/The LIFE Images Collection/Getty Images; p. 121: © Erica Simone Leeds; p. 126: © Chris Ratcliffe/Bloomberg via Getty Images; **Chapter 6 Opener:** © FocusDigital/Alamy; p. 137: The Granger Collection, NYC—All rights reserved.; p. 138 (top): © Time & Life Pictures/Getty Images; p. 138 (bottom): © Margaret Bourke-White/Time & Life Pictures/Getty Images; p. 140: © Bettmann/Getty Images; p. 142: © FocusMedia/Alamy; p. 146: © niloo/Shutterstock.com; p. 150 (top): © Mark Zemnick; p. 150 (bottom): © w85/ZUMA Press/Newscom; **Chapter 7 Opener:** © Mario Tama/Getty Images; p. 160: © Geoffrey Clements/Corbis Historical/Getty Images; p. 161: © Hulton-Deutsch Collection/Corbis Historical/Getty Images; p. 166: McGraw-Hill Companies; p. 171: © Michael Tullberg/Getty Images; p. 176: © Fancy Photography/Veer; p. 179: National Archives; p. 181 (top): © Camerique/Archive Photos/Getty Images; p. 181 (bottom): © CBS Photo Archive/Getty Images; p. 186 (top): © Kevin Winter/Getty Images; p. 186 (bottom): Brand X Pictures/Jupiter Images; p. 190: Courtesy of Carole Dominick; p. 191: © Johnny Nunez/WireImage/Getty Images; p. 193: © Scott Olson/Getty Images; **Chapter 9 Opener:** © Gustavo Caballero/WireImage/Getty Images; p. 207: Library of Congress Prints and Photographs Division [LC-DIG-cwpbh-04042]; p. 208: © Nina Leer/Timepix/Getty Images;

p. 209: © Getty Images; p. 210 (top): © Michael Stewart/WireImage/Getty Images; p. 210 (bottom): Everett Collection; p. 211 (left): Everett Collection; p. 211 (right): © Robert R. McElroy/Archive Photos/Getty Images; p. 212: © Shirlaine Forrest/WireImage/Getty Images; p. 217: © Mark Ralston/AFP/Getty Images; p. 221: © Joseph Branston/Future/Getty Images; **Chapter 10 Opener:** © David J. Green-Lifestyle/Alamy; p. 231: © Mary Evans Picture Library/Alamy; p. 234: Photofest; p. 235: Photofest; p. 236: Photofest; p. 237: © J. R. Eyerman//Time Life Pictures/Getty Images; p. 240: Photofest/Warner Bros. Pictures; p. 245: © Ken Wolter/Shutterstock.com; p. 246: © AF archive/Alamy; p. 252: © Columbia Pictures/Photofest; **Chapter 11 Opener:** © ABC/Photofest; p. 259: © Bettmann/Getty Images; p. 260: Everett Collection; p. 261: NASA; p. 268: © Cyrus McCrimmon/Denver Post/Getty Images; p. 270: © eldar nurkovic/Shutterstock; p. 273: © Fox Television / Courtesy: Everett Collection; p. 277: © Frederick M. Brown/Getty Images; p. 278: AP Photo/Paul Sakuma; **Chapter 12 Opener:** © Robert Stainforth/Alamy; p. 296: © C-SPAN KRT/Newscom; **Chapter 13 Opener:** © Paul Zimmerman/Getty Images; p. 311: © Mark Wilson/Getty Images; p. 316: © Gil C/Shutterstock; p. 320: © Jon C. Hancock/Bloomberg/Getty Image; p. 324: © U.S. Coast Guard photo by Petty Officer 3rd Class Patrick Kelley; **Chapter 14 Opener:** © Sean Gardner/POOL/EPA/Newscom; p. 333 (top): © Bettmann/Getty Images; p. 333 (bottom): Library of Congress Prints and Photographs Division LC-H25-49642-B; p. 337: © H.S. Photos/Alamy; p. 338: © teeranop/Shutterstock RF; **Chapter 15 Opener:** © Joseph Valenti/Bloomberg via Getty Images; p. 351: © Splash News/Newscom; p. 352: Image Courtesy of The Advertising Archives; p. 354: © Tony Freeman/PhotoEdit; p. 359: © Jack Dempsey/ AP Images for Papa John's International, Inc.; p. 362: Image Courtesy of The Advertising Archives; p. 363: © Clive Brunskill/Getty Images for Pepsi; p. 368: © Bill Aron/PhotoEdit; p. 370: Courtesy Caterpillar; **Chapter 16 Opener:** © Comstock/Jupiter Images; p. 378: AP Photo/Jim Wells; p. 382: © Red Huber/Tribune News Service/Getty Images; p. 395 (left): © Buyenlarge/Getty Images; p. 395 (right): © Classic Image/Alamy; p. 404: Image Courtesy of The Advertising Archives; **Chapter 17 Opener:** © London Stereoscopic Company/Getty Images; p. 412: © Ben Stansall/AFP/Getty Images; p. 418: AP Photo/Ric Francis; p. 419: © REUTERS/Alamy; p. 433: © FashionStock.com/Shutterstock.com; p. 435: © Lionsgate Films/Photofest. Photo by Alfeo Dixon; p. 437: © 20th Century Fox Film Corp. All rights reserved./Courtesy Everett Collection; p. 438: © Louisa Gouliamaki/AFP/Getty Images; p. 439: © Bettmann/Getty Images; p. 440: © Edouard Berne/Stone/Getty Images; p. 446: Everett Collection; p. 451: © BananaStock/Jupiter Images.

Text and Illustration Credits

Chapter 1: p. 10, Courtesy of Google; p. 13, Source: www.nmiupdate.blogspot.com; **Chapter 2:** p. 36, Source: www.craigslist.com; **Chapter 3:** p. 74, Source: www.facebook.com; **Chapter 4:** p. 90, Source: www .mashable.com; p. 91, Source: www.ecost.com; p. 92, Source: www.comscore.com; **Chapter 6:** p. 142, Source: www.zinio.com; p. 147, Used by permission; **Chapter 9:** p. 225, Source: Billboard; **Chapter 10:** p. 251, Source: Variety; p. 252, Source: Motion Picture Association of America; **Chapter 12:** p. 300, Source: www.youtube .com; p. 302, Used by permission of Alfred E. Fergerson, Fergerson Funeral Home, Inc.; **Chapter 14:** p. 343, Source: PRNewswire; **Chapter 15:** p. 348, courtesy of Groupon; p. 355, Courtesy of Google.

index

Credits

ISBN - 13: 978-1-307-17376-5
ISBN - 10: 1-307-17376-4